Psychology of Reasoning

Psychology of Reasoning
Theoretical and Historical Perspectives

edited by
Ken Manktelow & Man Cheung Chung

Psychology Press
Taylor & Francis Group
HOVE AND NEW YORK

First published 2004
by Psychology Press
27 Church Road, Hove, East Sussex BN3 2FA

Simultaneously published in the USA and Canada
by Psychology Press
270 Madison Avenue, New York, NY 10016

Psychology Press is a part of the Taylor & Francis Group

Copyright © 2004 Psychology Press

Typeset in Times by RefineCatch Limited, Bungay, Suffolk
Printed and bound in Great Britain by TJ International Ltd,
Padstow, Cornwall
Cover design by Hybert Design

All rights reserved. No part of this book may be reprinted or
reproduced or utilized in any form or by any electronic, mechanical, or
other means, now known or hereafter invented, including photocopying
and recording, or in any information storage or retrieval system,
without permission in writing from the publishers.

The publisher makes no representation, express or implied, with regard
to the accuracy of the information contained in this book and cannot
accept any legal responsibility or liability for any errors or omissions
that may be made.

This publication has been produced with paper manufactured to strict
environmental standards and with pulp derived from sustainable
forests.

British Library Cataloguing in Publication Data
A catalogue record for this book is available from the British Library

Library of Congress Cataloging-in-Publication Data
Psychology of reasoning: theoretical and historical perspectives /
edited by Ken Manktelow and Man Cheung Chung.—1st ed.
     p. cm.
  Includes bibliographical references and index.
  ISBN 1-84169-310-3 (hbk)
  1. Reasoning (Psychology) I. Manktelow, K., 1., 1952–
  II. Chung, Man Cheung, 1962–

  BF442.P79 2004
  153.4′3–dc22
                                                                    2004016579

ISBN 1-84169-310-3

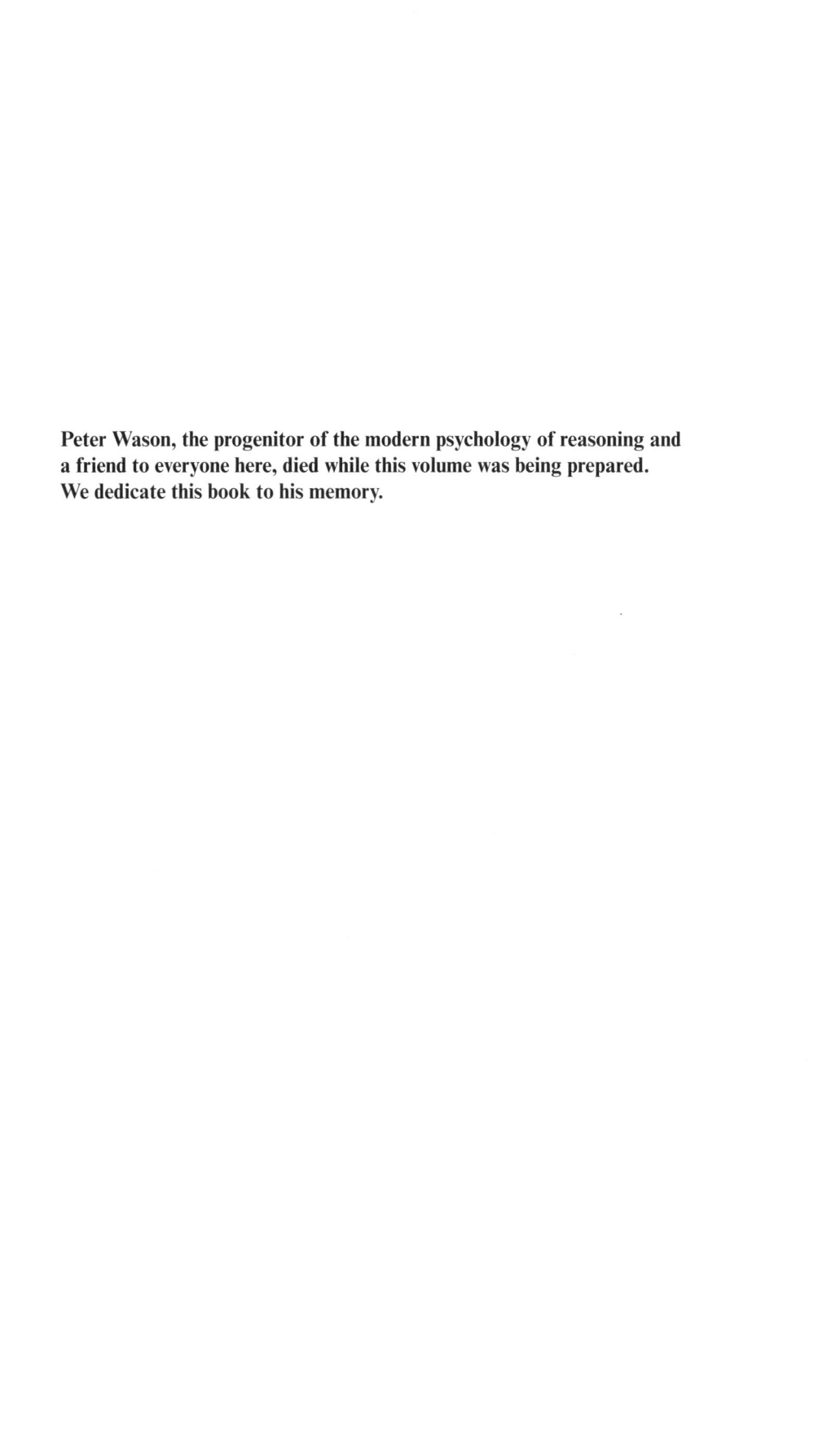

Peter Wason, the progenitor of the modern psychology of reasoning and a friend to everyone here, died while this volume was being prepared. We dedicate this book to his memory.

Contents

List of contributors   ix

1 The contextual character of thought: Integrating themes from the histories and theories of the study of reasoning   1
KEN I. MANKTELOW AND MAN C. CHUNG

2 Reasoning and task environments: The Brunswikian approach   11
MICHAEL E. DOHERTY AND RYAN D. TWENEY

3 Rationality, rational analysis, and human reasoning   43
NICK CHATER AND MIKE OAKSFORD

4 The psychology of conditionals   75
DAVID OVER

5 Violations, lies, broken promises, and just plain mistakes: The pragmatics of counterexamples, logical semantics, and the evaluation of conditional assertions, regulations, and promises in variants of Wason's selection task   95
DAVID P. O'BRIEN, ANTONIO ROAZZI, MARIA G. DIAS, JOSHUA B. CANTOR, AND PATRICIA J. BROOKS

6 The natural history of hypotheses about the selection task: Towards a philosophy of science for investigating human reasoning   127
KEITH STENNING AND MICHIEL VAN LAMBALGEN

7 Reasoning and rationality: The pure and the practical   157
KEN I. MANKTELOW

8 The history of mental models   179
PHILIP N. JOHNSON-LAIRD

9	**Some precursors of current theories of syllogistic reasoning** GUY POLITZER	**213**
10	**History of the dual process theory of reasoning** JONATHAN ST. B. T. EVANS	**241**
11	**Coherence and argumentation** DAVID W. GREEN	**267**
12	**Reasoning about strategic interaction: Solution concepts in game theory** ANDREW M. COLMAN	**287**
13	**What we reason about and why: How evolution explains reasoning** GARY L. BRASE	**309**
14	**The proof of the pudding is in the eating: Translating Popper's philosophy into a model for testing behaviour** FENNA H. POLETIEK	**333**
15	**Constructing science** SANDY LOVIE	**349**
	Author index	**371**
	Subject index	**381**

Contributors

Gary L. Brase, Department of Psychological Sciences, University of Missouri–Columbia, 210 McAlester Hall, Columbia, MO 65211, USA.

Patricia J. Brooks, Department of Psychology, College of Staten Island, City University of New York, 2800 Victory Blvd., 4S-108, Staten Island, NY 10314, USA.

Joshua B. Cantor, Department of Rehabilitation Medicine, Mount Sinai School of Medicine, 1 Gustave L. Levy Place, New York NY, USA.

Nick Chater, Department of Psychology, University of Warwick, Coventry CV4 7AL, UK.

Man Cheung Chung, Department of Psychology, University of Plymouth, Drake Circus, Plymouth PL4 8AA, UK.

Andrew M. Colman, Department of Psychology, Astley Clarke Building, University of Leicester, University Road, Leicester LE1 7RH, UK.

Maria G. Dias, Universidade Federal de Pernambuco, Av. Acad. Hélio Ramos, s/n – CFCH, 8° Andar, Recife 50670–901, PE Brazil.

Michael E. Doherty, Bowling Green State University, Bowling Green, Ohio, USA.

Jonathan St. B. T. Evans, Centre for Thinking and Language, University of Plymouth, Drake Circus, Plymouth PL4 8AA, UK.

David W. Green, Department of Psychology, University College London, Gower Street, London WC1E 6BT, UK.

Philip N. Johnson-Laird, Department of Psychology, Princeton University, Green Hall, Princeton, NJ 08544, USA.

Sandy Lovie, Department of Psychology, University of Liverpool, Eleanor Rathbone Building, Bedford Street South, Liverpool L69 7ZA, UK.

Ken Manktelow, Division of Psychology, School of Applied Sciences, University of Wolverhampton, Millennium City Building, Wulfruna Street, Wolverhampton WV1 1SB, UK.

Contributors

Mike Oaksford, School of Psychology, Cardiff University, P.O. Box 901, Cardiff CF1 3YG, Wales, UK.

David O'Brien, Baruch College and the Graduate School of the City University of New York, 55 Lexington Avenue, New York NY, USA.

David Over, Department of Psychology, University of Sunderland, Sunderland SR6 0DD, UK.

Fenna H. Poletiek, Unit of Experimental and Theoretical Psychology, University of Leiden, P.O. Box 9555, 2300 RB Leiden, The Netherlands.

Guy Politzer, CNRS: Laboratoire "Cognition et Activités Finalisées", Université de Paris 8, 2 Rue de la Liberté, 93526 Saint-Denis, France.

Antonio Roazzi, Universidade Federal de Pernambuco, Av. Acad. Hélio Ramos, s/n – CFCH, 8° Andar, Recife 50670–901, PE Brazil.

Keith Stenning, Human Communication Research Centre, Dept. of Psychology, Edinburgh University, 2 Buccleuch Place, Edinburgh EH8 9LW, UK.

Ryan D. Tweney, Bowling Green State University, Bowling Green, Ohio, USA.

Michiel van Lambalgen, Department of Philosophy, Amsterdam University, Plantage Muidergracht 24, 1018 TV Amsterdam, The Netherlands.

1 The contextual character of thought

Integrating themes from the histories and theories of the study of reasoning

K. I. Manktelow and M. C. Chung

The study of reasoning, unlike what was once said about psychology as a discipline, has both a long past and a long history. Indeed, it would not be too far-fetched to claim that people have been studying and reporting on their reasoning abilities for as long as they have been studying anything. So the shadow cast by this history is probably longer than in any other field of the cognitive sciences: modern authors still regularly appeal to the writings of their ancient philosophical forebears, most notably Aristotle, who lived over 2300 years ago. Even within the confines of contemporary empirical psychology, a long line can be traced back: the earliest such reference in this book is a near century old, from 1908.

All the more curious, then, that present-day students of the psychology of reasoning can find their attempts to situate the field rather an arduous business. While you will often find such material in the introduction sections of empirical papers, and in the background sections of theoretical reviews, you can feel rather like an archaeologist piecing together an object from various fragments you happen upon. One aim of this book is to enable those interested in the psychology of reasoning to apprehend more of its general historical base, and hence get a better appreciation of the direction in which the ideas are flowing, by finding more of these pieces in one place. We will have a better idea of where we are going if we are clearer about where we have come from.

In addition to the rich strata of history on which the psychology of reasoning stands, there has been an increasing acknowledgement, as it has turned from a task-based data-gathering enterprise to a deeper and wider theoretical one, that there are connections to be made both to other aspects of the study of human thought, and to cognitive science in general. Psychologists studying reasoning have often made appeals for engagement with these other fields and have increasingly gone out looking for it in recent years. Every recent major theoretical statement has been made in these terms, as several of the present chapters portray, although sometimes, as Stenning and van Lambalgen argue here, there has been a step in the other direction and a detrimental split has opened up. A second aim of this book is to present some of these theoretical extensions and contacts.

The third aim of the book was something of an act of faith on the part of its editors. We have 14 contributions here, taken from a wide range of areas of study; some of these areas will be familiar to and expected from people already interested in the psychology of reasoning, some perhaps less so. We believed (hoped) that it would be possible to identify emergent themes, from both the historical and theoretical strands, that would enable both ourselves and you, the reader, to form the more grounded view of the field that is one of the benefits of its progress towards being a more integrated science. That faith has been amply repaid, and in the rest of this introduction we shall set out some of these themes (you may well find others); they have informed the way the chapters have been organized.

One of the first true empirical psychologists, Hermann Ebbinghaus, devoted his life's work to the attempt to explain memories from their cradles to their graves, as it were: from their acquisition to their loss. He realized that in order to accomplish the first of these tasks, the material to be remembered had to be free of all prior associations, otherwise he could not be sure he was looking at the very start of an act of memory. Hence the development of his famous nonsense syllables. Something like this idea has also been applied in the psychology of reasoning: if one wants to study an inference, it had better not be contaminated by memory, otherwise any interesting effects could be attributed to knowledge rather than thought. This was the nub of Mary Henle's (1978) famous objection, that she had never found errors that could unambiguously be attributed to faulty reasoning. The answer seems obvious: strip out, as Ebbinghaus thought he had done, all possibility of other influences, and study only reasoning. Thus a research programme grew up based around the study of responses to various abstract tasks. This programme is reviewed in greatest detail in older texts such as Wason and Johnson-Laird (1972) and Evans (1982), although it is also at the core of later ones such as Evans, Newstead, and Byrne (1993), Garnham and Oakhill (1994), and Manktelow (1999).

However, the assumption that one can study reasoning directly by using abstract tasks has been replaced by a realization that, if one strips out content, one is losing something essential about reasoning (as one is about memory). This is far from a new idea in itself, as **Mike Doherty and Ryan Tweney** relate; it was at the heart of Brunswik's approach to psychology. (It was also acknowledged by Wason and Johnson-Laird, in both the title and the substance of their 1972 book.) Brunswik was guided by the principle of representative design: that the essential elements of the environment in question must figure in research design. If this principle is taken on board, certain consequences follow as to the way you go about designing experiments and interpreting their findings, as Doherty and Tweney show. Brunswik's ideas are probably most familiar to students of reasoning through the work of Gigerenzer and colleagues on fast and frugal heuristics and probabilistic mental models (see Gigerenzer, Todd, & the ABC Research Group, 1999), but they are becoming more influential more widely: a whole issue of the journal *Thinking and Reasoning* was devoted to this approach in 1996.

The need to acknowledge the relation between the task and the natural cognitive ecology of research participants has also been the fundamental concern of the "rational analysis" approach to cognition, as **Nick Chater and Mike Oaksford** demonstrate. They turn Brunswik's principle around, and ask of a given reasoning task, what environment is that task reflecting? In common with Brunswik, rational analysis thus requires a specification of the cognitive environment. A scientist might design a task assuming that the participant's response to it reflects one kind of cognition, but as Porgy said, it ain't necessarily so. The participants might be coming at it from quite another direction, in which case our evaluation of their performance is under serious question. Chater and Oaksford take the example of tasks ostensibly designed to assess logical deduction, but on which there is evidence that participants may be attempting optimal information gain. This approach is one of the most important recent theoretical and methodological innovations in the psychology of reasoning, and can only gain in influence in the future. It chimes with the standpoint of the philosopher Gilbert Harman (e.g., 1999), who argues that reasoning is all about belief revision, and hence that "deductive reasoning" is not reasoning, since deduction is concerned only with finding proofs, and so does not increase information. Chater and Oaksford remind us of this position when they declare that, since much of the experimental study of deductive reasoning does not seem to engage it, the term "psychology of deductive reasoning" may be a misnomer.

These are fundamental ideas about the way research into reasoning is and ought to be done, and the sorts of theories that ought to be compiled, but the acknowledgement of the importance of the contexts of thought can be cashed out in other ways. Much of our thinking – and almost all of the thinking that has been studied by psychologists – is verbal, and so the linguistic context comes to the fore. And at the heart of reasoning, as **David Over** emphasizes, is the conditional, usually expressed using sentences containing "if". This is reflected in the experimental study of human reasoning, where studies of conditional reasoning far outweigh any other kind. Over points out problems with "logicism", the idea that the study of conditionals must be restricted to those that embody statements expressing certainties. Most of the statements we make about the world are uncertain to some degree, and so most real-world conditional arguments cannot strictly be deductively valid. Adherence to a strong logicist approach to conditionals leads to some long-recognized, jarring paradoxes. Furthermore, many of our conditional expressions concern counterfactual or deontic situations, and so are not amenable to a strict deductive analysis in the first place. Over traces the history of the study of conditionals both in psychology (through the theories of natural deduction and mental models) and philosophy (focusing on the work of Ramsey and Stalnaker). He concludes that considerations of utility and probability are necessary in explaining reasoning with all types of conditional, with the hitherto "standard" indicative conditional being usefully seen as a special case of the deontic conditional. This decision-theoretic approach to conditional reasoning is shared by Chater and Oaksford, although they take a radically different theoretical stance.

The semantics and pragmatics of conditionals are also the focus of **David O'Brien, Antonio Roazzi, Maria Dias, Joshua Cantor, and Patricia Brooks**; they reflect on what a close analysis of these factors implies for research using the most well-known experimental paradigm on conditional reasoning, the Wason selection task. They concentrate on the indicative–deontic distinction, which has been the locus of much contemporary theorizing. It has often been held that when we evaluate an indicative conditional, in the selection task and elsewhere, we are dealing with its possible falsification, whereas when we evaluate a deontic conditional, we are dealing with possible violations of it. So in the former case, the status of the sentence is in question but in the latter it is not. Using a large range of task scenarios, O'Brien and colleagues show that it is easy to be simplistic about this, for instance in falsely assuming that deontic rules cannot be falsified, or in distinguishing lies and mistakes. The solution is a precise specification of both the semantics and the pragmatics of the task in question (a Brunswikian moral). Such an analysis leads in their view to a unified conception of conditional reasoning, where differences in performance can be explained using pragmatic principles and general-purpose reasoning mechanisms, rather than domain-specific processes.

The importance of the reasoner's interpretation of task materials is also the starting point for **Keith Stenning and Michiel van Lambalgen**'s analysis. They also address the selection task, and like Over and O'Brien and colleagues, strongly contest the "standard" reading of the conditional as corresponding to the logic of material implication (which states that a conditional is true when its antecedent is false or its consequent is true). Unlike the more intuitive analysis of O'Brien and colleagues, they point to developments in logical semantics as a descriptive rather than normative discipline, and urge a reunification between psychology and logic, whose divorce, they argue, has hindered the progress of research. Similarly, selection task research has contained an outdated philosophy of science based on Popper's falsificationist doctrine, another area that has moved on in recent times. As with O'Brien and colleagues and Chater and Oaksford, Stenning and van Lambalgen argue that researchers should not blithely assume that participants in a selection task experiment are using an implication conditional and seeking possible falsifications, and they too go into detail about the indicative–deontic distinction. Rather, the participants' task is to discover how the researcher intends the task and rule to be understood. Without this basic semantic account, we are in no position to argue about mental processes. Thus, echoing a sentiment first expressed by Anderson (1978) and urged on the psychology of reasoning by Evans (1982), theories require an account of both representation and process.

As we have seen above, there has been a lot of attention devoted to the indicative–deontic distinction in recent times, and this is the concern of the chapter by **Ken Manktelow**. He also locates his analysis in research on the Wason selection task, completing a trilogy of chapters that do so; the reason for this is that the empirical base of the upsurge in interest in deontic reasoning lies in work using that problem. It was given its most powerful stimulus in the mid 1980s, in the widely known studies of Cheng and Holyoak and Cosmides. One of the offshoots of the direction of attention to deontic reasoning was the reawakening of a bipolar argument concerning the integrity of reasoning. Broadly speaking, an indicative statement concerns matters of fact, while a deontic statement prescribes an action. This difference has been acknowledged since Aristotle, as the difference between pure, or theoretical, reasoning and practical reasoning. Are they two sides of the same coin, or different currencies? Manktelow considers a variety of approaches to this fundamental question, and raises another: that there may be a further distinction to be made, as causal reasoning does not fit comfortably under either heading.

There have been many centuries of argument over whether the intuitive pure–practical distinction reflects a categorical distinction in human cognition, and recent empirical studies have led to a number of modern authors espousing that position. Two foregoing chapters here, by Over and by O'Brien and colleagues, however, come down on the side of a unified approach to reasoning. That being so, how is reasoning carried out in the human mind? One answer is alluded to by O'Brien et al. – that people use a kind of mental logic, allied to the pragmatic principles about which they go into detail. The major alternative to this proposal is reviewed by **Phil Johnson-Laird**, who traces the historical antecedents of the theory of mental models. This is unquestionably the most influential theoretical proposal in the field, as reflected in the volume of published research that appeals to the notion of mental models, and the range of its applications. These began outside the field of reasoning, and extend ever more widely within and beyond its conventional boundaries; some flavour of this breadth of application can be gained here. Johnson-Laird finds precedents in 19th-century science, but locates the theory's true ancestry in the work of the philosopher C. S. Peirce, the Mozartish psychologist Kenneth Craik, and his contemporary, the "Gestalt behaviourist" E. C. Tolman. Another measure of a theory's influence is, of course, the amount of criticism as well as support that it attracts, and you will find many such statements here, most notably in the chapters by Over and by Stenning and van Lambalgen.

Before the field's preoccupation with conditionals, the selection task, and other such delights, its territory was largely occupied by the classical syllogism. This once again reflects its ancient antecedents, as the syllogism was first systematized and extensively written about by Aristotle. Once again, then, we can look for a line of inquiry through a long stretch of time, and this is what **Guy Politzer** does. As with Johnson-Laird's history of mental models,

Politzer finds a rich fossil record and concludes, rather challengingly for present-day researchers, that the important psychological observations were made about a century ago. And, as with mental models, one can go back even further: students of the syllogism will already be familiar with the 18th century creations of Venn and Euler, though perhaps less so, surprisingly, with Leibniz's pre-emption of such devices. One can of course go all the way back to Aristotle, who made psychological as well as logical proposals whose echoes can still be heard in modern theorizing.

Modern theorizing brings us to the third of these avowedly historical chapters, this time focusing on a theory that has a more recent origin, but which, like the theory of mental models, has had a wide influence on research into reasoning. **Jonathan Evans** gives a personal historical account of the origins and development of this theory, going back to his work with Peter Wason in the 1970s. This is particularly apt given that Wason was responsible more than any other individual for the way that the psychology of reasoning looks today, and it is fitting that his direct as well as his indirect influence is represented here (other references to Wason's own research can be found in the chapters by Stenning and van Lambalgen and by Poletiek, and a number of his former associates figure among this book's contributors). The dual process theory began life as an explanation for some curious selection task findings, but has taken on much greater import in the years since then, most extensively in its revisions resulting from Evans' collaboration with Over. Along the way, it has been influenced by ideas from other areas of cognitive psychology, and interestingly has been paralleled by independent developments of a similar kind, again in other areas.

Within the psychology of reasoning, dual process ideas inform the stance of **David Green**, who reviews an approach to the study of reasoning that, while sharing some features and interests with the kinds of research we have been dealing with so far, goes into a different kind of territory: the use of reasoning. Green's concern is with argumentation, and as with so many areas of reasoning research, it has some direct philosophical ancestry, this time in the work of Stephen Toulmin. Green focuses on the dual representation of arguments: their structure and the mental models that comprise them (again showing the scope of influence of the theory of mental models). He also ventures into terrain that is relatively less explored not only in most research on reasoning, but in most of cognitive psychology: the interaction between affect and cognition. He argues that both need to be considered if argumentation is to be understood. Anyone who has ever been involved in argument, no matter how "reasoned" – that's anyone – will testify that it can become decidedly hot, and it is likely that the emotional context of reasoning will come increasingly into focus in future.

Green's chapter is an example of one that takes the psychology of reasoning into areas where it does not often go. This was an aim we stated at the outset: to show that the study of reasoning is an enterprise that connects with a wide range of fields of research into human mentality. Several of the previous chapters (e.g., Chater and Oaksford, Over, Manktelow) have made one connection in particular: that between reasoning and decision making. Some (e.g., Doherty and Tweney, O'Brien et al., Green) have alluded to the fact that thinking and reasoning often take place in a social context. **Andrew Colman** reviews an area where such issues are thrown into sharp relief: psychological game theory. As with the Brunswikian approach, this is a field of study that does not loom large in much of the mainstream literature on reasoning, but it should. Game theory is concerned with the kinds of thinking that go on between interdependent decision-makers, that is, when the decisions taken by one party affect the decisions taken by others. As with so many of the areas under review here, it has historical roots outside psychology, but which have raised important psychological questions. Colman deals with one in particular: that because of the actions of others, the "players" in a social interaction have incomplete control over the situation. This profoundly affects the normative question of what each one should do. Thus, while game theory poses important psychological questions, psychology has equally unsettling effects on game theory.

What people should do in situations of social interaction is a many-layered question, one that has been the central focus of theorists working in an evolutionary tradition. This approach arrived in the psychology of reasoning with a bang on the appearance of Leda Cosmides' famous paper on the application of evolutionary social contract theory to the explanation of behaviour on the selection task in 1989, and has had an enormous impact. **Gary Brase** reviews the evolutionary approach here, and it is interesting that even in his title, the normative question is confronted immediately. Evolutionary theorizing is driven by the empirical predictions made on the assumption that people (and other animals) will tend to behave in ways that reflect inclusive fitness, i.e., that increase the likelihood that they will survive and pass on their genes. Brase argues that this perspective leads inevitably to the idea that reasoning, along with all other parts of cognition, will be domain-specific and, hence, modular. If one accepts this, there then follows a debate about how these domains are arranged. Evolutionary theory provides us with some signposts about this, too. This approach to cognitive theory has been as controversial as it is influential, as Brase relates in his chapter and as can be seen not only elsewhere in this book (e.g., Over and O'Brien et al. reject the strict modularity that many evolutionary reasoning theorists espouse) but in others, such as the recent volume edited by Over (2003).

Theoretical, historical, and philosophical ideas clearly run through the study of reasoning like the veins in granite but, as we saw in the case of game theory, the flow is not all one way. For instance, Stenning and van Lambalgen base some of their argument on the philosophy of science; and of course reasoning, particularly conditional reasoning, is a large part of scientific thought. The influence has, as they contend, been mutual: ideas from the philosophy of science have found their way into the design and interpretation of reasoning research. Foremost among these has been the falsificationism of

Karl Popper. The chapter by **Fenna Poletiek** presents a close examination of falsificationism, not this time in terms of its use by the selection task coterie, but as a model for testing behaviour in general, both scientific and everyday. As always, the closer one looks at something, the more complex it appears. Falsification and confirmation turn out to be conjoined twins, in that the success of an attempt at falsification is tied in intimately with how severe the test is in the first place. If you give your hypothesis a very severe test, you go in expecting a falsification, so when you achieve it, you have not learned very much. Falsifications are more useful when confirmations are expected, and vice versa. Thus hypothesis testing can be seen, as can conditional reasoning in Over's scheme, as a decision problem. Two-valued testing is too stringent for the real world, both in the lab and outside it: one does not simply ask whether a hypothesis is true or false, one thinks about the usefulness of a test and the likelihood of its possible outcomes.

Science and life are alike in another complicating aspect as well, of course: they are both inherently social activities. That much can also be taken from the Brunswikian approach expounded by Doherty and Tweney, from the pragmatic perspective of O'Brien and colleagues, from Stenning and van Lambalgen's semantically based examination of the progress (or lack of it) in selection task research, and from the evolutionary and game-theoretic standpoints on reasoning set out for us by Brase and Colman respectively. Green explores how reasoning is used in argumentation, and Stenning and van Lambalgen urge a sociological analysis of how reasoning researchers have gone about their work. Something along those lines is provided by **Sandy Lovie**, although his scope is rather wider; in fact, it is probably safe to say that the kind of perspective he offers is not common in books on the psychology of reasoning. Lovie acknowledges from the start the central roles of reasoning and argumentation in the doing of science, and directs us to the rhetorical practice of science as a socially constructed activity. He echoes Poletiek's basic outline of the structure of hypothesis-testing situations – hypothesis, test, interpretation – but rejects the idea of an experimental psychology of science, arguing instead for psychologically informed but naturalistic studies. Science, from this viewpoint, is a set of texts of belief and action in context, with reasoning employed in the service of argumentation, persuasion, and change in belief. Once again, there are reminders here of philosophical crosscurrents that appear elsewhere in the book, such as Toulmin's views on the structure of argument, and Harman's idea that reasoning is about belief revision.

Context is the theme that runs through all the contributions to this book. Reasoning is an activity whose objects cannot be detached from their context, be they syntactic, semantic, or pragmatic; which takes place in a context, be it linguistic, interpersonal, biological, or cultural. The psychology of reasoning itself takes place in context: methodological, theoretical, historical. In turn, the psychology of reasoning provides findings and ideas that reflect back on how we view everyday thinking, human rationality, the practice of science and hence human culture in general. We hope that this volume will help you to better appreciate these matters, and thank all the contributors for their efforts in this.

REFERENCES

Anderson, J. R. (1978). Arguments concerning representations for mental imagery. *Psychological Review, 85*, 249–277.

Cosmides, L. (1989). The logic of social exchange: Has natural selection shaped how humans reason? Studies with the Wason selection task. *Cognition, 31*, 187–316.

Evans, J. St. B. T. (1982). *The psychology of deductive reasoning*. London: Routledge & Kegan Paul.

Evans, J. St. B. T., Newstead, S. E., & Byrne, R. M. J. (1993). *Human reasoning; the psychology of deduction*. Hove, UK: Lawrence Erlbaum Associates Ltd.

Garnham, A., & Oakhill, J. V. (1994). *Thinking and reasoning*. Oxford: Blackwell.

Gigerenzer, G., Todd, P., & the ABC Research Group. (1999). *Simple heuristics that make us smart*. Oxford: Oxford University Press.

Harman, G. (1999). *Reasoning, meaning and mind*. Oxford: Oxford University Press.

Henle, M. (1978). Foreword. In R. Revlin & R. E. Mayer (Eds.), *Human reasoning*. Washington, DC: Winston.

Manktelow, K. I. (1999). *Reasoning and thinking*. Hove, UK: Psychology Press.

Over, D. E. (Ed.). (2003). *Evolution and the psychology of thinking: The debate*. Hove, UK: Psychology Press.

Wason, P. C. & Johnson-Laird, P. N. (1972). *Psychology of reasoning: Structure and content*. London: Batsford.

2 Reasoning and task environments
The Brunswikian approach

Michael E. Doherty and Ryan D. Tweney

> If there is anything that still ails psychology in general, and the psychology of cognition specifically, it is the neglect of investigation of environmental or ecological texture in favor of that of the texture of organismic structures and processes.
>
> (Brunswik, 1957, p. 6)

BRUNSWIK'S INTELLECTUAL HERITAGE

Egon Brunswik (1903–1955), born in Hungary but educated mostly in Vienna, came of age as a psychologist in the Vienna Psychological Institute founded by Karl and Charlotte Bühler. Karl Bühler was his primary mentor, but Moritz Schlick, founder of the Vienna Circle, was also an important influence. After completing his doctoral dissertation in 1927, with Bühler and Schlick as his committee, Brunswik became laboratory assistant to Bühler, assuming responsibility for the perception lab.

Brunswik's functionalist orientation derived from Bühler and reflects a very different set of influences than the American functionalism associated with such figures as William James and John Dewey. Instead of a post-Darwinian adaptationist perspective, Bühler's position emphasized the primacy of "intentionality", a central concept in the act psychology of Franz Brentano (Kurz & Tweney, 1997; Leary, 1987). Brentano, seeking a criterion for what constituted mental phenomena, used this term for the referential character of thought. Bühler, who had participated in the "Imageless Thought" school of Külpe, Messer, Ach, and others (Humphrey, 1951), combined Brentano's intentionality with a phenomenological approach (based loosely on Husserl; see Kusch, 1995) and argued that psychology must establish the fundamental units of study in the intentional consciousness. In spite of his phenomenological emphasis, however, Bühler found himself at odds with the Gestalt psychologists, disagreeing in particular with their extension of Gestalt perceptual laws to thinking.

By the time Brunswik arrived as a student, Bühler was emphasizing the importance of "thoughts" as the fundamental units of experience. For

Bühler, this led to research on the nature of language (Bühler, 1934/1990), and an emphasis on the social environmental context within which language and thought developed (Bühler, 1930). Perception became Brunswik's niche within the overall Bühlerian framework and, encouraged by his mentor, he sought to understand the perceptual constancies using an experimental approach. If mental phenomena are "intentional" and object oriented, and if the units of mind are "thoughts", how can the gap be bridged between the world of objects, the perceptions that "represent" those objects, and the "thoughts" (or judgements, to use a modern term often associated with Brunswik) that are the results of the process?

Another Bühler student, Karl Popper, received his PhD in 1928, one year after Brunswik and also with Bühler and Schlick as his advisors (Kurz, 1996). Like Popper, the young Brunswik cannot be classified as a "logical positivist" in spite of the influence of Schlick and the Vienna Circle. For both, Bühler had posed a fundamental issue that they saw as resolved too simplistically by the logical positivists. No matter how one sought to put the formulations of science on a sound logical and empirical footing, there remained the problem of bridging the gap between the mental world of those formulations and the world of objects. Brunswik sought the solution in psychology, whereas Popper decided that psychology was a dead end for understanding science, turning to inductivist formulations and a falsificationist account of science. Popper did this only in the context of how scientists *justify* propositions. How they *discovered* those propositions was, for Popper, a problem for "mere" psychology (Popper, 1974; see also Kurz, 1996 for an account of Popper's rejection of the cognitive psychology he learned from Bühler).

For Brunswik in the 1920s and 1930s, the task at hand was to show how the perceptual constancies could be investigated in a way that did justice to the object orientation of the perceiver. Even his earliest work rejected the usual experimental approach to such issues, which manipulated one variable at a time while observing the effects on a dependent measure (usually a judgement of magnitude). Instead, to understand size constancy, Brunswik used "multi-dimensional psychophysics" (a term used by Brunswik, 1956a, to describe his earlier work); he manipulated a multiplicity of variables simultaneously during a size judgement task because isolating one variable in the laboratory failed to reflect the environments in which organisms actually perceive. For Brunswik, the most important outcome of this research was the finding that although distal and proximal stimuli, which he came to call "cues", were only weakly related, and proximal cues and the final judgements were also only weakly related, there was an extremely high correspondence between distal stimuli and judgements. Brunswik referred to this apparent paradox as the "perceptual achievement" of the organism, and the development of this theme animated the rest of his career.

In 1933, Brunswik met a like-minded American who was visiting Vienna, the young Edward Chace Tolman; each found something of value in the ideas of the other, and their collaborative paper (Tolman & Brunswik, 1935) reveals

The Brunswikian approach 13

the overlap between their views. The paper gave the first clear statement of the causal texture of the environment, and developed a theme important in the later work of both men, that the environmental cues available to an organism may be equivocal. The central concepts of the paper, local representation, means-objects, and – especially – hypotheses, blend Tolman and Brunswik, and establish the latter as neobehaviourist, like Tolman. Even so, hindsight permits us to see that there are deep differences as well. Tolman's later work focused on central processes and how these mediate behaviour, whereas Brunswik's later work emphasized the relation between behaviour and the distal world (Kurz & Tweney, 1997).

Following a reciprocal visit to Berkeley in 1935–36, Brunswik moved permanently to the University of California in 1937, just prior to the 1938 Nazi takeover of Austria. Else Frenkel also left Vienna, and their marriage in 1938 brought her to Berkeley as well. The move to the US marked a turning point in Brunswik's career, and he soon began the process of adapting his views to what, to him, must have seemed a very different intellectual milieu. In particular, he began to incorporate statistical views into his work. If behaviour was mediated by probabilistic cues (see Gigerenzer, 1997), then it made sense to conceptualize the organism as something of an intuitive statistician (Gigerenzer & Murray, 1987). It was not long before Brunswik had developed a first version of the lens model (see below) to capture this in formal terms.

In the late 1930s, American psychology was permeated by statistical notions, one consequence of the heavy emphasis on predicting and controlling the aggregated behaviour of many individuals (Danziger, 1990). For Brunswik, this meant that new tools were available – in particular, he was able to use correlation to capture the inexact relation between cues and objects (Brunswik, 1940). We will show how he did this in subsequent parts of this chapter, but it is worth noting that, in one respect, Brunswik remained European in his use of statistical representations. By contrast to the prevailing trend in America, Brunswik's work never emphasized aggregation of data across "subjects", the newly coined term used to distance the researcher from the object of study.

At Berkeley, Brunswik developed his theoretical system and the empirical studies that supported it, moving beyond the reliance on perception that characterized his Vienna research, and establishing his probabilistic functionalism as an important school of psychological thought. Yet the austere and intellectual Austrian, an uncompromising perfectionist, was often seen as intimidating and, perhaps as a result, left few followers to carry on his work. Among his American contemporaries, Brunswik's use of correlational statistics in an experimental context was novel – too novel, as it turned out. When, shortly after the war, statistical inference techniques became the touchstone of American psychology (Rucci & Tweney, 1980), Brunswik's approach began to be criticized for its use of correlation, which Hilgard called an "instrument of the devil" (Hilgard, 1955, p. 228; see also Kurz & Tweney, 1997). Nor was it merely a question of this or that statistical tool; as we note below, the post-war emphasis on a methodological canon, first stated by Woodworth (1938) as the rule of one variable, and the attendant reliance on experimental designs that required strict separation and balancing of factorial variables, made Brunswik's emphasis on capturing the causal structure of probabilistic environments seem wrong-headed to his peers.

It would be wrong to say that Brunswik was ignored by his American contemporaries; his papers were published in the best journals, his views were attacked by the most prominent experimentalists (see Hammond, 1966), and he participated in some seminal conferences, including a 1955 meeting at Colorado that is often cited as one of the precursors of the cognitive revolution (Brunswik, 1957). One early follower of Brunswik, Kenneth Hammond, became a powerful advocate and extender of Brunswik's ideas. Hammond was among the first to use Brunswik's lens model in judgement and decision-making tasks, was the leading advocate of the Brunswikian approach known as Social Judgement Theory (Doherty & Kurz, 1996), and the founding father of the Brunswik Society. In large part because of Hammond's advocacy, Brunswik's memory remains vivid.

Brunswik himself was not wedded to one statistical tool, nor to one methodological approach. In particular, but for his premature death in 1955, we might have seen him apply the new information theory of Claude Shannon and the cybernetics of Norbert Wiener to the understanding of the probabilistic relations among cues and behaviour. He noted both of these in sympathetic terms (Brunswik, 1952), and it is interesting to speculate on how he might have used such approaches to capture uncertainty in a formal model.

THE METHODOLOGICAL POSTULATE OF BEHAVIOUR–RESEARCH ISOMORPHISM

Brunswik had a deep interest in methodological issues. He believed that empirical research would be wasteful and inefficient unless it was based on methods appropriate to the investigation of psychological phenomena. The heritage of European functionalism is reflected in his methodological postulate of behaviour–research isomorphism, which asserted that "the 'order,' or pattern, of research 'ideas,' or design, should be the same as the pattern of 'things' studied, which for psychology is behaviour" (1952, p. 25).

The principle of behaviour–research isomorphism is a hard doctrine. It says that *research should focus wherever behaviour focuses*. In espousing it, Brunswik asserted that creating laboratory situations that lack the fundamental features an organism faces in its natural environment precludes generalization beyond the specific task studied. Brunswik was advocating a radical position, one antithetical to the Zeitgeist of his time. He saw that it would entail both conceptual and practical difficulties, in that the features of entities that were the foci of instrumental or perceptual behaviour were inevitably correlated with the features of other entities in the environment.

His emphasis on the correlational structure of the ecology had all too clear implications for "the rule of one variable" (Woodworth, 1938) and for the then burgeoning use of factorial design (Rucci & Tweney, 1980).

THE ENVIRONMENT HAS TEXTURE AND DEPTH

Brunswik maintained that psychology must investigate how the organism adapts to and functions in its normal environment. This was not a unique view, but Brunswik was virtually alone in his belief that for psychology to take its proper place in the sciences, it must envision both the organism and environment as systems in their own right, each with its own properties, each with surface and depth, each with a rich texture (Brunswik, 1943, 1952). He lamented what he saw as the encapsulation of psychology inside the head – the concentration on understanding psychological processes either without regard to the environment, or with a naive "constancy hypothesis" that postulated one-to-one relations between environmental events, proximal stimuli, brain events, and psychological events.[1]

As an alternative, Brunswik proposed a "psychology without a subject", that is, he advocated investigating the properties of the "textural ecology as a propaedeutic to functional psychology" (1956a, p. 119). Thus, Brunswik and Kamiya (1953) carried out a study with an "*n*" of zero, in which they analyzed photographs to establish whether the environmental conditions for learning Gestalt-like proximity relations were present. Brunswik and Kamiya concluded that they were, and that learning was therefore a plausible alternative to the innate processes postulated by the Gestaltists.

The premise that psychology must address the causal texture of the environment was highly unusual in the historical context in which Brunswik worked – and remains so today. The environment of interest to Brunswik was not, of course, the environment as conceived by the physicist, but rather the environment confronted by the organism, an environment with a proximal surface, or "skin", and extending in depth away from the organism in both time and space. Yet it is not knowledge of the "skin" of the environment that is relevant to survival; it is knowledge of *things* in depth, distal things rather than proximal cues, that matters. And things in the world cannot, in principle, be known with certainty because causes in the world scatter their effects "semi-erratically". Brunswik thus envisaged psychology in terms of two characteristics of the environment: (1) "The environment has a *causal texture* ... in which different events are regularly dependent upon each other" (Tolman & Brunswik, 1935, p. 43), and (2) "Such causal connections are probably always to some degree *equivocal*, that is, not connected in simple one-one, univocal ... fashion, with the types of entities represented" (p. 44). This implies that perceptual cues are partially intersubstitutable for one another, a central concept for Brunswik. It appears throughout his work, in the lens model and in the idea that vicarious functioning in the organism mirrors the vicarious mediation in the organism's ecology (see Brunswik, 1956a, p. 50, 1956b, p. 158).

Two of Brunswik's papers used manipulations in a fashion especially consistent with his conception that the environment was imperfectly knowable: *Probability as a determiner of rat behaviour* (1939) and *Probability learning of perceptual cues in the establishment of a weight illusion* (Brunswik & Herma, 1951). Each reflects his belief that the environment is, as far as the organism can know, probabilistic. The very first sentence of the 1939 paper is "In the natural environment of a living being, cues, means or pathways to a goal are usually neither absolutely reliable nor absolutely wrong" (p. 175). Thus, he varied the probabilities of reward on the two arms of a T-maze, the differences between the probabilities, the ratios of the probabilities, and which of the two sides presented ambiguous information. In this, his only rat study and one of the earliest studies of probability learning, Brunswik found that rats could not only learn in a probabilistic environment, but could discriminate between probabilities as well. He concluded that "the strength of response appears to follow rather a kind of compromise" of tendencies, an idea deeply entrenched in his thinking about perception, and closely related to the concept of vicarious functioning (see also Doherty, 2001, p. 15).

Brunswik and Herma (1951) dealt with probability learning in perception. They set up "an artificial miniature environment in which the relationship between cue and referent was probabilistic rather than absolute, that is, in which reinforcement is 'partial' ... rather than of the conventional unequivocal kind" (1951, p. 281). Björkman, in commenting on this paper, attributes its significance to "the fact that it represents an early effort (the experiments were conducted in Vienna in 1937) to construct a task that mirrored important aspects of the environment" (2001, p. 170).

THE BASIC FACT OF PERCEPTION IS DISTAL FOCUSING

Brunswik maintained that all behaviour, including perceptual behaviour, has a distal focus. It follows that behaviour is not concerned with (does not focus on) immediate sensory experiences resulting from proximal stimuli, but rather on *things* in the world that must be inferred from arrays of intercorrelated cues. Research that has any chance of illuminating how organisms achieve survival and success must involve intercorrelated cues to entities in the environment, and must investigate behavioural repertoires relevant to that achievement.

THING CONSTANCY MAKES HIGHER LIFE POSSIBLE

Brunswik held that cognitive structures paralleled whatever was important in the environment. Since distal entities in the world maintain their identities in changing circumstances, they must be perceived by the organism as maintaining those identities: "Thing constancy is nothing but the mechanism that makes the behavioural environment conform to the geographic environment to a considerable extent, especially in its biologically more distal aspects, thus making higher life possible" (Brunswik, 1956a, p. 62). Thus, perceptual constancies acted as "stabilization mechanisms", providing the organism with a stable external world in the face of constantly shifting proximal stimuli (1956a, p. 47f). Brunswik saw a close analogy between perceptual constancy and Piaget's concept of conservation, in that both constancy and conservation provided the developing organism with a picture of things in the world as unchanging in the face of changing appearances (Brunswik, 1944, p. 38; see also Smedslund, 1966). Thus, whereas the experimental psychology of the early 1900s focused on the detection or discrimination of proximate sensory continua, Brunswik devoted much of his early research to the perceptual constancies. We see a person who comes towards us from 20 feet away to 10 feet away as maintaining a constant height even as the retinal image doubles in size. Clearly, the organismic response is more highly correlated with the distal stimulus than with the proximal stimulus, in this case, the retinal image.

It is easy to dismiss perceptual constancy as a curiosity to which a sentence or two is dedicated in introductory psychology textbooks. But constancy is a truly fundamental achievement, one of a high order of complexity. Perceptual constancy is an effect "of extreme biological importance to the organism, since otherwise no orderly and self consistent 'world' of remote manipulable 'independents' could be established" (Brunswik, 1937, p. 229). Perceptual constancy epitomizes distal focusing, since the essence of the constancies is that the same percept is achieved across different situations.

Under normal viewing circumstances, humans have an extraordinary capacity to see things in their actual sizes. In Brunswik's early work, in which he analyzed the data using his "constancy ratio", he typically found constancy ratios for size perception near 1.0, indicating nearly perfect constancy. In a later laboratory study using systematic design, he reported the correlation between actual size and perceived size to be .97, whereas the correlation between bodily size and proximal stimuli was only .10 and that between proximal stimuli and perceptual response was just .26 (1940, p. 72). These results are represented schematically in Figure 2.1.

Even so, size constancy is not perfect. Perception involves a "compromise tendency between distal and proximal focusing" (1952, p. 15). This is a specific instance of the general tendency in Brunswik's thinking, noted above, concerning the role of compromise in behaviour. In size constancy, he considered compromise ". . . as primordial as any theoretical principle in psychology proper is ever apt to become" (1951, p. 215). Following Karl Bühler's "duplicity principle" that perception is determined not only by the focal stimulus but also immediately and inextricably by the context, Brunswik argued that context was not a "variable" that could be separated from the organism, event, or focal stimulus. Instead, context was an inextricable part

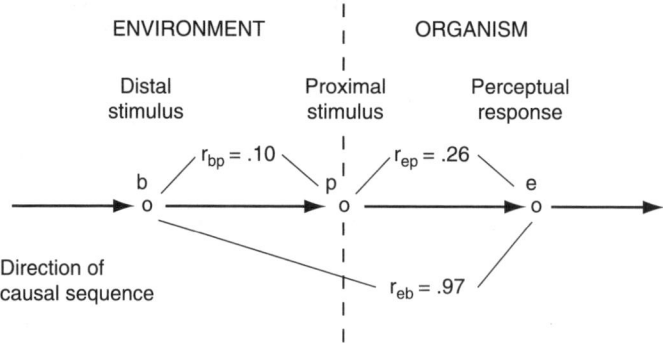

Figure 2.1 Figure 1. Correlations among distal stimuli, proximal stimuli, and perceptual responses. (After Brunswik, 1940.)

of the organism/environment system, part of the unit of analysis, and not a separable causal influence on the unit of analysis.

Further, those errors reflected in constancy ratios less than 1 or correlation coefficients less than 1.0 are better understood as errors *towards* something rather than as *away* from some "correct" value. In discussing his research on value constancy (with coins of varying values, sizes, and numerosities), Brunswik noted that "To those of us who see in functionalism mainly an avenue to the study of veridicality in perception the emphasis is shifted from the negative aspect of value-induced error to the positive aspect of value constancy" (1956a, p. 78). Thus, in a size constancy experiment, error is directed *to* the proximal focus of intention rather than *away* from the distal focus.[2] The ability to know that distal entities maintain their identities despite wildly varying proximal stimuli is a great cognitive achievement. This achievement can be properly investigated only by varying the conditions of experiments so that subjects can exercise and display it, which requires abandoning many uses of the "isolate a factor" method characteristic of current psychological research.

VICARIOUS FUNCTIONING IS OF THE VERY ESSENCE OF BEHAVIOUR

In his 1931 presidential address to the American Psychological Association, Walter S. Hunter, in defining the subject matter of psychology, asserted that "Typically, psychology deals with behaviour which although normally performed by certain bodily structures in certain ways need not be so performed" (Hunter, 1932, p. 18). Brunswik cited Hunter's address several times (e.g., 1952, p. 17; 1957, p. 9) and considered Hunter's "vicarious functioning" as "of the very essence of behaviour" (Brunswik, 1952, p. 92) and "the basic definiens of all behaviour" (1957, p. 9). In effect, the organism can attain perceptual and instrumental goals in a variety of ways. Here, Brunswik found common ground with his colleague and supporter, Edward Chace Tolman, and with his critic, Clark Hull and his concept of habit family hierarchy. Note that if vicarious functioning defines behaviour, then according to the behaviour–research isomorphy principle, psychological research must allow subjects to behave vicariously in attaining their goals. This consideration led Brunswik to the best known of his methodological innovations, representative design.

REPRESENTATIVE DESIGN IN THE STUDY OF DISTAL ACHIEVEMENT

If we wish to make principled generalizations to environments that are tangled webs of partial causes and partial effects, then we must represent the essential features of those environments in our research. If we wish to understand how people achieve accurate perceptions of the sizes of distal objects, we must allow the person the opportunity to use the multiple mediation of multiple proximal cues; we cannot learn how people perceive the sizes of things by presenting one size cue at a time. *Representative* design, not *factorial* design, is, according to Brunswik (1955a), the way to achieve these goals.

Representative design also requires situation sampling. If we wish to make principled generalizations concerning how organisms behave towards stable distal stimuli, the identities of which are mediated by a constant flux of changes in proximal stimuli, then our research must investigate behaviour across situations. Brunswik complained of a "double standard" (1956a, p. 39) in the experimental research of his day. Investigators would assiduously sample subjects from a carefully described population, present a single situation, then generalize over situations. The practice is not uncommon today, even though a two groups *t*-test with 50 subjects per group may have 98 df for populational generalization but 0 df for situational generalization.

The principle of behaviour–research isomorphism is a hard doctrine; so too is representative design. Yet it is required by Brunswik's conception of psychological science: for an experiment to be truly representative, experimental situations must reflect the essential features of the environment. But how does an investigator decide what features are essential? Hochberg pointed out that "representative sampling is no substitute for a theory of what to look for" (1966, p. 369). For Brunswik, psychological research had to begin with an ecological survey (Brunswik & Kamiya, 1953; see also Brehmer, 1984), after which representative environments might be instantiated in the research. Alternatively, an investigator might randomly sample situations in which measures of ecological success on the behaviour of interest could be correlated with measured features of the environment. Sampling situations randomly from the natural environment maintains both the substantive and formal features of the environment. That is, the features of the sample of situations that the subject confronts have about the same means, standard deviations, and cue intercorrelations, i.e., the same causal texture, as the population of situations to which the investigator wants to generalize.

"PSYCHOLOGY ... HAS TO BECOME STATISTICAL THROUGHOUT"

Brunswik argued that "psychology, as long as it wishes to deal with the vitally relevant molar aspects of adjustment and achievement, has to become statistical throughout, instead of being statistical where it seems hopeless to be otherwise ..." (1943, p. 262). In a 1940 paper, *Thing constancy as measured by correlation coefficients*, Brunswik took a radical step, proposing that experimental data should be analyzed by correlating responses with the stimuli. The correlational approach and the very idea of probabilistic laws were heresies to his contemporaries; Hilgard, as noted, expressed his animus for the idea by referring to correlation as an "instrument of the devil". For Brunswik, though, there could be no deterministic laws in psychology. Brunswik's exhortation that psychology become statistical throughout flew in the face of the orthodoxy of his (and, to a large extent, our own) day, the orthodoxy enshrined in Woodworth's 1938 *Experimental psychology*, the "Columbia Bible", which holds that the control of extraneous variables is a *sine qua non* of psychological science.

Note that Brunswik's position that can be contrasted with that of his otherwise sympathetic contemporary, James J. Gibson. Gibson shared Brunswik's belief that an ecological approach was essential for psychology, but disliked Brunswik's emphasis on unreliable cues and on cues that could be discrepant from one another. Instead, Gibson wanted to "concentrate on the theory of those spatial perceptions for which the determinants are supplementary to one another, not discrepant, and for which the stimulus conditions are optimal rather than impoverished or inadequate" (1950, p. 150f). As Kirlik (2001) noted, Gibson was uncomfortable with Brunswik's emphasis on singular objects, rather than field-like arrays, in his constancy experiments. Gibson's deterministic emphasis, suggests Kirlik, is the reason contemporary Gibsonians work on perception and action, whereas Brunswikians concentrate on social judgement and decision making.

Note that to have the data necessary to compute correlation coefficients such as those in Figure 2.1, there had to be multiple instances of the distal stimulus, b, varying in size. This entailed multiple instances of p, the size of the retinal image, and multiple responses, e, the subject's estimates of the size of the distal stimulus. The correlations for the subject's data in Figure 2.1 illustrate the idea that perception is distally focused, since the correlation between the distal stimulus and the perceptual response is far higher than the correlations between distal and proximal stimulus and between proximal stimulus and perceptual response.

BRUNSWIK'S DISTINCTION BETWEEN PERCEPTION AND THINKING

Brunswik sought an objective distinction between "perception" and "explicit reasoning". In a striking demonstration experiment, he had subjects judge size under two conditions. In one, subjects judged the size of an 8 cm object "in the laboratory, with the normal array of distance cues left intact" (1956a, p. 91). This condition represented perception, which he conceived as "uncertainty-geared" and characterized by multiple mediation with its organic multiplicity of factors involving rivalries and compromises (see also Brunswik, 1955b). The other condition represented thinking, which he conceived as "certainty-geared", and was characterized by single channel mediation. Here, subjects were given the numerical information necessary to make a precisely correct calculation of the size of the object. The results are shown in Figure 2.2.

The perceptual judgements fall in a "compact and fairly normal frequency distribution . . . with no particularly outstanding frequency of precisely correct answers" (Brunswik, 1956a, p. 91). The distribution of responses based on explicit reasoning is radically different. "Almost half of all the answers . . . are on-the-dot correct." But look at the distribution of errors! One error (64 cm) is an order of magnitude too high. Another (590 cm) is about two orders of magnitude too high, and a third (4800 cm) is almost three orders of magnitude too high! The secondary mode at 16 cm, which is the value of the retinal equivalent, "demonstrates one of the typical pitfalls of reasoning, namely, the going off in the wrong direction by being right about something else."

Brunswik argued that the multiple mediation characteristic of perception "must be seen as chiefly responsible for the above noted relative infrequency of precision. On the other hand, the organic multiplicity of factors entering the process constitutes an effective safeguard against drastic error" (1956a, p. 92). He went on,

> So long as we accept, with Hunter (1932) and Tolman (1932), vicariousness as the foremost objective criterion of behavioral purposiveness, perception must appear as the more truly behaviour-like function when compared with deductive reasoning with its machine-like, precariously one-tracked, tight-roped modes of procedure. The constantly looming catastrophes of the intellect would be found more often to develop into catastrophes of action were it not for the mellowing effect of the darker, more feeling-like and thus more dramatically convincing primordial layers of cognitive adjustment.
>
> (1956a, p. 93)

Brunswik also alluded in these pages to the "flash-like speed of perceptual responses," which he characterized as "a biologically very valuable feature,

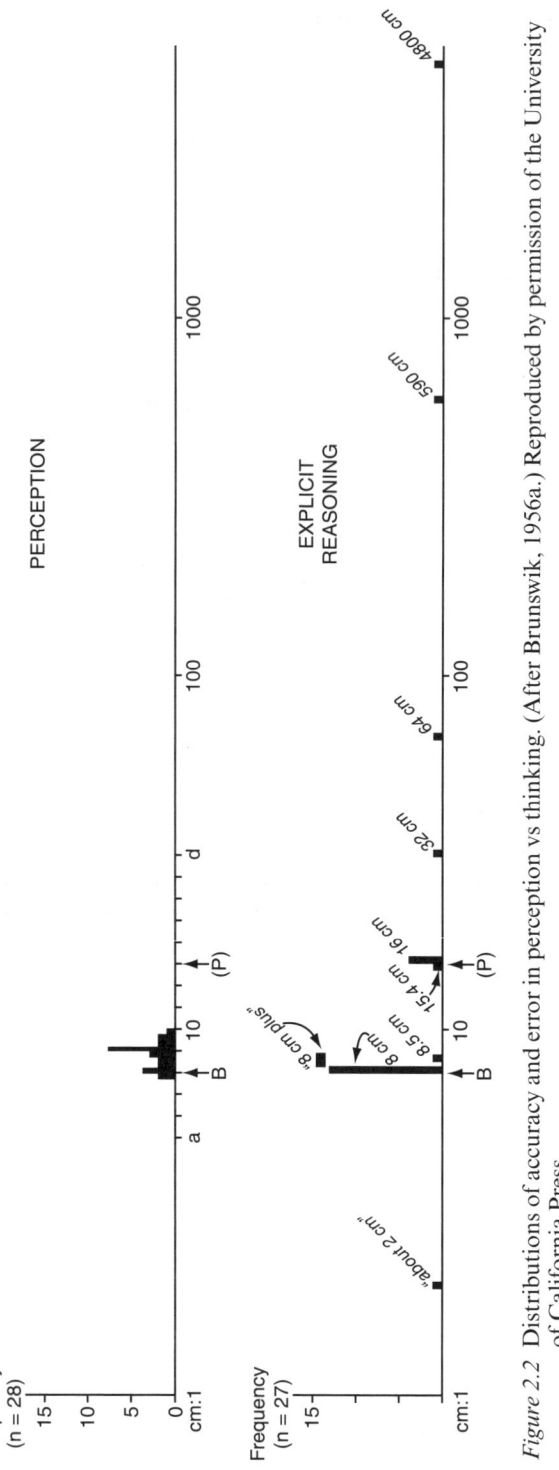

Figure 2.2 Distributions of accuracy and error in perception vs thinking. (After Brunswik, 1956a.) Reproduced by permission of the University of California Press.

especially where ... chances of success depend on quick action" (1956a, p. 92). Brunswik's distinction between perception and thinking illustrates his contention that psychology must become statistical throughout. When it came to showing the distinction objectively, he turned to an unequivocal statistical demonstration, one between the two distributions, not just between the means.

BRUNSWIK'S IDIOGRAPHIC STATISTICAL APPROACH

Brunswik's 1944 monograph exemplifies his call for psychology to be statistical throughout. At randomly selected times, a single subject estimated the size of what in her surroundings was in her focus of attention. "The surroundings ... included scenes on the street and campus, in the laboratory, at the desk, at home, and in the kitchen. An attempt was made to cover recreation and study, daytime and evening (including periods of artificial lighting) under conditions and in proportions representative of the daily routine" (1944, p. 5). Subsequent physical measurements of the distal stimuli provided the values necessary to assess achievement, and the data were analyzed by way of correlation coefficients. The subject achieved extraordinarily high levels of size constancy across a variety of situations, distances, and bodily sizes. Note that this study had multiple situations but a single subject. It involved an almost fully representative design that allowed for vicarious functioning, i.e., multiple mediation of size by a variety of cues, but did not directly assess multiple mediation.

How might Brunswik's idiographic statistical approach be implemented today? Consider an idealized study with a single subject. Assume that an investigator has identified an environment important to the organism's survival and success. That environment varies from situation to situation, hence is a theoretically infinite population of environments. Assume that the investigator has identified 10 features of the environment that are important to a perceptual or instrumental goal of the organism. The investigator has randomly sampled 100 instances of situations from the population of environments to which he or she wishes to generalize and confronted a subject with those 100 samples. The subject has responded to each one. Hence, the investigator has 100 measurements of the 10 features of potential ecological relevance to the organism, of the distal goal to be attained, and of the response to each situation. How can one make sense of the mass of data that results, even with a single subject? That is where the lens model comes into play.

THE LENS MODEL

The lens model is a simple, elegant representation that captures the essential features of representative design, including vicarious mediation, vicarious functioning, the duplicity principle, cue intercorrelation, and the distal focusing of perception. We will present two versions of the lens model – the first, Figure 2.3, from Brunswik (1952) and the second, Figure 2.4, a current version with the typical statistical indices shown.

The initial focal variable is the ecological object of either perception or an overt behavioural act. We describe the lens model in terms of perception. The initial focal variable scatters its effects semi-erratically. The cues, or proximal stimuli, come from the same initial focal variable, so they are intercorrelated with and intersubstitutable one for another, and can provide useful redundancy.

The multiple rays from the initial focal variable thus represent vicarious mediation, the re-collection of those rays into the terminal focal variable represents vicarious functioning. The heavy, wide arc at the top of the figure shows the relation between the organismic response and the ecological goal. That is, it measures achievement. The stray causes and stray effects arrows reflect the idea that the environment is complex and imperfectly knowable, and the feedback arrow indicates that the "lens patterns do not stand in isolation but are apt to reflect back upon the organism in a future state . . . such as when food is followed by satiation and reinforcement of the preceding behaviour . . ." (1952, p. 20).

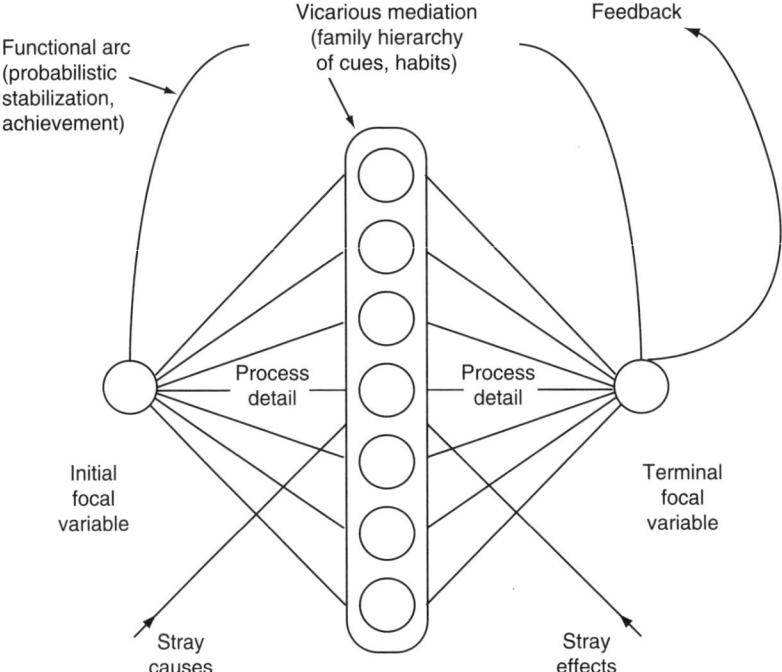

Figure 2.3 The lens model. (After Brunswik, 1952.) Reproduced with the permission of The University of Chicago Press.

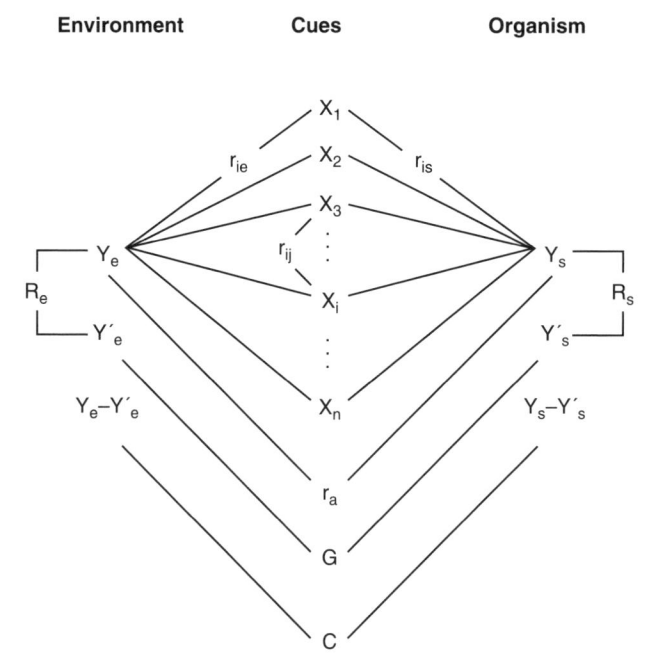

Figure 2.4 A contemporary lens model showing the typical notation for the indices that constitute an idiographic-statistical analysis.

A contemporary lens model, due essentially to the elaboration of Brunswik's system by Kenneth Hammond, is shown in Figure 2.4. The contemporary lens model is the conceptual and statistical framework for what has become "lens model methodology" (Doherty & Kurz, 1996). Consider how the lens model might be used to study diagnostic thinking. Suppose we are interested in assessing the diagnostic skills of a physician. Clearly we cannot make valid generalizations about his or her competence from a single case; there may be something unique about that case. We must observe the physician's behaviour in multiple cases sampled from the domain of cases to which we wish to generalize. Consider a physician who has made 50 diagnostic judgements (Y_s) of the presence or absence of a particular disease on the 50 cases, each case represented by 7 potential symptoms, or cues, (X_i). Subsequently, we ascertain the true ecological criterion value (Y_e) for each case, perhaps via post mortems. The physician's achievement is assessed by r_a, the correlation between the diagnoses and the criterion measures over the 50 cases.

The multiple correlation, R_s, which represents the degree to which the person's judgements are predictable, assuming a linear, additive model, should ideally be 1.0. Typically, linearity and additivity are assumed, though they need not be. The cue utilization coefficients (r_{is}) ought to match the ecological validities (r_{ie}), both of which are zero-order correlations. (The term "ecological validity" was, for Brunswik, a technical term meaning the correlation between a cue and distal stimulus, not the degree to which the experiment might be said to match some unspecified reality.) The G coefficient, the zero-order correlation between the predicted values of the two linear models, can be interpreted as the validity of the person's knowledge of the linear additive components of the environment. The C index, the zero-order correlation between the residuals from the two models, reflects the extent to which unmodelled aspects of the person's knowledge match unmodelled aspects of the environmental side of the lens, and can be partly interpreted as the validity of the person's configural knowledge.

All of the lens model indices are conceptually and statistically interrelated. The degrees to which r_{ie} and r_{is} are appropriate measures of relationship are influenced by whether we have specified the correct function forms and by the real strength of relationship. The degree to which the r_{ie} and r_{is} are ordinally related determines G. R_e and R_s are determined by how predictable the environment and the person are, and by how well we have specified the true model of each. Finally, achievement is influenced by all of the above, as expressed in Tucker's (1964) lens model equation:

$$r_a = R_e * R_s * G + C\,[(1 - R^2_e) * (1 - R^2_s)]^{1/2}.$$

In words, a person's achievement in predicting the world is determined by how predictable the world is, given the available data (R_e), how consistently the person uses those data (R_s), and how well the person understands the relevant causal texture of the environment (G and C).

The statistical indices that derive from the idiographic analyses can be tested for statistical significance. The domain of generalizability would be the physician-subject who had been confronted with the sample of situations, and the generalization would be to the population of situations from which the sample had been drawn. Of course, an investigation can include multiple individuals, the idiographic indices can themselves be subjected to nomothetic analyses, and generalizations across people as well as situations can be made (Schilling & Hogge (2001). Brunswik argued that the study of the environment is propaedeutic to the study of the organism. We might add that the study of the individual is propaedeutic to the study of individuals in general.

The lens model reflects many aspects of Brunswik's thinking, including the focus on achievement, vicarious mediation, and vicarious functioning, and the idea that correlation coefficients can be used to assess not only achievement but also the micro-mediational aspects of the organism's interaction with the environment. Perhaps the aspect of the lens model most directly reflecting the core of Brunswik's thinking is its symmetry, with the two sides, the environment and the person, being mirror images assessed with the same statistical tools.

Can a regression equation be considered a process model? Brunswik was aware of how multiple correlation might be used to explain how multiple cues of low ecological validities (r_{ie}) could be utilized (r_{is}) to arrive at high levels of functional validity (r_a). Referring to Else Frenkel-Brunswik's use of multiple correlation in her analysis of "clinical intuition", he wrote that "Prediction of response even from low utilization cues could be built up by such a procedure. And the same procedure could be used symmetrically for ecological validity so that eventually an understanding of the mechanism of the super ordinate functional achievement arcs ... could be obtained" (Brunswik, 1956a, p. 110). Hammond and Stewart (2001b) interpret this as showing that Brunswik considered multiple regression equations as "simulating" but not "duplicating" the form of cognitive activity that Brunswik termed quasirationality. For an extended discussion, see Doherty and Brehmer (1997).

CONTEMPORARY THEORY IN THE BRUNSWIKIAN TRADITION

Two main theoretical developments have built upon Brunswik's contributions. One is Cognitive Continuum Theory. The other derives from the study of fast and frugal heuristics, a programme referred to as "the adaptive toolbox".

Cognitive continuum theory

There is growing consensus that thinking is not a unitary phenomenon, susceptible of easy definition. There are variations on the theme, but the idea that there is a difference between analytic and intuitive thinking has been advanced by a variety of theorists (Doherty, 2003; Evans & Over, 1996). The long history of the distinction between intuition and analysis is traced by Hammond (1996a), who explored the behavioural markers of intuition vs analysis and the task conditions that elicit each. Hammond's Cognitive Continuum Theory holds that thinking lies on a continuum from intuition at one pole to analysis at the other, with most human cognitive activity being between the two, a type of cognition to which Hammond applied Brunswik's term "quasirationality". Hammond's postulate that most thinking is quasirational, a compromise between analysis and intuition, recalls Brunswik's emphasis on compromise. For an empirical assessment of Cognitive Continuum Theory and a further explication of the concepts of surface and depth see Hammond, Hamm, Grassia, and Pearson (1997).

A related contrast (Cooksey, 1996; Hammond, 1996a) is that between correspondence and coherence criteria for success. Correspondence is the same idea as Brunswik's achievement, r_a in the lens model. It is the functionalist's criterion of success or failure in interactions with the world. Coherence, by contrast, is the degree to which behaviour can be shown to be consistent with some normative model, such as modus tollens, Bayes' theorem, or the conjunction rule in probability theory. Researchers who adopt a coherence criterion are likely, because of the need to have a normative model against which to assess the behaviour studied, to investigate tasks that elicit analytic thinking. Correspondence theorists, especially those of a Brunswikian orientation, are likely to investigate tasks that confront the subject with multiple, probabilistic cues that elicit quasirational thinking. It is with respect to correspondence vs coherence criteria that Brunswikian approaches to research differ most sharply from the mainstream of thinking research.

Fast and frugal heuristics: The adaptive toolbox

Gerd Gigerenzer and his colleagues at the Max Planck Institute, (the Adaptive Behaviour and Cognition, or ABC, group), have developed a broad theoretical programme based on the premise that the organism has a set of simple heuristics that have evolved to achieve success in the environment. A favoured metaphor of the group is Simon's (1967/1996) description of bounded rationality as a pair of scissors, one blade being the cognitive limitations of the person, the other being the structure of the environment. "Minds with limited time, knowledge, and other resources can be nevertheless successful by exploiting structures in the environment" (Gigerenzer & Selten, 2001, p. 2).

In traditional lens model research, the term "intersubstitutability" implies weighting and averaging, typically implemented with multiple regression analysis, a compensatory model that processes all available information (but see Hammond, 1996b). Gigerenzer's fast and frugal models use a more literal meaning of intersubstitutability, assuming that people draw inferences in many circumstances by using a single cue at a time. The ABC approach follows Brunswik in positing that the environment has a structure such that multiple cues are probabilistically related to the distal criterion, and conceptualizes that uncertainty in terms of conditional probabilities. Their research programme has focused, in part, on discovering the cognitive heuristics that people use in dealing with such probabilistic cues, thus extending Simon's "bounded rationality" to an "adaptive rationality". The whole theoretical "adaptive toolbox" of special purpose heuristics proposed by Gigerenzer and his colleagues is accessible in Gigerenzer (2000), Gigerenzer and Todd (1999), and Gigerenzer and Selten (2001). For a brief treatment, see Gigerenzer and Kurz (2001).

CONTEMPORARY EMPIRICAL RESEARCH IN THE BRUNSWIKIAN TRADITION

Empirical investigations in this tradition range over many areas, including applied contexts. We considered as "Brunswikian" studies that included the following characteristics: (1) the subject is confronted with multiple samples from some population of uncertain environments; (2) the judgements made by the subject have a many–one character, i.e., vicarious functioning is possible; (3) the investigator has attempted to model and represent the causal texture of the environment.

Multiple Cue Probability Learning (MCPL)

In an MCPL study, a person learns a set of probabilistic cues (X_i in lens model notation) to some criterion (Y_e), then uses those cues in predicting that criterion. Hence, it is an investigation of how people think when combining cues. MCPL tasks typically involve a subject confronting an environment with several possibly intercorrelated cues with varying relationships to the criterion (i.e., the environment has a causal texture). The number of cues can be manipulated, as can the forms of the functions relating cues and criterion, whether the integration rule is additive or configural, and so forth. A subject is presented several blocks of trials, perhaps 25 per block, with each trial involving the presentation of the cues (X_i), a prediction (Y_s) of the criterion by the subject, then the presentation of the criterion value (Y_e). The latter operation is called outcome feedback. On the first trial of the first block, the subject's prediction is a guess. From then on, the subject takes account of the feedback and can discover, by inductive reasoning, the causal texture of the environment. The subject's performance is described by the lens model equation.

The question of whether subjects could even learn such probabilistic relationships was answered early on. They can. In relatively simple tasks, subjects' regression models at asymptotic performance levels are highly similar to those of the environment. We now know that people bring to the task an *a priori* hierarchy of function forms relating the cues to the criterion, from positive linear, to negative linear, inverse U, and finally U shaped (Brehmer, 1974). People have great difficulty learning if the function forms are nonlinear, but can profit greatly from "cognitive feedback", which might include a description of the nonlinearities and nonadditivies in the environment (Balzer, Doherty, & O'Connor, 1989; Doherty & Balzer, 1988). Empirical research using the MCPL paradigm peaked in the mid 1970s (Holzworth, 2001), and performance in the paradigm is so well understood that it has been used as a tool to study such diverse phenomena as the cognitive effects of psychoactive drugs (Gillis, 2001; Hammond & Joyce, 1975) and cognitive changes with ageing (Chasseigne & Mullet, 2001).

The single system case: Judgement analysis[3]

The MCPL paradigm directly incorporates two systems, the environment and the organism, represented by the two sides of the lens model. Judgement analysis directly involves just one, the organism, typically in the study of expert judgement. A single system paradigm may seem inconsistent with

Brunswik's fundamental approach, but the inconsistency is more apparent than real, because the investigator analyzes and represents the environment prior to the investigation. Judgement analysis entails having the subject judge multiple instances of multiattribute profiles. As in MCPL research, the default analysis is multiple regression. Judgement analysis is done when actual criterion data are unavailable or not of relevance to the research issue at hand (Cooksey, 1996).

For example, Ullman and Doherty (1984) used judgement analysis to investigate the diagnosis of hyperactivity. In Study 1, 11 mental health professionals made diagnostic judgements on 52 seven-cue profiles of boys, some of whom had been referred to the university clinic for assessment for hyperactivity. The individual differences in diagnoses of the same children were so great that the chapter reporting the research was called *Two determinants of the diagnosis of hyperactivity: The child and the clinician.*

Many of the subjects in Study 1 indicated that diagnoses should be based on more information, and listed the additional information they would have wanted. Consequently, Study 2 presented the diagnosticians with 95 hypothetical boys described in terms of 19 attributes. There were 74 subjects: 22 clinical and school psychologists, 15 paediatricians and child psychiatrists, 22 teachers and special educators, and 15 other mental health workers. The individual differences in cue usage and judgemental base rates were even greater than in Study 1, and swamped whatever group differences there may have been. The median interjudge correlation among diagnosticians was only .51. In both studies, the judges tended to use far less information than their subjective reports indicated, a commonly found mismatch between subjectively and statistically assessed measures of cue usage.

The individual differences found in Ullman and Doherty (1984) are commonly observed in judgement research. One source of those differences is that expert judgement is needed precisely in those domains where objective criteria are absent, domains such as psychodiagnosis, social policy formation, and employment interviewing. A second is that investigators tend to be interested in just those situations in which people will be expected to disagree. The evidence suggests, however, that the overwhelming individual differences in judgement research reflect real individual differences, which means that the best way to investigate expert judgement is idiographically. Otherwise, interesting individual differences are hidden in the error terms of group comparisons.

Judgement analysis studies with experts have routinely found that additive models account for virtually all of the predictable variance in the judgement. Configural (or, in ANOVA terminology, interaction) terms have repeatedly been found unnecessary. Part of the reason is statistical, in that the outputs of different models of the same dataset tend to be highly correlated, and parsimony dictates that we adopt the simpler model. A more powerful reason lies again in the selection of cues. Suppose two investigators are interested in investigating the factors influencing the choice of marital partners.

Investigator A uses a single set of multiple cue descriptions of potential mates to be used for both males and females; B uses separate sets of male and female profiles to be judged by female and male subjects, respectively. Serving as a subject for Investigator A, a heterosexual male would give a low rating to all male profiles without even looking at the other attributes. Conversely, this same subject, noting that the profile described a female, would examine the other cues and rate the profile accordingly. This is a configural policy, in that the impacts of the nongender cues depend on the level of the gender cue. To Investigator B, the same subject would appear additive. The difference shows up nicely in the scatterplots of the ratings against the cue values. Again, decisions made in good faith by experimenters who want their research to produce knowledge may lead to knowledge that is true in the laboratory, but leads to a serious overgeneralization beyond it. It is ironic that this occurs in research with Brunswikian origins, given Brunswik's insistence on representative design! Nevertheless, even when people describe their judgement polices as configural, additive models often predict their judgements remarkably well. It appears that people are capable of configural thinking, but claim to be thinking configurally even when additive models suggest otherwise.

Judgement analysis and extensions of the basic logic of the single system design to multiple systems have been used with a wide variety of issues, including the judgement of what police handgun ammunition would be acceptable to the diverse constituencies in Denver, Colorado (Hammond & Adelman, 1976), social perception (Funder, 2001; Gillis & Bernieri, 2001), highway design (Hammond, et al., 1997), medical ethics (Smith & Wigton, 1988), medical judgement (Wigton, 1988, 1996), fairness in faculty salaries (Roose & Doherty, 1978) and in graduate school admissions (Maniscalco, Doherty, & Ullman, 1980), scientists' assessment of the health risk associated with plutonium (Hammond & Marvin, 1981), the potential contribution of mediation to conflict resolution (Holzworth, 1983), self insight (Reilly & Doherty, 1989, 1992), and conflict resolution (Rohrbaugh, 1997). For summaries see Brehmer and Brehmer (1988) and Hammond and Stewart (2001a).

Many applications of judgement analysis involve decision making, e.g., Hammond and Adelman's (1976) "Denver bullet study", which artfully separated facts and values, so it might be useful to point out some of the distinctions between judgement analysis and a procedure known as decision analysis (e.g., von Winterfeldt & Edwards, 1986).

A decision analysis typically calls for a stakeholder to consider at length a single, complex problem, to decompose it into a set of prescribed categories (options for action, states of the world, attributes, probabilities, utilities), then aggregate the resulting values according to an algorithm that maximizes subjective expected utility. The externalization and decomposition of the problem are accomplished by analytical thought processes by the stakeholder, often with the aid of consultants.

In judgement analysis, a stakeholder makes holistic judgements on a large number of instances of the same sort of complex, multiattribute problem dealt with by the decision analyst. The decomposition is made via multivariate statistical analysis on a computer. Thus, judgement analysis is more attuned to the study of the sort of quasirational thinking that is a mix of intuitive and analytic processes, whereas decision analysis is supposed to be just that, analytic.

Probabilistic Mental Models (PMMs)

Gigerenzer and the ABC group focus on the basic cognitive processes involved in multiattribute judgement, We take as an example of their research one application from the adaptive toolbox, the "Take-The-Best" algorithm, which Gigerenzer, Hoffrage, and Kleinbölting (1991) proposed as a model of how people answer general knowledge questions. The task they presented German subjects was the choice of which of two randomly selected German cities was larger. PMM theory assumes that subjects have information available in memory concerning each city, ranging from not even having heard of the city to having a large number of cues of varying cue validities. These cue validities, coded as conditional probabilities rather than correlation coefficients, are analogous to cue utilization coefficients (r_{is}) in the lens model. In judgement analysis, the cues are presented to subjects in a profile format; in Take-The-Best, only the city names are presented; the cues are in memory.

Gigerenzer et al. illustrated the Take-The-Best approach with the question, "Which city has more inhabitants? (a) Heidelberg or (b) Bonn?". The first step in the algorithm is the construction of a local mental model (MM), i.e., whether the subject either knows the answer or has information from which the answer can be deduced with certainty. If a local MM cannot be brought to bear on the question, as is often the case, then a PMM is constructed that uses all relevant information known about the two cities. The cue with the highest cue validity might be as simple as whether the subject recognizes the name of one of the cities but not the other, the so-called recognition cue. Larger cities are mentioned more often in the environment, on the average, than smaller ones. Therefore recognition is correlated with population size, and is an ecologically valid cue. A person who is well adapted to the environment (in this regard) can therefore use recognition as a cue to size, but only if only one city name is recognized. If so, information search in memory is terminated and the decision is made based on this one best cue (hence the name, Take-The-Best). If both names are recognized, then the recognition cue cannot be used, and the cue of the next highest ecological validity is activated.

The cue with the next highest validity, say whether the city has a team in the German soccer league, is then activated and a comparison made. If this cue discriminates between Heidelberg and Bonn, the choice is made and the information search in memory is terminated. But neither of the cities has such a team, so the subject spontaneously drops down the cue hierarchy to the next best cue, and so forth. The postulated process proceeds until a cue discriminates or until a guess must be made. PMM also accounts for confidence in judgement, with the confidence judgement being determined by the cue validity of the discriminating cue.[4]

Social Judgement Theory and PMM may seem starkly different, but they are similar in deep ways. Both are in the Brunswikian tradition of probabilistic functionalism that focuses on cognitive successes in real environments, and for both, vicarious functioning is an essential feature of thinking. Both heed Brunswik's call for "the investigation of environmental or ecological texture".

A RECAPITULATION: BRUNSWIK IN THE 20TH CENTURY

Brunswik was concerned with everyday success in the world, a success mediated by perception and thinking. In his eyes, thinking, as well as perception, was distally focused; both thinking and perception were part of "psychology as a science of objective relations" (Brunswik, 1937). A fundamental idea of Brunswik's was that to understand a cognitive process one must understand the environment confronted by that process. That idea derives from Brunswik's functionalist orientation, and leads in turn to his insistence on probabilism. These ideas had, for Brunswik, inescapable methodological implications, including the principle of behaviour–research isomorphism, representative design, situation sampling, and his idiographic-statistical approach.

NEW DIRECTIONS: BRUNSWIK IN THE 21ST CENTURY

How are Brunswik's influences on the investigation of thinking and reasoning likely to play out in the future? To approach this question we note, first of all, the very wide scope of research now being carried out by those who consider themselves Brunswikians. Thus, studies of team decision making, interpersonal perception, the role of cognitive feedback in medical education, the relation between physicians' diagnostic judgements and treatment choices, and methodological studies modifying and extending representative design; these and many others appeared on the programme of a recent meeting of the Brunswik Society. In addition, Hammond (2000) has recently extended the concept of constancy, so fundamental to our understanding of perception, to play a central role in a theory of stress.

Second, we note that our own research, over the years, has shown a pervasive underlying Brunswikian theme – even when we were not aware of such a relation! Thus, together and separately, we have had a long-standing interest in the nature of scientific thinking. With hindsight, we see now that scientific thinking is a compelling case of distal focus. Scientists study a distal world inaccessible to perception and everyday thinking; their task, in Brunswik's terms, is to determine the relevant proximal cues, to assess their ecological validity, and to develop an explicit "lens model" (that is, a theory).

In science, vicarious functioning becomes deliberate and conscious rather than intuitive, but the processes by which this is achieved rely as much on intuitive thinking (analogies, metaphors, hunches) as on analytical thinking (deductive thinking, explicit mathematical reasoning). Brunswik's approach makes perfect sense as a framework for the study of science. In contrast to Popper (another student of Bühler's), such an approach is not "mere" psychology, of little or no interest to the true understanding of science!

Some of our own research has involved the kind of stripped-down laboratory simulations of scientific thinking introduced by Peter Wason in his 2–4–6 and selection tasks (1960, 1968; see, e.g., Tweney et al., 1980). In other research (e.g., Mynatt, Doherty, & Tweney, 1978) we used a more complex computer-based environment, a so-called artificial universe, asking a small number of subjects to conduct experiments in order to understand its laws. Since we designed the artificial universe, we understood the environmental laws and could assess the strategies used by the subjects as they sought to unravel its complexity by sampling different parts of the environment. Our idiographic descriptions of each subject were based on the portions of the environment that each subject had actually confronted. By matching drawings of the relevant portions with appropriate sections of taped think-aloud protocols, we were able to uncover many of the heuristics used by subjects and to relate this to what Brunswik would call the "achievement" of each subject. In other research, we extended the artificial universe paradigm by using probabilistic scenarios, that is, scenarios that met Brunswik's supposition about the actual universe, that its causal texture was proximally semi-erratic (e.g., O'Connor, Doherty, & Tweney, 1989). And, using traditional experimental designs, we explored the effect of varying base rates, varying semantic context, and varying task instruction on subjects' use of probabilistic information in inference tasks (e.g., Doherty, Chadwick, Garavan, Barr, & Mynatt, 1996).

In recent years, others have used an "artificial universe" approach to bridge the gap between the artificiality of the usual laboratory task and the complexity of real-world scientific thinking. Thus, David Klahr and his students used a programmable robot toy, "Big Trak", in a series of studies in which subjects had to determine experimentally the function of an obscure command within the otherwise simple programming language of the device (Klahr, 2000). Klahr showed that subjects searched separate "Experiment Spaces" and "Hypothesis Spaces" and described characteristic developmental differences in how such searches were carried out. Kevin Dunbar (1995) used a computerized model of gene interaction to conduct similar studies, then extended his inquiries by examining interactions among scientists in four molecular biology laboratories.

The use of "real" science as the object of study also characterizes studies of the work of Michael Faraday, whose extensive laboratory notebooks have long made him a favourite for cognitive historical studies (e.g., Gooding, 1990; Nersessian, 1984). In a series of studies, Tweney (e.g., 1985, 2001) has applied explicit cognitive models, some drawn from our artificial universe work, to the understanding of Faraday's research strategies. His current project, an attempt to understand Faraday's 1856 research on the optical properties of gold, illustrates clearly some of the central features of Brunswik's system (Tweney, 2002). Thus, in the case of the research on the optical properties of gold, over 600 of Faraday's microscope slides survive for study; these are "made objects" that can be related to Faraday's extensive laboratory notes. Faraday examined these richly complex slides in his effort to understand the underlying causal structure of the environment, much as a subject in a contemporary MCPL study examines numbers of multi-cue profiles to understand the underlying functional relations. We, too, can examine Faraday's slides and his reactions to them in our effort to understand Faraday's thought processes. And, since the artifacts themselves can be replicated, we can even determine something of the tacit knowledge that went into Faraday's construction of his "epistemic artifacts". Faraday himself was an agent in the making of these objects, and they provide insight into the way in which Faraday "danced" with nature; sometimes leading, sometimes following – always making, arranging, remaking, manipulating. Brunswik believed that to understand a cognitive process one must understand the environment confronted by that process; Faraday, in effect, constructed his environment, and the case provides an opportunity to see a side of scientific thinking that is usually too evanescent for examination.

Faraday sought to achieve understanding by methods that, if he were right, would together reveal a distal reality. The methods were partially intersubstitutable one for the other, and he thus self-consciously employed a version of vicarious functioning, much as Brunswik said we do in everyday life, a productive, creative admixture of thinking and perception. For Brunswik, the methods of science were an extension of the same psychological processes that underlie perception and judgement. The intensive study of Faraday's epistemic environment, and the reconstruction of his behaviour within that environment, promise to show just how such extension works.

CONCLUSION

At the beginning of this chapter, we noted the general lack of acceptance of Brunswik's views by his contemporaries; they respected his views but they did not, in the end, accept them. Even so, his ideas can now be seen to have permeated much of cognitive psychology in ways that suggest he was, in actuality, ahead of his time. And, of course, his death in 1955 was tragically premature, and we do not know how he would have responded to the seminal events that occurred just after his death. What might he have made of the cognitive revolution? As early as 1952, he had noted with approval the first stirrings of information theory and cybernetics. The information metrics developed by Shannon and applied by Miller and others to cognitive and perceptual questions were attempts to come to grips with uncertainty in the environment; and those metrics rely on the properties of statistical assemblages of signal and noise – in Brunswik's terms, they attempted to capture the causal texture of a semi-erratic environment. Brunswik, we suspect, would have been pleased to see the use made of such concepts as Simon's "bounded rationality" by later investigators (Simon, 1967/1996), or the way in which Bruner, Goodnow, and Austin (1956) used his notion of partially valid cues to extend their work on concept acquisition and utilization.

In the end, Brunswik remains a haunting figure whose work should nag at the conscience of psychology. Many of his ideas have become commonplace in cognitive psychology: tradeoffs between intuitive and analytic thinking, the need to empirically establish the generality of laboratory results, vicarious functioning, the importance of distinguishing between the proximal and the distal – all of these are now taken for granted by most cognitivists. Brunswik's writings are unique, however, in clarifying just how large a revolution of methodology will be required to take full advantage of these insights; the hard doctrines of behaviour–research isomorphism and representative design constitute still a moral imperative.

ACKNOWLEDGEMENTS

The authors would like to thank Kenneth Hammond, James Holzworth, Scott Highhouse, and Tom Stewart for comments on an earlier draft of this chapter.

NOTES

1 This is a quite different meaning of the term "constancy" than when the same word is used to denote perceptual constancy (Brunswik, 1944, p. 12f).
2 This conception of error presages much of the dispute in recent judgement and decision research (e.g., Gigerenzer, 1996; Kahneman & Tversky, 1996). In a prescient comment, Brunswik noted that "in the study of the limitations of ecological validity the more casuistic study of exceptions to the rule comes first; among them, those exceptions that can be produced artificially have exerted particular attraction . . ." (1957, p. 16).
3 A closely related term is "policy capturing". We reserve the term judgement analysis to refer to situations in which the investigator has carefully investigated and represented the structure of the environment.
4 Incidentally, Bonn has about twice the population of Heidelberg.

REFERENCES

Balzer, W. K., Doherty, M. E., & O'Connor, R. (1989). Effects of cognitive feedback on performance. *Psychological Bulletin*, *106*, 410–433.

Björkman, M. (2001). Probability learning or partial reinforcement? In K. R. Hammond & T. R. Stewart (Eds.), *The essential Brunswik: Beginnings, explications, applications*. (pp. 167–170). New York: Oxford University Press.

Brehmer, B. (1974). Hypotheses about relations between scaled variables in the learning of probabilistic inference tasks. *Organizational Behaviour and Human Performance*, *11*, 1–27.

Brehmer, B. (1984). Brunswikian psychology for the 1990s. In K. M. J. Lagerspetz & P. Niemi (Eds.), *Psychology in the 1990s* (pp. 383–398). Amsterdam: North-Holland Elsevier.

Brehmer, A., & Brehmer, B. (1988). What have we learned about human judgment from thirty years of policy capturing? In B. Brehmer & C. R. B. Joyce (Eds.), *Human judgment: The SJT view* (pp. 75–114). Amsterdam: North-Holland Elsevier.

Bruner, J. S., Goodnow, J. J., & Austin, G. A. (1956). *A study of thinking*. New York: John Wiley & Sons.

Brunswik, E. (1937). Psychology as a science of objective relations. *Philosophy of Science*, *4*, 227–260.

Brunswik, E. (1939). Probability as a determiner of rat behaviour. *Journal of Experimental Psychology*, *25*, 175–197.

Brunswik, E. (1940). Thing constancy as measured by correlation coefficients. *Psychological Review*, *47*, 69–78.

Brunswik, E. (1943). Organismic achievement and environmental probability. *Psychological Review*, *50*, 255–272.

Brunswik, E. (1944). Distal focusing of perception: Size constancy in a representative sample of situations. *Psychological Monographs*, Whole No. 254.

Brunswik, E. (1951). Note on Hammond's analogy between "relativity and representativeness". *Philosophy of Science*, *18*, 212–217.

Brunswik, E. (1952). *The conceptual framework of psychology*. Chicago: University of Chicago Press.

Brunswik, E. (1955a). Representative design and probabilistic theory in a functional psychology. *Psychological Review*, *62*, 193–217.

Brunswik, E. (1955b). "Ratiomorphic" models of perception and thinking. *Acta Psychologica*, *11*, 108–109.

Brunswik, E. (1956a). *Perception and the representative design of psychological experiments*. Berkeley, CA: University of California Press.

Brunswik, E. (1956b). Historical and thematic relations of psychology to other sciences. *Scientific Monthly*, *83*, 151–161.

Brunswik, E. (1957). Scope and aspects of the cognitive problem. In H. Gruber, R. Jessor, & K. R. Hammond (Eds.), *Contemporary approaches to cognition* (pp. 5–31). Cambridge, MA: Harvard University Press.

Brunswik, E., & Herma, H. (1951). Probability learning of perceptual cues in the establishment of a weight illusion. *Journal of Experimental Psychology*, *41*, 281–290.

Brunswik, E., & Kamiya, J. (1953). Ecological cue-validity of "proximity" and of other Gestalt factors. *American Journal of Psychology*, *66*, 20–32.

Bühler, K. (1930). *The mental development of the child* [trans. by O. Oeser from the 1929, 5th German edition]. New York: Harcourt Brace & Co.

Bühler, K. (1934/1990). *Theory of language: The representational function of language* [trans. by D.F. Goodwin]. Amsterdam: Benjamins.

Chasseigne, G., & Mullet, E. (2001). Probabilistic functioning and cognitive aging. In K. R. Hammond & T. R. Stewart (Eds.), *The essential Brunswik: Beginnings, explications, applications* (pp. 423–426). New York: Oxford University Press.

Cooksey, R. W. (1996). *Judgment analysis: Theory, methods and applications*. New York: Academic Press.

Danziger, K. (1990). *Constructing the subject: Historical origins of psychological research*. Cambridge: Cambridge University Press.

Doherty, M. E. (2001). Demonstrations for learning psychologists: "While God may not gamble, animals and humans do". In K. R. Hammond & T. R. Stewart (Eds.), *The essential Brunswik: Beginnings, explications, applications* (pp. 192–195). New York: Oxford University Press.

Doherty, M. E. (2003). Optimists, pessimists, and realists. In S. Schneider & J. Shanteau (Eds.), *Emerging perspectives on judgment and decision making research* (pp. 643–679). New York: Oxford University Press.

Doherty, M. E., & Balzer, W. K. (1988). Cognitive feedback. In B. Brehmer & C. R. B. Joyce (Eds.), *Human judgment: The SJT view* (pp. 163–197). Amsterdam: North-Holland Elsevier.

Doherty, M. E., & Brehmer, B. (1997). The paramorphic representation of human judgment: A 30 year retrospective. In W. M. Goldstein & R. M. Hogarth (Eds.), *Judgment and decision making: Currents, connections and controversies* (pp. 537–551). Cambridge: Cambridge University Press.

Doherty, M. E., Chadwick, R., Garavan, H., Barr, D., & Mynatt, C. R. (1996). On people's understanding of the diagnostic implications of probabilistic data. *Memory & Cognition, 24*, 644–654.

Doherty, M. E., & Kurz, E. M. (1996). Social judgement theory. *Thinking and reasoning, 2*, 109–140.

Dunbar, K. (1995). How scientists really reason: Scientific reasoning in real-world laboratories. In R. J. Sternberg & J. Davidson (Eds.), *Mechanisms of insight* (pp. 365–396). Cambridge, MA: MIT Press.

Evans, J. St. B. T., & Over, D. E. (1996). *Rationality and reasoning*. Hove, UK: Psychology Press.

Funder, D. C. (2001). The realistic accuracy model and Brunswik's approach to social judgment. In K. R. Hammond & T. R. Stewart (Eds.), *The essential Brunswik: Beginnings, explications, applications* (pp. 365–369). New York: Oxford University Press.

Gibson, J. J. (1950). *The perception of the visual world*. Boston: Houghton Mifflin.

Gigerenzer, G. (1996). On narrow norms and vague heuristics: A reply to Kahneman and Tversky. *Psychological Review, 103*, 592–596.

Gigerenzer, G. (2000). *Adaptive thinking: Rationality in the real world*. New York: Oxford University Press.

Gigerenzer, G., Hoffrage, U., & Kleinbölting, H. (1991). Probabilistic mental models: A Brunswikian theory of confidence. *Psychological Review, 98*, 506–528.

Gigerenzer, G., & Kurz, E. M. (2001). Vicarious functioning reconsidered: A fast and frugal lens model. In K. R. Hammond & T. R. Stewart (Eds.), *The essential*

Brunswik: Beginnings, explications, applications (pp. 342–347). New York: Oxford University Press.

Gigerenzer, G., & Murray, D. J. (1987). *Cognition as intuitive statistics*. Hillsdale, NJ: Lawrence Erlbaum Associates Inc.

Gigerenzer, G., & Selten, R. (Eds.). (2001). *Bounded rationality: The adaptive toolbox*. Cambridge, MA: The MIT Press.

Gigerenzer, G., & Todd, P. M. (1999). Fast and frugal heuristics: The adaptive toolbox. In G. Gigerenzer, P. M. Todd, & The ABC Research Group (Eds.), *Simple heuristics that make us smart* (pp. 3–34). New York: Oxford University Press.

Gillis, J. (2001). Understanding the effects of psychiatric drugs on social judgment. In K. R. Hammond & T. R. Stewart (Eds.), *The essential Brunswik: Beginnings, explications, applications* (pp. 393–400). New York: Oxford University Press.

Gillis, J. S., & Bernieri, F. (2001). The perception and judgment of rapport. In K. R. Hammond & T. R. Stewart (Eds.), *The essential Brunswik: Beginnings, explications, applications* (pp. 380–384). New York: Oxford University Press.

Gooding, D. (1990). *Experiment and the making of meaning: Human agency in scientific observation and experiment*. Dordrecht: Kluwer Academic Publishers.

Hammond, K. R. (Ed.). (1966). *The psychology of Egon Brunswik*. New York: Holt, Rinehart & Winston.

Hammond, K. R. (1996a). *Human judgment and social policy: Irreducible uncertainty, inevitable error, unavoidable injustice*. New York: Oxford University Press.

Hammond, K. R. (1996b). Upon reflection. *Thinking and Reasoning, 2*, 239–248.

Hammond, K. R. (2000). *Judgements under stress*. New York: Oxford.

Hammond, K. R., & Adelman, L. (1976). Science, values, and human judgment. *Science, 194*, 389–396.

Hammond, K. R., Hamm, R. M., Grassia, J., & Pearson, T. (1997). Direct comparison of the efficacy of intuitive and analytical cognition in expert judgment. In W. M. Goldstein & R. M. Hogarth (Eds.), *Research on judgment and decision making: Currents, connections and controversies* (pp. 144–180). Cambridge: Cambridge University Press.

Hammond, K. R., & Joyce, C. R. B. (Eds.). (1975). *Psychoactive drugs and social judgment: Theory and research*. New York: Wiley.

Hammond, K. R., & Marvin, B. A. (1981). *Report to the Rocky Flats Monitoring Committee concerning scientists' judgements of cancer risk* (Rep. No. 232). Boulder, CO: University of Colorado, Center for Research on Judgment and Policy.

Hammond, K. R., & Stewart, T. R. (Eds.). (2001a). *The essential Brunswik: Beginnings, explications, applications*. New York: Oxford University Press.

Hammond, K. R., & Stewart, T. R. (2001b). Introduction. In K. R. Hammond & T. R. Stewart (Eds.), *The essential Brunswik: Beginnings, explications, applications* (pp. 3–11). New York: Oxford University Press.

Hilgard, E. R. (1955). Discussion of probabilistic functionalism. *Psychological Review, 62*, 226–228.

Hochberg, J. (1966). Representative sampling and the purposes of perceptual research: Pictures of the world and the world of pictures. In K. R. Hammond (Ed.), *The psychology of Egon Brunswik* (pp. 361–381). New York: Holt, Rinehart & Winston.

Holzworth, R. J. (1983). Intervention in a cognitive conflict. *Organizational Behaviour and Human Performance, 32*, 216–231.

Holzworth, R. J. (2001). Multiple cue probability learning. In K. R. Hammond & T.

R. Stewart (Eds.), *The essential Brunswik: Beginnings, explications, applications* (pp. 348–350). New York: Oxford University Press.

Humphrey, G. (1951). *Thinking: An introduction to its experimental psychology.* London: Methuen & Co.

Hunter, W. S. (1932). The psychological study of behaviour. *Psychological Review, 39,* 1–24.

Kahneman, D., & Tversky, A. (1996). On the reality of cognitive illusions. *Psychological Review, 103,* 582–591.

Kirlik, A. (2001). Human factors. In K. R. Hammond & T. R. Stewart (Eds.), *The essential Brunswik: Beginnings, explications, applications* (pp. 400–403). New York: Oxford University Press.

Klahr, D. (2000). *Exploring science: The cognition and development of discovery processes.* Cambridge, MA: MIT Press.

Kurz, E. M. (1996). Marginalizing discovery: Karl Popper's intellectual roots in psychology, Or, How the study of discovery was banned from science studies. *Creativity Research Journal, 9,* 173–187.

Kurz, E. M., & Tweney, R. D. (1997). The heretical psychology of Egon Brunswik. In W. G. Bringmann, H. E. Lück, R. Miller, & C. E. Early (Eds.), *A pictorial history of psychology* (pp. 221–232). Carol Stream, IL: Quintessence Publishing.

Kusch, M. (1995). *Psychologism: A case study in the sociology of philosophical knowledge.* London: Routledge.

Leary, D. E. (1987). From act psychology to probabilistic functionalism: The place of Egon Brunswik in the history of psychology. In M. G. Ash & W. R. Woodward (Eds.), *Psychology in twentieth-century thought and society* (pp. 115–142). Cambridge: Cambridge University Press.

Maniscalco, C. I., Doherty, M. E., & Ullman, D. G. (1980). Assessing discrimination: An application of social judgment technology. *Journal of Applied Psychology, 65,* 284–288.

Mynatt, C. R., Doherty, M. E., & Tweney, R. D. (1978). Consequences of confirmation and disconfirmation in a simulated research environment. *Quarterly Journal of Experimental Psychology, 30,* 395–406.

Nersessian, N. (1984). *Faraday to Einstein: Constructing meaning in scientific theories.* Dordrecht: Nijhoff.

O'Connor, R., Doherty, M. E., & Tweney, R. D. (1989). The effects of system failure error on predictions. *Organizational Behaviour and Human Decision Processes, 44,* 1–11.

Popper, K. (1974). Autobiography of Karl Popper. In P. A. Schilpp (Ed.), *The philosophy of Karl Popper* (Vol. 1, pp. 2–181). LaSalle, IL: Open Court.

Reilly, B. A., & Doherty, M. E. (1989). A note on the assessment of self-insight in judgment research. *Organizational Behaviour and Human Decision Processes, 44,* 123–131.

Reilly, B. A., & Doherty, M. E. (1992). The assessment of self-insight in judgment policies. *Organizational Behaviour and Human Decision Processes, 53,* 285–309.

Rohrbaugh, J. (1997). Beyond the triple system case. In K. R. Fischer & F. Stadler (Eds.), *Wahrnemung und Gegenstandswelt: Zum Lebenswerk von Egon Brunswik (1903–1955)* (pp. 107–120). Vienna: Springer.

Roose, J. E., & Doherty, M. E. (1978). A social judgment theoretic approach to sex discrimination in faculty salaries. *Organizational Behaviour and Human Performance, 22,* 193–215.

Rucci, A. J., & Tweney, R. D. (1980). Analysis of variance and the "second discipline" of scientific psychology: A historical account. *Psychological Bulletin, 87*, 166–184.

Schilling, S. G., & Hogge, J. H. (2001). Hierarchical linear models for the nomothetic aggregation of idiographic descriptions of judgment. In K. R. Hammond & T. R. Stewart (Eds.), *The essential Brunswik: Beginnings, explications, applications* (pp. 332–341). New York: Oxford University Press.

Simon, H. A. (1969/1996). *The sciences of the artificial.* (3rd Ed.). Cambridge, MA: MIT Press.

Smedslund, J. (1966). Constancy and conservation: A comparison of the systems of Brunswik and Piaget. In K. R. Hammond (Ed.), *The psychology of Egon Brunswik* (pp. 382–404). New York: Holt, Rinehart & Winston.

Smith, D. G., & Wigton, R. S. (1988). Research in medical ethics: The role of social judgment theory. In B. Brehmer & C. R. B. Joyce (Eds.), *Human judgment: The SJT view* (pp. 427–442). Amsterdam: North-Holland Elsevier.

Tolman, E. C. (1932). *Purposive behaviour in animals and men.* New York: Appleton.

Tolman, E. C., & Brunswik, E. (1935). The organism and the causal texture of the environment. *Psychological Review, 42*, 43–77.

Tucker, L. R. (1964). A suggested alternative formulation in the developments by Hursch, Hammond, and Hursch and by Hammond, Hursch and Todd. *Psychological Review, 71*, 528–530.

Tweney, R. D. (1985). Faraday's discovery of induction: A cognitive approach. In D. Gooding & F. A. J. L. James (Eds.), *Faraday rediscovered: Essays on the life and work of Michael Faraday, 1791–1867* (pp.189–210). New York: Stockton Press/ London: Macmillan. [Reprinted, 1990, American Institute of Physics.]

Tweney, R. D. (2001). Scientific thinking: A cognitive-historical approach. In K. Crowley, C. D. Schunn, & T. Okada (Eds.) *Designing for Science: Implications from everyday, classroom, and professional settings* (pp. 141–173). Mahwah, NJ: Lawrence Erlbaum Associates Inc.

Tweney, R. D. (2002). Epistemic artifacts: Michael Faraday's search for the optical effects of gold. In L. Magnani & N. J. Nersessian (Eds.), *Model-based reasoning: Science, technology, values.* New York: Kluwer Academic/Plenum.

Tweney, R. D., Doherty, M. E., Worner, W. J., Pliske, D. B., Mynatt, C. R., Gross, K. A. et al. (1980). Strategies of rule discovery in an inference task. *Quarterly Journal of Experimental Psychology, 32*, 109–133.

Ullman, D. G., & Doherty, M. E. (1984). Two determinants of the diagnosis of hyperactivity: The child and the clinician. In M. Wolraich & D. K. Routh (Eds.), *Advances in developmental and behavioral pediatrics Vol. 5.* (pp. 167–219). Greenwich, CT: JAI Press.

von Winterfeldt, D., & Edwards, W. (1986). *Decision analysis and behavioral research.* Cambridge: Cambridge University Press.

Wason, P. C. (1960). On the failure to eliminate hypotheses in a conceptual task. *Quarterly Journal of Experimental Psychology, 12*, 129–140.

Wason, P. C. (1968). Reasoning about a rule. *Quarterly Journal of Experimental Psychology, 20*, 273–281.

Wigton, R. S. (1988). Applications of judgment analysis and cognitive feedback to medicine. In B. Brehmer & C. R. B. Joyce (Eds.), *Human judgment: The SJT view* (pp. 227–245). Amsterdam: North-Holland Elsevier.

Wigton, R. S. (1996). Social judgement theory and medical judgment. *Thinking and Reasoning, 2*, 175–190.

Woodworth, R. S. (1938). *Experimental psychology*. New York: Holt.

3 Rationality, rational analysis, and human reasoning

Nick Chater and Mike Oaksford

The idea of rationality is central to the explanation of human behaviour. Only on the assumption that people are at least typically rational can we attribute beliefs, motives, and desires to people – the assumption of rationality provides the "glue" that holds disparate beliefs, desires, and actions together in a coherent system. Imagine explaining a routine event, such a motorist slowing down when approaching a pedestrian crossing. The motorist, we might suggest, noticed that some people were near the crossing, believed that they were about to cross, wanted to avoid colliding with them, believed that collision might occur if the car continued at its current speed, and so on. The goal of such explanation is to provide a *rationale* for a person's behaviour, explaining how they understood and acted upon the world, from their point of view. But constructing a rationale for a piece of behaviour will only provide an explanation for it if we assume that people are sensitive to such rationales; that is, unless people exhibit rationality.

This style of explanation is, of course, ubiquitous in our everyday explanation of the thoughts and behaviour of ourselves and others – and it is embodied not merely in everyday discourse, but is also fundamental to explanation in the humanities and in literature. In attempting to *interpret* and *understand* other people's decisions and utterances, we are attempting to provide rationales for those decisions and utterances. The historian explaining the actions of a military general, the scholar interpreting a Biblical text, and the novelist conjuring up a compelling character all rely, fundamentally, on the assumption that people are, by and large, rational (Davidson, 1984; Quine, 1960).

The rationales that we provide for each other's behaviour are typically extremely subtle and elaborate, but at the same time incomplete and unsystematic. For example, in explaining why the general made a particular military decision, the historian may spell out some of the general's relevant beliefs and desires, e.g., beliefs concerning the location of enemy forces, the desire to be viewed as a hero by future generations. But the explanation will inevitably be partial. The historian will leave out beliefs such as the background assumptions that future generations will admire victory more than defeat, that to weaken enemy forces, shelling should be directed at them rather than at the surrounding countryside, that shells travel in the direction of fire and explode on impact, that explosions are injurious to those nearby, that people fight less well when deprived of supplies, and so on. To reconstruct a rationale for the general's actions in full detail would appear to be an intractable task. This is because explaining the basis for any aspect of the general's thought appears to draw on still further beliefs and desires. Thus, the general's beliefs about the motion of shells will depend on endless beliefs about naïve physics, about the approximate weight and size of a shell (e.g., that shells are denser than balloons), about how shells are fired and so on. Understanding how shells are fired leads on to understanding the properties of the gun, the properties of gunpowder, and so on indefinitely. The historian need not, of course, bother to enunciate this apparently endless store of knowledge in order to communicate with the reader – because this indefinitely large store of knowledge can be assumed to be *common knowledge* between historian and reader. But the fact that we can and do rely on common knowledge to underpin everyday explanation of human behaviour can obscure just how partial and incomplete everyday explanations are.

In this informal, and somewhat ill-defined everyday sense, most of us, most of the time, are remarkably rational. In daily life, of course, we tend to focus on occasions when reasoning or decision making breaks down. But our failures of reasoning are only salient because they occur against the background of rational thought and behaviour that is achieved with such little apparent effort that we are inclined to take it for granted. Rather than thinking of our patterns of everyday thought and action as exhibiting rationality, we tend to think of them as just plain common sense – with the implicit assumption that common sense must be a simple thing indeed. People may not think of themselves as exhibiting high levels of rationality – instead, we think of each other as "intelligent", performing "appropriate" actions, being "reasonable", or making "sensible" decisions. But these labels refer to human abilities to make the right decisions, or to say or think the right thing in complex, real-world situations – in short, they are labels for everyday rationality.

Indeed, so much do we tend to take the rationality of commonsense thought for granted, that realizing that commonsense reasoning is immensely difficult, and hence our everyday rationality is thereby immensely impressive, has been a surprising *discovery*, and a discovery made only in the latter part of the twentieth century. The discovery emerged from the project of attempting to formalize everyday knowledge and reasoning in artificial intelligence, where initially high hopes that commonsense knowledge could readily be formalized were replaced by increasing desperation at the impossible difficulty of the project. The nest of difficulties referred to under the "frame problem" (see, e.g., Pylyshyn, 1987), and the problem that each aspect of knowledge appears inextricably entangled with the rest (e.g., Fodor, 1983) so that commonsense does not seem to break down into manageable "packets" (whether schemas, scripts, or frames, Minsky, 1977; Schank & Abelson, 1977), and the deep problems of defeasible, or non-monotonic reasoning (e.g., McDermott, 1987), brought the project of formalizing commonsense effectively to a standstill. So the discovery is now made – it is now clear that everyday, commonsense reasoning is remarkably, but mysteriously, successful in dealing with an immensely complex and changeable world and that no existing artificial computational system begins to approach the level of human performance.

Let us contrast this informal, everyday sense of rationality concerning people's ability to think and act in the real world, with a concept of rationality originating not from human behaviour, but from mathematical theories of good reasoning. These mathematical theories represent one of the most important achievements of modern thought: Logical calculi formalize aspects of deductive reasoning; axiomatic probability formalizes probabilistic reasoning; a variety of statistical principles, from sampling theory (Fisher, 1922, 1925/1970) to Neyman–Pearson statistics (Neyman, 1950), to Bayesian statistics (Keynes, 1921; Lindley, 1971), aim to formalize the process of relating hypotheses to data; utility and decision theory attempt to characterize rational preferences and rational choice between actions under uncertainty; game theory and its variants (e.g., Harsanyi & Selten, 1988; von Neumann & Morgenstern, 1944) aim to provide a precise framework for determining the rational course of action in situations in which the reasoning of other agents must be taken into account. According to these calculi, rationality is defined, in the first instance, in terms of conformity with specific formal principles, rather than in terms of successful behaviour in the everyday world.

How are the general principles of formal rationality related to specific examples of rational thought and action described by everyday rationality? This question, in various guises, has been widely discussed – in this chapter we shall outline a particular conception of the relation between these two notions, focusing on a particular style of explanation in the behavioural sciences, *rational analysis* (Anderson, 1990). We will argue that rational analysis provides an attractive account of the relationship between everyday and formal rationality, which has implications for both. Moreover, this view of rationality leads to a re-evaluation of the implications of data from psychological experiments which appear to undermine human rationality. A wide range of empirical results in the psychology of reasoning have been taken to cast doubt on human rationality, because people appear to persistently make elementary logical blunders. We show that, when the tasks people are given are viewed in terms of probability, rather than logic, people's responses can be seen as rational.

The discussion falls into four main parts. First, we discuss formal and everyday rationality, and various possible relationships between them. Second, we describe the programme of rational analysis as a mode of explanation of mind and behaviour, which views everyday rationality as underpinned by formal rationality. Third, we apply rational analysis to re-evaluating experimental data in the psychology of reasoning, from a probabilistic standpoint. Finally, we consider implications, problems, and prospects for project of building a more adequate psychology of reasoning.

RELATIONS BETWEEN FORMAL AND EVERYDAY RATIONALITY

Formal rationality concerns formal principles of good reasoning – the mathematical laws of logic, probability, or decision theory. At an intuitive level, these principles seem distant from the domain of everyday rationality – how people think and act in daily life. Rarely, in daily life, do we accuse one another of violating the laws of logic or probability theory, or praise each other for obeying them. Moreover, when people are given reasoning problems that explicitly require use of these formal principles, their performance appears to be remarkably poor, a point we touched on above. People appear to persistently fall for logical blunders (Evans, Newstead, & Byrne, 1993) and probabilistic fallacies (e.g., Tversky & Kahneman, 1974), and to make inconsistent decisions (Kahneman, Slovic, & Tversky, 1982; Tversky & Kahneman, 1986). Indeed, the concepts of logic, probability, and the like do not appear to mesh naturally with our everyday reasoning strategies: these notions took centuries of intense intellectual effort to construct, and present a tough challenge for each generation of students.

We therefore face a stark contrast: the astonishing fluency and success of everyday reasoning and decision making, exhibiting remarkable levels of everyday rationality; and our faltering and confused grasp of the principles of formal rationality. What are we to conclude from this contrast? Let us briefly consider, in caricature, some of the most important possibilities, which have been influential in the literature in philosophy, psychology, and the behavioural sciences.

The primacy of everyday rationality

This viewpoint takes everyday rationality as fundamental, and dismisses the apparent mismatch between human reasoning and the formal principles of logic and probability theory as so much the worse for these formal theories.

This standpoint appears to gain credence from historical considerations – formal rational theories such as probability and logic emerged as attempts to systematize human rational intuitions, rooted in everyday contexts. But the resulting theories appear to go beyond, and even clash with, human rational intuitions – at least if empirical data that appear to reveal blunders in human reasoning are taken at face value.

To the extent that such clashes occur, the advocates of the primacy of everyday rationality argue that the formal theories should be rejected as inadequate systematizations of human rational intuitions, rather than condemning the intuitions under study as incoherent. It might, of course, be granted that a certain measure of tension may be allowed between the goal of constructing a satisfyingly concise formalization of intuitions and the goal of capturing every last intuition successfully, rather as, in linguistic theory, complex centre-embedded constructions are held to be grammatical (e.g., "the fish the man the dog bit ate swam"), even though most people would reject them as ill-formed gibberish. But the dissonance between formal rationality and everyday reasoning appears to be much more profound than this. As we have argued, fluent and effective reasoning in everyday situations runs alongside halting and flawed performance on the most elementary formal reasoning problems.

The primacy of everyday rationality is implicit in an important challenge to decision theory by the mathematician Allais (1953). Allais outlines his famous "paradox", which shows a sharp divergence between people's rational intuitions and the dictates of decision theory. One version of the paradox is as follows. Consider the following pair of lotteries, each involving 100 tickets. Which would you prefer to play?

A.

10 tickets worth £1,000,000
90 tickets worth £0

B.

1 ticket worth £5,000,000
8 tickets worth £1,000,000
91 tickets worth £0

Now consider which you would prefer to play of lotteries C and D:

C.

100 tickets worth £1,000,000

D.

1 ticket worth £5,000,000
98 tickets worth £1,000,000
1 ticket worth £0

Most of us prefer lottery B to lottery A – the slight reduction in the probability of becoming a millionaire is offset by the possibility of the really large prize. But most of us also prefer lottery C to lottery D – we don't think it is worth losing what would otherwise be a certain £1,000,000, just for the possibility of winning £5,000,000. This *combination* of responses, although intuitively appealing, is inconsistent with decision theory, as we shall see. Decision theory assumes that people should choose whichever alternative has the maximum expected utility. Denote the utility associated with a sum of £X by U(£X). Then the preference for lottery B over A means that:

$$10/100.U(£1,000,000) + 90/100.U(£0) < 1/00.U(£5,000,000) + 8/100.U(£1,000,000) + 91/100.U(£0) \quad (1)$$

and, subtracting 90/100.U(£0) from each side:

$10/100.U(£1,000,000) < 1/100.U(£5,000,000) + 8/100.U(£1,000,000) + 1/100.U(£0)$ (2)

But the preference for lottery C over D means that:

$100.U(£1,000,000) > 1/100.U(£5,000,000) + 98/100.U(£1,000,000) + 1/100.U(£0)$ (3)

and, subtracting $90/100.U(£1,000,000)$ from each side:

$10.U(£1,000,000) > 1/100.U(£5,000,000) + 8/100.U(£1,000,000) + 1/100.U(£0)$ (4)

But (2) and (4) are in contradiction.

Allais's paradox is very powerful – the appeal of the choices that decision theory rules out is considerable. Indeed, rather than condemning people's intuitions as incorrect, Allais argues that the paradox undermines the normative status of decision theory – that is, Allais argues that everyday rational intuitions take precedence over the dictates of a formal calculus.

Another example arises in Cohen's (1981) discussion of the psychology of reasoning literature. Following similar arguments of Goodman (1954), Cohen argues that a normative or formal theory is "acceptable . . . only so far as it accords, at crucial points with the evidence of untutored intuition," (Cohen, 1981, p. 317). That is, a formal theory of reasoning is acceptable only in so far as it accords with everyday reasoning. Cohen uses the following example to demonstrate the primacy of everyday inference. According to standard propositional logic the inference from (5) to (6) is valid:

If John's automobile is a Mini, John is poor, and (5)
if John's automobile is a Rolls, John is rich

Either, if John's automobile is a Mini, John is rich, or (6)
if John's automobile is a Rolls, John is poor

Clearly, however, this violates intuition. Most people would agree with (5) as at least highly plausible; but would reject (6) as absurd. *A fortiori*, they would not accept that (5) *implies* (6) – otherwise they would have to judge (6) to be at least as plausible as (5). Consequently, Cohen argues that standard logic simply does not apply to the reasoning that is in evidence in people's intuitions about (5) and (6). Like Allais, Cohen argues that rather than condemn people's intuitions as irrational, this mismatch reveals the inadequacy of propositional logic as a rational standard. That is, everyday intuitions have primacy over formal theories.

But this viewpoint is not without problems. For example, how can rationality be assessed? If formal rationality is viewed as basic, then the degree to which people behave rationally can be evaluated by comparing performance against the canons of the relevant normative theory. But if everyday rationality is viewed as basic, assessing rationality appears to be down to intuition. There is a danger here of losing any normative force to the notion of rationality – if rationality is merely conformity with each other's predominant intuitions, then being rational is like a musician being in tune. On this view, rationality has no absolute significance; all that matters is that we reason harmoniously with our fellows. But there is a strong intuition that rationality is not like this at all – that there is some absolute sense in which some reasoning or decision making is good, and other reasoning and decision making is bad. So, by rejecting a formal theory of rationality, there is the danger that the normative aspect of rationality is left unexplained.

One way to re-introduce the normative element is to define a procedure that derives normative principles from human intuitions. Cohen appealed to the notion of reflective equilibrium (Goodman, 1954; Rawls, 1971) where inferential principles and actual inferential judgements are iteratively bought into a "best fit" until further judgements do not lead to any further changes of principle (narrow reflective equilibrium). Alternatively, background knowledge may also figure in the process, such that not only actual judgements but also the way they relate to other beliefs are taken into account (wide reflective equilibrium). These approaches have, however, been subject to much criticism (e.g., Stich & Nisbett, 1980; Thagard, 1988). For example, there is no guarantee that an individual (or indeed a set of experts) in equilibrium will have accepted a set of *rational* principles, by any independent standard of rationality. For example, the equilibrium point could leave the individual content in the idea that the Gambler's Fallacy is a sound principle of reasoning.

Thagard (1988) proposes that instead of reflective equilibrium, developing inferential principles involves progress towards an optimal system. This involves proposing principles based on practical judgements and background theories, and measuring these against criteria for optimality. The criteria Thagard specifies are (i) robustness: principles should be empirically adequate; (ii) accommodation: given relevant background knowledge, deviations from these principles can be explained; and (iii) efficacy: given relevant background knowledge, inferential goals are satisfied. Thagard's (1988) concerns were very general: to account for the development of scientific inference. From our current focus on the relationship between everyday and formal rationality, however, Thagard's proposals seem to fall down because the criteria he specifies still seem to leave open the possibility of inconsistency, i.e., it seems possible that a system could fulfil (i) to (iii) but contain mutually contradictory principles. The point about formalization is of course that it provides a way of ruling out this possibility and hence is why a tight relationship between formality and normativity has been assumed since Aristotle. From the perspective of this chapter, accounts like reflective equilibrium and Thagard's account, which attempts to drive a wedge between formality and normativity, may not be required. We argue that many of the mismatches observed between human inferential performance and formal theories are a product of using the wrong formal theory to guide expectations about how people should behave.

An alternative normative grounding for rationality seems intuitively appealing: good everyday reasoning and decision making should lead to *successful action*; for example, from an evolutionary perspective, we might define success as inclusive fitness, and argue that behaviour is rational to the degree that it tends to increase inclusive fitness. But now the notion of rationality appears to collapse into a more general notion of adaptiveness. There seems to be no particular difference in status between cognitive strategies that lead to successful behaviour, and digestive processes that lead to successful metabolic activity. Both increase inclusive fitness; but intuitively we want to say that the first is concerned with rationality, which the second is not. More generally, defining rationality in terms of outcomes runs the risk of blurring what appears to be a crucial distinction – between minds, which may be more or less rational, and stomachs, which are not in the business of rationality at all.

The primacy of formal rationality

Arguments for the primacy of formal rationality take a different starting point. This viewpoint is standard within mathematics, statistics, operations research, and the "decision sciences" (e.g., Kleindorfer, Kunreuther, & Schoemaker, 1993). The idea is that everyday reasoning is fallible, and that it must be corrected by following the dictates of formal theories of rationality.

The immediate problem for advocates of the primacy of formal rationality concerns the *justification* of formal calculi of reasoning: Why should the principles of some calculus be viewed as principles of good reasoning, so that they may even be allowed to overturn our intuitions about what is rational? Such justifications typically assume some general, and apparently incontrovertible, cognitive goal; or seemingly undeniable axioms about how thought or behaviour should proceed. They then use these apparently innocuous assumptions and aim to argue that thought or decision making must obey specific mathematical principles.

Consider, for example, the "Dutch book" argument for the rationality of the probability calculus as a theory of uncertain reasoning (de Finetti, 1937; Ramsey, 1931; Skyrms, 1977). Suppose that we assume that people will accept a "fair" bet: that is, a bet where the expected financial gain is 0, according to their assessment of the probabilities of the various outcomes. Thus, for example, if a person believes that there is a probability of 1/3 that it will rain tomorrow, then they will be happy to accept a bet according to which they win two dollars if it does rain tomorrow, but they lose one dollar if it does not. Now, it is possible to prove that, if a person's assignment of probabilities to different possible outcomes violates the laws of probability theory in any way whatever, then the following curious state of affairs holds. It is possible to offer the person a combination of different bets, such that they will happily accept each individual bet as fair, in the above sense. But, despite being happy that each of the bets is fair, it turns out that *whatever the outcome* the person will lose money. Such a combination of bets – where one side is certain to lose – is known as a Dutch book; and it is seems incontrovertible that accepting a bet that you are certain to lose must violate rationality. Thus, if violating the laws of probability theory leads to accepting Dutch books, which seems clearly irrational, then obeying the laws of probability theory seems to be a condition of rationality.

The Dutch book theorem might appear to have a fundamental weakness – that it requires that a person willingly accepts arbitrary fair bets. But in reality of course this might not be so – many people will, in such circumstances, be risk aversive, and choose not to accept such bets. But the same argument applies even if the person does not bet at all. Now the inconsistency concerns a hypothetical – the person believes that if the bet were accepted, it would be fair (so that a win, as well as a loss, is possible). But in reality the bet is guaranteed to result in a loss – the person's belief that the bet is fair is guaranteed to be wrong. Thus, even if we never actually bet, but simply aim to avoid endorsing statements that are guaranteed to be false, we should follow the laws of probability.

We have considered the Dutch book justification of probability theory in some detail to make it clear that justifications of formal theories of rationality can have considerable force. Rather than attempting to simultaneously satisfy as well as possible a myriad of uncertain intuitions about good and bad reasoning, formal theories of reasoning can be viewed, instead, as founded on simple and intuitively clear-cut principles, such as that accepting bets that you are certain to lose is irrational. Similar justifications can be given for the rationality of the axioms of utility theory and decision theory (Cox, 1961; von Neumann & Morgenstern, 1944; Savage, 1954). Moreover, the same general approach can be used as a justification for logic, if avoiding inconsistency is taken as axiomatic. Thus, there may be good reasons for accepting formal theories of rationality, even if, much of the time, human intuitions and behaviour strongly violate their recommendations.

If formal rationality is primary, what are we to make of the fact that, in explicit tests at least, people seem to be such poor probabilists and logicians? One line would be to accept that human reasoning is badly flawed. Thus, the heuristics and biases programme (Kahneman & Tversky, 1973; Kahneman et al., 1982), which charted systematic errors in human probabilistic reasoning and decision making under uncertainty, can be viewed as exemplifying this position (see Gigerenzer & Goldstein, 1996), as can Evans' (1982, 1989) heuristic approach to reasoning. Another line follows the spirit of Chomsky's (1965) distinction between linguistic competence and performance – the idea is that people's reasoning competence accords with formal principles, but in practice, performance limitations (e.g., limitations of time or memory) lead to persistently imperfect performance when people are given a reasoning task.

Reliance on a competence/performance distinction, whether implicitly or explicitly, has been very influential in the psychology of reasoning: for example, mental logic (Braine, 1978; Rips, 1994) and mental models (Johnson-Laird, 1983; Johnson-Laird & Byrne, 1991) theories of human reasoning assume that classical logic provides the appropriate competence theory for deductive reasoning; and flaws in actual reasoning behaviour are explained in terms of "performance" factors.

Mental logic assumes that human reasoning algorithms correspond to proof-theoretic operations (specifically, in the framework of natural deduction, e.g., Rips, 1994). This viewpoint is also embodied in the vast programme of research in artificial intelligence, especially in the 1970s and 1980s, which attempted to axiomatize aspects of human knowledge and view reasoning as a logical inference (e.g., McCarthy, 1980; McDermott, 1982; McDermott & Doyle, 1980; Reiter, 1980, 1985). Moreover, in the philosophy of cognitive science, it has been controversially suggested that this viewpoint is basic to the computational approach to mind: the fundamental claim of cognitive science, according to this viewpoint, is that "cognition is proof theory" (Fodor & Pylyshyn, 1988, pp. 29–30; see also Chater & Oaksford, 1990).

Mental models concurs that logical inference provides the computational-level theory for reasoning, but provides an alternative method of proof. Instead of standard proof theoretic rules, this view uses a "semantic" method of proof. Such methods involve searching for models (in the logical sense) – a semantic proof that A does not imply B might involve finding a model in which A and B both hold. Mental models theory uses a similar idea, although the notion of model in play is rather different from the logical notion. How can this approach show that A does imply B? The mental models account assumes that the cognitive system attempts to construct a model in which A is true and B is false; if this attempt fails, then it is assumed that no counter-example exists, and that the inference is valid (this is similar to "negation as failure" in logical programming; Clark, 1978).

Mental logic and mental models assume that formal principles of rationality – specifically classical logic – (at least partly) define the standards of good reasoning. They explain the nonlogical nature of people's actual reasoning behaviour in terms of performance factors, such as memory and processing limitations.

Nonetheless, despite its popularity, the view that formal rationality has priority in defining what good reasoning is, and that actual reasoning is systematically flawed with respect to this formal standard, suffers a fundamental difficulty. If formal rationality is the key to everyday rationality, and if people are manifestly poor at *following* the principles of formal rationality (whatever their "competence" with respect to these rules), even in simplified reasoning tasks, then the spectacular success of everyday reasoning in the face of an immensely complex world seems entirely baffling.

Everyday and formal rationality are completely separate

Recently, a number of theorists have suggested what is effectively a hybrid of the two approaches outlined above. They argue that formal rationality and everyday rationality are entirely separate enterprises. For example, Evans and Over (1996a, 1997) distinguish between two notions of rationality (1997, p. 2):

> Rationality$_1$: Thinking, speaking, reasoning, making a decision, or acting in a way that is generally reliable and efficient for achieving one's goals.
>
> Rationality$_2$: Thinking, speaking, reasoning, making a decision, or acting when one has a reason for what one does sanctioned by a normative theory.

They argue that "people are largely rational in the sense of achieving their goals (rationality$_1$) but have only a limited ability to reason or act for good reasons sanctioned by a normative theory (rationality$_2$)" (Evans & Over, 1997, p. 1). If this is right, then one's goals can be achieved without following a formal normative theory, i.e., without there being a *justification* for the actions, decisions, or thoughts that led to success: rationality$_1$ does not require rationality$_2$. That is, Evans and Over are committed to the view that thoughts, actions, or decisions that cannot be normatively justified can, nonetheless, consistently lead to practical success.

But this hybrid view does not tackle the fundamental problem we outlined for the first view sketched above. It does not answer the question: *why* do the cognitive processes underlying everyday rationality consistently work? If everyday rationality is somehow based on formal rationality, then this question can be answered, at least in general terms. The principles of formal rationality are provably principles of good inference and decision making; and the cognitive system is rational in everyday contexts to the degree that it approximates the dictates of these principles. But if everyday and formal rationality are assumed to be unrelated, then this explanation is not available. Unless some alternative explanation of the basis of everyday rationality can be provided, the success of the cognitive system is again left entirely unexplained.

Everyday rationality is based on formal rationality: An empirical approach

We seem to be at an impasse. The success of everyday rationality in guiding our thoughts and actions must somehow be explained; and it seems that there are no obvious alternative explanations, aside from arguing that everyday rationality is somehow based on formal reasoning principles, for which good justifications can be given. But the experimental evidence appears to show that people do not follow the principles of formal rationality.

There is, however, a way out of this impasse. Essentially, the idea is to reject the notion that rationality is a monolithic notion that can be defined *a priori*, and compared with human performance. Instead, we treat the problem of explaining everyday rationality as an empirical problem of explaining why people's cognitive processes are successful in achieving their goals, given the constraints imposed by their environment. Formal rational theories are used in the development of these empirical explanations for the success of cognitive processes – however, which formal principles are appropriate, and how they should be applied, is not decided *a priori* but in the light of the empirical success of the explanation of the adaptive success of the cognitive process under consideration.

According to this viewpoint, the apparent mismatch between normative theories and reasoning behaviour suggests that the wrong normative theories may have been chosen; or the normative theories may have been misapplied. Instead, the empirical approach to the grounding of rationality aims to "do the best" for human everyday reasoning strategies – by searching for a rational characterization of how people actually reason. There is an analogy here with rationality assumptions in language interpretation (Davidson, 1984; Quine, 1960). We aim to interpret people's language so that it makes sense; similarly, the empirical approach to rationality aims to interpret people's reasoning behaviour so that their reasoning makes sense.

Crucially, then, the formal standards of rationality appropriate for explaining some particular cognitive processes or aspect of behaviour are not prior to, but are rather developed as part of, the explanation of empirical data. Of course, this is not to say that, in some sense, formal rationality may be prior to, and separate from, empirical data. The development of formal principles of logic, probability theory, decision theory, and the like may proceed independently of attempting to explain people's reasoning behaviour. But which element of this portfolio of rational principles should be used to define a normative standard for particular cognitive processes or tasks, and how the relevant principles should be applied, is constrained by the empirical human reasoning data to be explained.

It might seem that this approach is flawed from the outset. Surely, any behaviour can be viewed as rational from *some* point of view. That is, by cooking up a suitably bizarre set of assumptions about the problem that people think they are solving, surely their rationality can always be respected; and this suggests the complete vacuity of the approach. But this objection ignores the fact that the goal of empirical rational explanation is to provide an empirical account of data on human reasoning. Hence, such explanations must not be merely possible, but also simple, consistent with other knowledge, independently plausible, and so on. In short, such explanations are to be judged in the light of the normal canons of scientific reasoning (Howson & Urbach, 1989). Thus, rational explanations of cognition and behaviour can be treated as on a par with other scientific explanations of empirical phenomena.

This empirical view of the explanation of rationality is attractive, to the extent that it builds in an explanation of the success of everyday rationality. It does this by attempting to recruit formal rational principles to explain why cognitive processes are successful. But how can this empirical approach to rational explanation be conducted in practice? And can plausible rational explanations of human behaviour be found? The next two sections of the chapter aim to answer these questions. First, we outline a methodology for the rational explanation of empirical data – *rational analysis*. We also illustrate a range of ways in which this approach is used, in psychology, and the social and biological sciences. We then use rational analysis to re-evaluate the psychological data that have appeared to show human reasoning performance to be hopelessly flawed, and argue that, when appropriate rational theories are applied, reasoning performance may, on the contrary, be rational.

RATIONAL ANALYSIS

As with all good ideas, rational analysis has a long history. The roots of rational analysis derive from the earliest attempts to build theories of rational thought or choice. For example, probability theory was originally developed as a theory of how sensible people reason about uncertainty (Gigerenzer, Swijtnik, Porter, Daston, Beatty & Krüger, 1989). Thus, the early literature on probability theory treated the subject both as a description of human psychology and as a set of norms for how people ought to reason when dealing with uncertainty. Similarly, the earliest formalisations of logic (Boole, 1951/1854) viewed the principles as describing the laws governing thought, as well providing a calculus for good reasoning. This early work in probability theory and logic is a precursor of rational analysis, because it aims both to describe how the mind works, and to explain why the mind is rational.

The twentieth century, however, saw a move away from this "psychologism" (Frege, 1879; Hilbert, 1925) and now mathematicians, philosophers, and psychologists sharply distinguish between normative theories, such as a probability theory and logic, which are about how people *should* reason, and descriptive theories of the psychological mechanisms by which people actually *do* reason. Moreover, a major finding in psychology has been that the rules by which people *should* and *do* reason are not merely conceptually distinct; but they appear to be empirically very different (Kahneman & Tversky, 1973; Kahneman et al., 1982; Wason, 1966; Wason & Johnson-Laird, 1972). Whereas very early research on probability theory and logic took their project as codifying how people think, the psychology of reasoning has suggested that probability theory and logic are profoundly at variance with how people think. If this viewpoint is correct, then the whole idea of rational models of cognition is misguided: cognition simply is not rational.

Rational analysis suggests a return to the earlier view of the relationship between descriptive and normative theory, i.e., that a single theory can, and should, do both jobs. A rational model of cognition can therefore explain both how the mind works and why it is successful. But why is rational analysis not just a return to the conceptual confusion of the past? It represents a psychological proposal for explaining cognition that recognizes the conceptual distinction between normative and descriptive theories, but explicitly suggests that in explaining cognitive performance a single account that has both functions is required. Moreover, contemporary rational analyses are explicit scientific hypotheses framed in terms of the computer metaphor, which can be tested against experimental data. Consequently a rational model of cognition is an empirical hypothesis about the nature of the human cognitive system and not merely an a priori assumption.

The computational metaphor is important because it suggests that rational analyses should be described in terms of a scheme for computational explanation. The most well-known scheme for computational explanation was provided by Marr (1982). At Marr's highest level of explanation, the *computational* level the function that is being computed in the performance of some task is outlined. This level corresponds to a rational analysis of the cognitive task. The emphasis on computational explanation makes two points explicit. First, that in providing a computational explanation of the task that a particular device performs there is an issue about whether the computational-level theory is correct. Second, there is a range of possible computational-level theories that may apply to a given task performance, and which one is correct must be discovered and cannot be assumed a priori.

Let us consider an example. Suppose you find an unknown device and wonder what its function might be. Perhaps, observing its behaviour, you hypothesize that it may be performing arithmetical calculations. To make this conjecture is to propose a particular rational model of its performance. That is, this is a theory about what the device *should* do. In this case, the device should provide answers to arithmetical problems that conform to the laws of arithmetic, i.e., arithmetic (or some portion of it) provides the hypothesized rational model. On this assumption, you might give the device certain inputs, which you interpret as framing arithmetical problems. It may turn out, of course, that the outputs that you receive do not appear to be interpretable as solutions to these arithmetical problems. This may indicate that your rational model is inappropriate. You may therefore search for an alternative rational model – perhaps the device is not doing arithmetic, but is solving differential equations. Similarly, in rational analysis, theorists cannot derive appropriate computational-level theories by reflecting on normative considerations alone, but only by attempting to use those theories to describe human performance. For example, it is not controversial that arithmetic is a good normative account of how numbers should be manipulated – the question is: does this device do arithmetic?

This leads to the second difference between the modern programme of rational analysis and early developments of logic and probability: that the goal is not merely to capture people's intuitions, but rather to model detailed experimental data on cognitive function. Rational models aim to capture experimental data on the rate at which information is forgotten; on the way people generalize from old to new instances; on performance on hypothesis-testing tasks; on search problems; and so on. Rational analysis as a programme in cognitive science is primarily aimed at capturing these kinds of empirical phenomena, while explaining how the cognitive system is successful. Nonetheless, rational analysis shares with early views the assumption that accounts of the mind must be both normatively justified and descriptively adequate.

So far, we have considered rationality in the abstract – as consisting of reasoning according to sound principles. But the goals of an agent attempting to survive and prosper in its ecological niche are more concrete – it must decide how to act in order to achieve its goals. So a crucial issue is how normative principles can be combined with analysis of the structure of the environment in order to provide rational explanations of successful cognitive performance. Recent research indicates that many aspects of cognition can be viewed as optimized (to some approximation) to the structure of the environment. For example, the rate of forgetting an item in memory seems to be optimized to the likelihood of encountering that item in the world (Anderson & Milson, 1989; Anderson & Schooler, 1991; Schooler, 1998); categorization may be viewed as optimizing the ability to predict the properties of a category member (Anderson, 1991b, 1998); searching computer menus (Young, 1998), parsing (Chater, Crocker, & Pickering, 1998), and selecting evidence in reasoning (Oaksford & Chater, 1994, 1996, 1998a; Over & Jessop, 1998) may all be viewed as optimizing the amount of information gained. This style of explanation is similar to optimality-based explanations that have been influential in other disciplines. In the study of animal behaviour (Stephens & Krebs, 1986), foraging, diet selection, mate selection and so on, have all been viewed as problems, which animals solve more or less optimally. In economics, people and firms are viewed as more or less optimally making decisions in order to maximize utility or profit.

Models based on optimizing, whether in psychology, animal behaviour, or economics, need not, and typically do not, assume that agents are able to find the perfectly optimized solutions to the problems that they face. Quite often, perfect optimization is impossible even in principle, because the calculations involved in finding a perfect optimum are frequently computationally intractable (Simon, 1955, 1956), and, moreover, much crucial information is typically not available. The agent must still act, even in the absence of the ability to derive the optimal solution (Chater & Oaksford, 1996; Gigerenzer & Goldstein, 1996; Oaksford & Chater, 1991; Simon, 1956). Thus, there may be a tension between the theoretical goal of the rational analysis and the practical need for the agent to be able to decide how to act in real time, given the partial information available. This leads directly into the area of what Simon (1955, 1956) calls *bounded rationality*. We believe that rational analysis can be reconciled with the boundedness of cognitive systems in a number of ways.

First, the cognitive system may, in general, approximate, perhaps very coarsely, the optimal solution. Thus, the algorithms that the cognitive system uses may be fast and frugal heuristics (Gigerenzer & Goldstein, 1996) which generally approximate the optimal in the environments that an agent normally encounters. In this context, the optimal solutions will provide a great deal of insight into why the agent behaves as it does. However, an account of the algorithms that the agent uses will be required to provide a full explanation of the agent's behaviour – including those aspects that depart from the predictions from a rational analysis (Anderson, 1990, 1994).

Second, even where a general cognitive goal is intractable, a more specific cognitive goal, relevant to achieving the general goal, may be tractable. For example, the general goal of moving a piece in chess is to maximize the chance of winning, but this optimization problem is known to be completely intractable because the search space is so large. But optimizing local goals, such as controlling the middle of the board, weakening the opponent's king, and so on, may be tractable. Indeed, most examples of optimality-based explanation, whether in psychology, animal behaviour, or economics, are defined over a local goal, which is assumed to be relevant to some more global aims of the agent. For example, evolutionary theory suggests that animal behaviour should be adapted to increase an animal's inclusive fitness, but specific explanations of animals' foraging behaviour assume more local goals. Thus, an animal may be assumed to forage to maximize food intake, on the assumption that this local goal is generally relevant to the global goal of maximizing inclusive fitness. Similarly, explanations concerning cognitive processes may concern local cognitive goals such as maximizing the amount of useful information remembered, maximizing predictive accuracy, or acting to gain as much information as possible. All of these local goals are assumed to be relevant to more general goals, such as maximizing expected utility (from an economic perspective) or maximizing inclusive fitness (from a biological perspective). At any level, it is possible that optimization is intractable; but it is also possible that by focusing on more limited goals, evolution or learning may have provided the cognitive system with mechanisms that can optimize or nearly optimize some more local, but relevant, quantity.

The importance that the local goals be relevant to the larger aims of the cognitive system raises another important question about providing rational models of cognition. The fact that a model involves optimizing *something* does not mean that the model is a *rational* model. Optimality is not the same as rationality. It is crucial that the local goal that is optimized must be relevant to some larger goal of the agent. Thus, it seems *reasonable* that animals may attempt to optimize the amount of food they obtain, or that the categories used by the cognitive system are optimized to lead to the best predictions. This is because, for example, optimizing the amount of food obtained is likely to enhance inclusive fitness, in a way that, for example, maximizing the amount of energy consumed in the search process would not. Determining whether some behaviour is rational or not therefore depends on more than just being able to provide an account in terms of optimization. Therefore rationality requires not just optimizing something but optimizing something reasonable. As a definition of rationality, this is clearly circular. But by viewing rationality in terms of optimization, general conceptions of what are reasonable cognitive goals can be turned into specific and detailed models of cognition. Thus, the programme of rational analysis, while not answering the ultimate question of what rationality is, nonetheless provides the basis for a concrete and potentially fruitful line of empirical research.

This flexibility of what may be viewed as rational, in building a rational model, may appear to raise a fundamental problem for the entire rational analysis programme. It seems that the notion of rationality may be so flexible that, whatever people do, it is possible that it may seem rational under some description. So, for example, it may be that our stomachs are well adapted to digesting the food in our environmental niche, indeed they may even prove to be optimally efficient in this respect. However, we would not therefore describe the human stomach as rational, because stomachs presumably cannot usefully be viewed as information processing devices. Stomachs may be well or poorly adapted to their function (digestion), but they have no beliefs, desires, or knowledge, and hence the question of their rationality does not arise.

Optimality approaches in biology, economics, and psychology assume that the agent is well adapted to its normal environment. However, almost all psychological data are gained in a very unnatural setting, where a person performs a very artificial task in the laboratory. Any laboratory task will recruit some set of cognitive mechanisms that determine the participants' behaviour. But it is not obvious what problem these mechanisms are adapted to solving. Clearly, this adaptive problem is not likely to be directly related to the problem given to the participant by the experimenter, precisely because adaptation is to the natural world, not to laboratory tasks. In particular, this means that participants may fail with respect to the task that the experimenter thinks they have set. But this may be because this task is unnatural with respect to the participant's normal environment. Consequently participants may assimilate the task that they are given to a more natural task, recruiting adaptively appropriate mechanisms which solve this, more natural, task successfully.

This issue is most pressing in reasoning tasks where human performance has been condemned as irrational. For example, hypothesis-testing tasks, where people do not adopt the supposedly "logical" strategy of falsification, have been taken to demonstrate the irrationality of human reasoning (Stich, 1985, 1990; Sutherland, 1992). However, recently a number of theorists have suggested that human reasoning should be judged against probabilistic standards, as opposed the norms of logic (e.g., Evans & Over, 1997; Fischhoff & Beyth-Marom, 1983; Kirby, 1994; Oaksford & Chater, 1994, 1998c; Over & Jessop, 1998). One powerful argument for this position is that the complex and uncertain character of the everyday world implies that real-world everyday reasoning is inevitably uncertain (Chater & Oaksford, 1996; Oaksford & Chater, 1998c), and hence better modelled by probability, the calculus of uncertain reasoning, than by logic, the calculus of certain reasoning. From this point of view, people's behaviour in laboratory reasoning tasks is (to an approximation at least) rational, even though it violates the standards set by the experimenter – but this can only be appreciated once the standard of correct performance is reconceptualized in probabilistic terms.

RE-EVALUATING HUMAN REASONING: A PROBABILISTIC APPROACH

This section focuses on our recent attempts to develop a probabilistic analysis of laboratory reasoning tasks (Chater & Oaksford, 1999a, 1999b, 1999c, 2000; Oaksford & Chater, 1994, 1995a, 1995b, 1996, 1998a, 1998b, 1998c; Oaksford, Chater, & Grainger, 1999; Oaksford, Chater, Grainger & Larkin, 1997; Oaksford, Chater, & Larkin, 2000). But to appreciate what is distinctive about the probabilistic approach, we must first begin by considering logic-based theories in the psychology of reasoning, which have been dominant since the inception of the field. Logic-based theories of reasoning fall into two types.

According to the *mental models* view (Johnson-Laird, 1983; Johnson-Laird & Byrne, 1991), people construct one or more concrete models of the situation that is described by the premises with which they are presented, and derive conclusions from "reading off" conclusions that follow in one or more of these models. There are procedures for building, checking, and reading from models that should allow the reasoner, if all goes well, to conform with the dictates of deductive logic. According to the *mental logic* view, people reason by directly performing calculations in a particular logical system – typically assumed to be some kind of natural deduction system (Braine, 1978; Rips, 1983, 1994).

According to these viewpoints, people are rational in principle but err in practice – that is, we have sound procedures for deductive reasoning but the algorithms that we use can fail to produce the right answers because of cognitive limitations such as working memory capacity. Such an approach seems hard to reconcile with two facts. First, these faulty algorithms can lead to error rates as high as 96% (in Wason's selection task) compared to the standard provided by formal logic. Second, our everyday rationality in guiding our thoughts and actions seems in general to be highly successful. How is this success to be understood if the reasoning system people use is prone to so much error?

As we discussed above, we attempt to resolve this problem by arguing that people's everyday reasoning can be understood from the perspective of probability theory and that people make errors in so-called deductive tasks because they generalize their everyday strategies to these laboratory tasks. The psychology of deductive reasoning involves giving people problems that the experimenters conceive of as requiring logical inference. But people consistently respond in a non-logical way, thus calling human rationality into question (Stein, 1996; Stich, 1985, 1990). In our view, everyday rationality is founded on uncertain rather than certain reasoning (Oaksford & Chater, 1991, 1998c) and so probability provides a better starting point for an account of human reasoning than logic. It also resolves the problem of explaining the success of everyday reasoning: it is successful to the extent that it approximates a probabilistic theory of the task. Second, we suggest that a probabilistic analysis of classic "deductive" reasoning tasks provides an excellent empirical fit with observed performance. The upshot is that much of the experimental research in the "psychology of deductive reasoning" does not engage people in deductive reasoning at all but rather engages strategies suitable for probabilistic reasoning. According to this viewpoint, the field of research appears to be crucially misnamed!

We illustrate our probabilistic approach in the three main tasks that have been the focus of research into human reasoning: conditional inference, Wason's selection task, and syllogistic inference.

Conditional inference

Conditional inference is perhaps the simplest inference form investigated in the psychology of reasoning. It involves presenting participants with a conditional premise, *if p then q*, and then one of four categorical premises, *p*, *not-p*, *q*, or *not-q*. Logically, given the categorical premise *p* participants should draw the conclusion *q* and given the categorical premise *not-q* they should draw the conclusion *not-p*. These are the logically valid inferences of modus ponens ("MP") and modus tollens ("MT") respectively. Moreover, given the categorical premise *not-p* participants should *not* draw the conclusion *not-q* and given the categorical premise *q* they should *not* draw the conclusion *p*. These are the logical fallacies of denying the antecedent ("DA") and affirming the consequent ("AC") respectively. So, logically, participants should endorse MP and MT in equal proportion and they should refuse to endorse DA or AC. However, they endorse MP significantly more than MT and they endorse DA and AC at levels significantly above zero.

Following a range of other researchers (Anderson, 1995; Chan & Chua, 1994, George, 1997; Liu, Lo, & Wu, 1996; Stevenson & Over, 1995), Oaksford, Chater, and Larkin (2000) proposed a model of conditional reasoning based on conditional probability. The greater the conditional probability of an inference the more it should be endorsed. On their account the meaning of a conditional statement can be defined using a 2 by 2 contingency table as in Table 3.1 (see Oaksford & Chater, 1998c).

Table 3.1 Contingency table for a conditional rule

	q	$not\text{-}q$
p	$a(1-\varepsilon)$	$a\varepsilon$
$not\text{-}p$	$b - a(1-\varepsilon)$	$(1-b) - a\varepsilon$

This table represents a conditional rule, if p then q, where there is a dependency between the p and q that may admit exceptions (ε) and where a is the probability of the antecedent, $P(p)$, b is the probability of the consequent, $P(q)$, and ε is the probability of exceptions, i.e., the probability that q does not occur even though p has, $P(not\text{-}q|p)$. It is straightforward to then derive conditional probabilities for each inference. For example, the conditional probability associated with MP, i.e., $P(q|p) = 1 - \varepsilon$, only depends on the probability of exceptions. If there are few exceptions the probability of drawing the MP inference will be high. However, the conditional probability associated with MT, i.e.,

$$P(not\text{-}p|not\text{-}q) = \frac{1 - b - a\varepsilon}{1 - b}$$

depends on the probability of the antecedent, $P(p)$, and the probability of the consequent, $P(q)$, as well the probability of exceptions. As long as there are exceptions ($\varepsilon > 0$) and the probability of the antecedent is greater than the probability of the consequent not occurring ($P(p) > 1 - P(q)$), then the probability of MT is less than MP ($P(not\text{-}p|not\text{-}q) < P(q|p)$). For example, if $P(p) = .5$, $P(q) = .8$ and $\varepsilon = .1$, then $P(q|p) = .9$ and $P(not\text{-}p|not\text{-}q) = .75$. This behaviour of the model accounts for the preference for MP over MT in the empirical data. In the model conditional probabilities associated with DA and AC also depend on these parameters, which means that they can be non-zero. Consequently the model also predicts that the fallacies should be endorsed to some degree.

Oaksford et al. (2000) argue that this simple model can also account for other effects in conditional inference. For example, using Evans' Negations Paradigm in the conditional inference task leads to a bias towards negated conclusions. Oaksford and Stenning (1992; see also Oaksford & Chater, 1994) proposed that negations define higher-probability categories than their affirmative counterparts, e.g., the probability that an animal is not a frog is much higher than the probability that it is. Oaksford et al. (2000) show that according to their model the conditional probability of an inference increases with the probability of the conclusion. Consequently the observed bias towards negated conclusions may actually be a rational preference for high-probability conclusions. If this is right then, when given rules containing high- and low-probability categories, people should show a preference to draw conclusions that have a high probability analogous to negative conclusion bias, a prediction later confirmed experimentally (Oaksford et al., 2000).

Wason's selection task

The probabilistic approach was originally applied to Wason's selection task, which we introduced above (Oaksford & Chater, 1994, 1995b, 1996, 1998a, 1998c; Oaksford et al., 1999; Oaksford et al., 1997). According to Oaksford and Chater's (1994) optimal data selection model people select evidence (i.e., turn cards) to determine whether q depends on p, as in Table 3.1, or whether p and q are statistically independent (i.e., the cell values would simply be the products of the marginal probabilities, rather than as in Table 3.1). What participants are looking for in the selection task is evidence that gives the greatest probability of discriminating between these two possibilities. Initially participants are assumed to be maximally uncertain about which possibility is true, i.e., a prior probability of .5 is assigned to both the possibility of a dependency (the dependence hypothesis, H_D) and to the possibility of independence (the independence hypothesis, H_I). The participants' goal is to select evidence (turn cards) that would be expected to produce the greatest reduction in this uncertainty. This involves calculating the posterior probabilities of the hypotheses, H_D or H_I, being true given some evidence. These probabilities are calculated using Bayes' theorem, which requires information about prior probabilities ($P(H_D) = P(H_I) = .5$) and the likelihoods of evidence given a hypothesis, e.g., the probability of finding an A when turning the 2 card assuming H_D ($P(A|2, H_D)$). These likelihoods can be calculated directly from the contingency tables for each hypothesis: for H_D, Table 3.1, and for H_I, the independence model. With these values it is possible to calculate the reduction in uncertainty that can be expected by turning any of the four cards in the selection task. Oaksford and Chater (1994) observed that assuming that the marginal probabilities $P(p)$ and $P(q)$ were small (their "rarity assumption"), the p and the q cards would be expected to provide the greatest reduction in uncertainty about which hypothesis was true. Consequently, the selection of cards that has been argued to demonstrate human irrationality may actually reflect a highly rational data selection strategy. Indeed this strategy may be optimal in an environment where most properties are rare, e.g., most things are not black, not ravens, and not apples (but see Klauer, 1999, and Chater & Oaksford, 1999b, for a reply).

Oaksford and Chater (1994) argued that this model can account for most of the evidence on the selection task, and Oaksford and Chater (1996) defended the model against a variety of objections. For example, Evans and Over (1996b) criticized the notion of information used in the optimal data selection model and proposed their own probabilistic model. This model made some predictions that diverged from Oaksford and Chater's model and these have been experimentally tested by Oaksford et al. (1999). Although the results seem to support the optimal data selection model, there is still much room for further experimental work in this area. Manktelow and Over have been exploring probabilistic effects in deontic selection tasks (Manktelow, Sutherland, & Over, 1995). Moreover, Green and Over have also been exploring the probabilistic approach to the standard selection task (Green, Over, & Pyne, 1997; see also Oaksford, 1998; Green & Over, 1998). They have also extended this approach to what they refer to as "causal selection tasks" (Green & Over, 1997, 2000; Over & Green, 2001). This is important because their work develops the link between research on causal estimation (e.g., Anderson & Sheu, 1995; Cheng, 1997) and research on the selection task suggested by Oaksford and Chater (1994).

Syllogistic reasoning

Chater and Oaksford (1999c) have further extended the probabilistic approach to the more complex inferences involved in syllogistic reasoning, which we discussed in looking at mental models. In their probability heuristics model (PHM), they extend their probabilistic interpretation of conditionals to quantified claims, such as, All, Some, None, and Some . . . not. In Table 3.1, if there are no exceptions, then the probability of the consequent given the antecedent, ($P(q|p)$), is 1. The conditional and the universal quantifier "All" have the same underlying logical form: $\forall x(P(x) \Rightarrow Q(x))$. Consequently Chater and Oaksford interpreted universal claims such as All Ps are Qs as asserting that the probability of the predicate term (Q) given the subject term (P) is 1, i.e., $P(Q|P) = 1$. Probabilistic meanings for the other quantifiers are then easily defined: None, $P(Q|P) = 0$; Some, $P(Q|P) > 0$; Some . . . not, $P(Q|P) < 1$. Given these probabilistic interpretations it is possible to show which conclusions follow probabilistically for all 64 syllogisms (i.e., which syllogisms are "p-valid"). Moreover, given these interpretations and again making the rarity assumption (see above on the selection task), the quantifiers can be ordered in terms of how informative they are: All > Some > None > Some . . . not. It turns out that a simple set of heuristics defined over the informativeness of the premises can successfully predict the *p*-valid conclusion, if there is one. The most important of these heuristics is the *min*-heuristic, which states that the conclusion will have the form of the least informative premise. So for example, a *p*-valid syllogism such as, *All B are A, Some B are not C*, yields the conclusion *Some A are not C*. Note that the conclusion has the same form as the least informative premise. This simple heuristic captures the form of the conclusion for most *p*-valid syllogisms. Moreover, if overgeneralized to the invalid syllogisms, the conclusions it suggests match the empirical data very well. Other heuristics determine the confidence that people have in their conclusions and the order of terms in the conclusion.

Perhaps the most important feature of PHM is that it can generalise to syllogisms containing quantifiers such as Most and Few that have no logical interpretation. In terms of Table 3.1 the suggestion is that these terms are used instead of All when there are some (Most) or many (Few) exceptions. So the meaning of Most is: $1 - \Delta < P(Q|P) < 1$, and the meaning of Few is: $0 < P(Q|P) < \Delta$, where Δ is small. These interpretations lead to the following order of informativeness: All > Most > Few > Some > None > Some ... not. Consequently, PHM uniquely makes predictions for the 144 syllogisms that are produced when Most and Few are combined with the standard logical quantifiers. Chater and Oaksford (1999c) (i) show that their heuristics pick out the *p*-valid conclusions for these new syllogisms, and (ii) they report experiments confirming the predictions of PHM when Most and Few are used in syllogistic arguments.

There has already been some work on syllogistic reasoning consistent with PHM. Newstead, Handley, and Buck (1999) found that the conclusions participants drew in their experiments were mainly as predicted by the *min*-heuristic, although they found little evidence of the search for counter-examples predicted by mental models theory for multiple model syllogisms. Evans, Handley, Harper, and Johnson-Laird (1999) also found evidence consistent with PHM, indeed they found that an important novel distinction they discovered between strong and weak possible conclusions could be captured as well by the *min*-heuristic as by mental models theory. A conclusion is necessarily true if it is true in all models of the premises, a conclusion is possibly true if it is true in at least one model of the premises, and a conclusion is impossible if it is not true in any model of the premises. Evans et al. (1999) found that some possible conclusions were endorsed by as many participants as necessary conclusions and that some were endorsed by as few participants as impossible conclusions. According to mental models theory this happens because strong possible conclusions are those that are true in the initial model constructed but not in subsequent models, and weak possible conclusions are those that are only true in non-initial models. Possible strong conclusions all conform to the *min*-heuristic, i.e., they either match the *min*-premise or are less informative than the *min*-premise. Possible weak conclusions all violate the *min*-heuristic (bar one), i.e., they have conclusions that are more informative than the *min*-premise. In sum, PHM would appear to be gaining some empirical support.

WHERE NEXT FOR THE PSYCHOLOGY OF REASONING?

Despite the intensive research effort over the last 40 years, human reasoning remains largely mysterious. While there is increased understanding of some aspects of laboratory performance, deep puzzles over the nature of everyday human reasoning processes remain. We suggest that three key issues may usefully frame the agenda for future research: (1) establishing the relation between reasoning and other cognitive processes; (2) developing formal theories that capture the full richness of everyday reasoning; (3) explaining how such theories can be implemented in real-time in the brain.

Reasoning and cognition

From an abstract perspective, almost every aspect of cognition can be viewed as involving inference. Perception involves inferring the structure of the environment from perceptual input; motor control involves inferring appropriate motor commands from proprioceptive and perceptual input, together with demands of the motor task to be performed; learning from experience, in any domain, involves inferring general principles from specific examples; understanding a text or utterance typically requires inferences relating the linguistic input to an almost unlimited amount of general background knowledge. Is there a separate cognitive system for *reasoning*, or are the processes studied by reasoning researchers simply continuous with the whole of cognition? A key sub-question concerns the modularity of the cognitive system. If the cognitive system is non-modular, then reasoning would seem, of necessity, to be difficult to differentiate from other aspects of cognition. If the cognitive system is highly modular, then different principles may apply in different cognitive domains. Nonetheless, it might still turn out that, even if modules are informationally sealed off from each other (e.g., Fodor, 1983), the inferential principles that they use might be the same; the same underlying principles and mechanisms might simply be reused in different domains. Even if the mind is modular, it seems unlikely that there could be a module for *reasoning* in anything like the sense studied in psychology. This is because everyday reasoning (in contrast to some artificial laboratory tasks) requires engaging arbitrary world knowledge. Consequently, understanding reasoning would appear to be part of the broader project of understanding central cognitive processes and the knowledge they embody in full generality.

This is an alarming prospect for reasoning researchers because current formal research is unable to provide adequate tools for capturing even limited amounts of general knowledge, let alone reasoning with it effectively and in real-time, as we shall discuss below. Reasoning researchers often attempt to seal off their theoretical accounts from the deep waters of general knowledge, by assuming that these problems are solved by other processes – e.g., processes constraining how mental models are "fleshed out" (Johnson-Laird & Byrne, 1991) or when particular premises can be used in inference (Politzer & Braine, 1991), what information is relevant (Evans, 1989; Sperber, Cara, & Girotto, 1995) or how certain probabilities are determined (Oaksford & Chater, 1994). Whether or not this strategy is methodologically appropriate in the short term, substantial progress in understanding everyday reasoning will require theories that address, rather than avoid, these crucial issues, i.e., theories that explicate, rather than presupposing, our judgements concerning what is plausible, probable, or relevant. Moreover, as we have seen, recent empirical work seems to strongly suggest that progress in understanding human reasoning even in the laboratory requires the issue of general knowledge to be tackled.

Formal theories of everyday reasoning

Explaining the cognitive processes involved in everyday reasoning requires developing a formal theory that can capture everyday inferences. Unfortunately, however, this is far from straightforward, because everyday inferences are *global*: whether a conclusion follows typically depends not just on a few circumscribed "premises" but on arbitrarily large amounts of general world knowledge (see, e.g., Fodor, 1983; Oaksford & Chater, 1991, 1998c). From a statement such as *While John was away, Peter changed all the locks in the house*, we can provisionally infer, e.g., that Peter did not want John to be able to enter the house; that John possesses a key; that Peter and John have had a disagreement, and so on. But such inferences draw on background information, such as that the old key will not open the new lock, that locks secure doors, that houses can usually only be entered through doors, and a host of more information about the function of houses, and the nature of human relationships, and the law concerning breaking and entering. Moreover, deploying each piece of information requires an inference that is just as complex as the original one. Thus, even to infer that John's key will not open the new lock requires background information concerning the way in which locks and keys are paired together, the convention that when locks are replaced, they will not fit the old key, that John's key will not itself be changed when the locks are changed, that the match between lock and key is stable over time, and so on. This is what we call the "fractal" character of commonsense reasoning (Oaksford & Chater, 1998c) – just as, in geometry, each part of a fractal is as complex as the whole, each part of an everyday inference is as complex as the whole piece of reasoning.

How can such inferences be captured formally? Deductive logic is inappropriate, because everyday arguments are not deductively valid, but can be overturned when more information is learned. The essential problem is that these methods fail to capture the global character of everyday inference successfully (Oaksford & Chater, 1991, 1992, 1993, 1998c). In artificial intelligence, this has led to a switch to using probability theory, the calculus of *un*certain reasoning, to capture patterns of everyday inference (e.g., Pearl, 1988). This is an important advance, but only a beginning. Probabilistic inference can only be used effectively if it is possible to separate knowledge into discrete chunks – with a relatively sparse network of probabilistic dependencies between the chunks. Unfortunately, this just does not seem to be possible for everyday knowledge. The large variety of labels for the current impasse – the "frame" problem (McCarthy & Hayes, 1969; Pylyshyn, 1987), the "world knowledge" problem or the problem of knowledge representation (Ginsberg, 1987), the problem of non-monotonic reasoning (Paris, 1994), the criterion of completeness (Oaksford & Chater, 1991, 1998c) – is testimony to its fundamental importance and profound difficulty. The problem of providing a formal calculus of everyday inference presents a huge intellectual challenge, not just in psychology, but in the study of logic, probability theory, artificial intelligence, and philosophy.

Everyday reasoning and real-time neural computation

Suppose that a calculus which captured everyday knowledge and inference could be developed. If this calculus underlies thought, then it must be implemented (probably to an approximation) in real-time in the human brain. Current calculi for reasoning, including standard and non-standard logics, probability theory, decision theory, and game theory, are computationally intractable (Garey & Johnson, 1979; Paris, 1994). That is, as the amount of information that they have to deal with increases, the amount of computational resources (in memory and time) required to derive conclusions explodes very rapidly (or, in some cases, inferences are not computable at all, even given limitless time and memory). Typically, attempts to extend standard calculi to mimic everyday reasoning more effectively make problems of tractability *worse* (e.g., this is true of "non-monotonic logics" developed in artificial intelligence). Somehow, a formal calculus of everyday reasoning must be developed that, instead, eases problems of tractability.

This piles difficulty upon difficulty for the problem of explaining human reasoning computationally. Nonetheless, there are interesting directions to explore. For example, modern "graphical" approaches to probabilistic inference in artificial intelligence and statistics (e.g., Pearl, 1988) are very directly related to connectionist computation; and more generally, connectionist networks can be viewed as probabilistic inference machines (Chater, 1995; MacKay, 1992; McClelland, 1998). To the extent that the parallel, distributed style of computation in connectionist networks can be related to the parallel, distributed computation in the brain, this suggests that the brain may be understood, in some sense, as directly implementing rational calculations. Nonetheless, there is currently little conception either of how such probabilistic models can capture the "global" quality of everyday reasoning, or of how these probabilistic calculations can be carried out in real-time to support fluent and rapid inference, drawing on large amounts of general knowledge, in a brain consisting of notoriously slow and noisy neural components (Feldman & Ballard, 1982).

Where do we stand?

This chapter has focused on the relationship between mathematical theories of good reasoning and the everyday rational explanations of thought and behaviour. We have argued for a particular relationship between the informal and formal rationality – that patterns of informal reasoning can be explained as approximating the dictates of formal, rational theories. Rational analysis of a particular pattern of inference can serve both a descriptive and a normative role. It can describe the broad patterns of human reasoning performance; but at the same time explain why these patterns of reasoning are adaptively successful in the real world. We have also given a range of concrete examples of how this approach can be applied, showing that many aspects of human laboratory reasoning that appear to be unsystematic and irrational when viewed from the perspective of deductive logic, appear systematic and rational when re-conceptualized in terms of probability theory. But we have cautioned that the project of building a more adequate and general psychology of reasoning faces, nonetheless, enormous difficulties – most fundamentally because the performance of human everyday reasoning radically exceeds the performance of any current formal theories of reasoning. Thus, we believe that the project of understanding human reasoning requires the construction of richer normative theories of good reasoning. Hence, the apparently narrow project of the psychology of reasoning is, in fact, a joint project for disciplines that have fundamentally normative concerns (philosophy, probability theory, decision theory, artificial intelligence) in concert with the experimental, descriptive, study of human thought that has been the traditional territory of the psychologist.

REFERENCES

Allais, M. (1953). Le comportement de l'homme rationnel devant le risque: Critique des postulats et axiomes de l'école américaine. *Econometrica*, *21*, 503–546.

Anderson, J. R. (1990). *The adaptive character of thought*. Hillsdale, NJ: Lawrence Erlbaum Associate Inc.

Anderson, J. R. (1991a). Is human cognition adaptive? *Behavioral and Brain Sciences*, *14*, 471–517.

Anderson, J. R. (1991b). The adaptive nature of human categorization. *Psychological Review*, *98*, 409–429.

Anderson, J. R. (1994). *Rules of the mind*, Hillsdale, NJ: Lawrence Erlbaum Associates Inc.

Anderson, J. R. (1995). *Cognitive psychology and it implications*. New York: W. H. Freeman & Company.

Anderson, J. R., & Matessa, M. (1998). The rational analysis of categorization and the ACT-R architecture. In M. Oaksford & N. Chater (Eds.), *Rational models of cognition* (pp. 197–217). Oxford, UK: Oxford University Press.

Anderson, J. R., & Milson, R. (1989). Human memory: An adaptive perspective. *Psychological Review, 96*, 703–719.

Anderson, J. R., & Schooler, L. J. (1991). Reflections of the environment in memory. *Psychological Science, 2*, 396–408.

Anderson, J. R., & Sheu, C-F. (1995). Causal inferences as perceptual judgements. *Memory and Cognition, 23*, 510–524.

Boole, G. (1951). *An investigation into the laws of thought*. New York: Dover. [Originally published in 1854.]

Braine, M. D. S. (1978). On the relation between the natural logic of reasoning and standard logic. *Psychological Review, 85*, 1–21.

Chan, D., & Chua, F. (1994). Suppression of valid inferences: Syntactic views, mental models, and relative salience. *Cognition, 53*, 217–238.

Chater, N. (1995). Neural networks: The new statistical models of mind. In J. P. Levy, D. Bairaktaris, J. A. Bullinaria, & P. Cairns (Eds.), *Connectionist models of memory and language* (pp. 207–227). London: UCL Press.

Chater, N., Crocker, M., & Pickering, M. (1998). The rational analysis of inquiry: The case of parsing. In M. Oaksford, & N. Chater (Eds.), *Rational models of cognition* (pp. 441–468). Oxford: Oxford University Press.

Chater, N., & Oaksford, M. (1990). Autonomy, implementation and cognitive architecture: A reply to Fodor and Pylyshyn. *Cognition, 34*, 93–107.

Chater, N., & Oaksford, M. (1996). The falsity of folk theories: Implications for psychology and philosophy. In W. O'Donohue & R. Kitchener (Eds.), *The philosophy of psychology* (pp. 244–256), London: Sage Publications.

Chater, N., & Oaksford, M. (1999a). Ten years of the rational analysis of cognition. *Trends in Cognitive Sciences, 3*, 57–65.

Chater, N., & Oaksford, M. (1999b). Information gain vs. decision-theoretic approaches to data selection: Response to Klauer. *Psychological Review, 106*, 223–227.

Chater, N., & Oaksford, M. (1999c). The probability heuristics model of syllogistic reasoning. *Cognitive Psychology, 38*, 191–258.

Chater, N., & Oaksford, M. (2000). The rational analysis of mind and behaviour. *Synthese*, 93–131.

Cheng, P. W. (1997). From covariation to causation: A causal power theory. *Psychological Review, 104*, 367–405.

Chomsky, N. (1965). *Aspects of the theory of syntax*. Cambridge, MA: MIT Press.

Clark, K. L. (1978). Negation as failure. In *Logic and databases* (pp. 293–322). New York: Plenum Press.

Cohen, L. J. (1981). Can human irrationality be experimentally demonstrated? *Behavioral and Brain Sciences, 4*, 317–370.

Cox, R. T. (1961). *The algebra of probable inference*. Baltimore: The Johns Hopkins University Press.

Davidson, D. (1984). *Inquiries into truth and interpretation*. Oxford: Clarendon Press.

de Finetti, B. (1937). La prévision: Ses lois logiques, ses sources subjectives (Foresight: Its logical laws, its subjective sources). *Annales de l'Institute Henri Poincaré, 7*, 1–68.

[Translated in H. E. Kyburg & H. E. Smokler (Eds.) (1964). *Studies in subjective probability*. Chichester, UK: Wiley.]
Evans, J. St. B. T. (1982). *The psychology of deductive reasoning*. London: Routledge & Kegan Paul.
Evans, J. St. B. T. (1989). *Bias in human reasoning: Causes and consequences*. Hove, UK: Lawrence Erlbaum Associates Ltd.
Evans, J. St. B. T., Handley, S. J., Harper, C. N. J., & Johnson-Laird, P. N. (1999). Reasoning about necessity and possibility: A test of the mental model theory of deduction. *Journal of Experimental Psychology: Learning, Memory, and Cognition*, *25*, 1495–1513.
Evans, J. St. B. T., Newstead, S. E., & Byrne, R. M. J. (1993). *Human reasoning*. Hove, UK: Lawrence Erlbaum Associates Ltd.
Evans, J. St. B. T., & Over, D. (1996a). *Rationality and reasoning*. Hove, UK: Psychology Press.
Evans, J. St. B. T., & Over, D. (1996b). Rationality in the selection task: Epistemic utility vs. uncertainty reduction. *Psychological Review*, *103*, 356–363.
Evans, J. St. B. T., & Over, D. (1997). Rationality in reasoning: The problem of deductive competence. *Cahiers de Psychologie Cognitive*, *16*, 1–35.
Feldman, J., & Ballard, D. (1982). Connectionist models and their properties. *Cognitive Science*, *6*, 205–254.
Fischhoff, B., & Beyth-Marom, R. (1983). Hypothesis evaluation from a Bayesian perspective. *Psychological Review*, *90*, 239–260.
Fisher, R. A. (1922). On the mathematical foundations of theoretical statistics. *Philosophical Transactions of the Royal Society of London, Series A*, *222*, 309–368.
Fisher, R. A. (1925/1970). *Statistical methods for research workers* (14th Ed.). Edinburgh: Oliver & Boyd.
Fodor, J. A. (1983). *Modularity of mind*. Cambridge MA: MIT Press.
Fodor, J. A., & Pylyshyn, Z. W. (1988). Connectionism and cognitive architecture: A critical analysis. *Cognition*, *28*, 3–71.
Frege, G. (1879). *Begriffschrift*. Halle, Germany: Nebert.
Garey, M. R., & Johnson, D. S. (1979). *Computers and intractability: A guide to the theory of NP-completeness*. San Fransisco: W. H. Freeman.
George, C. (1997). Reasoning from uncertain premises. *Thinking and Reasoning*, *3*, 161–190.
Gigerenzer, G., & Goldstein, D. (1996). Reasoning the fast and frugal way: Models of bounded rationality. *Psychological Review*, *103*, 650–669.
Gigerenzer, G., Swijtnik, Z., Porter, T., Daston, L., Beatty, J., & Krüger, L. (1989). *The empire of chance*. Cambridge: Cambridge University Press.
Ginsberg, M. L. (Ed.). (1987). *Readings in nonmonotonic reasoning*. Los Altos, CA: Morgan Kaufman.
Goodman, N. (1954). *Fact, fiction and forecast*. Cambridge, MA: Harvard University Press.
Green, D. W., & Over, D. E. (1997). Causal inference, contingency tables and the selection task. *Current Psychology of Cognition*, *16*, 459–487.
Green, D. W., & Over, D. E. (1998). Reaching a decision: A reply to Oaksford. *Thinking and Reasoning*, *4*, 231–248.
Green, D. W., & Over, D. E. (2000). Decision theoretic effects in the selection task. *Current Psychology of Cognition*, *19*, 51–68.

Green, D. W., Over, D. E., & Pyne, R. A. (1997). Probability and choice in the selection task. *Thinking and Reasoning, 3,* 209–235.

Harsanyi, J., & Selten, R. (1988). *A general theory of equilibrium selection in games.* Cambridge, MA: MIT Press.

Hilbert, D. (1925). Über das unendliche. *Mathematische Annalen, 95,* 161–190.

Howson, C., & Urbach, P. (1989). *Scientific reasoning: The Bayesian approach.* La Salle, IL: Open Court.

Johnson-Laird, P. N. (1983). *Mental models.* Cambridge: Cambridge University Press.

Johnson-Laird, P. N., & Byrne, R. M. J. (1991). *Deduction.* Hillsdale, NJ: Lawrence Erlbaum Associates Inc.

Kahneman, D., Slovic, P., & Tversky, A. (Eds.). (1982). *Judgement under uncertainty: Heuristics and biases.* Cambridge: Cambridge University Press.

Kahneman, D., & Tversky, A. (1973). On the psychology of prediction. *Psychological Review, 80,* 237–251.

Keynes, J. M. (1921). *A treatise on probability.* London: Macmillan.

Kirby, K. N. (1994). Probabilities and utilities of fictional outcomes in Wason's four card selection task. *Cognition, 51,* 1–28.

Klauer, K. C. (1999). On the normative justification for information gain in Wason's selection task. *Psychological Review, 106,* 215–222.

Kleindorfer, P. R., Kunreuther, H. C., & Schoemaker, P. J. H. (1993). *Decision sciences: An integrated perspective.* Cambridge: Cambridge University Press.

Lindley, D. V. (1971). *Bayesian statistics: A review.* Philadelphia, PA: Society for Industrial & Applied Mathematics.

Liu, I., Lo, K., & Wu, J. (1996). A probabilistic interpretation of "If-then." *Quarterly Journal of Experimental Psychology, 49*A, 828–844.

MacKay, D. J. C. (1992). Information-based objective functions for active data selection. *Neural Computation, 4,* 590–604.

Manktelow, K. I., Sutherland, E. J., & Over, D. E. (1995). Probabilistic factors in deontic reasoning. *Thinking and Reasoning, 1,* 201–220.

Marr, D. (1982). *Vision.* San Francisco: W. H. Freeman.

McCarthy, J. M. (1980). Circumscription: A form of nonmonotonic reasoning. *Artificial Intelligence, 13,* 27–39.

McCarthy, J. M., & Hayes, P. (1969). Some philosophical problems from the standpoint of Artificial Intelligence. In B. Meltzer, & D. Michie (Eds.), *Machine intelligence, Volume 4* (pp. 463–502). Edinburgh: Edinburgh University Press.

McClelland, J. L. (1998). Connectionist models and Bayesian inference. In M. Oaksford & N. Chater, (Eds.), *Rational models of cognition* (pp. 21–53). Oxford: Oxford University Press.

McDermott, D. (1982). Non-monotonic logic II: Nonmonotonic modal theories. *Journal of the Association for Computing Machinery, 29,* 33–57.

McDermott, D. (1987). A critique of pure reason. *Computational Intelligence, 3,* 151–160.

McDermott, D., & Doyle, J. (1980). Non-monotonic logic I. *Artifical Intelligence, 13,* 41–72.

Minsky, M. (1977). Frame system theory. In P. N. Johnson-Laird, & P. C. Wason (Eds.), *Thinking: Readings in cognitive science* (pp. 355–376). Cambridge: Cambridge University Press.

Newstead, S. E., Handley, S. J., & Buck, E. (1999). Falsifying mental models: Testing the

predictions of theories of syllogistic reasoning. *Memory & Cognition*, *27*, 344–354.
Neyman, J. (1950). *Probability and statistics*. New York: Holt.
Oaksford, M. (1998). Task demands and revising probabilities in the selection task. *Thinking and Reasoning*, *4*, 179–186.
Oaksford, M., & Chater, N. (1991). Against logicist cognitive science. *Mind & Language*, *6*, 1–38.
Oaksford, M., & Chater, N. (1992). Bounded rationality in taking risks and drawing inferences. *Theory and Psychology*, *2*, 225–230.
Oaksford, M., & Chater, N. (1993). Reasoning theories and bounded rationality. In K. I. Manktelow, & D. E. Over (Eds.), *Rationality* (pp. 31–60). London: Routledge.
Oaksford, M., & Chater, N. (1994). A rational analysis of the selection task as optimal data selection. *Psychological Review*, *101*, 608–631.
Oaksford, M., & Chater, N. (1995a). Theories of reasoning and the computational explanation of everyday inference. *Thinking and Reasoning*, *1*, 121–152.
Oaksford, M., & Chater, N. (1995b). Information gain explains relevance which explains the selection task. *Cognition*, *57*, 97–108.
Oaksford, M., & Chater, N. (1996). Rational explanation of the selection task. *Psychological Review*, *103*, 381–391.
Oaksford, M., & Chater, N. (1998a). A revised rational analysis of the selection task: Exceptions and sequential sampling. In M. Oaksford & N. Chater (Eds.), *Rational models of cognition* (pp. 372–398). Oxford: Oxford University Press.
Oaksford, M., & Chater, N. (Eds.). (1998b). *Rational models of cognition*. Oxford: Oxford University Press.
Oaksford, M., & Chater, N. (1998c). *Rationality in an uncertain world*. Hove, UK: Psychology Press.
Oaksford, M., Chater, N., & Grainger, B. (1999). Probabilistic effects in data selection. *Thinking and Reasoning*, *5*, 193–243.
Oaksford, M., Chater, N., Grainger, B., & Larkin, J. (1997). Optimal data selection in the reduced array selection task (RAST). *Journal of Experimental Psychology: Learning, Memory and Cognition*, *23*, 441–458.
Oaksford, M., Chater, N., & Larkin, J. (2000). Probabilities and polarity biases in conditional inference. *Journal of Experimental Psychology: Learning, Memory and Cognition*, *26*, 883–899.
Oaksford, M., & Stenning, K. (1992). Reasoning with conditionals containing negated constituents. *Journal of Experimental Psychology: Learning, Memory & Cognition*, *18*, 835–854.
Over, D. E., & Green, D. W. (2001). Contingency, causation, and adaptive inference. *Psychological Review*, *108*, 682–684.
Over, D. E., & Jessop, A. (1998). Rational analysis of causal conditionals and the selection task. In M. Oaksford & N. Chater (Eds.), *Rational models of cognition* (pp. 399–414). Oxford: Oxford University Press.
Paris, J. (1994). *The uncertain reasoner's companion*. Cambridge: Cambridge University Press.
Pearl, J. (1988). *Probabilistic reasoning in intelligent systems: Networks of plausible inference*. San Mateo, CA: Morgan Kaufman.
Politzer, G., & Braine, M. D. S. (1991). Responses to inconsistent premises cannot count as suppression of valid inferences. *Cognition*, *38*, 103–108.
Pylyshyn, Z. W. (Ed.). (1987). *The robot's dilemma: The frame problem in artificial intelligence*. Norwood, NJ: Ablex.

Quine, W. V. O. (1960). *Word and object.* Cambridge, MA: MIT Press.
Ramsey, F. P. (1931). *The foundations of mathematics and other logical essays.* London: Routledge & Kegan Paul.
Rawls, J. (1971). *A theory of justice.* Cambridge, MA: Harvard University Press.
Reiter, R. (1980). A logic for default reasoning. *Artificial Intelligence, 13,* 81–132.
Reiter, R. (1985). One reasoning by default. In R. Brachman, & H. Levesque (Eds.), *Readings in knowledge representation* (pp. 401–410). Los Altos, CA: Morgan Kaufman. [First published in 1978.]
Rips, L. J. (1983). Cognitive processes in propositional reasoning. *Psychological Review, 90,* 38–71.
Rips, L. J. (1994). *The psychology of proof.* Cambridge, MA: MIT Press.
Savage, L. J. (1954). *The foundations of statistics.* New York: Wiley.
Schank, R. C., & Abelson, R. P. (1977). *Scripts, plans, goals, and understanding.* Hillsdales, NJ: Lawrence Erlbaum Associates Inc.
Schooler, L. J. (1998). Sorting out core memory processes. In M. Oaksford & N. Chater (Eds.), *Rational models of cognition* (pp. 128–155). Oxford: Oxford University Press.
Simon, H. A. (1955). A behavioral model of rational choice. *Quarterly Journal of Economics, 69,* 99–118.
Simon, H. A. (1956). Rational choice and the structure of the environment. *Psychological Review, 63,* 1298–1138.
Skyrms, B. (1977). *Choice and chance.* Belmont: Wadsworth.
Sperber, D., Cara, F., & Girotto, V. (1995). Relevance theory explains the selection task. *Cognition, 57,* 31–95.
Stein, E. (1996). *Without good reason.* Oxford: Oxford University Press.
Stephens, D. W., & Krebs, J. R. (1986). *Foraging theory.* Princeton, NJ: Princeton University Press.
Stevenson, R. J., & Over, D. E. (1995). Deduction from uncertain premises. *Quarterly Journal of Experimental Psychology, 48*A, 613–643.
Stich, S. (1985). Could man be an irrational animal? *Synthese, 64,* 115–135.
Stich, S. (1990). *The fragmentation of reason.* Cambridge, MA: MIT Press.
Stich, S., & Nisbett, R. (1980). Justification and the psychology of human reasoning. *Philosophy of Science, 47,* 188–202.
Sutherland, N. S. (1992). *Irrationality: The enemy within.* London: Constable.
Thagard, P. (1988). *Computational philosophy of science.* Cambridge, MA: MIT Press.
Tversky, A., & Kahneman, D. (1974). Judgement under uncertainty: Heuristics and biases. *Science, 125,* 1124–1131.
Tversky, A., & Kahneman, D. (1986). Rational choice and the framing of decisions. *Journal of Business, 59,* 251–278.
von Neumann, J., & Morgenstern, O. (1944). *Theory of games and economic behaviour.* Princeton, NJ: Princeton University Press.
Wason, P. C. (1966). Reasoning. In B. Foss (Ed.), *New horizons in psychology.* Harmondsworth, UK: Penguin.
Wason, P. C., & Johnson-Laird, P. N. (1972). *The psychology of reasoning: Structure and content.* Cambridge, MA: Harvard University Press.
Wilson, E. O. (1975). *Sociobiology: The new synthesis.* Cambridge, MA: Belknap Press.
Young, R. (1998). Rational analysis of exploratory choice. In M. Oaksford & N. Chater (Eds.), *Rational models of cognition* (pp. 469–500). Oxford: Oxford University Press.

4 The psychology of conditionals

David Over

The use of conditionals is central to human reasoning, and any psychological theory of reasoning worthy of the name must have an adequate account of conditionals in natural language. Yet even taking the first steps towards a theory of the ordinary indicative conditional immediately entangles the psychologist in formidable logical and philosophical, as well as psychological, problems. It is a good test of any psychological theory of reasoning to go straight to its account of ordinary indicative conditionals. The theory is in serious trouble if it does not have an adequate account of this conditional, and it is very easy to fail this test, as I will try to show in what follows. Further challenges are presented by counterfactual and deontic conditionals.

Present psychological theories of all these conditionals suffer from what has been called logicism (Evans, 2002; Oaksford & Chater, 1998). One way to characterize logicism is that it is the attempt to account for a significant aspect of human reasoning by using logic alone. Logicism restricts itself to the study of logical inference from assumptions, i.e., premises that are supposed to be taken, in effect, as certain. But inference in the real world is usually from premises that people rightly think of as uncertain to some degree. Effective reasoning from premises, whether scientific or everyday, essentially depends on judgements of probability, and sometimes of utility, even when it partly consists of logically valid inferences. Conditional premises are prominent in both scientific and everyday inference, and consequently psychological theories of reasoning should include an acceptable account of the subjective probability of conditionals. More generally, the psychological study of conditional reasoning (as well as of other types of reasoning) should be fully integrated with research on probability, utility, and decision making (Evans & Over, 1996; Evans & Over, 2004). Psychological theories of the ordinary conditional will be severely limited until this fact is fully appreciated.

INDICATIVE CONDITIONALS AND MENTAL MODELS

Many psychologists have assumed that the ordinary indicative conditional *if p then q* is logically equivalent to the material conditional of standard propositional logic. This is at least the presupposition of most of the experiments on conditional reasoning that have been run until fairly recently (see the review in Evans, Newstead, & Byrne, 1993). The material conditional has a precise truth table analysis and is logically equivalent to *not-p or q*. Suppose that *if p then q* is a material conditional. This conditional is true when p is false, true when q is true, and false only when p is true and q is false. Table 4.1 is a truth table and, as it shows, there are four exhaustive and exclusive logically possible states of affairs for the propositions p and q: s1, s2, s3, and s4. A material conditional is false in s2, when p is true and q is false, and is true in the other three possibilities. Clearly, by this table, the material conditional is truth functional and is logically equivalent to *not-p or q*: this conditional and this disjunction are both true in the logically possible states s1, s3, and s4, and both false in s2.

For the material conditional, Modus Ponens (MP) and Modus Tollens (MT) are valid inferences, and Affirmation of the Consequent (AC) and Denial of the Antecedent (DA) are invalid inferences. Table 4.2 displays these inferences, which have been much studied by psychologists (Evans et al., 1993). As can be seen in Table 4.1, the truth table analysis proves MP and MT to be valid: there is no possible state, s1–s4, in which the premises of either MP or MT are true and the conclusion false. And it proves AC and DA to be invalid: there is a possible state, s3, in which the premises of AC and DA are

Table 4.1 Truth values for a material conditional *if p then q*

Possible states	pq	Material conditional
s1	TT	T
s2	TF	F
s3	FT	T
s4	FF	T

Table 4.2 Conditional inferences

Inference	Major premise	Minor premise	Conclusion
Modus Ponens	If p then q	p	q
Modus Tollens	If p then q	not-q	not-p
Affirmation of the Consequent	If p then q	q	p
Denial of the Antecedent	If p then q	not-p	not-q

true and the conclusions false. Intuitively, MP and MT are also valid for the ordinary indicative conditional, and AC and DA invalid. To this extent, the material conditional could be said to be a reasonable substitute for the ordinary indicative conditional.

However, there are the so-called paradoxes of the material conditional. These are not paradoxes that infect the material conditional itself, but rather the assumption that the ordinary conditional is a material conditional. Consider this first paradoxical inference with a single premise:

> The Prime Minister is not in London today.
> Therefore, if he is in London today, then he is in France.

This inference is trivially valid for a material conditional, when it is equivalent to inferring *not-p or q* from *not-p*. But it is intuitively invalid for the ordinary conditional, suggesting that this conditional is not equivalent to a material conditional and *not-p or q*. Consider as well this second paradoxical inference with a single premise:

> The Prime Minister is in France.
> Therefore, if he is in London, then he is in France.

Again, this inference is trivially valid for the material conditional, when it is simply inferring *not-p or q* from *q*, but intuitively invalid for the ordinary conditional. This reinforces the suggestion that the ordinary conditional is not a material conditional. In fact, it is easy to see that accepting both inferences as valid for the ordinary conditional is logically equivalent, by trivial steps, to holding that this conditional is a material conditional. If we do not think that these paradoxical inferences are valid for the ordinary conditional, then we must conclude that the ordinary conditional is not a material conditional. If we believe that the paradoxes are only apparent, and the inferences are valid for the ordinary conditional, then we must accept that this conditional is a material conditional.

By the argument we have just rehearsed, Johnson-Laird and Byrne (1991, pp. 73–74) were right to stress that one must either give up a truth table analysis of the ordinary conditional or accept the validity of the paradoxes for this conditional. Their choice was to take the second alternative in their mental model theory of reasoning, and to try to explain the paradoxes away as only an apparent problem. According to their theory, the three fully explicit mental models for the ordinary conditional represent the three possible states in which the material conditional is true: s1, s2, and s3. These models are:

> p   q
> not-p   q
> not-p   not-q

However, Johnson-Laird and Byrne claim that many people will not usually have fully explicit models for conditionals, but will only have shortened, initial models, represented in this way:

    p   q
       . . .

The three dots in the above stand for implicit models. Johnson-Laird (1995) calls these dots a "mental footnote" that there are implicit models in which *not-p* holds.

Johnson-Laird and Byrne (2002) continue to give this analysis as their "core semantics" for what they call "basic conditionals", which have a "... neutral content that is as independent as possible from context and background knowledge, and which have an antecedent and consequent that are semantically independent apart from occurrence in the same conditional" (p. 648). A major change in their theory is that they now deny that the ordinary conditional or other sentential connectives in natural language, such as *or*, are truth functional (p. 673). One way to interpret this position is that *if p then q* is still supposed to be logically equivalent in natural language to *not-p or q*, but that neither of these propositions is truth functional. As it stands, this position is inconsistent with their continued unqualified claim that the two paradoxical inferences are valid (p. 651). They accept (Johnson-Laird, personal communication) that *not* is truth functional in natural language. But then the truth values of the propositions *if p then q* and *not-p or q* will be determined in the four possible truth table cases, s1–s4, and the two propositions will be truth functional. For *q* is true in s1, and so are *if p then q* and *not-p or q* by the second paradox above and a trivial inference, and in s3 and s4, both propositions are true by the first paradox above and another trivial inference. Finally, in s2 both propositions are trivially false. Hence, if Johnson-Laird and Byrne continue to hold that the paradoxes are valid for the ordinary conditional, then they must give up claiming that *if p then q* and *not-p or q* are not truth functional. Alternatively, they could be interpreted as holding that the paradoxes are valid for "basic conditionals", which are truth functional, but invalid for non-basic conditionals, which are not truth functional. But this interpretation is, on the face of it, inconsistent with their unqualified claim that the paradoxes are valid, apparently for all ordinary conditionals.

Johnson-Laird and Byrne (1991, 2002) try to explain some of the results of experimental studies on conditional inferences. For example, these studies have found that MP is endorsed with a greater frequency than MT (Evans et al., 1993). Johnson-Laird and Byrne point out that people would endorse MP on the basis of the initial models alone, in which *p* is the minor premise for MP. But people would have to expand this initial model to the fully explicit models, in which the minor premise of MT *not-q* occurs, to endorse MT. Expanding the initial models to the fully explicit models would require extra effort. Some people do not go to this extra trouble, Johnson-Laird and Byrne claim, and so do not endorse MT. A big drawback of this analysis, however, is that Johnson-Laird and Byrne (2002) cannot explain why people would endorse MT for non-basic conditionals. Only basic conditionals are given the fully explicit mental models, and any conditional that has these fully explicit models is truth functional. A basic conditional is supposed to be independent of context and background knowledge, but few ordinary conditionals that are actually used in everyday discourse have these properties. Most of these conditionals will then be non-basic and non-truth functional, and thus they cannot be given the fully explicit mental models. It is totally unclear what mental models these non-basic, non-truth functional conditionals have and how MT can be valid for them.

Another problem for Johnson-Laird and Byrne (1991, 2002) is to justify their claim that the paradoxical inferences are valid for the ordinary conditional. Their attempt to do this is best illustrated by considering a conditional with a negated antecedent, as in their example (Johnson-Laird & Byrne, 1991, pp. 74–75):

If Shakespeare didn't write the sonnets then Bacon did.

As they pointed out, their account of the ordinary conditional as the truth functional, material conditional implies that this example is logically equivalent to:

Shakespeare wrote the sonnets or Bacon did.

They went on to argue that both of the following inferences are valid and only seem paradoxical or odd for the same reason:

Shakespeare wrote the sonnets.
Therefore, if Shakespeare didn't write the sonnets then Bacon did.

Shakespeare wrote the sonnets.
Therefore, Shakespeare wrote the sonnets or Bacon did.

Their point was that both of these inferences "throw semantic information away", in that the single premise is more informative than the conclusion, and doing that violates "one of the fundamental constraints on human deductive competence" (Johnson-Laird & Byrne, 1991, p. 74). This argument that the paradoxes are only an apparent problem for mental model theory has been a constant theme of the theory (Johnson-Laird, 1995; Johnson-Laird & Byrne, 1991, 2002).

However, Johnson-Laird and Byrne's attempt to explain the paradoxes away is unpersuasive when the premises of the inferences are uncertain, as they almost always are in ordinary and scientific reasoning. Few useful premises can just be assumed to be true. Except in an exercise in pure logic, we cannot usually assume that a proposition is true when it has some probability that is less than certainty. We must take account of that degree of probability in our assertions and our inferences, if we are not to mislead ourselves as well as other people. Indeed, logicist psychological theories of reasoning were severely limited by covering only inferences from assumptions and not from premises uncertain to some degree (Evans, 2002; Evans & Over, 1996, 2004). This aspect of logicism is now starting to be abandoned in response to experiments in which valid inferences are suppressed by uncertainty in the premises (see Byrne, 1991; Politzer & Braine, 1991; Politzer & Bourmaud, 2002; Stevenson & Over, 1995, 2001). Some inferences should be suppressed by uncertainty in the premises, so that one can avoid believing or asserting an improbable conclusion, but other inferences should be encouraged by uncertainty in the premises, particularly those in which information is "thrown away".

Consider people who have heard that there is some dispute over whether Shakespeare or Bacon wrote the sonnets, but who know little about it. They are not completely confident that Shakespeare wrote the sonnets. With this uncertain belief, it will be rational for them to infer and to assert the disjunction: that Shakespeare wrote the sonnets or Bacon did. That is the safer inference and assertion for them to make, given their subjective probability judgements. With those judgements, they could rightly fear misleading their hearers by making the statement that Shakespeare wrote the sonnets. That categorical statement, if it were true, would admittedly be more informative than the disjunction, but it is also more likely to be false. Throwing information away in an inference is ruled out in Johnson-Laird and Byrne's mental model theory by one of their "fundamental constraints". But this constraint should not always apply. It is sometimes better to infer a less informative disjunction than to assert a more improbable categorical statement. On the other hand, it is truly paradoxical to infer, *merely* from the premise that Shakespeare wrote the sonnets, that Bacon wrote them if Shakespeare did not write them.

Although Johnson-Laird and Byrne (2002) continue to claim, without qualification, that the paradoxical inferences are valid, they have a new line (pp. 659–661) on the form of inference called strengthening the antecedent, which is:

If p then q
Therefore, if p & r then q

Strengthening the antecedent is a valid inference for the material conditional, when it is, in effect, a matter of inferring *not-(p & r) or q* from *not-p or q*. But Johnson-Laird and Byrne imply, with apparent inconsistency, that this inference is invalid for the ordinary conditional. This appears

The psychology of conditionals 81

inconsistent as the validity of strengthening the antecedent follows directly from the paradoxes. From *if p then q*, we may infer *not-(p & not-q)*, and so *not-p or q*, by any reasonable account of the ordinary conditional. So suppose that *if p then q* holds, and infer *not-p or q*. We may now infer *not-p* holds or *q* holds. If *not-p* holds, then *not-(p & r)* trivially holds and we get by *if p & r then q* by the first paradox above. And if *q* holds, then we get *if p & r then q* by the second paradox above.

We might try to interpret Johnson-Laird and Byrne (2002) as having the view that strengthening the antecedent is valid for basic conditionals, which are truth functional, but invalid for non-basic conditionals, which are not truth functional. However, their paper is inconsistent about what is, and what is not, a basic conditional. On strengthening the antecedent, they discuss this example (pp. 659–660):

SL   If a match is struck properly, then it lights

They describe how their computer program, which is supposed to follow the way the human mind constructs mental models, represents SL. This program produces these initial models for SL:

Match-struck   Match-lights
             . . .

The three dots above are supposed to denote implicit mental models of the two *not-p* possibilities: s3 and s4. That would make SL a truth functional, basic conditional. Yet SL should not be a "basic conditional" by the definition, which specifies a ". . . neutral content that is as free as possible from context and background knowledge . . ." (Johnson-Laird & Byrne, 2002, p. 648). Most of us have background knowledge about matches, and it transpires that the computer program has this as well.

Johnson-Laird and Byrne suppose that an assertion of SL is followed by this statement:

The match is soaked in water and then struck.

Their computer program combines the mental model for this conjunction with the initial models for SL to get this mental model:

Match-soaked   Match-struck   Match-lights

The computer has background knowledge of this conditional:

WNL   If a match is soaking wet, then it will not light

Johnson-Laird and Byrne say that the program's models for WNL are:

Match-soaked	¬Match-lights
¬Match-soaked	¬Match-lights
¬Match-soaked	Match-lights

These mental models would make WNL a "basic conditional", and yet WNL does not fit the definition either.

Johnson-Laird and Byrne have a principle of "pragmatic modulation", according to which precedence is given to background knowledge in constructing mental models. This principle has the effect that combining all the above mental models produces this inference in the computer:

Match-soaked, and match-struck, so it is not the case that the match lights.

This inference is the last step in supposedly explaining how the principle of pragmatic modulation prevents strengthening the antecedent, which would be to infer, from SL, that the match lights if it is soaked in water and struck. Of course, strengthening the antecedent is intuitively invalid for the ordinary conditional and indeed could be called another paradox of identifying the ordinary conditional with the material conditional. But the point is that Johnson-Laird and Byrne imply that SL is a basic conditional, and basic conditionals are material conditionals. Strengthening the antecedent is a valid form of inference for SL given that SL is a basic conditional. Therefore, Johnson-Laird and Byrne have not given us an example in which strengthening the antecedent is invalid by their mental model theory, but rather an example in which, by that theory, their computer program commits a fallacy.

There are still further problems with consistency in what Johnson-Laird and his collaborators have said about the probability of ordinary conditionals (see also Over, 2004). Johnson-Laird, Legrenzi, Girotto, Legrenzi, and Caverni (1999) repeated that the initial models of *if p then q* contain not only what is in effect the conjunction *p & q* but also the mental footnote of the three dots, indicating that there are models left implicit. In Experiment 2 in their paper, they predicted that some participants would take account of the three dots when judging the probability of *if p then q*, P(*if p then q*), on the basis of the initial models. More precisely, their prediction was that some participants would assign equal probability to *p & q* and to the three dots when making a probability judgement about the conditional, and they claimed to find some evidence that this is so. They also found that other participants forgot about the three dots and identified P(*if p then q*) with P(*p & q*). However, Johnson-Laird and Byrne (2002), in describing an experiment on the probability of conditionals by Girotto and Johnson-Laird, make no mention of a probability for the three dots. The modal response in this experiment is that of giving P(*p & q*) when asked for P(*if p then q*), and Johnson-Laird and Byrne explain this in terms of the explicit part, *p & q*, of the initial models. The three dots do not come into it at all. There is apparently no evidence in this experiment that any participants take account of the three dots in their probability judgements.

It is unclear what mental model theory predicts about participants' responses when they are asked for a judgement about P(*if p then q*). Some may reply with P(*p & q*), and some other participants, in some experiments, may reply with P(*p & q*) plus some probability for the three dots, while a small number will supposedly respond with P(*not-p or q*). But we can derive one specific prediction about P(*if p then q*) from mental model theory. Consider only participants who endorse MT and, after this endorsement, ask them for P(*if p then q*). By mental model theory, these people should have fully explicit models of *if p then q* and so should give us as its probability P(*not-p or q*). However, it appears most unlikely that these people will make this response. There is very strong evidence (Evans, Handley, & Over, 2003; Oberauer & Wilhelm, 2003; Over & Evans, 2003) against the hypothesis that a significant number of people will ever judge P(*if p then q*) to be P(*not-p or q*).

SUPPOSITIONS AND CONDITIONALS

Philosophical logicians have long attacked the idea that the ordinary indicative conditional is the truth functional, material conditional (Edgington, 1995). Some have developed other systems of logic and formal semantics for the ordinary conditional that have influenced some psychologists. The theory of Stalnaker (1968) has been one of the most influential in this respect, and we will describe it briefly here (see also Lewis, 1973). It is best to return to Table 4.1 to compare what we can call the Stalnaker conditional with the material conditional. A Stalnaker conditional *if p then q* is true in possibility s1, where *p* and *q* are true, and false in possibility s2, where *p* is true *q* is false. Up to this point then, the Stalnaker conditional is the same as the material conditional. But in the *not-p* possibilities, s3 and s4, where the material conditional is automatically true, the Stalnaker conditional can be either true or false. What determines whether the Stalnaker conditional is true at a *not-p* possibility? Stalnaker's answer is that *if p then q* is true at a *not-p* possibility like s3 or s4 if and only if *q* is true at the closest possible state of affairs, or "possible world", to s3 or s4 in which *p* is true.

Return as well to the example:

If the Prime Minister is in London then he is in France.

Suppose that the Prime Minister is out of London at Chequers, i.e., that the actual state of affairs can be represented by s4. That makes the material conditional automatically true. But this example is false if it is a Stalnaker conditional, and that obviously agrees with intuition and indeed common sense. The closest possible state of affairs in which the Prime Minister returns to London is not one in which London has become part of France. There are possibilities in which London is part of France, e.g., ones in which Napoleon successfully invaded Britain, but these are too distant for us to consider when thinking about the example as a Stalnaker conditional. Stalnaker's analysis will also work for the following counterfactual, which is false by his analysis and by common sense:

If the Prime Minister were in London then he would be in France.

Some psychologists have been impressed by how the Stalnaker conditional is intuitively much more like the ordinary conditional than the material conditional is. Other psychologists have been worried about what kind of psychological reality possible states of affairs, or "possible worlds", could have. Johnson-Laird and Byrne (1991, 2002) have expressed this worry, but supporters of mental model theory could identify mental models as schematic, or partial, representations of these possible states of affairs. However, the psychologists most sympathetic to the Stalnaker conditional have rejected mental model theory for other reasons. Rips has the most developed and rigorous of such positions. (See Rips & Marcus, 1977, and Rips, 1994, but also Over & Evans, 2003, and Evans & Over, 2004, for a discussion of another major psychological account of the ordinary conditional, that of Braine & O'Brien, 1991.)

Rips and Marcus (1977) looked for a psychological "analogue" for the "possible worlds" in Stalnaker's formal semantics for the ordinary conditional. They suggested that what fulfils this role are suppositions that people naturally make. Assume we hear the above counterfactual about the Prime Minister, when we believe that he is at Chequers and not in London. In that case, we believe that we are in a *not-p* state of affairs, specifically one of the form s4, in which the Prime Minister is not in London and is not in France. To make a judgement about the counterfactual, Stalnaker asks us, as we have explained, to consider the "closest" possible state of affairs in which the Prime Minister is in London. This corresponds, according to Rips and Marcus, to our making the supposition that the Prime Minister is in London and taking this as a "seed" proposition for hypothetically modifying our beliefs. Their proposal is that we rank the mental propositions in our belief "data base" in terms of their importance for describing the current state of affairs as we take it to be. Of the highest rank are to be beliefs that we can easily give up hypothetically, such as ones based on our memory of a news report that the Prime Minister is at Chequers. Very far down the ranking will be our beliefs that Napoleon lost the battle of Waterloo and failed to conquer Britain. We are to expand our supposition by forming the largest consistent subset, or subsets, of the "seed" proposition and the beliefs of the highest rank. We ideally proceed through all the ranks in this way, expanding the consistent subset or subsets, until we exhaust the ranks, leaving out at each step only beliefs of the given rank that are inconsistent with the expanding subset or subsets. In our example, we would end up with an expanded supposition, i.e., an expanded consistent subset, in which the Prime Minister returns to London for some reason and news reports are altered accordingly, but in which Napoleon did not conquer Britain and London is not in France. For this reason, we would reject the counterfactual as clearly false.

Consider this new example of a counterfactual:

> If the Prime Minister were in London then he would be in Downing Street.

We might conclude that this counterfactual was true after running through the procedure Rips and Marcus describe. That would be our conclusion if we ended up with one consistent suppositional subset in which the Prime Minister returns to London and in that he goes to Downing Street. However, we might also generate, say, three different suppositional ways in which the Prime Minister returns to London, perhaps for three different reasons – and in two of these he might be in Downing Street and in one at Parliament. In this case, we would judge that the above counterfactual was *probably* true. Rips and Marcus's precise proposal is that the probability of the counterfactual is given by the proportion of suppositional subsets in which the antecedent and consequent hold, out of the total of generated suppositional subsets in which the antecedent holds. In other words, Rips and Marcus relate the probability of an ordinary conditional, P(*if p then q*), to this way of determining the conditional probability of its consequent given its antecedent, $P(q/p)$. They discuss (1977, pp. 213–214) some other work that made a link between the probability of conditionals and conditional probability, and this suggested link has become much more important as a result of very recent research, which we will discuss below.

Rips and Marcus did not apparently consider the possibility of different probability weightings for the generated suppositional subsets, but this would be a necessary extension to their proposal. It would correspond to different probability weightings for different possible states of affairs, which is clearly necessary to take full account of uncertainty about them. For example, the two suppositional subsets in which the Prime Minister returns to London to go to Downing Street might both be much more implausible than the one in which he goes to Parliament, and the counterfactual would then be improbable rather than probable. The different weightings could derive from heuristics or some kind of frequency information, say, as a result of recalling that the Prime Minister almost never suddenly returns to London from Chequers except when there is important business in Parliament to attend to. Of course, in order to be psychologically plausible, these weightings, and for that matter the whole business of suppositions in Rips and Marcus's approach, would have to be the product of a much more bounded system than Rips and Marcus describe.

What Rips and Marcus say about suppositional subsets can be seen as a development of comments made by Stalnaker, who does not restrict to himself to formal semantics and a philosophical theory of possible states of affairs. In fact, Stalnaker (1968) referred to a view briefly stated by Ramsey (1931) that can be interpreted as psychological in nature (Evans & Over, 2004; Over & Evans, 2003). Ramsey said that people who are arguing about *if p then q* are trying to determine what their degree of belief in *q* given *p* should be, and they do that by "adding *p* hypothetically to their stock of knowledge and arguing on that basis about *q*" (p. 247). What Ramsey seemed to be suggesting in this passage came to be known, among philosophers, as the "Ramsey test" for determining whether one should believe a conditional, and for how strongly one should believe it. Stalnaker (1968) generalized this "test" to contexts in which we are confident that *p* does not hold. In that case, Stalnaker tells us that, to assess the believability of *if p then q*, we should "add the antecedent (hypothetically) to your stock of beliefs, make whatever adjustments are necessary to preserve consistency, and consider whether or not the consequent is then true." (p. 102). Stalnaker held that, by engaging in this mental process, we are trying to determine whether *q* holds in the nearest possible world in which *p* holds. In this way, he himself tried to connect his formal and philosophical theory of conditionals with what can be seen as a psychological hypothesis about how people make a conditional probability judgement.

A consequence of the Ramsey test is that the subjective probability of a conditional, P(*if p then q*), is identical to the corresponding conditional degree of belief, or conditional subjective probability, P(*q*/*p*). Stalnaker (1968), in trying to base his analysis of conditionals on the Ramsey test, endorsed this identity, and as we have seen above, Rips and Marcus (1977) also in effect follow Stalnaker in this respect. Identifying P(*if p then q*) with P(*q*/*p*) is certainly far more intuitive than the paradoxical view we discussed above of holding that P(*if p then q*) should be equal to P(*not-p or q*). To return to our example above, if P(*if p then q*) is P(*q*/*p*), and not P(*not-p or q*), then it is extremely improbable, as it clearly is intuitively, that the Prime Minister is in France if he is in London. Philosophical logicians (Adams, 1975; Edgington, 1995) have argued for a relation between P(*if p then q*) and P(*q*/*p*), there is mounting psychological evidence for it (Evans et al., 2003; Hadjichristidis, Stevenson, Over, Sloman, Evans, & Feeney, 2001; Oberauer & Wilhelm, 2003; Over & Evans, 2003), and many psychological results can potentially be explained if the relation holds (Oaksford, Chater, & Larkin, 2000; Stevenson & Over, 1995).

However, if P(*if p then q*) is P(*q*/*p*) for the ordinary conditional, then this conditional cannot, it turns out, be the Stalnaker conditional, in spite of Stalnaker's original claim. This is one of the consequences of a famous proof in philosophical logic by Lewis (1976). As we saw above, a Stalnaker conditional *if p then q* sometimes holds in the possible states s3 and s4, in which *not-p* is true. Such a Stalnaker conditional must then have some probability added to it for the s3 and s4 possibilities. The probabilities of s3 and s4, P(s3) and P(s4), add together to give P(*not-p*), but the probabilities of P(s3) and P(s4), and so of P(*not-p*), are irrelevant for determining P(*q*/*p*), which is fixed only by the relative probabilities of s1 and s2, P(s1) and P(s2), where *p* is true. P(s1) is the same as P(*p* & *q*) and P(s2) is the same as P(*p* & *not-q*), and P(*q*/*p*) is fully determined, in probability theory, by the relative values of P(*p* & *q*) and P(*p* & *not-q*). The result is that P(*if p then q*) cannot usually be identified with P(*q*/*p*), where *if p then q* is the Stalnaker conditional (Edgington, 1995; Evans & Over, 2004).

Some philosophical logicians have proposed unified accounts of ordinary indicative and counterfactual conditionals purely in terms of conditional probability, but the detailed psychological investigation of this possibility is only just beginning. A way forward might be to extend mental model theory to include weighted mental models or, at least, mental models ordered in terms of relative probability (Johnson-Laird et al., 1999; Stevenson & Over, 1995). Then the weighted or ordered mental models of s1 and s2 could be compared to yield a judgement about P(*q*/*p*) in a kind of Ramsey test (Evans et al., 2003; Evans & Over, 2004; Over & Evans, 2003). However, Johnson-Laird and Byrne's current mental model theory has further problems in its accounts of ordinary conditionals that are counterfactuals or deontic conditionals.

COUNTERFACTUALS AND MENTAL MODELS

We have discussed above the problems of the current mental model theory of ordinary indicative conditionals. Its account of counterfactuals is not satisfactory either.

Johnson-Laird and Byrne (2002) criticize the Ramsey test and Stalnaker's extension of it, and they would be equally critical of Rips and Marcus's proposal on the same grounds. Johnson-Laird and Byrne point out that it can be extremely difficult to find a unique way to modify our mental state in order to make a judgement about a counterfactual when we disbelieve its antecedent. They ask us to consider an example from philosophical logic:

> If Verdi and Bizet had been compatriots then they would both have been Italian.
>
> If Verdi and Bizet had been compatriots then they would both have been French.

We would be puzzled in trying to decide, when we hypothetically suspend our belief in *not-p* here, whether we should make Verdi and Bizet both Italian or both French. However, this is an odd objection to make to Stalnaker and Rips and Marcus, who can reply that they can explain why these counterfactuals are hard to make a judgement about. After all, the counterfactuals are intuitively difficult to come to a conclusion about, and it could be argued that that is precisely because it is difficult to apply the generalized Ramsey test, or Rips and Marcus's procedure, to them.

This possible reply would be especially effective against Johnson-Laird and Byrne (2002), whose own theory of counterfactuals does not explain the difficulty at all. In their account, some of the states s1–s4 are designated "counterfactual possibilities", and a counterfactual conditional like our example,

> If the Prime Minister were in London then he would be in Downing Street

has the mental models:

Fact:	not London	not Downing Street
Counterfactual possibility:	London	Downing Street

In this Johnson-Laird and Byrne analysis, by asserting the counterfactual, we state that the Prime Minister is not in London and not in Downing Street, but also that there is one counterfactual possibility in which the Prime Minister is in London and in Downing Street. (Another counterfactual in which the Prime Minister is not in London but is in Downing Street is ruled out by background knowledge.) One immediate problem with this analysis is that, in it, the counterfactual logically implies that the Prime Minister is not, in fact, in London and not in Downing Street. This is counterintuitive. We would not intuitively feel that we stated a falsehood by asserting the counterfactual if we found out later that, unknown to us, the Prime Minister has returned to London and gone to Downing Street. We would rather claim that the core of what we had asserted was true, although we had unintentionally used a pragmatically misleading subjective form in which to express it.

Another problem with the analysis of Johnson-Laird and Byrne (2002) is that, in it, the above counterfactual is perfectly compatible with:

> If the Prime Minister were in London then he would be in Parliament.

For this second counterfactual has the mental models:

Fact:	not London	not Parliament
Counterfactual possibility:	London	Parliament

Thus the second counterfactual states that the Prime Minister is not in London and not in Parliament, and also that there is one counterfactual possibility in which the Prime Minister is in London and in Parliament. Clearly, it is perfectly consistent to assert that there is one counterfactual possibility in which the Prime Minister is in London and in Downing

Street and another counterfactual possibility in which he is in London and in Parliament. Johnson-Laird and Byrne reject the notion that one counterfactual possibility may be "closer" or "nearer" to the actual state of affairs than another, although there is considerable psychological evidence that ordinary people do have this notion (Kahneman & Miller, 1986; Roese, 1997; Teigen, 1998). But then Johnson-Laird and Byrne do not have the means, as Stalnaker has with his notion of closeness, to explain why the first and second counterfactuals about the Prime Minister make incompatible claims about counterfactual possibilities. Nor do Johnson-Laird and Byrne give an account of how one of these counterfactuals could be more probable than the other by relating the counterfactuals to the relevant conditional probabilities. Johnson-Laird and Byrne do not assign weights to the mental models that represent counterfactual possibilities, or order these in terms of relative probability. If they did, they could base some notion of relative closeness on that. For example, a counterfactual possibility in which the Prime Minister returns to London to go to Parliament might be relatively more plausible, in some context, than one in which he goes to go to Downing Street. That would make the former counterfactual possibility "closer" than the latter one in this context.

Johnson-Laird and Byrne's analysis implies that the mental models for

> If Verdi and Bizet had been compatriots then they would both have been Italian.

are:

| Fact: | not compatriots | not Italian |
| Counterfactual possibility: | compatriots | Italian |

and implies that the mental models for

> If Verdi and Bizet had been compatriots then they would both have been French.

are:

| Fact: | not compatriots | not French |
| Counterfactual possibility: | compatriots | French |

It is very easy to construct these mental models for these two counterfactuals, and thus Johnson-Laird and Byrne do not explain why we should find them so problematic. At least Stalnaker's generalization of the Ramsey test and Rips and Marcus's procedure imply that these counterfactuals are incompatible, and suggest why we should have difficulty in deciding which one to assent to and in assigning a probability to them. The mere hypothetical supposition that Verdi and Bizet were born in the same country gives us no basis for inferring that they were both born in France or that they were both born in Italy, nor even that one of these counterfactual probabilities is more probable than the other.

DEONTIC CONDITIONALS AND MENTAL MODELS

The deontic modals, "must" (in one sense), "should", "ought to", and "may" (in one sense), are used to express moral, legal, social, and prudential obligations and permissions. Deontic conditionals, which explicitly or implicitly contain these modals, are commonly used to lay down rules that are supposed guide our actions, according to some moral, legal, social, or prudential principles. For example, a moral principle of honesty supports the deontic conditional in the ethics of science that, if we run an experiment, then we should report the results accurately. A prudential principle about the underlying value of good health justifies the deontic conditional that we ought to take a break and go for walk if we have been working at our desk for a long time. Deontic conditionals could hardly be more important for reasoning and decision making in the real world. The study of these conditionals in psychology has, however, been rather restricted by an almost exclusive reliance on Wason's selection task as the experimental paradigm (following the seminal paper by Cheng & Holyoak, 1985).

Johnson-Laird and Byrne (2002), in their mental model theory of deontic conditionals, appeal to unexplained concepts of deontic possibility and impossibility. Consider, for instance, this deontic conditional as a general moral rule for guiding behaviour:

If you are asked for directions, then you ought to help.

To understand this conditional, we set up, according to Johnson-Laird and Byrne, mental models representing the following "deontic possibilities", i.e., permissible actions:

asked   help
not-asked   help
not-asked   not-help

We will also, in their view, have a mental model in some contexts for the "deontic impossibility" that violates the rule:

asked   not-help

A problem with this approach becomes apparent when we consider this new moral rule:

If you can prevent a crime, then you should do so.

The "deontic impossibility" that violates this rule will be:

crime   not-prevent

If our mental models were limited to the above for the two rules, we would be unable to make a decision when someone who was obviously going to commit a crime asked us for directions. But clearly most of us would be able to decide that not preventing a crime was a far more serious, and in a sense more "costly" (morally), violation of a rule than not giving help when asked.

We have used conditional moral rules in our examples, but we could have equally used legal, social, or prudential rules instead. The underlying point would be the same. To engage in realistic reasoning and decision making that appeals to deontic rules, we must have (moral, legal, social, or prudential) preferences among different possible outcomes and particularly between possible states of affairs of the form s1 and s2. We must think of these possible outcomes or states as potentially leading to certain "costs" and "benefits", or in still more technical language, we must make judgements about differences in subjective expected utility (based on our moral, legal, social, or prudential preferences) about the states s1 and s2. To cover this type of reasoning and decision making in a mental model theory, mental models must be ordered, not only in terms of relative probability but also in terms of our (moral, legal, social, or prudential) preferences among the possible outcomes that the models represent (Evans & Over, 1996, 2004; Manktelow & Over, 1991, 1992, 1995).

As we have discussed above, there appears to be some connection between the probability of ordinary indicative, and perhaps counterfactual, conditionals and conditional probability. It can also be plausibly argued that the corresponding relation for a deontic conditional is with a judgement of conditional expected utility (Evans & Over, 2004; Manktelow & Over, 1995). The evidence is that an ordinary indicative conditional, *if p then q*, will be confidently used in reasoning and decision making when $P(q/p)$ is appropriately high for the context (Evans et al., 2003; Oberauer & Wilhelm, 2003; Over & Evans, 2003). In that case, P(*if p then q*) will be high when P(s1) is higher than P(s2) and low when P(s1) is lower than P(s2). The suggestion is that there is a similar relation between a deontic conditional and conditional expected utility. That is, a deontic conditional of the form, *if p then q should hold*, will be confidently used in reasoning and decision making when the relevant subjective expected utility judgements are appropriate for the context. That will be when the subjective expected utility of *q* given *p* is appropriately higher than the subjective expected utility of *not-q* given *p*. And that will in turn depend on whether the subjective expected utility of s1 is appropriately higher than the subjective expected utility of s2. For example, we would assert the ordinary deontic conditional

If a friend asks us for advice, then we should give it.

as a result of our preference for giving a friend advice who asks for it, an s1 state, over not giving a friend advice who asks for it, an s2 state. This preference implies (in technical terms) that the s1 state has higher expected utility for us than the s2 state. There are not yet experimental investigations of this possible relation between deontic conditionals and conditional expected utility, simply because the empirical study of deontic conditionals is in its infancy (but see Over, Manktelow, & Hadjichristidis, in press).

CONCLUSION

Current psychological theories of ordinary conditionals are all seriously inadequate (see Evans & Over, 2004, for further support of this conclusion). Progress in understanding these basic forms in reasoning will mean finally, and decisively, giving up logicism. Valid inference, including that with conditionals, is a part of human reasoning, but little progress can be made in studying this reasoning independently of judgements of probability and utility. It will perhaps be possible to represent these judgements in mental model theory by introducing a relative ordering of mental models in terms of probability and different kinds of (moral, legal, social, prudential, or epistemic) preferences. But we will get better psychological theories of ordinary conditionals when we have a deeper understanding of the relations between these conditionals and probability and utility judgements, and we can incorporate this understanding into unified theories of reasoning and decision making.

REFERENCES

Adams, E. W. (1975). *The logic of conditionals.* Dordrecht: Reidel.
Braine, M. D. S., & O'Brien, D. P. (1991). A theory of if: A lexical entry, reasoning program, and pragmatic principles. *Psychological Review, 98,* 182–203.
Byrne, R. M. J. (1991). Can valid inferences be suppressed? *Cognition, 39,* 71–78.
Cheng, P., & Holyoak, K. (1985). Pragmatic reasoning schemas. *Cognitive Psychology, 17,* 391–416.
Edgington, D. (1995). On conditionals. *Mind, 104,* 235–329.
Evans, J. St. B. T. (2002). Logic and human reasoning: An assessment of the deductive paradigm. *Psychological Bulletin, 128,* 978–996.
Evans, J. St. B. T., Handley, S. H., & Over, D. E. (2003). Conditionals and conditional probability. *Journal of Experimental Psychology: Learning, Memory, and Cognition, 29,* 321–335.
Evans, J. St. B. T., Newstead, S.E., & Byrne, R. M. J. (1993). *Human reasoning: The psychology of deduction.* London: Lawrence Erlbaum Associates Ltd.

Evans, J. St. B. T., & Over, D. E. (1996). *Rationality and reasoning*. Hove, UK: Psychology Press.
Evans, J. St. B. T., & Over, D. E. (2004). *If*. Oxford: Oxford University Press.
Hadjichristidis, C., Stevenson, R. J., Over, D. E., Sloman, S. A., Evans, J. St. B. T., & Feeney, A. (2001). On the evaluation of "if p then q" conditionals. *Proceedings of the 23rd Annual Meeting of the Cognitive Science Society, Edinburgh*. Retrieved from http://www.cognitivesciencesociety.org/
Johnson-Laird, P. N. (1995). Inference and mental models. In S. E. Newstead & J. St. B. T. Evans (Eds.), *Perspectives on thinking and reasoning: Essays in honour of Peter Wason*. Hove, UK: Lawrence Erlbaum Associates Ltd.
Johnson-Laird, P. N., & Byrne, R. (1991). *Deduction*. Hove, UK: Lawrence Erlbaum Associates Ltd.
Johnson-Laird, P. N., & Byrne, R. (2002). Conditionals: A theory of meaning, pragmatics and inference. *Psychological Review, 109*, 646–678.
Johnson-Laird, P. N., Legrenzi, P., Girotto, V., Legrenzi, M., Caverni, J-P. (1999). Naive probability: A mental model theory of extensional reasoning. *Psychological Review, 106*, 62–88.
Kahneman, D., & Miller, D. (1986). Norm theory: Comparing reality to its alternatives. *Psychological Review, 93*, 136–153.
Lewis, D. (1973). *Counterfactuals*. Oxford: Basil Blackwell.
Lewis, D. (1976). Probabilities of conditionals and conditional probabilities. *Philosophical Review, 85*, 297–315.
Manktelow, K. I., & Over, D. E. (1991). Social roles and utilities in reasoning with deontic conditionals. *Cognition, 39*, 85–105.
Manktelow, K. I., & Over, D. E. (1992). Utility and deontic reasoning: Some comments on Johnson-Laird & Byrne. *Cognition, 43*, 183–186.
Manktelow, K. I., & Over, D. E. (1995). Deontic reasoning. In S. E. Newstead & J. St. B. T. Evans (Eds.), *Perspectives on thinking and reasoning: Essays in honour of Peter Wason*. Hove, UK: Lawrence Erlbaum Associates Ltd.
Oaksford, M., & Chater, N. (1998). *Rationality in an uncertain world: Essays on the cognitive science of human reasoning*. Hove, UK: Psychology Press.
Oaksford, M., Chater, N., & Larkin, J. (2000). Probabilities and polarity biases in conditional inference. *Journal of Experimental Psychology: Learning, Memory and Cognition, 26*, 883–889.
Oberauer, K., & Wilhelm, W. (2003). The meaning(s) of conditionals: Conditional probabilities, mental models, and personal utilities. *Journal of Experimental Psychology: Learning, Memory, and Cognition, 29*, 680–693.
Over, D. E. (2004). Naive probability and its model theory. In V. Girotto & P. N. Johnson-Laird (Eds.), *The shape of reason: Essays in honour of Paolo Legrenzi*. Hove, UK: Psychology Press.
Over, D. E., & Evans, J. St. B. T. (2003). The probability of conditionals: The psychological evidence. *Mind & Language, 18*, 340–358.
Over, D. E., Manktelow, K. I., & Hadjichristidis, C. (in press). What makes a good rule? Conditions for the acceptance of deontic conditionals. *Canadian Journal of Experimental Psychology*.
Politzer, G., & Bourmaud, G. (2002). Deductive reasoning from uncertain conditionals. *British Journal of Psychology, 93*, 345–381.
Politzer, G., & Braine, M. D. S. (1991). Responses to inconsistent premises cannot count as suppression of valid inferences. *Cognition, 38*, 103–108.

Ramsey, F. (1931). *The foundations of mathematics*. London: Routledge & Kegan Paul.

Rips, L. J. (1994). *The psychology of proof*. Cambridge, MA: MIT Press.

Rips, L. J., & Marcus, S. L. (1977). Suppositions and the analysis of conditional sentences. In M. A. Just & P. A. Carpenter (Eds.), *Cognitive processes in comprehension*. Hove, UK: Lawrence Erlbaum Associates Ltd.

Roese, N. J. (1997). Counterfactual thinking. *Psychological Bulletin, 121*, 133–148.

Stalnaker, R. (1968). A theory of conditionals. *American Philosophical Quarterly Monograph Series, 2*, 98–112.

Stevenson, R. J., & Over, D. E. (1995). Deduction from uncertain premises. *The Quarterly Journal of Experimental Psychology, 48*A, 613–643.

Stevenson, R. J., & Over, D. E. (2001). Reasoning from uncertain premises. Effects of expertise and conversational context. *Thinking and Reasoning, 7*, 367–390.

Teigen, K. H. (1998). When is the unreal more likely than the real: Post hoc probability judgements and counterfactual closeness. *Thinking and Reasoning, 4*, 147–177.

5 Violations, lies, broken promises, and just plain mistakes

The pragmatics of counterexamples, logical semantics, and the evaluation of conditional assertions, regulations, and promises in variants of Wason's selection task

David P. O'Brien, Antonio Roazzi, Maria G. Dias, Joshua B. Cantor, and Patricia J. Brooks

Wason's selection task (Wason, 1966, 1968), which requires identification of potential counterexamples to conditionals, has been among the most investigated of laboratory reasoning tasks.[1] We believe, however, that much of the literature about this task has relied on mistaken assessments both of the pragmatics of counterexamples to conditionals and of the logical semantics of conditionals, and we address these two topics in this chapter. Our motive is not to present any new theoretical proposals, but to point out how the literature has taken wrong directions and to suggest directions in which the literature should be moving.

We begin by considering the following scenarios, each of which includes a conditional statement of the form *if p then q*, together with its counterexample, an instance of *p and not q*:

Scenario 1
Maira was a tourist arriving at the airport in Porto Velho. When she rented a car, the rental agent told her that according to Rondônia's traffic regulations, if someone drives on highway BR-364, their speed must not exceed 100 kilometres per hour. Later, as Maira drove on highway BR-364, she observed that the other drivers were going well above 100 kilometres per hour.

Scenario 2
Bruna stopped at a petrol station and asked for directions to the City Museum. After complaining to Bruna that the petrol station was not a tourist information booth, the petrol-station worker told her that if she took the Monroe Street exit, the museum would be right there. She took the Monroe Street exit, but discovered that the museum was not there.

What would the protagonists in these two scenarios be likely to conclude? Our intuition is that Maira in Scenario 1 would think that the other drivers were violating the speeding regulation, but would not think that what the rental agent told her was false; people violate such regulations with regularity, and ordinarily one does not think that this demonstrates the falsity of the regulation. Thus a counterexample can be a violating instance without being a falsifying one. Bruna in Scenario 2 is likely to conclude that what the petrol-station worker had told her was false, but she is unlikely to think that anything had been violated (except, perhaps, that her Gricean expectation that the petrol-station worker would tell her the truth had been violated). Thus a counterexample can be falsifying without being violating. As illustrated in these two scenarios, the conjunction of *p and not q* is incompatible with *if p then q*. The implications of this incompatibility can vary, however, and whether an instance of *p and not q* violates or falsifies *if p then q* has to do with the content of *p* and of *q* and with the context of utterance of the conditional, *if p then q*, and the nature of its counterexample, *p and not q*.

What is illustrated in these two scenarios corresponds to an observation conveyed by Evans and Over (1996), Griggs and Cox (1993), and Jackson and Griggs (1990) that the research literature has presented two distinct species of the selection task that are defined by two different kinds of conditionals and two different corresponding kinds of instructions. Scenario 1 presents a type of conditional referred to as *deontic*, which conveys a conditional duty or a conditional obligation to act in a certain way; given that Maira would interpret the counterexamples to the deontic conditional in Scenario 1 as violating but not falsifying the deontic conditional, we are not surprised that Evans and Over reported that selection task versions that have presented a deontic conditional have been presented with instructions to check whether the conditional is being obeyed. Scenario 2 illustrates a type of conditional referred to as *indicative*, which conveys a conditional matter of fact, and given that Bruna would interpret the counterexample to the indicative conditional in Scenario 2 as falsifying but not as violating the conditional, we are not surprised that Evans and Over reported that selection task versions that have presented an indicative conditional have been presented with instructions to test the truth status of the conditional.

The literature generally has reported that when a task version has contained a deontic conditional with instructions to find potential violators, it has succeeded in eliciting selection of potentially violating cases, but when a task version has contained an indicative conditional with instructions to test the truth of the conditional, it typically has failed to elicit selection of such potentially falsifying cases (see discussions in Evans, Newstead, & Byrne, 1993; Noveck & O'Brien, 1996). Such findings have often been interpreted as supporting the contention that reasoning is governed by content-specific processes, for example, some inductively acquired pragmatic schemas (e.g., Cheng & Holyoak, 1985) or an innate reasoning module that checks for violators of social contracts (e.g., Cosmides, 1989; Gigerenzer & Hug, 1992). Those who have championed such content-specific reasoning processes have been united in asserting that reasoning does not proceed by any content-general logical processes, which, they have argued, is why task versions that have required testing the truth status of an indicative conditional typically have not been solved. We turn first to the claims of content-dependent reasoning processes and to the evidence for such claims from versions of the selection task; later we will turn to the assumptions about the logical semantics of conditionals that have provided a foundation for interpretation of performances on the selection task as evidence against the presence of any logical processes in reasoning.

TYPES OF CONDITIONALS AND THE INTERPRETATIONS OF COUNTEREXAMPLES TO CONDITIONALS

In its standard form the selection task requires identification of potential falsifying evidence for an indicative conditional. Participants are shown four cards – for example, showing A, D, 4, and 7, respectively – are told that each card has a letter on one side and a number on the other, and are told that there is a rule for the four cards, e.g., *If a card has a vowel on one side then it has an even number on the other side*. Finally, participants are told that the rule might be true or might be false, and they are required to turn over those cards, but only those cards, that are needed to find out whether the rule is true. Tasks of this sort rarely lead successfully to selection of potential counterexamples because hardly anyone selects the card showing 7. In comparison, for example, Cheng and Holyoak (1985) reported that 61% of their participants solved a version of the task (when this version was presented first in a within-subjects design) that instructed them to take the role of an authority checking for violators of a rule that *if one is to take Action A then one must first satisfy Precondition P*. The four cards showed *has taken Action A, has not taken Action A, has fulfilled Precondition P*, and *has not fulfilled Precondition P*. The finding that Cheng and Holyoak's permission-rule version of the problem was solved by a majority of their participants was particularly impressive given that the problem shared with the standard version of the task the presentation of abstract content – that is, it was presented with algebraically designated actions and preconditions, rather than with familiar content. Cheng and Holyoak argued that the task was solved because the pragmatic nature of its permission rule elicited the use of a pragmatic schema for permissions, whereas no pragmatic schema was available for the standard task version.

The various theoretical accounts that propose content-specific processes to explain such differences in rates of selections of potential cases of counterexamples have differed from one another in the extent to which they have viewed a special role for conditionals with deontic content *per se*, although all have proposed that deontic conditionals elicit content-specific processes that lead to selections of potential counterexamples. At one extreme is social-contract theory; Cosmides' (1989) cheater-detection module is set up only to find violators of a particular sort of deontic regulation (i.e., those deontic regulations that relate social costs and benefits), and the cheater-detection module seems to have no obvious applicability to any possible broader range of content types or to other types of propositional operators. The pragmatic schemas theory allows for a perhaps limitless number of pragmatic schemas (see Holyoak & Cheng, 1995), but as yet no pragmatic schemas have been described that apply to anything but two highly related sorts of deontic conditionals for permissions and obligations, so how pragmatic schemas might operate, for example, for alternatives, is not clear. At the other end of the spectrum of theoretical possibilities are the utilities theorists (e.g., Evans & Over, 1996; Oaksford & Chater, 1994, 1996), who seem the most willing of the content-dependent approaches to allow for extension of their proposals. Evans and Over, for example, have allowed for the possibility that the sorts of utilities they propose could, in principle, be extended to a broader range of types of content, but as yet they have provided little that is specific about how the sorts of utilities they proposed can be assigned without presentation of a deontic regulation.

Given that the abstract-content task version described above, with its deontic conditional and its instructions to find potential violating instances, was presented by Cheng and Holyoak (1985), let us discuss their theoretical explanation of how this task is solved as a way of viewing the interaction of theory and data for these deontic-specific approaches. Cheng and Holyoak's account of their abstract-rule problem was provided in terms of a pragmatic reasoning schema for permissions. In brief, they proposed that as a result of repeated exposure to various regulations for permissions and obligations, people inductively acquire an operational schematic understanding of the actions and preconditions of such regulations. A permission schema, for example, contains the following four production rules:

Rule 1. If the action is to be taken, then the precondition must be satisfied.
Rule 2. If the action is not to be taken, then the precondition need not be satisfied.
Rule 3. If the precondition is satisfied, then the action may be taken.
Rule 4. If the precondition is not satisfied, then the action must not be taken.

Once the problem solver has understood that the problem requires checking whether a permission rule is being violated, the permission schema is elicited, and each card is checked against the four production rules. The first and fourth rules apply when the cards showing *has taken Action A* and *has not fulfilled Precondition P*, respectively, are encountered, and since these two production rules convey deontic necessity with *must be* and *must not be*, the reasoner judges that the corresponding cards must be inspected. The second and third rules are applicable when the cards showing *has not taken Action A* and *has fulfilled Precondition P* are encountered, and the language *need not be* and *may be*, respectively, signals that these two cards need not be inspected.

In a subsequent literature (e.g., Jackson & Griggs, 1990; Noveck & O'Brien, 1996), it became clear that the presentation of a permission rule, or an obligation rule, together with instructions to find a rule violator, is not sufficient to elicit selections of *p* and *not q*. These authors noted several confounds in the original comparisons presented by Cheng and Holyoak (1985); for example, Cheng and Holyoak had presented the cards in the permission-rule task with explicit negatives (*had* not *taken Action A*, *had* not *fulfilled Precondition P*), but had presented negatives with a mixture of implicit and explicit negatives in their control problem (D, i.e., not A). Further, the permission-rule problem included instructions to assume the role of an authority checking whether the regulation is being obeyed, whereas the control problem with the standard sort of rule about letters and numbers on cards did not provide any sort of context, pragmatic or otherwise. Subsequent investigations (e.g., Girotto, Mazzocco, & Cherubini, 1992; Griggs & Cox, 1993; Kroger, Cheng, & Holyoak, 1993; Noveck & O'Brien, 1996) reported that task versions presenting deontic conditionals led to normatively appropriate selections only when the tasks also presented such features, as well as instructions to select potential violating cards rather than cards that can test whether the conditional is true.

However, Girotto et al. (1992), Kroger et al. (1993), and Griggs and Cox (1993) argued that the required presence of such task features is consistent with the claims of pragmatic reasoning schemas theory, as follows: Solution of the task requires a pragmatic regulation, such as a conditional permission or a conditional obligation, which allows a pragmatic schema to be engaged. They noted that the pragmatic schema that can be engaged when the pragmatic rule concerns permissions consists of four production rules, and the two production rules that refer to negative information can be applied only when the negative information in the cards is expressed explicitly; pragmatic reasoning schemas theory thus accounts for the necessity of explicitly presented negatives. The pragmatic schema is set up to detect violators and not to assess the truth or falsity of rules, so findings that the task is not solved when it requires testing the truth of a deontic regulation are viewed by pragmatic schemas theorists as confirmation of the theory. Instructions to assume the role of a checking authority can assist in elicitation of the pragmatic schema, because such instruction helps to clarify that the task requires exactly what the schema is set up to accomplish. Kroger et al. argued that such task features will not facilitate solution unless the problem presents a pragmatic rule, and because presentation of a non-pragmatic conditional will not engage any pragmatic schema, problem solution will not be forthcoming even when such task features are included unless a task presents a pragmatic rule.

Another task feature that seems to influence solution of task versions that present deontic conditionals is inclusion of the word *must* in the regulation's consequent, e.g. *if the action is to be taken, the precondition* must *be fulfilled*. Most authors have referred to *must* as a modal particle, a term that was adopted from logicians who developed modal-logic systems for possibility and necessity operators. Platt and Griggs (1995), for example, reported that inclusion of the term strongly influences task solution on problems with deontic conditionals, and Holyoak and Cheng (1995) noted that inclusion of the term in a problem with a non-deontic conditional does not seem to facilitate task solution.[2] Again, from the perspective of the content-specific approach the inclusion of the modal particle is thought to facilitate solution because it plays a role in cueing the use of a content-specific reasoning process, such as a pragmatic schema. Thus, although matters appear to be somewhat more complicated for the content-specific theorists than they did at the beginning of the 1990s, proponents of content-specific reasoning processes have continued to view selection of potential counterexamples on problems presenting deontic conditionals as evidence for special content-specific reasoning processes, even though successful application of these processes requires some particular task features, such as the presentation of explicit negatives and instructions to find rule violators rather than rule falsifiers.

The data are not entirely consistent in assessing the necessity of each of these task features. For example, although Jackson and Griggs (1990) found that removal of the instructions to assume the role of a checking authority led to failure to select potential counterexamples even when the problem presented a deontic rule, Griggs and Cox (1993) found that its removal did not suppress solution. Jackson and Griggs also reported that presentation of negatives implicitly rather than explicitly suppressed the *p* and *not q* response pattern, and Griggs and Cox, and Noveck and O'Brien (1996) replicated this finding. However, Kroger et al. (1993) reported a significant minority solving the problem even with implicitly presented negatives, and Girotto et al. (1992) reported such selections so long as the negative nature of the information was salient. Several investigations have addressed whether a task with a deontic conditional will lead to selection of *p* and *not q* only when it requires finding rule violators rather than rule falsifiers (Chrostowski & Griggs, 1985; Griggs, 1984; Jackson & Griggs, 1990; Kroger et al., 1993, Noveck & O'Brien, 1996; Yachanin, 1986; Yachanin & Tweney, 1982). These studies consistently reported that the *p* and *not q* response pattern occurred significantly more often when the task required a search for violators rather than a search for falsifiers, and most found that this response pattern occurred only when the task required a search for violators (see review in Noveck & O'Brien, 1996). In summary, based on the previous literature, if one wants to construct a version of the task with a deontic conditional that has a reasonable chance of leading to selections of p and *not q*, one ought to include instructions to assume the role of a checking authority, to present the negatives in the cards explicitly, and to require identification of potential rule violators rather than rule falsifiers.

Given this discussion of the necessity that a selection task present a deontic conditional together with instructions to find potential violating instances, consider the following Scenario 3:

Scenario 3
George and Ruth Herman rented a car when they arrived at the airport in Lingala. When they got in the car, Ruth asked George whether he knew the driving rules in Lingala. "George," she said, "don't you think we should at least ask what side of the road you're supposed to drive on?" George told his wife not to worry; he knew that if someone drives in Lingala, they must drive on the left side of the road. When they pulled out onto the road, they saw that the other cars were not driving on the left side of the road.

Our intuition is that George and Ruth Herman would not conclude that the other drivers were violating the driving regulation, in spite of the fact that the conditional is deontic and the other drivers are providing instances of *p and not q*, that is, counterexamples. A more reasonable interpretation, we believe, is that the Hermans would conclude that George was wrong about the rule. Thus, a counterexample to a deontic regulation need not be understood as a violating instance, but reasonably can be interpreted as a falsifying instance.

If our intuition about the counterexamples to the deontic conditional in Scenario 3 is correct, then our expectation is that one could construct a version of the selection task that people would solve which presents a deontic conditional (the driving regulation concerning on which side of the road one is required to drive in Lingala) together with instructions to find potential rule falsifiers (asking about the sorts of situations that could reveal whether George was wrong about the regulation). Note that a theory like Cheng and Holyoak's would explain neither our intuition about how counterexamples are interpreted in Scenario 3, nor the success that we predict in solving the falsifier-checking task version based on Scenario 3, because, as Kroger et al. (1993) and Holyoak and Cheng (1995) argued, the inclusion in a task of a pragmatic rule should be beneficial only when a task requires finding potential violators of that pragmatic rule. Note also that the sort of content-specific reasoning processes proposed by Cosmides (1989) and Gigerenzer and Hug (1992) would not be helpful here either, because such processes are also applicable only for violation checking.

We have conducted an empirical test of our intuition about how counterexamples of the sort that are found in Scenario 3 are understood, using what we refer to as a *counterexample interpretation task*. This task presents a conditional, together with its counterexample, and requires a judgement about whether the counterexample falsifies or violates the conditional. For example, following the paragraph in Scenario 3, the counterexample interpretation task asked whether: (i) The cars they saw were violating the driving regulation, or (ii) George was wrong about the driving regulation. We presented the task to 25 Baruch College students in New York City (we refer henceforth to the population of Baruch College students as the Americans) and to 25 students at the Federal University of Pernambuco in Recife, Brazil (we refer to this population of Federal University students henceforth as the Brazilians). A total of 68% of the Americans and 88% of the Brazilians judged the counterexamples as falsifying rather than as violating the deontic regulation. These data thus confirmed our intuitions about Scenario 3 that the counterexamples would be understood as falsifying rather than violating the deontic driving regulation. These results can be compared to those obtained with a companion counterexample interpretation task that presented a car-rental agent telling George and his wife that the local highway in Lingala has a speed limit of 100 kilometres per hour, and with the couple then observing that the other drivers were exceeding that limit. In this case, a different set of 25 Americans and 25 Brazilians decided on a counterexample interpretation task that the counterexamples indicated that the regulation was being violated rather than that the car-rental agent was wrong in his assertion (92% and 96%, respectively).

In a between-subjects design, four versions of the selection task that were based on these scenarios were each then presented to new groups of 25 American and 25 Brazilian university students. Two task versions presented the regulation about the side of the highway on which one must drive, with one of these two versions asking for selection of those cards that could find potential violators and the other asking for selection of those cards that could test whether the regulation might be false. (On both versions of the task the four cards showed [*p*] a car on a highway in Lingala, [*not p*] a car on a highway outside Lingala, [*q*] a car driving on the left-hand side of the road, and [*not q*] a car driving on the right-hand side of the road.) The other two task versions each presented the regulation about the speed limit to which drivers must keep, with one of the two asking for selection of those cards that could find potential violators of the regulation and the other version asking for selections that could test whether the regulation might be false. (On both versions of the task the four cards showed [*p*] a car on the Lingala highway, [*not p*] a car on a highway outside Lingala, [*q*] a car driving under the speed limit, and [*not q*] a car exceeding the speed limit.) On the problems that referred to the speeding regulation stated by the car-rental agent, when asked to find potential violators 76% of 25 Americans and 64% of 25 Brazilians selected either both *p* and *not q* or just *not q*, but when asked to find potential falsifying instances, no one chose either of these response patterns. These findings, of course, are similar to those reported by previous researchers showing solution rates that are high only on task versions requiring checking for violators of deontic regulations. On the problems based on the scenario about George's assertion concerning the side of the road on which one is required to drive, however, 72% of the Americans and 80% of the Brazilians selected either both *p* and *not q* or just *not q* when asked to find potentially falsifying instances; these rates dropped to 36% and 40% for the Americans and Brazilians, respectively, when asked to find potential rule violators.[3] Clearly, selections of *p* and *not q* or of just *not q* were not limited to those task versions that required checking for violators of deontic conditionals. Indeed, significantly more selections of *p* and *not q* or of just *not q* were made when participants were asked to check whether the rule about the requisite side of the road on which to drive was false than when asked to check for violators of that rule, $z = 3.84, p < .01$.

These results cannot be explained by the pragmatic schemas theory; Cheng and Holyoak (1985), Holyoak and Cheng (1995), and Kroger et al. (1993) were clear that the beneficial effects of presentation of a permission or obligation rule in a selection-task problem are available only to task versions that require searching for potential rule violators, and the pragmatic schemas theorists have been clear that the inductively acquired pragmatic schemas are not equipped to test whether such rules are true. Similarly, the violator-checking skills described by Cosmides (1989) and Gigerenzer and Hug (1992) are not applicable when a task requires that one check whether a deontic rule is true, but are applicable only to find violators of an existing rule that is assumed to be true.

Although the previous literature has matched deontic conditionals with instructions to search for potential violators and indicative conditionals with instructions to search for potential falsifiers (with only the former leading successfully to selection of potential counterexamples), the results just described demonstrate that this correspondence of a deontic conditional with violator-checking instructions need not be the case in order to elicit selection of potential counterexamples. Indeed, we discovered that the task version presenting a deontic conditional with instructions to find potentially falsifying information led to higher rates of solution than did the comparable task version requiring identification of potential violators of the same deontic regulation – a result that can only be odd when viewed from the perspective of the existing content-specific theories.

The following conclusion seems obvious to us: The literature has been on the wrong tack in trying to deal with matters in terms of classifications of different sorts of conditionals. The fact that the conditional in Scenario 3 is deontic probably had little to do with why the participants in our study judged its counterexamples as falsifying rather than as violating. After all, it was George's assertion of the regulation that was being judged as false, and not merely the regulation itself, and George might make all sorts of erroneous assertions about all sorts of things other than deontic conditionals.

This finding is consistent with a point made by Noveck and O'Brien (1995) that the deontic-violations task versions and the indicative-falsifier task versions that typically are presented in the literature make fundamentally different demands about how participants must view the status of the conditional. In the standard version, with its indicative conditional and its instructions to find potentially falsifying evidence, a participant cannot assume that the conditional is true – indeed one is told explicitly that the conditional may be true or it may be false, and the point of the task is to find out about the truth status of the conditional. For the participant to make sense of the deontic-violator task version as it is intended by the researcher, however, the conditional must be accepted as a rule that truly exists – after all, a rule can hardly be violated when it does not exist, that is, when an assertion about its existence is false. (Imagine, for example, being arrested for speeding when one is driving at 100 kilometres per hour and the speed limit is 150 kilometres per hour.) Thus, to construct a selection task from Scenario 3, where the status of the conditional rule is cast into doubt by the existence of a counterexample, it makes sense to require finding potentially falsifying instances rather than to require finding potentially verifying instances. Note, however, that this distinction in which type of instruction is reasonable has nothing at all to do with any particular type of conditional. The doubt that is cast in Scenario 3 has to do with George's assertion, and such a doubt could just as easily have been cast on an assertion of an indicative conditional as on an assertion of a deontic conditional or of any other sort of conditional. To illustrate this point, consider the following Scenario 4, which presents an indicative conditional:

Scenario 4
George and Ruth Herman rented a car when they arrived at the airport in Lingala. When they got in the car, George told Ruth that he knew an interesting fact about the drivers in Lingala. George told his wife that he knew that because of local cultural norms, if someone drives in Lingala, they always maintain a speed that is well below the speed limit. When they pulled out onto the road, however, George and his wife saw that the other cars were not driving below the speed limit.

In our intuitions, the counterexamples show both that the regulation is being violated and that George's assertion is wrong. Our expectation thus was that people would select potential counterexamples for both violation-checking and falsification-checking versions of a selection task based on Scenario 4, and so we constructed two such versions and presented them to university students both in America and in Brazil. Both versions were introduced with descriptions of George and Ruth Herman arriving in Lingala and with George asserting that he knew that if someone drives in Lingala, they always maintain a speed that is well below the speed limit. The truth-testing version then said that George might be wrong and asked participants to choose those cases that could test whether George was wrong; the violation-testing version also said that George might be wrong but asked participants to chose those cases that could find potential rule breakers. For the truth-testing version, 68% of Americans and 76% of Brazilians selected both *p* and *not q* or just *not q*, and for the violation-checking version, 60% of Americans and 72% of Brazilians made such selections. Thus, both the violator-checking and the falsifier-checking instructions led to selections of potential counter-examples for selection task versions based on Scenario 4.

In order to ascertain that the rate of selections of potential counter-examples on the falsifier-checking version of the selection task based on Scenario 4 had not been dependent on the reference to a deontic regulation concerning the speed limit, we also constructed two additional versions that used falsifier-checking instructions which made no such reference, and we presented these two versions to two groups of American university students. In one of these versions, George told Ruth that he knew that drivers in Lingala were extremely cautious so there was no need for a regulation about a speed limit, and so if someone drove in Lingala they always maintained a speed below 50 kilometres per hour. The second version was identical except that it made no reference to the presence or to the absence of a speeding regulation but stated simply that drivers in Lingala always maintained a speed below 50 kilometres per hour because of their extremely cautious and conservative nature. On these two versions, 60% and 84%, respectively, of the Americans made selections of both *p* and *not q* or of just *not q*. Thus, selections of potential counterexamples did not rely on any reference to a deontic regulation. When faced with a clear opportunity to judge what sort of evidence would demonstrate that George's assertions were wrong, a strong majority of participants in both American and Brazilian universities were able to make selections of potential counterexamples, whether George was asserting an indicative conditional or a deontic conditional and whether or not there was a reference to a deontic regulation.

It thus seems that it was George's assertion of the deontic regulation in Scenario 3, rather than the conditional obligation itself, that was being evaluated upon encountering the counterexample in Scenario 3, and counter-examples falsify assertions whether they refer to deontic content or not. Although some researchers have proposed a crucial importance for recognition of when a conditional is deontic, knowing that the conditional in Scenario 3 is deontic seems irrelevant to task solution; furthermore, knowledge that the conditional is deontic does not allow one to know what implication its counterexample will have. Why the counterexamples to the deontic conditional in Scenario 3 falsify an assertion about a regulation rather than violate the regulation, whereas the counterexamples to the deontic conditional in Scenario 1 violate a regulation rather than falsify an assertion about it, is far from obvious, although one can speculate about such matters at great length. Perhaps the difference stems from the differential potential effects of violating a speeding regulation when compared to the potential effects of violating a regulation about the side of the road to which one should keep – although in Scenario 3, when a speeding regulation rather than a locative regulation was presented, the change did not seem to influence rates of selections of potential counterexamples. Perhaps the difference in counterexamples to the deontic conditionals in Scenarios 1 and 3 stems from the many specific experiences people have with situations like that in Scenario 1 compared to the relatively few experiences they have with situations like that in Scenario 3, although this also seems at odds with the additional task versions in which speeding cars were seen as falsifying rather than as violating. Perhaps the difference between Scenarios 1 and 3 stems from the believability of the car-rental agent when compared to the believability of Ruth's husband, George – a difference that might rely on epistemic knowledge about husbands and wives, for example, on knowledge of the stereotypes that men are notoriously reticent to ask for directions or advice, and that Ruth might not be hesitant to point this out to her husband. Perhaps, in the case of Scenario 3, the context of Ruth's question indicates a doubt about matters, whereas in Scenario 1 the conditional is presented without being in response to any question at all. (Of course, one could add a similar question in Scenario 1, which would be posed by Maira to the car-rental agent, although our intuition is that this probably would not create the same atmosphere of doubt that seems to exist in Scenario 3.) In sum, explaining what it is about Scenarios 1 and 3 that leads to the differences in how their counterexamples are understood is not a simple matter, and the difference seems to rely on as yet unspecified parameters. Whatever the reason(s) for the difference, whether a conditional is understood as being violable or as being falsifiable by its counterexamples clearly is not simply a matter of whether it is deontic or indicative, and both sorts of conditionals seem open to falsification at least some of the time.

An additional problem for theoretical accounts that focus on matching types of conditionals with types of instructions is the fact that the categories of deontic and indicative are not exhaustive for the sorts of conditionals that exist, and other sorts of conditionals do not necessarily behave in quite the same ways as do the deontic and indicative conditionals we have been discussing in terms of whether they are violated or falsified by their counterexamples. Consider, for example, the promissory conditional in the Scenario 5:

Scenario 5
Eugene bought a used car. The salesman told him that if he paid cash, the car dealer would put new tyres on the car. Eugene was concerned about safety, so he paid cash. Later, as he drove the car on the Expressway, the front right tyre blew out. Eugene discovered that the tyres were retreads.

Eugene reasonably could conclude that the used car salesman had lied to him – used car salesmen have notorious reputations for such behaviours, and the salesman had a clear motivation to be deceitful. Eugene just as reasonably could conclude, however, that the car dealership had violated its agent's promise to him. A counterexample to a promissory conditional thus can be both falsifying and violating. In this, the promissory conditional in Scenario 5 is unlike the deontic conditional in Scenario 1, which is only violable, or the indicative conditional in Scenario 2, which is only falsifiable. It is also unlike the deontic conditional is Scenario 3, which the counterexample interpretation task revealed is falsifiable, but is similar to the situation in Scenario 4, where counterexamples both violated the deontic regulation and falsified the assertion about the regulation. Our intuition, however, is that the promise made by the car salesman in Scenario 5 is both violated (one concludes that there has been a broken promise) and falsified (one concludes that the salesman lied) in a fairly direct way; it is not merely that the assertion of the existence of a regulation that is being falsified, but the promise itself that is a lie. In terms of our distinction between obligations and assertions of obligations, a promise is an assertion of an obligation within the agency of the asserter, which allows its counterexamples to be equally violations and falsifications.

Our intuitions that the promise made to Eugene in Scenario 5 is both a false promise and a broken promise lead us to expect that selection task versions based on Scenario 5 and its promissory conditional would be solved both when presented with instructions to find potential falsifiers and when presented with instructions to find potential violators. In this, the expectations were different from those based on the deontic and indicative conditionals in Scenarios 1, 2, and 3, and were more like those based on Scenario 4. Indeed, when we presented selection task versions based on Scenario 5 to Americans, a majority selected both *p* and *not q* or just *not q* when the task was presented with an instruction to identify those instances that could show that the salesman had lied to Eugene (56%) or those instances that could show that the promise to Eugene had been broken (76%). Debriefing of participants revealed that the fact that the rate of such selections was somewhat higher when the broken-promises instructions were used than when the false-promises instructions were used seems to have occurred because some participants were reluctant to conclude that the salesman had intentionally lied (perhaps the salesman thought the dealer would put new tyres on the car, but other employees of the dealer then failed to do so – that is, that fulfilling the promise was outside the agency of the salesman), although most of our research participants agreed that a counterexample was sufficient to conclude that the promise had been broken.

The question of how many sorts of conditionals there are may not be resolvable. In addition to indicative conditionals that convey states of affairs, and deontic conditionals that convey regulations, conditionals can convey promises, threats, predictions, warnings, advice, mathematical implications, tautologies, and so forth. Further, where the boundaries reside between any two sorts of conditionals is not always clear, and not all authors have agreed even about where the boundaries are between deontic and indicative conditionals; Almor and Sloman (1996), for example, presented conditionals that they labelled as non-deontic, but Oaksford and Chater (1996) argued that these conditionals were, in fact, deontic. We believe that this sort of disagreement concerning category boundaries was bound to occur because a difference between types of conditionals – such as deontic and indicative – is not always informative about how research participants will approach a task requiring evaluation of a conditional and its counterexamples. Further, as was shown in Scenario 3, even when one seems to have a conditional that is fairly clearly of one sort or another – in Scenario 3 the conditional seems to us unambiguously deontic – it cannot be known on that basis alone how its counterexamples will be interpreted.

Our discussion of counterexamples to conditionals in the scenarios above reveals that the cues as to whether a counterexample is thought to be violating or falsifying can be quite subtle, and there can be further subtle variations within the categories of violation and falsification. For example, a falsifying case can be labelled either as a lie or as a plain mistake, a violating case can be labelled either as a felony or as a simple oversight, and so forth. Consider the following scenario:

Scenario 6
Francine was an astronaut on the first trip to Ganymede, one of Jupiter's moons. The scientists told her that if she dropped a weight to the surface of Ganymede, it would fall at an accelerating rate of 5 metres per second per second. When she arrived on Ganymede she dropped a weight to the surface, but found that it fell at a different rate.

Whereas Bruna in Scenario 2 might well think that she had been told a lie (following the complaint of the petrol-station worker about not working in a tourist information booth), and Ruth might think that her husband George is a mistaken idiot, Francine in Scenario 6 is unlikely to think that the scientists told her a lie or that they are idiots. A more reasonable interpretation is simply that the scientists made a mistake (e.g., that their calculations were wrong because their estimate of Ganymede's mass on which the calculations were based was wrong). Concluding that a lie has been told, rather than that a simple mistake made, or vice versa, requires making an inference about the intentions of a speaker, and thus seems to require a theory of mind to infer a state of a speaker's mind. Thus, Scenario 6 conveys an assertion that is open to falsification, but it shows that not all labels for falsification are equally reasonable.

How counterexamples to other sorts of conditionals should be interpreted can also be open to considerable debate. Consider the following scenario with its promissory conditional:

Scenario 7
When Celestine's company sent him on a business trip to Katangani, he was worried because a recent civil war had left the area controlled by various warlords who made a practice of kidnapping foreign businessmen. The chief of security for his company, Mr Kabasale, told him not to worry because, "If you arrive in Katangani, I will keep you safe from kidnappers." Unfortunately, when Celestine arrived in Katangani he discovered that Mr Kabasale himself had been kidnapped, as was Celestine shortly thereafter.[4]

The counterexample in this scenario falsifies Mr Kabasale's conditional promise. In what sense one can say that Mr Kabasale violated his promise, however, is not clear. On the one hand, Celestine could reasonably feel that a commitment that had been made to him had not been kept; on the other hand, the fact that Mr Kabasale was not in a position to fulfil his promise makes it unclear whether it is fair to hold him to it. The unfortunate events that happened to Mr Kabasale also make it unclear how one should think about the falsifying nature of the counterexample; should one conclude that Mr Kabasale lied to Celestine, or merely that he was overconfident in his abilities and therefore was mistaken? This sort of ambiguity in making pragmatic assessments about how to understand the meaning of a counterexample doubtless is widespread in everyday circumstances. People have numerous disagreements in assigning responsibility and blame in both significant and trivial situations, and decisions about how to resolve such ambiguities often rely on judgements about one's abilities to fulfil one's obligations. None of this has anything obvious to do with a role for logic in reasoning, and all of it has to do with various pragmatic considerations that we think are common in ordinary judgements about how to interpret counterexamples. Further, we suspect that such subtle differences would have an impact if one were to vary the wording of instructions in the construction of reasoning tasks that present conditionals and require identification of potential counterexamples.

Let us propose a simple *counterexample correspondence principle* for such things: A selection task version is apt to result in selections of potential counterexamples only if its instructions correspond to how counterexamples to its conditional would be interpreted if encountered. When a counterexample would be interpreted only as violating, but not as falsifying, a selection task with instructions to find potentially falsifying cases is unlikely to lead to selections of potential counterexamples. Likewise, when a counterexample would be interpreted only as falsifying, but not as violating, a selection task with instruction to find potentially violating cases is unlikely to lead to selections of potential counterexamples. The likelihood that a set of instructions will succeed in eliciting selections of potential counterexamples is unlikely to exceed the likelihood that a counterexample would be interpreted in a way that is consistent with the instructions. If the instructions refer to finding evidence that someone lied, but a counterexample is likely to be interpreted as evidence only that a simple mistake has been made, potential counterexamples are unlikely to be selected. Of course, none of this is within the scope of any existing theory of the pragmatics. Indeed, as yet there is no theory of the pragmatics of counterexamples to conditionals, and clearly such a theory would be needed to make clear and consistent predictions about which task instructions are appropriate for any particular selection task version. In part, such a theory would need to address when the basis for evaluation of a counterexample for a deontic conditional will be on an act of assertion about an obligation or on an obligation itself. In the meantime, perhaps the best that we can do is to make empirical estimates based on data from a counterexample interpretation task.

A PSYCHOLOGICALLY APPROPRIATE LOGICAL SEMANTICS FOR CONDITIONALS

Previous investigators have generally proceeded from the assumption that a normative logical semantics for conditionals is provided by the material conditional, and thus that the logical semantics for a universally quantified conditional of the sort presented in selection task versions is provided by $(\forall x)(Px \supset Qx)$, which is the normal disjunctive form of the material conditional. Given this perspective, the universally quantified conditional is rendered false only by instances of *p and not q*, that is, $(\forall x)(Px \supset Qx) \equiv \sim(\exists x)(Px \wedge \sim Qx)$. Another way of expressing this definition is that $(\forall x)(Px \supset Qx)$ is equivalent to *for all x, (p and q) or (not-p and q) or (not-p and not-q)*. From the assumption that the material conditional provides the appropriate logical semantics for *if*, many researchers apparently think that the selection task should be solved easily, for testing the truth of a conditional would only require making certain that there is no instance of *p and not q*. The fact that people rarely make selections of *p* and *not q* when asked to solve the standard version of the task therefore has been interpreted to show that people are lacking an adequate grasp of the logical semantics for *if*.

We propose instead that $(\forall x)(Px \supset Qx)$ does not provide a plausible logical semantics for a psychological model for reasoning about conditionals, in which case there must be some other logical semantics that provides a more plausible psychological model. Note first that $(\forall x)(Px \supset Qx)$ does not imply any particular psychological reasoning processes, and thus it is not obvious what the psychological implications would be in assuming that the semantics of the material conditional ought to provide a normative standard. One could imagine, for example, that something akin to a truth table exists in the mind, together with some mechanism for scanning the truth table against propositional input, although the choices of how such a mechanism might operate are extremely open ended. Alternatively, one could imagine that the mind possesses some inference schemas that are consistent with the semantics of material implication, for example, the set of inference schemas proposed by Gentzen (1935); as O'Brien (1995) noted, however, even a mind containing the set of inference schemas that were presented by Gentzen would not find a straightforward line of reasoning using those schemas that would determine which cards to select. A set of inference schemas of a Gentzen type can be applied to premise sets, that is, to sets of propositions that are assumed to be true, in order to make inferences and draw conclusions, but the standard selection task does not present a premise set. The conditional is presented only as a hypothesized assertion that cannot be assumed true, thus making straightforward application of any schemas impossible.

Moreover, several difficulties exist for any proposal that uses material implication as a psychological model. For more than two millennia philosophical logicians have written about the paradoxes of material implication (e.g., Kneale & Kneale, 1962); for example, following from the semantics of material implication, any conditional with a necessarily false antecedent is true. Thus, the conditional *if 42 is an odd number, then England won the world cup in 2002* would be true, although surely no supporter either of English or Brazilian football would find this a sensible conclusion.

More crucially, we think, material implication does not provide a model for evaluating conditionals that corresponds to ordinary intuitions about how conditionals are falsified. Consider Scenario 8:

> *Scenario 8*
> Kathleen was in Gotham City as a tourist. She wanted to visit Gideon's Department Store, and asked a passerby on the sidewalk for directions. He told her that if she took a left on Third Street, she would find Gideon's Department Store on the corner of Fifth Avenue. Kathleen walked down Second Street to Fifth Avenue, and then walked one block over to Third Street. Gideon's Department Store was not there.

Kathleen reasonably would conclude that what she had been told was not true, even though the scenario does not include a counterexample, i.e., an instance of *p and not q*. Why, then, would Kathleen conclude that the assertion was wrong? Quite simply, the truth or falsity of the passerby's conditional assertion does not depend on whether Kathleen actually goes left on Third Street or on whether she actually finds the department store on that corner. From what she was told, Kathleen can infer that Gideon's Department Store *must* be on the corner of Third Street and Fifth Avenue. Discovering that Gideon's Department Store is *not* at that location allows her to work out that *if* she had taken a left on Third Street she *would not* have found Gideon's Department Store on that corner. The fact that she did not take the suggested route would not change that conclusion. Falsification of a conditional thus *does not necessarily* require finding an instance of *p and not q*, revealing the need for a different account of the semantics of conditionals.

Philosophical writers such as Gentzen (1935), Quine (1960), Block (1987), Peacocke (1992), Harman (1982), Loar (1981), Woods (1981), Fodor and Lepore (1991) and Field (1977) have proposed an inferential-role (or conceptual-role) approach to semantics in which the meaning of a word is provided by the pattern of inferences that it sanctions, and advocates of this approach point to logical connectives as the paradigmatic cases of how meanings can come from patterns of implication. We have doubts about whether this approach can suffice for language as a whole, but we see no reason that it cannot provide a semantics for logical connectives. For logical terms such as *if, not, and, or, all, some*, and so forth, an inferential-role semantics needs to specify empirically testable inference procedures, and the mental-logic theory of Braine and O'Brien (e.g., Braine & O'Brien, 1991/1998; O'Brien, Dias, Roazzi, & Braine, 1998a) provides such descriptions for conditionals. (For the most complete presentation of mental-logic theory, see Braine & O'Brien, 1998.) What distinguishes the mental-logic proposal from other inferential-role semantics is its integration of inference schemas and the reasoning routines that apply these schemas in lines of reasoning – a matter that is particularly important for conditionals, and for this reason we have referred to it as a procedural semantics (Braine & O'Brien, 1991/1998; O'Brien et al. 1998a).[5]

The basic semantics for a logic particle, its lexical entry, is provided by the schemas that are relevant to it as they are implemented by the reasoning routine.[6] Indeed, it is the way the schemas are implemented by the reasoning routine that deflects the approach from falling into the same difficulties that result from adopting the material conditional as a logical semantics. The procedure that is directly relevant to evaluating the truth or falsity of a conditional consists of a *schema for conditional proof* and a *direct-reasoning routine* that applies the schema. The schema for conditional proof holds that to assert *if p then q*, add *p* as a suppositional premise to other information assumed true; when *q* is derived in a line of reasoning under the supposition, one can assert *if p then q*.[7] A direct-reasoning routine applies the conditional-proof schema when there is a conditional to evaluate: To evaluate *if p then q*, add *p* (as an additional suppositional premise) to other background premises and then treat *q* as a conclusion to be evaluated. When *q* is derived, *if p then q* is judged true; when the negation of *q* is derived, *if p then q* is judged false. Note that this latter judgement that *if p then q* is judged false when the supposition of its antecedent leads to the derivation of *not q* is not valid on the material conditional of standard logic (because *p* might be false); the judgement made on the procedural semantics of mental-logic theory thus is not the same as that which would be made on the semantics of the material conditional of standard logic.[8]

There are empirical reasons to think that the procedural semantics we are describing provides a better fit with psychological reality that does the semantics of material implication. In studies with adults, Braine, Reiser, and Rumain (1984/1998) reported judgements about when conditional conclusions were judged false that were consistent with the mental-logic procedural semantics, and this is a result that has been replicated with primary-school children (O'Brien et al., 1998a). For example, among some reasoning problems in which children were asked to evaluate the truth or falsity of conclusions from premise sets, they were shown a box containing toy animals and fruits and told that *there is either a cat or a banana in the box*. In one problem they were then asked to evaluate whether *if there is not a cat then there is a banana* was true or false (which was almost always judged true), and in another problem with the same premise they were asked to evaluate *if there is not a cat then there is not a banana* (which was almost always judged false, although this judgement is not warranted on the semantics of the material conditional of standard logic). There thus are empirical data to support our predictions about the circumstances in which conditionals are judged false. The data thus support our proposal for a procedural semantics for *if*, and, in particular, the data show that such judgements are not consistent with what would be predicted from the logical semantics of the material conditional.

Nothing in the mental-logic procedure (nor anything we know of in the pragmatics associated with assertion) provides any reason to seek falsifying rather than verifying evidence when one is asked to evaluate a conditional – that is, there is no *a priori* reason to expect *not q* rather than *q* as a response unless a research participant is provided with a special interest in falsification rather than in mere evaluation. We expect, therefore, that selection of *not q* in a selection task requiring identification of relevant cases for evaluation of an indicative conditional assertion, will require a reason to realize that the experimenter is interested in identification of potential routes to falsification, rather than in mere evaluation of a conditional's truth status.

Oaksford and Stenning (1992) reported that the truth-checking versions of the task are solved more often when instructions ask to find falsifying cases rather than merely to test whether the conditional is true. We have collected data on several task versions presenting indicative conditionals and requiring identifications of potential falsifiers that show almost no one makes selections of *not q* unless specifically asked to find falsifying evidence rather than merely testing whether the conditional is true. We have presented several task versions that compare specific instructions to find falsifying cases to instructions simply to find out whether the conditional is true. We present two such versions here to illustrate. One problems stated,

> Eldridge was trying to assemble a new exercise bicycle that he just bought and was having trouble getting the handlebars attached. His friend, Bobby, was reading the owner's manual and said, "If you use the bracket with a square head, the handle bars will fit." Below are four cards. One side of each card shows whether or not Eldridge used the bracket with a square head, and the other side shows whether or not the handlebars fit. To find out whether what Bobby said was mistaken, which card or cards would you need to turn over?

The companion problem asked instead, "To find out whether what Bobby said was right. ...." When specific falsifier instructions were given, 72% of 25 Americans provided the *p* and *not q* selections or just the *not q* selection, but this dropped to 8% when the instructions asked only to find whether Bobby was right.

A second version stated,

> Dagvar was the chief of a Danish tribe in the 10th century. He was very ambitious and wanted to challenge an even more powerful chief, Eric Thorkold. Dagvar told his warriors that "although we might not be able to beat Eric Thorkold by ourselves, if we join forces with my cousin, Rolf, we will beat Eric Thorkold." Unfortunately for Dagvar, he was wrong. Below are pictures of four cards. One side of each shows whether or not Dagvar and Rolf joined forces, and the other side of each card shows whether or not Eric Thorkold was beaten. Which card or cards would you need to turn over to find evidence that Dagvar was wrong?

The companion problem asked participants to find evidence about whether Dagvar was right. A total of 64% made the *p* and *not q* or the *not q* selections when asked to find falsifying information, but only 4% did so when asked to find out whether Dagvar was right.

These data, and similar data from similar problems that we have presented, are consistent with our realization that the procedures of the direct-reasoning routine and the schema for conditional proof would not lead one to look specifically for falsifying information, but that one can identify falsifying cases when asked to do so. Clearly, when not given specific instructions to find falsifying information, most of our participants did not seek to do so, but when asked to do so, most knew exactly what those cases were.

We return now to Scenario 8 and to Kathleen's conclusion that the passerby's conditional assertion (that if she took a left on Third Street, she would find Gideon's Department Store on the corner of Fifth Avenue) is false, even though Kathleen never took a left on Third Street. Because there is no counterexample, that is, no instance of *p and not q*, Kathleen's judgement is problematic when viewed from the perspective of the standard semantics for the material conditional; the conclusion is straightforwardly sensible, however, when viewed from the perspective of the procedural semantics for evaluating a conditional that we advocate. One begins by supposing Kathleen taking a left on Third Street, even though she actually took a left on Second Street. The supposition leads to the realization that such a journey would result in not finding the store on the corner of Fifth Avenue, even though Kathleen actually took an alternative route to get to the crucial destination. This is sufficient under the procedure of the direct-reasoning routine to judge the conditional assertion false, even though there has been no instance of *p and not q*. Note, then, that although the discovery of a counterexample falsifies a conditional assertion (because if a counterexample exists, after one supposes *p*, one can then assert the counterexample, *p and not-q*, which leads to the derivation of *not-q* under the supposition, thus falsifying the conditional), on our procedural semantics the existence of a counterexample does not provide the sole means to falsification.

Braine et al. (1984/1998) found that the supposition step of the procedure takes relatively little cognitive effort. They reported, for example, that an argument with a single premise of the form *p or q* and with *if not p then q* as a conclusion to be evaluated is judged to take only marginally more effort than a problem with the two premises of the form *p or q* and *not p* and requiring evaluation of the conclusion *q*. Further, once this supposition step has been accomplished, it is the consequent, *q*, that becomes the conclusion to be evaluated; thus, the real effort (and therefore the focus of attention) that occurs while evaluating a conditional is on the construction of a line of reasoning towards the consequent (or its negation). Given that (a) the likely focus of a reasoner in evaluating the truth or falsity of a conditional is on constructing a line of reasoning towards the consequent, and (b) that the truth of the antecedent may not be required to evaluate the truth or falsity of a conditional, when a reasoner is asked to evaluate a conditional, the focus typically will be on the conditional's consequent, that is, either on *q* or on *not q*, rather than on its antecedent.

Given that a reasoner who is evaluating a conditional under a suppositional line of reasoning is focused on what follows under the supposition rather than on the proposition that has been supposed, consider how the focus of reasoning for Scenario 8 might differ if the conditional had presented, for example, *if she goes to the corner of Third Street and Fifth Avenue she will find Gideon's Department Store*, rather than *if she takes a left on Third Street she would find Gideon's Department Store on the corner of Fifth Avenue*. In both cases, one will conclude that the antecedent implies that she will find the store on the corner of Third Street and Fifth Avenue. How might the two conditionals differ in their likelihoods of selecting instances of *p* in order to falsify? In the original version, with the antecedent, *she takes a left on Third Street*, our intuition is that *p* is incidental in the discovery that the conditional is wrong; the antecedent merely plays a role in ascertaining what must be the case given the supposition, that is, that the store must be on the corner of Third Street and Fifth Avenue, and the location of the store becomes the important proposition that needs to be tested. A response to a selection task based on the original Scenario 8 thus reasonably *could* exclude selection of *p*. For the conditional in the revised version, however, *p* takes on a central importance; one needs to discover that the store is not on the corner of Third Street and Fifth Avenue, which is the proposition in the antecedent clause. A response to a selection task based on the revised conditional for Scenario 8 thus reasonably would include selection of *p*. Note that in both cases, Scenario 8 with the original conditional or with the revised conditional, the line of reasoning begins by supposing *p* and then constructing a line of reasoning about what follows thereafter. In both cases, when one is asked to identify potentially falsifying information, one comes to realize that not finding the store on the corner of Third Street and Fifth Avenue is crucial to falsification of the conditional assertion made by the passerby, but in the original version the antecedent plays a role only in terms of deciding what the crucial evidence is, whereas with the revised conditional the antecedent itself conveys a crucial piece of information. It is not the logic alone that determines how one views these cases; in the mental-logic procedure the antecedent is merely used to set up a line of reasoning that follows under its supposition. How one judges the importance of the pieces of information that are in the line of reasoning following the supposition is likely to be a matter of the context of utterance of the conditional claim, of background knowledge about the subject matter, and so forth. This realization is consistent with what Braine and O'Brien (1991/1998) described of how lines of reasoning are constructed under the supposition of p: such lines of reasoning can be constructed using a wide variety of inferential means, such as scripts, story grammars, and so forth, and the soundness of any inference that follows from such processes can be open to dispute and negotiation between interlocutors. Logical inference schemas do not provide the sole basis for making inferences under a supposition and they do not provide the means for deciding which pieces information in a line of reasoning are of crucial importance.

We have constructed selection task versions using both the original and revised conditionals for Scenario 8. One version stated that Kathleen asked a passerby where she could find Gideon's Department Store. He told her that if she took a left on Third Street she would find the store on the corner of Fifth Avenue. The task then told participants that each of the four cards stated on one side whether or not Kathleen took a left on Third Street and on the other side whether or not she found the store on the corner of Fifth Avenue. Participants were asked to select the card or cards needed to reveal that what the passerby told her was wrong. The cards showed (p) she took a left on Third Street, (*not p*) she did not take a left of Third Street, (q) she found the store on the corner of Fifth Avenue, and (*not q*) she did not find the store of the corner of Fifth Avenue. A second version of the task stated that the passerby told her that if she went to the corner of Third Street and Fifth Avenue, she would find the store. The cards showed (p) she went to the corner of Third Street and Fifth Avenue, (*not p*) she did not go to the corner of Third Street and Fifth Avenue, (q) she found the store, and (*not q*) she did not find the store. On the first task version, 16% of 25 Americans selected both p and *not q*, and 48% selected only *not q*; on the second task version, 64% of 25 Americans selected both p and *not q*, and only 8% selected only *not q*. These findings thus were consistent with our expectations, with p selected more often on the problem in which it seemed to us to be a crucial piece of falsifying information, and not being selected on the problem in which it seemed a piece of incidental information on the way to discovering the location of the store.

We found similar results with other problem versions. For example, one problem stated,

> Some American tourists in Bangkok had become tired of eating nothing but Thai food, and decided they would like to find a MacDonalds. The manager of their hotel told them, "If you take the Number 16 bus to the Siam Square Mall, there is a MacDonalds in the food court." The tourists became upset when they concluded that what the manager said was wrong.

This problem was expected to elicit selection of the *not q* card and without selection of the *p* card more often than would a companion problem which was identical except that the manager told the tourists, "If you go to the Siam Square Mall, my cousin will show you where to find a MacDonalds," which was expected to encourage selection of both of the *p* card together and the *not q* card. On the first of these two problems, only 16% of 25 Americans chose both *p* and *not q*, whereas 60% chose only *not q*; on the second of these problems, however, 52% of 25 Americans chose both *p* and *not q*, and only 16% chose only *not q*.

We do not believe that these data should be interpreted as showing that the procedural semantics of mental-logic theory are correct; they were in no way intended as a test of our approach. They do show, however, that it is simplistic and inaccurate to accept the truth-table assignments of the material conditional as providing an accurate account of the reasoning processes that govern how people select potentially falsifying cases, whereas the procedure we describe does seem consistent with the data we are presenting. Further, we constructed such problems because the mental-logic procedure for evaluating a conditional led us to realize that it is the consequent that will be the focus of the process, so at times the antecedent will be of only incidental interest to the reasoner, as though it were merely setting up a context for the inferences to follow. As yet, we are not prepared to suggest a principle with which to make predictions about when *p* will be selected on such versions of a selection task, and when *p* will not be selected. Nonetheless, the phenomenon itself is problematic for any approach that assumes the material conditional as a psychological model.

RELATIONS AMONG THE VARIOUS SORTS OF TASK VERSIONS AND REASONING PROCESSES

A set of obvious questions exists concerning the reasoning processes that apply to the various sorts of conditionals we have considered deontic, indicative, promissory, and so forth, and their interactions with instructions to find potentially violating or falsifying instances. What relations, if any, are there between the sorts of reasoning processes that apply when a problem requires finding potential violators of a deontic regulation and those that apply when a problem requires finding a potential falsifier of an indicative conditional? Do falsification instructions lead to the same reasoning processes regardless of the sentence type? Are the processes the same when one needs to falsify an assertion about a deontic regulation and to find violators of that regulation? Do deontic sentences lead to the same reasoning processes regardless of instruction types? Are the processes the same when one seeks to discover whether a conditional promise has been broken or whether that promise was false in the first place? If the processes that are applied in these various tasks and other similar such tasks are different from one another, what determines which process is used in any particular case?

Noveck and O'Brien (1996) argued that instructions to find potential violators and instructions to find potential falsifiers require very different roles for the conditionals in the respective tasks. When one is asked to find a violator of a regulation, one needs to assume that the regulation is true (at least in the sense that there truly is such a regulation), whereas when one is asked to find a falsifier of an assertion, one sensibly can make no such assumption – indeed, to assume that the assertion is true would make the task absurd. In other words, tasks that instruct one to find violators of a rule require reasoning *from* a rule assumed true, whereas tasks that instruct one to find falsifiers of an assertion require reasoning *about* whether an assertion is true.[9]

When a task requires finding potential falsifiers of an indicative conditional requiring reasoning about a conditional, we propose that people typically seek to evaluate the proposition in the consequent clause of the conditional after supposing the proposition in the antecedent clause. When a task requires reasoning from a conditional that is assumed to be true, however, there is no basis to undertake the same sort of line of suppositional reasoning. Only one schema can be applied by the direct-reasoning routine when one needs to reason from a conditional that is assumed true: modus ponens. This schema holds that when one has premises of the form *if p then q* and *p*, one can assert *q*. The version of the schema that applies when there is a universally quantified conditional holds that if all members of a class have Property P and α is a member of that class, then α has Property P.

Application of modus ponens, however, is not sufficient by itself to select any cards in a violator-checking task. Of the four cards, only one card can lead directly to an application of modus ponens. For example, for the universally quantified permission rule presented in Cheng and Holyoak (1985), If one is to take Action *A*, then one must fulfil Precondition *P*, a line of reasoning upon encountering the card showing someone who has taken Action *A* can be described as follows: Given that obligation *P* is a property of all members of the class *A* of those who take Action *A* and that A_1 is a member of the class *A*, then A_1 has obligation *P*. Note, however, that this application of the modus ponens schema does not provide a reason to select any card; the reasoner still needs to make the inference that finding (on the other side of the card) that obligation *P* was not fulfilled violates the inference that A_1 must fulfil obligation *P*. The basic mental-logic skills of the direct-reasoning routine thus are not by themselves sufficient to decide to select any card on a task requiring finding potential violators of a conditional regulation that is assumed true.

There is, however, a straightforward reason for someone to select the *p* card after modus ponens has been applied and also to select the *not q* card, with both selections based on a pragmatically based realization that the task is to discover instances in which the obligation has not been fulfilled.[10] Obligation is attached to the consequent of a conditional obligation, and the consequent clause often is deontically marked by the modal term, *must*; the *not q* card thus straightforwardly has the potential of providing discovery of a violation of the obligation, as does the *p* card after one realizes from application of modus ponens, for example, that person A_1 has obligation *P*. The contribution of logic when one is searching for potential violators of a deontic conditional is thus limited to the realization, based on modus ponens, that if a conditional obligation is the property of all members of a group, it is the property of the individual member of the group under consideration. Beyond this, decisions are based on the pragmatically based realizations that: (i) an authority typically wants to find those who are violating, rather than those who are obeying, the regulation, and (ii) an obligation is attached to the consequent term in the conditional (whether modally marked or not).

The analysis we have just proposed in terms of two processes – one process for finding potential falsifiers when an indicative conditional is presented with instructions to find potential falsifiers and another for finding potential violators when a deontic conditional is presented with instructions to find potential violators – is complicated by Scenario 3 when a deontic conditional is falsified and by Scenario 5 when a promissory conditional is both violated and falsified. We turn first to Scenario 3, where George and Ruth Herman would conclude that George was wrong about the side of the road to which one must keep if driving in Lingala. Construction of a suppositional line of reasoning when assessing George's assertion in Scenario 3 is unlikely. More likely is a process in which one realizes that the cars are not meeting the obligation that George asserted, which then requires a decision about how to interpret this evidence. In Scenario 3 it is the assertion of a conditional obligation rather than the conditional obligation itself that is judged the focus of evaluation, but this judgement is based not on logic, but on a pragmatic evaluation of regulations and behaviours. Similarly, in Scenario 5 with its conditional promise made to Eugene by the used-car salesman, the judgements both that the salesman lied, and that he violated his promise, do not follow only from an application of a logic schema. Rather, there is a recognition that a conditional obligation has not been met. Whether one then judges this as a lie or as a broken promise, or both, depends on a complex set of pragmatic considerations that have to do with what the salesman knew and intended when the promise was made, and these judgements are not the result of any logical process *per se*.

Those who are not favourably disposed towards the mental-logic approach will not find comfort in the materials presented here. The fact that logic plays a limited role in accounting for performance on the selection task is not unexpected; we have argued repeatedly that one should not look to the selection task to find logic in human reasoning (e.g., Braine & O'Brien, 1991/1998; O'Brien, 1995). Moreover, the existing content-specific theories do not provide an account of the data we have presented. The pragmatic schemas theory and the social contract theory describe processes that are appropriate for violation checking, but not for making judgements about when deontic regulations are false; yet the data presented here reveal that people have no difficulty in judging when a deontic conditional is falsified.

Because the content-specific proposals account for content effects with the selection task in terms of reasoning processes that are exclusive for identifying violators of deontic conditionals, such as permissions, obligations, or social contracts, those theories are too limited to account for the sorts of judgements we have examined here about when indicative conditionals ranging over many sorts of content are falsified. Cosmides (1989), Fiddick, Cosmides, and Tooby (2001), and Cheng, Holyoak, Nisbett, and Oliver (1986), for example, have stated extremely serious doubts about any explanatory role for any content-general reasoning processes that go beyond violation checking. Yet there is mounting evidence that a wide variety of sorts of content and a widening set of types of conditionals can lead to appropriate responses with the selection task. Several new versions of the task have been presented here, and they add to those presented by other authors (e.g., Almor & Sloman, 1996; Green, 1995; Green & Larking, 1995; Platt & Griggs, 1993, 1995; Sperber, Cara, & Girotto, 1995). Note that the presence of such data shows that task solution need not rely on reasoning processes that are particular to deontic regulations or to instructions to check for violators. Additional empirical support for our expectation that conditionals can be evaluated appropriately even when they are not deontic comes from reports by Bowerman (1986) and Reilly (1986) of conditional assertions in the spontaneous speech of 2-year-olds. These assertions seem to have been made appropriately, and were consistent with sorts of lines of reasoning one would expect from application of the schema for conditional proof (see discussions in Braine & O'Brien, 1998; O'Brien et al., 1998); even young children thus have some way of knowing how to assert conditionals and thus should have a way to evaluate them. Further, O'Brien, Dias, Roazzi, and Cantor (1998b) reported that when 3- and 4-year-olds were asked to identify which instances falsified indicative conditionals, violated deontic conditionals, and both violated and falsified promissory conditionals, they chose instances of *p and not q* on an evaluation task. The indicative problems, for example, presented a Pinocchio puppet who made assertions about what children in a park were wearing, e.g., *If a boy is playing basketball, he is wearing red sneakers*, together with four pictures showing a child playing basketball in red sneakers, a child playing basketball in green sneakers, a child playing tennis in red sneakers, and a child playing tennis in green sneakers. When asked to point to the picture that would make Pinocchio's nose grow, the 3- and 4-year-olds had no difficulty in pointing to the picture of a child playing basketball in green sneakers. Such judgements, of course, are not explained in any obvious way in terms of reasoning processes that rely on presentation of deontic conditionals. Note that such responses indicate an appreciation at an early age both of the logic of conditionals and of the sorts of pragmatic concerns we have been describing here.

In their present forms none of the content-specific theories include any description, at least in anything approaching a clearly developed form of reasoning processes, that would apply to the selection task constructed from Scenario 2 with its indicative conditional and with its invitation to use falsifier instructions. Indeed, those theories are not equipped to provide explanations for any of the selection task versions stemming from situations like those in Scenarios 3–8, even though we constructed a wide variety of tasks from many of these scenarios that led to appropriate selections. We are not claiming that we have falsified any of those content-dependent theories, and we did not set out to do so; we have discovered, however, that the content-specific theories are not adequate in their current states of development to explain the extant data for the selection task, including the data presented here.

An adequate theory of pragmatics as it pertains to the selection task is needed, and such a theory needs to explain the ways in which counterexamples to conditionals are understood. People can make decisions about whether a counterexample is a violator or a falsifier of a conditional, and such decisions are not explained by classifying conditionals as deontic or indicative. People make judgements about how to interpret violations that range, for example, from inadvertent oversights to felonious criminal acts, and they make judgements about how to interpret false assertions that can range from innocent misunderstandings to wicked mendacities. We have shown that such variations in interpretations influence whether, and how, people search for potentially falsifying evidence or for potential rule violators. We know of no pragmatic principle that has been put forth to explain any of these things, nor do we know of any other sort of psychological explanation that has been offered. Researchers can rely on their intuitions about each case – which is essentially what we have done in discussing the scenarios we have presented – to predict whether violator or falsifier instructions should be provided when a selection task is constructed. To assess how a counterexample to any particular conditional is understood can be examined empirically with what we refer to as a *counterexample interpretation task*, which presents a conditional together with its counterexample and requires a judgement about whether this means that the conditional has been violated or falsified. Finding a principle with which one can predict how counterexamples to conditionals will be judged, however, is apt to be a difficult task.

ACKNOWLEDGEMENTS

This material is based on work supported by the National Science Foundation under Grant No. 0104503 to David P. O'Brien and Patricia J. Brooks and by a grant from Convênio de Cooperação Bilateral CNPq do Brazil to Antonio Roazzi and Maria G. Dias (Proc. número 910023/01–8).

NOTES

1 Guy Politzer conveyed to us that his systematic effort to catalogue the deductive-reasoning literature confirms the prevalence of research on conditionals, but shows more studies presenting the conditional syllogisms than presenting the selection task.
2 We add a note of caution about whether the selection-task literature should have fallen into the habit of thinking about "must" only as a modal operator. As a modal, "must" emphasizes the obligatory nature of the consequent in a conditional regulation. In ordinary language usage, as Karttunen (1972) noted, "must" also has an epistemic usage that weakens an assertion. "It is raining", for example, makes a stronger claim than "It must be raining". The latter ordinarily indicates that the speaker is making an inference from some secondary evidence, whereas the former indicates that the claim is made from direct observation (see discussion in Braine & O'Brien, 1991/1998). The presence of "must" in the consequent of an indicative conditional thus has a quite different role from the presence of "must" in a deontic conditional.
3 We shall return later to a discussion of selection of only the *not q* card without also selecting the *p* card. Given that the most salient feature of wrong answers reported in the previous literature is the failure to select *not q*, we include the *not-q only* response pattern in our counts of appropriate falsifying and violating responses.
4 Note that the promissory conditional in this scenario differs from the deontic conditionals we have considered in that the addition of the word "must" to the consequent term would not strengthen Mr Kabasale's obligation; "If you arrive in Katangani, I must keep you safe from kidnappers" would have weakened rather than strengthened Celestine's expectation that he would be kept safe. In this, it is more like the use of "must" with an indicative conditional.
5 This notion of a procedural semantics is similar to a proposal made by Johnson-Laird (1977) that meaning can be understood in terms of procedures operating on information.
6 Braine and O'Brien (1991/1998) also described various pragmatic principles for conditionals, but we need not address them here.
7 Braine and O'Brien (1991/1998) proposed a constraint such that no proposition can be admitted in a line of reasoning under a supposition that leads to a conditional conclusion unless that proposition would still be true under the supposition. The constraint plays little role in the issues presented here, so we shall say no more about it here. The constraint does contribute to differences between the procedural semantics of our approach and the semantics of the material conditional.
8 For simplicity, we have described here the conditional-proof schema for the unquantified propositional *if*. In order to assert a universally quantified conditional, $(\forall x)(Px \supset Qx)$, one applies a slightly modified version of the schema: One supposes an arbitrarily chosen member (or members), α, of the class P, and derives that α

has property *Q*. One can then assert that any member of the class has property *Q*. So long as there are members of the class, one can assert that *all the Ps have property Q*. The same constraint applies that was mentioned in Note 7 concerning which propositions are admissible under the supposition.

9 The title of Wason's (1968) seminal article was "Reasoning about a rule". From this perspective, none of the tasks that require reasoning from a rule assumed to be true truly are versions of the selection task.

10 The task of an authority checking whether a regulation is being obeyed is usually to look for rule violators rather than to seek out those who are obeying a rule. For example, the police typically have little interest in attending to those who are drinking legally or driving within the speed limit. We assume that when a task includes instructions to assume the role of an authority, such instructions signal that one is to find those breaking the rule. Of course, there are obvious exceptions to this generalization; Nazi authorities were interested in finding those who obeyed the regulation that *if one is a Jew one must wear the Star of David* just as they were interested in finding those who were violating the regulation. We take it that this is not typical of how people view authorities who are enforcing regulations, and the default expectation is that an authority is interested in identifying violators.

REFERENCES

Almor, A., & Sloman, S. A. (1996). Is deontic reasoning special? *Psychological Review*, *103*, 374–380.

Block, N. (1987). Functional role and truth conditions. *Proceedings of the Aristotelian Society*, *61*, 157–181.

Bowerman, M. (1986). First steps in acquiring conditionals. In E. Traugott, A. ter Meulen, J. S. Reilly, C. A. Ferguson (Eds.), On conditionals (pp. 285–307) Cambridge, UK: Cambridge University Press.

Braine, M. D. S., & O'Brien, D. P. (1998). (Eds.). *Mental logic*. Mahwah, NJ: Lawrence Erlbaum Associates Inc.

Braine, M. D. S., & O'Brien, D. P. (1991/1998). A theory of *if*: A lexical entry, reasoning program, and pragmatic principles. *Psychological Review*, *98*, 182–203. [Reprinted in M. D. S. Braine & D. P. O'Brien (Eds.), *Mental logic*. Mahwah, NJ: Lawrence Erlbaum Associates Inc.]

Braine, M. D. S., Reiser, B. J., & Rumain, B. (1984/1998). Some empirical justification for a theory of natural propositional logic. In G. Bower (Ed.), *The psychology of learning and motivation*. New York: Academic Press. [Reprinted in M. D. S. Braine & D. P. O'Brien (Eds.), *Mental logic*. Mahwah, NJ: Lawrence Erlbaum Associates Inc.]

Cheng, P., & Holyoak, K. J. (1985). Pragmatic reasoning schemas. *Cognitive Psychology*, *17*, 391–416.

Cheng, P., Holyoak, K. J., Nisbett, R., & Oliver, L. (1986). Pragmatic vs. syntactic approaches to training deductive reasoning. *Cognitive Psychology*, *18*, 293–328.

Chrostowki, J. J., & Griggs, R. A. (1985). The effects of problem content, instructions and verbalization procedure on Wason's selection task. *Current Psychological Research and Reviews*, *4*, 99–107.

Cosmides, L. (1989). The logic of social exchange: Has natural selection shaped how humans reason? Studies with the Wason selection task. *Cognition*, *31*, 187–276.

Evans, J. St. B. T., Newstead, S., & Byrne, R. M. J. (1993). *Human reasoning: The psychology of deduction.* Hove, UK: Lawrence Erlbaum Associates Ltd.

Evans, J. St. B. T., & Over, D. E. (1996). Rationality in the selection task: Epistemic utility versus uncertainty reduction. *Psychological Review, 103,* 356–363.

Fiddick, L., Cosmides, L., & Tooby, J. (2001). No interpretation without representation: The role of domain-specific representations and inferences in the Wason selection task. *Cognition, 77,* 1–79.

Field, H. (1977). Logic, meaning and conceptual role. *Journal of Philosophy, 69,* 379–408.

Fodor, J. A. (1980). Methodological solipsism as a research strategy in psychology. *Behavioral and Brain Sciences, 3,* 63–73.

Fodor, J., & Lepore, E. (1991). Why meaning (probably) isn't conceptual role. *Language and Mind, 6,* 328–343.

Gentzen, G. (1964/1935). Investigations into logical deduction. *American Philosophical Quarterly, 1,* 288–306. [Original work published in 1935.]

Gigerenzer, G., & Hug, K. (1992). Domain-specific reasoning: Social contracts, cheating and perspective change. *Cognition, 42,* 127–171.

Girotto, V., Mazzocco, A., & Cherubini, P. (1992). Judgements of deontic relevance in reasoning: A reply to Jackson and Griggs. *Quarterly Journal of Experimental Psychology, 45*A, 547–574.

Green, D. (1995). Externalization, counter-examples, and the abstract selection task. *Quarterly Journal of Experimental Psychology, 48*A, 424–446.

Green, D., & Larking, R. (1995). The locus of facilitation in the abstract selection task. *Thinking and Reasoning, 1,* 183–199.

Griggs, R., & Cox, J. R. (1993). Permission schemas and the selection task. *Quarterly Journal of Experimental Psychology, 46*A, 637–651.

Griggs, R. A. (1984). Memory cueing and instructional effects on Wason's selection task. *Current Psychological Research and Reviews, 3,* 3–10.

Harman, G. (1982). Conceptual role semantics. *Notre Dame Journal of Formal Logic, 28,* 252–256.

Holyoak, K. J., & Cheng, P. (1995). Pragmatic reasoning from multiple points of view. A response. *Thinking and Reasoning, 1,* 373–388.

Jackson, S., & Griggs, R. (1990). The elusive pragmatic reasoning schemas effect. *Quarterly Journal of Experimental Psychology, 42*A, 353–373.

Johnson-Laird, P. N. (1977). Procedural semantics. *Cognition 5,* 189–214.

Karttunen, L. (1972). Possible and must. In J. P. Kimball (Ed.), *Syntax and semantics 1,* New York: Seminar Press.

Kneale, W., & Kneale, M. (1962). *The development of logic.* Oxford: Clarendon Press.

Kroger, J. K., Cheng, P. W., & Holyoak, K. J. (1993). Evoking the permission schema: The impact of explicit negations and a violations-checking context. *Quarterly Journal of Experimental Psychology, 46*A, 615–635.

Loar, B. (1981). *Mind and meaning.* Cambridge: Cambridge University Press.

Noveck, I. A., & O'Brien, D. P. (1996). To what extent are pragmatic reasoning schemas responsible for performance on Wason's selection task? *Quarterly Journal of Experimental Psychology, 49*A, 463–489.

Oaksford, M., & Chater, N. (1994). A rational analysis of the selection task as optimal data selection. *Psychological Review, 101,* 608–631.

Oaksford, M., & Chater, N. (1996). Rational explanation of the selection task. *Psychological Review, 103,* 381–391.

Oaksford, M., & Stenning, K. (1992). Reasoning with conditionals containing negated consitituents. *Journal of Experimental Psychology: Learning, Memory, and Cognition*, *18*, 835–854.

O'Brien, D. P. (1995). Finding logic in human reasoning requires looking in the right places. In S. E. Newstead & J. St. B. T. Evans (Eds.), *Perspectives on thinking and reasoning: Essays in honour of P.C. Wason*. Hove, UK: Lawrence Erlbaum Associates Ltd.

O'Brien, D. P., Dias, M. G., Roazzi, A., & Braine, M. D. S. (1998a). Conditional reasoning: The logic of supposition and children's understanding of pretense. In M. D. S. Braine & D. P. O'Brien (Eds.), *Mental logic*. Mahwah, NJ: Lawrence Erlbaum Associates Inc.

O'Brien, D. P., Dias, M. G., Roazzi, A., & Cantor, J. B. (1998b). Pinocchio's nose knows: Preschool children recognize that a pragmatic rule can be violated, and indicate conditional can be falsified, and that a broken promise is a false promise. In M. D. S. Braine & D. P. O'Brien (Eds.), *Mental logic*. Mahwah, NJ: Lawrence Erlbaum Associates Inc.

Peacocke, C. (1992). *A theory of concepts*. Cambridge, MA: MIT Press.

Platt, R. D., & Griggs, R. A. (1993) Facilitation in the abstract selection task: The effects of attentional and instructional factors. *The Quarterly Journal of Experimental Psychology*, *46*A, 637–651.

Platt, D. P. & Griggs, R. A. (1995) Facilitation and matching bias in the abstract selection task. *Thinking and Reasoning*, *1*, 55–70.

Quine, W. V. (1960). *Word and object*. Cambridge, MA: MIT Press.

Reilly, J. S. (1986). The acquisition of temporals and conditionals. In E. Traugott, A. ter Meulen, J. S. Reilly & C. A. Ferguson (Eds.), *On conditionals*. Cambridge, UK: Cambridge University Press.

Sperber, D., Cara, F., & Girotto, V. (1995). Relevance theory explains the selection task. *Cognition*, *52*, 3–39.

Wason, P. C. (1966). Reasoning. In B. M. Foss (Ed.), *New horizons in psychology*. Harmonsworth, UK: Penguin Books.

Wason, P. C. (1968). Reasoning about a rule. *Quarterly Journal of Experimental Psychology*, *20*, 273–281.

Woods, W. (1981). Procedural semantics as a theory of meaning. In A. Joshi, B. Webber, & I. Sag. (Eds.), *Elements of discourse understanding*. New York: Cambridge University Press.

Yachanin, S. A. (1986). Facilitation in Wason's selection task: Content and instructions. *Current Psychological Research and Reviews*, *5*, 20–29.

Yachanin, S. A., & Tweney, R. D. (1982). The effect of thematic content on cognitive strategies in the four-card selection task. *Bulletin of the Psychonomic Society*, *19*, 87–90.

6 The natural history of hypotheses about the selection task

Towards a philosophy of science for investigating human reasoning

*Keith Stenning and
Michiel van Lambalgen*

Wason's selection task is as interesting for what the history of its study tells us about psychological experimenters, as for what it tells us about subjects' reasoning. In both cases the task is a rich source of insights. This chapter reprises some of what has been revealed under both headings in the 35 years since Wason invented the task. The purpose of studying history is, of course, to avoid reliving those parts of it we would sooner have avoided the first time around.

The initial publication of the selection task (Wason, 1966) was contemporaneous with Chomsky's (1965) *Aspects of the theory of syntax* in linguistics, Montague's (1970, reprinted 1974) *English as a formal language* in semantics, Kuhn's (1962) *Structure of scientific revolutions* in the philosophy and sociology of science, and Goodman's (1965) *Fact, fiction and forecast*[1] in the philosophy of induction. In those intervening 35 years, our conceptualization of language in general and its cognitive implementations; of the semantics of conditional statements; and of how evidence is weighed in the adjudication of statements of regularities, have each been substantially transformed by these, among many other, landmark works. But by that curious relativistic time warping that only academic disciplines can achieve, the speed and direction of progress in the psychological study of deductive reasoning, viewed from points outside, has appeared incommensurable with these other progresses. Our contemporary understanding of natural language semantics, conditional semantics in particular, tells us that there is a range of possible interpretations available for sentences of the form in which Wason chose to couch his rule, and a range of different expressions for each of these conditional relations. Our contemporary understanding of the relationship between evidence and generalization in the process of developing and testing theory tells us that these processes are extremely knowledge rich and socially embedded, and that lawlike generalizations come with environments of possibly implicit background conditions, which require complex bridging inferences for them to be brought to bear on data. Even nearer to home within cognitive psychology, 35 years of psycholinguistics have taught us that interpretation and reasoning are highly interactive processes.

Nevertheless, psychological experiment on the selection task, with one or two honourable and instructive exceptions, has universally assumed that a single logical model of the conditional provides not only the experimenter with a yardstick of correct performance in the task, but also the subjects with their model of the meaning of Wason's rule; that the relation between evidence and rule is uniform and as Wason assumed it to be; that a particular rather simplistic interpretation of Popper's philosophy of science defines subjects' only proper course of action; and that the question of the origin of hypotheses has no bearing on how we should measure them against evidence.

The selection task has in fact been used as a weapon *against* the application of linguistic and semantic theory in understanding subjects' reasoning. Famously, Wason and Johnson-Laird (1972) used the variability of performance with what they claimed to be rules of the same form, to argue that human reasoning operated in virtue of content rather than of form. Johnson-Laird continues this line of argument today (e.g. Johnson-Laird & Byrne, 2002). This call to arms against logical accounts was taken up by Cosmides' "evolutionary psychology" (e.g., Cosmides 1989). The ramifications of this argument can be traced even in the most recent and various theories of selection task performance.

The historical reasons why psychology might clash with logic on this ground are well known. Psychology and logic had an acrimonious parting of the ways at the end of the 19th century, usually traced to the twin influences of Frege's anti-psychologism and the invention of psychological experiment. This divorce was no doubt necessary for both disciplines to establish their identities and methods. That this divorce should prove such an enduring barrier to communication is regrettable, particularly for the psychology of reasoning. Logic, semantics, and most parts of psychology have changed out of all recognition in the meantime. Specifically, the field that has come to be known as "formal semantics" applies the techniques of logic to the *descriptive* study of the meaning of natural language sentences and so constitutes a body of knowledge about what interpretations of sentences like Wason's rule are likely to be entertained by subjects. It is the thesis of this chapter that the 35 years of history of investigation of the selection task can only be understood in terms of the baleful effects of this divorce, and that the children need to re-establish a dialogue.

PSYCHOLOGICAL INTERPRETATION OF POPPER'S VIEW OF SCIENCE

Popper (1963) argued against a positivist view of science that held that theories could be shown to be true by recourse to observations recorded in "observation sentences" and measured for their implications against theoretical sentences. He proposed that there could be no easy division between observation and theoretical statements. Theories had to be tested against the evidence, found wanting, and revised in the light of their falsifications. If no falsification was in principle possible, no theory existed. The truth could be successively approached by continual falsification and revision, but might forever remain beyond our grasp. Theory, or the smaller unit, the hypothesis, could be tested against evidence, in the process of justification, but this process was to be carefully distinguished from the processes by which hypotheses came to be entertained – the processes of discovery. Although much could be said about "the logic of justification" (and this is where Popper's efforts were expended) there was, he claimed, no analogous "logic of discovery", despite the English title.

Popper's philosophy of science has been remarkably influential amongst psychologists studying reasoning, although it undergoes some transformation in crossing the disciplinary boundary. I understand that Wason himself resisted the inference that the selection task was inspired by Popper's philosophy of science and that Popper attended early presentations by Wason at UCL and denied the relevance of the selection task to his philosophical concerns (Manktelow, personal communication). In fact, somewhat later, Wason chooses Kuhn as his philosophical referent in concluding an overview of his "selection task" paradigm for *The Oxford Companion to the Mind* (Wason, 1987, p. 644):

> Our basic paradigm has the enormous advantage of being artificial and novel; in these studies we are not interested in everyday thought, but in the kind of thinking that occurs when there is minimal meaning in the things around us. On a much smaller scale, what do our students' remarks remind us of in real life? They are like saying "Of course, the earth is flat", "Of course, we are descended from Adam and Eve", "Of course, space has nothing to do with time". The old ways of seeing things now look like absurd prejudices, but our highly intelligent student volunteers display analogous miniature prejudices when their premature conclusions are challenged by the facts. As Kuhn has shown, old paradigms do not die in the face of a few counterexamples. In the same way, our volunteers do not often accommodate their thought to new observations, even those governed by logical necessity, in a deceptive problem situation. They will frequently deny the facts, or contradict themselves, rather than shift their frame of reference. Other treatments and interpretations of problem solving could have been cited. For

instance, most problems studied by psychologists create a sense of perplexity rather than a specious answer. But the present interpretation, in terms of the development of dogma and its resistance to truth, reveals the interest and excitement generated by research in this area.

This quote brings out just how strongly Wason believed that his student subjects were deluded, and this belief continues today in several of the most prominent treatments of the selection task (evolutionary psychology, mental models, matching theory . . .). It is certainly true that there is a considerable gap between the psychological and and philosophical uses of Popper's theory. Nevertheless, it is equally clear on the psychological side of the fence that the influence was strong, and is still very much alive, even if, as we will argue here, some of the parts of the theory are more honoured in the breach.

Psychologists in studying reasoning have placed enormous emphasis on the testing of hypotheses and much less on where hypotheses come from. For a contemporary example, Poletiek (2001) in a review that is far more theoretically informed than much of the literature, still can accurately characterize the field in stating that "I do not go into detail about how the idea [of the hypothesis] has come to the subject's mind" (p. 2).

Meantime, back in the philosophy of science, the relations between logic, discovery, and justification have received much scrutiny. The processes of justification are no longer seen as narrowly logical, even if some logical foundations may be required for the study of all these processes. Induction is not analogous to deduction, and while logics are systems for deduction there is no comparable "logic of induction".

If the idea of a "logic of justification" has taken a drubbing in the intervening years, what about the absence of a "logic of discovery"? Philosophers of science such as Hanson (1958) and the "friends of discovery" had already pioneered the study of historical scientific discoveries. They showed that it was possible to make systematic studies of discovery although these should not be regarded as "logics" anymore than should the processes of justification. The fact that highly personal psychological processes may be involved in discovery does not rule out that discovery also involves systematic processes, both psychological and sociological.

It is worth concretely illustrating the relation between idiosyncratic and systematic aspects of discovery. Take even one of the most extreme cases of "irrational" processes of invention – Kekulé's famous discovery of the ring structure of the benzene molecule through a dream in which a snake seized its own tail.[2] Notice what part the dream plays in the discovery of Kekulé's hypothesis. Kekulé and chemists of his time were trying to discover the structure of the benzene molecule from a starting point in which the other known organic carbon molecules were all structured as linear carbon chains. This generalization that carbon compound molecules were composed of linear chains of carbon atoms with other groups hanging off them seems to have been so well embedded in the scientific community that alternatives such as ring structures were unconsciously but never explicitly ruled out. Kekulé's dream appears to have dislodged this assumption and started him thinking about the possibility of a ring structure. Once this hypothesis was entertained, it could be seen to account for existing data and to guide further experiment to discriminate it from the linear hypothesis.

Dreaming may be an irrational process, but notice exactly what the dream does and doesn't achieve in this process. It is only because there is a highly structured pre-existing space of hypotheses about the structure of benzene (that it is a linear chain of six carbon atoms with other groups attached) that Kekulé could interpret his dream as indicating a radical new hypothesis (that benzene is a six-atom carbon ring). Anyone not party to the reigning hypothesis-space of the day could not have interpreted the dream in the way that Kekulé did. That hypothesis-space was the result of the complex state of chemical knowledge involving a large body of theory and data, as well as the social relations in the community of chemists of the day. There is an essential level at which the phenomenon is systematic even when there are levels that are idiosyncratic. I do not wish to decry the importance of idiosyncratic psychological processes in creative thought, but they must be interpreted against the theoretical background in which they play their part.

Notice also that the idiosyncratic level is not unique to the processes of discovery. Other scientists may just as well have been influenced by their dreams in their invention of ways of *justifying* hypotheses. The relation between dream and hypothesis is the same in both cases. It would not justify a hypothesis simply to dream that the hypothesis was true, but it could be of great use to dream how a proof or experimental demonstration could be achieved. Just as Kekulé could not have interpreted his dream of discovery without the systematic background of the hypothesis-space of the day, so a dream of a method of justification would require an interpretable relation to the field's existing methods of justification to be of any use.

In summary, Popper's (and other philosophers of science) rejection of a "logic of discovery" needs to be reassessed in a landscape in which the logic of justification has been so thoroughly reappraised. One can agree with Popper that there is no "logic of discovery" on the same grounds that there is no logic of justification. Neither process is of the kind that logic is now understood to capture. Both discovery and justification are highly systematic processes, both at the psychological and the sociological levels. Nevertheless, parts of both the processes of discovery and justification may also at times consist of highly idiosyncractic psychological processes such as dreaming. So understanding discovery is just as important for understanding science as is understanding justification. Even if this is the state of understanding in philosophy of science, Popper's backgrounding of discovery is still very much alive in the psychology of reasoning.

INCURIOUS NATURALISTS

What has been the impact on the psychology of reasoning of its particular interpretations of Popper's philosophy? Especially their impact on understanding of the selection task? In the selection task, from the subject's point of view, a hypothesis arrives out of the blue, a message in a bottle on the beach so to speak. The subject's task is interpreted as one of justification (or dismissal) of the rule from the blue. But we will argue that the subject is faced with a task of discovery that is just as central to our understanding of what happens in Wason's task. This task is the discovery of how the experimenter intends the task and rule to be understood. This discovery process needs to give rise to hypotheses (about interpretations) before any policy of testing can be designed, although discovery and testing may well take place iteratively. Our argument is that problems with this necessary discovery are what drive the mental processes of subjects, especially in the original descriptive (as opposed to the later deontic) versions of Wason's task.

Popper's distinction is also required to understand the behaviour of the experimenters over the ensuing years. The experimenter's task *should* also be seen as consisting of one task of discovery and one of justification. Experimenters need to engage in descriptive explorations in order to discover what subjects are doing in the task and, thereafter, to engage in processes of justification (or dismissal) of the resulting explanatory hypotheses.

We have identified two strands to Popper's prescriptions for science. One is that science must proceed by testing hypotheses: the other is that hypotheses must be tested by seeking to falsify these hypotheses. Psychologists' interpretation of Popper as writing off discovery as beyond systematic study, and his downgrading of the role of exploration in the formulation of hypotheses, appear to have led them to omit the descriptive and exploratory research one might expect as a prelude to justifying hypotheses about how their subjects reason. Psychologists could, with some justification, blame these errors on their master.

With regard to Popper's second prescription, the great bulk of the work in the psychology of deductive reasoning has consisted of attempts to find positive evidence for models of performance which have arrived, just like the rule in the selection task, like messages in bottles on the beach. Looking for positive cases is, at least on the psychological interpretation of Popper, a very un-Popperian activity, even if it is seen to be required at some stages in theoretical development by other philosophies of science. Here the master is surely not to blame.

What might one have expected scientists to do in response to Wason's publication of his original findings in the selection task? What are the obvious exploratory questions that one might have expected to come first, and to have constituted the process of discovery? What would have been reasonable exploratory questions to have asked first with the conceptual resources available in 1969? Remember, we are dealing with a field of investigators who consider themselves first and foremost to be empirical experimenters, who might be expected to revel in the stage of observation and exploration of a startling new empirical phenomenon. What is most surprising is that rather few researchers spent rather little effort on the simple descriptive questions one might expect to have dominated the field initially. Questions such as, what range of possible interpretations might subjects reasonably have of the rule? Is Wason's logical competence model a reasonable interpretation of what we know about the meaning of the rules used? How does the original descriptive task differ informationally from the easy deontic tasks? How do subjects construe the task? Do they all construe it the same way? What is the difference between the subjects who respond in different ways? What range of explanations could distinguish the hard and the easy versions of the task? There are of course honourable exceptions to this generalization and we will consider some of their contributions to the debate. But the debate has not been organized by these descriptive questions. The debate has been organized by attempts to justify a set of extremely specific hypotheses about performance in the task. The field has, in Newell's (1973) memorable phrase, been playing twenty questions with nature, and it hasn't been winning.

First let us briefly review the outline history of hypotheses. Of all the researchers into selection task performance, Wason ranks as by far the most exploratory. He did explore sources of difficulty. One of his earliest exploratory papers (Wason & Shapiro, 1971) in fact lists for future exploration most of the factors that have subsequently been shown to be significant, even down to the possibility of entertaining a statistical information-based model of the task. Wason did use alternative experimental paradigms such as socratic tutoring (e.g., Wason, 1969). But even Wason could not resist the allure of the testing of a narrow hypothesis, and his early investigations are dominated by the hypothesis that subjects attempt to find cards the rule is true of, rather than ones it is false of – Wason's interpretation of the Popperian account of irrationality.

When several demonstrations of good reasoning with more "concrete" materials were presented (among them some of Wason's own), attention shifted to the role of the familiarity of materials. Griggs and Cox (1982) showed that a drinking-age rule produced excellent performance, but also showed that Johnson-Laird, Legrenzi, and Legrenzi's (1972) UK postal regulation did not facilitate performance unless the subject was familiar with the rule as a post office regulation. Manktelow and Evans (1979) then showed that familiarity *per se* was not sufficient to produce good performance, in that perfectly familiar material was as hard as abstract material if the nature of the *relation* between antecedent and consequent was not clear.

Meanwhile Evans (1972) pursued the hypothesis that subjects were responding in the abstract task by merely choosing the cards that "matched" antecedent and consequent of the rule. This hypothesis is of course nothing but a redescription of the modal response in the original abstract task, until it is taken together with the "negations paradigm" evidence that negations are ignored in the process of matching. Matching of a negated consequent version of the rule to the positive instance card was deemed the logically correct choice. The matching hypothesis construed this as the subject making a correct choice for the wrong reason, because matching was a superficial process unrelated to logical reasoning. Evans continued his pursuit of the matching hypothesis by looking at inspection times of cards and showing that subjects made fast decisions about which cards to select and then spent large amounts of time considering these choices without further inspection of any others (an exactly analogous pattern we are here arguing researchers show with regard to their favourite hypotheses).

Cheng and Holyoak (1985) developed from Griggs' observations their "pragmatic reasoning schema" account of deontic selection task performance. Their work shines out as trying to maintain the generality of reasoning. Pragmatic reasoning schemas are best interpreted as a fragment of a deontic logic and its attendant theorem prover which defines reasoning goals. When these authors contrast their theory with a logic-based theory, they must be read as contrasting it with a descriptive (non-deontic) logical theory. But their work does not contrast the semantics of the descriptive and deontic tasks, nor propose an analysis of descriptive task performance.

Cosmides (1989) built her evolutionary hypothesis on Griggs and Cox's observations of good performance with drinking-age laws. She hypothesized that where performance was good it was achieved by cheating detector modules evolved in the Pleistocene era for policing social contracts. This is a rather specific hypothesis and Cosmides' efforts have gone into finding evidence to support it. Some very obvious opportunities to falsify it have been completely ignored. To fit drinking-age laws into the category of social contracts, the laws had to be considerably bent. Cosmides and Tooby (1992) claimed that the drinking age law "expresses a social contract in which one is entitled to a benefit (beer) only if one has satisfied a requirement (being a certain age)" (p. 183). Undergraduate heaven! Perhaps the authors intended that the benefit was the *right* to buy beer rather than the beer, but even here, a very elaborate and rather particular political philosophy is required to bring drinking-age laws under the rubric of social contracts. Besides, there were already well known cases of easy materials in the selection task that were clearly not social contracts, such as Wason and Green's (1984) inspector scenarios. Even the internal coherence of the hypothesis is dubious. For example, it is not clear why cheating detectors should not serve also to detect lying, which is a form of cheating more plausibly based on a "social contract" than drinking-age laws. Detecting lying *ought* to be enough to perform the descriptive selection task. All a subject with "cheating (lying) detectors" has to do is to ask herself, about each card, whether the source of the rule *could* be cheating by giving false information. Yet even explicit instructions to take this stance do not help much with the task, as Wason had already showed (Hughes, 1966; Wason, 1968). So the hypothesis is not even able to explain why the descriptive (abstract) selection task is so hard (see Stenning, 2002, for further discussion).

Johnson-Laird (e.g., 1983; Johnson-Laird & Byrne, 2002) has pursued the hypothesis that selection task reasoning is done by applying the apparatus of mental models. Again this is intended to be a very specific hypothesis, even if it is less specific than it is intended to be. It is not clear that mental models, as a representational theory, is distinct from mental logic theory (Stenning, 1992; Stenning & Yule, 1997). However, for present purposes of understanding the selection task, the most distinctive property of mental models theory (and mental logic theory) is the insistence that a single basic semantic interpretation of the "if ... then" rule as a material implication is adequate as a competence model of correct reasoning, *and* is the interpretation spontaneously adopted by subjects. Even in the course of a paper arguing for the multiplicity of interpretations of "if ... then", Johnson-Laird and Byrne (2002) invoke a single semantic reading for their explanations of descriptive selection task performance. Although it is slightly too simple to say that this reading is the material conditional of classical logical treatment because the latter paper employs an obscure ontology of "possibilities", it is in all essential respects, as far as the selection task is concerned, the material conditional. Crucially, it shares with the material conditional the same definition of competent card turnings (see Stenning & van Lambalgen, 2004).[3]

This attribution of a single interpretation to subjects is a very strong hypothesis. Semantic accounts of natural language "if ... then" are uniformly agreed that material implication is a difficult or impossible reading to induce in naive reasoners. In fact a good deal of scorn from outside the field has been poured on the selection task precisely because Wason assumed that material implication is the right competence model for the task, and this has been thought to make the task hopelessly artificial. We will return below to the significance of the artificiality of the task. Here the point is that while much effort has been expended on finding evidence to support the mental models hypothesis, little has been expended on attempting to falsify this central assumption, even though the evidence against the assumption was already available elsewhere and not unknown to the experimenters concerned. We argue below that this attribution of a single interpretation to the conditional rules in the descriptive selection task stems from Johnson-Laird's sustained confusion about the implications of the formality of logic. This confusion is one example of the ramifications of the divorce between psychology and logic described above.

Chater and Oaksford's (1994) application of a Bayesian optimal experiment framework as a competence model for the selection task made the valuable contribution of challenging the hegemony of Wason's choice of competence model, an assumption inherited by all other preceding authors. The Bayesian model assumes that subjects make certain plausible assumptions about the cards being a certain kind of sample from a larger population, and that subjects' likelihood of turning cards is in proportion to the information value of the cards as determined by these assumptions. Nevertheless, despite rejecting the purely deductive treatments of the task, Chater and Oaksford's competence model shares with the other theories one very strong hypothesis about selection task performance. Most distinctively, this model assumes the same semantic interpretation of "if ... then" that all other models assume – namely the material conditional interpretation (see Stenning & van Lambalgen, 2001). The focus on the statistical superstructure of the theory may divert attention from the necessary semantic foundations, but the relevant probabilities are probabilities of the truth of propositions, and those propositions have to be specified in a language with a semantics. The semantics Chater and Oaksford choose is the same material implication.

Finally, Sperber, Cara, and Girotto (1995) argued that relevance theory explains subjects' selections. Relevance theory is a broadly based linguistic/cognitive theory about the pragmatics of natural languages. For relevance theory the selection task is a testing ground rather than the ground on which the theory was developed, and so the degree to which relevance theory permits or encourages exploratory research as opposed to focusing on a specific hypothesis has to be assessed on broader grounds, which are beyond the scope of this paper. We certainly applaud Sperber and his colleagues' arguments that subjects' reasoning in the task should, on the whole, be seen as rational, and that the assessment of their rationality rests primarily on the pragmatics of the situation. However, as far as relevance theory is applied to the selection task, it shares with the other hypotheses described here the feature that it assumes the same semantic interpretation of the rule, and, for this reason, it fails to relate problems that subjects have in the task to the specific interactions between semantic interpretations and the task.

Each of these approaches to the selection task adopted the extremely specific hypothesis that subjects' interpretation of the rule used was adequately characterized by material conditionals. Each of these approaches to the selection task is thoroughly Popperian in focusing on the justification of a hypothesis to the exclusion of asking where that hypothesis comes from and whether it is a reasonable or effective starting place for investigations into Wason's initial startling results. Each of these approaches is thoroughly un-Popperian in its search for verifying evidence and their failure to systematically attempt to falsify their considerable assumptions.

From our vantage point that sees Popper's estimation of the merits of falsification as overdone, one might have some sympathy with the approach of looking for positive cases for hypotheses, so these approaches may be better justified in some other philosophy of science. However, we will argue that this can hardly exonerate them from ignoring the problem of the subjects' interpretation of the materials. We return below to an alternative explanation for researchers' lack of exploration and this particular failure to falsify.

THE COMPLEAT ANGLER

Although these have been the prominent approaches to the selection task, there has been a sceptical undercurrent of more descriptive empirical work throughout its study.[4] We have already mentioned Wason's own exploratory work looking for materials that make the task easy, and Manktelow and Evans' (1979) demonstration that familiarity, if it was a factor at all, operated on the relation between antecedent and consequent rather than on the contents of either. One might add Wason and Green's (1984) work on the reduced array selection task, showing how restricting material on the visible sides of the cards to information relevant to the consequent of the rule made the task much easier. Hoch and Tschirgi (1985) made concerted efforts to analyze and demonstrate sources of difficulty operating in the abstract selection task. Margolis's (1988) work drawing attention to the importance of how subjects interpret the available response categories also belongs here.

Although Wason did entertain the possibility that subjects adopted a biconditional interpretation of the rule, and failed to understand the intended reversibility of the cards, Gebauer and Laming (1997) were almost alone in empirically investigating the assumed semantic interpretations of the rule in the selection task. They used a repetition technique to show that a large proportion of subjects' selections are consistent with one or other of four interpretations of the rule attained by combining conditional and biconditional readings of the connective, with constant and variable readings of the anaphors in Wason's rule. However, Gebauer and Laming still assumed that subjects each make single interpretations of the rule and reason perfectly from their adopted interpretation.[5] Beside the issue of interactions between interpretation and reasoning, all the interpretations investigated share with the rest of the field the assumption that conditional and biconditional are to be read materially.

The major truly exploratory psychological work on subjects' frequencies of interpretation of conditionals and other connectives was by Fillenbaum (1978) but the variety of interpretations Fillenbaum exposed were not entertained as hypotheses about subjects' interpretations in the selection task literature. For one example, Fillenbaum showed that a substantial number of subjects interpret "if ... then" *conjunctively*, but this interpretation was not taken seriously as a possibility in the selection task (see Stenning & van Lambalgen, 2004) for some exploration of this possibility and its implications).

What alternative was available to this history of attempts to test highly specialized hypotheses? Obviously, if there was no available alternative, then it is impolite to carp. But there was an alternative. The logic and semantics literature represents a huge body of descriptive work on the meanings of English sentences of the form "If ... then" and other expressions of conditionality. The methodology of this literature is to systematize the intuitions of native speakers of the language in question. This methodology is notoriously weak when it comes to making fine distinctions about exactly when certain structures are used, but it has considerable strength in enumerating possible readings of natural language sentences, together with some information about kinds of contexts that enable the interpretations. One might argue that this literature had failed to find some readings because of its restrictions to the data of intuition, but it is rather implausible to argue that natural language sentences could *not* have readings that are described therein. One might be sceptical about the relation of the theoretical apparatus this literature uses for describing semantics, perhaps believing that it is unimplementable. But this hardly argues against the existence of the data that semanticists describe.

Is this reading of the situation in 1966 anachronistic? It might be argued that the semantics literature, which self-consciously treats its aim as the *characterization* of natural language semantics (rather than the prescription of good reasoning), postdates Montague's work. But it is nevertheless true that the preceding logical literature contains extensive discussion and cataloguing of the divergences between natural language conditionals and those of propositional calculus. A tradition of rejection of the application of formal logic to natural language was already well developed (e.g., Toulmin 1958; Wittgenstein 1953). These arguments centre on the non-truth functionality of natural language conditionals.

There is here an interesting paradox. One might expect that a field with strong allergies to logical treatments of reasoning might reach for the kinds of arguments that had been produced by the philosophical opponents of formal logic. But allergy is sometimes closely related to addiction. The psychologists, despite their allergies to logical treatments, were simultaneously addicted to an earlier logical view that classical logic provided a single monolithic standard against which to *evaluate* reasoning. One sees the seductive power of this simple standard in Piaget's treatments of the development of reasoning in a logical framework. Notably, Piaget steadfastly ignores the role of language in communication – the role that brings problems of interpretation to the fore. The plot takes even a further twist in that Piaget is the favourite target of Wason and Johnson-Laird in their arguments that reasoning is context sensitive. Despite the fact that Piaget's entire edifice of developmental theory is designed to explain how formal operations emerge from contentful experience, Wason and Johnson-Laird dismiss his work on the achievement of formal operations as claiming an insensitivity to content.

In summary, it is true that there is a crucial shift in the logical literature between a primarily prescriptive stance, in which what is important is seen as the clarified reasoning specified in the calculus, to one that sees natural language as another (range of) systems for reasoning. This shift comes with Montague, and it is missing this shift that is critical in psychologists' subsequent course. But it is still true that the disparities between the material conditional and the interpretations plausibly imposed by subjects were well known in 1966. Indeed, it is doubly paradoxical that psychologists should happily accept an essentially early 20th-century view of logic's model of the conditional as a *prescription* for their subjects' reasoning.

This acceptance of the *prescriptions* of a simple reading of logic and the simultaneous rejection of available *descriptions* of semantics cannot be entirely put down to ignorance on the part of the psychologists working on the selection task. The competence model that they entertained was derived from the logical literature, and the difficulties inherent in ascribing material conditional interpretations to natural language conditionals had been discovered and discussed at great length in that literature since the early 20th century (Lewis, 1912). Indeed, the paradoxes of material implication were current in the introductory texts in logic in 1966 (e.g. Copi, 1961 [already a second edition]; Lemmon, 1965). The lack of correspondence between material interpretations and lawlike conditionals had already received much discussion in the philosophy of science literature to which Popper's contributions belonged (e.g., Hempel, 1965). We know that Wason was alerted to these issues by his graduate student Wetherick (1970, 1971).

So a descriptive and exploratory approach to the selection task in 1966 could very well have entertained the kinds of exploratory questions listed above. To put some flesh on the argument, we will now give a very brief description of what such a programme looks like, before returning to the question of why this was not the course taken by the field.

Somewhat belatedly, Stenning and van Lambalgen (2001, 2004) have been pursuing an exploratory programme of research designed to find out what is going on when subjects do the original abstract selection task. They start from a consideration of the difference in the semantics of descriptive and deontic rules, and how the semantics of descriptive rules interact with the circumstances of the selection task to throw up difficulties for subjects. Using only simple model-theoretic differences between descriptive and deontic semantics, differences that have been well known since the classical Greeks and which are taught in most introductory logic classes, they show first that the task interpreted descriptively presents a whole range of problems that the task interpreted deontically does not. They then go on to generate initial exploratory but nevertheless strongly suggestive evidence, from Socratic tutoring of the kind that Wason used, to the effect that subjects do experience the proposed problems in performing the task. They go on to present evidence from conventional non-interactive experiments to demonstrate that indeed these problems are also experienced in the original form of the task.

Of course this work was not the first to point out the semantic differences between descriptive and deontic conditionals. Manktelow and Over (1990) observed the logical differences between descriptive and deontic interpretation of rules. They showed how additional assumptions likely to be made by subjects about the intentions of the utterers of deontic rules gave rise to the so-called "perspective" differences observed by those who had been arguing against logical accounts of the task. They argued from this analysis that the deontic and descriptive rules posed quite different reasoning tasks. But perhaps surprisingly, what they did not do was to use the semantic accounts available to them of descriptive conditionals to predict the set of problems that descriptive conditionals uniquely posed in the selection task.

The root semantic difference between descriptive interpretations and deontic interpretations of rules is simple. Because deontic rules are about the compliance of cases, and the compliance of cases has no bearing on the truth of the rules, the semantic relation between each card and the rule is independent of the relation of all other cards to the rule. Whether this drinker is obeying the law has no impact on the law, and therefore does not interact in its impact with whether any other drinker is obeying the law. Whether this card complies with a descriptive rule *may* affect the truth of the rule and *may* interact with other cards' compliance or non-compliance in the effect it has. This is just the notorious asymmetry of compliant and non-compliant cases in their effects on the truth value of descriptive generalizations. Compliant cases can only make rules true in combination with other cases: single non-compliant cases can make rules false (at least under some circumstances). The descriptive semantics of generalizations is complicated. It is a central topic in the philosophy of science.

This simple semantic difference gives rise to several problems for subjects reasoning in selection tasks with descriptively interpreted generalizations that do not arise with deontically interpreted rules. We will review them briefly here. More adequate discussions are available in Stenning and van Lambalgen (2001, 2004).

In the descriptive but not in the deontic task, there are several semantic relations between rule and cases that are distinct, asymmetrical, but readily confused. Rules apply or fail to apply to cases. Cases comply with or fail to comply with rules. Some cases may make rules false and some sets of cases may make rules true. None of these relations is identical (or even exactly inverse) and yet they are all sometimes described in the vernacular in terms of "truth" and it is easy to confuse them.

In the descriptive but not in the deontic task, rules may be interpreted as brittle or robust with regard to exceptions. Most natural language generalizations are robust to at least some exceptions. If the rule is interpreted as robust, then it is not clear how to interpret the rest of the selection task. This is a central problem with material conditionals as accounts of natural language conditionals.

In the descriptive but not in the deontic task, it is crucial what the domain of interpretation of the rule is taken to be. Although the original instructions tell the subject that the rule only applies to the four cards, it has often been pointed out that it is unclear whether they assimilate this instruction, or rather think of the cards as a sample from a larger population. This tendency is encouraged by and encourages robust interpretations of the rule. Such an interpretation is also encouraged by the use of "if ... then" and the term "rule". "If ... then" is more naturally used for making open-ended generalizations than contingent descriptions, and it is odd to describe a statement about four particular cards as a "rule". It is true that some experiments have used "each" plus a relative clause rather than "if ... then" and found no difference (e.g., Wason & Shapiro, 1971). But one of the morals of our approach is that there are multiple problems, which undoubtedly interact with each other, and merely showing that one controlled manipulation in isolation has no effect does not rule out its contributing to results in other circumstances.

In the descriptive materials but not in the materials usually used in the deontic task, there are anaphors ("one side of the card" ... "the other side") which are intended to be interpreted as variable anaphors, but which are often interpreted as constant anaphors (equivalent to "the front" ... "the back"). This reading changes the appropriate card choices.

Because the descriptive semantics (but not in the deontic semantics) involves sets of cards, subjects are faced with a problem about contingencies of card turnings. They are intended to imagine that they have to turn all the cards they *might* need to turn before getting any feedback, but they are not told this. If they do not assume this, then their choices should be contingent on what they find on the backs of their previous choices. The instruction not to make unnecessary turns should be expected to exacerbate this problem.

In the descriptive but not in the deontic task, the subject is put in what may be a rather socially uncomfortable position of doubting the veracity of the experimenter. To find the rule false is to suggest the experimenter is a liar, but to find some drinkers breaking the law does not reflect on the experimenter.

We make no claim that this list of difficulties peculiar to the interaction between descriptive interpretation of the rule and the rest of the task is exhaustive. Some of these factors have been investigated before and some have not, but even where they have been investigated they have not generally been related systematically to the semantics of descriptive rules. Because syntactic mood (indicative/subjunctive) is such an unreliable guide to descriptive and deontic interpretation, subjects have every reason to entertain the possibility of either kind of interpretation and to settle the issue on the basis of global fit to pragmatic and semantic constraints rather than through sentence characteristics. One sees this problem arising with experimenters' failure to note that their scenarios with indicative rules often demand deontic interpretations.

For example, Johnson-Laird et al.'s (1972) postal regulation was stated indicatively and was most likely to invoke a descriptive reading in any audience that was unaware of the somewhat arcane deontic basis for the rule. Similarly, when a quality inspector applies an indicatively stated rule to the items on a production line, he or she makes a deontic interpretation about what they *ought to be* like, rather than an indicative one about what they *are* like. Note that, however many items are duff, the regulation still remains in force – one hallmark of deontic semantics.

To point out these issues is, of course, not to demonstrate that they cause subjects any problems or account for differences between descriptive and deontic performance. Stenning and van Lambalgen (2001) sought *prima facie* exploratory evidence about what problems students have with the task by using Wason's socratic tutoring method. Although Wason first applied the technique to the problem, he was strongly channelled in his interpretation of his results by his specific hypothesis that students' problem was their failure to seek falsification. Our technique of tutoring was similar to Wason's but our analysis of the data took a much more exploratory approach. We attempted to elicit subjects' views on some aspects of their interpretation of the semantics of the rules, but we also combed the transcripts of the video tapes for *any* evidence that spoke to their interpretations.

This approach brought to light plenty of evidence that subjects do encounter most of the problems listed above. They misinterpret anaphors; are confused as to whether they will get feedback from early choices before making later choices; bow to the authority of the experimenter and assume the rule is true, treating the task as to choose which cards demonstrate this; treat the cards as a sample from a larger population; are unclear about what implications the possibility of exceptions has for their choices; and above all show frequent confusions about the many different semantic relations that hold between examples and rule in the descriptive case. The cited papers contain extensive quotations of examples of confusions arising, traceable to one or more of the problems listed. The dialogues produce ample evidence that subjects' state of confusion is dynamic. They frequently show one difficulty while being clear on another at one point, only to reverse themselves on both what they had been wrong about and what they had been right about at the next point. We believe this vacillation is a good guide to the kind of processes that go on in subjects' reasoning. In these dialogues subjects are *not* reporting earlier reasoning. They are reasoning interactively. But of course the interaction of externalized dialogue may affect their reasoning, and so we need further evidence that these problems really are experienced in the standard task, and to estimate their impacts on reasoning performance.

Some of these problems with the descriptive selection task are already known to cause difficulties. Gebauer and Laming (1997) interpret their evidence as showing that a large majority of subjects adopt a constant anaphora reading, which is identified by incorrect choices. A sequence of task and instructional manipulations designed to remove other problems from the descriptive task is reported in Stenning and van Lambalgen (2004). They observed 3.7% of subjects choosing the P and the not-Q cards in the classical baseline task. A two-rule task designed to decrease the likelihood of robust readings of the conditional instructed subjects that one rule was false and one true, and set subjects the task of selecting cards to find out which rule is which. This task enabled 20% more subjects to make the selections predicted by the logical competence model even though no "matching" response is correct in this task. Similarly, instructions that explicitly state that all selections must be made before any feedback is received enable 14% more subjects to succeed in the standard descriptive task. Deflecting the social conflict of having to impute falsehood to the experimenter enables 9% more subjects to make correct selections.

Our experimental programme of exploring difficulties with the original descriptive selection task is not yet complete, and by its nature is open-ended. It is hard to be sure that all difficulties of the descriptive task have been found, and hard to analyze what combinations of difficulties different subjects experience and how they interact. Nevertheless, the programme has already revealed substantial problems of the kinds predicted on semantic grounds. What is most startling about the approach is that it so easily unearths such a list of difficulties that are unique to the descriptive selection task, and how many of them had not been experimentally explored.

The empirical generalization that arises most strongly from this approach is that interpreting the descriptive selection task is inherently hard, and that almost all the materials that are easy turn out to invoke deontic readings. So for example, as mentioned above, Sperber et al.'s scenarios designed to make false-consequent cards relevant (which are similar to those originally designed by Wason & Green, 1984) invoke deontic readings. These inspection line scenarios, in which an inspector examines cards to ensure a quality regulation is enforced, require a deontic reading. Our findings strongly suggest, for another example, that what is crucial for Johnson-Laird et al.'s (1972) postal regulation to facilitate reasoning is that subjects recognize that it has deontic force, rather than that they are familiar with the rule. It is just that familiarity with the regulation is the only evidence subjects can have about the need for deontic interpretation.

Cummins (1996) has proposed that deontic reasoning is an especially easy kind of reasoning because we are evolutionarily equipped to perform it. Are we to suppose that descriptive selection task performance is carried out by an innate module once it is made easy by removing all the obscurities presented by the task? Chater and Oaksford (1996) rebut Cummins' claims of innateness and modularity for deontic reasoning. But neither party to the debate draws attention to the simplicity of deontic semantics as it interacts with *the specific demands of the selection task* as an explanation for the observations.

The picture that emerges from this exploratory empirical approach to what is happening as subjects reason in the descriptive selection task is one of subjects struggling to decide how it is that the experimenter intends them to interpret a range of conflicting information. Finding an interpretation that fits all the task's constraints is not easy, and subjects are, on this view, for the most part, thinking in highly reasonable ways, even though they stumble from one interpretation to another, each conflicting with some constraints, in doing so. It is not that all solutions are equally good fits to all the constraints. Nor that Wason's particular chosen classical logical competence model isn't an important solution – perhaps even arguably the best. And quite likely an educationally important one too.

On this view of the descriptive selection task, it is important because it places subjects in a kind of communicational vacuum, deprived of most of the cues that they would normally exploit in understanding the semantics and pragmatics of communications. The rationale for this experiment is then just like the rationale for most laboratory experiments. By studying behaviour in abstracted environments it is possible to expose mental processes in a way that observations in natural environments cannot achieve. As such, the approach runs the dangers that all such laboratory approaches run – of producing behaviour that is artificial and unsystematically related to behaviour in more "natural" environments. The defence of the results in this case is just as the defence always has to be – that the relations between what subjects do here and what they do naturally are sufficiently transparent that they can be analyzed. The distance between the mental processes exposed in the Socratic dialogues and the mental processes shown to be going on in the standard non-interactive version of the task is shown to be much smaller than was widely believed. The problems that show up in the first are demonstrated to be at work in the second.

Unnaturalness is a slippery notion. The selection task is highly representative of tasks that are prominent in late secondary and early tertiary education which combine the need for cooperative interpretation of constraints (for example, believing the background rule that there are letters on one side of the cards and numbers on the other) and adversarial testing of other parts of information from the same source. Seen in this light, these are exciting results. We can study the learning involved in subjects' acquisition of explicit control of the classical logical interpretation of the task, and the ramifications this has in their reasoning in other circumstances (see Stenning, 2002). The selection task becomes a window onto important processes in learning to think, processes that are central to late secondary and tertiary education. A whole vista of empirical explorations opens up.

Why did such an exploratory empirical programme not take root much earlier? The answer we would give is one in terms of the original divorce of psychology and logic. Logic was dismissed by psychologists as a necessarily prescriptive study of reasoning. Nevertheless, they honoured an out-of-date logic in this evaluative role by adopting it as a monolithic competence model. But this move also meant that they simultaneously had to incorporate the same particularly simple logical model as their account of how people actually interpret the experimental materials. The only alternative would have been to acknowledge the multiplicity of interpretation, and they felt this acknowledgement would threaten their aspiration to be natural scientists. This complex of ideas explains their simultaneous embrace of a particularly simple logical model at the heart of psychological theory, coupled with the vehement rejection of logic as having anything to contribute to understanding human reasoning. And of course dismissing logic on the grounds of prescriptiveness is hopelessly simplistic. Subjects themselves have prescriptive standards that they apply to their own reasoning processes. One has only to listen to the Socratic dialogues to hear subjects upbraiding themselves for what they judge to be lapses in their standards of reasoning. These standards have causal consequences. There is no way for psychology to escape the description of prescriptions.

But the rejection of logic has not been merely on the grounds that it is a prescriptive theory of reasoning. The rejection goes much deeper and affects the details of the psychological theories offered in its place. Two essentially similar examples are Cosmides' and Johnson-Laird's rejections of logic as essentially universal and context-insensitive.

"On this view, reasoning is viewed as the operation of content-independent procedures, such as formal logic, applied impartially and uniformly to every problem, regardless of the nature of the content involved" (Cosmides & Tooby, 1992, p. 166).

"Formal rules are, by definition, blind to content. . ." (Johnson-Laird & Byrne, 2002, p. 665).

Both quotes betray a fixation with the operation of rules applied to sentences in virtue of form, but simultaneously a denial of the whole apparatus of logical interpretation. Logic gains its grasp on context and on content through its specification of the local interpretation of arguments. Most obviously, what assumptions are made affects what conclusions are valid in an argument. Assumptions may change at any point in an argument. Logic classically gives no account of how assumptions should change, although it provides the essential framework for formulating a psychological theory of how these non-logical processes might work.

Many more fundamental changes in interpretation may be invoked interactively during argument as the participants come to understand more about each others' or their own interpretations. Mental models theory just as certainly needs a level at which its operations are formal, and a level at which changes in assumptions take place. It is just that mental models theory jumbles these together in a way that makes the theory difficult to evaluate, and has led it to miss the most important differences between descriptive and deontic tasks. The fact that logic separates out the theoretical levels of interpretation and reasoning does not mean that the mental processes corresponding to interpretation and reasoning have to take place in that order, and without cycling. The Socratic dialogues provide examples to rapidly disabuse anyone of such a theory.

This repression of the processes of interpretation betrays a belief that logic is a theory of processing of a language that has a universal interpretation, fixed for all time, if modulated locally in processing. Curiously, Johnson-Laird and Byrne appear to believe that once reinterpretation during the course of argument is allowed, any theory becomes vacuous. A full discussion of the ramifications of this construal of logic is beyond the present scope. The arguments are presented in Stenning (2002) and Stenning and van Lambalgen (2004). The point here is that it is this view of logic as insensitive to context which has been used systematically for 35 years to shore up the isolation of the two fields.

Despite inventing an alternative semantic theory (Johnson-Laird & Byrne, 2002) that proposes a large number of readings for conditionals, their account of the selection task still ascribes to subjects the least likely reading of the conditional known to science. When this is pointed out in criticism of arguments such as those for "deductive illusions" (Johnson-Laird & Savary, 1999) the authors argue that the materiality of implication cannot be the problem because the illusions arise with exclusive disjunction. But this misses the point that each of the connectives can be interpreted "materially" or, alternatively, as having some non-truth functional element, and the exclusive disjunction used in Johnson-Laird, Legrenzi, Girotto, and Legrenzi (2000) generates the same choices of interpretation as the conditional (see Stenning & van Lambalgen (2004) for the argument).

IF YOU SO CLEVER, HOW COME YOU AIN'T RICH?

One psychologist colleague, presented with the argument that the careful comparison of the semantics of descriptives with the semantics of deontics is capable of predicting a whole range of difficulties in the selection task, responded that this was a powerful case of hindsight. This riposte reveals an interesting temporal perspective. The characterization of descriptive and deontic semantics at the granularity required for this exercise was achieved in classical Greek logic. Reasoning about how the world *is* was well understood to have different features from reasoning about how it *ought to be*, is *planned to be*, or we are *commanding it to be*.

These insights are alive and well in logic teaching even today. The charge of hindsight is wide of the mark. The problem is not one of hindsight but one of rejection of old insights of other disciplines – a not-invented-here syndrome perhaps. A more justifiable accusation would be one of tardiness. The first author had known about the selection task since 1968 and even taught it regularly as part of courses on cognitive psychology since 1976. The inadequacies of the available accounts were fairly clear, as his students would attest, and the topic was always presented as a scandal ripe for research. So why did it take so long to design an empirical programme?

The first author's own mistake, he now believes, was to overestimate the distance between the student subjects and the semantic theories – being too ready to believe that the task was an artificial one that failed to engage with subjects' knowledge of their language, and elicited only superficial behaviour. It was obvious that the deontic versions of the task were simply logically different and much easier tasks, and besides, the extravagant evolutionary claims founded on them seemed so ill-anchored as to be best left to natural selection. The ill-argued evolutionary case distracted attention from the explicitly deontic versions of the task and delayed a detailed analysis of the implications of the differences between deontic and descriptive interpretations of rules.[6]

The mistake was to doubt that the mental processes of subjects in the original descriptive task could be related so directly to specifiable semantic problems with which the subjects actually struggled. The social psychology of the experiment was also a source of confusion. The students debriefed after teaching about the selection task usually reported that they now saw the error of their initial responses. But then they would, to the professor, wouldn't they? And besides, they generally could not recapture their own state of innocence at the time they were debriefed. By that time they had forgotten the thought processes they had themselves gone through just before, especially since they had no conceptual system for explicitly recording them. As the current predicament testifies, remembering what you thought before you understood something is a tricky business.

But it really was obvious that the robustness to exceptions of natural rules which arises from their non-truth functional interpretation had a major part to play in any adequate explanation. Similarly, problems of what subjects took to be the domain of interpretation was an obvious source of issues. Why otherwise would one teach about the applicability of the Ravens Paradox (and its involvement of assumptions about the size of sets in the domain) to the selection task?

But enough biography. Why did the field not adopt this exploratory approach? A response encountered from psychologist colleagues is that this account of the selection task in terms of the semantic complexities of descriptive conditionals is merely a negative spoiling of the existing positive psychological accounts, which leaves us with no psychological theory of reasoning. This perception of the situation should be rejected, although it is revealing about how the field came to be in its current condition. This response only makes sense if semantic and psychological accounts are seen as accounts competing for the same explanatory space. But semantic accounts do not compete with processing accounts, and this semantic account is used as the basis for making a series of predictions about unexplored factors affecting processing. There can be no processing accounts without a semantic foundation, because without such a foundation there is no specification of what is processed with what result. This is why mental models theory has to reinvent semantic accounts of its own, and why the Bayesian theory has to have an underlying semantic account.

Far from competing, semantic research needs to be integrated into psychological research, and when it is integrated, it provides a radically different conceptualization of psychological problems. Instead of subjects processing with a fixed interpretation, within a single system of reasoning, they are seen as, wittingly or unwittingly, making metalogical choices between alternative systems, and changing those choices interactively as they encounter new clashes with problem constraints. The content of processing is radically different as well as the outcome.

With this change in conceptualization comes a shift to an interest in individual differences in reasoning. Even subjects who make the same card selections can be seen to be making them for quite different reasons, and the different interpretations of rule and task reflected in different selections also become targets for explanation. A far richer cognitive psychology results from a richer view of the semantics (Stenning, 2002; Stenning & Monaghan, 2003). Once individual differences are acknowledged as a worthwhile focus of explanation, that immediately makes learning and the change of patterns of response an interesting topic, and reconnects the field to educational interests. It even suggests that deduction's primary importance in everyday life is its involvement whenever issues of interpretation come to the fore – interpretation of others' communications or of our own thoughts (see Stenning & Monaghan, 2003).

So why has the psychology of reasoning been impoverished by premature hypothesis testing research strategies? The explanation can only be the perception that logic and psychology are mutually exclusive. This perception leads to the feeling that if psychology is to establish itself as a proper science of reasoning then it must present theories of reasoning that are not based on logical conceptualizations. These theories should preferably be counterintuitive, and they must explain some "fundamental human reasoning" mechanism.

But all mental models theory's programme does is to reinvent the 19th-century logical programme of rediscovering the laws of thought. Modern logic moved on from this programme a long time ago. Logics are not mechanisms, whether fundamental or not; whether presented as proof-theory or model-theory. Logic now sees itself as the mathematics of information systems, whether artificial or natural. It provides an information system hypermarket from which one can choose an appropriate system for modelling whatever informational phenomenon takes one's interest, and one expects to be able to find at least fragments of subjects' behaviour that are best explained by assuming they have adopted one or other of these systems as their interpretation of the task at hand. Logic is to human reasoning roughly what geometry is to human visual perception, the mathematics and conceptualization that is required for any empirical research programme, but something quite distinct from the empirical programme itself. In Marr's terminology it is the mathematics for defining the computational level – *what is processed with what result* – when things are working right.

THE RELATION BETWEEN LOGIC AND PSYCHOLOGY IN COGNITIVE SCIENCE

From a logical point of view, the psychology of reasoning is about how the many systems that logic characterizes are implemented in the mind, often as fragments or approximations. This statement should *not* conjure up images of the brain processing representations that are squiggly sentences punctuated by *modus ponens* ... Logics, and more plausibly fragments of logics, can be implemented in diagrams or in feelings just as well as in sentences, and the "rules" of most direct interest to psychologists are the regularities in the theorem provers, which are bits of non-logical apparatus, whose content may be just about anything – probabilities of diagrams, just as likely as squiggly sentences. Psychologically they may be habits of thought as often as "rules of inference". To try to overcome these preconceptions, we will consider one illustrative example, Cosmides' cheating detectors, and compare the picture that emerges from a logical approach with that which Cosmides' anti-logical approach presents. A fuller treatment is available in Stenning (2002).

We argued above that Cosmides' cheating detectors cannot plausibly explain why the descriptive selection task is so hard, because cheating detectors should be applicable to the descriptive task. Lying is a form of cheating on informational exchange. All the subjects have to do is ask themselves whether the utterer of the rule *could* be lying about the cards. Of course there is more to lying than uttering falsehoods, just as there is more to breaking contracts than not supplying benefit or paying cost, but if the statement is true then the speaker cannot be lying (even if they could still be misleading).

Here we focus instead on the relation between affective responses to cheating/lying and subjects' reasoning. In order to get as far as possible from the idea that theories based on logic should posit mechanisms processing squiggles, let us assume that the psychological implementation of cheating/lying detectors are our emotional reactions to cheating/lying – our gut feelings about good and bad intentions of parties.

There is no reason why a logical approach has to feel any conflict with the idea that reasoning is at least partially implemented in emotional reactions. Cosmides might or might not be right about the involvement of our feelings about cheating in people's reasoning about social contracts. We are personally inclined to think she has the makings of a plausible story, even if it is a different story from the one she has told, and even if she has not pursued the empirical programme one might expect to validate it.

It might be that at a certain stage of development/education subjects find it easy to reason with material that has the right sort of content for them to engage their feelings about cheating/lying. It might even be that when subjects have passed this stage (perhaps due to extensive education about reasoning) the implementation of their extended abilities has been achieved by broadening the range of materials that they can get to engage these underlying affective reactions, even though these materials are now "abstract", and the affective nature of the intuitions involved may have gone underground. That is, their gut feelings are still involved, rather than having been replaced by some symbol-twiddling device.

Given a proposition about vowels and consonants, subjects achieving the ability to deal with decontextualized material might have a strategy of asking themselves "*Could* the source of this sentence be telling me a lie?". If they can do this, then they should be able to solve the descriptive task, at least provided they can settle all the other imponderables about the experimenter's intentions mentioned above. If the statement is true then the source cannot be using it to tell a lie, although of course they might still be using it to mislead. And we know from construction and evaluation tasks that subjects are generally well aware that a 7 with an A on the back is an exception or a counterexample to the intended reading of the rule, even if they may not know that that reading is the one intended in the selection task.

This "simulationist" (as opposed to theory-based) account we find quite conducive. But it is completely consistent with a logically based psychology of reasoning. A logically based psychology of reasoning would expect intimate interactions between content of materials (and interpretation of the task generally) and the logical forms (semantic interpretations) subjects assign to sentences. In fact logic is exactly a theory about how non-logical assumptions (domain- and context-specific assumptions) interact with the generalities of language to determine what is valid reasoning in particular contexts. If affective reactions play some role in subjects' reasoning in these situations, then their status in theory is as implementations of logical systems in subjects' minds.

Some psychologists' reaction to this argument is that if logic with all its formal squiggles and inference rules is only a specification of what has to be implemented, then once more we can forget about logic and just study the affective implementation. But this is to miss the point of cognitive theories of mind. Cognitive theory, because it is computational, is always about relations between a systemic level and an implementational level. Just studying the cheating detectors has led to the missing of the most powerful behavioural regularity in these observations – that humans have an intuitive understanding of the difference between reasoning about how the world *is* and reasoning about how the world *ought to be* quite independently of the specifics of their cheating detectors, and the selection task makes one easy and the other hard.

Further psychological investigation of the deontic vs descriptive distinction could still benefit from the guidance of logical insight. Current developmental work on the relation between deontic reasoning and theory-of-mind abilities raises the interesting question of whether it is the mental topic of reasoning about other minds that make false-belief tasks hard, or whether it is the counterfactuality that is the source of difficulty. Logically, deontic reasoning is one species of modal reasoning, although there are many species of modal reasoning that are not deontic, for example reasoning about the possibility and necessity of situations. For instance, Peterson and Riggs (1999) provide some evidence that the difficulty of false-belief tasks may be more to do with modality than mentality. Again age-old logical knowledge could provide valuable guidance to empirical programmes, if it were seen not as an alternative but as a source of conceptual foundations.

CONCLUSION

Where does all this leave Popper and the impact of his teachings on our understanding of subjects and experimenters? Popper's advice had two strands: the focus on justification rather than discovery, and the invocation to attempt to falsify hypotheses rather than to seek supporting evidence. To take experimenters first, they do seem to have focused on hypotheses, with little attention to where hypotheses originate or how they relate to other bodies of knowledge about reasoning. But this strand of Popper's philosophy has been least supported by developments in the philosophy of science. Understanding how hypotheses are embedded in existing knowledge plays a vital role in understanding where they come from, which are worth pursuing, and how they can best be investigated. The result has been a focus on over-specific hypotheses and a neglect of the exploratory and descriptive research that must play such an important part in developing sciences, and which constitutes the most important contribution of empirical work.

As far as falsification of these hypotheses goes, this principle seems to have been more honoured in the breach than in compliance. The preponderance of research has sought supporting evidence for experimenters' over-specific hypotheses. We have argued here that the explanation for the acceptance of an extremely specific hypothesis about the semantics of rules, as well as all the even more specific superstructures built on that acceptance, can only be explained by a rejection of logical insight as inherently competitive with psychological explanation.

If we are to capture the 35-year interlude in scientific research constituted by research on Wason's selection task in a philosophical framework, it seems that Kuhn's theories are much more readily applicable than Popper's. It has been the researchers' insistence on the divorce of logical and psychological research, an essentially socially based segregation of disciplines, that has been the most powerful force in shaping the course of research. Insights straddling the disciplinary boundary have been steadfastly ignored, just as Kuhn's analyses of historical episodes in science show that available counter-evidence is always ignored unless its relevance is socially supported. There is also the issue of the relative social status of the natural and social sciences; psychologists' eagerness to be classified with the former rather than the latter; and the importance this brings with it of proposing apparently new theories untainted by any past history in the social sciences or, worse still, the humanities. The whole episode is ripe for a sociological analysis.

How about the subjects – all those anonymous students who have contributed their time to the progress of science? What light have the 35 years of research on the selection task thrown on the relevance of the philosophy of science to understanding their mental processes? Our argument here has been that Wason's task above all has to be understood as a communication between experimenter and subject, though one that is cryptic in the extreme. It is the cryptic nature of the communication that invokes the effort after meaning that we observe in the Socratic dialogues, and these dialogues appear to be rather good initial guides to the mental processes taking place in the standard task, at whatever level of awareness.

The intriguing observation is that experimenters have continued for the most part unaware of the multiplicity of things they might reasonably be taken to mean by their instructions, and generations of students have been persuaded to have the insight into the intended competence model without generally appreciating the reasonableness of their initial confusions. So the competence model has been handed from generation to generation, so to speak, without much challenge as to its uniqueness or adequacy – perhaps just what Kuhn would have predicted during periods of "normal science"? But what Kuhn did not pay so much attention to is the effective insulation achievable between contemporary scientific communities by the erection of discipline boundaries.

So have we found an effective philosophy of science for the practice of the psychology of reasoning? And what does it tell us about how our direction in the field should change? Of course, there is no reason why practising scientists would be signed up to one or another particular philosophy of science. But they should be aware of the main findings and able to recognize the phenomena philosophers describe as transferred to their own specific branch of science. They should know, for example, that all sciences have conceptual and mathematical foundations which are generally maintained by non-empirical work using the methods of philosophy and mathematics. These foundations are often referred to by the practitioners as "theory". Sciences use a range of empirical methods to make observations, explorations, and experiments. There is a balance to be kept between curiosity-driven empirical exploration, and theory testing. And there should be intimate interactions between experiment and theory. Experimentalists and theoreticians are often folk of rather different temperament. Not everyone necessarily engages in both activities, but at the level of a scientific community, a coordination of theory and experiment has to be achieved.

The situation in the study of human reasoning has been one in which the community has been split by its methods into groups of people who do not even see themselves as studying the same phenomenon. This was most vividly brought home to me when a prominent member of the mental models community responded to a conference paper I had given on equivalence-mappings between mental models theory and mental logic theory, with the pronouncement that I may have my theorems but mental models theory had its experiments. All scientists ought to know that theorems and experiments have to be brought into some accommodation. Just the one or just the other isn't science.

The result of this splitting of what should be a single community is that psychology of reasoning has reinvented crypto-semantic theories and aped the high prestige practices of mature sciences in its testing of extremely specific hypotheses. Physics is possessed of a huge accumulation of bridging theory which enables this kind of approach. Logic and semantics (and more generally other mathematical theories of reasoning such as probability theory and game theory) could supply both conceptual frameworks and some of the requisite bridging required for psychology to contribute to cognitive science what every young empirical endeavour should contribute – the exploration and description of phenomena ripe for explanation and the stimulation of theory. Wason's selection task, I believe, is an outstanding contribution of just the kind one might expect – discovery of an easily replicable yet profoundly challenging phenomenon of human reasoning capable of stretching the best that semantic theory has to offer. The social arrangements in academic psychology in the last 35 years have militated against this contribution having its full impact on the cognitive science of human reasoning. Restoration of a dialogue between semantics and psychology would enable a truly exciting empirical exploration of the phenomena of human reasoning, and especially learning to reason. Of course, a dialogue takes two partners, and the semantic community has its own share of responsibility in the arrangements that have prevailed – but that is an entirely other paper.

NOTES

1 At least the second edition.
2 Some doubt has been cast on the role of the dream in the discovery, but for our purposes, the most extreme hypothesis about its causal efficacy is the most informative one to examine. Even if the extreme role were true, our argument is that a rational level of analysis is still available and required.
3 Johnson-Laird and Byrne explain some content effects in the selection task in terms of "semantic and pragmatic modulation" and they describe these effects as leading to the non-truth functionality of their interpretation of the conditional. However, as we shall see, these effects are not the central effects of non-truth-functionality, which we will show create problems for subjects specifically in the descriptive task, nor do they suggest this interpretation challenges the standard competence model.
4 We echo here the title of Izaak Walton's original work in praise of exploration: *The compleat angler, or, The contemplative man's recreation: being a discourse of fish and fishing, not unworthy of the perusal of most anglers* (Walton, 1815).
5 Stenning and van Lambalgen (2001) present evidence that interpretation and reasoning interact iteratively, and that constant anaphor readings of the rule are invoked by memory demands that result from reasoning with a variable interpretation.
6 The first author would also like to acknowledge here the contribution of the second author in setting him straight.

REFERENCES

Chater, N., & Oaksford, M. (1994). A rational analysis of the selection task as optimal data selection. *Psychological Review, 101,* 608–631.

Chater, N., & Oaksford, M. (1996). Deontic reasoning, modules and innateness: A second look. *Mind and Language, 11*(2), 191–202.
Cheng, P., & Holyoak, K. (1985). Pragmatic reasoning schemas. *Cognitive Psychology, 17*, 391–416.
Chomsky, N. (1965). *Aspects of the theory of syntax*. Cambridge, MA: MIT Press
Copi, I. (1961). *Introduction to logic* (2nd Edn.) New York: Macmillan.
Cosmides, L. (1989). The logic of social exchange: Has natural selection shaped how humans reason? Studies with the Wason selection task. *Cognition, 31*, 187–276.
Cosmides, L., & Tooby, J. (1992). Cognitive adaptations for social exchange. In J. Barkow, L. Cosmides, & J. Tooby (Eds.), *The adapted mind: Evolutionary psychology and the generation of culture* (pp. 163–228). New York: Oxford University Press.
Cummins, D. (1996). Evidence for the innateness of deontic reasoning. *Mind and Language, 11*, 160–190.
Evans, J. (1972). Interpretation and "matching bias" in a reasoning task. *Quarterly Journal of Experimental Psychology, 24*, 193–199.
Fillenbaum, S. (1978). How to do some things with if. In J. W. Cotton & R. L. Klatzky (Eds.), *Semantic functions in cognition*. Hove, UK: Lawrence Erlbaum Associates Ltd.
Gebauer, G., & Laming, D. (1997). Rational choices in Wason's selection task. *Psychological Research, 60*, 284–293.
Goodman, N. (1965). *Fact, fiction and forecast* (2nd Ed.). Indianapolis: Bobbs-Merrill.
Griggs, R. A., & Cox, J. R. (1982). The elusive thematic materials effect in Wason's selection task. *British Journal of Psychology, 73*, 407–420.
Hanson, N. R. (1958). *Patterns of discovery: An inquiry into the conceptual foundations of science*. Cambridge: Cambridge University Press.
Hempel, C. (1965). *Aspects of scientific explanation, and other essays in the philosophy of science*. New York: Free Press.
Hoch, S., & Tschirgi, J. (1985). Logical knowledge and cue redundancy in deductive reasoning. *Memory and Cognition, 13*, 453–476.
Hughes, M. (1966). *The use of negative information in concept attainment*. PhD thesis, University of London.
Johnson-Laird, P. N. (1983). *Mental models*. Cambridge, UK: Cambridge University Press.
Johnson-Laird, P., & Byrne, R. (2002). Conditionals: A theory of meaning, pragmatics and inference. *Psychological Review, 109*, 646–678.
Johnson-Laird, P., Legrenzi, P., Girotto, V., & Legrenzi, M. (2000). Illusions in reasoning about consistency. *Science, 288*, 531–532.
Johnson-Laird, P., Legrenzi, P., & Legrenzi, S. (1972). Reasoning and a sense of reality. *British Journal of Psychology, 63*, 395–400.
Johnson-Laird, P., & Savary, F. (1999). Illusory inferences: A novel class of erroneous deductions. *Cognition, 71*(3), 191–229.
Kuhn, T. (1962). *The structure of scientific revolutions*. Chicago: Chicago University Press.
Lemmon, E. (1965). *Beginning logic*. London: Nelson.
Lewis, C. I. (1912). Implication and the algebra of logic. *Mind, 21*, 522–531.
Manktelow, K., & Evans, J. (1979). Facilitation of reasoning by realism: Effect or non-effect? *British Journal of Psychology, 70*, 477–488.

Manktelow, K., & Over, D. (1990). *Inference and understanding: A philosophical perspective*. London: Routledge.

Margolis, H. (1988). *Patterns, thinking and cognition*. Chicago: University of Chicago Press.

Montague, R. (1974). English as a formal language. In R. Thomason (Ed.), *Formal philosophy: Selected papers of Richard Montague* (pp. 108–221).

Newell, A. (1973). You can't play twenty questions with nature and win. In W. C. Chase (Ed.), *Visual information processing*. New York: Academic Press.

Peterson, D. M., & Riggs, K. (1999). Adaptive modeling and mind reading. *Mind and Language, 14*, 80–112.

Poletiek, F. (2001). *Hypothesis-testing behaviour*. Hove, UK: Psychology Press.

Popper, K. (1963). *Conjectures and refutations: The growth of scientific knowledge*. London: Routledge & Kegan Paul.

Sperber, D., Cara, F., & Girotto, V. (1995). Relevance theory explains the selection task. *Cognition, 57*, 31–95.

Stenning, K. (1992). Distinguishing conceptual and empirical issues about mental models. In Y. Rogers, A. Rutherford & P. Bibby (eds.) *Models in the mind* (pp. 29–48) Academic Press

Stenning, K. (2002). *Seeing reason: language and image in learning to think*. Oxford, UK: Oxford University Press.

Stenning, K., & Monaghan, P. (2003). Strategies and knowledge representation. In R. Sternberg & J. P. Leighton (Eds.) *The nature of reasoning*. Cambridge, UK: Cambridge University Press.

Stenning, K., & van Lambalgen, M. (2001). Semantics as a foundation for psychology: A case study of Wason's selection task. *Journal of Logic, Language and Information, 10*(3), 273–317.

Stenning, K., & van Lambalgen, M. (2004). A little logic goes a long way: basing experiment on semantic theory in the cognitive science of conditional reasoning. *Cognitive Science, 28*(4), 481–529.

Stenning, K., & Yule, P. (1997). Image and language in human reasoning: A syllogistic illustration. *Cognitive Psychology, 34*, 109–159.

Toulmin, S. (1958). *The uses of argument*. Cambridge: Cambridge University Press.

Walton, I. (1815). *The compleat angler, or, The contemplative man's recreation: being a discourse of fish and fishing, not unworthy of the perusal of most anglers. Bagster's 2nd ed., being the 8th of this work, with improvements and additions*. London: Printed for S. Bagster by R. Watts.

Wason, P. (1966). Reasoning. In B. Foss (Ed.), *New horizons in psychology*. Harmondsworth, UK: Penguin.

Wason, P. (1968). Reasoning about a rule. *Quarterly Journal of Experimental Psychology, 20*, 273–281.

Wason, P. (1969). Regression in reasoning? *British Journal of Psychology, 60*, 471–480.

Wason, P. (1987). Problem solving. In R. Gregory (Ed.), *The Oxford companion to the mind* (pp. 641–644). Oxford: Oxford University Press.

Wason, P. C., & Green, D. W. (1984). Reasoning and mental representation. *Quarterly Journal of Experimental Psychology, 36*A, 598–611.

Wason, P., & Johnson-Laird, P. (1970). A theoretical analysis of insight into a reasoning task. *Cognitive Psychology, 1*, 134–148.

Wason, P., & Johnson-Laird, P. (1972). *The psychology of reasoning: Structure and content*. London: Batsford.

Wason, P. C., & Shapiro, D. (1971). Natural and contrived experience in a reasoning paradigm. *Quarterly Journal of Experimental Psychology, 23*, 63–71.

Wetherick, N. E. (1970). On the representativeness of some experiments in cognition. *Bulletin of the British Psychological Society, 23*, 213–214.

Wetherick, N. E. (1971). 'Representativeness' in a reasoning problem: A reply to Shapiro. *Bulletin of the British Psychological Society, 24*, 213–214.

Wittgenstein, L. (1953). *Philosophical investigations* [translated by G. E. M. Anscombe]. Oxford: Blackwell.

7 Reasoning and rationality
The pure and the practical

K. I. Manktelow

Dualities abound in the contemporary study of reasoning, and it is striking how this kind of theoretical structure has characterized so much of recent research. For instance, we have the dual-process theory of thought, which began with Evans and Wason in the 1970s (Evans & Wason, 1976; Wason & Evans, 1975) and has cropped up in similar forms in a number of different and independent fields in rough synchrony (see Evans, chapter 10 this volume; Evans & Over, 1996; Stanovich, 1999). Then there is dual rationality theory, in which there is a broad divide between rationality conceived as adherence to (or justification by) an appropriate normative system, and rationality as doing the right thing in the circumstances, i.e., as optimal goal attainment. Evans and Over (1996) and Stanovich (1999; Stanovich & West, 2000) again provide extensive surveys of this second duality.

In this chapter, we examine a third duality, to do with the kind of reasoning that has formed the prime focus of psychological enquiry. That focus has largely been on people's ability to draw inferences about matters of truth and falsity, for instance in the assessment of validity in categorical syllogisms or propositional inferences, or the judgement of what items make a conditional sentence true or false. However, that is not the only kind of reasoning one can explore, and more recently, effort has been directed at the study of the kinds of reasoning people engage in when determining the actions they or others should or should not perform.

Thus, if you want a nice jingle, we can think about what is true or about what to do. Assessing the truth of statements against the facts, or assessing the soundness of arguments, is an exercise of what has traditionally been called pure reasoning or theoretical reasoning, while determining appropriate action is an exercise of practical reasoning. This tradition is very long-standing: the theoretical–practical distinction goes back over more than two millennia, and has been the subject of much philosophical debate. In this chapter we shall examine some of these historical ideas alongside the more contemporary empirical research, and assess how they might be related. We begin with a brief review of the turn taken towards practical reasoning by psychological research in recent decades. This has generated debates about whether categorically different types of reasoning can be identified, a debate that has ancient echoes. We therefore track back and examine some of these ideas about pure and practical reasoning. From there, we revisit the more recent research, and consider where this leaves the characterization of these two forms of thought. Are they really psychologically distinct types, are they the same type in different guises, or can a different distinction be drawn?

FROM CONTENT TO CONTEXT IN REASONING RESEARCH

The study of reasoning may have a long philosophical past but it has a short psychological history. The most often cited old reference in the empirical literature is undoubtedly of Minna Wilkins' (1928) paper on syllogistic reasoning. Rather arrestingly, this paper concerns itself with the effects of content, what she called "changed material", on people's ability to assess the validity of conclusions in the classical quantified or categorical syllogism. Wilkins presented her participants with four kinds of content: thematic (using everyday terms), abstract (using single letters), unfamiliar (using made-up or weird words), and belief bias (using thematic contents either where the valid conclusion conflicted with belief in what was empirically true, or where an invalid conclusion was consistent with belief). The participants had to choose their preferred conclusion from a set of alternatives. Performance was generally good (in excess of 75% logically correct choices overall, higher than one tends to find in more recent studies), but was best in the thematic condition, as expected. Performance in the belief bias condition was less good, but still better than with the abstract and unfamiliar materials, indicating that while the thematic nature of this condition helped, the conflict of validity with belief did produce some error.

So the role of the content of reasoning problems in people's inferences and evaluations has been right at the heart of psychological reasoning research more or less from the beginning. Wilkins' pioneering work set in motion a line of research on belief bias that is still being pursued. That is, for several decades psychologists have attempted to assess the extent to which people's attitudes to the premises and conclusions of a syllogistic argument affect their appreciation of its logical soundness. This very long story can now be cut reasonably short. The assessment of performance simply as logically correct or incorrect masks an important statistical pattern that consistently emerges in the data (see Evans, Newstead, & Byrne, 1993; Evans & Over, 1996; Garnham & Oakhill, 1994; Manktelow, 1999, for reviews): the biasing effect of belief is far stronger on invalid than on valid syllogisms. While there is a slight tendency for people to accept valid syllogisms that have believable conclusions more than those that have unbelievable conclusions, there is a massive tendency to reject invalid syllogisms with unbelievable conclusions compared to those with believable conclusions (e.g., Evans, Barston, & Pollard, 1983). Note that in both cases, the pull of the bias is in the right direction as far as logic is concerned: you should accept valid conclusions and reject invalid conclusions, and belief helps you do this. Thus belief bias is really having a *debiasing* effect (cf. Evans, 1989), a fact that has enabled it to be recruited in arguments about dual rationality (e.g., Evans, Over, & Manktelow, 1993).

The revival of interest in the belief bias effect on syllogistic reasoning that occurred in the 1980s overlapped with an upsurge of interest in a similar effect in research on conditionals. The motor for this second wave of concern with content was the introduction of the Wason selection task in the 1960s. It was found early in the history of research on this problem, which now runs into several hundred published reports and who knows how many unpublished, that, just as Wilkins had found in her study of syllogisms, thematic content had significant effects on performance.

We are not dealing with "belief" here in the same way, though: thematic syllogisms involve people's beliefs in the sense of their empirical knowledge about the state of the world. The manipulation of content in the selection task is not so much about people's knowledge in this sense, but about the more general role of knowledge in reasoning; specifically, its possible role in enabling or disabling inference, rather than deflecting it. The selection task, in its original form, was not about attitudes but about people's appreciation of the conditions under which a stated claim (usually in conditional form) could be put to the test. People are not asked to arrive at or evaluate a conclusion, and so have nothing to agree or disagree with. The selection task literature therefore talks of content *effects* rather than biases. Shortly after the first systematic report of the task (by Wason, 1968), Wason and Shapiro (1971) presented the first evidence that thematic content facilitated performance.

Wason and Shapiro presented their participants with a claim about four (and only four) journeys said to have been made by the experimenter: that, for instance, "Every time I go to Manchester I travel by car". Details of the four journeys were written on four cards, each having the destination on one side and the means of transport on the other. Two cards showed city names uppermost (Manchester and Leeds) and two showed means of transport uppermost (car and train). Which cards should be examined to see whether the experimenter's claim was true or false? The standard normative answer (this cagey wording is now necessary because of questions that have arisen over the status of the norms for this task; see Chater & Oaksford, chapter 3 this volume; Stenning, chapter 6 this volume; Stanovich, 1999) is that you should point to the card showing Manchester, in case it has a means of transport other than Car on its reverse side, and the one showing Train, in case it has Manchester on its reverse, and no other. Going to Manchester other than by car would show the claim to be false, and the two cards referred to are the only ones that could bear that combination. Of the 16 people given this task, 10 produced this solution, compared to 2 out of 16 given an isomorphic abstract version about letters and numbers. As with syllogistic belief bias, then, we see once again how thematic content has facilitated logical performance. Indeed, the effect in the selection task is often referred to simply as the facilitation effect.

But what is its source? The resemblance to belief bias is purely superficial. The participants are not asking themselves whether they agree with the conclusion of an argument. In the selection task, we ask them to reason *about* a rule, as Wason (1968) stated at the outset. Their task is to think about the conditions under which a certain type of claim would be true or false, and apply this judgement to the question of what might lurk on the hidden sides of the cards before them. In 1971, it seemed that thinking about journeys made this easier than did thinking about letters and numbers, but no one was quite sure how. Was it the lexical content – towns, transport? Was it the relation between them – journeys? The first true pointer came from Johnson-Laird, Legrenzi, and Legrenzi the following year (1972), but it was another decade before its real significance was recognized.

Johnson-Laird et al. had their subjects assume the role of workers sorting the mail. Their rule was "If a letter is sealed, then it has a 50 lire stamp on it", although the subjects were British, not Italian. Five envelopes were presented: one with a 50 lire stamp, one with a 40 lire stamp, one with no stamp at all (you could not tell whether these were sealed or not), one that was sealed and one that was unsealed (whose stamps were hidden). The task was to select those envelopes that might violate the rule. Clearly, one should be on the lookout for sealed letters without the proper (50 lire) stamp on, and the subjects of 30 years ago thought so too: 21 out of 24 selected the appropriate envelopes, compared to 2 out of 24 when given a similar letter–number rule (they were the same subjects).

The title of the Johnson-Laird et al. paper was "Reasoning and a sense of reality", something they thought might be "no more than a sense of familiarity" (p. 400). This idea was further explored by Manktelow and Evans (1979) who, after several abortive attempts to reproduce the facilitation effect using a variety of materials, proposed that the success of the participants in the postal experiment and others like it might be due to familiarity – that is memory – and nothing else. This contrasted with the then prevailing explanation in terms of the familiarity enabling them (by some means) to achieve insight into the logical structure of the task, and reason their way to the answer. Perhaps people were simply remembering situations they had been in: two-tier postal regulations for sealed and unsealed mail were part of the experience of the British population from which the postal participants were drawn at the time. Solution would then reduce to little more than pattern recognition. Thematic contents that were not familiar in this way should not facilitate.

This was named the memory-cueing hypothesis by Griggs and Cox (1982) who tested it in an elegant series of experiments: they surveyed their participant population for materials with which the participants were familiar, and hit upon the drinking-age task. People played the role of a police officer given the rule that "If a person is drinking beer then the person must be over

19 years of age". Cards showed a person's age on one side and their drink on the other side. Three-quarters of the participants chose the 16-year-old drinker (who might have been drinking beer) and the beer drinker (who might have been under 19). However, attributing this performance, impressive as it and that on the postal task are, to "memory-cueing" is not taking us very far down the explanatory road. What kind of memory, what kind of cueing?

With the research of Cheng and Holyoak (1985), a better answer began to emerge. They explicitly invoked the notion of *deontic* reasoning, and proposed that it was familiarity with this form of thought, not with post offices or bars *per se*, that was the material factor. Thus the explanation shifted from thematic content to deontic context: people were getting the thematic task right because they were familiar with reasoning about rules in the sense of regulations, not in the sense of descriptive generalizations. From this stance, we can recognize the research of Johnson-Laird et al. (1972) as the first study of the deontic selection task. Cheng and Holyoak's theoretical explanation, that people acquired schemas for such reasoning through their life experiences, found an immediate competitor in the evolutionarily based social contract theory of Cosmides (1989), and the rise of these theories brought about another surge of interest in the selection task. This time, it had found a new role as a – or rather the – vehicle for empirical research into deontic reasoning.

Repeated demonstrations appeared of people's facility with deontic reasoning, and two aspects of this research are worth picking out at this point. First, the apparently facilitating effect of deontic materials began to extend back down the age range. Girotto, Light, and Colbourn (1988) showed that children aged 9 and 10 reliably selected the right items (plastic model bees) in a reduced deontic selection task. Then, most startlingly of all, Cummins (1996a) found the same effect in 3- and 4-year-olds. Given that fewer than 10% of adults (undergraduate students) typically find the right cards in the standard abstract descriptive selection task, something different is clearly happening in the deontic task. Second, a new cast on what constituted the "right" solution was necessitated by reports of a new phenomenon: the social perspective effect.

For instance, Manktelow and Over (1991) argued that in some cases, the mirror image of the standard correct solution would be the right one. In the standard task, the rule is usually a conditional in the logical form "*If p then q*", with the "correct" solution (remember those cagey words) being *p* (e.g., Manchester, sealed, drinking beer) with *not-q* (e.g., not by car, less than 50 lire, under 19). Now consider a task used by Manktelow and Over, concerning a promotional rule aimed at increasing sales in a shop: "If a you spend more than £100, then you may take a free gift". What counts as a violation of this rule depends on who is doing the violating, the shop or the customer: violation is available to both. The shop cheats the customer when it takes more than £100 and does not dispense the gift (one comes across such events quite often in consumer columns and TV programmes); the customer cheats the shop when she takes the gift without spending enough money. In selection task terms, these would be the *p*, *not-q* values in the first case, but the *not-p*, *q* values in the second case. But as Manktelow and Over and others (e.g., Gigerenzer & Hug, 1992; Politzer & Nguyen-Xuan, 1992) have stressed, there is nothing irrational about the second solution, although it might appear illogical, if one adheres to the standard logic of the descriptive conditional.

This is one reason why we now need to be cagey about specifying what is the right answer. The deontic selection task is not the selection task as it was originally designed and used, if the kinds of reasoning called for in the case of the deontic and the descriptive/indicative task are not the same. Even with the standard task, what is normative is controversial. And we are on even shakier ground if we extend one kind of norm from the indicative task and apply it to the deontic task. We should not therefore talk about facilitation effects when comparing indicative reasoning with deontic reasoning, and the observation by Johnson-Laird et al. (1972) that the apparently excellent performance on the postal task did not transfer to the abstract task fits nicely with this proposal. We should not expect it to transfer: it would be like expecting long-jumping to facilitate pole-vaulting. Indicative reasoning is a form of theoretical reasoning, of thinking about the way the world is. Deontic reasoning is a form of practical reasoning, wherein people consider what actions should be performed. That is what rules as regulations are all about: the regulation of action. Let us therefore look more closely at the division between practical and theoretical reasoning, and see what justification there is for the notion that they comprise two categorically different types of reasoning. Psychologists have turned their gaze on this question in the last decade and begun to wonder about the indicative–deontic, or theoretical–practical, distinction. For example, they have asked whether there is something "special" about deontic reasoning, given that people seem to be so naturally good at it (e.g., Almor & Sloman, 1996; Chater & Oaksford, 1996; Cosmides, 1989; Cosmides & Tooby, 1992; Cummins, 1996b, 1998).

ACROSS THE GREAT DIVIDE: THEORETICAL AND PRACTICAL REASONING

The theoretical–practical divide is not the sole province of psychologists and philosophers: everybody recognizes it, at least implicitly. As Johnson-Laird et al. (1972) presciently noted in explaining the "facilitation effect" of their postal task, the participants were "not required to test a rule, but to test whether or not objects conform to a rule whose truth is guaranteed" (p. 399). On the roads, it is commonly understood that if the speed limit sign says X, you must not exceed X. On being pulled up by the police for driving at X + 20, you might try the argument that your instantiation of the *p*, *not-q* case makes the speed rule false, but you won't get very far; about as far as the nearest police station. One difference between the indicative and deontic tasks, then, is the difference between reasoning *about* a rule (to establish its truth status) and reasoning *from* a rule (to assess compliance to it).

As we have noted, however, there is also a difference between theoretical and practical reasoning, which goes beyond this: in the former, one is reasoning about the what is true, in the latter one is reasoning about what to do. That was the essential difference between the abstract task and the postal task, as it is between all indicative and deontic selection tasks. Whether and to what extent these are or are not different categories of thinking has been debated since Aristotle, so it will be helpful to turn at this point to the treatment of the debate by the ancients.

Aristotle's consideration of theoretical and practical reasoning was an outgrowth of the revolution in human knowledge brought about in previous generations by work in fields such as geometry (Aristotle lived between 384 and 322 BC). Euclid's beautiful demonstrations of the lawful relations between lines, angles, and figures rested on pure deduction about their forms and the relations between them. Geometry became the paradigm case of the prospect of being able to encompass the whole of nature and experience within a sound and complete system of laws. Such aspirations are not an ancient conceit, of course, and echoes of such grand ambition can still be found; witness, within psychology, the aims and claims of 20th-century behaviourism.

Aristotle questioned whether such an enterprise was possible, and reflected that thought could be seen as occupying different domains with very different purposes and characteristics. Scientific thought, or *episteme* in Aristotle's terminology, concerned universal truths about idealized types. For instance, in geometry, one deals with "the isosceles triangle" as an abstraction. One's reasoning about such things is not bound up with concrete exemplars, such as triangles cut out of paper or drawn in the sand, and what is true of an isosceles triangle here today will still be true elsewhere tomorrow; geometrical axioms and proofs know no spatial or temporal boundaries. That being so, arguments can be drawn strictly deductively: true conclusions necessarily follow from true premises properly arranged and consistently interpreted.

These abstract properties, Aristotle realized, did not extend to matters of everyday experience where, he argued, one's wisdom is of a different kind; he called this *phronesis* (practical wisdom, or prudence). Practical arguments are not about idealized abstractions but about particular cases; they are not detached from time and place but embodied in them; and their premises are "presumptive", i.e., they have meanings that can be presumed to hold for present purposes, but cannot be assumed to be fixed. Practical wisdom was a matter of experience, not quasi-geometrical law. (A second kind of practical wisdom, which Aristotle called *technai*, knowledge of how to do things, will not be considered here.)

In making this basic division, Aristotle does not argue that rational thought is possible in episteme but not in phronesis, and so sets out to specify how one can reason about practical matters in a reasonable and rational manner. The relation between theory and practice has also been returned to repeatedly since Aristotle's time, and we shall return to it later in this chapter as well. Aristotle's account of justifiable practical reasoning brings us the first instance of the practical syllogism. We can compare the practical syllogism with the more familiar kind of syllogism involving quantified categorical premises (which Aristotle also systematized). Aristotle's version of the practical syllogism seems to be distinct from theoretical syllogisms primarily in virtue of its contents. Thus a practical syllogism concerns practical matters, i.e., the particulars of an everyday situation, as opposed to the universal statements about the world that are the constituents of a theoretical syllogism.

To illustrate, here is an example of a practical syllogism based on one given by Aristotle himself (adapted from the version in Anscombe, 1957):

Dry food suits any human
Muesli is a type of dry food
I am human
This is a bowl of muesli.

Aristotle rarely stated the conclusions to his syllogistic examples, and as Anscombe points out, the problem with this one is that the conclusion that is necessitated is something like "muesli suits me". This is not an answer to the question, "what should I do?": "muesli suits me" is not an action. What we have here is, therefore, a theoretical argument concerning what can be included as instances of the classes "suits" and "humans"; that the contents of the syllogism are practical, in that they concern day-to-day matters of experience rather than quasi-geometrical laws, is beside the point. You could (indeed should) arrive at this conclusion, but are still not compelled to perform the action of eating muesli. However, Aristotle was concerned with action, and wrote as if the conclusion of a piece of practical reasoning would be an action (Anscombe, 1957; Audi, 1989; Jonsen & Toulmin, 1988), or at least an intention to act (Harman, 1976).

Later authors have addressed this problem by getting away from the kinds of arguments originated by Aristotle, for instance by changing the grammar of the constituent sentences from indicative to imperative. Imperatives are about actions. However, Anscombe argued that this manoeuvre still does not enable us to derive necessary conclusions about actions from practical syllogisms. She uses the following example, again based on Aristotle (and adapted here to fit our modern tastes):

Vitamin X is good for all men over 50
Muesli is full of vitamin X
I am a man over 50
Here is a bowl of muesli.

This does not entail the conclusion "So I'd better eat it"; one should still conclude something like "What is here is good for me". And this is still a theoretical argument with practical, in the sense of everyday, experienced, content. To derive an action, then, one might change the first premise to a universal imperative form, such as "All men over 50 must eat all foods containing vitamin X that they ever come across". But Anscombe argues that such premises are "insane" (p. 58), because they cannot be complied with, and therefore could not ever form the basis of a prescription for action. Thus the Aristotelian practical syllogism cannot give us the answer to the essential practical question, What should I do? As Audi (1989) puts it, the Aristotelian practical syllogism only yields a conclusion *in favour of* an action.

Aristotle established that there are different universes of reasoning, if you like, but left us with a puzzle. The Aristotelian practical syllogism consists entirely of propositions: each can be true or false, and the conclusion can be arrived at or assessed therefore in terms of its validity, just as in any theoretical argument. There is thus from this viewpoint no fundamental difference in the processes by which we reason theoretically or practically, so they should both be accounted for by the same logic. A practical argument is practical only in that its contents are practical. However, practical reasoning should be about action, and actions are not propositions; an action is not something that can be said to be true or false. Even if we accepted Aristotle's perspective on the practical syllogism, there would still have to be something intervening between the conclusion (muesli suits me) and a truly practical inference (so I should eat this bowl of muesli), and also between this inference and actually doing it.

Aristotle's approach to practical reasoning does, however, embody an idea that has found echoes, as so many of his ideas have, in contemporary explanations of practical reasoning: the idea that what is at issue is the relation between ends and means. The first premise of the syllogism, in particular or universal form, expresses an end that the reasoner is supposed to have, although in the above examples it is implicit (so the arguments are enthymematic): the end here would be to attain something good. The minor premises describe conditions under which one may approach this end. (As we shall see later, the idea that practical reasoning can be explained in means–end terms is one that has resurfaced in psychological research.) The question arises as to where the ends come from, and whether reasoning can be a means to them.

This question was addressed in the 18th century by the philosophers David Hume (1711–1776) and Immanuel Kant (1724–1804). Hume attacked the question of whether reasoning can tell us what to do, and his answer is encapsulated in his most famous quotation: "Reason is, or ought to be the slave of the passions, and can never pretend to any other office than to serve and obey them" (in *A Treatise on Human Nature*, 1739). Hume did not mean, of course, that we should put aside thought in favour of impulse whenever there is some kind of contest between the two. Rather, he takes reason to have no intrinsic motivating role in action. This is the doctrine of instrumentalism: reason is (one of) the means by which passions can be satisfied; reason can direct you along the route to satisfaction. Reason can also arouse passions in the first place, for instance by determining that something exists that we would desire to have or to avoid. Thus, for instance, you might be travelling in a wild place, and reckon, from your knowledge gained through watching survival programmes on TV, that the tree in the distance might well have some edible fruits on it. It occurs to you that you quite fancy some of this fruit (you don't have to have some pre-existing biological state of hunger for this passion to arise). You then figure out how best to reach the tree and then get at the fruit. Reason has delivered you the object of desire and the means by which to assuage the desire, but it has not delivered you the desire (passion) itself. In this sense, reason is, in another of Hume's phrases, "perfectly inert": it does not promote action directly. It also does not seem, on this account, in any way practical, in so far as reasoning seems once again to be about matters of fact: existences and means. The missing element behind the question What should I do? (Why should I want to do it?) is given by the passions, in whose interests reason acts only as a servant – or a slave.

Kant came to a very different conclusion about the relation between reason and the motivation of action. Part of the explanation for this seems to be that Kant's concern was principally with moral reasoning, or ethics, a particular form of practical reasoning and one that has not been the prime focus either of this chapter or of the psychology of reasoning in general. (There is a large literature in developmental psychology on moral reasoning, mostly stemming from the Piagetian approach of Kohlberg, e.g., 1963, but it has made almost no contact with the psychology of reasoning, and vice versa. Fiddick, 2003 is a welcome exception.) Focusing on ethics and morality leads to a different emphasis in framing the question What should I do? compared to, say, the question of whether I should eat muesli or cross a river and climb a fruit tree.

For Kant, the major premise of a practical argument was a special kind of universal statement: a maxim. More than this, these maxims had to be consistent with his celebrated "categorical imperative": one should only act according to maxims that one would set down as a law for everyone. Hence action should be based on duty, duty being determined by (universal) laws. The minor premise of a practical argument would, as in Aristotle's scheme, concern the means of fulfilling the maxim. So we are once again back with the idea of practical reasoning being about ends and means, although Kant departs from Hume in that he allows such reasoning to give us these ends and compel us to attempt them: reason can, for Kant, directly motivate action without appeal to some detachable "passion". For Kant, the idea of what constitutes duty, and hence moral imperatives themselves, was a product of the will, and hence of practical reason, and therefore reason is autonomous (Audi, 1989) in its motivational force for action. Duty does not reduce to desire, to the pursuit of pleasure or the avoidance of pain, and hence practical reasoning does not need passion to motivate action.

Kant therefore sees practical reasoning as essentially rule-based, in contrast to Aristotle's emphasis on the wisdom accrued through experience. Kant assumed, like Aristotle, that the distinction between practical and theoretical reasoning was not one of type or form, but of content or object: practical reasoning is practical because its object is human conduct. There is a contrast here between these philosophical views and those that have emerged from psychological research and which have been taken to imply that there is a qualitative difference between practical and theoretical reasoning; this contrast will figure again later in the chapter.

Kant's rule-based approach also implies the possibility of some kind of ethical "geometry": given that maxims for action should always be stateable as universal laws, it must be the case that all (practically) rational people should adopt and adhere to them. However, life is not like that and, as Kant himself recognized, there was the occasional need to engage in casuistry: allowing the circumstances of the case to bear upon the judgement made (Jonsen & Toulmin, 1988). Jonsen and Toulmin deny that Kant's aim was to locate ethics in the realm of theoretical reasoning, and give the example of medicine as an area of contemporary life in which it is important to maintain the distinction between theory and practice. Medical *science* depends on theoretical reasoning, about the nature and causes of disease, but medical *practice* depends, as its name implies, on practical wisdom also. What you, as a clinician, should do (prescribe) depends not only on your theoretical knowledge but also on your judgement of the particulars of this patient and his or her circumstances. Kantian ethics can supply us with one kind of moral certainty, but a casuistical analysis tempers this with regard to the case in hand.

Casuistry was shattered as a reputable philosophical enterprise, as Jonsen and Toulmin relate, by what must be one of the most effective satires in history, Blaise Pascal's *Provincial Letters* of 1656. Pascal lampooned what he regarded as its inevitable consequence: that of utter moral laxity as all principles were opened to question. However, Jonsen and Toulmin mount a noble attempt to rehabilitate "case analysis" of ethical judgements, and it is interesting to note that the role of circumstances and excuses has begun to be explored by psychologists researching deontic reasoning (Fairley, Manktelow, & Over, 1999; Manktelow, Fairley, Kilpatrick, & Over, 2000) and causal reasoning (Cummins, 1995; Fairley et al., 1999). Case analysis is indispensable to civil jurisprudence as well as medical practice, and various governmental and supra-governmental bodies have been established, such as the US National Commissions and the European Court of Human Rights, to engage in it on behalf of the rest of us.

IS PRACTICAL REASONING SPECIAL?

Audi (1989) brings together these various considerations to produce what he calls the simple basic schema for practical reasoning, residing in a "cognitive-motivational" conception. This term embodies the central idea of practical reasoning as reasoning about means to ends. The schema has the following form:

> Major premise – the motivational premise: I want X
> Minor premise – the cognitive premise: My doing A would contribute to realizing X
> Conclusion – the practical judgement: I should do A.

The constituent terms are broadly defined: "want" does not only mean what it means in everyday language, but includes that X which one feels obliged to approach, such as in adhering to a prudential, moral, or legal injunction (you might not want to eat muesli, put money in a collection box, or keep to the speed limit, but you acknowledge that you ought to). Similarly, "should" contains various possible types of force, for instance, again, prudential, moral, or legal. And "doing A" can mean any number of things, not just performing a single action, but formulating plans or defining sub-goals. Audi allows that there can be many different types of conclusion, all of which can be taken as an answer to the practical question: for instance, one might make a practical judgement, form an intention to act, make a decision, or perform the action itself.

However, Audi continues the Aristotelian position of denying that practical and theoretical reasoning are to be distinguished on a formal (logical) basis. Both are processes of inference that involve deriving justified conclusions from premises expressed as propositions. The difference between them arises in the conclusion, and hence in the objective of the reasoning: it should be possible to perform a theoretical inference and a practical inference from the same premises.

Jonsen and Toulmin (1988) argue along similar lines using their example of medicine, but their example seems to point up problems for the thesis that theoretical and practical reasoning are formally indistinguishable. Consider their example of a case in which an elderly woman presents with an array of ailments common in old age; it is hard to tell which of her signs and symptoms are caused by which ailments. Now consider the responses of a clinical practitioner versus a research gerontologist. The clinician wants to do what is best for the patient, and will engage in some prudent satisficing, looking to stabilize her condition before attempting to sort out which of her pathologies to treat, and what her prescription should be. This is clearly an exercise of practical reasoning. The medical scientist, on the other hand, wants to find out about the ailments of old age for theoretical reasons, and such a case may be of no interest or relevance: the symptoms and ailments are so tangled that trying to sort them out would literally be a waste of time.

It seems, then, that not only are the objects of reasoning different from these two perspectives, but, all down the line, the kinds of reasoning each doctor will engage in will be different. This is contrary to the Aristotelian position espoused by Audi. The clinician will engage in a form of decision making, where the costs and benefits of various treatments will be assessed alongside their prospects of success, while the task of the scientist is a form of belief revision (cf. Harman, 1995; Chater & Oaksford, chapter 3 this volume) in which the scientist must determine how best to conduct tests of various hypotheses. This continues right down to the question of whether to spend any time with this patient at all, i.e., even to begin to think about her.

We can also see this difference in an example given by the philosopher Anthony Kenny (1975) to illustrate the point that either logic, or the use of logic, must be different in theoretical and practical cases:

I'm to be in London at 4.15
If I catch the 2.30 I'll be in London at 4.15
So I'll catch the 2.30.

If this were a theoretical argument, the conclusion would be invalid: it is an example of the fallacy of affirming the consequent (q; If p then q; therefore p). However, as a practical argument it seems perfectly sound: the antecedent is sufficient for the consequent, and the consequent represents a goal. However, the antecedent is not necessary given the consequent, and we can see the practical nature of the argument signalled in the subtle changes in mood between the minor and major premises and the consequent (I'm to be/I'll be) and in tense between the antecedent of the conditional and the conclusion (I catch/I'll catch).

Examples such as these are interesting because they reveal that theoretical and practical reasoning can not only be distinguished, they can also be quite intimately related. Instances of this relationship are available from both the philosophical and psychological literatures. Thus Harman (1995) shows how it is possible to have practical reasons for theoretical beliefs – indeed, as he says (p. 187), there is a practical aspect to all reasoning. We can see that in the earlier example of the medical scientist, who has to make the practical judgement of whether to devote his cognitive resources to a theoretical question. We can recognize this also as a form of decision making: the doctor considers the costs and benefits of his options, together with the probabilities of these results, and attempts to trade off the one (a gain in theoretical knowledge) against the other (the costs arising from the effort that would be required to unravel this patient's pathologies). Harman goes further than this, though, and adds that it is possible for beliefs themselves to be driven by practical considerations. The most famous example of this in the philosophical annals is Pascal's wager, in which Pascal set out a practical argument for believing in God. This again has, from our contemporary viewpoint, a clear decision-theoretic aspect. There are costs involved in believing in God (such as those incurred through pious acts and self-denial) and benefits and costs depending on whether God really exists or not. If there is the slightest possibility that God exists, then you should believe, says Pascal, since the payoffs (an eternity in Heaven for the believer, eternal damnation in Hell for the unbeliever) so vastly outweigh the costs of belief.

Theoretical and practical reasoning are conjoined in another way, as argued by Chater and Oaksford (1996); Kenny (1975) has made a similar point. They were responding to Cummins' (1996b) thesis that deontic reasoning was "special", in an evolutionary sense. Her case was that the deontic–indicative (i.e., practical–theoretical) distinction was not just a matter of philosophical debate, but "a primitive in the cognitive architecture" (p. 160). In other words, it reflects a fact about human biology as well as psychology, determined by our evolutionary history. She marshals psychological, neurological, and cultural evidence in support of this claim. Chater and Oaksford dispute much of Cummins' interpretation of the scientific evidence, but also argue that it is implausible to contend that there is a special "module" for deontic reasoning that is not present for indicative reasoning, since efficient theoretical reasoning is a prerequisite for effective practical reasoning. We need to know what is true before we decide what to do: as Kenny (1975, p. 179) put it, "one cannot reason practically about Communist China without accepting its existence".

We have seen from this brief discussion of some of the foundational ideas in the philosophical study of practical reasoning some key points of connection with the contemporary psychology of reasoning: that practical and theoretical reasoning can be distinguished by their form and their content, although a debate ensues as to whether form or content is the proper distinguishing mark; that theoretical and practical reasoning, though distinct, are linked; that practical reasoning concerns thinking about means and ends; that there is a question as to the relation between reasoning and the causes (motivation) of behaviour; that practical reasoning is concerned with the circumstances in which an inference is made; that there are rule-based and experienced-based theoretical perspectives; and that practical reasoning is about action.

PSYCHOLOGICAL EVIDENCE AND THE PURE–PRACTICAL DIVIDE

We shall now work back through these points and focus on the psychological literature, leaving the first (the great divide) until last. The idea that reasoning is about action, involves means–end deliberation, and is concerned with circumstances, has correspondents in a programme of research into deontic reasoning conducted by Manktelow and Over and colleagues since the early 1990s. As we saw in the first section of this chapter, this work emerged from a concern with deontic reasoning that had been established by Cheng and Holyoak's (1985) pioneering demonstrations of a deontic "facilitation" effect in the Wason selection task, and Cosmides' (1989) theoretical argument as to the source of this effect, based in evolutionary psychology. Cheng and Holyoak and Cosmides both produced rule-based theories of deontic reasoning, although neither was in the Kantian tradition, whereby these rules are themselves the product of reason. For Cheng and Holyoak, we abstract schemas for deontic reasoning out of our everyday experience, and use their rule structures to determine our conclusions about actions in novel situations. Cosmides argued that our rules for deontic reasoning comprise a mental module given to us by our species' evolutionary history, necessitated by our need as individuals to recognize when we and others comply with or violate the core social contract rule that enables us to survive: that if you take a benefit, you must pay a cost. Thus each of these theories has an Aristotelian flavour to it, with the library of experience located in individual learning by Cheng and Holyoak, and in the human gene pool by Cosmides.

As we have set out in detail elsewhere (e.g., Manktelow & Over, 1991, 1995), there are aspects of deontic reasoning with which these rule theories are not as comfortable in dealing as they might be. For instance, they do not say why regulations exist in the first place, or why a person should be concerned with some kinds of violations and not others – there are many more ways to violate a deontic conditional than those recognized by the schemas. We put forward an essentially decision-theoretic alternative to the rule theories, in which people represent mental models (Johnson-Laird & Byrne, 1991) of the situation at hand, and think about the preferences they hold between the possible states of affairs they describe. This enables an answer to the question of what motivates deontic reasoning. For instance, in the example of the shop rule given earlier in the chapter, the shop owners consider the case in which the customers spend over £100 and are given a free gift against one in which they spend less than £100 and get a gift. They prefer the former to the latter, since it is in their material interest to do so. The owners will therefore be on the lookout for the latter, as a violation of the rule is against their interests. The same process can be followed through from the customers' perspective: they prefer the model in which they get a gift for their lavish spending to the one where they do not, and so watch for the latter case as an instance of sharp practice by the shops, which entails a potential loss to them.

This scheme has the advantage of explaining why rules are made in the first place, something not directly addressed by the schema theories (Cosmides' theory contains an account of why we should have a general social contract schema, but not why particular rules might be effective; and many deontic rules do not fit this general schema). Rules are formulated by agents with the aim of inducing actors to deliver something they value, such as a higher rate of spending in a shop. The agent makes use of the actor's assumed values in doing so – say, that customers appreciate free gifts. If the agent's preference were absent, the rule would not be uttered, and if the actor's did not hold, the rule would not work. Furthermore, regarding deontic reasoning as a form of decision making opens up other questions. Decision theory is about *expected* utility, and so deontic reasoning should show an influence of subjective probability as well as utility: it does, as people tend not to look for violations that, although equally serious, are seen as less likely (Manktelow, Sutherland, & Over, 1995). People should also engage in a form of "case analysis" in their practical reasoning, in that they should be sensitive to the circumstances in which rules are seen to be broken, since these will affect the utilities assigned to such acts: they do (Manktelow et al., 2000). For example, people are less inclined to punish speeding compared to drunken driving, while breaking the speed limit when taking a woman in labour to a maternity ward is scarcely seen as an offence at all.

As we have seen, there has been a long-running philosophical debate on the question of the causal role played by practical reason in motivating action. For Aristotle, it was almost taken as read that the ultimate product of a practical argument would be an action, although he seemed to assume this rather than state how it would come about. The poles of the debate are occupied by the Humean tradition on the one hand, with its insistence that reason does not, in itself, give rise to action; and by the Kantian tradition on the other, which regards practical reason as autonomous, i.e., as capable of motivating action directly, without recourse to an independent passion. More recently, Harman (1976) states that reason can only give rise to intentions, with the connection between intention and action not being completely clear (also Harman, 1995).

Psychological research on deontic reasoning shows how causality plays a complex and integral role in practical reasoning. Deontic utterances themselves contain causal or quasi-causal connotations with regard to behaviour. For instance, when a shop declares that "If you spend over £100, you may take a free gift", a causal enabling relation is implied, in the same way as it might be said that if you turn the ignition key, you may drive down the road. The illocutionary force of deontic utterances is also causal: the shop states its promise with the purpose of inducing, i.e., causing, its customers to spend more money, and that is the purpose of all conditional promises: to function as inducements. You utter a threat with the intention of preventing, i.e., causing not to happen, an undesired action.

This observation implies that there may be a deep psychological connection between causal and deontic reasoning. One way of assessing this was explored by Fairley et al. (1999). They used the constructs of alternative and disabling conditions (introduced by Cummins, 1995; Cummins, Lubart, Alksnis, & Rist, 1991, to explain causal conditional reasoning) to produce perspective effects with non-deontic materials. Alternative and disabling conditions affect people's construals of the condition relations in a causal conditional, i.e., the perceptions of necessity and sufficiency between antecedent and consequent. As an example, consider a conditional stating that "If you turn the ignition key, then the car starts". An alternative condition is one that brings about the consequent (the car starting) in the absence of the antecedent (turning the key). If such conditions are available (as they are: hot-wiring, jump-starting), then they undermine the idea that the antecedent is causally necessary for the consequent: an alternative condition shows that the consequent is possible without the original antecedent. Similarly, disabling conditions undermine the perception of sufficiency of the antecedent for the consequent. For instance, an empty fuel tank would disable the relation between the ignition key and the car starting. Fairley et al. introduced these factors into a large-array version of the selection task, and found that when cued to think about alternative conditions, participants would search for instances of consequent without antecedent, but when cued to think about disabling conditions, they would search for instances of antecedent without consequent. This effect parallels the classic deontic perspective effect, and Fairley at al. proposed that the latter could be explained in similar terms, i.e., invoking perceived necessity and sufficiency.

Causal statements thus resemble deontic statements, and so causal reasoning is like practical reasoning, in this respect. However, causal reasoning is not (necessarily) about human behaviour, whereas practical reasoning is, by definition. Moreover, causal statements and arguments are about the way the world is, or more exactly, how it works: they are therefore about matters of fact, and so should belong in the world of episteme. Causal arguments therefore should resemble other factual arguments, and indeed, they are usually taken to do so; a recent example occurs in the extended mental model theory of conditionals presented by Johnson-Laird and Byrne (2002). They incorporate the traditional great divide between the theoretical and the practical into their theory, by developing it with respect to two kinds of possibilities that conditionals can be held to express: factual possibilities and deontic possibilities. Representations of these two sorts of possibilities can be modulated by knowledge and by the semantics and pragmatics of arguments to yield 10 possible interpretations, defined by 10 sets of these possibilities. The 10 sets are essentially the same for both factual and deontic possibilities, with slight modifications: deontic possibilities are defined as those that are permissible, while deontic necessities are defined as those that are obligatory. These glosses are then used as tags in the models, but beyond this, Johnson-Laird and Byrne do not go any more deeply into the indicative–deontic, or theoretical–practical, distinction.

Johnson-Laird and Byrne's modulation theory is thus fully consistent with the idea, stretching back over the centuries, that there is no real great divide between theoretical and practical reasoning after all; that they differ with regard to content, not type. However, factual statements are not all of the same stripe. And we still have those differences in reasoning performance between tasks of different kinds. These two facts pull in different directions when considering the psychological status of the divide. Factual conditional statements themselves contain a duality: they can describe attributes and causes. For example, conditionals can be used to state relations between classes, as in the case of a statement such as "If a car is German, then it is reliable". Being German does not cause reliability, and other countries also produce reliable cars. The statement, if true, expresses the fact that German cars are a member of the class "reliable". Many of Johnson-Laird and

Byrne's examples of "factual" conditionals are causal rather than non-causal.

Evidence of the relation between causal and deontic conditionals implies that their theory may need to be supplemented to deal with a possible distinction between causal and non-causal conditionals. This distinction does not rest on a few empirical demonstrations: there are formal differences too, and people seem to have an implicit knowledge of them. These centre on the condition relations of necessity and sufficiency. In the case of the standard indicative inferential conditional, the antecedent is sufficient for the consequent while the consequent is necessary for the antecedent. Thus given that the antecedent occurs, the consequent must occur, and if the consequent does not occur, the antecedent cannot occur either. This is another way of expressing material implication, and hence the standard valid forms of inference, modus ponens and modus tollens respectively. On this logic, there is no sense in which the antecedent can be necessary but not sufficient for the consequent. However, causal conditionals do allow this possibility, as we have seen. It is perfectly possible for a cause to be necessary but not sufficient for an effect, as when we assert that if there is fuel in the tank, then the engine will start (in which case we are specifying an enabling condition). Fairley et al. (1999) argued that causal and deontic sentences can be modulated in the same way by additional conditions, so that the deontic perspective effect is a double misnomer: it is not specifically deontic, and not necessarily to do with social perspective. Johnson-Laird and Byrne's analysis is consistent with this claim, but relies for its explanation of deontic perspective effects on people's reading of deontic conditionals as biconditionals (cf. Johnson-Laird & Byrne, 1995). This is an unnecessary step if we accept a deep relation between causals and deontics, and a distinction between these and non-causal (inferential) arguments. The analysis of these forms of reasoning in terms of condition relations offers a way of explaining how knowledge modulates conditionals, requiring only an acceptance of a distinction within the class of "factual" expressions between causal and non-causal statements.

This benefit comes at a price, though. The historic divide has been between theoretical and practical reasoning, with theoretical reasoning concerning what is true and practical reasoning concerning what to do. Perhaps it is this great divide itself that needs re-examining. Causal reasoning is problematic both from the philosophical and the psychological standpoints. Causal statements are about facts, and yet they are about behaviour – of things, as much as people. Practical reasoning is also about behaviour. In experiments, people treat causal inferences in similar ways to deontic inferences, and they treat deontic inferences differently from indicative inferences. We are left with a number of possibilities, and rather reluctantly, we must conclude that the jury may need to retire again to consider its verdict on them (yes, further research is necessary). One is that there is a tripartite rather than bipartite division in reasoning, between theoretical but non-causal, causal, and practical. Alternatively, perhaps the definition of practical should extend to include causal, so that practical reasoning is a class of reasoning concerning events and outcomes while theoretical reasoning is to do with properties and classes. Third, perhaps there is, as has been argued down the ages and is still being argued, no divide at all, merely differences in the object of reasoning. Psychological research has helped to introduce new ways of characterizing the long-standing divide between the pure and the practical, and to point to the kinds of evidence that might in future help us settle this age-old philosophical question.

ACKNOWLEDGEMENTS

Thanks to Neil Fairley and David Over for comments on an earlier draft.

REFERENCES

Almor, A., & Sloman, S. A. (1996). Is deontic reasoning special? *Psychological Review, 103*, 374–380.

Anscombe, G. E. M. (1957). *Intention*. Oxford: Blackwell.

Audi, R. (1989). *Practical reasoning*. London: Routledge.

Chater, N., & Oaksford, M. R. (1996). Deontic reasoning, modules and innateness: A second look. *Mind and Language, 11*, 191–202.

Cheng, P. W., & Holyoak, K. J. (1985). Pragmatic reasoning schemas. *Cognitive Psychology, 17*, 391–416.

Cosmides, L. (1989). The logic of social exchange: Has natural selection shaped how humans reason? Studies with the Wason selection task. *Cognition, 31*, 187–316.

Cosmides, L., & Tooby, J. (1992). Cognitive adaptations for social change. In J. Barkow, L. Cosmides, & J. Tooby (Eds.), *The adapted mind*. Oxford: Oxford University Press.

Cummins, D. D. (1995). Naïve theories and causal deduction. *Memory and Cognition, 23*, 646–658.

Cummins, D. D. (1996a). Evidence of deontic reasoning in 3- and 4-year-old children. *Memory and Cognition, 24*, 823–829.

Cummins, D. D. (1996b). Evidence for the innateness of deontic reasoning. *Mind and Language, 11*, 160–190.

Cummins, D. D. (1998). Social norms and other minds; the evolutionary roots of higher cognition. In D.D. Cummins & C. Allen (Eds.), *The evolution of mind*. Oxford: Oxford University Press.

Cummins, D. D., Lubart, T., Alksnis, O., & Rist, R. (1991). Conditional reasoning and causation. *Memory and Cognition, 19*, 274–282.

Evans, J. St. B. T. (1989). *Bias in reasoning: Causes and consequences*. Hove, UK: Lawrence Erlbaum Associates Ltd.

Evans, J. St. B. T. (1993). Bias and rationality. In K. I. Manktelow & D. E. Over (Eds.), *Rationality: Psychological and philosophical perspectives*. London: Routledge.

Evans, J. St. B. T. Barston, J. L., & Pollard, P. (1983). On the conflict between logic and belief in syllogistic reasoning. *Memory and Cognition, 11*, 295–306.

Evans, J. St. B. T., Newstead, S. E., & Byrne, R. M. J. (1993). *Human reasoning; the psychology of deduction.* Hove, UK: Lawrence Erlbaum Associates Ltd.

Evans, J. St. B. T., & Over, D. E. (1996). *Rationality and reasoning.* Hove, UK: Psychology Press.

Evans, J. St. B. T., Over, D. E., & Manktelow, K. I. (1993). Reasoning, decision making, and rationality. *Cognition, 49,* 165–187.

Evans, J. St. B. T., & Wason, P. C. (1976). Rationalisation in a reasoning task. *British Journal of Psychology, 67,* 205–212.

Fairley, N., Manktelow, K. I., & Over, D. E. (1999). Necessity, sufficiency, and perspective effects in causal conditional reasoning. *Quarterly Journal of Experimental Psychology, 52*A, 771–790.

Fiddick, L. (2003). Domains of deontic reasoning: Resolving the discrepancy between the cognitive and moral reasoning literatures. *Quarterly Journal of Experimental Psychology, 57*A, 447–474.

Garnham, A., & Oakhill, J. V. (1994). *Thinking and reasoning.* Oxford: Blackwell.

Gigerenzer, G., & Hug, K. (1992). Domain-specific reasoning: Social contracts, cheating and perspective change. *Cognition, 43,* 127–171.

Girotto, V., Light, P., & Colbourn, C. (1988). Pragmatic schemas and conditional reasoning in children. *Quarterly Journal of Experimental Psychology, 40*A, 469–472.

Griggs, R. A., & Cox, J. R. (1982). The elusive thematic-materials effect in Wason's selection task. *British Journal of Psychology, 73,* 407–420.

Harman, G. (1976). Practical reasoning. *Review of Metaphysics, 29,* 431–463.

Harman, G. (1995). Rationality. In E. E. Smith & D. N. Osherson (Eds.), *Thinking: Invitation to cognitive science, Vol. III.* Cambridge, MA: MIT Press. [Reprinted in G. Harman (Ed.), *Reasoning, meaning and mind.* Oxford, Oxford University Press, 1999.]

Johnson-Laird, P. N., & Byrne, R. M. J. (1991). *Deduction.* Hove, UK: Lawrence Erlbaum Associates Ltd.

Johnson-Laird, P. N., & Byrne, R. M. J. (1995). A model point of view. *Thinking and Reasoning, 1,* 339–350.

Johnson-Laird, P. N., & Byrne, R. M. J. (2002). Conditionals: A theory of meaning, pragmatics and inference. *Psychological Review, 109,* 646–678.

Johnson-Laird, P. N., Legrenzi, P., & Legrenzi, M. S. (1972). Reasoning and a sense of reality. *British Journal of Psychology, 63,* 395–400.

Jonsen, A. R., & Toulmin, S. E. (1988). *The abuse of casuistry.* London: University of California Press.

Kenny, A. J. P. (1975/1978). Practical reasoning and rational appetite. In J. Raz (Ed.), *Practical reasoning.* Oxford: Oxford University Press.

Kohlberg, L. (1963). The development of children's orientations toward a moral order. 1. Sequence in the development of human thought. *Vita Humana, 6,* 11–33.

Manktelow, K. I. (1999). *Reasoning and thinking.* Hove, UK: Psychology Press.

Manktelow, K. I., & Evans, J. St. B. T. (1979). Facilitation of reasoning by realism: Effect or non-effect? *British Journal of Psychology, 70,* 477–488.

Manktelow, K. I., Fairley, N., Kilpatrick, S. G., & Over, D. E. (2000). Pragmatics and strategies for practical reasoning. In W. Schaeken, G. de Vooght, A., Vandierendonck, & G. D'Ydewalle (Eds.), *Deductive reasoning and strategies.* Mahwah, NJ: Lawrence Erlbaum Associates Inc.

Manktelow, K. I., & Over, D. E. (1991). Social roles and utilities in reasoning about deontic conditionals. *Cognition, 39,* 85–105.

Manktelow, K. I., & Over, D. E. (1995). Deontic reasoning. In S. E. Newstead & J. St. B. T. Evans (Eds.), *Perspectives on thinking and reasoning: Essays in honour of Peter Wason*. Hove, UK: Lawrence Erlbaum Associates Ltd.

Manktelow, K. I., Sutherland, E. J., & Over, D. E. (1995). Probabilistic factors in deontic reasoning. *Thinking and Reasoning, 1*, 201–220.

Politzer, G., & Nguyen-Xuan, A. (1992). Reasoning about conditional promises and warnings: Darwinian algorithms, mental models, relevance judgements or pragmatic schemas? *Quarterly Journal of Experimental Psychology, 44*A, 401–412.

Stanovich, K. E. (1999). *Who is rational?* Mahwah, NJ: Lawrence Erlbaum Associates Inc.

Stanovich, K. E., & West, R. W. (2000). Individual differences in reasoning: Implications for the rationality debate. *Behavioral and Brain Sciences, 23*, 645–726.

Wason, P. C. (1968). Reasoning about a rule. *Quarterly Journal of Experimental Psychology, 20*, 273–281.

Wason, P. C., & Evans, J. St. B. T. (1975). Dual processes in reasoning? *Cognition, 3*, 141–154.

Wason, P. C., & Shapiro, D. A. (1971). Natural and contrived experience in a reasoning problem. *Quarterly Journal of Experimental Psychology, 23*, 63–71.

Wilkins, M. C. (1928). The effect of changed material on ability to do syllogistic reasoning. *Archives of Psychology, 102*.

8 The history of mental models

P. N. Johnson-Laird

> Deduction is that mode of reasoning which examines the state of things asserted in the premises, forms a diagram of that state of things, perceives in the parts of the diagram relations not explicitly mentioned in the premises, satisfies itself by mental experiments upon the diagram that these relations would always subsist, or at least would do so in a certain proportion of cases, and concludes their necessary, or probable, truth.
>
> (C. S. Peirce, 1931–1958, 1.66)

What is the end result of perception? What is the output of linguistic comprehension? How do we anticipate the world, and make sensible decisions about what to do? What underlies thinking and reasoning? One answer to these questions is that we rely on mental models of the world. Perception yields a mental model, linguistic comprehension yields a mental model, and thinking and reasoning are the internal manipulations of mental models. The germ of this answer was first proposed during World War II by the remarkable Scottish psychologist and physiologist, Kenneth Craik. In a short but prescient book, *The nature of explanation*, he sketched such a theory. He wrote:

> If the organism carries a "small-scale model" of external reality and of its own possible actions within its head, it is able to try out various alternatives, conclude which is the best of them, react to future situations before they arise, utilize the knowledge of past events in dealing with the present and the future, and in every way to react in a much fuller, safer, and more competent manner to the emergencies which face it.
>
> (Craik, 1943, Ch. 5, p. 61)

Craik would have developed his sketch into a thoroughgoing theory and tested its empirical consequences. But, on the eve of VE day in 1945, he was cycling in Cambridge when a car door opened in front of him and he was thrown into the path of a lorry. He was 31 years old. It was left to others to follow up his ideas.

Where did the notion of a mental model come from? And how have Craik's successors brought his ideas to fruition? This chapter aims to tell you. There are several historical precursors, although they probably had no direct influence on Craik. The present author confesses that for many years his knowledge of mental models went no further back than 1943. It was a shock to discover that there were important antecedents, particularly certain 19th-century physicists and the great American logician and philosopher, Charles Sanders Peirce. The chapter begins with these precursors, and then describes Craik's hypothesis and some similar ideas about "cognitive maps" proposed by Tolman. It outlines theories of mental representation in the 20th century, which presaged the revival of mental models. It then explains their role in perception, comprehension, and the representation of knowledge. It turns to the mental model theory of deductive reasoning, and describes the application of this theory to reasoning with quantifiers such as "all" and "some" and to reasoning with sentential connectives such as "if" and "or". It outlines the role of models in different strategies for reasoning. It concludes with an assessment of the theory.

THE PRECURSORS

Several 19th-century thinkers anticipated the model theory. The physicist Lord Kelvin stressed the importance to him of the construction of mechanical models of scientific theories. In his 1884 Baltimore lectures, he asserted:

> I never satisfy myself until I can make a mechanical model of a thing. If I can make a mechanical model I can understand it. As long as I cannot make a mechanical model all the way through I cannot understand; and that is why I cannot get the electro-magnetic theory.
>
> (cited by Smith & Wise, 1989, p. 464)

Indeed, he never quite accepted Maxwell's equations for electro-magnetism, because he could not construct a mechanical model of them. Ironically, Maxwell did have a mechanical model in mind in developing his theory (Wise, 1979). This use of models in scientific thinking is characteristic of 19th-century physics. Ludwig Boltzmann (1890) argued that all our ideas and concepts are only internal pictures. And he wrote:

> The task of theory consists in constructing an image of the external world that exists purely internally and must be our guiding star in thought and experiment; that is in completing, as it were, the thinking process and carrying out globally what on a small scale occurs within us whenever we form an idea.
>
> (Boltzmann, 1899)

These notions became obsolescent in the 20th century with the development of quantum theory. As the late Richard Feynman (1985) has remarked, no one can have a model of quantum electrodynamics. The equations make unbelievably accurate predictions, but they defy commonsense interpretation.

A principle of the modern theory of mental models is that a model has the same structure as the situation that it represents. Like an architect's model, or a molecular biologist's model, the parts of the model and their structural relations correspond to those of what it represents. Like these physical models, a mental model is also partial because it represents only certain aspects of the situation. There is accordingly a many-to-one mapping from possibilities in the world to their mental model. Maxwell (1911) in his article on diagrams in the *Encyclopaedia Britannica* stressed the structural aspect of diagrams. But the theory's intellectual grandfather is Charles Sanders Peirce.

Peirce formulated the major system of logic known as the predicate calculus and published its principles in 1883 (3.328; this notation, which is standard, refers to paragraph 328 of Volume 3 of Peirce, 1931–1958). Frege (1879) independently anticipated him. Peirce made many other logical discoveries, and he also devised two diagrammatic systems for logic, which were powerful enough to deal with negation, sentential connectives such as "if", "and", and "or", and quantifiers such as "all", "some", and "none", i.e., with the predicate calculus (see, e.g., Johnson-Laird, 2002). He anticipated semantic networks, which were proposed in the 20th century to represent the meanings of words and sentences (Sowa, 1984), the recent development of discourse representation theory in linguistics (Kamp, 1981), and the theory of mental models.

Peirce distinguished three properties of signs in general, in which he included thoughts (4.447). First, they can be iconic and represent entities in virtue of structural similarity to them. Visual images, for example, are iconic. Second, they can be indexical and represent entities in virtue of a direct physical connexion. The act of pointing to an object, for example, is indexical. Third, they can be symbolic and represent entities in virtue of a conventional rule or habit. A verbal description, for example, is symbolic. The properties can co-occur: a photograph with verbal labels for its parts is iconic, indexical, and symbolic. Diagrams, Peirce believed, ought to be iconic (4.433). He meant that there should be a visible analogy between a diagram and what it represents: the parts of the diagram should be interrelated in the same way that the entities that it represents are interrelated (3.362, 4.418, 5.73). The London tube map is a wonderful iconic representation of the city's subway system. Its designer, Harry Beck, realized that underground travellers need to know only the order of stations on each tube line, and where they can change from one line to another. His map captures these relations in a pleasingly transparent way, but it makes no attempt to capture distances systematically. It is an old joke to suggest to out-of-towners that they go by tube from Bank to Mansion House. The map calls for a change from one line to another, and a journey through several stations. Bank and Mansion House are about a 5-minute walk apart.

In his early work, the philosopher Ludwig Wittgenstein (1922) defended a "picture" theory of meaning, which was inspired by the use of model cars in the reconstruction of an accident. It can be summarized in a handful of propositions from his Tractatus:

2.1   We make to ourselves pictures of facts.
2.12 The picture is a model of reality.
2.13 To the objects [in the world] correspond in the picture the elements of the picture.
2.15 That the elements of the picture are combined with one another in a definite way, represents that the things [in the world] are so combined with one another.
2.17 What the picture must have in common with reality in order to be able to represent it after its manner – rightly or falsely – is its form of representation.

The Gestalt notion that vision creates an isomorphism between brain fields and the world (Köhler, 1938) is yet another version of the same idea. Peirce, however, had anticipated Maxwell, Wittgenstein, and Köhler. His concept of an iconic representation contrasts, as he recognized, with the syntactical symbols of a language. The iconic nature of diagrams made possible Peirce's (1.66) thesis in the epigraph to the present chapter. He argued that the inspection of an iconic diagram reveals truths to be discerned over and above those of the propositions that were used in its construction (2.279, 4.530). This property of iconicity is fundamental to the modern theory of mental models (Johnson-Laird, 1983, pp. 125, 136).

THE FIRST MODEL THEORISTS

Craik's (1943) book, *The nature of explanation*, addresses philosophical problems, and argues against both scepticism and an a priori approach to the existence of the external world. The core of the book, however, is its fifth chapter, which is about thought. Craik argues that its fundamental property is its power to predict events. This power depends on three steps:

(1) The translation of an external process into words, numbers, or other symbols, which can function as a model of the world.
(2) A process of reasoning from these symbols leading to others.
(3) The retranslation back from the resulting symbols into external processes, or at least to a recognition that they correspond to external processes.

Stimulation of the sense organs translates into neural patterns, reasoning produces other neural patterns, and they are retranslated into the excitation of the motor organs. The process is akin, Craik writes, to one in which the final result was reached by causing actual physical processes to occur. Instead of building a bridge to see if it works, you envisage how to build it. The brain accordingly imitates or models the physical processes that it is trying to predict. Craik makes the prescient claim that the same process of imitation can be carried out by a mechanical device, such as a calculating machine, an anti-aircraft "predictor", or Kelvin's machine for predicting the tides. The programmable digital computer had yet to be invented, although its precursor at Bletchley Park was in use to crack the German Enigma cipher.

One difference between Craik's views and the modern theory of mental models concerns iconicity. Craik eschews it. He writes (pp. 51–2):

> the model need not resemble the real object pictorially; Kelvin's tide-predictor, which consists of pulleys on levers, does not resemble a tide in appearance, but it works in the same way in certain essential respects – it combines oscillations of various frequencies so as to produce an oscillation which closely resembles in amplitude at each moment the variation in tide level at any place.

So, for Craik, a model parallels or imitates reality, but its structure can differ from the structure of what it represents. In contrast, mental models are now usually considered to mirror the structure of what they represent (for a Craikian view, see Holland, 1998). A model of the world can have a three-dimensional structure for high-level processes such as spatial reasoning. But it does not necessarily call for a three-dimensional layout in the brain (or a computer). Its physical embodiment has merely to support a representation that functions as three dimensional for reasoning. Underlying the high level of representation, there might be – as Craik supposed – something as remote from it as Kelvin's tidal predictor is from the sea.

Craik was among the first to propose a philosophy of mind now known as "functionalism" (Putnam, 1960). This doctrine proposes that what is crucial about the mind is not its dependence on the brain, but its functional organization. Craik wrote (1943, p. 51):

> By a model we thus mean any physical or chemical system which has a similar relation-structure to that of the process it imitates. By "relation-structure" I do not mean some obscure non-physical entity which attends the model, but the fact that it is a physical working model which works in the same way as the process it parallels, in the aspects under consideration at any moment.

He added (p. 57):

> My hypothesis then is that thought models, or parallels, reality – that its essential feature is not "the mind", "the self", "sense-data", nor

propositions but symbolism, and this symbolism is largely of the same kind as that which is familiar to us in mechanical devices which aid thought and calculation.

Hence Craik likens the nervous system to a calculating machine capable of modelling external events, and he claims that this process of paralleling is the basic feature of thought and of explanation (pp. 120–121).

Craik has little to say about reasoning, the process that leads from the input to the output symbols. He implies, however, that it is a linguistic process: "[language] must evolve rules of implication governing the use of words, in such a way that a line of thought can run parallel to, and predict, causally determined events in the external world" (p. 81).

An American contemporary of Craik's, Edward C. Tolman, independently developed a similar idea. Tolman was a behaviourist who was influenced by Gestalt theory. His research concerned rats running mazes, and he and his colleagues showed that they tend to learn the spatial location of the reward rather than the sequence of required responses to get there. Tolman's hypotheses were couched, not in mentalistic terms, but in the language of neo-behaviourism, i.e, in terms of variables that intervened between stimuli and responses (Tolman, 1932, 1959). Some maze studies had shown that animals appeared to be able to reason, i.e., they could learn two paths on separate occasions and, if necessary, combine them in order to reach a goal (e.g., Maier, 1929; Tolman & Honzik, 1930). This performance could be explained in behaviourist terms by the mediation of "fractional anticipatory goal responses". But, in an influential paper, Tolman (1948) introduced the concept of a "cognitive map". He suggested that the rat's brain learns something akin to a map of the environment. This map governs the animal's behaviour. For instance, if it learns a complicated dog-legged route to food, then when this route is blocked, it chooses a path directly to a point close to the food box. Students of ethology will know von Frisch's (1966) similar findings about the dance of the honey bees. After they have flown a dog-leg to nectar, their dance signals the direct route.

How much of the environment does a cognitive map cover? Tolman's study showed that rats could acquire not merely a narrow strip, but "a wider comprehensive map to the effect that the food was located in such and such a direction in the room" (1948, p. 204). Tolman argued that what militates against comprehensive maps are inadequate cues, repetitive training, and too great a motivation. He speculated that regression to childhood, fixation, and hostility to an "out-group" are expressions of narrow cognitive maps in human beings. What is missing from his account is any extrapolation from cognitive maps to human spatial representations and navigation. That extrapolation was left to others (e.g., Kitchin, 1994; Thorndyke & Hayes-Roth, 1982). In short, neither of the original model theorists addressed the puzzle of how models underlie reasoning.

MENTAL REPRESENTATIONS

Mentalistic psychologists investigated visual imagery around the end of the 19th century (e.g., Binet, 1894; Perky, 1910). In a study of syllogistic reasoning, Störring (1908) reported that his participants used either visual images or verbal methods to reason. The study of imagery, however, fell into neglect during the era of behaviourism. With the revival of mentalism, cognitive psychologists again distinguished between visual and verbal representations (Bower, 1970; Paivio, 1971). Shepard and his colleagues demonstrated that individuals can transform objects mentally in a variety of ways. In one of their experiments (Shepard & Metzler, 1971), the participants saw two drawings of a "nonsense" figure assembled out of 10 blocks glued together to form a rigid object with right-angled joints. They had to decide whether the pictures depicted one and the same object. Their decision times increased linearly with the angular difference between the orientations of the object in the two pictures. This result held for rotations in the picture plane, but also held for rotations in depth. As Metzler and Shepard (1982, p. 45) wrote: "These results seem to be consistent with the notion that ... subjects were performing their mental operations upon internal representations that were more analogous to three-dimensional objects portrayed in the two-dimensional pictures than to the two-dimensional pictures actually presented." In other words, the participants were rotating mental models of the objects.

Kosslyn and his colleagues asked experimental participants to scan from one landmark to another in their image of a map that they had committed to memory (Kosslyn, Ball, & Reiser, 1978). In another study, participants had to form an image of, say, an elephant and then to imagine walking towards it until the image began to overflow their mind's eye. In this way, Kosslyn (1980) was able to estimate the size of the mental "screen" on which the participants project their images. It is about the same size for an image as for a visual percept. Other investigations of visual imagery – from its mnemonic value (Luria, 1969) to its need for a special short-term memory store (Baddeley & Hitch, 1974) – implied that it is a distinct medium of mental representation.

Sceptics such as Pylyshyn (1973) rejected this view. A distinct medium of representation would be part of the functional architecture of the mind and so its properties could not be affected by an individual's beliefs or attitudes. The case is comparable, Pylyshyn claimed, to the architecture of a computer: the design of its hardware cannot be modified by a program that the computer is running. Mental architecture is thus "cognitively impenetrable", whereas imagery is influenced by an individual's beliefs. And, Pylyshyn argued, the results of the rotation and scanning experiments might merely show that individuals can simulate how long it would take to rotate an actual object, or to scan an actual map. Such simulations therefore reveal nothing about the real nature of mental representations. In Pylyshyn's view, the mind makes no use of images. They occur as subjective experiences, but they play no causal role in mental processes. The mind carries out formal computations on a single medium of representation, so-called "propositional representations", that is, syntactically structured expressions in a mental language. This claim dovetailed with the then orthodox theory of reasoning, which postulated that formal rules of inference akin to those of logic are applied to representations of the logical form of assertions (see below).

There appear to be two ways to resolve the argument between the "imagists" and "propositionalists" (Johnson-Laird, 1983, ch. 7). In one sense of propositional representation, the propositionalists are right. The mind depends on the brain's "machine code", i.e., everything must be reduced to nerve impulses and synaptic events, just as the execution of any computer program reduces to the shifting of bits from one memory register to another. Yet, in another sense of propositional representation, the imagists are right. Images and propositional representations are both high-level representations within the same computational medium, just as arrays and lists are distinct data-structures in a high-level programming language.

Recent theorists have argued against propositional representations (Barsalou, 1999; Markman & Dietrich, 2000). These authors claim that both theory and evidence suggest that cognitive science should eschew such abstract representations in favour of representations rooted in perception. As these investigators show, perceptual representations such as visual or kinaesthetic images are powerful. Yet not everything can be represented iconically. No image can alone capture the content of a negation, such as:

The circle is not to the right of the triangle.

Even if you form an image of a cross superimposed on your image of the un-negated situation, you have to know that the cross denotes negation, and you have to know the meaning of negation, that it reverses the truth value of the corresponding, un-negated assertion. No image can capture this meaning (Wittgenstein, 1953). Defenders of imagery might argue that negation can be represented by a contrast class, e.g., the case of the circle to the left of the triangle. Individuals do indeed envisage contrast classes (Oaksford & Chater, 1994; Schroyens, Schaeken, & d'Ydewalle, 2001). But to capture the full meaning of negation, you need to envisage a disjunction of all the sorts of possibility in the class. An affirmative assertion that is true, such as:

The circle is to the right of the triangle

is compatible with one sort of possibility. Its falsity is compatible with many sorts of possibility. In contrast, a negative assertion that is true, such as:

The circle is not to the right of the triangle

is compatible with many sorts of possibility. Its falsity is compatible with only one sort of possibility. (This pattern may explain why people are faster to evaluate true affirmatives than false affirmatives, but faster to evaluate false negatives than true negatives, see Clark & Chase, 1972; Wason, 1959). Negations could be spelt out in the form of disjunctions, but the representation of disjunctions cannot be iconic. You cannot perceive whether two signs denote a conjunction or a disjunction of alternatives (Johnson-Laird, 2001).

The moral is that the use of conventional symbols is necessary to represent negation and disjunction, and that in principle at least three distinct sorts of mental representation could exist:

- Propositional representations, which are strings of syntactically structured symbols in a mental language.
- Images, which are two-dimensional visualizable icons, typically of an object or scene from a particular point of view.
- Mental models, which are also iconic as far as possible, but which can contain elements, such as negation, that are not visualizable (Johnson-Laird & Byrne, 1991; Newell, 1990). They can also represent three-dimensional objects and scenes (as in Shepard's studies of mental rotation described earlier).

THE INHERITORS: THE REVIVAL OF MENTAL MODELS

The original model theorists' most immediate influence was on cybernetics (e.g., McCulloch, 1965). But in the 1970s a revival of mental models in psychology occurred in three research areas, which this section explores: vision, knowledge representation, and discourse. The late David Marr (1982) argued that vision depends on an unconscious inference from the structure of an image to a mental model that makes explicit the three-dimensional structure of the scene. The inference makes use of a series of mental representations. Pure vision begins with the physical interaction between light focused on the retinae and the visual pigment in retinal cells. It ends with the "two-and-a-half dimensional" sketch, which makes explicit the relative distance and orientation (with respect to the observer) of each visible surface in the scene. In order to move about safely, however, you need to know what things are where in the world. You need a representation of the world that is independent of your point of view. When you walk into a wood and recognize that it contains trees, shrubs, and plants, you can readily navigate your way through it to a particular goal – say, to a distant landmark – even if you have never been in the wood before. You can do so because vision solves three problems: it constructs a mental model that makes explicit the three-dimensional shapes of everything in the scene, it uses these shapes to identify the objects, and it makes explicit their locations in relation to one another.

Marr and his colleagues postulated that the recognition of objects from their shape depends on two steps. First, the visual system represents the shape of an object in terms of its own canonical axes, e.g., a pencil is a long thin cylinder. Second, the system compares this shape with a mental catalogue of the shapes of all known objects. Each entry in the catalogue is itself a model, which decomposes the object into the shapes of its component parts and their interrelations. At the highest level, the gross shape of the object is made explicit, but at lower levels the detailed shapes of its parts are fleshed out. The matching of a percept to a catalogued model is complicated and not well understood. One possibility is that a cue about the shape of an object may trigger access to a model in the catalogue, which is then used to try to match the rest of the percept (cf. Biederman, 1987).

In the late 1970s, cognitive scientists began to talk of general knowledge as represented in mental models, but without any commitment to a particular sort of structure. For example, Hayes (1979) used assertions in the predicate calculus to describe the naïve physics of liquids. His aim was to capture the content of everyday knowledge, and he was not concerned with how inferential processes use this knowledge. Other researchers in artificial intelligence tried to model everyday qualitative reasoning, and de Kleer (1977) distinguished between envisioning a model and running it to simulate behaviour. To envision a model of a device, you have to consider how each component works in isolation, and to combine this knowledge with the structure of the device to infer how it works. Forbus (1985) implemented a program that constructs two-dimensional spatial models in order to draw inferences about the behaviour of bouncing balls. Such models are simpler than the theory of mechanics, and they have an iconic structure that reflects our qualitative experience of the world, although they also contain conventional symbols. They allow the program to determine the relations among objects just as humans can from a diagram (cf. Glasgow, 1993; Kuipers, 1994; Larkin & Simon, 1987).

Psychologists similarly began to study naïve and expert models of various domains, such as mechanics (McCloskey, Caramazza, & Green, 1980), handheld calculators (Young, 1981), and electrical circuits (Gentner & Gentner, 1983). At the heart of these studies is the idea that people learn how to make mental simulations of phenomena (e.g., Hegarty, 1992; Schwartz & Black, 1996), either in a series of dynamic images in the mind's eye or in more abstract mental models. Researchers studied how children develop mental models (e.g., Halford, 1993; Vosniadou & Brewer, 1992), how models of one domain can serve as analogies for another domain (Holland, Holyoak, Nisbett, & Thagard, 1986), and how to design artifacts and computer systems for which it is easy for users to acquire models (e.g., Ehrlich, 1996; Genter & Stevens, 1983; Moray, 1990, 1999). They studied the role of models in the diagnosis of faults (e.g., Rouse & Hunt, 1984), and algorithms for diagnosis (e.g., Davis & Hamscher, 1988; de Kleer & Williams, 1987). Knowledge indeed appears to be represented in mental models that are as iconic as possible.

Humans construct models of the world, as do other species, but humans also communicate the content of such models. Discourse accordingly enables individuals to experience the world by proxy. The inklings of this idea are in the following passage:

> It is possible that from the meanings of sentences in connected discourse, the listener implicitly sets up a much abbreviated and not especially linguistic model of the narrative ... Where the model is incomplete, material may even be unwittingly invented to render the memory more meaningful or more plausible – a process that has its parallel in the initial construction of the model. A good writer or raconteur perhaps has the power to initiate a process very similar to the one that occurs when we are actually perceiving (or imagining) events instead of merely reading or hearing about them.
> (Johnson-Laird, 1970, p. 269)

Other psychologists had similar intuitions (e.g., Bransford, Barclay, & Franks, 1972), and experiments showed that individuals rapidly forget the surface form of sentences (Sachs, 1967), their underlying syntax (Johnson-Laird & Stevenson, 1970), and even the gist or meaning of individual sentences (Garnham, 1987).

The present author was aware of some of these developments and intrigued by the possibility that reasoning might be based on a representation of the meaning of discourse, and so he tried to integrate comprehension, reasoning, and consciousness in his book on mental models (Johnson-Laird, 1983). He argued that when individuals understand discourse, they can use its meaning to construct a mental model of the situation to which it refers (see Van Dijk & Kintsch, 1983). This representation is remote from the syntactic structure of sentences. It is iconic in the following ways: it contains a token for each referent in the discourse, each token has properties corresponding to the properties of the referent, and the tokens are interrelated according to the relations among the referents. Hence, an indefinite noun phrase that introduces an individual into the discourse, such as: "an ancient monarch", leads to the insertion of a corresponding token into the discourse model, and subsequent references to the same individual, either direct ("the ancient monarch") or indirect ("the old king"), are used to address the same token in order to attach new information to it. Similar ideas were advanced by workers in formal semantics (Kamp, 1981), linguistics (Karttunen, 1976), psycholinguistics (Stenning, 1977), and artificial intelligence (Webber, 1978). That, perhaps, is why the notion of mental models as representations of discourse is uncontroversial. Although many aspects of discourse models remain puzzling, psycholinguists have made progress in discovering how they are constructed as individuals understand discourse (e.g., Garnham, 2001; Garnham & Oakhill, 1996; Glenberg, Meyer, & Lindem, 1987; Stevenson, 1993). The construction of these models depends on the meaning of sentences, on background knowledge, and on knowledge of human communication.

MENTAL MODELS AND REASONING WITH QUANTIFIERS

Piaget and his colleagues were the first modern psychologists to address the question of how people reason. They argued that intellectual development reaches a stage in which, by about the age of 12, children have acquired a set of formal procedures akin to those of a logical calculus (e.g., Inhelder & Piaget, 1958). Subsequent theorists postulated that the mind is equipped with a set of formal rules of inference (Johnson-Laird, 1975; Macnamara, 1986; Osherson, 1974–6), and this view still has its adherents (e.g., Braine & O'Brien, 1998; Rips, 1994). But, if mental models are the end result of vision and the comprehension of discourse, what is more natural than that reasoning should be based on them? This intuition lay behind an attempt to unify discourse and deduction (first mooted in Johnson-Laird, 1975). It adopted the fundamental semantic principle of validity: an inference is valid if its conclusion holds in all the possibilities consistent with the premises. And it aimed to explain reasoning about syllogisms, i.e., those inferences first formulated by Aristotle that are based on two premises that each contain a single quantifier, such as "all", "some", or "none". The following sort of syllogism is child's play:

Some of the parents are chemists.
All the chemists are drivers.
What follows?

Young children can deduce a valid conclusion:

Some of the parents are drivers.

In contrast, the following sort of syllogism is very difficult:

None of the readers is a cyclist.
All the cyclists are women.
What follows?

Many people draw the invalid conclusion:

None of the readers is a woman.

Others suppose that there is no valid conclusion. Only the best of adult reasoners draw the valid conclusion:

Some of the women are not readers.

In the traditional Scholastic account of syllogisms, each premise is in one of four moods:

All X are Y.
Some X are Y.
No X is a Y.
Some X are not Y.

The terms in the premises can have four arrangements (known as "figures"):

1.	2.	3.	4.
A – B	B – A	A – B	B – A
B – C	C – B	C – B	B – C

where B denotes the term common to both premises, e.g., "cyclist" in the example above. Hence, there are 64 possible pairs of premises (4 moods for the first premise, 4 moods for the second premise, and 4 figures). The syllogisms in figure 2 are identical to those in figure 1 apart from the order of the premises, and, allowing for this factor, the premises in figures 3 and 4 each yield only 10 logically distinct syllogisms, i.e., there are 36 logically distinct syllogistic premises. Granted that As, Bs, and Cs exist in the domain of discourse, only 27 out of the 64 forms of premises yield valid conclusions (Johnson-Laird, 1983, pp. 102–103).

Although syllogisms had been investigated for many years, the first study of the inferences that individuals drew from all 64 possible pairs of premises was not carried out until 1971 – a study done in collaboration with Janellen Huttenlocher, but not reported until later (Johnson-Laird & Steedman, 1978). The patterns of performance were robust, and stood in need of explanation. One hypothesis was accordingly that people imagined the possibilities compatible with the premises and drew whatever conclusion, if any, that held in all of them. Johnson-Laird (1975) outlined such an account based on Euler circles. But there was a problem. Euler circles represent each possibility compatible with syllogistic premises. Thus, a premise of the form *All the A are B* has two Euler diagrams: in one the circle representing A is included within the circle representing B corresponding to the proper inclusion of A within B, and in the other the two circles lie one on top of the other to represent that the two sets are co-extensive. There are 16 possible Euler diagrams for the easy inference above but only 6 for the difficult inference. Granted that the number of possibilities ought to correlate with difficulty, either reasoners are not considering all the possibilities compatible with the premises, or their mental models somehow coalesce different possibilities into a single representation. Erickson (1974) accepted the first alternative, suggesting that reasoners never represent more than four Euler diagrams; others chose the second alternative arguing that a single mental model could represent more than one sort of possibility (Johnson-Laird & Bara, 1984; Johnson-Laird & Steedman, 1978). For example, for easy premises of the form:

Some of the A are B.
All the B are C.

reasoners construct a single model in which only one sort of individual must exist:

A [B] C

where the square brackets indicate that the set of Bs has been exhaustively represented in relation to Cs. This model is consistent with the 16 alternative possibilities, i.e., allowing that there may, or may not, be As that are not Bs, for example, and that the only constraint is that Bs must be Cs. The model yields the conclusion:

Some of the A are C.

or its converse, although the figure biases reasoners to the conclusion shown. A difficult syllogism of the form:

None of the A is a B.
All the B are C.

yields an initial model:

[A] ¬ B
[A] ¬ B
         [B] C
         [B] C
  . . .

where "¬" denotes a symbol for negation, and each line denotes a different individual. This model yields the conclusion: *None of A is a C*, or its converse. But these conclusions are refuted by an alternative model created by adding additional tokens of the set that is not exhaustively represented:

[A] ¬ B C
[A] ¬ B
         [B] C
         [B] C
  . . .

The two models together support the conclusion: *Some of the A are not C*, or its converse. The first of these conclusions is refuted by a third model:

[A] ¬ B   C
[A] ¬ B   C
         [B] C
         [B] C
  . . .

Only the converse conclusion survives unscathed: *Some of the C are not A*.

There are, of course, other possible procedures for reasoning with models. For example, Johnson-Laird and Bara (1984) described a procedure in which one predicate is substituted for another under the control of models. Thus, given a model of the premise, *Some of the A are B*, such as:

A   B
A

The model of second premise, *All the B are C*, is used to substitute Cs for Bs in the model:

A   C
A

and hence to draw the conclusion: *Some of the A are C*.

Theorists have argued that some individuals use images, whereas other individuals use verbal methods – a view that goes back to Störring (1908). Thus, Ford (1995) vigorously defends the hypothesis that reasoners use either Euler circles or verbal substitutions based on rules of inference. Reasoners could represent syllogisms as Euler circles, especially when they are used with procedures that prevent an explosion in the number of possible diagrams. They then become difficult to distinguish from the mental models above (Stenning, 2002; Stenning & Oberlander, 1995). A study of the external models that reasoners construct yields a more radical possibility: individuals use a variety of strategies (Bucciarelli & Johnson-Laird, 1999). They systematically overlook possible models of individual premises, e.g., they often treat *All X are Y* as referring to two co-extensive sets, which yields an invalid conclusion for the difficult syllogism above. Granted the variety of strategies, which differ from individual to individual and even within individuals, there is a robust generalization: those syllogisms that call for only a single mental model are reliably easier than those that call for more than one model (see also Espino, Santamaria, Meseguer, & Carreiras, 2000). The generalization suggests that the strategies themselves rely on mental models.

One reason for wondering whether naïve individuals spontaneously use Euler circles is that they are likely to have learned about them in school.

Another reason is that the standard system of circles cannot cope with simple inferences based on multiple quantifiers, for example:

Someone has read all these books.
Therefore, all these books have been read by someone.

The converse inference is invalid on the normal interpretation of these assertions (see Wason & Johnson-Laird, 1972). In contrast, mental models can represent these assertions. The first step is to show how they cope with relations. Consider, for example, the following problem (from Byrne & Johnson-Laird, 1989):

The cup is on the right of the spoon.
The plate is on the left of the spoon.
The knife is in front of the cup.
The fork is in front of the plate.
What's the relation between the fork and the knife?

The premises call for the model:

plate   spoon   cup
fork   knife

which represents the entities as though they were arranged symmetrically on top of a table. The model yields the answer to the question:

The fork is on the left of the knife.

If one word in the second premise is changed:

The plate is on the left of the cup.

the premises are consistent with at least two possible layouts:

plate   spoon   cup
fork   knife

or:

spoon   plate   cup
        fork   knife

In either case, however, the same conclusion follows as before:

The fork is on the left of the knife.

As the theory predicts, the first problem, which calls for one model, is easier than the second problem, which calls for at least two models. The theory was subsequently extended to temporal and other relations (Carreiras & Santamaria, 1997; Schaeken, Johnson-Laird, & d'Ydewalle, 1996; Vandierendonck & De Vooght, 1996, 1997), and to reasoning based on multiply-quantified relations (Johnson-Laird, Byrne, & Tabossi, 1989). An assertion, such as: *Someone has read all these books*, has the following sort of model:

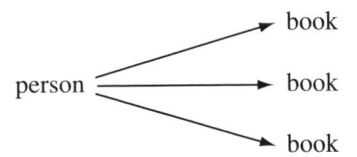

```
                    → book
person  ⇄           → book
                    ↘ book
```

where the arrows denote the relation of "reading". The assertion: *All these books have been read by someone*, is true in this model, but it also has the following model:

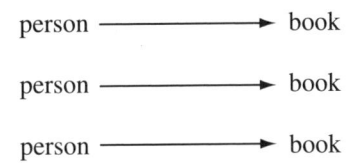

```
person  ─────→ book
person  ─────→ book
person  ─────→ book
```

The salient interpretation of the first assertion is false in this model, and so the converse inference is valid.

Reasoners might rely on visual images rather than more abstract models to make relational and quantified inferences. One datum, however, suggests that they use models. Relations that are easy to visualize, but hard to envisage spatially, such as "cleaner than" and "dirtier than", impede reasoning. These relations probably elicit images with vivid details that are irrelevant to reasoning. Hence, they slow the process down in comparison with other sorts of relation, including those that invoke spatial or abstract matters (Knauff & Johnson-Laird, 2002). They are also the only such relations to elicit activity in the areas of the brain that mediate visual associations (Knauff, Fangmeir, Ruff, & Johnson-Laird, 2003).

MENTAL MODELS AND SENTENTIAL REASONING

When the model theory was first formulated, it accounted for relational and quantified reasoning, but not for sentential reasoning, i.e., reasoning that hinges on negation and sentential connectives. A collaboration with Ruth Byrne filled in the lacuna. A disjunctive assertion, such as:

There is a circle or a triangle, or both

calls for models of three possibilities (shown here on separate lines):

    o
       △
    o △

whereas the conjunction:

There is a circle and a triangle

calls only for one model (the third of the preceding ones). What was problematic was the representation of conditional assertions, such as:

If there is a circle then there is a triangle.

It was clear that individuals focus on the possibility in which the antecedent is true, and do not think much about other possibilities. We therefore hypothesized that they normally construct two models:

    o △
    . . .

where the second model is a place-holder standing in for the possibilities in which the antecedent of the conditional (there is a circle) is false.

The theory explained the main phenomenon concerning two standard forms of conditional inference. One form is known as *modus ponens*:

If there is a circle then there is a triangle.
There is a circle.
Therefore, there is a triangle.

and the other form is known as *modus tollens*:

If there is a circle then there is a triangle.
There is not a triangle.
Therefore, there is not a circle.

Modus ponens is reliably easier than modus tollens (for a review, see Evans, Newstead, & Byrne, 1993). Yet individuals *can* make a modus tollens inference. So, how is that possible? Plainly, they must be able on occasion to represent explicitly the possibilities in which the antecedent of the conditional is false (see Barrouillet, Grosset, & Lecas, 2000; Barrouillet & Lecas, 1999; Girotto, Mazzocco, & Tasso, 1997; Markovits, 2000). They flesh out their representation into fully explicit models, corresponding either to those of a biconditional (if there is a circle then there is a triangle, and if there isn't a circle then there isn't a triangle):

    o   △
  ¬o   ¬△

or to those of a regular conditional (if there is a circle then there is a triangle and if there isn't a circle then there may, or may not, be a triangle):

    o   △
    o   △
  ¬o   ¬△

where "¬" denotes a symbol for negation. We therefore distinguished between mental models and fully explicit models. But how do reasoners get from one to the other?

We argued that individuals must make mental footnotes on their models of the conditional (Johnson-Laird & Byrne, 1991), and we adopted a rather cumbersome notation to represent them, akin to the notation for showing that a set has been exhaustively represented (see above). Later, we introduced a more efficient representation in a computer implementation of the theory, which makes footnotes on mental models to indicate what is false in them. For example, the mental models for a conditional of the form:

If A and B then C

are as follows:

  A   B   C
  . . .

and the footnote on the implicit model is that it represents the possibilities in which the conjunction, A and B, is false. The models can therefore be fleshed out to represent the seven fully explicit possibilities compatible with this conditional. Naïve reasoners are unable to enumerate these possibilities correctly (Barres & Johnson-Laird, 2002). In general, more models mean more work, and less chance of a correct conclusion (Johnson-Laird & Byrne, 1991; Klauer & Oberauer, 1995). Reasoners tend to focus on as few mental models as possible, and often just on a single model (Richardson & Ormerod, 1997; Sloutsky & Goldvarg, 1999; Sloutsky & Johnson-Laird, 1999). Hence, another possibility is that they use the meaning of the conditional to construct this or that model depending on the circumstances (Johnson-Laird & Byrne, 2002).

The theory of sentential reasoning formulated in Johnson-Laird and Byrne (1991) abided by a principle, whose importance was not realized at first: mental models represent only what is true, not what is false. This principle of truth applies both to premises as a whole and to clauses within them. For premises as a whole, models represent only the possibilities that are true. For each clause in the premises, mental models represent the clause only when it is true in a possibility. For example the exclusive disjunction:

There isn't a circle or else there is a triangle

has the mental models:

¬o
   Δ

The mental models do not represent clauses, whether affirmative or negative, if they are false. Fully explicit models, however, do represent false clauses, using negation where relevant. Hence, the fully explicit models of the preceding disjunction are:

¬o ¬Δ
o   Δ

Some commentators have argued that the principle of truth is misnamed, because individuals merely represent those propositions that are mentioned in the premises. This view is mistaken. The same propositions can be mentioned in, say, a conjunction and a disjunction, but the mental models of these assertions are very different.

Reasoners focus on what is true and neglect what is false. One consequence is the difficulty of Wason's (1966) selection task. In this task, reasoners have to select evidence relevant to the truth or falsity of an assertion. Given a conditional, such as:

If there is an A on one side of a card then there is a 2 on the other side

they tend to select only an instance of an A, or else instances of an A and of a 2. What they neglect is an instance of a 3. Yet if a 3 occurred in conjunction with an A, the conditional would be false. Any manipulation that helps reasoners to bring to mind the falsifying instance of the conditional improves performance in the selection task (Johnson-Laird, 2001).

The history of mental models 199

Another consequence of the principle of truth was discovered by chance in the output of the program implementing the theory. The neglect of falsity leads to systematic illusions in reasoning. Here is one example (from Goldvarg & Johnson-Laird, 2000):

> Only one of the following premises is true about a particular hand of cards:
> There is a king in the hand or there is an ace, or both.
> There is a queen in the hand or there is an ace, or both.
> There is a jack in the hand or there is a 10, or both.
> Is it possible that there is an ace in the hand?

Intelligent reasoners tend to respond: "Yes". In fact, it is impossible for an ace to be in the hand, because both of the first two premises would then be true, contrary to the rubric that only one premise is true. Most sorts of inference are not illusory, because the neglect of falsity does not affect their validity. But, as the theory predicts, many sorts of illusion do occur in every domain of deduction (e.g., Johnson-Laird & Savary, 1999; Yang & Johnson-Laird, 2000). Experts succumb too. They propose ingenious alternative explanations for their errors. The problems are so complicated, or so artificial, they say, that people are confused. Such explanations, however, overlook that individuals do very well with control problems that are syntactically identical to the illusions.

The illusions corroborate the model theory, but seem wholly inconsistent with other theories of reasoning. Their occurrence is a litmus test for mental models. Certain manipulations alleviate the illusions (e.g., Santamaría & Johnson-Laird, 2000), but the search for a perfect antidote to them has so far been in vain.

Because meaning is central to models, the content of inferences and background knowledge can modulate reasoning (Johnson-Laird & Byrne, 2002). To account for the phenomena, the theory postulates that knowledge takes the form of fully explicit models of those possibilities that are known in detail. The semantic content of a premise is likely to trigger pertinent knowledge of this sort, which is conjoined with the mental models of the assertion, although knowledge normally takes precedence in the case of contradiction. One consequence is the addition of temporal, spatial, and other information to models of assertions. But another important consequence is that knowledge can block the construction of models. The following inference is in the form of a valid modus tollens:

> If Pat is not in Rio then she's in Brazil.
> Pat is not in Brazil.
> Therefore, she is in Rio.

But individuals are reluctant to draw this conclusion. They know that Rio is in Brazil, and so if a person is not in Brazil, then that person cannot be in Rio. Hence, the conditional refers to only two possibilities:

¬ Rio Brazil
Rio Brazil

In contrast, the following inference is easy:

If Pat is in Rio then she is in Brazil.
Pat is not in Brazil.
Therefore, she is not in Rio.

Knowledge readily allows one to draw the conclusion (Johnson-Laird & Byrne, 2002). Analogous phenomena occur as a result of the meaning of clauses, and they extend to disjunctions (Ormerod & Johnson-Laird, 2002).

In logic, connectives such as "if" and "or" have idealized meanings that are truth-functional, that is, the truth or falsity of a sentence they form depends only on the truth or falsity of the clauses they interconnect (Jeffrey, 1981). The preceding examples show that natural language is not truth-functional: the interpretation of a conditional depends on the meanings of its individual clauses and background knowledge. The conditional, *If Pat is not in Rio then she is in Brazil*, rules out the possibility in which both its antecedent and consequent are false, but the conditional, *If Pat is in Rio then she is in Brazil*, does not. Knowledge can also influence the process of reasoning. Reasoners search harder for counterexamples to conclusions that violate their knowledge. This search is compatible with a robust phenomenon: knowledge and beliefs have a bigger effect on invalid inferences than on valid inferences (e.g., Cherubini, Garnham, Oakhill, & Morley, 1998; Evans, 1989; Oakhill, Johnson-Laird, & Garnham, 1989; Santamaría, García-Madruga, & Johnson-Laird, 1998).

STRATEGIES AND COUNTEREXAMPLES

When reasoners make a series of inferences, they develop strategies for coping with them. Different individuals develop different strategies – in sentential reasoning (Byrne & Handley, 1997; Dieussaert, Schaeken, Schroyens, & d'Ydewalle, 2000), in relational reasoning (Roberts, 2000), and in reasoning with quantifiers (Bucciarelli & Johnson-Laird, 1999). Our hypothesis is that individuals develop strategies by trying out different sequences of inferential tactics based on mental models (Van der Henst, Yang, & Johnson-Laird, 2002). Consider, for example, the following problem about marbles in a box:

There is a red marble if and only if there is a green marble.
Either there is a green marble or else there is a blue marble, but not both.
There is a blue marble if and only if there is brown marble.
Does it follow that if there is not a red marble then there is a brown marble?

The history of mental models 201

One strategy is based on following up the consequences of a supposition. Such reasoners say, for instance:

> Assuming there is not a red marble, it follows from the first premise that there is not a green marble. It then follows from the second premise that there is a blue marble. The third premise then implies there is a brown marble. So, yes, the conclusion does follow.

A different strategy is to construct a chain of conditionals leading from one clause in the conditional conclusion to the other. This strategy calls for immediate inferences to convert premises into appropriate conditionals. A "think aloud" protocol contained the following chain, which started invalidly from the consequent of the conditional in the example above:

> If there is a brown marble then there is a blue marble.
> [Immediate inference from premise 3]
> If there is a blue marble then there is not a green marble.
> [Immediate inference from premise 2]
> If there is not a green marble then there is not a red marble.
> [Immediate inference from premise 1]

At this point, the reasoner said that the conclusion followed from the premises.

The strategy that corresponds most directly to the use of mental models is to construct a diagram that integrates all the information from the premises. For example, a participant drew a horizontal line across the middle of the page, and wrote down the two possibilities compatible with the premises in the example above:

Red   Green
―――――――――――――――――
            Blue   Brown

Such reasoners work through the premises in whatever order they are stated, taking into account irrelevant premises. When Victoria Bell taught naïve reasoners to use this strategy in a systematic way (in unpublished studies), their reasoning was both faster and more accurate.

Although some strategies are surprising, they can all be based on mental models, and some of them are difficult to explain in any other way. As the model theory predicts, disjunctive premises tend to elicit the incremental diagram strategy, whereas conditional premises tend to elicit the suppositional strategy. Regardless of strategy, however, one-model problems are easier than two-model problems, which in turn are easier than three-model problems. This trend occurs in the correct evaluations of conclusions, and in the validity of conclusions that reasoners draw for themselves (Van der Henst et al.,

2002). It supports the hypothesis that all strategies make an underlying use of models.

A rare experimental result contrary to the model theory is Rips's (1994) finding that an inference based on a conjunction was no easier than one based on a disjunction. Rips compared an inference with an initial conjunction, which calls for only one model:

> A and B.
> If A then C.
> If B then C.
> Therefore, C.

with an inference with an initial disjunction, which calls for at least two models:

> A or B.
> If A then C.
> If B then C.
> Therefore, C.

The participants evaluated the conclusions, and there was no reliable difference between the two sorts of inference. However, in a recent study (García-Madruga, Moreno, Carriedo, Gutiérrez, & Johnson-Laird, 2001) reasoners drew their own conclusions from such premises, and the conjunctive problems were easier than the disjunctive problems. The results also corroborated the model theory when the premises were presented one at a time, and the participants had to evaluate the conclusions. Rips's procedure may therefore have elicited a different strategy from those that the participants developed in the García-Madruga studies.

From its inception, the model theory has postulated that reasoners could reject invalid conclusions on the basis of counterexamples, i.e., models in which the premises are true but the conclusion is false (see also Halpern & Vardi, 1991). But such a model violates the principle of truth, and reasoners do not invariably search for counterexamples (Newstead, Thompson, & Handley, 2002; Polk & Newell, 1995). One way to elicit them is to ask reasoners to evaluate given conclusions that are invalid, for example:

> More than half the people in the room speak English.
> More than half the people in the room speak Italian.
> Does it follow that more than half the people in the room speak both languages?

A typical response is that there could be five people in the room, three speak one language, three speak the other language, but only one person speaks both languages (Neth & Johnson-Laird, 1999).

The use of counterexamples is just one strategy in refuting invalid inferences (Johnson-Laird & Hasson, 2003). With an inference of the following form, for example:

If A then not B.
B or C.
Therefore, A or C.

all the participants in an experiment constructed a counterexample: not-A, B, not-C. But, given an inference of the form:

If A then B.
If B then C.
Therefore, C.

the participants remarked that nothing definite could follow from two conditionals. In other cases, they pointed out the need for a missing premise, or generated a valid conclusion that they contrasted with the given conclusion. As the theory predicts, however, the use of counterexamples is more frequent when an invalid conclusion is consistent with the premises rather than inconsistent with them.

The competence to use counterexamples is contrary to theories of reasoning in which invalidity is established solely by a failure to find a proof (Braine & O'Brien, 1998; Rips, 1994). But it is consistent with the model theory's claim that human rationality rests on the fundamental semantic principle of validity: an inference is valid if its conclusion holds in all the possibilities – the models – consistent with the premises. An application of this principle to invalidity is to construct counterexamples.

CONCLUSIONS

If Craik (1943) is right, then mental models underlie all sorts of thinking from induction to creation. So far, however, the theory has focused on deduction (see the web page maintained by Ruth Byrne and her colleagues at www.tcd.ie/Psychology/Ruth_Byrne/mental_models/). Its three main principles owe something to Craik, something to his precursors, and something to those who inherited his ideas:

(1) Reasoners use the meaning of premises and their knowledge to construct mental models of the possibilities compatible with the premises.
(2) Mental models are iconic as far as possible, but certain components of them are necessarily symbolic.
(3) Mental models represent what is true, but not what is false. Reasoners can – with some difficulty – flesh them out into fully explicit models.

The theory provides a single psychological mechanism for deductions about necessary, probable, and possible conclusions. A conclusion that holds in all possible models of the premises is necessary given the premises. It is not necessary if it has a counterexample, i.e., a model of the premises in which the conclusion is false. A conclusion that holds in most of the models of the premises is probable. Reasoners can estimate the probability of a conclusion based on the proportion of equipossible models in which it holds, or from calculating its probability from models tagged with numerical frequencies or chances of occurrence (Girotto & Gonzalez, 2001; Johnson-Laird, Legrenzi, Girotto, Legrenzi, & Caverni, 1999). A conclusion that holds in at least one model of the premises is possible.

In recent years, the model theory has been extended to many domains:

- Counterfactual reasoning (Byrne & McEleney, 2000; Byrne & Tasso, 1999).
- Reasoning based on suppositions (Byrne & Handley, 1997).
- Modal reasoning about possibilities (Bell & Johnson-Laird, 1998; Evans, Handley, Harper, & Johnson-Laird, 1999).
- Deontic reasoning about obligations (Bucciarelli & Johnson-Laird, 2002; Manktelow & Over, 1995).
- Causal reasoning (Goldvarg & Johnson-Laird, 2001).
- The detection of inconsistencies and their resolution (Girotto, Johnson-Laird, Legrenzi, & Sonino, 2000; Johnson-Laird, Legrenzi, Girotto, & Legrenzi, 2000).
- Strategic reasoning in games (Steingold & Johnson-Laird, 2002).
- The construction of arguments (Green & McManus, 1995).

Opponents of the theory have often criticized it in helpful ways. Many of its details do need to be clarified. And, despite some steps in the right direction (Bara, Bucciarelli, & Lombardo, 2001), its single biggest weakness is its lack of a comprehensive account of reasoning based on the interplay between quantifiers and connectives.

Yet the theory seems to be on the right lines. Perhaps the best evidence in its favour comes from its unexpected prediction of illusory inferences, which have now been confirmed for many sorts of reasoning. Other theories seem to have no way to account for such systematic errors short of postulating invalid rules of inference – a step with disastrous implications for human rationality. In contrast, failures to construct the correct models are predictable from the principle of truth, but do not impugn rationality based on the semantic principle of validity. The model theory does not imply that reasoners never rely on rules of inference. Intelligent individuals may develop rules spontaneously as a result of experience with many inferences of a similar form. And this step, in principle, can lead to the development of formal logic.

ACKNOWLEDGEMENTS

Preparation of this article was supported by a grant from the National Science Foundation (Grant BCS 0076287) to study strategies in reasoning. The author thanks the community of researchers on deductive reasoning for their help. Their names are in the following section.

REFERENCES

Baddeley, A. D., & Hitch, G. (1974). Working memory. In G. H. Bower (Ed.), *The psychology of learning and motivation, Vol. 8*. London: Academic Press.

Bara, B. G., Bucciarelli, M., & Lombardo, V. (2001). Model theory of deduction: A unified computational approach. *Cognitive Science*, 25, 839–901.

Barres, P., & Johnson-Laird, P. N. (2002). On imagining what is true (and what is false). *Thinking & Reasoning*, 9, 1–42.

Barrouillet, P., & Lecas, J.-F. (1999). Mental models in conditional reasoning and working memory. *Thinking & Reasoning*, 5, 289–302.

Barrouillet, P., Grosset, N., & Lecas, J.-F. (2000). Conditional reasoning by mental models: Chronometric and developmental evidence. *Cognition*, 75, 237–266.

Barsalou, L. W. (1999). Perceptual symbol systems. *Behavioral and Brain Sciences*, 22, 577–660.

Bell, V., & Johnson-Laird, P. N. (1998). A model theory of modal reasoning. *Cognitive Science*, 22, 25–51.

Biederman, I. (1987). Recognition by components: A theory of human image understanding. *Psychological Review*, 94, 115–147.

Binet, A. (1894). *Psychologie des grands calculateurs et joueurs d'echecs*. Paris: Hachette.

Boltzmann, L. (1890/1974). On the significance of physical theories. In B. McGuiness (Ed.), *Ludwig Boltzmann: Theoretical physics and philosophical problems* (pp. 33–36). Boston: Reidel. [Originally published, 1890.]

Boltzmann, L. (1899/1974). On the fundamental principles and equations of mechanics. In B. McGuiness (Ed.), *Ludwig Boltzmann: Theoretical physics and philosophical problems* (pp. 101–128). Boston: Reidel. [Originally published, 1899.]

Bower, G. H. (1970) Analysis of the mnemonic device. *American Scientist*, 58, 496–501.

Braine, M. D. S., & O'Brien, D. P. (Eds.) (1998). *Mental logic*. Mahwah, NJ: Lawrence Erlbaum Associates Inc.

Bransford, J. D., Barclay, J. R., & Franks, J. J. (1972). Sentence memory: A constructive versus an interpretive approach. *Cognitive Psychology*, 3, 193–209.

Bucciarelli, M., & Johnson-Laird, P. N. (1999). Strategies in syllogistic reasoning. *Cognitive Science*, 23, 247–303.

Bucciarelli, M., & Johnson-Laird, P. N. (2002). *Foundations of deontic meaning and reasoning*. Manuscript submitted for publication.

Byrne, R. M. J., & Handley, S. J. (1997). Reasoning strategies for suppositional deductions. *Cognition*, 62, 1–49.

Byrne, R. M. J., & Johnson-Laird, P. N. (1989). Spatial reasoning. *Journal of Memory and Language*, 28, 564–575.

Byrne, R. M. J., & McEleney, A. (2000). Counterfactual thinking about actions and failures to act. *Journal of Experimental Psychology: Learning, Memory, and Cognition*, *26*, 1318–1331.

Byrne, R. M. J., & Tasso, A. (1999). Deductive reasoning with factual, possible, and counterfactual conditionals. *Memory & Cognition*, *27*, 726–740.

Carreiras, M., & Santamaría, C. (1997). Reasoning about relations: Spatial and nonspatial problems. *Thinking & Reasoning*, *3*, 191–208.

Cherubini, P., Garnham, A., Oakhill, J., & Morley, E. (1998). Can any ostrich fly? Some new data on belief bias in syllogistic reasoning. *Cognition*, *69*, 179–218.

Clark, H. H., & Chase, W. G. (1972). On the process of comparing sentences against pictures. *Cognitive Psychology*, *3*, 472–517.

Craik, K. (1943). *The nature of explanation*. Cambridge: Cambridge University Press.

Davis, R., & Hamscher, W. (1988). Model-based reasoning: Troubleshooting. In H. E. Shrobe & AAAI (Eds.), *Exploring artificial intelligence: Survey talks from the National Conferences on Artificial Intelligence*. San Mateo, CA: Morgan Kaufmann.

de Kleer, J. (1977). Multiple representations of knowledge in a mechanics problem-solver. *International Joint Conference Artificial Intelligence*, 299–304.

de Kleer, J., & Williams, B. C. (1987). Diagnosing multiple faults. *Artificial Intelligence*, *32*, 97–130.

Dieussaert, K., Schaeken, W., Schroyens, W., & d'Ydewalle, G. (2000). Strategies during complex conditional inferences. *Thinking & Reasoning*, *6*, 125–160.

Ehrlich, K. (1996). Applied mental models in human–computer interaction. In J. Oakhill & A. Garnham (Eds.), *Mental models in cognitive science*. Mahwah, NJ: Lawrence Erlbaum Associates Inc.

Erickson, J. R. (1974). A set analysis theory of behaviour in formal syllogistic reasoning tasks. In R. Solso (Ed.), *Loyola Symposium on Cognition, Vol. 2*. Hillsdale, NJ: Lawrence Erlbaum Associates Inc.

Espino, O., Santamaría, C., Meseguer, E., & Carreiras, M. (2000). Eye movements during syllogistic reasoning. In J. A. García-Madruga, N. Carriedo, & M. J. González-Labra (Eds.), *Mental models in reasoning* (pp. 179–188). Madrid: Universidad Nacional de Educación a Distancia.

Evans, J. St. B. T., (1989). *Bias in human reasoning: Causes and consequences*. Mahwah, NJ: Lawrence Erlbaum Associates Inc.

Evans, J. St. B. T., Handley, S. J., Harper, C. N. J., & Johnson-Laird, P. N. (1999). Reasoning about necessity and possibility: A test of the mental model theory of deduction. *Journal of Experimental Psychology: Learning, Memory, and Cognition*, *25*, 1495–1513.

Evans, J. St. B. T., Newstead, S. E., & Byrne, R. M. J. (1993). *Human reasoning: The psychology of deduction*. Mahwah, NJ: Lawrence Erlbaum Associates Inc.

Feynman, R. P. (1985). *QED: The strange theory of light and matter*. Princeton, NJ: Princeton University Press.

Forbus, K. (1985). Qualitative process theory. In D. G. Bobrow (Ed.), *Qualitative reasoning about physical systems*. Cambridge, MA: MIT Press.

Ford, M. (1995). Two modes of mental representation and problem solution in syllogistic reasoning. *Cognition*, *54*, 1–71.

Frege, G. (1879). *Begriffsschrift, eine der Arithmetischen nachgebildete Formelsprache des reinen Denkens*. Halle: Nebert.

García-Madruga, J. A., Moreno, S., Carriedo, N., Gutiérrez, F., & Johnson-Laird, P. N. (2001). Are conjunctive inferences easier than disjunctive inferences? A comparison of rules and models. *Quarterly Journal of Experimental Psychology, 54*A, 613–632.

Garnham, A. (1987). *Mental models as representations of discourse and text*. Chichester, UK: Ellis Horwood.

Garnham, A. (2001). *Mental models and the interpretation of anaphora*. Hove, UK: Psychology Press.

Garnham, A., & Oakhill, J. V. (1996). The mental models theory of language comprehension. In B. K. Britton & A. C. Graesser (Eds.), *Models of understanding text* (pp. 313–339). Hillsdale, NJ: Lawrence Erlbaum Associates Inc.

Gentner, D., & Gentner, D. R. (1983). Flowing waters or teeming crowds: Mental models of electricity. In D. Gentner & A. L. Stevens (Eds.), *Mental models*. Hillsdale, NJ: Lawrence Erlbaum Associates Inc.

Gentner, D., & Stevens, A. L. (Eds.). (1983). *Mental models*. Hillsdale, NJ: Lawrence Erlbaum Associates Inc.

Girotto, V., & Gonzalez, M. (2001). Solving probabilistic and statistical problems: A matter of question form and information structure. *Cognition, 78*, 247–276.

Girotto, V., Johnson-Laird, P. N., Legrenzi, P., & Sonino, M. (2000). Reasoning to consistency: How people resolve logical inconsistencies. In J. A. García-Madruga, N. Carriedo & M. J. González-Labra (Eds.), *Mental models in reasoning* (pp. 83–97). Madrid: Universidad Nacional de Educación a Distancia.

Girotto, V., Mazzocco, A., & Tasso, A. (1997). The effect of premise order in conditional reasoning: A test of the mental model theory. *Cognition, 63*, 1–28.

Glasgow, J. I. (1993). Representation of spatial models for geographic information systems. In N. Pissinou (Ed.), *Proceedings of the ACM Workshop on Advances in Geographic Information Systems* (pp. 112–117). Arlington, VA: Association for Computing Machinery.

Glenberg, A. M., Meyer, M., & Lindem, K. (1987). Mental models contribute to foregrounding during text comprehension. *Journal of Memory and Language, 26*, 69–83.

Goldvarg, Y., & Johnson-Laird, P. N. (2000). Illusions in modal reasoning. *Memory & Cognition, 28*, 282–294.

Goldvarg, Y., & Johnson-Laird, P. N. (2001). Naïve causality: A mental model theory of causal meaning and reasoning. *Cognitive Science, 25*, 565–610.

Green, D. W., & McManus, I. C. (1995). Cognitive structural models: Perception of risk and prevention in coronary heart disease. *British Journal of Psychology, 86*, 321–335.

Halford, G. S. (1993). *Children's understanding: The development of mental models*. Hillsdale, NJ: Lawrence Erlbaum Associates Inc.

Halpern, J. Y., & Vardi, M. Y. (1991). Model checking vs. theorem proving: A manifesto. In J. A. Allen, R. Fikes & E. Sandewall (Eds.), *Principles of knowledge representation and reasoning: Proceedings of the Second International Conference* (pp. 325–334). San Mateo, CA: Kaufmann.

Hayes, P. J. (1979). Naive physics I – ontology for liquids. Mimeo, Centre pour les études Semantiques et Cognitives, Geneva. [Reprinted in Hobbs, J., & Moore, R. (Eds.), *Formal theories of the commonsense world*. Hillsdale, NJ: Lawrence Erlbaum Associates Inc.]

Hegarty, M. (1992). Mental animation: Inferring motion from static diagrams of mechanical systems. *Journal of Experimental Psychology: Learning, Memory, and Cognition, 18,* 1084–1102.

Holland, J. H. (1998). *Emergence: From chaos to order.* Reading, MA: Perseus Books.

Holland, J. H., Holyoak, K. J., Nisbett, R. E., & Thagard, P. R. (1986). *Induction: Processes of inference, learning, and discovery.* Cambridge, MA: MIT Press.

Inhelder, B., & Piaget, J. (1958). *The growth of logical thinking from childhood to adolescence.* London: Routledge & Kegan Paul.

Jeffrey, R. (1981). *Formal logic: Its scope and limits* (2nd Ed.). New York: McGraw-Hill.

Johnson-Laird, P. N. (1970). The perception and memory of sentences. In J. Lyons (Ed.), *New horizons in linguistics* (pp. 261–270). Harmondsworth, UK: Penguin Books.

Johnson-Laird, P. N. (1975). Models of deduction. In R. Falmagne (Ed.), *Reasoning: Representation and process.* Hillsdale, NJ: Lawrence Erlbaum Associates Inc.

Johnson-Laird, P. N. (1983). *Mental models: Towards a cognitive science of language, inference, and consciousness.* Cambridge: Cambridge University Press.

Johnson-Laird, P. N. (2001). Mental models and deduction. *Trends in Cognitive Science, 5,* 434–442.

Johnson-Laird, P. N. (2002). Peirce, logic diagrams, and the elementary operations of reasoning. *Thinking & Reasoning, 8,* 69–95.

Johnson-Laird, P. N., & Bara, B. G. (1984). Syllogistic inference. *Cognition, 16,* 1–61.

Johnson-Laird, P. N., & Byrne, R. M. J. (1991). *Deduction.* Hillsdale, NJ: Lawrence Erlbaum Associates Inc.

Johnson-Laird, P. N., & Byrne, R. M. J. (2002). Conditionals: A theory of meaning, pragmatics, and inference. *Psychological Review, 109,* 646–678.

Johnson-Laird, P. N., Byrne, R. M. J., & Tabossi, P. (1989). Reasoning by model: The case of multiple quantification. *Psychological Review, 96,* 658–673.

Johnson-Laird, P. N., & Hasson, U. (2003). *Counterexamples in sentential reasoning. Memory & Cognition, 31,* 1105–1113.

Johnson-Laird, P. N., Legrenzi, P., Girotto, V., & Legrenzi, M. S. (2000). Illusions in reasoning about consistency. *Science, 288,* 531–532.

Johnson-Laird, P. N., Legrenzi, P., Girotto, V., Legrenzi, M., & Caverni, J.-P. (1999). Naive probability: A mental model theory of extensional reasoning. *Psychological Review, 106,* 62–88.

Johnson-Laird, P. N., & Savary, F. (1999). Illusory inferences: A novel class of erroneous deductions. *Cognition, 71,* 191–229.

Johnson-Laird, P. N., & Steedman, M. J. (1978). The psychology of syllogisms. *Cognitive Psychology, 10,* 64–99.

Johnson-Laird, P. N., & Stevenson, R. (1970). Memory for syntax. *Nature, 227,* 412.

Kamp, H. (1981). A theory of truth and semantic representation. In J. A. G. Groenendijk, T. M. V. Janssen & M. B. J. Stokhof (Eds.), *Formal methods in the study of language* (pp. 277–322). Amsterdam: Mathematical Centre Tracts.

Karttunen, L. (1976). Discourse referents. In J. D. McCawley (Ed.), *Syntax and semantics, Vol. 7: Notes from the linguistic underground.* New York: Academic Press.

Kitchin, R. M. (1994). Cognitive maps: What are they and why study them? *Journal of Environmental Psychology, 14,* 1–19.

Klauer, K. C., & Oberauer, K. (1995). Testing the mental model theory of propositional reasoning. *Quarterly Journal of Experimental Psychology, 48*A, 671–687.

Knauff, M., Fangmeir, T., Ruff, C. C., & Johnson-Laird, P. N. (2003). Reasoning, models, and images: Behavioral measures and cortical activity. *Journal of Cognitive Neuroscience, 4*, 559–573.

Knauff, M., & Johnson-Laird, P. N. (2002). Imagery can impede inference. *Memory & Cognition, 30*, 363–371.

Köhler, W. (1938). *The place of value in a world of facts*. New York: Liveright.

Kosslyn, S. M. (1980). *Image and mind*. Cambridge, MA: Harvard University Press.

Kosslyn, S. M., Ball, T. M., & Reiser, B. J. (1978). Visual images preserve metric spatial information: Evidence from studies of image scanning. *Journal of Experimental Psychology: Human Perception and Performance, 4*, 47–60.

Kuipers, B. (1994). *Qualitative reasoning: Modeling and simulation with incomplete knowledge*. Cambridge, MA: MIT Press.

Larkin, J., & Simon, H. (1987). Why a diagram is (sometimes) worth 10,000 words. *Cognitive Science, 11*, 65–99.

Luria, A. R. (1969). *The mind of a mnemonist*. London: Cape.

Macnamara, J. (1986). *A border dispute: The place of logic in pychology*. Cambridge, MA: Bradford Books, MIT Press.

Maier, N. R. F. (1929). Reasoning in white rats. *Comparative Psychology Monographs, 6*, No. 29.

Manktelow, K. I., & Over. D. E. (1995). Deontic reasoning. In S. E. Newstead & J. St.B. T. Evans (Eds.), *Perspectives on thinking and reasoning: Essays in honour of Peter Wason* (pp. 91–114). Hove, UK: Psychology Press.

Markman, A. B., & Dietrich, E. (2000). Extending the classical view of representation. *Trends in Cognitive Science, 4*, 470–475.

Markovits, H. (2000). A mental model analysis of young children's conditional reasoning with meaningful premises. *Thinking & Reasoning, 6*, 335–347.

Marr, D. (1982). *Vision: A computational investigation into the human representation and processing of visual information*. San Francisco: W. H. Freeman.

Maxwell, J. C. (1911). Diagram. *The Encyclopaedia Britannica, Vol. XVIII*. New York: The Encylopaedia Britannica Company.

McCloskey, M., Caramazza, A., & Green, B. (1980). Curvilinear motion in the absence of external forces: Naïve beliefs about the motions of objects. *Science, 210*, 1139–1141.

McCulloch, W. S. (1965). *Embodiments of mind*. Cambridge, MA: MIT Press.

Metzler, J., & Shepard, R. N. (1982). Transformational studies of the internal representations of three-dimensional objects. In R. N. Shepard & L. A. Cooper (Eds.), *Mental images and their transformations*. Cambridge, MA: MIT Press. [Originally published in Solso, R. L. (Ed.), *Theories in cognitive psychology: The Loyola Symposium*. Hillsdale, NJ: Lawrence Erlbaum Associates Inc, 1974.]

Moray, N. (1990). A lattice theory approach to the structure of mental models. *Philosophical Transactions of the Royal Society of London B, 327*, 577–583.

Moray, N. (1999). Mental models in theory and practice. In D. Gopher & A. Koriat (Eds.), *Attention & performance XVII: Cognitive regulation of performance: Interaction of theory and application* (pp. 223–358). Cambridge, MA: MIT Press.

Neth, H., & Johnson-Laird, P. N. (1999). The search for counterexamples in human reasoning. *Proceedings of the Twenty First Annual Conference of the Cognitive Science Society*, 806.

Newell, A. (1990). *Unified theories of cognition*. Cambridge, MA: Harvard University Press.
Newstead, S. E., Thompson, V. A., & Handley, S. J. (2002). Generating alternatives: A key component in human reasoning? *Memory & Cognition, 30*, 129–137.
Oakhill, J. V., Johnson-Laird, P. N., & Garnham, A. (1989). Believability and syllogistic reasoning. *Cognition, 31*, 117–140.
Oaksford, M., & Chater, N. (1994). A rational analysis of the selection task as optimal data selection. *Psychological Review, 101*, 608–631.
Ormerod, T. C., & Johnson-Laird, P. N. (2002). *How pragmatics modulates the interpretation of sentential connectives*. Manuscript submitted for publication.
Osherson, D. N. (1974–6). *Logical abilities in children, Vols. 1–4*. Hillsdale, NJ: Lawrence Erlbaum Associates Inc.
Paivio, A. (1971). *Imagery and verbal processes*. New York: Holt, Rinehart & Winston.
Peirce, C. S. (1931–1958). C. Hartshorne, P. Weiss & A. Burks (Eds.), *Collected papers of Charles Sanders Peirce, 8 Vols*. Cambridge, MA: Harvard University Press.
Perky, C. W. (1910). An experimental study of imagination. *American Journal of Psychology, 21*, 422–452.
Polk, T. A., & Newell, A. (1995). Deduction as verbal reasoning. *Psychological Review, 102*, 533–566.
Putnam, H. (1960). Minds and machines. In S. Hook (Ed.), *Dimensions of mind*. New York: New York University Press.
Pylyshyn, Z. W. (1973). What the mind's eye tells the mind's brain: A critique of mental imagery. *Psychological Bulletin, 80*, 1–24.
Richardson, J., & Ormerod, T. C. (1997). Rephrasing between disjunctives and conditionals: Mental models and the effects of thematic content. *Quarterly Journal of Experimental Psychology, 50*A, 358–385.
Rips, L. J. (1994). *The psychology of proof*. Cambridge, MA: MIT Press.
Roberts, M. J. (2000). Strategies in relational inference. *Thinking & Reasoning, 6*, 1–26.
Rouse, W. B., & Hunt, R. M. (1984). Human problem solving in fault diagnosis tasks. In W. B. Rouse (Ed.), *Advances in man–machine systems research*. Greenwich, CN: JAI Press.
Sachs, J. S. (1967). Recognition memory for syntactic and semantic aspects of connected discourse. *Perception & Psychophysics, 2*, 437–442.
Santamaría, C., García-Madruga, J. A., & Johnson-Laird, P. N. (1998). Reasoning from double conditionals: The effects of logical structure and believability. *Thinking & Reasoning, 4*, 97–122.
Santamaría, C., & Johnson-Laird, P. N. (2000). An antidote to illusory inferences. *Thinking & Reasoning, 6*, 313–333.
Schaeken, W., Johnson-Laird, P. N., & d'Ydewalle, G. (1996). Mental models and temporal reasoning. *Cognition, 60*, 205–234.
Schroyens, W., Schaeken, W., & d'Ydewalle, G. (2001). The processing of negations in conditional reasoning: A meta-analytic case study in mental model and/or mental logic theory. *Thinking & Reasoning, 7*, 121–172.
Schwartz, D., & Black, J. B. (1996). Analog imagery in mental model reasoning: Depictive models. *Cognitive Psychology, 30*, 154–219.
Shepard, R. N., & Metzler, J. (1971). Mental rotation of three-dimensional objects. *Science, 71*, 701–703.

Sloutsky, V. M., & Goldvarg, Y. (1999). Effects of externalization on representation of indeterminate problems. *Proceedings of the Twenty First Annual Conference of the Cognitive Science Society*, 695–700.

Sloutsky, V. M., & Johnson-Laird. P. N. (1999). Problem representations and illusions in reasoning. *Proceedings of the Twenty First Annual Conference of the Cognitive Science Society*, 701–705.

Smith, C., & Wise, M. N. (1989). *Energy and empire: A biographical study of Lord Kelvin*. Cambridge: Cambridge University Press.

Sowa, J. F. (1984). *Conceptual structures: Information processing in mind and machine*. Reading, MA: Addison-Wesley.

Steingold, E., & Johnson-Laird, P. N. (2002). Naïve strategic thinking. In W. Gray & C.D. Schunn (Eds), Proceedings of the Twenty-Fourth Annual Conference of the Cognitive Science Society, Fairfax, VA (pp. 845–849). Mahwah, NJ: Lawrence Erlbaum Associates Inc.

Stenning, K. (1977). Articles, quantifiers, and their encoding in textual comprehension. In M. Halle, J. Bresnan & G. A. Miller (Eds.), *Linguistic theory and psychological reality*. Cambridge, MA: MIT Press.

Stenning, K. (2002). *Seeing reason: Image and language in learning to think*. Oxford: Oxford University Press.

Stenning, K., & Oberlander, J. (1995). A cognitive theory of graphical and linguistic reasoning: Logic and implementation. *Cognitive Science*, 19, 97–140.

Stevenson, R. J. (1993). *Language, thought and representation*. New York: Wiley.

Störring, G. (1908). Experimentelle Untersuchungen über einfache Schlussprozesse. *Archiv für die gesamte Psychologie*, 11, 1–27.

Thorndyke, P. W., & B. Hayes-Roth. (1982). Differences in spatial knowledge acquired from maps and navigation. *Cognitive Psychology*, 14, 560–589.

Tolman, E. C. (1932). *Purposive behaviour in animals and men*. New York: The Century Co.

Tolman, E. C. (1948). Cognitive maps in rats and men. *Psychological Review*, 55, 189–208. [Reprinted in Tolman, E. C. (1958). *Behaviour and psychological man: Essays in motivation and learning*. (Originally published as *Collected papers in psychology*, 1951) Berkeley: University of California Press.]

Tolman, E. C. (1959). Principles of purposive behaviour. In S. Koch (Ed.), *psychology: A study of a science, Study 1. Conceptual and systematic, Vol. 2. General systematic formulations, learning, and special processes* (pp. 92–157). New York: McGraw-Hill.

Tolman, E. C., and Honzik, C. H. (1930). "Insight" in rats. *University of California Publications in Psychology*, 4, 257–275.

Van der Henst, J.-B., Yang, Y., & Johnson-Laird, P. N. (2002). Strategies in sentential reasoning. *Cognitive Science*, 26, 425–468.

Vandierendonck, A., & De Vooght, G. (1996). Evidence for mental model based reasoning: A comparison of reasoning with time and space concepts. *Thinking & Reasoning*, 2, 249–272.

Vandierendonck, A., & De Vooght, G. (1997). Working memory constraints on linear reasoning with spatial and temporal contents. *Quarterly Journal of Experimental Psychology*, 50A, 803–820.

Van Dijk, T. A., & Kintsch, W. (1983). *Strategies of discourse comprehension*. New York: Academic Press.

von Frisch, K. (1966). *The dancing bees* (2nd Ed.). London: Methuen.

Vosniadou, S., & Brewer, W. F. (1992). Mental models of the earth: A study of conceptual change in childhood. *Cognitive Psychology, 24*, 535–585.

Wason, P. C. (1959). The processing of positive and negative information. *Quarterly Journal of Experimental Psychology, 21*, 92–107.

Wason, P. C. (1966). Reasoning. In B. M. Foss (Ed.), *New horizons in psychology*. Harmondsworth, UK: Penguin.

Wason, P. C., & Johnson-Laird, P. N. (1972). *The psychology of reasoning*. London: Batsford. Cambridge, MA: Harvard University Press.

Webber, B. L. (1978). Description formation and discourse model synthesis. In D. L. Waltz (Ed.), *Theoretical issues in natural language processing, 2*. New York: Association for Computing Machinery.

Wise, M. N. (1979). The mutual embrace of electricity and magnetism. *Science, 203*, 1310–1318.

Wittgenstein, L. (1922). *Tractatus logico-philosophicus*. London: Routledge & Kegan Paul.

Wittgenstein, L. (1953). *Philosophical investigations*. New York: Macmillan.

Yang, Y., & Johnson-Laird, P. N. (2000). Illusory inferences in quantified reasoning: How to make the impossible seem possible, and vice versa. *Memory & Cognition, 28*, 452–465.

Young, R. (1981). The machine inside the machine: Users' models of pocket calculators. *International Journal of Man Machine Studies, 15*, 51–85.

9 Some precursors of current theories of syllogistic reasoning

Guy Politzer

Syllogisms have a long logical and philosophical history. At first sight, one might wonder whether this history would be of any interest to experimental psychologists. Respect for the autonomy of psychology and the fear of logicism might explain such a negative attitude. Still, as will be shown in this chapter, investigators of human reasoning have a great deal to learn from an examination of logical and philosophical theories of the syllogism because, through the exposition of their principles and methods of resolution, these often make use of, and disclose, processes that are psychological in nature.

The work of the German psychologist, G. Störring, published in 1908, which in all likelihood contains the first series of psychological experiments on syllogistic reasoning ever published, will be taken as a point of departure and reference. Indeed it is interesting, if only for the sake of curiosity, to go back to the origins, but this is only a secondary motivation. The main reason to comment on the Störring study is that it contains a few ideas of capital importance, which either passed unnoticed or have been forgotten. And it turns out that the main current approaches to syllogistic reasoning are based on a resurrection of the same ideas which can, in turn, be traced back to the writings of philosophers and logicians of the past, including Aristotle. In brief, the logico-philosophical and psychological histories of syllogistic reasoning and its psychological explanation are intertwined.

THE STÖRRING STUDY

In 1908, Störring published a 127-page article devoted to the experimental study of two areas in deductive reasoning: relational and syllogistic. We will consider only the latter.[1] The paper has a very short introduction showing psychologism to be the author's implicit frame of reference; he presents his experimental study as an attempt to provide an answer to two questions debated *between logicians:* Is every conclusion inferred on the basis of spatial representations? Does the conclusion result from a synthesis of the terms in the premises, or does it result from a process of comparison?

The method is succinctly described: the administration was individual; premises were visually presented and remained visible until the participants had responded. They were asked to answer with absolute certainty, an instruction repeated on every trial. The response times were measured and then a clinical interview started, the aim of which was to make the participants specify, from a descriptive point of view, how they understood each premise and generated the conclusion. The propositions had an abstract content: letters of the alphabet stood for the three classes and the formulation adopted was such that a syllogism like EI-1 (see Appendix) would be: *no A belong [German Gehören] to class D; some T belong to class A* ∴ *?*.[2]

The paper has no explicit hypotheses, no experimental design, and no statistical treatment, and there were only four participants. Although this seems irredeemable by our current standards, after closer examination it appears that the paper contains a number of essential observations, reviewed below, that certainly put it abreast with modern studies.

The figural effect

First, the author noticed longer response times when the major premise is in the first position as compared with the case where it is in the second position. This inversion amounts to comparing the first and the fourth figures.[3] Three quarters of a century later, this difference in difficulty was observed by Johnson-Laird and Bara (1984) who showed that fewer errors and shorter latencies occurred on the fourth figure than on the others. They also observed that most of the problems in the first and fourth figures produce a response bias, namely all the subjects tended to give a response following the SP order on the first figure and the PS order on the fourth figure. Störring's explanation (1908) for the increase in response time was that

> when the major premise is in the first position, the identification of the elements that function as a middle term can occur only after reading the premises. When the major premise occupies the second place, it occurs while reading and comprehending.

In brief, there is a difference in difficulty in integrating the premises, and this explanation foreshadows that of the mental model theory and its interpretation of the figural effect in terms of the ease of integration of the premises in working memory.

Strategies

The next discovery made by Störring is far more important. Throughout his paper he emphasizes that people adopt *strategies* to solve syllogisms, and he distinguishes two of them. The first one is a visual representation of the premises: often people imagine circles standing for classes, sometimes they imagine clusters of letters standing for members of classes;[4] then the conclusion is read off these configurations. The other strategy is verbal: it concerns the reformulation of the premises and efforts to identify two terms with each other, on which more below.

In fact, Störring described the two types of strategy rediscovered by Ford (1995) with a similar method (interview and verbal report). She observed two kinds of participants: some made drawings such as circles or squares to represent the classes; some others made transformations on the terms, such as replacing a term by another, rewriting a syllogism in the form of an equation, or drawing arrows to relate terms. Nowadays it seems very likely that not all individuals tackle syllogisms in the same manner: some rely on a semantic or analogical strategy of the type hypothesized by mental model theory; some rely on a syntactic treatment. One moral of the Störring experiments is that investigators have much to gain from looking for possible individual processes and differences; from this point of view, the administration of paper-and-pencil questionnaires seems of little use. Indeed, Newell (1981) criticized what he called the "fixed-method fallacy" but this was avoided in only a few studies such as Ford's and Bucciarelli and Johnson-Laird's (1999).

The process of "insertion"

Unlike the two previous observations, which can by now be considered well-known established phenomena, the third one has been recognized only recently by a few authors. It will be argued later that this observation might well be the most important ever made on the psychology of syllogisms, because it reveals the essence of syllogisms and possibly the way they are solved, according to one major theoretical approach.

Let us follow the reports of Störring's subjects who had to solve the IA-4 syllogism: *some P belong to class M; all the M belong to class S ∴ ?* One participant said: "all the M, including some P, belong to class S". Another one commented: "these M, to which some P belong, belong to class S". Or take a syllogism in the first figure with a negative premise, EA-1: *no M belong to class P; all the S belong to class M ∴ ?* One participant commented: "One can say the same thing about S as about M" and he went on saying that he "inserted" (his own word) S in the place of M, hence the conclusion "no S belong to class P". The same participant reported for IE-4 *(some P belong to class M; no M belong to class S ∴ ?)*: "What is said of M can also be said of some P" to conclude correctly "some P do not belong to class S".

These are instances of the various ways of expressing a common process by which subjects select the end term of one premise and insert it next to the middle term in the other premise. And to reach the conclusion it will suffice to extract it from the composite expression: "the concluding sentence is obtained by abstraction of a part of what has been asserted as a result of the insertion", that is, in the first example, from *all the M, including some P, belong to class S*, one extracts the conclusion *some P belong to class S*.

Thus, Störring observed the process of insertion in all his four subjects and it was the only clearly identifiable strategy when it was at all possible for participants to report in some detail. Only recently has this process been identified by other investigators: As we will see later, Ford (1995), Stenning and Yule (1997), and Braine (1998) essentially described the same process, each of them formulating it within his or her own framework.

We leave the Störring investigation only to note that the most important psychological phenomena associated with syllogism solving were discovered nearly 100 years ago by a careful investigator but, sadly enough, were soon forgotten. It has already been mentioned that they have been rediscovered, the last one only very recently. We will engage in an enquiry that will take us much farther back in time, in search of the origins of the concepts underlying Störring's three main observations, which we will consider in turn.

THE FIGURAL EFFECT

Compare the two syllogisms in the first and fourth figure, respectively, AI-1: *all M are P; some S are M ∴ some S are P*, and IA-4: *some P are M; all M are S ∴ some P are S*. Although they are logically equivalent (as a change in the order of the premises shows) there is general agreement that the conclusion of the latter follows more "naturally", or more fluently, than the conclusion of the former. As we have seen, greater ease of the fourth figure is nothing mysterious: it is linked with the contiguity of the two occurrences of the middle term.

Could this have influenced logicians of the past? One would expect a negative answer because logic is a formal matter, and logicians are not expected to be influenced by performance factors. However, most surprisingly, the question has a positive answer, to be found in the father of the syllogisms himself. Before this, a brief historical foray into the formulation of syllogisms is in order. Lukasiewicz (1958) points out that the current formulation of syllogisms, which follows a tradition fixed a long time ago,[5] differs sharply from Aristotle's. Only one difference will concern us: our current use of the copula *IS A/ARE* in categorical sentences such as in *some S are M*, differs from Aristotle's formulation, which used either *M is predicated of some S*, or *M belongs to some S*. Consequently, we state the terms in an order that is the reverse of Aristotle's formulation. The same obtains for the three other categorical sentences. This inversion has a remarkable consequence. Take for instance the AI syllogism in the first figure. While it is nowadays expressed as *all M are P; some S are M*, the original syllogism was *P is predicated of all M; M is predicated of some S*, so that the occurrences of the middle term appeared in contiguity in the first figure, not in the fourth figure as is the case in the tradition. Notice that the first figure is the only one in which such a contiguity occurs.

We are now in a position to answer our question and will concern ourselves with Aristotle's notion of perfect syllogism. As we will see later, Aristotle's main method of proof is to transform the syllogism under study into one belonging to a small set, the perfect syllogisms, whose truth is regarded as evident. The perfect syllogisms are essential because, in modern terms, they play the role of axioms of the system. Patzig (1968) discusses at length Aristotle's reasons for considering the truth of some syllogisms as evident; in other words, the question is, what are the formal properties that qualify a syllogism to be regarded as evident by Aristotle? Now, it turns out that all the perfect syllogisms are in the first figure, but logically they need not be in the first figure because there are alternative possible axiomatic choices. Patzig's answer is that the formal property consists in the immediate connection between the premises offered by the middle term, a feature possessed only by the first figure.

So, we reach this remarkable conclusion: in all likelihood, Aristotle based the perfect–imperfect partition of syllogisms on a formal property, namely the contiguity of the occurrences of the middle term, which has a psychological import rather than a logical one: it is this contiguity that provides the syllogism with greater evidence.

In summary, the identification of the role of the figure as a source of difficulty (or rather, of easiness) is to be found in Aristotle himself, a fact that has been concealed because of the choice made after him to formulate the relational term that links the subject and the predicate of categorical sentences: this formulation resulted in removing the characteristic feature of the first figure and in transferring it to the fourth figure instead (a figure that, in addition, was discarded by Aristotle for reasons that are beyond the scope of this paper).

THE ANALOGICAL STRATEGY AND THE REPRESENTATION OF CATEGORICAL PROPOSITIONS

Many people, starting with Störring's subjects, associate diagrams with syllogism solving. Since the 17th century, various kinds of diagram have been proposed by logicians to represent syllogisms and how to solve them. Although Euler is often credited with the invention of the circles that are named after him, he was in fact preceded by Leibniz, who developed not only the circles, but also a straight lines representation. Bochenski (1970) mentions that both kinds of diagram can even be traced back to earlier logicians in the 17th century.[6]

Since then, there have been various kinds of diagrams to represent and solve syllogisms (for a survey of some methods developed in the 19th century, see Gardner, 1958). The most famous, and no doubt the most practical method, are Venn diagrams (which are made of three mutually intersecting circles whose overlapping parts and common borders are shaded or marked by a cross in order to encode the mood of the syllogism). But Venn diagrams

218 *Politzer*

are an automatized method to encode the premises, work out a solution, and decode it. They have two characteristics: they are external representations, and they support an algorithmic method of resolution (and in this sense are operative). No claim of psychological validity (as internal representation) has been made for Venn diagrams. Such a claim does not seem tenable because it is hard to see how the eight areas defined by the three overlapping circles and the areas obtained by addition or subtraction of these could ever be kept in working memory; it is precisely the power of the graphical method to help visualize so many areas that makes the method efficacious.

Leibniz's straight line diagrams

Leibniz's diagrams are described in an undated 18-page opuscule (1988). In the line diagrams, a class is represented by a straight line, and the two classes of a categorical sentence by two parallel lines whose ends are determined by the relation that the two classes entertain. The four basic categorical sentences are represented in Figure 9.1. The vertical dotted lines indicate that a statement is made relating the two classes.

To represent a syllogism, the major premise is placed on lines one and two (with the middle term on line two) and the minor premise on lines two and three. By considering lines one and three, which represent the relation

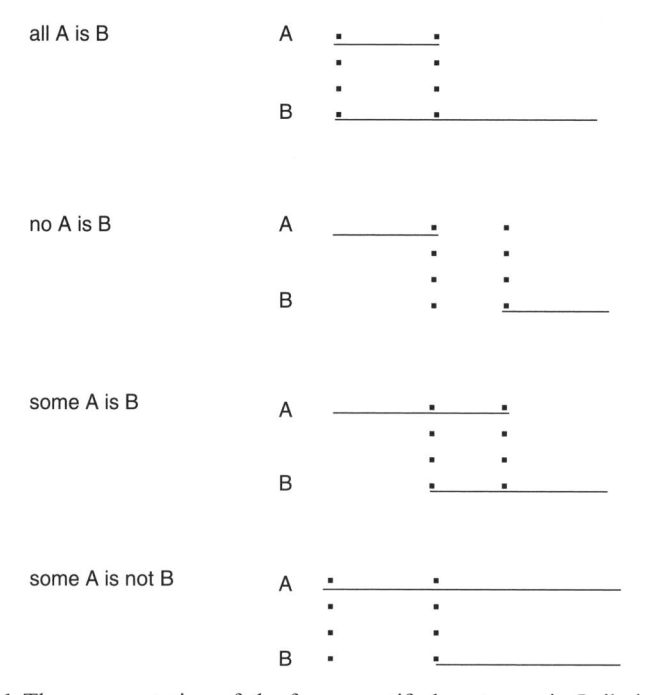

Figure 9.1 The representation of the four quantified sentences in Leibniz's straight lines system.

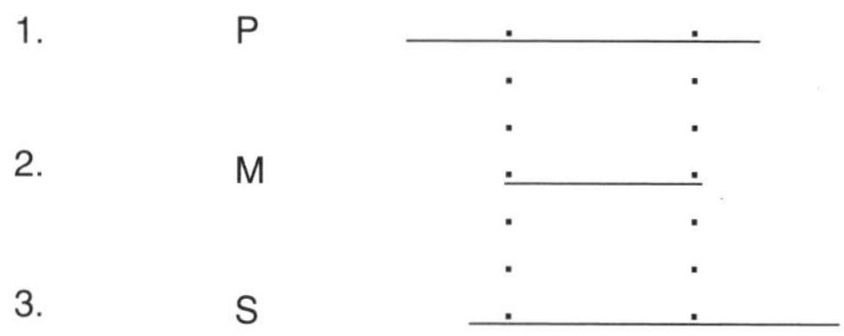

```
1.      P       _____   .      .
                          .      .
2.      M         ._____.
                          .      .
                          .      .
3.      S             ._____
```

lines 1 & 2: all M is P
lines 2 & 3: all M is S
lines 1 & 3: some S is P

Figure 9.2 Leibniz line diagram for the AA-3 syllogism.

between the end terms, one produces the vertical dotted lines if necessary, and reads off the solution. An example is given in Figure 9.2, in which it can be seen how easy it is to read the solution.

There is a remarkable feature in Leibniz's lines: whereas a horizontal line represents the extension of a class, a vertical line represents a single member; consequently, the intersecting points of a vertical line with the three horizontal lines describe one single entity that can be considered from the point of view of its belonging to either one of the classes or to more than one class (when there is more than one intersection). The same obtains of course with circle diagrams: one point in the common part of, say, S and M can be viewed as an S individual or an M individual. The important idea underlying Leibniz's representation, whether in lines or in circles, is that an individual (e.g., a point in A) that is considered *qua* A can also be considered *qua* B whenever the two classes A and B intersect: it enables a multiple characterization, and a subsequent change in perspective (the topic, or subject shifting from one class to another one).

What use did Leibniz make of his diagrams? The answer is the same for the straight lines and for the circles, as they are isomorphic: they were used for illustration purposes, each concluded syllogism being accompanied by one single line diagram together with its unique circle diagram counterpart. To some extent, Leibniz chose for each syllogism one prototypical diagram (often the only possible one, of course); the point is that he did not envisage the possible multiple configurations for each syllogism.

The current psychological theory that makes extensive use of diagrams is the mental model theory. Leibniz's lines share two important features with diagrams used by mental model theory: (i) the extension of a class is represented along a line (a graphical line in the former case, an alignment of a number of tokens in the latter case); and (ii) the relation between two classes is captured by the relative position or shift of the two lines along their common direction, allowing for the presence or the absence of members common to the two classes on a perpendicular line.

Euler's circles

The definition of Euler's circles and how he used them can be found in a few of his *Lettres à une Princesse d'Allemagne*, written in 1761 (Euler, 1842). The author's aim is essentially a didactical exposition of the theory of the syllogism (and indeed it is a remarkable achievement from this point of view). It is doubtful that the author had a stronger objective in mind, such as offering a method of proof. Referring to his way of representing propositions, he says: "this way will disclose [French *nous découvrira*] the correct forms of all the syllogisms", an ambiguous expression which, as we will see, should be interpreted in its loose sense: Euler's aim is more to illustrate than to demonstrate. Another consequence of this genre of exposition (letters written by a tutor do not constitute a treatise) is that what is gained in clarity is often lost in conceptual depth: Euler seldom elaborates to justify his method.

After remarking that

> since a general notion contains an infinity of individual objects, it is regarded as a space in which all these individuals are enclosed (p. 410),

Euler gives the representation of the four propositions as in Figure 9.3. Notice that the A proposition is given a strict inclusion representation. For the I proposition,

> a part of space A will lie inside space B, as it is well visible that some thing that is contained in notion A is also contained in notion B (p. 411).

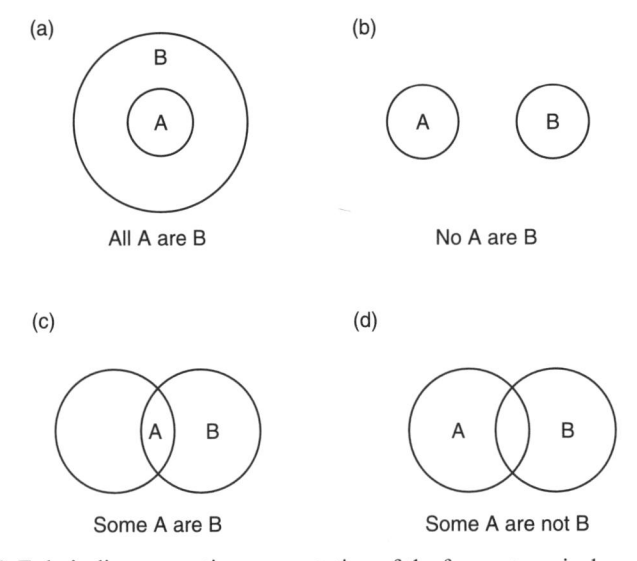

Figure 9.3 Euler's diagrammatic representation of the four categorical propositions.

Accordingly, the letters A and B in the diagram (Figure 9.3c) denote two spaces which do not have the same status: while B labels the B class (or notion), A marks the area that captures the concept of a common part to two notions (and foreshadows the concept of set intersection). Similarly, the representation of the O proposition is defined as follows:

> a part of space A must lie out of space B [. . .]; here it will be noticed chiefly that there is something in notion A which is not comprised in notion B, or which lies out of this notion (p. 411).

and while the letter B in the diagram (Figure 9.3d) just labels the B class, the letter A marks the area crucial to represent the concept of the part of A that is not B (the difference between A and B in set-theoretical terms) which may be all or only part of the A class. This distinction is confirmed by the fact that in Figure 9.3d, A and B are symmetrical, which by parity would invite the unfortunate interpretation that some B are not A, were the notational difference just mentioned not kept in mind. It is with these four diagrams only that Euler tackles the task of identifying the valid syllogisms (and showing in passing how to identify the invalid ones). A century earlier, Leibniz had made exactly the same choice for the representation of the four basic sentences.

Euler's method is the following. First, make the single diagram that represents the major premise (so representing the relation between M and P). Second, integrate the minor premise by (i) placing S with respect to M, which is easy because there is only one way of representing a proposition, while (ii) considering at the same time whether S can have different positions in relation to P. These relative positions are among the following three: the notion S is either entirely contained in the notion P (inclusion), or partly contained (overlapping), or outside (exclusion). In brief, for any syllogism, it will be necessary to draw one, or two, or at most three diagrams.

Let us illustrate with the EI-1 syllogism: *no M are P; some S are M*. Given that the notion M is entirely out of the notion P, if the notion S has a part contained in the notion M, this part will certainly lie out of the notion P, like in Figure 9.4a; or in that way (Figure 9.4b), or yet in (Figure 9.4c).

Although this explanation is clear and convincing (so much so that, in fact, one could almost dispense with the diagrams) the usage of the diagrams is somehow incoherent. In effect, we could expect Euler to look for the conclusion by trying to identify in each diagram, in terms of S and P, one of the four basic propositional relations that he has defined. For instance in Figure 9.4c, the definitional pattern of an O sentence appears between S and P. However, Euler does not exploit this. Instead, he makes a non-definitional, intuitive use of the diagrams to support his demonstration (based on a container-content interpretation of the sentences). In the present case, the part common to M and S (in which S is aptly written) is considered in isolation and shown to lie necessarily out of P because it is part of M; but being also part of S it can be designated as *some S*, hence the conclusion *some S is not P*.

222 Politzer

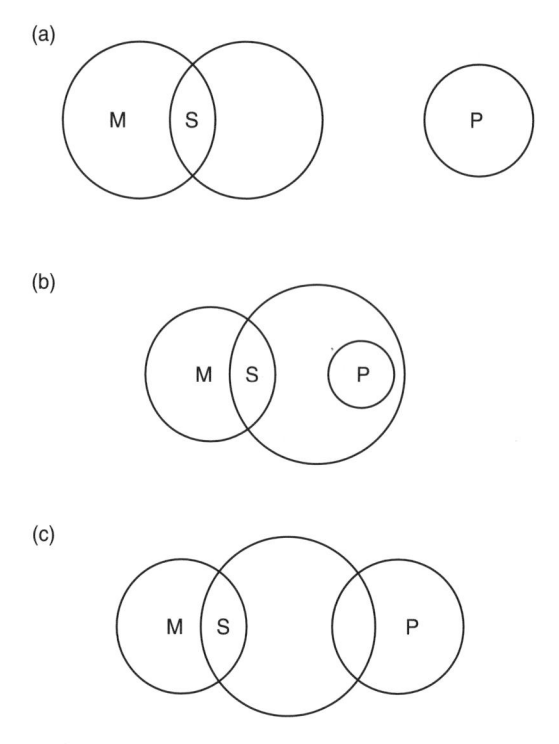

(a)

[Diagram: two overlapping circles labeled M and S, and a separate circle labeled P]

(b)

[Diagram: two overlapping circles labeled M and S, with a smaller circle labeled P inside the S region but outside M]

(c)

[Diagram: two overlapping circles labeled M and S, and a circle labeled P overlapping with S]

Figure 9.4 Euler's diagrams for the EI-1 syllogism.

This applies to all three diagrams (9.4a, b, and c). There is one good reason for this usage of the diagrams, which appears clearly in Figure 9.4a and b: these exhibit respectively the two interpretations of the O sentence that Euler has not considered in his definitional diagram; as a consequence he is prevented from reading the O relation between S and P off each diagram; rather, as just seen, he argues in terms of the relation between the intersection labelled S, and P.

Notice that in Euler's usage of the diagrams, it is not even necessary to draw more than one diagram. For instance, even an undetermined diagram such as the one given in Figure 9.5 demonstrates that P and M lying entirely out of each other, any part of M cut out by S will remain out of P (assuming the border of S to be closed and convex).[7] Interestingly, Leibniz gives exactly the same diagram as Euler's (Figure 9.4a) for EI-1, and he always restricts himself to a single diagram whatever the syllogism under consideration.

Thus, one can wonder why Euler took the trouble to represent multiple diagrams of syllogisms. This is necessary in order to be exhaustive only if diagrams are used as a search procedure to identify the conclusion in terms of each basic proposition. For example, for the EI-1 syllogism, one can interpret the relation between the S and P terms and notice that the only solution compatible with the three diagrams is the O sentence. This is very much

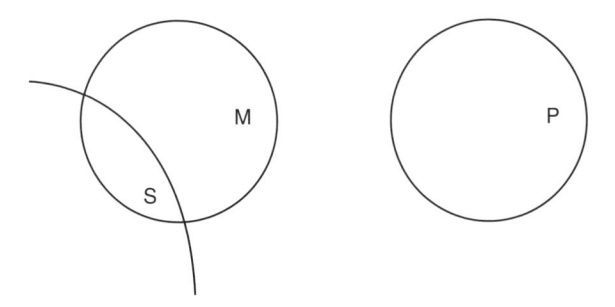

Figure 9.5 A single diagram summarizing diagrams 4a, 4b, and 4c.

reminiscent of the mental model theory, and indeed the three diagrams are identical with those produced by this theory. However, this agreement does not always obtain. There are several reasons for that. One is just some carelessness on the part of the author; for example, for the OA-2 syllogism, Euler gave two diagrams (the same ones as mental model theory) but in the preceding letter he gave only one diagram for the AO-2 syllogism even though he recognized that it was the same as OA-2 (the latter being non-standard), which he discarded as redundant for that reason. Another reason is that there are optional parts in the diagrams of mental model theory, which on some occasions yield fewer diagrams than Euler's method (e.g., one diagram instead of two for IA-4). Yet another, more fundamental, reason is due to the restriction imposed by having a single diagram for each sentence, which cuts the combinatorial analysis. Interestingly, on only four occasions does this lead to an ambiguous conclusion: on AO-2 for the reason noticed earlier, and on OA-3, IA-3, and IA-4 the two diagrams support both an O and an I solution. The unwarranted solution would be eliminated if the O (resp. I) premise was allowed a possible exclusion (resp. inclusion) interpretation.

To return to the question raised, we can speculate that although Euler made a figurative usage of his diagrams, he must have recognized the potential operative usage of them *as a method of proof*. The necessity of the combinatorial exploitation that such a usage implies must have been so compelling that he could not refrain from applying it even though his figurative usage of the diagrams did not require it.

There is, however, one domain where it was appropriate to look for alternative diagrams, namely the identification of the invalid forms. Here the method is straightforward: try to show that the relation of S to P can be either an exclusion, or an overlap, or an inclusion. For this, three diagrams are required. Euler provided the demonstration for IA-1 and IA-3 together, for II-1 and II-3, and also for the non standard IE-1 and IE-3 considered from a standard point of view. He did not review the other cases, including the cases (the EO and OE syllogisms) where the method fails (yielding an

O solution) again for lack of considering the exclusive interpretation of the O sentence.

To summarize, Euler did not develop an algorithmic use of the diagrams that would enable one to identify the valid syllogisms and provide their conclusion. This would have required different definitions of the basic diagrams (about which more below). To such an operative usage of diagrams, he preferred a figurative usage supporting the interpretation of the various syllogisms. This interpretation in turn reflects the interpretation of the *IS A* relation in terms of container-content which he chose for didactical reasons:

> the foundation of all these forms [of syllogisms] consists, in short, in these two principles on the nature of container and content: (i) all that is in the content is also in the container. (ii) all that is out of the container is also out of the content (p. 421).

The extraordinary ease with which syllogisms seem to be understood, and even most of the time solved, under a container-content construal of them is certainly of great psychological interest. Consider for instance the OA-3 syllogism which is very seldom passed, and let us follow the royal tutor:

> Assume [. . .] that a part of the notion A lies out of the notion B. In that case, if the third notion C contains the notion A entirely, it will certainly also have a part out of notion B [. . .], hence this syllogism: some A are not B; all A are C; therefore some C are not B (pp. 419–420).

Euler's explanations consist in reformulating the argument, replacing all ARE, no ARE, some ARE, some ARE NOT with *is entirely contained in, is entirely out of, is partly in, is partly out* respectively, and this seems enough to deeply modify the task. Apparently, the human being who (as shown by nearly a century of experiments and over two millennia of painful exposition to logic treatises) is not cognitively equipped to solve the majority of the syllogisms worded with the underdetermined IS A relation, seems to become an expert (admittedly, experimental data are missing) at solving the same syllogisms worded in container-content terms. A possible reason for this will be considered later.

Gergonne's circles

We have noticed Euler's choice of one, and only one, diagrammatic representation for each proposition (and the unfortunate consequences of this choice from a proof-oriented point of view). The consideration of the five possible relative positions of two circles in the same plane (the circles representing two "ideas", one being a subject and the other a predicate) is due to Gergonne (1816–1817).[8] He expounded the correspondence between the four propositions of the natural language and the five logical relations, which by now

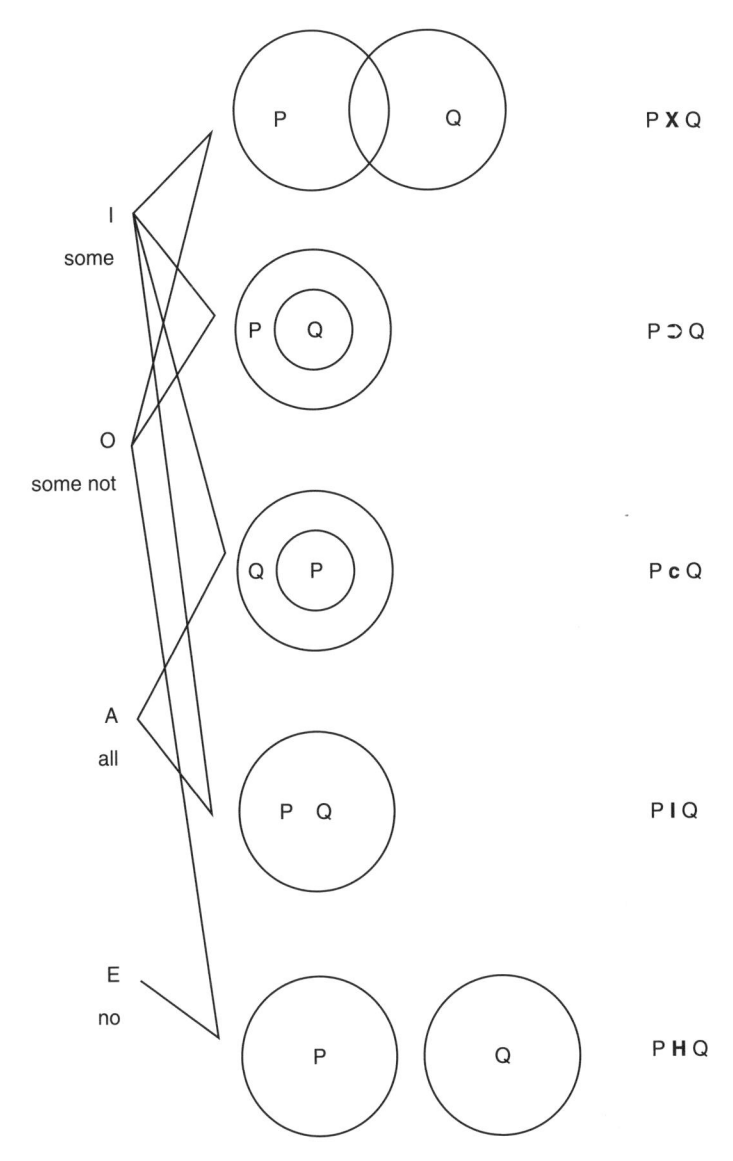

Figure 9.6 Gergonne's diagrams and their mapping onto the four categorical propositions.

has become familiar, not by giving the mapping of the former onto the latter, but in the form of two tables. The mapping between the four propositions and the five diagrams is given in Figure 9.6 using the symbols proposed by Gergonne for each of the five relations.[9]

The relations can be paraphrased as follows (notice the explicit quantification of the predicate):

226   *Politzer*

- P X Q: a part of P is part of Q;
- P ⊃ Q: a part of P is the whole of Q
- P c Q: the whole of P is a part of Q;
- P I Q: the whole of P is the whole of Q;
- P H Q: no part of P is a part of Q.

The Gergonne correspondence displays the semantics of quantified sentences and it is far more complicated than a one-to-one correspondence. It poses the following questions: (i) the semantic question: Why is the mapping not one-to-one? (ii) the pragmatic question: How does one restrict the number of choices from diagram to propositions and from proposition to diagrams? (iii) the psycholinguistic question: Given a proposition, are all its related diagrams psychologically equivalent?

The first question is why natural languages have not evolved to produce one and only one expression for each relation. One putative answer, based on the general assumption that language reflects cognitive constraints, is the following. Given any two concepts, in the absence of a priori knowledge about the world, an individual is not in a position to express a judgement coinciding with any of the five basic states or relations, but this state of ignorance changes with experience. Take some of our ancestors who may have had no a priori judgement about the relative extension of mushrooms and poisonous things. One of them has a bad experience, and it may be important to communicate belief in this newly discovered state of the world where there are poisonous mushrooms; this can be communicated by a unique expression, namely, in our evolved language, *some*. At this stage, the fifth relation is eliminated but there is not enough information to know which of the four diagrams for *some* obtains: this is matter of further experience or of systematic enquiry. Only after more data have been gathered will it be possible to know (or at least start knowing) which is the state of the world.[10] In brief, because there is not enough information, the new belief, *some mushrooms are poisonous*, has to be communicated without qualification. Now, some more experience may reveal two different states of the world:

- One, that there are occasions when no poisoning occurs after eating mushrooms. Communicating this revised belief may have survival interest if mushrooms are the only food available. This can be done by qualifying *some* either (i) by *only:* only *some mushrooms are poisonous;* or (ii) by using a negation: *some mushrooms are poisonous* but some are not. Either of diagrams 1 and 2 refer to this state. Which one is the case again may still not be decidable for lack of information but nevertheless the judgement that both represent can be communicated as indicated.
- Two, that there is always poisoning after eating mushrooms, in which case there is a need to extend *some;* the linguistic device *all* does just that: *all mushrooms are poisonous* communicates this new belief compatible

only with diagrams 3 and 4 (and again this will suffice pending new information). It seems that there is no lexical device in English to further distinguish the two diagrams for *all* and also (in the background knowledge that *some* is the case) the two diagrams for *only some* (or *some are not*).

To summarize: after the very first experience, in a language lexicalized with the five relations, one would have to state: *P X Q or P ⊃ Q or P c Q or P I Q* in order to express the important belief that there are P that are Q: *some P are Q* fulfils this purpose much more economically. Similarly, by iteration of the same principle, in a situation of emergency it is more appropriate to state *only some P are Q* than *P X Q or P ⊃ Q*, and also *all P are Q* than *P c Q or P I Q*. In brief, the mapping between relative extensions of properties in the world and natural language seems optimal from the viewpoints of ease and efficiency in communicating information: natural language is well adapted as it is.

The second question concerns the pragmatics of quantifiers and it will be treated succinctly. Consider first the mapping from right to left: on each of the five cases it is one to two. The problem is to decide which of the two verbal expressions to choose and we shall see that this choice is determined by considerations of relevance (Sperber & Wilson, 1986), which in turn depend on the background assumptions about the hearer's beliefs. We assume each time that the speaker is knowledgeable, i.e., that she has obtained enough evidence to support the relation under consideration.

The first two relations, P X Q and P ⊃ Q, are mapped onto I and O and will be treated together. The relevant information is that which helps the hearer to eliminate states of the world. The speaker chooses a *some* sentence or a *some are not* sentence on the basis of her assumptions about the hearer's beliefs regarding the states of the world that obtain. Suppose an initial background where P H Q is already known to be false (i.e., where, by elimination, the background is made of the first four relations); then the relevant contrast is between the first two and the next two relations, so that a *some not* sentence is appropriate because it eliminates the third and fourth states. On the contrary, in an initial background of uncertainty with regard to P H Q, the relevant contrast is between all first four relations on the one hand and P H Q on the other hand, and a *some* sentence is appropriate because it eliminates P H Q. (The speaker may even use the awkward *some are and some are not* sentence if both pieces of information are estimated useful to the hearer as an additional contrast against P c Q and P I Q when P H Q is uncertain.) Logically, the choice amounts to a detachment from I&O: detach I or detach O, whichever is relevant. The same applies to the P ⊃ Q relation.

Suppose now the speaker believes one of the next two relations (P c Q or P I Q); there is a similar choice to be made, but this time between *all* and *some:* in an initial background where P H Q is known to be false, an *all* sentence is appropriate because it enables the hearer to eliminate the first two relations. Whereas in an initial background where P H Q is uncertain, both *all* and *some* are *logically* appropriate: *some* eliminates P H Q, and *all* eliminates P H Q and also P X Q and P ⊃ Q.

For instance, suppose the wizard has made many trials and concludes that the local mushrooms and poisonous food are related as per P c Q or P I Q. In order to convey this discovery to someone who believes that some mushrooms are poisonous, he will say that *all mushrooms are poisonous*, so contrasting P I Q (or P c Q) with the other three relations, thereby eliminating them. But if the hearer's background knowledge is ignorance, there are logically two possible utterances: *all mushrooms are poisonous*, because it contrasts with P H Q and also with P X Q and P ⊃ Q, and *some mushrooms are poisonous*, because it contrasts with P H Q. However, while the *all* sentence, which eliminates the most states of the world, is optimally relevant to express the P c Q (or the P I Q) relation, the *some* sentence is not, because it eliminates fewer states (only the P H Q state). This means that, given a presumption of optimal relevance, a *some* sentence is not appropriate to express the P c Q (or the P I Q) relation. Therefore, if a *some* sentence is used, the hearer can infer that among the relations mapped onto *some*, only the relations other than P c Q (or the P I Q), namely P X Q (or P ⊃ Q) are being expressed. This inference is the source of the well-known conversational implicature (Grice, 1975; Horn, 1989) which gives to *some* its interpretation *some but not all* and countermands its use to express an *all* state of the world.[11] The same situation obtains, *mutatis mutandis*, for the *no/some not* opposition as for the *all/some* opposition, for the same reasons and needs no specific treatment; there is only a change in the background assumption, which is (P c Q or P I Q) instead of P H Q.

Before taking up the psycholinguistic question, it will be useful to complement the correspondence with the *converse* propositions. The mathematical formalism, with P in the first position and Q in the second one, conceals that in ordinary language the converses are very natural: for instance, the **X** relation can be characterized as naturally by *some Q are not P* as by *some P are not Q*; still, such converses do not appear in Gergonne's first two tables. (They appear later in another form.) So, at this stage, the mapping fails to exhaust the meaning of the diagrams. This is why a more complete mapping is presented in Figure 9.7, in which *some Q are not P* (noted O′) and *all Q are P* (noted A′) have been introduced.

Now, on the right of Figure 9.7 there appears a formula for each relation, which shows that they all are a conjunction of three propositions. For example, an exhaustive description of the first diagram P **X** Q is: *some P are Q and some P are not Q and some Q are not P*. It will be noticed that across the first four relations, I is an invariant, as expected since they all are mapped onto I; similarly, O is an invariant across relations **X**, ⊃, and H; and A is invariant across relations **c** and **I**; while E is of course invariant for its single relation H; similar invariance obtains for A′ and O′.

For each proposition type in turn, we can now ask the question, Is there a diagram, that is, a formula, more fundamental than the others? The answer is

$P \mathbf{X} Q = \underline{I} \& \underline{O} \& \underline{O}'$

$P \supset Q = I \& \underline{O} \& A'$

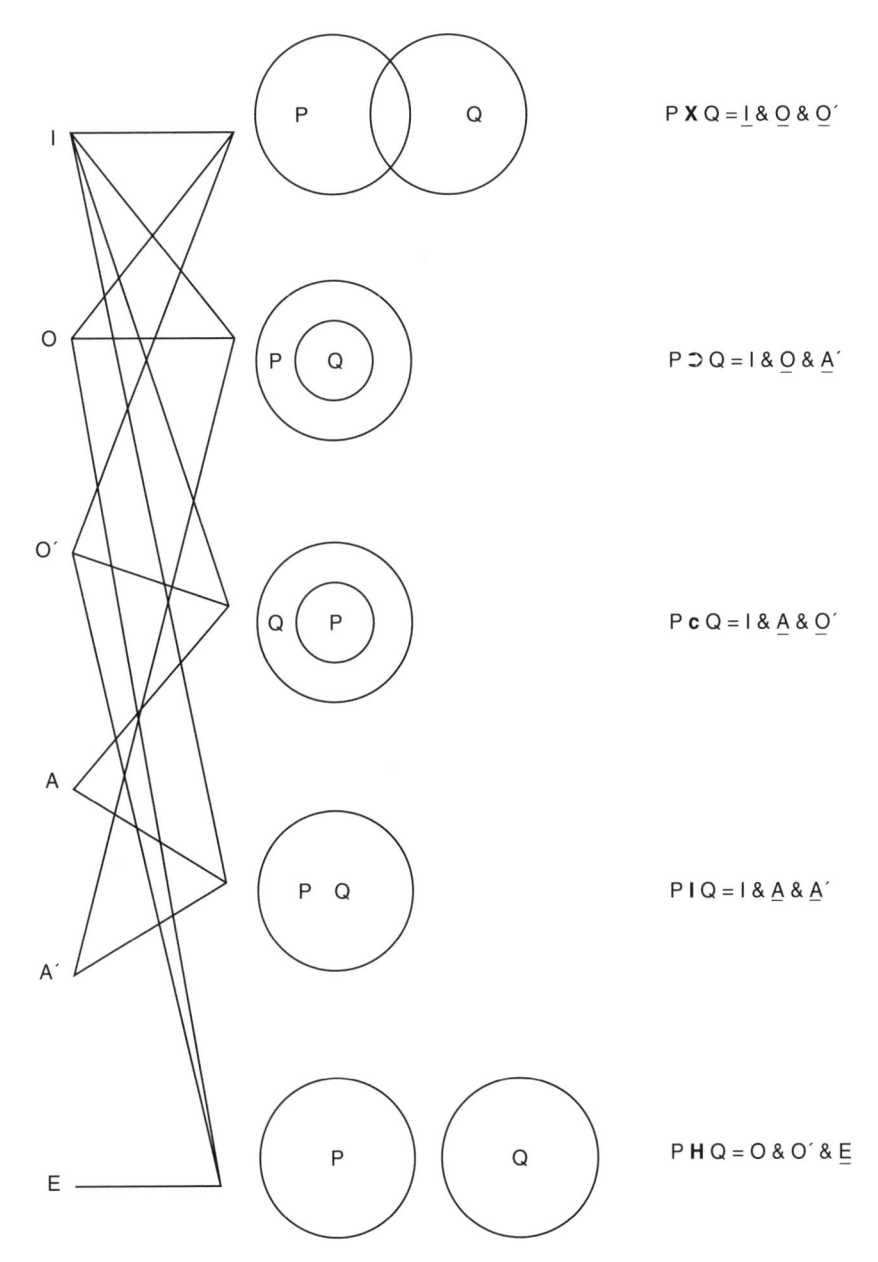

$P \mathbf{c} Q = I \& \underline{A} \& \underline{O}'$

$P I Q = I \& \underline{A} \& \underline{A}'$

$P H Q = O \& O' \& \underline{E}$

Figure 9.7 Gergonne's diagrams complemented with converse propositions and their formulas.

easy, and it is affirmative. It results from the observation that for each formula except the first, one or two of the components are logically implied by another one: I is implied by A as well as by A', and O and O' are implied by E. The definitional sentential components of each relation have been underlined accordingly.

The simplest case is the E proposition for which there is nothing to add: it has only one diagram. Next, the A proposition has two equally fundamental diagrams: in both the **c** and the **I** diagrams, A is a definitional component. Contrary to what is generally claimed, there is not one single logically "correct" diagram to represent the A sentence (supposed to be the strict inclusion **c**, while the identity **I** would result from a conversion error): there are two equally correct representations differing by their third components, which negate each other: in one case it is A', the converse of A, and in the other case it is O'. A testable consequence of this claim is that people should be willing to identify A sentences with both diagrams equally (provided, of course, that the sentence does not refer to known states of the world in which one, and only one, of the diagrams obtains).

The O proposition has three diagrams but in the last one (**H**) the O component is obtained by inference, so that for *some not* there are two diagrams that do not require an inference and are fundamental for that reason, **X** and ⊃. Again, a testable consequence is that people should be reluctant to identify the **H** diagram with *some not*, whereas they should equally accept **X** and ⊃ as representations for it.

Finally, the I proposition has four diagrams but only in the **X** relation is the I component not inferred, so that although the four diagrams are logically correct, one of them is psychologically more fundamental than the others because it does not require an inference for the concept of "common part" to be identified in the diagram. The testable consequence is that people should show a preference for the overlap relation.[12]

Studies of the comprehension of quantified sentences confirm that the overlapping position plays a more fundamental role, similar to that of a prototype. For example, in Begg and Harris's (1982) study, when people were asked to distribute 100 points over the five Gergonne diagrams, for the I sentence the overlapping position received the absolute majority of the points (63%) while the next choice (P **c** Q) received only 21% of the points. Interestingly, for the O sentence, the points were equally shared by the overlapping (45%) and the B included in A (44%) diagrams, as predicted by the inferential analysis just proposed. And similarly for the A sentence, people's choices were not far from equality between identity (**I** : 57%) and inclusion (**c**: 43%).

Coming back to Euler's choice of diagrams to represent propositions, one is better able to explain what must have motivated it. His didactical obligations may have recommended a single diagram for the sake of simplicity, but why precisely the overlapping configuration for the I proposition? Our analysis answers this question: the I proposition has one diagram provided with the property of greater ease for judgement of representation, namely the overlapping position. For the O and A propositions, Euler's choice coincides with one of the diagrams that we have identified as equally easy. Notice that Leibniz's choice for representing the four basic sentences was exactly the same; this is interesting because in all likelihood Euler was not aware of Leibniz's diagrams, which were discovered and published only in the first years of the 20th century.

Finally, what is the psychological plausibility that the Gergonne diagrams be the basis for a mental representation of quantified propositions? The one-to-several mapping between linguistic quantifiers and diagrams is a common argument against this plausibility (Johnson-Laird & Bara, 1984) because of a "combinatorial explosion" when integrating two propositions. However, the argument is not compelling: people might limit their usage of the correspondence to the preferred diagrams (just as Euler did), or they could have a more flexible representation in which there is, for each proposition, one basic diagram marked with compulsory and optional parts; this proposal was made by Wetherick (1993) and applied by Stenning and Oberlander (1995). For instance, in Wetherick's representation, a *some* sentence is based on the basic overlapping position; but only the central "lens" is drawn with a continuous line, while the left and right arcs are drawn with a dotted line whose limits indicate optional areas. With reference to Figure 9.7, this diagram shows an **X** relation underlining the invariance of I (the common part); suppressing the left dotted line, or the right one, or both, amounts to negating O, or O', or both in the formula I&O&O', so changing the diagram into I&A&O' (P c Q), or I&O&A' (P ⊃ Q), or I&A&A' (P I Q), respectively.

THE VERBAL STRATEGY

Recent investigations

We will consider first the modern versions of Störring's insertion strategy and begin with Ford (1995). About one half of her subjects exhibited on the majority of the syllogisms what she calls a "substitution behaviour", that is, replacing one term in a premise with another, as if solving an algebraic problem. The substitution also appeared in the form of arrows linking terms in the premises, or in the form of terms crossed and replaced with another term. Using the IA-4 syllogism as an example *(some P are M; all M are S)*, Ford says that the second premise allows one to give the value of S to M; the value of S can be substituted for M in the first premise, giving the conclusion. This amounts to collapsing Störring's insertion and abstraction processes.[13]

Ford formalizes the substitution procedure as follows. The premise that provides the replacement term plays the role of a rule relating membership of class C and property P, while the premise that contains the term to be replaced provides specific objects whose status with regard to C or P is known. The following rules guide the process of substitution (Ford, 1995, p. 21):

> A. If a rule exists affirming of every member of the class C the property P then (1) whenever a specific object, O, that is a member of C is encountered it can be inferred that O has the property P, and (2) whenever a specific object, O, that lacks property P is encountered it can be inferred that O is not a member of C.
>
> B. If a rule exists denying of every member of the class C the property P then (1) whenever a specific object, O, that is a member of C is encountered it can be inferred that O does not have the property P, and (2) whenever a specific object, O, that possesses the property P is encountered it can be inferred that O is not a member of C.

Notice that individual objects are introduced, an important point about which more will be said later. Apart from this novelty, there is formally nothing new in these rules. They were already spelled out (in their universal formulation) 300 years ago in the Logic of Port-Royal. In the chapter on syllogisms, Arnauld and Nicole (1978, p. 21) formulate the *principle of the affirmative moods* for the first figure as follows: "that which applies to an idea taken universally, also applies to all that of which this idea is affirmed". Using Ford's names for classes, the property P which applies to all the C also applies to the object O of which C is affirmed: this is rule A1. Similarly, the *principle of the negative moods* (still for the first figure) says that "that which is denied of an idea taken universally is denied of all that of which this idea is affirmed." In other words, the property P denied of all the C is also denied of the object O of which C is affirmed: this is rule B1. In fact, these two principles of the first figure have a much longer history: they were referred to by the Scholastic logicians, in a more synthetic formulation including both of them, as the *dictum de omni et nullo*. Finally, the *principle of the AEE and AOO moods* for the second figure given by the Port-Royal logic expresses rule A2: "whatever is included in the extension of a universal idea does not apply to any of the subjects of which it is denied." That is, being part or whole of those C which have the property P does not apply to those O of which P is denied.[14] In brief, Ford claims that her rules, which are the singular counterparts of formal principles identified by logicians of the past, have psychological reality, and she relates her claim to the fact that A1 and B1 are equivalent to modus ponens, and A2 and B2 are equivalent to modus tollens.

We now turn to Braine's (1998) contribution. In his essay on mental-predicate logic, he deals very shortly with categorical syllogisms. He only considers the reasons for individual differences in performance and identifies one of these reasons with possessing or not a strategy for choosing a *secondary topic* (p. 321):

Syllogistic reasoning 233

The strategy is to choose as secondary topic the subset of the subject of which the middle term can or cannot be predicated (the S that are, or are not, M, as determined by the premise relating S and M).

Once a secondary topic is chosen, it is transferred into the other premise: this executes Störring's insertion process. The resolution then proceeds in two steps: one is the application of either a generalization of modus ponens for predicate logic (equivalent to Ford's rules A1 and B1), or, by a *reductio ad absurdum*, of a modus tollens (equivalent to Ford's rules A2 and B2); the other is a schema of universal or existential generalization. Braine offers this example (EA-3): *none of the M are P; all of the M are S*. The secondary topic, *the S that are M*, is provided by the second premise; according to the first premise, *the S that are M are not P* (by modus ponens), hence: *some S are not P* (by existential generalization).

The notion that the verbal strategy hinges upon the insertion process, followed by the operation of modus ponens and modus tollens, also appears in one of the main hypotheses of Stenning and Yule's (1997) theoretical approach. They propose that syllogisms exist and are soluble owing to one of their structural properties, namely the *identification of individual cases*. An individual can be characterized by the fact that it possesses, or does not possess, the properties defined by three categories, S, M, and P which constitute the premises, so that there are eight types of individual: $S^+M^+P^+$; $S^+M^+P^-$; $S^+M^-P^+$; $S^+M^-P^-$; $S^-M^-P^+$; $S^-M^+P^-$; $S^-M^-P^+$; $S^-M^-P^-$. For each syllogism, the joint premises warrant or do not warrant the existence of such individuals: in the affirmative, the syllogism has a conclusion. The authors describe two procedures for identifying individual cases, one analogical by models, the other by rules, which constitute two different implementations of a common underlying abstract individual identification algorithm.

For the analogical procedure, the authors apply the graphical algorithm defined by Stenning and Oberlander (1995). As mentioned above, a "combinatorial explosion" ensuing from the use of Gergonne diagrams is not obliged: each diagram has a minimal representation defined by the "critical regions", that is, those that must exist if the premise is true (these correspond to the invariants in the Gergonne formulas mentioned above). A simple procedure follows to integrate the premises. If there remains a critical region in the diagram restricted to the end terms, this is the diagram of the conclusion; if not, there is no conclusion.

The verbal procedure is described in the form of a three-step algorithm. At the first step, a "source premise" is selected: this is the premise that will provide the first two terms of the individual description. One of these is necessarily the middle term M. At the next step, it is compared with its occurrence in the other premise from the viewpoint of quality. There are three possible cases: (i) if the qualities match and M is subject of the other premise, a modus ponens is applied whose conclusion (which is the predicate of the other premise) provides the third term of the individual description; (ii) if the qualities do not match, and M is the predicate of the other premise, this means that there is a M^+ and a M^-, which allows a modus tollens whose conclusion (which is the subject of the other premise) again provides the third term of the individual description; (iii) if none of the two previous cases occurs, there is no conclusion. At the third step, the M term is eliminated and a quantifier is introduced. We exemplify with AO-2: *all the P are M; some S are not M*. The source premise is the second premise, which contains a negated M (M^-); this provides S^+M^- for the first two terms of the individual description. Since in the first premise M is predicate and affirmative, modus tollens applies: *all the P are M; not-M* yields *not-P*, that is P^-, which completes the individual description to yield $S^+M^-P^-$, hence the conclusion: some S are not P.

In summary, Stenning and Oberlander's verbal algorithm specifies in detail Störring's insertion and abstraction process. It highlights the commonality in the approaches that we have considered: the first step is equivalent to, and specifies, Braine's choice of a secondary topic; the second and third steps coincide with, and specify Ford's substitution process and application of rules, as well as Braine's application of inference schemas.

It has been mentioned that Stenning and Yule claim that both of their algorithms are implementations of a more abstract algorithm for individual case identification. Thus, this concept would be at the heart of syllogism solving, and in particular it would account for the process of insertion in the verbal strategy. The rest of this chapter will be devoted to showing that Störring's insertion process and its more recent variants appear explicitly in Aristotle's writings, and that Stenning and Yule's concept of individual case identification, which seems to capture the essence of the syllogism, is implicitly present in one of Aristotle's methods of proof.

Aristotle's methods of proof and ecthesis

As is well known, in order to identify the concluding modes, Aristotle distinguished two methods of proof, and a subsidiary one. Since the first two involve a "reduction" in two different senses, it is wise to follow Bochenski (1970) and call them the *direct* and the *indirect method*, respectively. The *direct method* consists of the transformation of the syllogism into a perfect one by the conversion of one or both premises; in addition, depending on the syllogism, it may be necessary to apply one or both of the following operations: the transposition of the premises, and the conversion of the conclusion. Thus, this method (often called *method of conversion* for that reason) requires knowledge of the conversion of I and E propositions: *some A are B* to *some B are A; no A are B* to *no B are A;* and *all A are B* to *some B are A* (called *conversion by limitation*).

Not all syllogisms can be proved by conversion, and a complementary method is needed. This second method, the *indirect method* applies a *reductio ad impossibile*. Given a syllogism $P, Q \therefore C$, it consists of conjoining the negation of the conclusion *(not-C)* to one of the premises, say *P*, and showing that *P, not-C*/*not-Q* is a perfect syllogism. It is a fairly sophisticated method for non-logicians, and one should not expect to find participants in psychological experiments applying it (especially when the conclusion is not provided). In contrast, the direct method, in the simple cases where only one or two conversions are involved, is easy to execute. Since the rules of I and E conversion are mastered by a majority of people (Begg & Harris, 1982; Newstead & Griggs, 1983; Politzer, 1990), one could expect that some individuals have a strategic use of the direct method. Unluckily, the usual methodology does not allow its identification; think-aloud protocols might be useful to look for this possibility.

All valid syllogisms can be solved by the direct or the indirect method. However, Aristotle mentions a third method, *ecthesis* (also called by classical authors the *method of exposition*), which he applies only a few times and always in a rather allusive manner. This lack of precision, and also the fact that such an alternative method of proof was not necessary, has aroused many comments and speculations about Aristotle's motivation (Kneale & Kneale, 1978). Here is the passage with the most explicit use of ecthesis, aiming to give the proof of AAI-3 (*all M are P; all M are S ∴ some S are P*):

> ... if both P and S belong to every M, should one of the Ms, e.g. N, be taken, both P and S will belong to this, and thus P will belong to some S.
>
> (*Analytica Priora*, 6, 28a; transl. Ross. Names of classes changed to fit this chapter's notations)

Here Aristotle executes the extraction (which is the meaning of *ecthesis*) of "one of the Ms", calls it N, of which P and S are still predicated, and states that from this it follows that P is predicated of S. Lukasiewicz points out that, as objected in the 3rd century AD by Alexander of Aphrodisias (one of Aristotle's greatest commentators), in order for the conclusion to follow, one would have to assume N to be a sub-class of M and apply AAI-3 to *all N are P; all N are S*, again an AAI-3 syllogism, which is entirely circular. Rather, Alexander proposed a non-logical interpretation of the passage, according to which N is an *individual* of which it is easy, *through perception*, to predicate both P and S, and so realize that *some P is S*.

In brief, this is a *psychological* interpretation of Aristotle's obscure passage, which is of great interest to us because it shows how the intuition of a logician in antiquity meets the heuristic followed by logically naïve individuals in the 20th century, captured by the first step of Störring's insertion process: *to solve syllogisms, try first to extract an* individual *out of one premise*.

But is there not a *logical* interpretation of Aristotle's passage above? Modern analysts of Aristotle's syllogistic agree to answer affirmatively (Lear, 1980; Lukasiewicz, 1958; Patzig, 1968; Thom, 1981). A logical interpretation can be given on the assumption that in the present case, as on many other occasions, Aristotle limited himself to giving the sketch of a proof. The analyses diverge, in that for Lukasiewicz and Patzig the logical proof requires an existential quantification over a term; Patzig proposes the following law for ecthesis:

some B are A ≡ (∃C) [(all C are A) & (all C are B)]

(and a similar one, *mutatis mutandis*, for the *some not* case) from which the proof for AAI-3 follows easily. However, formally, there are difficulties linked with the fact that such laws insert syllogistic logic into propositional logic and second-order predicate logic.

The other interpretation of ecthesis, based on the extraction of an individual variable rather than of a class variable, does not have these shortcomings and Thom (1981) shows that it results in a simple system which contains singular and universal syllogisms. The only two singular syllogisms in the first figure are axioms. They are (**a** being an arbitrary instance of A, **b** of B, etc.) *all B are A; c is a B ∴ c is an A*, and *no B are A; c is a B ∴ c is not an A*. From the rule of proof *per impossibile*, taken as an axiom, and the previous two syllogisms, the only two singular syllogisms in the second figure follow: *all B are A; c is not an A ∴ c is not a B*, and *no B are A; c is an A ∴ c is not a B*. It will be noticed that these four syllogisms are identical with Ford's rules A1, B1, A2, B2, respectively. Adding the axiom *a is an A*, there follow from the two singular syllogisms in the first figure the following theses: *all A are B ∴ a is a B* and its negative counterpart *no A are B ∴ a is not a B* which both capture the concept of extraction of the individual **a** out of A. By an application of the first one to *b is an A; b is a C ∴ some C are A* (which is provable *per impossibile* applied to the second singular syllogism in the first figure) one reproduces Aristotle's proof of AAI-3. It can be seen that this proof explains Aristotle's by providing the missing step (the latter syllogism) that made it obscure, while justifying Alexander's intuitive rendering of it.

In brief, ecthesis is a logically correct method of proof, and comments such as Alexander's reflect, besides the lack of logical tools to justify it, the intuitive appeal of the logical principles on which it is based. In didactical situations, proof by ecthesis is very convincing, a sufficient indication that it captures something psychologically essential to solve syllogisms. Nevertheless, classical logicians lost interest and sight of it, and this had the unfortunate consequence that it has escaped psychologists' attention, at least consciously.

In agreement with Stenning and Yule's theory, the operative use of diagrams (whether Stenning & Oberlander's algorithm or Venn diagrams) and the container-content analogy enable one to solve syllogisms because they all enable the reasoner to catch *simultaneously* the three properties affirmed or denied of an individual (or of a set of individuals) and this probably captures the essence of syllogism solving. The container-content analogy is powerful in that it exploits our capacity to view simultaneously an individual as an A, a B, a C or their negation through a spatial interpretation of the abstract relation *IS A*. Now, with respect to this conceptualization, ecthesis can be viewed as a crucial step in that it primes the process of identification by providing an individual together with the first term of the description (a role played by Stenning & Yule's source premise). Störring's description of his participants' insertion process is the counterpart of this logical process observable among those participants who possess the strategy.

What about ecthesis within Aristotle's writings? It is fascinating that what seems to be at the heart of the *psychology* of syllogisms, namely the capability of extracting an entity in order to make a subsequent multiple affirmative or negative attribution, surfaces in the writings of the founder of the syllogistic. The fact that ecthesis was logically unnecessary (that is, unnecessary to prove the validity of syllogisms in his system), that Aristotle knew this (having proved all the syllogisms by the two main methods), but nevertheless used it, attests to its importance from a point of view different from logical. We can surmise that Aristotle must have recognized by introspection its role in reasoning, that is, in the mental process by which he himself, without any doubt a particularly skilled individual capable of using such a strategy, probably worked out the solution of some of them. Admittedly, this is pure speculation, but a psychologist involved in the study of syllogistic reasoning cannot refrain from considering such a hypothesis.

NOTES

1 The major part of the article is occupied by relational reasoning. It includes different kinds of two-premise arguments: spatial (e.g., S is to the left of D, R is to the right of D ∴ ?); temporal (e.g., action A is posterior to action C, action D is anterior to action C ∴ ?); linear (F is longer than K; L is shorter than K ∴ ?); and of equality (e.g., A = K; P = K ∴ ?).
2 A description of syllogisms is given in the Appendix.
3 The first figure being MP; SM, the inversion of the premises yields SM; MP which coincides with the fourth figure, as shown by the position of the middle term (the labels P and S are immaterial).
4 There is also, while solving an AA-4 syllogism (*all the P are M; all the M are S*) a report of a three-step stair configuration, with S, M, and P terms on the top, middle, and bottom steps, respectively.
5 Possibly by Boethius (6th century AD) according to Patzig (1968).
6 Straight lines can be found in Alstedius' (1614) work and circles in Sturm (1661).
7 Remarkably, one of Ford's participants did just that for IE-3 (1995, p. 61). This supports the hypothesis that people who use diagrams may have a figurative, rather than operative, use of them: in that case, the diagram operates in support of their verbal strategy to illustrate the principles that they apply at a metacognitive level.
8 In view of this, the expression "Euler circles", often used to refer to Gergonne's five diagrams, is a clear historical mistake. Although Gergonne himself explicitly refers to Euler, he correctly remarks that Euler failed to fully exploit his own idea.

9 Gergonne's paper actually does not contain any diagram!
10 In terms of causality (but this point of view is in no way obligatory) **P c Q** is a sufficient condition, **P ⊃ Q**, a necessary one, **P I Q** a necessary and sufficient condition, and **P X Q** a statistical correlation whose value depends on the extent of overlapping.
11 Horn (1989) notes that the Gricean view was anticipated by philosophers and logicians, starting with J. S. Mill who pointed out the *not all* inference made in natural language when interpreting I sentences.
12 Another prediction concerns reaction times: it should take people equal times to make *all* judgements on **c** and **I** diagrams; reaction times for *some not* judgements should be equal on **X** and **⊃** diagrams, and shorter than on **H** diagrams; and they should be shorter for *some* judgements on the **X** diagram than in **⊃**, **c**, and **I**.
13 Ford notes that this strategy must be used with care because equating two terms should not imply their universal equivalence: for example, in EA-4 (*no P are M; all M are S*), substituting S for M without precaution would yield *no P are S*, which is erroneous. She describes a "sophisticated substitution" applicable to similar cases.
14 Arnauld and Nicole did not give the counterpart of this principle for the moods EAE-2 and EIO-2 (the equivalent of B2) for reasons of economy: they prefer to justify them by appeal to the principle of the negative moods for the first figure applied after the conversion of the E premise (which turns these two syllogisms into the first figure).

REFERENCES

Arnauld, A., & Nicole, P. (1978). *La logique ou l'art de penser*. Paris: Flammarion. [*Logic, or the art of thinking*; originally published 1683.]
Barnes, J. (Ed.). (1984). *The complete works of Aristotle: The revised Oxford translation*. Princeton, NJ: Princeton University Press.
Begg, I., & Harris, G. (1982). On the interpretation of syllogisms. *Journal of Verbal Learning and Verbal Behaviour, 21*, 595–620.
Bochenski, I. M. (1970). *A history of formal logic*. New York: Chelsea Publishing Co. [Original German edn. 1956.]
Braine, M. D. S. (1998). Steps toward a mental-predicate logic. In M. D. S. Braine & D. P. O'Brien (Eds.), *Mental logic* (pp. 273–331). Mahwah, NJ: Lawrence Erlbaum Associates Inc.
Bucciarelli, M., & Johnson-Laird, P. N. (1999). Strategies in syllogistic reasoning. *Cognitive Science, 23*, 247–307.
Euler, L. (1842). *Lettres à une Princesse d'Allemagne sur divers sujets de physique et de philosophie*. Paris: Hachette. [*Letters to a princess of Germany on various subjects in physics and philosophy*; originally published 1768–1772.]
Ford, M. (1995). Two modes of mental representation and problem solution in syllogistic reasoning. *Cognition, 54*, 1–71.
Gardner, M. (1958). *Logic machines and diagrams*. Brighton, UK: Harvester Press.
Gergonne, J. (1816/1817). Essai de dialectique rationnelle [Essay on rational dialectic.] *Annales de Mathématiques Pures et Appliquées, 7*, 189–228.
Grice, H. P. (1975). Logic and conversation. In P. Cole & J. L. Morgan (Eds.), *Syntax and semantics, Vol 3: Speech acts* (pp. 41–58). New York: Academic Press.

Horn, L. R. (1989). *A natural history of negation*. Chicago: Chicago University Press.
Johnson-Laird, P. N., & Bara, B. G. (1984). Syllogistic inference. *Cognition*, 16, 1–61.
Kneale, W., & Kneale, M. (1978). *The development of logic* (1st Edn. 1962). Oxford: Clarendon Press.
Lear, J. (1980). *Aristotle and logical theory*. Cambridge: Cambridge University Press.
Leibniz, G. W. (1988). *Opuscules et fragments inédits*. Hildesheim: Georg Olms Verlag. [*Opuscula and unpublished fragments*, original edn. 1903, L. Couturat (Ed.), Paris: Alcan.]
Lukasiewicz, J. (1958). *Aristotle's syllogistic* (1st Edn. 1951). Oxford: Clarendon Press.
Newell, A. (1981). Reasoning, problem solving and decision processes: The problem space as a fundamental category. In R. Nickerson (Ed.), *Attention and performance, Vol. 8* (pp. 693–718). Hillsdale, NJ: Lawrence Erlbaum Associates Inc.
Newstead, S. E., & Griggs, R. A. (1983). Drawing inferences from quantified statements: A study of the square of opposition. *Journal of Verbal Learning and Verbal Behaviour*, 22, 535–546.
Patzig, G. (1968). *Aristotle's theory of the syllogism*. Dordrecht: Reidel. [Original German edn, 1958.]
Politzer, G. (1990). Immediate deduction between quantified sentences. In K. J. Gilhooly, M. T. G. Keane, R. H. Logie, & G. Erdos (Eds.), *Lines of thinking. Reflections on the psychology of thought* (pp. 85–97). London: Wiley.
Sperber, D., & Wilson, D. (1995) *Relevance: Communication and cognition* (1st Edn. 1986). London: Blackwell.
Stenning, K., & Oberlander, J. (1995). A cognitive theory of graphical and linguistic reasoning: Logic and implementation. *Cognitive Science*, 19, 97–140.
Stenning, K., & Yule, P. (1997). Image and language in human reasoning: A syllogistic illustration. *Cognitive Psychology*, 34, 109–159.
Störring, G. (1908). Experimentelle untersuchungen über einfache Schlussprozesse. *Archiv für die Gesamte Psychologie*, 11, 1–127.
Thom, P. (1981). *The syllogism*. München: Philosophia Verlag.
Wetherick, N. E. (1993). Psychology and syllogistic reasoning: Further considerations. *Philosophical Psychology*, 6, 423–440.

APPENDIX: A TRADITIONAL DESCRIPTION OF CATEGORICAL PROPOSITIONS AND OF SYLLOGISMS

Categorical propositions

From an extensional point of view, they affirm or deny that a class S is included in a class P in whole or in part, which gives four types of proposition:

all S are P (universal affirmative, called an A proposition)
no S are P (universal negative, called an E proposition)
some S are P (particular affirmative, called an I proposition)
some S are not P (particular negative called an O proposition)

Categorical syllogisms

They are deductive arguments made of three categorical propositions: the two premises and the conclusion. The three propositions taken together involve three classes, each of which occurs in two propositions. The three classes are labelled S, P, and M, (called the *terms* of the syllogism). P (the *major* term) occurs in the first premise (called the *major premise*) and as the predicate of the conclusion. S (the *minor* term) occurs in the second premise (called the *minor premise*) and as the subject of the conclusion, and M (the *middle term*) occurs in each premise but not in the conclusion. These constraints determine the following four dispositions, called *figures*:

	1	2	3	4
major premise	M P	P M	M P	P M
minor premise	S M	S M	M S	M S
conclusion	S P	S P	S P	S P

For each figure, there are 4(proposition types)$^{3\text{(propositions)}}$ = 64 manners of constituting a syllogism, called *moods*. Combining with the four figures, this yields 256 syllogisms designated by their abbreviated propositions and their figure number. For instance, EIO-1 designates: no M are P; some S are M ∴ some S are not P.

In psychology, the term *mood* is often used to refer only to the two premises presented to the participant. In this special sense, there are only $4^2 = 16$ moods. Investigators select their problems among 4 (figures) × 16 (moods) = 64 problems called *syllogisms* although they are only pairs of premises. (In this sense, the previous example will be called an EI-1 syllogism, omitting the conclusion O.)

With the conventional constraint that the conclusion should have the S term as a subject and the P term as a predicate (SP conclusion) there are only 19 valid syllogisms. But this constraint is hard to maintain when participants are required to produce their own response: they are free to give conclusions with P as a subject and S as a predicate as well (PS conclusions). After relaxing this constraint, there are 27 valid syllogisms, that is, syllogisms whose conclusion cannot be false if the premises are true.

10 History of the dual process theory of reasoning

Jonathan St. B. T. Evans

The authors of journal articles – conditioned as they are by the rewards and punishments handed out in editorial letters – present their research to the academic world in a stylized format. A student reading such articles must think that research starts with a full and balanced survey of the literature, the careful identification of unresolved issues and missing experiments, and the deduction of research hypotheses and experimental designs. There are good reasons for this convention – journals must contribute knowledge to their disciplines in an objective and collective manner. As a picture of the research process, however, it is a complete sham. The literature from which the research so logically follows was often unknown to the authors (unread or not yet published) at the time research was actually designed. The well-crafted journal article is a masterpiece of rationalization and post-hoc justification.

The unfortunate consequence of this convention is that one learns almost nothing about the process of research from reading the journals. It is therefore constitutes a rare – in my case unique – opportunity to be asked by the editors of this volume to present the history of the dual process theory of reasoning in personal terms: as it actually happened. Of course, the process will seem disorganized and chaotic, as I recall 30 years of trying to understand what goes on in people's heads when they take part in reasoning experiments in the psychological laboratory. In the process, I was assisted by many colleagues and collaborators with whom I worked directly, by findings of my own experiments which more often surprised and puzzled me than conformed to my prior predictions, and by reading as best I could the increasing numbers of reasoning papers that were produced by reasoning researchers around the world. In 1970, when I started, the field was quite small, much of it revolving around my PhD supervisor, Peter Wason. The field has grown exponentially over the years and changed its character and purpose almost out of recognition (Evans, 2002).

Authors have been proposing dualities and dichotomies for the classification of human thought since the time of Aristotle. The dual process theory of reasoning with which we are concerned here is broadly that published by Evans and Over (1996b) with distinct similarities to the distinctions argued for by Sloman (1996) and a non-coincidental congruence with the dual process theory of learning presented by Reber (1993) – a relatively late, but critical influence on my own thinking. The theory has since been further developed by Stanovich (1999) in his very impressive programme of research into individual differences in reasoning, in ways that I find (almost) entirely congenial. For a recent orthodox review of the theory and the evidence that has been accumulated for it, see Evans (2003).

In its contemporary form, the theory envisages the operation of two distinct cognitive systems described as tacit and explicit by Evans and Over, and by the more generic labels System 1 and System 2 by Stanovich. System 1 is variously described as implicit, associative, pragmatic, evolutionarily primary, shared with other animals, computationally powerful, and independent of general intelligence. System 2 by contrast is described as explicit, symbolic, limited by working memory capacity, related to general intelligence, evolutionarily late, and uniquely human. What – for me at least – was confined for many years to attempts to account for the findings of reasoning experiments, has somehow turned into a grandiose account of the structure of the mind and the evolution of human consciousness.

Stanovich (1999, p.145), in presenting his generic version of the dual process theory, cites a number of other partially compatible dualities that have been presented by psychologists in related fields. It is relevant to our current purpose (if humbling) to admit that I knew of none of these (apart from Sloman and Reber) before reading Stanovich's book. They certainly had no influence on the development of theory presented by Evans and Over (1996). In the 1970s when the germs of the dual process theory were born I was, however, aware of some other dualities that may have had an influence. There was the idea embodied in associationist philosophy (see Mandler & Mandler, 1964) that some thinking was goal directed and other thinking free associative. I was aware of Freud's related distinction between primary and secondary process thinking, the primary process of the id being responsible for fantasy and the secondary process of the ego developing to allow problem solving in conformity with the reality principle. Whilst sceptical about the notion of an unconscious *mind* – suggesting an homunculus – I was aware of the limits of consciousness and sceptical of the viewpoint then described as mentalism and nowadays as "folk psychology". I had read Galton (1879, 1893) on the limits of the introspective method and was familiar with the behaviouristic philosophy of mind of Ryle (1949). I was definitely interested in the idea of unconscious thinking.

In the 1970s it was quite unclear that the psychology of reasoning had very much to do with the emerging disciplines of cognitive psychology – then dominated by studies of short-term memory, semantic memory, lexical access, dichotic listening, and pattern recognition (Neisser, 1967). I was interested in these subjects but could find little point of contact with reasoning research. The psychology of thinking had a long tradition of its own with roots in philosophy and in experimental psychological studies dating from the 19th century. This field was well documented by textbooks of the time (for example, Bolton, 1972; Radford & Burton, 1974) with established topics such as concept identification and problem solving whose roots predated by many years the exciting new metaphor of the mind as computer that led to the foundation of cognitive psychology and cognitive science. The context for reasoning research was set by logicism – the idea that logic forms the basis for rational thought (Henle, 1962) – especially as manifest in the developmental theories of Jean Piaget, a monumental influence on psychology at that time. According to the theory of formal operations (Inhelder & Piaget, 1958) adults eventually develop abstract reasoning based on an inherent mental logic. Research on deduction was born as an attempt to demonstrate the extent to which people reasoned logically, and hence – according to the view of the time – rationally.

The biggest early influence on my own thinking was, of course, that of Peter Wason, who was not just my PhD supervisor but the leading creative force behind the modern psychological study of reasoning. Wason accepted the normative framework of logicism, but vigorously rejected the theories of Piaget, claiming in his early papers that people were both illogical and irrational (see Evans, 2002, for relevant quotes). He was writing his famous book on the psychology of reasoning with Phil Johnson-Laird (Wason & Johnson-Laird, 1972) while I was carrying out my doctoral research. Wason was interested in Freudian ideas and this influenced a number of his papers, including his collaboration with me in which the term "dual processes" was first used (Wason & Evans, 1975). This collaboration forms one of two distinct roots of the modern dual process theory of reasoning. The other, with which I will start, was the "two-factor" theory of Evans (1982).

THE TWO-FACTOR THEORY: LOGICAL AND NON-LOGICAL PROCESSES

In my PhD studies with Wason, I worked on conditional reasoning, but not yet the Wason selection task. I devised what has become known as the "negations paradigm" (Oaksford & Stenning, 1992) in which participants are asked to reason in turn with four conditional sentences of the following form:

If p then q
If p then not q
If not p then q
If not p then not q

Actually, as I was later to discover, I was not the first to use this method – I had been anticipated by Roberge (1971, 1974), working in an educational context. Fortunately (for me), Roberge had not analyzed and interpreted his data in such a way as to discover the trends that I reported in my early papers

(Evans, 1972a; 1972b; 1977a). The negations paradigm was critical in the development of the two-factor theory, so I will take time to explain its application.

The paradigm is based on the idea that the polarity (affirmative/negative) of logical premises or assertions can be varied orthogonally with the logical case (see Table 10.1). Hence, any biases associated with the processing of negations can be demonstrated with logic held constant. Conversely, any effect of logic can be demonstrated with biases held constant. The paradigm was thus used to demonstrate the influence of logical and non-logical factors on reasoning: the two-factor theory. For example, with the conditional inference task, people are given an assertion about the truth or falsity of one premise of the conditional statement and asked to evaluate a conclusion about the other. Hence, the modus tollens (MT) inference for an *affirmative* conditional rule might read:

If the letter is A then the number is 4
The number is not 4
Therefore, the letter is not A

Table 10.1a The negations paradigm as applied to the conditional inference task

Rule	MP Prem	Conc	DA Prem	Conc	AC Prem	Conc	MT Prem	Conc
If p then q	p	q	not-p	not-q	q	p	not-q	not-p
If p then not q	p	not-q	not-p	q	not-q	p	q	not-p
If not p then q	not-p	q	p	not-q	q	not-p	not-q	p
If not p then not q	not-p	not-q	p	q	not-q	not-p	q	p

Table 10.1b The negations paradigm as applied to the truth table task

Rule	TT	**TF**	FT	FF
If p then q	pq	p¬q	¬pq	¬p¬q
If p then not q	p¬q	pq	¬p¬q	¬pq
If not p then q	¬pq	¬p¬q	pq	p¬q
If not p then not q	¬p¬q	¬pq	p¬q	pq

Table 10.1c The negation paradigm as applied to the selection task

Rule	TA	**FA**	TC	FC
If p then q	p	not-p	q	not-q
If p then not q	p	not-p	not-q	q
If not p then q	not-p	p	q	not-q
If not p then not q	not-p	p	not-q	q

If only affirmative conditionals are used, then the two inferences that affirm the truth of one component (modus ponens, affirmation of the consequent) would always have affirmative premises and conclusions. Similarly, the denial inferences (denial of the antecedent, modus tollens) would always have negative premises and conclusions. This is deconfounded by using the negation paradigm as Table 10.1a shows. I discovered early on (Evans, 1977a; see also Evans, Clibbens, & Rood, 1995) that the polarity of the conclusion biased reasoning with logic held constant. For example, whilst most people (correctly) endorse the MT inference shown above, significantly and substantially fewer agree that the following argument is valid:

If the letter is not G then the number is 4
The number is not 4
Therefore, the letter is G

This was termed *negative conclusion bias* by Evans (1982) on the grounds that people overall endorsed more negative than affirmative conclusions. According to the logic of two-factor theory, the true (logical component) inference rates for these four conditional inferences could only be revealed by averaging across the four rules and hence balancing the effects of polarity biases.

A better known phenomenon, described as *matching bias* was discovered by applying the negations paradigm first to the truth table task (Evans, 1972a) and subsequently to the Wason selection task (Evans & Lynch, 1973). The full history of research on matching bias has been recorded (Evans, 1998) and I will just briefly illustrate the effect here. In the truth table task (Table 10.1b) people are shown every logical case for each rule and asked whether it conforms to or contradicts the rule or is irrelevant to it. It was argued by Wason (1966) that people would see conditional rules as irrelevant when their antecedents were false – the "defective truth table" hypothesis. These are the cases labelled FT and FF in Table 10.1b, meaning false antecedent–true consequent, false antecedent–false consequent. Evidence for this was found by Johnson-Laird and Tagart (1969) using affirmative rules, but first investigated using the negations paradigm by Evans (1972a). Averaging across the four rules, I found support also for the defective truth table. Within logical cases, however, the matching bias effect emerged.

For example, the correct falsifying case of the conditional is TF – true antecedent–false consequent. On the rule

If the letter is P then the number is not 7

the TF case corresponds to the double affirmative (or matching) case of P and 7. Almost everyone can discover this case. Given the rule

If the letter is not G then the number is 6

however, the TF case is the double mismatch in which both letter and number have to be set to alternative values, for example: B4. Far fewer people give the TF case here, and many give the FT case instead, which is also the matching case G6.

The power of the negations paradigm is perhaps best illustrated by the paper of Evans and Lynch (1973) who first applied the negations paradigm to the Wason selection task. The standard abstract version of the task as initially investigated in a series of experiments described by Wason and Johnson-Laird (1972) takes the following form. Participants are shown four cards whose visible sides display the symbols

>   A   D   3   7

and told that each has a capital letter written on one side and single digit number on the other side. They are told that the following rule applies to these four cards and may be true or false:

> If there is an A on one side of the card, then there is 3 on the other side of the card

The task is to choose those cards, and only those cards, that need to be turned over in order to test whether the rule is true or false. The generally agreed correct answer to this problem is A and 7, but this is typically chosen by only 10% or so of student participants (Evans, Newstead, & Byrne, 1993). This is because logically such a rule can be disproved but not proved. The counter-example required is a card that has an A one side and does not have a 3 on the other side. Only turning the A and the 7 could lead to discovery of such a card. The typical answers given, however, are A alone or A and 3. In general for a rule of the form "if p then q", the correct answer is p and not-q, but the typical answer is p, or p and q.

Wason and Johnson-Laird (1972) interpreted this robust phenomenon as a "verification bias". They suggested that people were trying to confirm the rule by finding a card with an A and a 3. After running the original matching bias experiment with the truth table task, however (Evans, 1972), I realized that there was a confound between the logical and matching case when only an affirmative rule was used. Instead of calling the four cards p, not-p, q, and not-q, we could refer to them as true antecedent (TA), false antecedent (FA), true consequent (TC), and false consequent (FC). The p and q cards are the matching cards (same lexical content as in the rule) whereas the not-p and not-q cards are mismatching cards. As Table 10.1c shows, the logical and matching cases can be deconfounded using the negations paradigm.

The first experiment to apply the negations paradigm to the selection task was reported by Evans & Lynch (1973) and was decisive. On all four logical cases, TA, FA, TC, and FC, comparisons across rules showed that matching cards were selected significantly more often than mismatching cards. When averaged across the four rules, the difference between TC and FC cases disappeared. The order was TA > TC = FC > FA. Hence, verification bias – it appeared – was due to the confound of logical and matching cases. On the standard task people choose more q than not-q cards not because they are verifying but because they are matching. Naturally, Peter Wason was the first to hear of the results of this new experiment. Good Popperian that he was, he immediately and graciously abandoned the verification bias hypothesis.

From these beginnings the two-factor theory of Evans (1982) was born. The idea was that orthogonal logical and non-logical processes influenced behaviour on reasoning tasks. Biases such as negative conclusion bias and matching bias needed to be controlled by the negations paradigm, before underlying logical processing could be determined. The theory was formalized by me (Evans, 1977b) as an additive stochastic model, but failed to capture the deterministic flow-chart mood of the time and was almost entirely ignored (but see Krauth, 1982). Much more influential was a manifestation of the two-factor theory on a different task – the investigation of belief biases in syllogistic reasoning reported by Evans, Barston, and Pollard (1983).

The belief bias effect was first reported by Wilkins (1928) and is generally described as a tendency to accept as valid, arguments that have believable rather than unbelievable conclusions. Prior to the Evans et al. (1983) paper, the phenomenon had been mostly investigated in social psychology but with rather questionable methodology (see Evans, 1982, pp. 107–111). In our study, we applied all relevant controls and succeeded in showing substantial influence of both belief and logical validity on participants' willingness to accept the conclusion of a presented syllogism as valid. The two-factor methodology was employed here, so that logical validity and conclusion believability were varied orthogonally. Example syllogisms and conclusion acceptance rates are shown in Table 10.2.

The Evans et al. (1983) paper was entitled "On the conflict between logic and belief in syllogistic reasoning" which is indicative of the interpretation we offered. The results were portrayed as a within-participant conflict between logical and non-logical processes. An analysis of think-aloud protocols showed that premise-centred protocols were more often associated with logically correct responses and conclusion-centred protocols with belief-based responses. However, we showed that this was not due to two kinds of participants: individuals could show either type of response pattern and then associate the appropriate protocol on a given problem. The analysis and interpretation here is extremely similar to the formal two-factor theory of the selection task (Evans, 1977b) with the emphasis on probabilistic responding and within-participant competition between the two factors.

The two-factor theory was (as colleagues pointed out at the time) essentially descriptive, with no real attempt to posit underlying mental processes to account for these findings. That was to begin with the development of

Table 10.2 Evidence of belief bias in reasoning: Example syllogisms with % acceptance of conclusions as valid

Valid-Believable No police dog are vicious Some highly trained dogs are vicious Therefore, some highly trained dogs are not police dogs	**89%**
Valid-Unbelievable No nutritional things are inexpensive Some vitamin tablets are inexpensive Therefore, some vitamin tables are not nutritional	**56%**
Invalid-Believable No addictive things are inexpensive Some cigarettes are inexpensive Therefore, some addictive things are not cigarettes	**71%**
Invalid-Unbelievable No millionaires are hard workers Some rich people are hard workers Therefore, some millionaires are not rich people	**10%**

From Evans et al. (1983).

the heuristic-analytic theory (Evans, 1984a) described later. First, however, I must report the other main origin of the modern dual process theory.

WASON AND EVANS' "DUAL PROCESS THEORY" AND THE PROBLEM OF INTROSPECTION

It may seem strange that the current dual process theory has origins in two different aspects of my work in the 1970s that I did not connect at the time. The easiest way to understand this is to appreciate that the two-factor theory described above was developed as a descriptive model of reasoning experiments whose purpose was to separate out logical reasoning from biases. It was basically a research programme aimed at establishing the main phenomena to be explained, rather than a test of theory. My other – and then separate – interest in the 1970s and early 1980s was with the problem of conscious thinking and introspection. This was an interest that was by no means confined to research on reasoning. I was very interested, for example, in the debate about mental imagery, and a strong Pylyshyn supporter in his famous debate with Kosslyn (see Evans, 1980). This led me to an epiphenomenalist view of conscious thinking and a very critical perspective on introspective reporting. I remain sceptical to the present day about the latter for methodological reasons, but I eventually abandoned my epiphenomenalist stance in order to develop the modern version of the dual process theory with David Over (Evans & Over, 1996).

The original dual process theory of Wason and Evans (1975) came about as Wason and I tried to resolve some apparently contradictory findings. Johnson-Laird and Wason (1970) had presented a model of the selection task in which different response patterns were associated with three degrees of insight. With no insight, people tried to verify the rule and chose either p, or p and q. With partial insight, people tried to both verify and falsify and chose p, q, and not-q. Full insight participants would try only to falsify the rule and choose the correct p and not-q. Whilst the standard task mostly produced responses with no insight, training and therapeutic procedures induced relatively high frequencies of the p, q, not-q, (partial insight), and p, not-q (full insight), patterns. In apparent confirmation of this theory, Goodwin and Wason (1972) reported an experiment in which people were asked to write down reasons for their card choices. These verbal reports revealed verification and falsification motives that appeared to match the predicted degree of insight for the choices made.

Following the publication of the Evans and Lynch (1973) paper, however, Peter Wason had accepted that matching bias seemed to account better for standard choices than verification bias. He and I discussed this paradox, and decided to run an experiment in which we used Goodwin and Wason's verbal reporting, but with two selection tasks. One used the standard "If p then q" rule, and the other a rule with a negated consequent, "If p then not q". We knew that participants would tend to choose the matching cards, p and q, on both tasks and thus give the classical no insight response on the affirmative rule, but the logically correct choice on the negative rule. The question was how would they reconcile this in their verbal accounts of the reasons for their card selections?

The participants in the Wason and Evans (1975) experiment obligingly showed strong matching bias on both rules and no transfer of performance. That is, those who did the negative rule first and gave the correct (and matching) answer did no better as a result on the affirmative rule that followed. What was fascinating was that, as in the Goodwin and Wason study, reports showed the correct degree of insight. For example, a participant given the rule "If A then not 3" might choose A and 3 with the following justifications:

A: because a 3 on the back could disprove the rule
3: because an A on the back could prove the rule false

The same participant then given a rule "If B then 4" would then choose B and 4 and justify these as follows:

B: because a 4 on the back would show the rule to be true
4: because a B on the other side would prove the rule

In other words, the same participant would show "full insight" when matching led them to the correct answer, but "no insight" when it led them astray. We argued that it was grossly implausible that people could lose insight in this way and that what was being observed were *rationalizations* of unconsciously motivated choices. We posited a distinction between type 1 processes, such as matching bias, that unconsciously biased reasoning, and type 2 conscious processes that rationalized these choices – the original dual processes. In a second paper, Evans and Wason (1976) showed that participants given at random one of several alternative "correct" solutions to the selection task and asked to explain them (the *only* time I have ever used deception in an experiment) would happily endorse it and explain why it was the right answer.

Two years after publication of the Wason and Evans paper, Nisbett and Wilson (1977) published their famous critique of introspective reporting in cognitive and social psychology in the premier journal *Psychological Review*. They argued that people could not tell what they did not know – that people lacked direct access to the processes underlying their behaviour. They also argued that when asked to produce reasons or justifications post hoc, people would respond with a priori theories about their own behaviour, often supplied by the culture. I was more than a little put out at the time that this paper did not cite Wason and Evans, and that few people noticed that we had published very similar arguments (albeit in a much more limited domain) in *Cognition* two years earlier. Nevertheless, I was a great fan of the Nisbett and Wilson paper and its conclusions, and recommended its wisdom to my students and in my publications at every opportunity.

I was equally interested in the follow-up paper by Ericsson and Simon (1980) who advocated the method of think-aloud protocols, and were worried that Nisbett and Wilson's paper would lead people to throw these out along with retrospective verbal reports. I liked their paper just as much as Nisbett and Wilson's, and was one of the few authors at that time who saw no conflict between them (see Evans, 1989, Chapter 5). Retrospective reporting of reasons for behaviour encourages rationalizations in line with the findings of Wason and Evans, and of Nisbett and Wilson. Think-aloud protocols are different because (a) they are concurrent with the thinking, (b) they report the locus of attention, and (c) it is the experimenter not the participant who interprets the protocols with regard to underlying processes. Hence, I was happy to use such protocols in the Evans et al. (1983) study of belief bias and saw no inconsistency with the claims of Wason and Evans (1975). The frequent references of other authors in the 1980s to Ericsson and Simon's "refutation" of Nisbett and Wilson were a source of great irritation.

In retrospect, I think my campaign against mentalism and introspectionism in cognitive psychology (for example, Evans, 1980), while sound, led me into an incorrectly epiphenomenalist view of conscious thinking. Thus paradoxically, while this interest helped to develop the original Wason and Evans dual process theory, it also obstructed the mapping of type 1 and type 2 processes on to the two-factor theory, which would have required some equation of logicality with conscious reasoning. However, significant progress was made in next step: development of the heuristic-analytic theory.

THE HEURISTIC-ANALYTIC THEORY OF REASONING

Received wisdom these days is that journal articles are more important and influential than books. My experience with the heuristic-analytic (H-A) theory was quite the opposite. The original publication of theory as a journal article (Evans, 1984b) provoked little reaction at the time, although it did provide a firm basis for my own thinking about reasoning phenomena for a decade and more to come. The theory only penetrated the consciousness of the field following publication of my book *Bias in human reasoning* (Evans, 1989), which is often cited as though it were the original source of the theory.

The H-A theory provided a bridge between the two origins described above and the dual process theory of Evans and Over (1996). It was mostly provoked by the research programme structured around the two-factor theory as an attempt to explain the co-existence of reasoning biases with deductive competence. Theoretical developments were mostly focused on the explanation of biases via heuristic processes. My 1989 book had specified no process by which "analytic" processes actually produced the logical component of performance, an omission that drew much criticism from reviewers and other researchers, especially my friends in the mental models camp.

The heuristic-analytic theory did feature a kind of unconscious–conscious thinking distinction, but one that was structured sequentially rather in parallel as implied by Wason and Evans. In this theory, heuristics are by definition preconscious and their function is to selectively represent "relevant" information. The processes involved here are essentially *pragmatic*, although it was some years before I started using this term. Heuristic processes both selectively represent information presented, and also retrieve and add relevant prior knowledge from memory. People then reason with these personalized representations of relevance. I attempted (Evans, 1989) to use this framework to account for a wide range of biases in reasoning and judgement. The theory also explained why people may exhibit apparent deductive competence on one task and fail to apply it on another. If preconscious heuristics filter out logically relevant information or add in logically irrelevant information, then biases will inevitably result, regardless of how effective the mysterious "analytic" processes may be.

As an example of H-A theorizing, let us return to the selection task and the matching bias effect. I argued (Evans, 1989, 1995b) that the selection task was a special case in which analytic processes played no role in the choice of cards that were determined purely by relevance. Whilst analytic processes influenced reasoning on other tasks, they served only to rationalize choices on the selection task, in the manner observed by Wason and Evans (1975). This is because the instructions ask people to choose cards that need to be turned over – which appears only to require a judgement of relevance. I argued that on the abstract selection task two linguistically based heuristics determined the perceived relevance of cards: the if-heuristic and the not-heuristic – which I now prefer to call the matching-heuristic (see Evans, 1998). The matching-heuristic reflects the use of negation in natural language, which is to deny presuppositions rather than to assert new information. Both the statements "the letter is A" and the "the letter is not A" are *about* the letter A. It is the A that seems relevant, not some unspecified exemplar of the not-A category. The if-heuristic explains the preference for TA over FA cards when matching bias is controlled by the negations paradigm. The word "if" is used to provoke hypothetical thinking about a possible state of affairs specified by the antecedent. Hence, it makes TA appear relevant and FA irrelevant.

Evidence for the H-A account was adduced by several indirect means. I predicted that the use of explicit negatives would remove the matching bias effect. For example, on the truth table task people should be able to identify the TF case for the rule "If the letter is not B then the number is 5" if presented as

A letter which is not B and a number which is not 5

rather than in the usual implicit form

The letter G and the number 1

This prediction was confirmed first in an experiment reported by Evans (1983), and later replicated and extended to the selection task by Evans, Clibbens, and Rood (1996), and then to the conditional inference task (introducing implicitly negative premises) by Evans and Handley (1999). I eventually came to the view that matching bias was little more than difficulty in processing implicit negations (Evans, 1998). The theory was also supported by protocol analyses showing that while people did think about the hidden sides of the cards on the selection task, they thought about the matching cases that might be there, and this thought did not change their selections (Evans, 1995b). I then introduced a novel methodology of asking people to point with a mouse at the cards they were thinking of selecting on a computer screen (Evans, 1996). As predicted, people spent far longer thinking about cards they ended up selecting, and there was little evidence that cards were rejected due to analytic reasoning. (For subsequent work on this see Ball, Lucas, Miles, & Gale, 2003; Roberts, 1998; Roberts & Newton, 2002.)

The heuristic-analytic theory has been incorporated into the modern dual process theory rather than superseded by it. A limitation of the theory, however – as already noted – was that it did not specify how the component of deductive competence (the logical factor in the dual factor theory) was actually achieved. Around about 1990 I was ready to give some serious thought to this issue, which is when I started to get interested in mental model theory.

THE INFLUENCE OF MENTAL MODEL THEORY

After his early collaboration with Wason, Johnson-Laird concentrated mostly on psycholinguistics for some years before launching his mental models research programme in the early 1980s (Johnson-Laird, 1983). By the end of the decade mental models research was established as major framework in the study of reasoning (Johnson-Laird & Byrne, 1991) which was to have a lasting influence on European cognitive psychology (see recent volumes by Garcia-Madruga, Carriedo, & Conzales-Labra, 2000; Schaeken, DeVooght, Vandierendonck, & d'Ydewalle, 2000). In the 1980s I saw this work more as a parallel than a rival research programme. While my colleagues and I were concentrating on explaining biases, Johnson-Laird and his colleagues were concerned with addressing the issue of deductive competence and their arguments with rule-based mental model theorists (see Braine & O'Brien, 1998; Rips, 1994, for recent work in this tradition). In terms of the current dual process theory, we were examining System 1 questions and they were looking at System 2. This is an oversimplification, however, as mental model theorists were also trying to explain phenomena such as belief bias (Oakhill & Johnson-Laird, 1985; Oakhill, Johnson-Laird, & Garnham, 1989). I also knew that I could not defer much longer the question of how logical competence was achieved.

Having never been much attracted to the mental logic approach, I started to wonder whether the semantic reasoning procedure proposed by Johnson-Laird might provide the missing link in the heuristic-analytic theory. This specified that people reason not by applying inference rules, but by imagining states of affairs (mental models) consistent with the premises of an argument and deriving possible conclusions that held (non-trivially) in those models. If no counterexample were discovered (a model where the premises but not the conclusion held true) then the argument would be considered valid. Could this account for the unspecified analytic component of reasoning? I also perceived a complementary weakness in the model theory at that time in that it had very little say about pragmatic influences – the main topic of study in the H-A research programme. Perhaps the two theories could be merged to mutual advantage.

When model theorists started writing about people attending to information explicitly represented in models as "focusing effects" (for example, Legrenzi, Girotto, & Johnson-Laird, 1993), the similarity to pre-attentive heuristics was striking. Suppose, I thought, that we equate my notion of relevance with Johnson-Laird's idea of explicit representation in models (Evans, 1993c). Then the kinds of heuristics that I had been working on might account for what became represented in mental models, adding power of explanation on pragmatic influences to the existing model theory. At the same time, the semantic reasoning principle of the model theory might account for the competence factor. Perhaps such model-theoretic notions as "search for counterexamples" and "fleshing-out of implicit models" might account for analytic reasoning.

The two research programmes have never formally merged in this way, although they have grown closer together in the past decade or so. The fact that Simon Handley – who completed a model theory PhD under the supervision of Ruth Byrne – joined the Plymouth group and became regular collaborator was an obvious influence. My experimentation with trying to merge the two theories certainly played a part in developing (with David Over and Simon Handley) contemporary ideas about hypothetical thinking discussed later. When I started to look closely at the model theory, however, I found a number of things that I did not agree with, although these were more a matter of detail than of general principle. I published a critical appraisal and attempted reformulation of the model theory of conditional and propositional reasoning (Evans, 1993b). David Over and I later reviewed the mental models versus mental rules debate (Evans & Over, 1996b, ch. 6, 1997), and argued that neither approach was sufficiently well formulated as to be strictly testable. Nevertheless we favoured the models approach as more plausible and useful.

It is probably fair to say that the two research programmes were at their closest during the early to mid-1990s during which time I participated in several papers based around the mental models framework. At the current time, our paths seem to be diverging somewhat again. Very recently, we have formulated a further critique of the model theory of conditional reasoning (Evans, Handley, & Over, 2003; Evans, Over, & Handley, 2003b) focused on the most recent proposals of Johnson-Laird and Byrne (2002) which reflects significant disagreement with some basic aspects of their current theoretical approach. I will return to some of the salient issues below. However, there is one more major influence to acknowledge before I turn to the work of Evans and Over (1996).

THE INFLUENCE OF REBER AND IMPLICIT LEARNING RESEARCH

In 1993 two books appeared at more or less the same time on the topic of implicit learning (Berry & Dienes, 1993; Reber, 1993). I had always thought this topic to be vaguely interesting and so volunteered to write a review of them for *Thinking and Reasoning*. When I read the books, I was absolutely fascinated and ended up returning a 5000 word feature review (Evans, 1995a). The review focused on something that none of the authors actually mentioned in the books (!), namely the relationship of the field to the study of thinking and reasoning. To me, the connections leapt out on almost every page and Reber's ideas in particular struck a chord that was to resonate through Evans and Over's (1996) reformulation of the dual process theory of reasoning. There is a lesson here for the development of scientific thinking. Had I not happened to read these books at this time, and failed to make connections with an apparently separate research field, what followed might have been very different. The unfortunate fact is that keeping up with the literature in one's own chosen fields is such a demanding task that reading of peripheral fields of interest occurs patchily, if at all.

Both books explored the hypothesis (which has since become very controversial) that implicit and explicit learning were separate processes reflecting distinct cognitive systems. From Berry and Dienes, I learned that there were distinct psychological differences in the nature of knowledge acquired through implicit as opposed to explicit learning. For example, implicitly acquired knowledge tended to be domain-specific. It was also relatively robust to disruption by time, competing tasks, or neurological insult. What really excited me, though, was Reber's dual process account. He argued for an implicit cognitive system that was evolutionarily primary, shared with other animals, largely independent of age and general intelligence, and providing functions that showed little variability across individuals and populations. He also argued that humans had evolved late a distinct explicit system providing reflective consciousness and the capacity for explicit learning. The major influence that these books had on my thinking was to direct me to the idea of distinct cognitive systems, as opposed to simply different kinds of cognitive processes underlying reasoning performance. Moreover, the systems they were describing seemed to map on to reasoning distinctions remarkably well. In the review (Evans, 1995a), I drew connections with the heuristic-analytic theory and my recently formulated distinction between personal and normative rationality (Evans, 1993a) discussed below.

Much though I admired Reber's theoretical insights, I was also struck by a curious asymmetry and caution in his treatment of the two systems. His main purpose seemed to be to argue for the "primacy of the implicit" as he termed it and he seemed reluctant to attribute much in the way of functionality to the explicit system. This put me uncomfortably in mind of my own history of epiphenomenalist thinking about consciousness. I started to think that human beings surely must have evolved this second system for a purpose linked to our unique cognitive facilities such as language and hypothetical thinking. I noticed, however, that the concept of consciousness was playing little or no part in the psychology of reasoning generally. For example, it was scarcely mentioned in the major exposition of mental model theory presented by Johnson-Laird and Byrne (1991). In particular, there was no commitment to the apparently reasonable idea that the content of mental models should be available to concurrent verbal reporting, such that a process like searching for counterexamples should be detectable through protocol analysis. In fact, Johnson-Laird and Byrne (1991, p. 39) explicitly ruled this out when they stated that:

The tokens of mental models may occur in a visual image, or they may not be directly accessible to consciousness. What matters is not the phenomenal experience, but the structure of the models.

In my later work with David Over (see below) in which we tried to explain the properties of the explicit thinking system and the nature of hypothetical thinking, I believe that we have started to address aspects of consciousness at least in the process of reasoning.

RATIONALITY$_1$ AND RATIONALITY$_2$

The final precipitating factor in the development of the dual process theory of Evans and Over (1996) came from an apparently unrelated theoretical exercise. In the early 1990s, Ken Manktelow and David Over were editing together a book on rationality and asked me to write a chapter. I had become increasingly irritated by references to my work as showing or claiming that people were irrational. This was on account of being typed as a "bias researcher". As the counter-revolution against the heuristics and biases research programme led by Gigerenzer got under way in the late 1980s (see, for example, Gigerenzer's chapter in the same edited book, Gigerenzer, 1993), rationality came back into fashion and I suffered guilt by association. The problem was that I have never used the term "bias" in a pejorative sense nor claimed that people were irrational. In fact, I thought the heuristic processes I was studying would normally be quite adaptive. On reflection, I realized that this meant that I was dissociating the idea of rationality from logicality.

In my chapter (Evans, 1993a), I analyzed the various critiques of bias research and classified them into three categories, which I termed the normative system problem, the interpretation problem, and the external validity problem (all of these were originally argued by Cohen, 1981). The first argument was that people were using the wrong normative system to assess rationality. I found myself in some sympathy with this, as it seemed evident to me that logic provided a poor account of effective reasoning in the real world. The second argument was that people reasoned logically but from a personalized representation of the problem information, leading to apparent biases. The difficulty I had with this was that its proponents used ambiguity of interpretation to argue for perfect logicality (Henle, 1962; Smedslund, 1970), whereas I did not believe in logic as either a descriptive or normative system for human reasoning. However, I had applied heuristic-analytic theory in a rather similar way, when explaining biases in terms of preconscious heuristics leading to selective representations of relevance (Evans, 1989). I had argued, for example, that people's deductive competence is underestimated on certain tasks, such as the selection task, because they think about the wrong information.

The argument for which I had least sympathy was that reasoning experiments were artificial and unrepresentative of real life. Laboratories are part of the real world, and just as the laws of physics apply inside labs as well as out, so do the laws of psychology. The idea that psychologists had somehow contrived by incompetence or malevolence to consistently provide evidence of bias in normally bias-free people in many hundreds of independent experiments was frankly ridiculous. I was also aware that most of the main judgemental biases had been demonstrated with expert groups. Hence, I focused most interest on the first two arguments.

In the same chapter, I described the paradox of rationality, namely that people were on the one hand a highly adaptive and effective species, and on the other hand chronically prone to biases in reasoning and judgement research. In an attempt to resolve this paradox, I suggested that people were using the word "rationality" in two different senses which I termed rationality$_1$ (achieving everyday goals) and rationality$_2$ (conforming to a normative system). I then argued that behaviour could be rational$_1$ whilst being irrational$_2$, as is the case with many cognitive biases. The editors of the volume, Ken Mantkelow and David Over, were most interested in this distinction, as it made connections with their own recent work, viewing reasoning as a form of decision making (Manktelow & Over, 1991). It was then that I started talking with David Over, a philosophical logician by training who had been working for several years with Manktelow on psychological studies of reasoning.

While this book was in press, Phil Johnson-Laird invited the three of us to write a paper together for a special issue of *Cognition*. This was an inspiration of near telepathic nature on his part, as I had never worked with Over and had not collaborated with Manktelow since he left Plymouth in the early 1980s. The three of us found it remarkably easy to integrate our recent ideas (Evans, Over, & Manktelow, 1993) and developed further the notion of rationality 1/2. For example, we gave an account of how the belief bias reflected mental processes that were highly adaptive in everyday life, but gave rise to bias in the context of an experimental instructions to assume premises and deduce necessary conclusions. Even the external validity argument was taking its toll.

At this point I must acknowledge – with apology – a rather odd unconscious influence. Anderson (1990) had earlier made a similar distinction between normative and adaptive rationality, applied to a different domain of cognitive tasks. This work is not cited by Evans (1993a) and neither is a relevant paper in *Behavioral and Brain Sciences* (Anderson, 1991), despite the fact that I had written a commentary on it (Evans, 1991). Strange as it may sound, I completely forgot about both Anderson's paper and my own commentary, and was not consciously aware of either when writing the 1993a paper on rationality. In fact, it was several years later that I came across (to my chagrin and amazement) my 1991 commentary and discovered the roots of the rationality 1/2 distinction clearly in place. Anderson's ideas evidently were an important influence, although unacknowledged by me at the time.

EVANS AND OVER (1996a)

Following the 1993 papers, David Over and I decided to write a book on *Rationality and reasoning* (Evans & Over, 1996a). There were some creative tensions in this collaboration, which probably show in the book but which were extremely helpful in developing my own thinking about the psychology of reasoning. In particular, Over led me away from my epiphenomenonalist thinking about consciousness (though not my scepticism about introspective reports – see Evans & Over, 1996a, pp. 155–157). For example, he insisted that the definition of rationality$_2$ included the phrase "acting when one has a reason for what one does sanctioned by a normative theory". His point was that to be termed rational in this sense, one had to be following rules explicitly, not simply complying with rules in the manner of a bumblebee apparently maximizing expected utility in its observed behaviour (Real, 1991).

The book started out as detailed examination of these two notions of rationality in reasoning and decision making, but ended up with the revised and elaborated dual process theory, the broad nature of which was mentioned at the outset of this article. This came about as we developed examples of behaviours in cognitive tasks that violated normative systems, but appeared to be rational$_1$. We noticed that such behaviour appeared to be governed by implicit processes, developing also the idea of preconscious heuristics in the heuristic-analytic theory. As an example, consider belief bias. We argued that it was adaptive in real life to reason from *all relevant belief* and that problem information was hence automatically contextualized against prior knowledge. This led to inferences that would normally be adaptive but appeared irrational$_2$ in the context of experimental instructions to assume the premises and reason only from the information given. The pragmatic processes underlying this must be extremely computationally powerful, but they are not consciously controllable. We drew an analogy with vision. If someone instructs you to look around a room and *not* see the colour blue, you cannot comply. This does not mean that your visual system is non-adaptive. In reasoning experiments, we suggested, people are accused of being irrational for doing much the same kind of thing.

Where the analogy with vision breaks down, however, is that people *can* control these pragmatic processes to an extent. For example, the degree to which reasoning is based on prior belief or on deductions drawn from the premises can be manipulated to a significant extent by the kinds of instructions given (Evans, Allen, Newstead, & Pollard, 1994; George, 1995; Stevenson & Over, 1995). Deduction is maximized and belief bias reduced (but not eliminated) when strong instructional emphasis on assuming the premises and drawing necessary conclusions is present. In later work

Stanovich (1999) showed that the ability to decontextualize and find normative solutions to reasoning problems is associated with individuals of high general intelligence (confirming an hypothesis in Reber's 1993 dual process theory). However, even high-intelligence participants will reason pragmatically in the absence of clear instructions to reason deductively. I later suggested (Evans, 2000) that deductive reasoning resulted from a strategy that bright people could be persuaded by the right instructions to adopt, rather than a reflection of any inbuilt logicality.

Just as our accounts of rational$_1$ behaviour led us to the idea of implicit cognitive processes, so our analyses of the requirements of rational$_2$ reasoning, identifying normative solutions, required the idea of explicit processing. We realized that these explicit resources were constrained by working memory and much more limited in capacity than the associative neural-net type of processes that we envisaged in the implicit system. We argued that while rationality$_1$ was universal, there was but a limited human capability to be rational$_2$. We had not yet made the link with individual differences, although we should have, as not only had Reber pointed to the relationship between explicit learning and IQ, but it was also known that working memory capacity and reasoning ability were closely linked (Kyllonen & Christal, 1990).

What did happen in the course of writing *Rationality and reasoning* was the integration of all the previous ideas discussed in this chapter. The logical and non-logical components of the two-factor theory, the Wason and Evans type 1 and 2 processes, and the heuristic-analytic distinction all fell into place. Reasoning experiments often exhibit two orthogonal factors because participants wrestle with a conflict between an attempt to comply with instructions and their natural pragmatic processes. Wason and Evans were right to postulate two kinds of process, but wrong to confine the role of their type 2 (explicit) processes to rationalization. The heuristic-analytic theory was right to point to the influence of preconscious pragmatic factors in our representation and thought about problem information. However, this theory failed to develop the idea of implicit thought processes that could lead to response without any intervention from the explicit reasoning system, and was wrong to convey an idea of sequential ordering in which one type of process followed the other.

RECENT DEVELOPMENTS

Perhaps the most significant development of dual process theory in recent years has been in the individual differences programme of Keith Stanovich and Richard West (Stanovich, 1999; Stanovich & West, 2000). In their generic theory, System 1 corresponds to the tacit of implicit system of Evans and Over and System 2 to the explicit system. While their view of dual processes is very similar to ours, their discussion of rationality is rather different.

Following their idea that System 1 evolved early, they attribute evolutionary rationality to its functions. This they contrast with normative (or individual) rationality that serves the purpose of individuals. (Our rationality$_1$ and rationality$_2$ are both regarded by them as forms of normative rationality.) Because System 2 was evolved for general problem solving it is a "long-leash" system not directly controlled by genes (Stanovich & West, 2003). Thus individuals can use it to pursue their own goals (such as long life and happiness) that are of little interest to their genes.

Unlike many contemporary evolutionary psychologists, Stanovich does not assume that evolutionary rationality, designed for the evolving environment, necessarily confers advantage in a modern technological society. Instead he argues that it leads to a fundamental computational bias (Stanovich, 1999) in which people compulsively contextualize all information. However, in a series of large-scale studies of individual differences in reasoning and judgement, he and West have shown that individuals high in general intelligence are much more likely to find normative solutions, in part because they can suppress pragmatic influences. He therefore sees it as an educational challenge to develop System 2 thinking and to train people to counter the fundamental computational bias.

This line of argument leads to a puzzle. If System 2 thinking is advantageous to individuals – and surely it is – why is it so highly heritable? Highly adaptive functions tend to become fixed to optimal levels in the population by evolution, as seems to be the case with System 1 processes (for example, language comprehension, pattern recognition). IQ, on the other hand, is highly variable and strongly linked with the particular genes passed from parents to offspring. One possible solution is that System 2 thinking allows individuals who are good at it to provide leadership and technological solutions for the society in which they live. Once the ability to develop knowledge explicitly and pass it on to others by use of language developed, the evolution of intelligence by natural selection would have greatly diminished (Over & Evans, 2000).

Another exciting recent development lies in the use of neuroimaging techniques to track brain activity during reasoning. Vinod Goel and his colleagues, using fMRI, have shown that responses attributed to System 1 light up different areas from those attributed to System 2, for example, within the belief bias paradigm (Goel, Buchel, Rith, & Olan, 2000; Goel & Dolan, 2003). The same has been shown for the competition between matching bias and logical responding on the selection task, using PET scan methods (Houde et al., 2000, 2001). Both research groups implicate the frontal cortex in System 2 processing, which makes sense of the evolutionary aspect of the dual process theory (this is the new brain area mostly developed in humans).

My own recent work in collaboration with David Over and Simon Handley has been mostly motivated by one aspect or another of dual process theory. For example, we have argued against the idea that the facilitation of probability judgements (Cosmides & Tooby, 1996; Gigerenzer & Hoffrage,

1995) by use of frequency formats is due to the presence of an innate frequency processing module. Our argument (Evans, Handley, Perham, Over, & Thompson, 2000) is that although such a mechanism might have evolved, it would operate through the System 1 and would not assist reasoning on statistical word problems. Instead we identified an artefact in the procedure, such that the frequency formats used explicate the set–subset relationships involved in Bayesian reasoning and hence facilitate System 2 reasoning by cueing a helpful mental model of the task (see also Girotto & Gonzales, 2001).

We have been working on a theory of *hypothetical thinking* (Evans, Over, & Handley, 2003a) developed from Evans and Over's (1996) attempts to understand the function of the explicit thinking system. Hypothetical thinking involves the imagination of possible states of affairs and is required for such matters as forecasting, consequential decision making, hypothesis testing, and deductive reasoning – assuming a semantic mental models approach to the last. We argue that all forms of hypothetical thinking require System 2 thinking, as opposed – for example – to routine decisions made on the basis of past experience, which can operate easily at the implicit level without conscious intervention. We have suggested that hypothetical thinking involves processing mental models corresponding to possibilities, and proposed some principles for how this is done. For example, people consider only one model (hypothesis, possibility) at a time and maintain it until there is good reason to give it up, leading to satisficing in decision making.

IN CONCLUSION

I hope that this unusually personal account of the development of the dual process theory may have provided some insights for readers into how research actually happens – a process so skilfully disguised in the orthodox scientific writing of journal articles. I have tried to convey the process as accurately as I can, acknowledging all major influences of which I am aware. I suspect, however, that Anderson's forgotten paper is indicative of a host of other influences from articles read or conversations with colleagues that I could never hope to recall and document over a 30-year period of work. It is therefore to these many unsung and unknown heroes of the dual process theory of reasoning that I dedicate this chapter.

REFERENCES

Anderson, J. R. (1990). *The adaptive character of thought*. Hillsdale, NJ: Lawrence Erlbaum Associates Inc.
Anderson, J. R. (1991). Is human cognition adaptive? *Behavioral and Brain Sciences*, *14*, 471–517.

Ball, L. J., Lucas, E. J., Miles, J. N. V., & Gale, A. G. (2003). Inspection times and the selection task: What do eye-movements reveal about relevance effects. *Quarterly Journal of Experimental Psychology*, *56*A, 1053–1077.

Berry, D. C., & Dienes, Z. (1993). *Implicit learning*. Hove, UK: Lawrence Erlbaum Associates Ltd.

Bolton, N. (1972). *The psychology of thinking*. London: Methuen.

Braine, M. D. S., & O'Brien, D. P. (Eds.). (1998). *Mental logic*. Mahwah, NJ: Lawrence Erlbaum Associates Inc.

Cohen, L. J. (1981). Can human irrationality be experimentally demonstrated? *Behavioral and Brain Sciences*, *4*, 317–370.

Cosmides, L., & Tooby, J. (1996). Are humans good intuitive statisticians after all? Rethinking some conclusions from the literature on judgment under uncertainty. *Cognition*, *58*, 1–73.

Ericsson, K. A., & Simon, H. A. (1980). Verbal reports as data. *Psychological Review*, *87*, 215–251.

Evans, J. St. B. T. (1972a). Interpretation and matching bias in a reasoning task. *Quarterly Journal of Experimental Psychology*, *24*, 193–199.

Evans, J. St. B. T. (1972b). Reasoning with negatives. *British Journal of Psychology*, *63*, 213–219.

Evans, J. St. B. T. (1977a). Linguistic factors in reasoning. *Quarterly Journal of Experimental Psychology*, *29*, 297–306.

Evans, J. St. B. T. (1977b). Toward a statistical theory of reasoning. *Quarterly Journal of Experimental Psychology*, *29*, 297–306.

Evans, J. St. B. T. (1980). Thinking: Experiential and information processing approaches. In G. Claxton (Ed.), *Cognitive psychology: New directions* (pp. 275–299). London: Routledge.

Evans, J. St. B. T. (1982). *The psychology of deductive reasoning*. London: Routledge.

Evans, J. St. B. T. (1983). Linguistic determinants of bias in conditional reasoning. *Quarterly Journal of Experimental Psychology*, *35*A, 635–644.

Evans, J. St. B. T. (1984a). Heuristic and analytic processes in reasoning. *British Journal of Psychology*, *75*, 451–468.

Evans, J. St. B. T. (1984b). In defense of the citation bias in the judgment literature. *American Psychologist*, *39*, 1500–1501.

Evans, J. St. B. T. (1989). *Bias in human reasoning: Causes and consequences*. Hove, UK: Lawrence Erlbaum Associates Ltd.

Evans, J. St. B. T. (1991). Adaptive cognition: The question is how. *Behavioral and Brain Sciences*, *14*, 403–404.

Evans, J. St. B. T. (1993a). Bias and rationality. In K. I. Manktelow & D. E. Over (Eds.), *Rationality: Psychological and philosophical perspectives* (pp. 6–30). London: Routledge.

Evans, J. St. B. T. (1993b). On the relation between cognitive psychology and social cognition. In J. P. P. M. F. Caverni (Ed.), *Studies on the self and social cognition*. Singapore: World Scientific.

Evans, J. St. B. T. (1993c). The mental model theory of conditional reasoning: Critical appraisal and revision. *Cognition*, *48*, 1–20.

Evans, J. St. B. T. (1995a). Implicit learning, consciousness and the psychology of thinking. *Thinking and Reasoning*, *1*, 105–118.

Evans, J. St. B. T. (1995b). Relevance and reasoning. In S. E. Newstead & J. St. B. T.

Evans (Eds.), *Perspectives on thinking and reasoning* (pp. 147–172). Hove, UK: Lawrence Erlbaum Associates Ltd.

Evans, J. St. B. T. (1996). Deciding before you think: Relevance and reasoning in the selection task. *British Journal of Psychology, 87*, 223–240.

Evans, J. St. B. T. (1998). Matching bias in conditional reasoning: Do we understand it after 25 years? *Thinking and Reasoning, 4*, 45–82.

Evans, J. St. B. T. (2000). What could and could not be a strategy in reasoning. In W. Schaeken, G. DeVooght, & A. d. G. Vandierendonck (Eds.), *Deductive reasoning and strategies* (pp. 1–22). Mahwah, NJ: Lawrence Erlbaum Associates Inc.

Evans, J. St. B. T. (2002). Logic and human reasoning: An assessment of the deduction paradigm. *Psychological Bulletin, 128*, 978–996.

Evans, J. St. B. T. (2003). In two minds: Dual process accounts of reasoning. *Trends in Cognitive Sciences, 7*, 454–459.

Evans, J. St. B. T., Allen, J. L., Newstead, S. E., & Pollard, P. (1994). Debiasing by instruction: The case of belief bias. *European Journal of Cognitive Psychology, 6*, 263–285.

Evans, J. St. B. T., Barston, J. L., & Pollard, P. (1983). On the conflict between logic and belief in syllogistic reasoning. *Memory and Cognition, 11*, 295–306.

Evans, J. St. B. T., Clibbens, J., & Rood, B. (1995). Bias in conditional inference: Implications for mental models and mental logic. *Quarterly Journal of Experimental Psychology, 48*A, 644–670.

Evans, J. St. B. T., Clibbens, J., & Rood, B. (1996). The role of implicit and explicit negation in conditional reasoning bias. *Journal of Memory and Language, 35*, 392–409.

Evans, J. St. B. T., & Handley, S. J. (1999). The role of negation in conditional inference. *Quarterly Journal of Experimental Psychology, 52*A, 739–769.

Evans, J. St. B. T., Handley, S. H., & Over, D. E. (2003). Conditionals and conditional probability. *Journal of Experimental Psychology: Learning, Memory and Cognition, 29*, 321–355.

Evans, J. St. B. T., Handley, S. H., Perham, N., Over, D. E., & Thompson, V. A. (2000). Frequency versus probability formats in statistical word problems. *Cognition, 77*, 197–213.

Evans, J. St. B. T., & Lynch, J. S. (1973). Matching bias in the selection task. *British Journal of Psychology, 64*, 391–397.

Evans, J. St. B. T., Newstead, S. E., & Byrne, R. M. J. (1993). *Human reasoning: The psychology of deduction*. Hove, UK: Lawrence Erlbaum Associates Ltd.

Evans, J. St. B. T., & Over, D. E. (1996a). *Rationality and reasoning*. Hove, UK: Psychology Press.

Evans, J. St. B. T., & Over, D. E. (1996b). Rationality in the selection task: Epistemic utility versus uncertainty reduction. *Psychological Review, 103*, 356–363.

Evans, J. St. B. T., & Over, D. E. (1997). Rationality in reasoning: The case of deductive competence. *Current Psychology of Cognition, 16*, 3–38.

Evans, J. St. B. T., Over, D. E., & Handley, S. H. (2003a). A theory of hypothetical thinking. In D. Hardman & L. Maachi (Eds.), *Thinking: Psychological perspectives on reasoning, judgement and decision making* (p. 3–21). Chichester, UK: Wiley.

Evans, J. St. B. T., Over, D. E., & Handley, S. H. (2003b). Rethinking the model theory of conditionals. In W. Schaeken, A. Vandierendonck, W. Schroyens, & G. d'Ydewalle (Eds.), *The mental model theory of reasoning: Refinements and extensions*. Hove, UK: Psychology Press.

Evans, J. St. B. T., Over, D. E., & Manktelow, K. I. (1993). Reasoning, decision making and rationality. *Cognition*, *49*, 165–187.

Evans, J. St. B. T., & Wason, P. C. (1976). Rationalisation in a reasoning task. *British Journal of Psychology*, *63*, 205–212.

Galton, F. (1879). Psychometric experiments. *Brain*, *2*, 148–162.

Galton, F. (1893). *Inquiries into human faculty and its development*. London: Macmillan.

Garcia-Madruga, J., Carriedo, N., & Conzales-Labra, J. (Eds.). (2000). *Mental models in reasoning*. Madrid: Universidad Nacional ed Education a Distanca.

George, C. (1995). The endorsement of the premises: Assumption based or belief-based reasoning. *British Journal of Psychology*, *86*, 93–111.

Gigerenzer, G. (1993). The bounded rationality of probabilistic mental models. In K. I. Manktelow & D. E. Over (Eds.), *Rationality: Psychological and philosophical perspectives* (pp. 284–313). London: Routledge.

Gigerenzer, G., & Hoffrage, U. (1995). How to improve Bayesian reasoning without instruction: Frequency formats. *Psychological Review*, *102*, 684–704.

Girotto, V., & Gonzales, M. (2001). Solving probabilistic and statistical problems: A matter of information structure and question form. *Cognition*, *78*, 247–276.

Goel, V., Buchel, C., Rith, C., & Olan, J. (2000). Dissociation of mechanisms underlying syllogistic reasoning. *NeuroImage*, *12*, 504–514.

Goel, V., & Dolan, R. J. (2003). Explaining modulation of reasoning by belief. *Cognition*, *87*, B11–B22.

Goodwin, R. Q., & Wason, P. C. (1972). Degrees of insight. *British Journal of Psychology*, *63*, 205–212.

Henle, M. (1962). On the relation between logic and thinking. *Psychological Review*, *69*, 366–378.

Houde, O., Zago, L., Crivello, F., Moutier, S., Pineau, A., Mazoyer, B. et al. (2001). Access to deductive logic depends upon a right ventromedial prefrontal area devoted to emotion and feeling: Evidence from a training paradigm. *NeuroImage*, *14*, 1486–1492.

Houde, O., Zago, L., Mellet, E., Moutier, S., Pineau, A. et al. (2000). Shifting from the perceptual brain to the logical brain: The neural impact of cognitive inhibition training. *Journal of Cognitive Neuroscience*, *12*, 721–728.

Inhelder, B., & Piaget, J. (1958). *The growth of logical thinking*. New York: Basic Books.

Johnson-Laird, P. N. (1983). *Mental models*. Cambridge: Cambridge University Press.

Johnson-Laird, P. N., & Byrne, R. M. J. (1991). *Deduction*. Hove, UK: Lawrence Erlbaum Associate Ltd.

Johnson-Laird, P. N., & Byrne, R. M. J. (2002). Conditionals: A theory of meaning, pragmatics and inference. *Psychological Review*, *109*, 646–678.

Johnson-Laird, P. N., & Tagart, J. (1969). How implication is understood. *American Journal of Psychology*, *2*, 367–373.

Johnson-Laird, P. N., & Wason, P. C. (1970). A theoretical analysis of insight into a reasoning task. *Cognitive Psychology*, *1*, 134–148.

Krauth, J. (1982). Formulation and experimental verification of models in propositional reasoning. *Quarterly Journal of Experimental Psychology*, *34*A, 285–298.

Kyllonen, P., & Christal, R. E. (1990). Reasoning ability is (little more than) working memory capacity!? *Intelligence*, *14*, 389–433.

Legrenzi, P., Girotto, V., & Johnson-Laird, P. N. (1993). Focusing in reasoning and decision making. *Cognition, 49*, 37–66.
Mandler, J. M., & Mandler, G. (1964). *Thinking: From association to Gestalt*. New York: Wiley.
Manktelow, K. I., & Over, D. E. (1991). Social roles and utilities in reasoning with deontic conditionals. *Cognition, 39*, 85–105.
Neisser, U. (1967). *Cognitive psychology*. New York: Appleton.
Nisbett, R. E., & Wilson, T. D. (1977). Telling more than we can know: Verbal reports on mental processes. *Psychological Review, 84*, 231–295.
Oakhill, J., & Johnson-Laird, P. N. (1985). The effects of belief on the spontaneous production of syllogistic conclusions. *Quarterly Journal of Experimental Psychology, 37*A, 553–569.
Oakhill, J., Johnson-Laird, P. N., & Garnham, A. (1989). Believability and syllogistic reasoning. *Cognition, 31*, 117–140.
Oaksford, M., & Stenning, K. (1992). Reasoning with conditional containing negated constituents. *Journal of Experimental Psychology: Learning, Memory and Cognition, 18*, 835–854.
Over, D. E., & Evans, J. St. B. T. (2000). Rational distinctions and adaptations. *Behavioral and Brain Sciences, 23*, 693–694.
Radford, J., & Burton, A. (1974). *Thinking: Its nature and development*. Letchworth, UK: Wiley.
Real, L. A. (1991). Animal choice behaviour and the evolution of cognitive architecture. *Science, 253*, 980–979.
Reber, A. S. (1993). *Implicit learning and tacit knowledge*. Oxford: Oxford University Press.
Rips, L. J. (1994). *The psychology of proof*. Cambridge, MA: MIT Press.
Roberge, J. J. (1971). Some effects of negation on adults' conditional reasoning abilities. *Psychological Reports, 29*, 839–844.
Roberge, J. J. (1974). Effects of negation on adults' comprehension of fallacious conditional and disjunctive arguments. *Journal of General Psychology, 91*, 287–293.
Roberts, M. J. (1998). Inspection times and the selection task: Are they relevant? *Quarterly Journal of Experimental Psychology, 51*A, 781–810.
Roberts, M. J., & Newton, E. J. (2002). Inspection times, the change task, and the rapid-response selection task. *Quarterly Journal of Experimental Psychology, 54*A, 1031–1048.
Ryle, G. (1949). *The concept of mind*. London: Hutchinson.
Schaeken, W., DeVooght, G., Vandierendonck, A., & d'Ydewalle, G. (2000). *Deductive reasoning and strategies*. Mahwah, NJ: Lawrence Erlbaum Associates Inc.
Sloman, S. A. (1996). The empirical case for two systems of reasoning. *Psychological Bulletin, 119*, 3–22.
Smedslund, J. (1970). Circular relation between understanding and logic. *Scandinavian Journal of Psychology, 11*, 217–219.
Stanovich, K. E. (1999). *Who is rational? Studies of individual differences in reasoning*. Mahwah, NJ: Lawrence Erlbaum Associates Inc.
Stanovich, K. E., & West, R. F. (2000). Individual differences in reasoning: Implications for the rationality debate. *Behavioral and Brain Sciences, 23*, 645–726.
Stanovich, K. E., & West, R. F. (2003). Evolutionary versus instrumental goals: How evolutionary psychology misconceives human rationality. In D. E. Over (Ed.),

Evolution and the psychology of thinking (pp. 171–230). Hove, UK: Psychology Press.

Stevenson, R. J., & Over, D. E. (1995). Deduction from uncertain premises. *The Quarterly Journal of Experimental Psychology, 48A*, 613–643.

Wason, P. C. (1966). Reasoning. In B. M. Foss (Ed.), *New Horizons in Psychology I* (pp. 106–137). Harmandsworth: Penguin

Wason, P. C., & Evans, J. St. B. T. (1975). Dual processes in reasoning? *Cognition, 3*, 141–154.

Wason, P. C., & Johnson-Laird, P. N. (1972). *Psychology of reasoning: Structure and content*. London: Batsford.

Wilkins, M. C. (1928). The effect of changed material on the ability to do formal syllogistic reasoning. *Archives of Psychology, 16*, no. 102.

11 Coherence and argumentation

David W. Green

In everyday life individuals consider arguments in order to reach many decisions. In organizational contexts groups of individuals present and consider arguments in order to agree a course of action or to understand a situation. The importance and relevance of argumentation to an understanding of both individual cognition and group cognition would seem self-evident. But a number of researchers have proposed that the role of arguments is overblown. For instance, Zajonc (1980) proposed that affect is primary and that the explicit reasons and arguments individuals provide for their actions are a side-show, mere rationalizations for the unconscious machinery of mind. Others have supposed that the decisions individuals reach are strongly influenced by implicit factors such as the ease of generating arguments that have nothing to do with the merits of the case. Clearly if these two objections are true, any theory of argument and decision will be circumscribed and the conditions under which any theory of argument and decision applies will need to be carefully charted.

The first section of this chapter discusses these two objections and proposes accounts of them. It also considers a further objection. Some have argued that accuracy-driven reasoning (cold cognition) is radically different from motivated reasoning (hot cognition) where individuals seek evidence for a favoured conclusion. If this objection is well founded, then it may be necessary to generate two distinct theories. The claim that different processes are used for hot versus cold cognition is undermined by recent evidence showing that even when individuals are engaged in being accurate their perceptions of arguments come to cohere with respect to the emerging decision. The second section explores the nature of such coherence using the concept of a mental model. It proposes that arguments are fundamentally about states of affairs and that coherence arises because individuals construct representations that parsimoniously explain the pattern of data. The final section discusses the issue of individual differences in building argument models and the implications for reasoning about controversial issues.

THE ROLE OF ARGUMENTS IN DECISION MAKING

Affective and cognitive processes

What role do arguments play in everyday decisions and opinions? Slovic, Finucane, Peters, and MacGregor (2001) claimed that reliance on affect and emotion is a quicker, easier, and more efficient way to navigate in a complex, uncertain, and sometimes dangerous world. In their work they presented participants with an issue and asked them to record in a word or a phrase any images, feelings, and thoughts that came to mind. Individuals then rated each one on a 5-point affect scale running from −2 (very negative) to +2 (very positive). In a number of studies they found that the affective value of these responses (either averaged or summed) was a good predictor of preferences for different cities, attitudes to different technologies (such as nuclear power), purchasing stock in new companies (MacGregor, Slovic, Dreman & Berry, 2000), and engaging in behaviours that either threaten health (e.g., smoking) or enhance it (e.g., exercise) (Benthin, Slovic, Moran, Severson, Mertz & Gerrard, 1995).

Slovic et al.'s proposal pits affect against reason. But are the representations that generate a set of elicited images, feelings, and thoughts disjoint from those used in arguments about the issue? Following the procedure developed by Slovic et al. (2001), I asked individuals ($N = 84$) to write down in a word or a phrase, images, feelings, and thoughts that came to mind about genetically modified crops (Green, in press). They then indicated which, if any, of these they would use as arguments about the issue in a discussion with a friend or colleague. They also wrote down any other arguments. Of the total set of arguments, 79% originated in the initial set of images and thoughts. The remaining 21% arose on further reflection. In fact, 68% of the initial reactions were endorsed as possible arguments. Initial reactions then also tend to reflect material that individuals would use in order to generate overt arguments about an issue.

Affective responses may also be the product of arguing about an issue and not simply an unthinking reaction. Consider a juror who reviews the proceedings of a court case and decides their previous decision was in error. This is not to say that affective reactions may not make an independent contribution to a decision or opinion. In a study by Green, McClelland, Muckli, and Simmons (1999) participants read about a person called Lucy who suffered food poisoning after eating a meal in a restaurant. They were asked to decide on the amount of fine the restaurant should pay, and recorded both their degree of sympathy for Lucy and the reason for their fine (such as restaurants have a duty of care to their customers or this was a one-off accident). Linear regression analyses showed that both the proffered reason and the degree of sympathy predicted the amount of fine awarded, although the proffered reason accounted for a substantially larger proportion of the variance. Sympathy can be thought of as an affective reason and so we can infer that both affective and cognitive reasons contribute to the decisions individuals reach. The precise contribution of these two reasons presumably depends on the topic and on other manipulations such as whether or not a participant adopts the perspective of the victim.

Any general claim that arguments are irrelevant to decisions is refuted by their causal role. When individuals deliberate about an issue, their decisions reflect the nature of the arguments they consider and the argumentative actions they carry out. Individuals are persuaded more by arguments that they rate as strong compared to arguments that they rate as weak (Green & McCloy, 2003, Experiment 2), and reach more extreme decisions when they are free to envisage a single reason for decision, compared to when they are required to consider two possible reasons and must either endorse one of them if it fits with their own reason, or generate another reason (Green et al., 1999; see also Lord, Lepper, & Preston, 1984).

Likewise, Kuhn, Weinstock, and Flaton (1994) showed that individuals who considered just one account of a mock legal case were more extreme in their verdict compared to those who envisaged an alternative account. On the other hand, if individuals are presented with two possible arguments for a decision and must explicitly rebut the non-preferred alternative, their judgements are more extreme compared to those who are not required to rebut the alternative (Green et al., 1999, Experiment 2).

Implicit and explicit processes

There is evidence that other factors besides the reasons or arguments that individuals generate determine their opinions. Attitudes or judgements might be retrieved from memory and represent some stable evaluation about some issue or person (Eagly & Chaiken, 1993). They may also be constructed on the spot (Hastie & Park, 1986; Iyengar & Ottati, 1994) and so should be affected by information that is temporarily accessible at the time of judgement (Wilson, Lindsey, & Schooler, 2000). In a study by Wänke, Bless, and Biller (1996) individuals wrote down either three or seven arguments either in favour of public transport or against public transport before reporting their attitude. Participants reported more favourable attitudes when they experienced an easy time in generating positive arguments or a difficult time in generating negative arguments.

How should the effects of accessibility be interpreted? It is important to note that these implicit effects are indirect and moderated by the nature of the reasons generated. If this were not the case, greater difficulty would simply be associated with a more negative outcome. Consistent with the role of arguments, individuals may treat accessibility as a proxy for the extent of support for one position over another. More directly, the effects of accessibility may be effects of argument strength. Those required to produce more arguments may typically produce weaker additional arguments. In the extreme, individuals may fail to produce an argument at all. Functionally, the strength of such arguments is zero. On this proposal, the strength of arguments would be less on average for those required to produce five arguments compared to two arguments. Granted a relation between argument strength and opinion (Green, 2000), opinion would be less favourable for five arguments compared to two. Likewise, the average strength of five negative arguments would be less than the average strength of two negative arguments. In consequence, opinion would be relatively more favourable for five arguments compared to two. This proposal can therefore explain the results of Wänke et al., 1996.

Interestingly, Haddock (2002) showed that accessibility affected opinion only for those individuals who had no strong prior interest in the topic – in his case Tony Blair, the British Prime Minister at the time. Such individuals might avoid the effects of accessibility, by retrieving an already-formed opinion. However, they might also be less susceptible, because they are better at producing five arguments of reasonable strength. This proposal awaits empirical investigation but the line of argument establishes that implicit processes do not inevitably challenge the importance of argument in the determination of opinion.

Hot vs cold cognition

Another line of attack on the view that opinion is reason-based is the idea that radically distinct processes are involved when individuals engage in motivated thinking (hot cognition) as compared with dispassionate thinking, cold cognition (Kunda, 1990). Research on motivated reasoning suggests that when individuals have a desired conclusion in mind (e.g., preservation of their self-image) they reason in such a way as to reach that desired conclusion. When their goal is to be accurate, reasoning is generally considered to be accurate. But there are limits to the impact of motivated thinking. As Kunda (1990, p. 483) acknowledges, people will come to believe what they want to believe only to the extent that reason permits.

But how different is motivated reasoning, i.e., reasoning with a specific conclusion in mind, from reasoning whose goal is accuracy? One possibility is that the former is a truncated version of the latter (Kruglanski & Ajzen, 1983). Individuals stop reasoning when a particular conclusion is reached. Another possibility is that reasoning processes and processes of argumentation are driven by the goal to achieve a coherent representation of a situation. Recent research (Holyoak & Simon, 1999; Simon, Pham, Le, & Holyoak, 2001), using a mock legal case, points to this deeper commonality. These researchers found changes in the evaluation of arguments in line with the verdict reached even though individuals were not driven by any motivational goal. The next few paragraphs describe these studies in some detail as the background to a discussion of the nature of coherence.

Holyoak and Simon (1999) asked students to reach a verdict in a case involving a software company, Quest, whose financial position collapsed after a dissatisfied shareholder, Smith, posted an internet message strongly critical of the management and the company's prospects. Quest went bankrupt and sued Smith for libel. I will describe the follow-up studies reported in Simon et al., 2001.

Prior to reading the case description, individuals rated their agreement with a set of independent questions. For instance, after describing circumstances leading to an investor spreading a negative message, individuals rated their agreement with a question indicating (a) that he was motivated by vindictiveness and (b) that he was motivated by a desire to protect other innocent victims. The questions mapped onto six points of dispute in the case. For instance, one concerned motive (Quest claimed that Smith's action was motivated by vindictiveness, whereas Smith claimed he only aimed to protect other innocent investors). Others points of dispute included the truth of the internet message, the real cause of Quest's downfall, and whether or not the law of libel applied.

Prior to reading the case, individuals under one set of orienting instructions were informed that they would have to reach a verdict (simulating the role of junior judge) but were advised to suspend reaching a judgement until after they had heard about the opinion of a senior judge adjudicating a similar case. In one condition (Simon et al., 2001, Experiment 1; see also Experiment 1, Holyoak & Simon, 1999), having read the case and the six points of dispute, individuals were asked to reach an interim verdict. They then rated their agreement with each of the questions used in the pre-test but now presented as part of the Quest case. In another condition, participants completed their ratings prior to giving their interim verdict. After this interim phase, individuals were told that the judge was not going to give a verdict after all and they should now provide their final verdict. They were free to look over the case once again. All participants then rated the critical questions once again (post-decision).

Despite the ambiguity of the case and split in the verdicts, most participants rated their confidence in the final verdict either high or moderately high. Simon et al. (2001, p. 1253) infer: This combination of ambiguity and relatively high individual confidence in decisions is consistent with constraint-satisfaction models of decision making which tend to resolve ambiguous situations by allowing one coherent set of beliefs to become highly activated while inhibiting the rival set. This increase in support for the chosen verdict increases confidence in the final stated verdict.

Constraint satisfaction models predict that the emergence of a decision will be accompanied by agreement ratings for each point of dispute cohering: e.g., individuals reaching a Quest verdict will come to agree with all statements favourable to their position. Holyoak and Simon (1999) and Simon et al. (2001) converted agreement ratings to Quest-scores (favourability to Quest's position). These range from −5 (minimal support) to +5 (maximal support). Relative to baseline test, those who eventually reached a Quest verdict showed an increase in Quest score both in the interim test and post-decision. Individuals reaching a Smith verdict showed the opposite pattern. Their Q-scores became more negative by the interim test and post-decision.

The important point is that agreement ratings for the arguments inter-correlated (i.e., their evaluations cohered) only once they had been presented in the context of the case. Holyoak and Simon (1999) had found that coherence emerged following an interim verdict, and before their final verdict was given, and so they argued that coherence was causally relevant to the decision. Simon et al. (2001) extended this line of research by showing that coherence emerged even before individuals expressed an interim verdict (Experiment 1). It is conceivable that only single a argument persuaded individuals. But if individuals used a constraint-satisfaction process to reach a verdict, then participants would be expected to shift their assessments of all the points at issue in the direction of their eventual verdict.

At baseline only 2 of the 21 correlations among the disputed points and verdict were significantly positive, at interim test all but 5 were significantly positive, and post-decision all but 3. Coherence had emerged by the interim test phase and was unaffected by whether or not individuals had made an explicit, if interim, decision.

In subsequent studies, coherence emerged under various orienting instructions: *memorization* (Experiment 2), where individuals were initially instructed to memorize the text and there was no mention that any decision would be required; *reception* (Experiment 3) where individuals were led to believe that more information was to be supplied later; and *communication* (Experiment 3) where they were told that the information would have to be communicated later. Crucially, there was no effect of whether or not individuals gave a preliminary judgement before or after their ratings on the interim test. In other words, the shift in coherence was not a product of having reached a decision. In addition, there was no difference between interim and final decision.

The fact that the same pattern of coherence emerged over a range of different orienting instructions indicates that a process common to all such tasks is involved. In all tasks, the material has to be comprehended. Such shifts might then be an outcome of comprehending material and the search after meaning. In understanding text individuals seek to build representations of meaning that are coherent both between successive sentences (by drawing bridging inferences, for example) and at the level of the text as a whole (i.e., what it is about – see Bransford & Johnson, 1973; Graesser, Singer, & Trabasso, 1994, p. 371). Coherence shifts arose even though these served no accuracy goal either. Instead, Simon et al. (2001, p. 1259) propose that the attainment of coherence can be viewed as a cognitively driven goal that guides reasoning processes ostensibly intended to achieve accuracy goals.

COHERENCE AND THE DUAL REPRESENTATION OF ARGUMENTS

Argument structure

What mediates shifts in coherence? Coherence could reflect the perceived structure of the presented arguments such that arguments pro a position are mutually excitatory and inhibit arguments counter to that position.

Arguments (minimally comprising a claim and a reason, Voss & Means, 1991) bear different relations to one another (see, for example, Baron, 1995; van Eemeren et al., 1996; Kuhn, 1991; Rips, 1999; Toulmin, 1958). One argument might support another by providing a further reason for the claim it makes. Alternatively, it may undercut the reason motivating the claim or else present an opposing claim (a counter-argument or rebuttal).[1]

A priori, individuals need to represent the structure of arguments. For instance, in a discussion individuals need to know which arguments are for, and which arguments are against, a particular view. They also need to keep track of who is committed to which arguments (see Rips, 1999). Individuals can certainly identify arguments in texts (e.g., Oestermeier & Hesse, 2000; Shaw, 1996), and although there has been little psychological work on this question they must also represent the structure of arguments. If coherence involves perception of the structure of arguments then changes in coherence should emerge during the course of processing case material. Such shifts in coherence should be observed when individuals rate the strength of the presented arguments (not simply their agreement with them) and the intercorrelations of these ratings should reflect the formal structure of the arguments. Together with Rachel McCloy, we examined changes in the perception of arguments as a case unfolded. The case was loosely based on that used by Simon and Holyoak (1999) and concerned two companies, Quest and Futura. Participants were presented with three blocks of arguments with the order of presentation counterbalanced.

Each argument block consisted of four different arguments. These were a principal argument in favour of the position (either pro Quest or pro Futura) advocated by the block, a counter-argument to the principal argument, an undercutting argument to the counter-argument, and a supporting argument to the principal argument. These categories are illustrated in the example given below. Within each argument block, the arguments were presented in the order (1) principal argument, (2) an argument undercutting the counter-argument, (3) the counter-argument, and (4) an argument supporting the principal argument. To create the two conditions of the experiment, we constructed three pairs of matched argument blocks. In each pair one block was pro Quest and one block was pro Futura. The blocks were matched in that the counter-argument in one block appeared as the principal argument in the other block and vice versa. The undercutting and supporting arguments were then tailored to match their corresponding counter-argument and principal argument. Here is an example (the numbers used here are used purely to aid explanation and did not appear in the text presented to participants):

> (1) Quest argues that Futura's action resulted directly in the collapse of the company by frightening the company's investors and creditors. (2) They further argue that the majority of investors who withdrew money from Quest cited Futura's message as the main reason for their unhappiness with Quest, contrary to (3) Futura's argument that Quest's poor performance was to blame. (4) Quest also argue that Futura was the only large investor to criticise Quest openly in this manner, suggesting that many people were not unhappy with Quest's performance.

In this block, which is pro Quest, argument number 1 is the principal argument, argument number 2 is the undercutting argument, argument number 3 is the counter-argument, and argument number 4 is the supporting argument. Comparable materials were devised that were pro Futura. In the pro Futura block, the original principal argument (1) appears as the counter-argument, whereas the original counter-argument (3) appears as the principal argument. The undercutting argument and the supporting argument changed in line with the changes in the counter-argument and the principal argument.

Individuals rated the strength of each presented argument before providing an interim verdict. If individuals are sensitive to the structure and to the content of these arguments, we should expect positive correlations of strength ratings among arguments that mutually support one another (the principal argument, the supporting argument, and the argument undercutting the counter-argument). Each of these strength ratings, in turn, should correlate negatively with the counter-argument. The mean Pearson correlations among the three supporting arguments increased over successive blocks, averaging +.101 in block 1, +.479 in block 2, and +.576 in block 3. The mean correlations of these arguments with the counter-argument increased and then decreased (−.182, −.403 and −.179, for blocks 1, 2, and 3, respectively). These results extend the results reported by Holyoak and Simon (1999) and Simon et al. (2001). Individuals are sensitive to the structure of arguments, and discriminate between supporting and undermining arguments in terms of their ratings of argument strength. Coherence amongst arguments, at least supporting arguments, increases during the course of processing material.

Examining the intercorrelation of ratings of argument strength provides an indirect method for examining perceived argument structure. One alternative direct method is to ask individuals to sort sets of arguments differing formally in various ways, to see if they sort them into groups corresponding to their formal properties. More pertinent is to understand how individuals perceive arguments in the context of a decision-making task. In one study Green and McCloy (2003) participants drew a diagram of how they perceived the interrelationship of the presented arguments and their connections to their decision.

Diagrammatic representations have been used by argumentation theorists (e.g., van Eemeren & Grootendorst, 1992, pp. 76–85) to capture the formal relations among arguments and, in previous work, I have found that diagrams offer an effective way of eliciting individual perceptions of complex issues (e.g., Green, 2000, Green & McManus, 1995; see also Torrens, Thompson, & Cramer, 1999 for the use of diagrams in understanding syllogistic reasoning performance). Green and McCloy (2003) presented individuals with two pairs of arguments in a version of the mock legal case described above. In each pair, one argument was nominally pro the plaintiff and the other pro the defendant (see below). After they had reached their decision and rated their confidence in it, participants drew a diagram indicating how they saw the various arguments relating to one another and to their decision.

The majority of individuals (81%) represented arguments in line with the experimenter-defined designation as pro plaintiff or pro defendant. However, as anticipated, individuals differed in their perceptions of argument structure. We expected such differences to yield differences in rated confidence. A total of 66% of participants represented arguments as linking only to their decision (direct-relations only diagrams); 25% represented a one-way relation between argument and counter-argument (one-way diagrams) and 9% represented a two-way relation between argument and counter-argument (two-way diagrams, i.e., they depicted the argument and counter-argument of each pair of arguments as mutually undermining one another). As predicted, individuals with two-way diagrams were less confident than those with one-way diagrams, and individuals with one-way diagrams were more confident than those with direct-relations-only diagrams, although only the latter difference was statistically significant.

Argument models: The dual representation of arguments

Individuals must certainly represent the relationship of arguments to one another, and so coherence shifts could reflect the perceived organization of the presented arguments. Alternatively, shifts in coherence could fundamentally reflect the states of affairs to which these arguments refer. Coherence among the agreement ratings or ratings of argument strength could reflect the interpretation of events. On this view, arguments are fundamentally about states of affairs, and the key to understanding how arguments relate to decisions is to understand the nature of the mental models that individuals construct. These possibilities are not exclusive. The core of the present proposal is that a comprehension process generates an argument structure and builds one or more mental models of the states of affairs relevant to the issue (Green, 2001). Individuals construct a dual representation.

The task, or a person's construal of it, determines the criteria for reaching a decision such as how arguments are to be evaluated. An argument can be evaluated *qua* argument. For instance, the evaluation could be in terms of the sheer number or complexity of the arguments expressed in favour of a given position irrespective of their quality (analogous to the peripheral route in the model of persuasion developed by Petty & Cacioppo, 1984). Alternatively, the quality of the data cited in the argument may be used to evaluate it. Such metrics or yardsticks are general. An alternative yardstick is to evaluate the support for a claim by assessing the extent to which the states of affairs referred to by the arguments give rise to the results proposed. So, for example, is it the case that some action on the part of the defendant caused the outcome? Such a claim may be assessed by mentally simulating the possibility (Kahneman & Tversky, 1982). The resulting model is justified or warranted by the mental simulation. It will be termed an argument model.

Exploring the notion of an argument model

In principle, individuals could reach a verdict by assessing the quality of arguments and not construct any representation of the causal possibilities. As a way to assess what individuals did, we asked them to provide reasons for their decisions and then analyzed the nature of these reasons. We also asked individuals explicitly whether or not they considered the possibility that the defendant's action was the cause of the bankruptcy and/or whether some action by the plaintiff was its cause. Participants first read the following background material:

> As you may know a company's current share price reflects the views of many investors and investment companies on the stream of profits the company will make in the future. Share prices rise if the market as a whole believes that there will be a strong stream of profits. Share prices fall in the expectation that profits will fall. The present case concerns Quest – a computer software company with an excellent track record and with a strong range of well-tested and innovative products. Innovation is important in the sector but a new product must also be well tested. At the time of the case, overall share prices within its sector had fallen dramatically and lost between 70% to 80% of their value. 4 out of 5 companies had suffered such declines. At such a time, a company's share price can be extremely sensitive to negative information. Futura is an investment company specializing in high technology companies but with no specific expertise in Quest's sector of the market. On its internet site, Futura criticised Quest's management. Two weeks later Quest filed for bankruptcy and is now suing Futura claiming that Futura's message caused investors to lose confidence in Quest. The key arguments of the case are summarised below. Your task is to reach a verdict on the case given these arguments.

Participants then read one pair of arguments that referred to Quest's share price and another that referred to a future product the company was developing.

1. Quest argued that their shares were trading at the average price of the shares in their sector prior to Futura's message.
2. Futura argued that Quest's shares had already lost three quarters of their value over the previous two weeks and were still falling sharply at the time of their message.
3. Quest argued that their new product was likely to be profitable and would have boosted their share price if they had been able to launch it.
4. Futura argued that Quest's new product was still a year away from being launched at the time of their message and was too late to improve the company's prospects.

Half the participants were informed in advance that they would need to justify their decisions (justification condition) and half were not (basic condition). The order of presenting the arguments was suitably counterbalanced over participants.

A reason was categorized as one of argument quality if it mentioned, for example, that the argument was weak and/or that the argument cited no facts or independent support for its claim. Individuals could also reach a verdict on the basis of their understanding of the causal possibilities. We expected individuals who found in favour of the plaintiff (Quest) either to mention that Futura's message caused Quest to become bankrupt (a direct causal reason) or to mention that Quest would not have become bankrupt if Futura had not posted its message (a counterfactual causal reason) indicated by expressions such as "if only Futura had not posted its message, Quest would (probably) have survived". A counterfactual mental representation presupposes the factual situation that the message was posted and that Quest became bankrupt. It represents the *conjectured* possibility that without the message being posted Quest survived (see Boninger, Gleicher, & Stratham, 1994; Byrne & Tasso, 1999; Fillenbaum, 1974; Johnson-Laird & Byrne, 1991). In contrast, individuals who found in favour of the defendant would provide a semifactual causal reason for their decision indicated by expressions such as "Even if Futura had not posted its message, Quest would (probably) have failed". The mental representation of a semifactual presupposes the factual situation and represents the *conjectured* possibility that without Futura's message, Quest failed (see McCloy & Byrne, 2002 for a further discussion of the role of counterfactual and semifactual thinking in causal judgements).

We expected that the instructions would modulate the proportion of individuals mentioning the quality of arguments as a reason for their decision. In the basic condition ($N = 39$), most participants (64%) provided a causal reason for their verdict, 15% mentioned argument quality, and none gave both a causal reason and argument quality reason. A final 21% mentioned some other reason (e.g., to do with motives). In the justification condition ($N = 38$), the figures for these types of reason were respectively, 42%, 29%, 18%, and 11%. If we ignore "other" reasons and contrast cases in which only a causal reason was mentioned with cases in which there is mention of the quality of argument (i.e, either an argument-only reason or reason combining a comment on argument quality and a causal reason) then significantly fewer participants commented on argument quality in the basic condition compared with the justification condition (19% vs 53%).

As expected, if we tabulate the data according to the type of causal reason mentioned, direct causal reasons (26%) or counterfactual reasons (41%) are prominent for those reaching a verdict in favour of the plaintiff. In contrast for those favouring the defendant, semifactual reasons are prominent (53%).

Individuals, it seems, generally provide causal arguments for their decisions and these arguments vary with the verdict. However, even those who reached a verdict based on an assessment of argument quality also reported envisaging one or two causal possibilities. So it is more correct to say that instructions increased the tendency to provide a specific kind of account for the decision. The basis of the decision was an assessment of the state of affairs that gave rise to the outcome.

What are the consequences of envisaging one versus two models? Conceivably individuals who envisage two models might be less confident in their verdicts (cf. Kuhn et al., 1994). In fact, in pilot work, this seemed to be the case but there was no overall difference in the present study. Consider the decision problem. Where individuals envisage a single model, they do not explore the alternative in detail. In such a case, confidence might decrease as a function of the strength of arguments for the other possibility (i.e., the counter-argument). In principle, those who envisage two causal possibilities could also endorse the possibility with the highest support (reflected in the ratings of argument strength). However, those who envisage two causal possibilities may actively reject the non-preferred alternative. If they choose to do so then they need an argument sufficient to undermine the counter-argument. Their confidence might then, apparently paradoxically, increase as a positive function of the strength of the counter-argument. Such an outcome should hold especially for those who report explicitly rejecting the alternative.

The results support these predictions. For those envisaging a single mental model ($N = 29$), confidence decreased as a function the rated strength of the counter-arguments with the strength of supporting arguments partialled out. The partial correlation of the rated strength of supporting arguments and confidence was not significant. In contrast, for those envisaging two mental models ($N = 48$) stronger counter-arguments were associated with *increased* confidence. This effect was most marked for those ($N = 12$) who reported explicitly rejecting the non-preferred alternative. As in the case of those envisaging a single model, there was no effect on confidence of the strength of the supporting arguments.

We have treated an envisaged model as the best account of the data. The best account of the data depends on what data are being considered. As noted above, the background material provided grounds for undermining the defendant's arguments. We expected therefore that individuals finding in favour of the plaintiff as opposed to the defendant would be more likely to mention background information in the reasons for their verdict. A total of 79% of those finding in favour of the plaintiff, Quest ($N = 34$), cited background information. In contrast, 80% finding in favour of Futura ($N = 43$) mentioned no background information.

Do individuals need to identify the best account of the data? In other circumstances, individuals might start off with an hypothesis and assess the extent to which the case material fits it. Conceivably then rather different effects would be observed if we presented individuals with a ready-made decision and asked them whether it should be endorsed or overturned. In this case, individuals might endorse the existing decision as long as it was supported more or less by case material. Such a strategy might lead individuals merely to question the quality of arguments for the other side.

In a follow-up study, participants were asked to imagine themselves as an appeal court judge hearing a case that concerns two companies. Their task was to decide whether or not there were grounds for endorsing, or for overturning, the original decision. Participants were assigned at random either to a condition where the prior verdict was in favour of Quest ($N = 41$) or in favour of Futura ($N = 43$). They then read the same material as participants in the original study under the justification instructions. Contrary to a satisficing strategy, participants were unaffected by the initial verdict. Participants mostly decided in favour of the defendant, Futura (63% given Quest and 77% given Futura). As previously, the main predictor of a verdict in favour of the plaintiff Quest was the use of background information.

Contrary to initial expectation, the majority (63%) gave causal reasons for their verdicts and these were linked consistently with the verdicts as in the previous study. Of those giving argument-only reasons ($N = 13$), over three-quarters (77%) found in favour of Futura, presumably because it is up to the plaintiff to prove that the defendant is at fault rather than up to the defendant to prove their innocence (Bailenson & Rips, 1996). However, as in the previous study, all participants envisaged a causal possibility rather than reaching a verdict based on the quality of the argument alone. Hence, judgements of argument quality did not curtail processing. Instead individuals used argument quality either to flesh-out one causal possibility or to adjudicate between two envisaged causal possibilities.

As previously, the majority of participants envisaged two mental models (63%). Curiously, those envisaging two models were slightly more confident (10% on average) in their verdicts than those who envisaged just one model. Of more interest is the extent to which a slight change in task altered the relation between strength of argument and confidence. Excepting participants ($N = 18$) who explicitly rejected an alternative model, participants who envisaged one or two models ($N = 66$) performed similarly whether they endorsed or overturned the prior verdict. In contrast to the earlier study, confidence increased significantly with the rated strength of supporting arguments and decreased with the rated strength of counter-arguments, although not significantly so. Only those who overturned the verdict and explicitly rejected the alternative possibility ($N = 10$) showed increased confidence as a function of the strength of the counter-argument. Those who endorsed the verdict and explicitly rejected the alternative ($N = 8$) showed decreased confidence as the strength of the counter-argument increased. In short, in this task, confidence was more strongly associated with support for the preferred possibility rather than with support of the non-preferred alternative. Only those who overturned *and* explicitly rejected the non-preferred alternative increased their confidence as a function of the strength of the counter-argument.

If individuals base their decisions on a causal explanation of the event, then perceptions of argument structure, as described above, may reflect operations on the envisaged models. That is, a diagrammatic representation in which individuals represent one argument as undermining another argument may be functionally equivalent to the case where an alternative model is explicitly rejected. Consistent with this possibility, individuals in the first study who rejected the alternative causal model were slightly more confident (1.70 scale points, on average) than those who did not explicitly reject the alternative. In the appeal study, where the verdict was overturned, explicit rejection of the alternative also led to a small increase in confidence by nearly two scale points on average. However, neither result was statistically robust. Pro tem, it is conceivable that the diagram task and the requirement to state whether the alternative was explicitly rejected are tapping into the same process. It follows that decisions are primarily determined by the judgements of the best fitting model.

COHERENCE, ARGUMENT MODELS, AND INDIVIDUAL DIFFERENCES

Individuals in the present studies differed in the number of envisaged causal models they reported. What accounts for this individual difference and how is it that individuals manage to favour one causal model over another? Consider the individual difference question first of all. One possibility is that envisaging more than one model reflects some general cognitive attribute such as the willingness to entertain alternatives. One area where this is likely to be revealed is the extent to which individuals consider future states of affairs. In the appeal study, participants also completed the Consideration of Future Consequences (CFC) questionnaire (Stratham, Gleicher, Boninger,

& Scott Edwards, 1994). This provides a validated measure of the extent to which individuals consider immediate or long-term consequences of behaviours. Individuals rate each of the questionnaire items on the extent to which it applies to them. One item reads: Often I engage in a particular behaviour in order to achieve outcomes that may not result for many years. A higher score indicates a greater concern with the future consequences. In the present case, scores on the questionnaire showed a small but significant positive correlation with the number of models envisaged (Pearson $r = .216$, $p < .05$). High-CFC participants were more likely to envisage two alternative causal models.

The willingness or motivation to think about future consequences may also reflect an interest or motivation to think about problems (as indexed, for instance, by the Need for Cognition Scale, Cacioppo, Petty, & Kao, 1984) and/or relate to measures of general intelligence (see also Kuhn, 1991). Torrens et al. (1999) showed that both factors predict the number of different alternative diagrams individuals draw to depict the states of affairs compatible with the premises of quantified syllogisms (e.g., Some of the A are not B and None of the B are C). In turn the number of envisaged alternatives predicts the extent to which individuals endorse invalid but believable conclusions.

The second question concerns the decision to prefer one causal model over another. Let us consider the possibility that individuals are seeking to make sense of the material. Pennington and Hastie (1993) proposed that individuals construct a story or narrative of the events. Such a story functions to generate the event in question. It functions in Peirce's terms (Feibleman, 1960; Green, 1994; Legrenzi, Legrenzi, Girotto, & Johnson-Laird, 2000) as an abductive explanation of an outcome such as Quest's bankruptcy.

Suppose individuals are trying to find the best fitting model. Now the best fitting model is the one that provides the simplest encoding of the data. The simplest encoding of a pattern of data is the shortest code to generate the data. Chater (1999) argued that the human perceptual system is geared to finding the most parsimonious description of the data. A parsimonious description is an important aspect of what is meant by a coherent representation (cf. Thagard, 1989). What counts as the simplest pattern depends on the kinds of data that are being considered and the weight attached to these data. Consider individuals who do or who do not mention background information in the two studies described above. Individuals who ignore the background and focus only on the arguments presented are effectively attaching zero weight to the background. For them the simplest encoding of the data will yield a verdict in favour of the plaintiff. A second important point is that there is a connection between simplicity and probability (Chater, 1999). The simplest pattern is also the most probable pattern. In short, the best fitting model is arguably the most parsimonious model as perceived by the individual and so will also be reckoned to be the most probable or likely model.

We have supposed so far that individuals are effectively concerned to establish the best fitting model. Which hypothesis best explains the facts? It is at least arguable that in everyday affairs individuals are not much interested in the best argument. Their primary goal is determining whether the arguments support the beliefs or opinions that they hold (e.g., Bartlett, 1958; Bereiter & Scardamalia, 1989, although see Kunda, 1990, discussed above). The second study showed that there are differences between the task of determining a verdict and endorsing or overturning a verdict. But these differences were primarily associated with the effects on confidence.

An important area is to examine how individuals respond in real-time to arguments that either support or undermine a previous position. Green et al. (1999 Experiment 3) showed that in the case of novel judgements individuals smoothly vary their opinions in the light of new arguments. Entrenched opinions may less susceptible to change because they are also part of a wider set of beliefs. It may be rational to avoid changing opinion because of the costs involved. But here the notion of an argument model may be relevant. It supposes that endorsement of a decision or opinion is an outcome of a process of mental simulation. The simulation explains the outcome. Individuals may become more committed to the extent that they engage in model building and mental simulation rather than merely appraising the quality of arguments. This notion fits well with the general observation that individual stories and narratives persuade individuals better than bare numbers.

CONCLUSIONS

The extent to which individuals act as deliberative or rational agents has provided fertile grounds for psychological research. The fact that affective evaluations predict opinion does not entail that such evaluations are based on representations distinct from those generating the arguments individuals would propose. The impact of the difficulty of generating an argument on opinion does not imply that some implicit process is at work. On the contrary, individuals may use the process of generating an argument as a proxy for the strength of arguments generated. The principal focus of this chapter has been to work through an example of deliberative thinking: reaching a verdict. Starting from the notion that individuals seek to establish a coherent representation, we have explored the nature of such coherence. The essential notion is that coherence can be understood as the construction of an argument model. The process of reaching such a model has effects on ratings of confidence. The idea of an argument model carries wider implications. For instance, it suggests that the process of persuading individuals is not simply a matter of presenting arguments that are well justified, but of presenting ones that can allow individuals to simulate, and to experience, the possibilities.

NOTE

1 Argumentation theorists have considered this matter and proposed various tests to establish the relationship among arguments. For instance, in a set of supporting arguments, one reason may be independent of a second reason if it provides a unique source of support for the claim or conclusion. Alternatively, the first reason might depend on the second. The independence of a pair of reasons may be tested by assuming that the second reason is false and then examining the extent to which this affects the degree of support for the claim offered by the first reason (e.g., van Eemeren & Grootendorst, 1992, pp. 76–85; Walton, 1996, pp. 119–120).

REFERENCES

Bailenson, J., & Rips, L. J. (1996). Informal reasoning and the burden of proof. *Applied Cognitive Psychology, 10*, S3–S16.

Baron, J. (1995). Myside bias in thinking about abortion. *Thinking and Reasoning, 1*, 221–235.

Bartlett, F. (1958). *Thinking: An experimental and social study*. London: Allen & Unwin.

Benthin, A., Slovic, P., Moran, P., Severson, H., Mertz, C. K., & Gerrard, M. (1995). Adolescent health-threatening and health-enhancing behaviors: A study of word association and imagery. *Journal of Adolescent Health, 17*, 143–152.

Bereiter, C., & Scardamalia, M. (1989). When weak explanations prevail. *Behavioral and Brain Sciences, 12*, 468–469.

Boninger, D. S., Gleicher, F., & Stratham, A. (1994). Counterfactual thinking: From what might have been to what may be. *Journal of Personality and Social Psychology, 67*, 297–307.

Bransford, J. D., & Johnson, M. K. (1973). Consideration of some problems of comprehension. In W. G. Chase (Ed.), *Visual information processing*. New York: Academic Press.

Byrne, R. M. J., & Tasso, A. (1999). Deductive reasoning with factual, possible and counterfactual conditionals. *Memory and Cognition, 27*, 726–740.

Cacioppo, J. T., Petty, R. E., & Kao, C. F. (1984). The efficient assessment of need for cognition. *Journal of Personality Assessment, 48*, 306–307.

Chater, N. (1999). The search for simplicity: A fundamental cognitive principle? *Quarterly Journal of Experimental Psychology, 52*A, 273–302.

Eagly, A. H., & Chaiken, S. (1993). *The psychology of attitudes*. Forth Worth, TX: Harcourt Brace Jovanovich.

Feibleman, J. K. (1960). *An introduction to Peirce's philosophy*. London: George Allen & Unwin.

Fillenbaum, S. (1974). Information amplified: Memory for counterfactual conditionals. *Journal of Experimental Psychology, 102*, 44–49.

Graesser, A. C., Singer, M., & Trabasso, T. (1994). Constructing inferences during narrative text comprehension. *Psychological Review, 101*, 371–395.

Green, D. W. (1994). Induction: Representation, strategy and argument. *International Studies in the Philosophy of Science, 8*, 45–50.

Green, D. W. (2000). Argument and opinion. In J. García-Madruga, N. Carriedo, & M. J. González-Labra (Eds.), *Mental models in reasoning* (pp. 57–67). Madrid: UNED.

Green, D. W. (2001). *A mental model theory of informal argument*. Paper presented to the Workshop on The Mental Models Theory of Reasoning: Refinements and Extensions, Brussels.

Green, D. W. (in press). Affect and argument. In V. Girotto & P. N. Johnson-Laird (Eds.), *The shape of reason*. Hove, UK: Psychology Press.

Green, D. W., McClelland, A., Muckli, L., & Simmons, C. (1999). Arguments and deontic decisions. *Acta Psychologica, 101*, 27–47.

Green, D. W., & McCloy, R. (2003). Reaching a verdict. *Thinking and Reasoning, 9*, 307–333.

Green, D. W., & McManus, I. C. (1995). Cognitive structural models: Perception of risk and prevention in coronary heart disease. *British Journal of Psychology, 86*, 321–336.

Haddock, G. (2002). It's easy to like or dislike Tony Blair: Accessibility experiences and the favourability of attitude judgements. *British Journal of Psychology, 93*, 257–267.

Hastie, R., & Park, B. (1986). The relationship between memory and judgement depends on whether the judgement is memory-based or on-line. *Psychological Review, 93*, 258–268.

Holyoak, K. J., & Simon, D. (1999). Bidirectional reasoning in decision making by constraint satisfaction. *Journal of Experimental Psychology: General, 128*, 3–31.

Iyengar, S., & Ottati, V. (1994). Cognitive perspective in political psychology. In R. S. Wyer Jr. & T. K. Srull (Eds.), *Handbook of social cognition* (Vol. 2, pp. 143–187). Hillsdale, NJ: Lawrence Erlbaum Associates Inc.

Johnson-Laird, P. N., & Byrne, R. M. J. (1991). *Deduction*. Hove, UK: Lawrence Erlbaum Associates Ltd.

Kahneman, D., & Tversky, A. (1982). The simulation heuristic. In D. Kahneman, P. Slovic, & A. Tversky (Eds.), *Judgment under uncertainty: Heuristics and biases* (pp. 201–208). New York: Cambridge University Press.

Kruglanski, A. W., & Ajzen, I. (1983). Bias and error in human judgement. *European Journal of Social Psychology, 13*, 1–44.

Kuhn, D. (1991). *The skills of argument*. Cambridge: Cambridge University Press.

Kuhn, D., Weinstock, M., & Flaton, R. (1994). How well do jurors reason? Competence dimensions of individual variation in a juror reasoning task. *Psychological Science, 5*, 289–296.

Kunda, Z. (1990). The case for motivated reasoning. *Psychological Bulletin, 108*, 480–498.

Legrenzi, M. S., Legrenzi, P., Girotto, V., & Johnson-Laird, P. N. (2000) Reasoning to consistency: A theory of naive nonmonotonic reasoning.

Lord, C. G., Lepper, M. R., & Preston, E. (1984). Considering the opposite: A corrective strategy for social judgment. *Journal of Personality and Social Psychology, 47*, 1231–1241.

MacGregor, D. G., Slovic, P., Dreman, D., & Berry, M. (2000). Imagery, affect, and financial judgment. *Journal of Psychology and Financial Markets, 1*, 104–110.

McCloy, R., & Byrne, R. M. J. (2002). Semifactual even if thinking. *Thinking and Reasoning, 8*, 41–67.

Oestermeier, U., & Hesse, F. W. (2000). Verbal and visual causal arguments. *Cognition, 75*, 65–104.

Pennington, N., & Hastie, R. (1993). Reasoning in explanation-based decision-making. *Cognition, 49*, 123–163.

Petty, R. E., & Cacioppo, J. T. (1984). The effects of involvement on responses to argument quantity and quality: Central and peripheral routes to persuasion. *Journal of Personality and Social Psychology, 46*, 69–81.

Rips, L. R. (1999). Reasoning and conversation. *Psychological Review, 105*, 411–441.

Russo, J. E., Medvec, V. H., & Meloy, M. G. (1996). The distortion of information during decisions. *Organizational Behaviour and Human Decision Processes, 66*, 102–110.

Shaw, V. (1996). The cognitive processes in informal reasoning. *Thinking and Reasoning, 2*, 51–80.

Simon, D., Pham, L. B., Le, Q. A., & Holyoak, K. J. (2001). The emergence of coherence over the course of decision-making. *Journal of Experimental Psychology: Learning, Memory and Cognition, 27*, 1250–1260.

Slovic, P., Finucane, M., Peters, E., & MacGregor, D. G. (2001). The affect heuristic. In T. Gilovich, D. Griffin, & D. Kahneman (Eds.), *Intuitive judgment: Heuristics and biases*. Cambridge: Cambridge University Press.

Stratham, A., Gleicher, F., Boninger, D. S., & Scott Edwards, C. (1994). The consideration of future consequences: Weighing immediate and distant outcomes of behaviour. *Journal of Personality and Social Psychology, 66*, 742–752.

Thagard, P. (1989). Explanatory coherence. *Behavioral and Brain Sciences, 12*, 435–467.

Torrens, D., Thompson, V. A., & Cramer, K. M. (1999). Individual differences and the belief bias effect: Mental models, logical necessity, and abstract reasoning. *Thinking and Reasoning, 5*, 1–28.

Toulmin, S. (1958). *The uses of argument*. Cambridge: Cambridge University Press.

van Eemeren, F. H., & Grootendorst, R. (1992). *Argumentation, communication and fallacies: A pragma-dialectical perspective*. Hillsdale, NJ: Lawrence Erlbaum Associates Inc.

van Eemeren, F. H., Grootendurst, R., Henkemans, F. S., et al. (1996). *Fundamentals of argumentation theory: A handbook of historical backgrounds and contemporary developments*. Mahwah, NJ: Lawrence Erlbaum Associates Inc.

Voss, J. F., & Means, M. L. (1991). Learning to reason via instruction in argumentation. *Learning and Instruction, 1*, 337–350.

Walton, D. N. (1996). *Argument structure: A pragmatic theory*. Toronto, Canada: University of Toronto Press.

Wänke, M., Bless, H., & Biller, B. (1996). Subjective experience versus content of information in the construction of attitude judgements. *Personality and Social Psychology Bulletin, 22*, 1105–1113.

Wilson, T. D., Lindsey, S., & Schooler, T. Y. (2000). A model of dual attitudes. *Psychological Review, 107*, 101–126.

Zajonc, R. B. (1980). Feeling and thinking: Preferences need no inferences. *American Psychologist, 35*, 151–175.

12 Reasoning about strategic interaction

Solution concepts in game theory

Andrew M. Colman

Game theory is concerned with rational choice in decisions involving two or more interdependent decision makers. Its range of applicability is broad, including all decisions in which an outcome depends on the actions of two or more decision makers, called *players*, each having two or more ways of acting, called *strategies*, and sufficiently well-defined preferences among the possible outcomes to enable numerical *payoffs* reflecting these preferences to be assigned.

Decision theory has a certain logical primacy in psychology, because decision making drives all deliberate behaviour, and game theory is the portion of decision theory dealing with decisions involving strategic interdependence. This chapter focuses on reasoning in games, and in particular on theoretical problems of specifying and understanding the nature of rationality in strategic interaction. These problems are far from trivial, because even simple games present deep and mysterious dilemmas that are imperfectly understood and have not been solved convincingly.

The notion of rationality underlying game theory is *instrumental rationality*, according to which rational agents choose the best means to achieve their most preferred outcomes. This means–end characterization of rational choice is conspicuously neutral regarding an agent's preferences or desires, a point that was stressed by the Scottish philosopher David Hume in a frequently quoted passage of his *Treatise of human nature*: "Reason is, and ought only to be the slave of the passions, and can never pretend to any other office than to serve and obey them. . . . A passion can never, in any sense, be call'd unreasonable, but when founded on a false supposition, or when it chuses means insufficient for the design'd end" (1739–40, 2.III.iii). Hume conceded only that preferences based on "false supposition" are unreasonable or irrational. Contemporary philosophers and game theorists take an even more permissive view, requiring only that preferences should be consistent. Although everyday language contains both internal reason statements (*P has a reason for doing x*) and external reason statements (*There is a reason for P to do x*), the philosopher Bernard Williams (1979) has shown that "external reason statements, when definitely isolated as such, are false, or incoherent, or really something else misleadingly expressed" (p. 26). A person's reasons for acting in a particular way are invariably internal, hence an action is instrumentally rational, *relative to the agent's knowledge and beliefs at the time of acting*, if it is the best means to achieve the most preferred outcome, provided only that the knowledge and beliefs are not inconsistent or incoherent. Thus, if I am thirsty, and I come upon a jar of powder that I believe to be cocoa but is actually rat poison, I act rationally, relative to my knowledge and beliefs, if I dissolve the powder in hot milk and drink the infusion, even though my preference for doing so is based on a false supposition.

Instrumental rationality is formalized in *expected utility theory*, introduced as an axiomatic system by von Neumann and Morgenstern (1947), in an appendix to the second edition of their book, *Theory of games and economic behaviour*. It is based on the idea that a rational agent has complete and consistent preferences among the available outcomes and also among gambles involving those outcomes. The theory assigns numerical utilities to the outcomes in such a way that players who always choose utility-maximizing options (strategies or gambles) can be shown to be acting in their own best interests and therefore to be instrumentally rational. In game theory, utilities are represented by payoffs, and the theory, as presented by von Neumann and Morgenstern, is primarily *normative*, inasmuch as its basic aim is to determine what strategies rational players should choose to maximize their payoffs. It is not primarily a *positive* or *descriptive* theory that predicts what strategies human players are likely to choose in practice. It can nonetheless be argued (Colman, 2003) that it becomes a positive theory by the addition of a bridging hypothesis of weak rationality, according to which people try to do the best for themselves in any given circumstances. Granted that deviations from perfect rationality are inevitable, because human decision makers have bounded rationality, the bridging hypothesis provides game theory with a secondary objective, that of making testable predictions, thus justifying the otherwise inexplicable enterprise of experimental gaming (reviewed by Camerer, 2003; Colman, 1995, chapters 5, 7, 9; Kagel & Roth, 1995, chapters 1–4; Pruitt & Kimmel, 1977).

The fundamental problem that we encounter when we attempt to determine rational play in games is that individual players have incomplete control over the outcomes of their actions. In individual decision making, expected utility theory provides a clear and unambiguous interpretation of rationality. A rational decision maker chooses the option with the highest expected utility or, if there is a tie for top place, one of the options with the highest expected utility. But a game does not generally have a strategy that is best in this straightforward sense, because a player's preferences range over outcomes, not strategies, and outcomes are determined partly by the choices of other players.

The remainder of this chapter will be devoted to the most prominent suggestions that have been put forward for solving this problem. I shall focus principally on *non-cooperative* games, except for a brief discussion of cooperative games near the end. The distinction between these two classes of games was introduced by Nash (1951). In non-cooperative games, the players act independently, whereas in cooperative games they are free to negotiate coalitions based on binding and enforceable agreements. The following sections are devoted to an examination of the ideas behind the major solution concepts – general principles designed to yield rational solutions to particular classes of games. These fundamental issues are seldom discussed in the game-theoretic literature.

NASH EQUILIBRIUM

The leading solution concept for non-cooperative games is undoubtedly *Nash equilibrium*. A Nash equilibrium (or *equilibrium point*, or *strategic equilibrium*, or simply *equilibrium*) is a profile of strategy choices, one for each of the n players in a game, such that each player's strategy is a *best reply* to the $n - 1$ others. A best reply is a strategy that maximizes a player's payoff, given the strategies chosen by the others. It follows from the definition that any non-equilibrium profile of strategies is necessarily self-destabilizing, inasmuch as at least one player has an incentive to deviate from it. It is often claimed, conversely, that an equilibrium point is self-supporting and self-enforcing, but we shall see that this is not always the case. An important psychological property of an equilibrium point is that it gives the players no cause to regret their strategy choices when those of their co-players are revealed.

The equilibrium concept can be illustrated by the Assurance Game, the payoff matrix of which is displayed in Figure 12.1. This is a simple two-person game, first introduced by Sen (1969), in which Player I chooses between the rows arbitrarily labelled *C* and *D*, Player II independently chooses between the columns labelled *C* and *D*, and by convention the pair of numbers in each cell are the payoffs to Player I and Player II in that order. What defines this game as the Assurance Game is the rank order of the payoffs rather than their absolute values – it is still an Assurance Game if the payoffs are 10, 0, –5, and –10, for example, provided that the highest payoff goes to each player in the (*C*, *C*) outcome, the second-highest payoff to each in the (*D*, *D*) outcome, and so on. The identities of other named games also depend on their ordinal structures.

```
                    II
              C          D
         ┌────────┬────────┐
       C │  4, 4  │  1, 2  │
    I    ├────────┼────────┤
       D │  2, 1  │  3, 3  │
         └────────┴────────┘
```

Figure 12.1 Assurance Game.

Sen (1969) gave the following interpretation to illustrate how the Assurance Game might arise in an everyday strategic interaction, at least in the dreaming spires of academia. Two people face the choice of going to a lecture or staying at home. Both regard being at the lecture *together* the best alternative; both, staying at home the next best; and the worst is for him or her to be at the ... lecture without the other (Sen, 1969, p. 4, footnote 5). Given these preferences, the strategic structure corresponds to Figure 12.1. It is clear that the (C, C) outcome in the top-left cell of the payoff matrix is an equilibrium point because, for Player I, C is the best reply to Player II's C, and for Player II, C is the best reply to Player I's C. But there is another equilibrium point at (D, D), where strategies are also best replies to each other. It yields lower payoffs for both players, and it seems intuitively obvious that rational players would choose their C strategies, because (C, C) is not only an equilibrium point but is the best equilibrium point for both players (technically, it is *payoff dominant*, and that is something we need to examine more closely later). In fact, (C, C) is uniquely *Pareto-efficient* in the sense that no other outcome gives either player a higher payoff without giving the other player a lower payoff.

The equilibrium concept was first formalized by Nash (1950a, 1951), who gave two separate proofs that every finite game – that is, every game with a finite number of players, each having a finite number of strategies – has at least one equilibrium point, provided that *mixed strategies* are brought into consideration. A mixed strategy is a probability distribution over a player's (pure) strategies. For example, if a player has two pure strategies, such as C and D in the Assurance Game, then one feasible mixed strategy involves choosing randomly between them with equal probabilities assigned to each, by tossing a coin, for example; another mixed strategy involves 60%–40% randomization, and so on. In fact, with the payoffs shown in Figure 12.1, it is easy to verify that if both players choose C and D with equal probability, these mixed strategies form a third Nash equilibrium, with expected payoffs of 2½ to each player. In the increasingly popular Bayesian interpretation of game theory, a mixed strategy is construed as uncertainty in the mind of a co-player about which pure strategy will be chosen (Harsanyi, 1973).

What makes Nash equilibrium so important is a theoretical discovery that if a game has a uniquely rational solution, then it must be an equilibrium point. This proposition was deduced by von Neumann and Morgenstern (1944, pp. 146–148), using a celebrated *Indirect Argument*, and prominently expounded by Luce and Raiffa (1957, pp. 63–65, 173). In its current interpretation, the Indirect Argument rests on the standard *common knowledge and rationality* assumptions of game theory. The first of these is that the specification of the game, embodied in a payoff matrix in the case of a two-person game, and everything that follows logically from it, are common knowledge among the players. The second is that the players are instrumentally rational, invariably choosing strategies that maximize their utilities or payoffs, relative to their knowledge and beliefs, and that this too is common knowledge in the game. The concept of *common knowledge* was introduced by Lewis (1969, pp. 52–68) and formalized by Aumann (1976). Roughly speaking, a proposition is common knowledge among a group of players if every player knows it to be true, knows that every other player knows it to be true, knows that every other player knows that every other player knows it to be true, and so on.

According to the standard assumptions, the specification of the game and the players' rationality are common knowledge in the game. From these assumptions, it can be proved that any uniquely rational solution must be an equilibrium point. First, an immediate implication of the common knowledge and rationality assumptions is that any conclusion that a player validly deduces about a game will be deduced by the co-player(s) and will be common knowledge in the game. This logical implication is called the *transparency of reason* (Bacharach, 1987). It implies that, if it is uniquely rational for Player 1 to choose Strategy s_1, Player 2 to choose Strategy s_2, ..., and Player n to choose Strategy s_n, then $s_1, s_2, \ldots, s_n$ must be best replies to one another because, by the transparency of reason, each player anticipates the others' strategies and, to maximize utility, chooses a best reply to them. Because $s_1, s_2, \ldots, s_n$ are best replies to one another, they are in Nash equilibrium by definition. This establishes that if a game has a uniquely rational solution, then that solution must necessarily be an equilibrium point. A deep and subtle problem that is often overlooked is that the converse does not necessarily hold, because the Indirect Argument rests on an unproved assumption that a game has a uniquely rational solution (Sugden, 1991). A Nash equilibrium, even if unique, is not necessarily a rational solution, because a game may have no uniquely rational solution.

Unstable equilibrium

If a particular outcome is a Nash equilibrium, that is not a sufficient reason for a rational player to choose the corresponding equilibrium strategy. This can be seen, first, in certain games with only mixed-strategy equilibrium points, such as the game shown in Figure 12.2. This game has no pure-strategy equilibrium point. Its unique equilibrium point is the mixed-strategy solution in which Player I randomizes between Strategies C and D with probabilities $\frac{2}{3}$ and $\frac{1}{3}$ respectively, and Player II randomizes between

		II	
		C	D
I	C	3, 3	4, 2
	D	5, 1	3, 3

Figure 12.2 Game with a unique mixed-strategy equilibrium point.

Strategies C and D with probabilities $\frac{1}{3}$ and $\frac{2}{3}$ respectively. If both players use these equilibrium strategies, then Player I's expected payoff is $3\frac{2}{3}$ and Player II's is $2\frac{1}{3}$, and neither player can benefit by deviating. The transparency of reason may seem to imply that each player will therefore expect the other to choose the prescribed equilibrium strategy. But if Player I expects Player II to choose ($\frac{1}{3}C$, $\frac{2}{3}D$), then this nullifies Player I's reason for choosing ($\frac{2}{3}C$, $\frac{1}{3}D$), because *any* pure or mixed strategy yields an identical expected payoff of $3\frac{2}{3}$ against Player II's mixed strategy, and the same argument applies, *mutatis mutandis*, to Player II. This is a valid deduction, and the transparency of reason ensures that it is common knowledge. It implies that neither player has any reason to expect the other to choose a mixed equilibrium strategy. In the mixed-strategy case, not only does the fact that a particular outcome is a Nash equilibrium fail to provide a player with a sufficient reason for choosing the corresponding equilibrium strategy but, on the contrary, it appears to vitiate any reason that a player might have for choosing it.

This suggests that the [($\frac{2}{3}C$, $\frac{1}{3}D$), ($\frac{1}{3}C$, $\frac{2}{3}D$)] mixed-strategy equilibrium solution in Figure 12.2 is unstable. A player can deviate from it unilaterally without suffering any penalty, although there is no positive incentive to do so. Harsanyi (1973) argued, however, that this instability is apparent rather than real, provided that an element of uncertainty is introduced into the modelling of the game. He suggested that a player should always be assumed to have a small amount of uncertainty about a co-player's payoffs. If games with solutions in mixed strategies are modelled by *disturbed games* with randomly fluctuating payoffs, deviating slightly from the values in the payoff matrix, then mixed-strategy equilibrium points disappear and are replaced by pure-strategy equilibrium points, and the fluctuating payoffs interact in such a way that rational players choose strategies with the probabilities prescribed by the original mixed-strategy solution. If the game shown in Figure 12.2 is disturbed, then it will no longer have a mixed-strategy solution. Player I will receive a higher payoff from either the C or the D strategy – C in $\frac{2}{3}$ of disturbed games and D in $\frac{1}{3}$ – and for Player II these proportions will be reversed. Thus, although rational players will simply choose their best pure strategies without making any attempt to randomize, they will choose them with the probabilities of the classical mixed-strategy solution.

Subgame-perfect equilibrium

There is worse to come for Nash equilibrium. Some equilibrium points require players to choose strategies that are arguably irrational. This anomaly was discovered by Selten (1965, 1975), who developed a refinement of Nash equilibrium, called the *subgame-perfect equilibrium*, specifically to eliminate it. A simple example of an imperfect equilibrium is shown in Figure 12.3.

In the payoff matrix shown in Figure 12.3(a), both (C, C) and (D, D) are equilibrium points, but (C, C) is subgame-perfect, in Selten's terminology,

Game theory 293

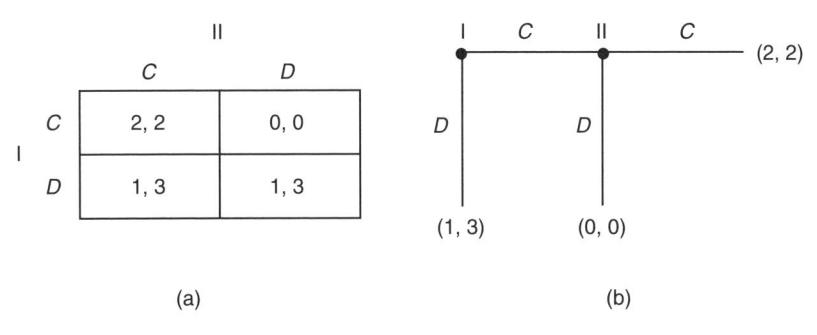

		II	
		C	D
I	C	2, 2	0, 0
	D	1, 3	1, 3

(a)

(b)

Figure 12.3 Game with an imperfect equilibrium point. (a) Normal form. (b) Extensive form.

and (D, D) is imperfect, requiring an irrational choice from one of the players. This emerges from an examination of the *extensive form* of the game shown in Figure 12.3(b), a graph depicting the players' moves as if they moved sequentially, starting with Player I on the left. If the game were played sequentially, and if the second decision node were reached, then a utility-maximizing Player II would choose C, to secure a payoff of 2, not D, yielding 0. Working backwards, Player I would anticipate Player II's reply and would therefore choose C rather than D, to secure 2 rather than 1. Thus we can conclude that (C, C) is the only rational equilibrium point of the extensive-form game, and it is therefore subgame-perfect. Because the (D, D) equilibrium point could not be reached by rational behaviour in the extensive form, it is imperfect in the normal form. A subgame-perfect equilibrium is one that induces payoff-maximizing choices in every branch or subgame of its extensive form.

Selten (1975) introduced the concept of *trembling-hand equilibrium* to identify and eliminate imperfect equilibria. At every decision node in the extensive form of a game there is assumed to be a small probability ε (epsilon) that the player's rationality will break down for some unspecified reason, resulting in a mistake or unintended move. The introduction of these small error probabilities produces a *perturbed game* – slightly different from Harsanyi's (1973) disturbed games, in which it is the payoffs rather than the players' actions that go astray. In Selten's theory, whenever a player's hand trembles, the erroneous move is assumed to be determined by a random process, and every move that could possibly be made at every decision node therefore has some positive probability of being played. Assuming that the players' trembling hands are common knowledge in a game, Selten proved that only the subgame-perfect equilibria of the original game remain equilibrium points in the perturbed game, and they continue to be equilibrium points as the probability ε tends to zero. According to this widely accepted refinement of the equilibrium concept, the standard game-theoretic assumption of rationality is reinterpreted as a limiting case of incomplete rationality.

PAYOFF DOMINANCE

Undoubtedly the most serious deficiency of Nash equilibrium as a solution concept is its systematic indeterminacy, arising from multiplicity of equilibrium points. We have already encountered this problem in the Assurance Game in Figure 12.1. Equilibrium points are convincing solutions to strictly competitive (finite, two-person, zero-sum) games in which one player's gain is invariably equal to the co-player's loss, because in such games, if there are multiple equilibrium points, then they are invariably *equivalent* and *interchangeable*. Two equilibrium points (E, F) and (E', F') are equivalent if the payoffs are the same in each, and they are interchangeable if (E, F') and (E', F) are also equilibrium points. Then it *makes no difference* which equilibrium strategies the players choose, because (it is easy to prove) the outcome is invariably an equilibrium point with the same payoffs. Figure 12.4, for example, shows a typical strictly competitive game. Following the convention for strictly competitive games, only Player I's payoffs are shown – Player II's are simply the negatives of these, Player I's gains being Player II's loses. The four outcomes $(C, D), (C, E), (D, D), (D, E)$ are all equilibrium points, and as long each player chooses an equilibrium strategy – C or D for Player I and D or E for Player II – the strategies are in equilibrium and payoffs are the same: 2 units to Player I and -2 to Player II.

The classic solution of strictly competitive games is widely accepted, although occasional sceptical voices have been raised against it from the beginning (see especially Ellsberg, 1956). But games that are not strictly competitive often have multiple equilibrium points that are non-equivalent and non-interchangeable, and as a consequence lack determinate equilibrium solutions. The Assurance Game shown in Figure 12.1 is a case in point: there are pure-strategy equilibrium points at (C, C) and (D, D), but they are non-equivalent because the payoffs are different in each, and non-interchangeable because if Player I chooses C and Player II D, for example, then the resulting (C, D) outcome is not an equilibrium point. In the Assurance Game, both players obviously prefer (C, C) to (D, D), but the Nash equilibrium criterion, on its own, is indeterminate, and games typically have several equilibrium points.

	II		
I	C	D	E
C	4	2	2
D	7	2	2
E	3	0	1

Figure 12.4 Strictly competitive game with multiple equilibrium points.

Game theory 295

In their influential book, *A general theory of equilibrium selection in games*, Harsanyi and Selten (1988) suggested a principle that they called the *payoff-dominance principle* to help solve the problem of Nash indeterminacy. (The also suggested a secondary *risk-dominance principle* that is not directly relevant to this discussion.) Given two equilibrium points in a game, one payoff-dominates (or Pareto-dominates) the other if it gives every player a higher payoff than the other. In the Assurance Game of Figure 12.1, (C, C) payoff-dominates (D, D), because it gives both players higher payoffs. The payoff-dominance principle is the proposition that if one equilibrium point payoff-dominates all others in a game, then rational players will choose the strategies corresponding to it. Harsanyi and Selten proposed that the payoff-dominance principle should be regarded as part of every player's concept of rationality and should be common knowledge among the players.

Payoff dominance is the leading principle of equilibrium selection, and its intuitive force is generally acknowledged (Colman, 1997; Colman & Bacharach, 1997; Crawford & Haller, 1990; Lewis, 1969; Sugden, 1995). But why is it intuitively compelling, and why should rational players use it? To expose the phenomenon in its starkest form, let us consider the Hi-Lo Matching Game shown in Figure 12.5(a).

The Hi-Lo Matching Game is really just a simplified version of Sen's Assurance Game with out-of-equilibrium payoffs stripped out. There are two pure-strategy equilibrium points at (C, C) and (D, D), and (C, C) obviously payoff-dominates (D, D). In spite of this, the standard common knowledge and rationality assumptions of game theory provide no rational justification for preferring C to D. That is why Harsanyi and Selten (1988) had to introduce the payoff-dominance principle as an axiom. A rational player would choose C rather than D if there were a reason to expect the co-player to choose C, but there is no such reason, because the co-player faces exactly the same quandary, and this leads to an infinite regress. It is impossible to derive a mandate for choosing C from the common knowledge and rationality assumptions. This point is widely misunderstood, presumably because choosing C seems intuitively rational, and it is therefore worth pausing to discuss two common fallacies.

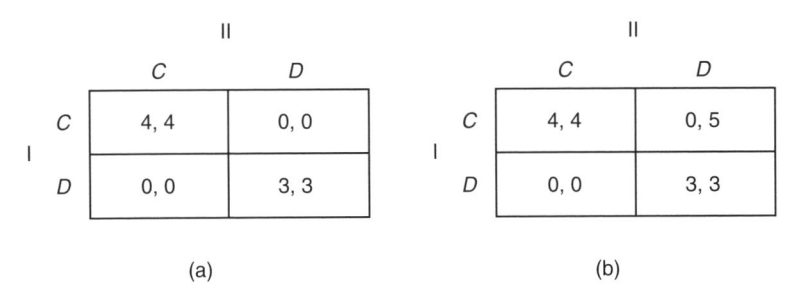

		II	
		C	D
I	C	4, 4	0, 0
	D	0, 0	3, 3

(a)

		II	
		C	D
I	C	4, 4	0, 5
	D	0, 0	3, 3

(b)

Figure 12.5 (a) Hi-Lo Matching Game. (b) Modified Hi-Lo Matching Game.

First, it is tempting to argue, as a referee of a journal article that I submitted once did, that C yields a payoff of 4 or zero, whereas D yields 3 or zero, therefore a rational player should choose C to maximize expected utility under uncertainty. This argument is easily refuted by considering the modified version in Figure 12.5(b). For Player I, C yields 4 or zero, whereas D yields 3 or zero, just as in the original version in Figure 12.5(a), but it is obvious that no rational Player I would choose C. In the modified game, Player II receives a higher payoff by choosing D than C against *both* of Player I's strategies and will therefore certainly choose D, if rational. By the transparency of reason, Player I knows this and, if rational, will therefore choose D in order to secure a payoff of 3 rather than zero. The only rational outcome in Figure 12.5(b), and of course the only Nash equilibrium, is (D, D).

The second fallacy is to assume that the Bayesian principle of insufficient reason can be used to assign equal probabilities to the co-player's strategies. According to this principle, we are entitled to consider two events as equally probable if we have no reason to consider one more probable than the other. If this were valid, then in the original Hi-Lo Matching Game of Figure 12.5(a), Player I might assume that Player II's strategies are equally probable, in which case it would certainly be rational for Player I to choose C, because it would yield a (subjective) expected utility of $(\frac{1}{2} \times 4) + (\frac{1}{2} \times 0) = 2$, whereas the expected utility of a D choice would be $(\frac{1}{2} \times 0) + (\frac{1}{2} \times 3) = 1\frac{1}{2}$. But then, by the transparency of reason, Player II would anticipate Player I's C strategy and, to maximize utility, would also choose C – with certainty. Player I would anticipate *this*, and we have a contradiction. Starting from the assumption that Player II's C and D strategies are equally probable, we have proved that their probabilities are 1 and 0 respectively. From the assumption that Player II is equally likely to choose C or D, we have proved that Player II is certain to choose C – *reductio ad absurdum*. No method of assigning subjective probabilities to co-players' strategies yields up a valid reason for choosing C in the Hi-Lo Matching Game.

There is simply no way of justifying the payoff-dominance principle in the Hi-Lo Matching Game, or in the Assurance Game of Figure 12.1, or in any other game, on the basis of the standard knowledge and rationality assumptions. Surprisingly, payoff dominance is not rationally justifiable, in spite of its intuitive appeal. But there is experimental evidence to show that human decision makers coordinate on payoff-dominant solutions with considerable ease, even in matching games with far more strategies than the Hi-Lo Matching Game (Mehta, Starmer, & Sugden, 1994) and that players are strongly influenced by payoff dominance in more complex games as well (Cooper, DeJong, Forsythe, & Ross, 1990). Various modifications of the assumptions have been suggested to account for this phenomenon, the most prominent being team reasoning and Stackelberg reasoning.

Team reasoning and Stackelberg reasoning

Team reasoning (Bacharach, 1999; Sugden, 1993) is based on the idea that, in certain circumstances, players act to maximize their collective payoff, relative to their knowledge and beliefs, rather than their individual payoffs. A team-reasoning player first identifies a profile of strategy choices that maximizes the collective payoff of the players, and if this profile is unique, plays the corresponding individual strategy that is a component of it. This involves a radical revision of the standard assumptions, according to which decision makers maximize individual payoffs. But examples of joint enterprises abound in which people appear to be motivated by collective rather than individual interests. On sports fields and battlefields, in commercial companies, university departments, and families, anecdotal evidence suggests that people sometimes choose actions according to what is good for "us", although their individual preferences may not coincide with the collective interest. In some circumstances de-individuation may even occur, with people tending to lose their sense of personal identity and accountability (Colman, 1991; Dipboye, 1977; Zimbardo, 1969). Team reasoning leads naturally to the selection of payoff-dominant equilibrium points such as (C, C) in Figures 12.1 and 12.5(a).

Experimental research has confirmed the intuition that there are circumstances in which decision makers prefer outcomes that maximize collective payoffs. Park and Colman (2001) reported an experiment in which 50 participants were presented with vignettes designed to elicit various social value orientations. In two vignettes, describing scenarios in which payoffs go into a common pool and the participants benefit jointly from cooperative outcomes, preferences were strongly and significantly biased towards joint rather than individual payoff maximization, and qualitative analysis of verbally expressed reasons for choices indicated that team-reasoning explanations, alluding directly or indirectly to collective payoff maximization, were invariably given in these two vignettes.

A second suggestion for explaining the payoff-dominance phenomenon is Stackelberg reasoning, suggested by Colman and Bacharach (1997). The assumption here is that players choose strategies that maximize their individual payoffs on the assumption that any choice will invariably be met by the co-player's best reply, as if players could read each others' minds. In the Hi-Lo Matching Game shown in Figure 12.5(a), for example, if the players assume that any strategy will always be correctly anticipated by the co-player, then Player I might reason that a C choice will be met with a C counter-strategy (because Player II prefers 4 to zero), and D will be met with by D (because Player II prefers 3 to zero). Player I would receive a payoff of 4 in the first case and 3 in the second, hence if the choice could be anticipated by Player II, then a rational Player I would choose C. If both players reason like this, then they choose the payoff-dominant (C, C) equilibrium point in the Hi-Lo Matching Game in Figure 12.5(a), or in the Assurance Game in Figure

12.1. Colman and Bacharach proved that Stackelberg reasoning results in coordination on a payoff-dominant equilibrium point in any game that has one. In some games, Stackelberg reasoning yields strategies that are not in equilibrium, and such games are not Stackelberg soluble. Stackelberg reasoning functions as a strategy generator and Nash equilibrium as a strategy filter.

Is there any evidence that people do, in fact reason in this way? Colman and Stirk (1998) reported an experiment in which 100 randomly paired players made one-off strategy choices in 12 different 2 × 2 games. Nine of the games were Stackelberg soluble and three were not. The players were motivated by substantial monetary payoffs. A significant bias towards Stackelberg strategies emerged in all Stackelberg-soluble games, with large effect sizes. In non-Stackelberg-soluble games, very small and non-significant effects were found. A protocol analysis of players' stated reasons for choices revealed joint payoff maximization to be a reason significantly more frequently in the Stackelberg-soluble games. These results provide strong evidence that Stackelberg reasoning influences players, at least in 2 × 2 games. Both Stackelberg reasoning and team reasoning probably contribute to the payoff-dominance phenomenon, and both require revision of the underlying assumptions of game theory.

STRATEGIC DOMINANCE

The concept of strategic dominance is illustrated in the familiar Prisoner's Dilemma Game (Figure 12.6). Each player chooses between cooperating (*C*) and defecting (*D*). Each receives a higher payoff from defecting than cooperating, irrespective of whether the other player cooperates or defects, but each receives a higher payoff if both cooperate than if both defect. The game's name derives from an interpretation devised by Albert W. Tucker for a seminar at Stanford University Psychology Department in 1950, a few months after the game was discovered at the RAND Corporation in Santa Barbara, California. Two people, charged with joint involvement in a serious crime, are arrested, prevented from communicating with each other, and interrogated separately. The police have insufficient information for a successful prosecution unless at least one of the prisoners discloses incriminating evidence. Each prisoner has to choose between cooperating with the other

		II *C*	II *D*
I	*C*	3, 3	0, 5
I	*D*	5, 0	2, 2

Figure 12.6 Prisoner's Dilemma Game.

prisoner by concealing the incriminating evidence (*C*) and defecting by disclosing it (*D*). If both cooperate, both are acquitted (the second-best payoff for each); if both defect, both are convicted (the third-best payoff for each); and if only one defects while the other cooperates, then according to a plea bargain offered to them, the one who defects is acquitted with a reward for helping the police (the best possible payoff), and the one who conceals the evidence receives an especially heavy sentence (the worst possible payoff).

The Prisoner's Dilemma is ubiquitous in everyday strategic interaction. It is a standard model of bilateral arms races (Brams, 1976, pp. 81–91) and of many similar interactions involving cooperation and competition, trust and suspicion. Rapoport (1962) found a poignant example in Puccini's opera *Tosca*, after Tosca's lover has been condemned to death, when the police chief, Scarpia, offers to save his life by ordering the firing squad to use blank cartridges if Tosca agrees to have sex with him. Tosca and Scarpia each face a choice between keeping their side of the bargain and double-crossing the other player, and the strategic structure corresponds to Figure 12.6. In the opera, Tosca and Scarpia both defect: Tosca stabs Scarpia as he is about to grab her, and Scarpia turns out not to have ordered the firing squad to use blank cartridges. The diabolically frustrating Prisoner's Dilemma game models cooperation versus competition, trust versus suspicion, and individualism versus collectivism. Multi-person social dilemmas with the same underlying strategic properties have also been extensively studied (see reviews by Colman, 1995, chapters 6, 7, 9; Foddy, Smithson, Schneider, & Hogg, 1999; Van Lange, Liebrand, Messick, & Wilke, 1992).

There is a certain logical inevitability about the unfolding tragedy in *Tosca*, and the unravelling of certain peace processes in political trouble spots. The reason is that *D* is a *dominant strategy* for both players, in the sense that each player receives a higher payoff from defecting than from cooperating, irrespective of the co-player's choice. If Player II chooses *C*, then Player I receives a higher payoff by playing *D* than *C* (Player I gets 5 rather than 3), and similarly if Player II chooses *D* (Player I gets 2 rather than 0). Defecting is thus the unconditionally best strategy for Player I, and by symmetry, the same applies to Player II. It is best for each player to defect whatever the other player does, but this entails a paradox, because each does better if both cooperate than if both defect. The (*D*, *D*) outcome, corresponding to dominant strategies, is the only Nash equilibrium, but if both players choose their dominated *C* strategies, then the outcome (*C*, *C*) is better for each. Rationality is thus self-defeating in the Prisoner's Dilemma Game.

In spite of strategic dominance, experimental evidence (reviewed by Colman, 1995, chapter 7) has shown that players frequently cooperate, to their mutual advantage. For example, in the largest experiment, in which the Prisoner's Dilemma Game was played repeatedly, approximately half of all strategy choices were cooperative (Rapoport & Chammah, 1965), and even in experiments using one-shot games, a substantial minority of choices tend

300 *Colman*

to be cooperative (e.g., Deutsch, 1960; Shafir & Tversky, 1992). Real players earn higher payoffs than they would have done had they followed the rational prescriptions of game theory. This is paradoxical, because rationality is defined as expected utility maximization.

As a solution concept, strategic dominance is warmly accepted by decision theorists and game theorists and, like motherhood and apple pie, it is seldom questioned. Its persuasive force seems overwhelming when dominance is strong – when a strategy yields a strictly better payoff than any alternative against all possible counter-strategies, as in the Prisoner's Dilemma Game. In those circumstances, it seems obvious that it is the uniquely rational way of acting. Attempts to justify cooperation in the one-shot Prisoner's Dilemma Game are laughed to scorn by game theorists (see Binmore, 1994, chapter 3). Even if a strategy only weakly dominates all other strategies – if it is at least as good against all counter-strategies and strictly better against at least one – that seems a knock-down argument for choosing it. But there are games that pose bigger challenges to the strategic dominance principle than the Prisoner's Dilemma Game.

The most notorious is Newcomb's problem, discovered by William A. Newcomb and published by Robert Nozick (1969), with the footnote: "It is a beautiful problem. I wish it were mine". For a detailed analysis of the problem from various angles, see Campbell and Sowden (1985). Here is a simple version of it. On the table is a transparent box containing £1000 and an opaque box containing either £1m or nothing. A player is offered the choice of taking both boxes or only the opaque box. The player is told, and believes, that a behavioural predictor, such as a sophisticated computer programmed with psychological information about the player, has already put £1m in the opaque box if and only if it has predicted that the player will take only that box, and not the transparent box as well. The player knows that the predictor is always correct or (if it is more credible) correct in 95% of cases, say, although the exact figure is not critical. The problem is summarized in Figure 12.7.

The predictor's payoffs are not shown in Figure 12.7, because they are assumed to play no part in the dilemma. The strategy of taking both boxes is strongly dominant, because it yields more than taking only one box against both of the predictor's counter-strategies – if the predictor has added £1m to the opaque box, then it yields £1m + £1000 rather than just £1000, and if the

	Predictor	
	Add £1m	No £1m
Player One box	£1m	£0
Both boxes	£1m + £1000	£1000

Figure 12.7 Newcomb's problem.

predictor has not added £1m to the opaque box, then it yields £1000 rather than nothing. That might seem to settle the matter, but the problem is that expected utility theory appears to require a rational player to take only one box. If the player takes both boxes, then the predictor will probably have left the opaque box empty, therefore the player will probably get only £1000, whereas if the player takes only one box, then the predictor will probably have left £1m in it. The player will therefore probably receive a much higher payoff by taking only one box. Thus seemingly irrefutable arguments appear to justify both the one-box and the two-box strategies – expected utility theory appears to justify taking only one box, and strategic dominance taking both. Most people, after pondering the problem, consider the rational strategy to be perfectly obvious, but they are divided as to which strategy that is (Nozick, 1969).

Rational players, by definition, maximize expected utility. Newcomb's problem represents a clash between two different ways of reasoning about expected utility, called *evidential* and *causal* expected utility respectively (Nozick, 1993, pp. 41–63). A player who maximizes evidential expected utility uses standard conditional probabilities (such as *the probability that the opaque box contains £1m given that it is chosen*) and infers that players who take only one box usually earn a fortune, whereas people who take both boxes usually do not. If you are a one-box type of person, then the conditional probability that the predictor has put £1m in it is high, and it follows that taking only one box is likely to net you a fortune, whereas if you are a two-box type of person, then there is probably nothing in the opaque box. According to evidential reasoning, the one-box strategy maximizes conditional expected utility and is therefore rational. A player who maximizes causal expected utility uses causally conditional probabilities, reasoning that taking only one box cannot cause £1m to appear in it, if it is not there already, therefore causal expected utility is maximized by taking both boxes. This is often illustrated with the *smoking gene* example. The statistician Ronald A. Fisher (1959) argued that cigarette smoking is a form of behaviour caused by a gene that also causes lung cancer. If this is true, then rational smokers should consider their smoking behaviour as unwelcome evidence that they probably have the gene and are likely to get lung cancer, but it would be futile for them to give up smoking on that account, because doing so would not cause the gene to disappear. On this view, it is equally futile to take only the opaque box in Newcomb's problem, because that cannot make money appear in it – the two-box strategy maximizes causal expected utility.

Although causal rather than evidential reasoning obviously applies in the smoking gene case, both evidential and causal reasoning can be defended in the right circumstances (Nozick, 1993). After Newcomb's problem was aired in *Scientific American* magazine in 1973, no fewer than 148 people wrote to the magazine, and 60% of them favoured the one-box strategy (Nozick, 1974). Experimental evidence (Anand, 1990) has confirmed that many intelligent and well-educated people favour the one-box strategy. Human decision makers evidently do not consider strong strategic dominance to be a knock-down argument in Newcomb's problem, and evidential reasoning has also been found in other problems (Quattrone & Tversky, 1984).

In some games, strategic dominance is more obviously irrational. These are games in which players' strategies are not independent of each other. I shall illustrate this with a game described in *Luke* 10: 30–37 that I shall call the Good Samaritan Game. An onlooker comes across a victim of a mugging. The onlooker has two available strategies, namely to help the victim, like the Good Samaritan, or pass by on the other side, like the Levite. The mugger is still lurking in the vicinity and may violently assault anyone who intervenes. The onlooker's utilities, taking into account the pain, suffering, and humiliation associated with being mugged (valued at –10 units of utility) and the warm glow that would arise from acting compassionately (worth 5 units of utility), are as shown in the Figure 12.8.

The onlooker's payoff from helping the victim is higher than the payoff from passing by on the other side *whether or not the mugger chooses the assaulting strategy*. This suggests that helping the victim is a strongly dominant strategy and must therefore be unconditionally best for a rational onlooker. The onlooker may reason as follows.

> The mugger may assault me whether or not I help the victim. If I'm to be assaulted, then I'm better off helping the victim than passing by on the other side, because then at least my bruises will not be in vain. On the other hand, if the mugger leaves me alone, I'm also better off helping the victim than passing by, because then I'll have done something good. I receive a higher payoff from helping in either case, therefore it must be rational for me to help the victim.

This argument is seductive but (alas) subtly flawed, because helping the victim may cause the onlooker to be assaulted, and passing by may result in the onlooker being left alone. The problem here is that the condition of *act independence* does not hold. As mentioned near the beginning of the section on Nash equilibrium, an explicit assumption of non-cooperative game theory is that the players choose their strategies independently. In the Good Samaritan Game, the onlooker's actions are not independent of the mugger's and may have the capacity to influence the mugger's. In the extreme, if the

		Mugger	
		Assault	Leave
Onlooker	Help	–5	5
	Pass	–10	0

Figure 12.8 Good Samaritan Game.

onlooker knew that helping the victim would certainly elicit an assault from the mugger and passing by would certainly not, then the outcomes (*Help, Assault*) and (*Pass, Leave*) on the main diagonal of the payoff matrix would be the only relevant ones and, given the onlooker's utility function, passing by would seem prudent, because (*Pass, Leave*) yields a better payoff to the onlooker than (*Help, Assault*) does.

Formally, according to evidential expected utility reasoning, if the conditional probabilities of the onlooker being assaulted are 1 if the onlooker helps the victim and 0 if the onlooker passes by, then *Prob*(*Assault* | *Help*) = 1, *Prob*(*Leave* | *Help*) = 0, *Prob*(*Assault* | *Pass*) = 0, *Prob*(*Leave* | *Pass*) = 1, and the conditional expected utility (CEU) of helping and of passing by can be calculated from the payoff matrix shown in Figure 12.8 using standard rules of probability:

CEU(*Help*) = [−5 × *Prob*(*Assault* | *Help*)] + [5 × *Prob*(*Leave* | *Help*)] = −5 + 0 = −5

CEU(*Pass*) = [−10 × *Prob*(*Assault* | *Pass*)] + [0 × *Prob*(*Leave* | *Pass*)] = 0 + 0 = 0

It is clear that passing by on the other side yields a higher conditional expected utility than helping. This shows why the argument from strong strategic dominance is fallacious when act independence does not hold. In my opinion, it also exposes the crux of Newcomb's problem. If the actions of the player and the predictor in Figure 12.7 are truly independent, then the dominance argument is valid and a rational player should take both boxes, whereas if act independence is violated by the specification of the problem, then evidential reasoning based on conditional expected utilities applies, and a rational player should take only the opaque box. Differences of opinion about Newcomb's problem seem to me to arise from disagreements about whether or not the specification of the problem implies act independence – if the predictor has paranormal powers, for example, then it might not.

STABLE SETS AND THE CORE

This chapter has been concerned mainly with non-cooperative games, but a few comments about cooperative games will help to place the earlier sections in perspective. In cooperative games, players are not constrained to choose strategies independently but are able to negotiate coalitions based on binding and enforceable agreements with one another.

The modern history of game theory is often traced to the publication of *Games and economic behaviour* by von Neumann and Morgenstern (1944). These pioneering theorists failed to derive a generalized equilibrium concept and devoted most of their attention to cooperative games, which they modelled in terms of different ways of dividing a payoff among the players, but it is fair to say that cooperative game theory is still poorly understood. Divisions of the payoff that satisfy conditions of individual and collective rationality are called *imputations*. These are divisions in which the individual players receive at least as much as they could guarantee for themselves by acting independently, and the grand coalition of all players receives the whole payoff, so that nothing is wasted. Von Neumann and Morgenstern struggled to find a solution concept that would prescribe a uniquely rational imputation for every cooperative game, but they succeeded only in showing that certain *stable sets* of imputations were rational in a specially defined sense. They interpreted these stable sets as standards of behaviour governed by social and moral conventions, providing no rational criteria for choosing particular imputations as solutions, and it subsequently transpired that there are games with no stable sets.

Nash (1950b) developed a more radical technique of modelling cooperative games as non-cooperative games and then applying his equilibrium solution concept. This proposed unification of game theory became known as the Nash programme, and it attracted considerable support, but its edge was blunted by Nash indeterminacy, as it emerged that reformulated non-cooperative games typically have multiple equilibrium points.

The most influential solution concept for cooperative games is the *core*, a natural extension of the imputation concept discovered by a postgraduate student (Gillies, 1953). The core of a cooperative game is an imputation in which every possible coalition of players receives at least as much as it could guarantee for itself by acting collectively. This would provide a convincing solution concept were it not for the unfortunate fact that many cooperative games gave empty cores, in the sense that no imputation satisfies all three requirements of individual, coalition, and collective rationality. The simplest example of this is the game of dividing a fixed sum of money among three players by majority vote. For every possible imputation, there is a coalition with the motive and the power to overturn it. For example, if Players I and II agree to take half the payoff each, then Player III can form a coalition with Player I in which Player I gets 60% and Player III 40%, and this coalition has the power to impose its will. I discussed a literary example of an empty core, taken from Harold Pinter's play, *The caretaker*, in Colman (1995, pp. 169–175).

CONCLUSIONS

A noted game theorist once warned that "the foundations of game theory are a morass into which it is not wise to wander if you have some place you want to get to in a hurry" (Binmore, 1994, p. 142). This is a salutary warning, but in this volume we are not in a hurry, and the foundations need to be secured to understand reasoning about interactive decision making. What can be seen clearly through the muddy waters of the morass is that the foundations are in need of maintenance work. The foundations should support whatever theoretical superstructure is required, but in their current state they cannot even support the payoff-dominance principle, leaving unexplained the intuitively obvious solutions to games such as the Hi-Lo Matching Game shown in Figure 12.5(a).

What is surprising and impressive is that we can make any progress at all in understanding reasoning in games. Instrumental rationality, which has a clear and simple interpretation in individual decision making, and can be defined rigorously in terms of expected utility maximization, is difficult to apply in interactive decision making, where the outcomes of a player's decisions depend partly on the decisions of other players. In spite of this, some progress has been made. I have outlined the major solution concepts, and I have discussed some of the problems that they raise.

The leading solution concept for non-cooperative games is undoubtedly Nash equilibrium. It follows logically from the standard knowledge and rationality assumptions of game theory that any uniquely rational solution to a game must be a Nash equilibrium. In the special case of strictly competitive games, this yields determinate and persuasive solutions, but in other classes of games, it narrows down the search for a rational solution without generally yielding determinate solutions. Application of the Nash equilibrium solution concept therefore leaves us with a residual problem of equilibrium selection.

The most compelling solution concept of all is strategic dominance. Nothing seems more obvious than the rationality of choosing a strategy that yields a higher payoff than any other against every possible counter-strategy or combination of counter-strategies. If one course of action is unconditionally best in all circumstances that might arise, then it seems obvious that a rational player will invariably choose it. Although this may seem controversial in certain special cases, such as Newcomb's problem, it is unassailable in games that clearly satisfy the condition of act independence. Provided that the players' actions are truly independent, this is therefore a good place to start when seeking a solution to a game. If a player has strategies that are even weakly dominated by others, then delete the dominated strategies. In the resulting reduced game, it may turn out that another player has dominated strategies that can be deleted, and if this process of iterated deletion of dominated strategies is continued, it sometimes converges on a unique solution. If act independence does not hold, then before beginning this process, the game should first be reformulated as a sequential game, with each player having perfect knowledge of any preceding move(s). It is useful to know that when simultaneous-choice games are reformulated as sequential games in this way, they often become soluble by iterated deletion of weakly dominated strategies.

The strategic dominance solution concept is not always helpful, however. In the Assurance Game of Figure 12.1 and the Hi-Lo Matching Game of Figure 12.5(a), for example, it gets us nowhere. In such cases, ad hoc methods of equilibrium selection such as the payoff-dominance principle may have to be applied. If a game with multiple equilibrium points has one yielding a higher payoff to every player than any other, then it seems obvious that rational players will play their parts in it. Team reasoning and Stackelberg reasoning provide possible mechanisms to explain the payoff-dominance principle, but the principle is not implied by the standard knowledge and rationality assumptions. Harsanyi and Selten (1988) introduced it into their general theory of equilibrium selection rather inelegantly as an axiom, though they did so with some reluctance (see their comments on pp. 355–363). In time, the fundamental assumptions of game theory may be amended to imply payoff dominance. But even that will not necessarily help us to understand strategic interactions in cooperative games in which binding and enforceable coalitions can be negotiated. When analysing a cooperative game, we can only hope that it has a core, because if it does not, then it may lack any determinate solution. Perhaps some games simply do not have uniquely rational solutions. If that is the case, it would be good to have a rigorous proof of it. Let us put on our wellington boots – there is work to be done.

ACKNOWLEDGEMENT

Preparation of this article was facilitated by a period of study leave granted to me by the University of Leicester.

REFERENCES

Anand, P. (1990). Two types of utility: An experimental investigation into the prevalence of causal and evidential utility maximisation. *Greek Economic Review*, *12*, 58–74.

Aumann, R. J. (1976). Agreeing to disagree. *Annals of Statistics*, *4*, 1236–1239.

Bacharach, M. (1987). A theory of rational decision in games. *Erkenntnis*, *27*, 17–55.

Bacharach, M. (1999). Interactive team reasoning: A contribution to the theory of co-operation. *Research in Economics*, *53*, 117–147.

Binmore, K. (1994). *Playing fair: Game theory and the social contract Volume I*. Cambridge, MA: MIT Press.

Brams, S. J. (1976). *Paradoxes in politics: An introduction to the nonobvious in political science*. New York: Free Press.

Camerer, C. F. (2003). *Behavioural game theory: Experiments in Strategic interaction*. Princeton, NJ: Russell Sage Foundation.

Campbell, R., & Sowden, L. (Eds.). (1985). *Paradoxes of rationality and cooperation: Prisoner's dilemma and Newcomb's problem*. Vancouver: University of British Columbia Press.

Colman, A. M. (1991). Crowd psychology in South African murder trials. *American Psychologist*, *46*, 1071–1079.

Colman, A. M. (1995). *Game theory and its applications in the social and biological sciences* (2nd Edn.). London: Routledge.

Colman, A. M. (1997). Salience and focusing in pure coordination games. *Journal of Economic Methodology, 4*, 61–81.
Colman, A. M. (2003). Cooperation, psychological game theory, and limitations of rationality in social interaction. *The Behavioral and Brain Sciences, 26*, 139–153.
Colman, A. M., & Bacharach, M. (1997). Payoff dominance and the Stackelberg heuristic. *Theory and Decision, 43*, 1–19.
Colman, A. M., & Stirk, J. A. (1998). Stackelberg reasoning in mixed-motive games: An experimental investigation. *Journal of Economic Psychology, 19*, 279–293.
Cooper, R. W., DeJong, D. V., Forsythe, R., & Ross, T. W. (1990). Selection criteria in coordination games: Some experimental results. *American Economic Review, 80*, 218–233.
Crawford, V. P., & Haller, H. (1990). Learning how to cooperate: Optimal play in repeated coordination games. *Econometrica, 58*, 571–595.
Deutsch, M. (1960). The effect of motivational orientation upon threat and suspicion. *Human Relations, 13*, 123–139.
Dipboye, R. L. (1977). Alternative approaches to deindividuation. *Psychological Bulletin, 85*, 1057–1075.
Ellsberg, D. (1956). Theory of the reluctant duellist. *American Economic Review, 46*, 909–923.
Fisher, R. A. (1959). *Smoking: The cancer controversy, some attempts to assess the controversy*. Edinburgh: Oliver & Boyd.
Foddy, M., Smithson, M., Schneider, S., & Hogg, M. (Eds.). (1999). *Resolving social dilemmas: Dynamic, structural, and intergroup aspects*. London: Psychology Press.
Gillies, D. B. (1953). *Some theorems on n-person games*. Unpublished doctoral dissertation, Princeton University, USA.
Harsanyi, J. C. (1973). Games with randomly distributed payoffs: A new rationale for mixed-strategy equilibrium points. *International Journal of Game Theory, 2*, 1–23.
Harsanyi, J. C., & Selten, R. (1988). *A general theory of equilibrium selection in games*. Cambridge, MA: MIT Press.
Hume, D. (1739–1740/1978) *A Treatise of Human Nature*. (2nd Edn., L. A. Selby-Bigge, Ed.). Oxford: Oxford University Press.
Kagel, J. H., & Roth, A. E. (Eds.). (1995). *Handbook of experimental economics*. Princeton, NJ: Princeton University Press.
Lewis, D. K. (1969). *Convention: A philosophical study*. Cambridge, MA: Harvard University Press.
Luce, R. D., & Raiffa, H. (1957). *Games and decisions: Introduction and critical survey*. New York: Wiley.
Mehta, J., Starmer, C., & Sugden, R. (1994). Focal points in pure coordination games: An experimental investigation. *Theory and Decision, 36*, 163–185.
Nash, J. F. (1950a). Equilibrium points in *n*-person games. *Proceedings of the National Academy of Sciences, USA, 36*, 48–49.
Nash, J. F. (1950b). The bargaining problem. *Econometrica, 18*, 155–162.
Nash, J. F. (1951). Non-cooperative games. *Annals of Mathematics, 54*, 286–295.
Nozick, R. (1969). Newcomb's problem and two principles of choice. In N. Rescher (Ed.), *Essays in honor of Carl Hempel* (pp. 114–146). Dordrecht: D. Reidl.
Nozick, R. (1974). Reflections on Newcomb's paradox. *Scientific American, 230*(3), 102–108.

Nozick, R. (1993). *The nature of rationality*. Princeton, NJ: Princeton University Press.

Park, J. R., & Colman, A. M. (2001). Team reasoning: An experimental investigation. Paper presented at the V Conference of the Society for the Advancement of Economic Theory, Ischia, 2–8 July.

Pruitt, D. G., & Kimmel, M. J. (1977). Twenty years of experimental gaming: Critique, synthesis, and suggestions for the future. *Annual Review of Psychology, 28*, 363–392.

Quattrone, G. A., & Tversky, A. (1984). Causal versus diagnostic contingencies: On self-deception and the voter's illusion. *Journal of Personality and Social Psychology, 46*, 237–248.

Rapoport, A. (1962). The use and misuse of game theory. *Scientific American, 207*(6), 108–118.

Rapoport, A., & Chammah, A. M. (1965). *Prisoner's dilemma: A study in conflict and cooperation*. Ann Arbor, MI: University of Michigan Press.

Selten, R. (1965). Spieltheoretische behandlung eines Oligopolmodells mit Nachfragetragheit. *Zeitschrift für die gesamte Staatswissenschaft, 121*, 301–324, 667–689.

Selten, R. (1975). Re-examination of the perfectness concept for equilibrium points in extensive games. *International Journal of Game Theory, 4*, 25–55.

Sen, A. K. (1969). A game-theoretic analysis of theories of collectivism in allocation. In T. Majumdar (Ed.), *Growth and choice: Essays in honour of U. N. Ghosal* (pp. 1–17). Calcutta: Oxford University Press.

Shafir, E., & Tversky, A. (1992). Thinking through uncertainty: Nonconsequential reasoning and choice. *Cognitive Psychology, 24*, 449–474.

Sugden, R. (1991). Rational bargaining. In M. Bacharach & S. Hurley (Eds.), *Foundations of decision theory* (pp. 294–315). Oxford: Blackwell.

Sugden, R. (1993). Thinking as a team: Towards an explanation of nonselfish behaviour. *Social Philosophy and Policy, 10*, 69–89.

Sugden, R. (1995). A theory of focal points. *Economic Journal, 105*, 533–550.

Van Lange, P. A. M., Liebrand, W. B. G., Messick, D. M., & Wilke, H. A. M. (1992). Social dilemmas: The state of the art. In W. B. G. Liebrand, D. M. Messick, & H. A. M. Wilke (Eds.), *Social dilemmas: Theoretical issues and research findings* (pp. 3–28). New York: Pergamon.

Von Neumann, J., & Morgenstern, O. (1944). *Theory of games and economic behaviour*. Princeton, NJ: Princeton University Press. [2nd Ed., 1947; 3rd Ed., 1953.]

Williams, B. (1979). Internal and external reasons. In R. Harrison (Ed.), *Rational action: Studies in philosophy and social science* (pp. 17–28). Cambridge: Cambridge University Press.

Zimbardo, P. G. (1969). The human choice: Individuation, reason, and order, vs deindividuation, impulse, and chaos. *Nebraska Symposium on Motivation, 17*, 237–307.

13 What we reason about and why

How evolution explains reasoning

Gary L. Brase

One of the more distinctive characteristics of evolutionary approaches to understanding human reasoning (or, indeed, to understanding the human mind in general) is its insistence on *domain specificity*. That is, evolutionary accounts of human reasoning propose that the vast bulk of reasoning that people normally engage in is done by cognitive processes that are specialized to work within a specific topic area (i.e., domain). The best known of these accounts is the work by Cosmides and Tooby (1989, 1992), that focuses on reasoning about social exchanges. A social exchange, briefly, is an exchange between two individuals that has the form of "If you take Benefit X, then you must pay Cost Y" – for example, "If you take this book, then you pay the cashier $20". A violation of this arrangement ("cheating") occurs when someone takes a benefit without paying the reciprocal cost (e.g., taking this book without paying for it), and this is a violation regardless of whether or not it is incorrect according to standards such as deductive logic. Other reasoning domains, involving other specialized cognitive processes, have been similarly proposed for reasoning about threats, precautions, social dominance hierarchies, social group memberships, objects, physical causality, artifacts, language, and mental states.

This domain specificity thesis is controversial for a number of reasons. It creates issues regarding how one should parse reasoning up into different domains. Domain specificity on the scale proposed by evolutionary psychologists also raises issues of how the mind can be organized to manage such a constellation of different and distinct mechanisms. For some traditional psychologists studying human reasoning, however, there may be a simpler cause for worry over the domain specificity thesis: Traditional theories of human reasoning are fundamentally based on extremely domain-*general* assumptions, which consider the reasoning process to be fundamentally the same across all subject matters. In a very real sense, then, domain-specific theories of human reasoning threaten the very foundations of some of the most prominent theories of human reasoning.

WHY NOT DEDUCTION AS THE DOMAIN?

Although the reasoning literature often labels certain theories as being domain specific or domain general, this is actually a false dichotomy. All theories are domain specific to some degree. Traditional reasoning theories such as the mental models approach, for instance, only cover reasoning; they do not address the areas of vision, motor movement, or interpersonal attraction. In fact, it is clear that the mind simply cannot be completely domain general or content independent. Such a general purpose system – with parameters open enough to accommodate vision, reasoning, courtship, and locomotion, to name but a few – would necessarily be a "weak" system (in the artificial intelligence sense; see Newell & Simon, 1972: a system in which the parameters are minimally constrained). Weak systems can solve certain well-defined problems (e.g., finding a pattern of letters in a database of text) and they can be quite powerful within such contexts, but they cannot deal with the ill-defined problems (e.g., finding a suitable spouse) that make up nearly all real-life problems (Simon, 1973). The debate is, therefore, not really if the mind has specific domains or not, but rather about *how specific* the domains are within the mind.

The conventional view of human reasoning has been that the only domain is that of deduction. The idea of studying deductive reasoning as a circumscribed area of inquiry is based on the notion that there are normative guidelines – typically formal deductive logic – about how reasoning is properly performed and that these guides transcend the particular contents or topics about which one is reasoning. For example, the conditional if p, then q allows certain deductive inferences (if p is true, then q is true, and if q is false, then p is false) regardless of what information is used to replace "p" and "q". Of course, one of the things everybody can agree on is that people do not always follow these guidelines. Some aspects of deductive logic are very difficult for people to apply in their reasoning, whereas other aspects of people's reasoning go far beyond what deductive logic would allow. Nevertheless, these theories assert that the computational problem for which reasoning exists is performing deductive logic, and the two systems – reasoning and deductive logic – should therefore be rather similar. The issues, then, became those of describing what aspects of reasoning mirror deductive logic, how those aspects are cognitively represented, and how those representations also lead to the deviations between human reasoning and formal logic. A classic division within deduction-based theories of human reasoning has to do with whether people reason with rules akin to (but not necessarily the same as) deduction (e.g., Braine, 1978; Braine et al., 1995; Rips, 1994), or people reason with more fluid representations, or models, of situations (Johnson-Laird, 1983, 2001; Johnson-Laird & Byrne, 1991, 1993).

Mental rules and mental models

Mental rule theories propose, in general, that the mind uses rule systems to reason. These rules may or may not be the rules of deductive logic, but they approximate deduction and attempt to serve the same purpose – finding the formal truth in situations. Deviations in reasoning from the results expected by deductive logic are considered the anomalies in need of explanations. Thus, the rules postulated in mental rules theories, while formal-logical in nature, also include additional assumptions to explain human reasoning behaviours. For example, the PSYCOP reasoning model proposed by Rips (1994) includes deductive inference rules such as "and" elimination, Double Negative Elimination, and Modus Ponens, but then adds that prior experiences may be used as the basis for some inferences. Other modifications and addenda to formal logic invoke various cognitive processing limitations, accessory processes, or constraints that interfere with (or augment) logical processing. Rule-based reasoning theories are generally quite well specified in terms of computational components, but as a class of theories they are difficult to conclusively invalidate. The reason for this situation is the large number of algorithm sets that could be used to satisfy the particular computational goals established for a rule-based theory. Any one set of rules or procedures is testable and potentially falsifiable, but the rules can merely be modified to avoid conclusive falsification as a class of reasoning theories (just as version 2.0 of a computer software program can be a disaster, but modifications to produce version 3.0 may result in a perfectly successful program; see Johnson-Laird, Byrne, & Schaeken, 1994).

A viewpoint traditionally given as the counter-theory to mental rule theories is the mental model theory, advocated by Johnson-Laird and colleagues (e.g., Johnson-Laird, 1983, 2001; Johnson-Laird & Byrne, 1991). Briefly, the mental models theory of reasoning proposes that people form an internal representation of the reasoning problem (a model), generate a tentative conclusion, and then search for alternative possible models that would falsify the original representation. As there is some uncertainty in these representations – that is, premises can be interpreted in more than one way – there is room for people to generate alternative models for a single syllogism. The theory of mental models is a Popperian hypothesis-falsification strategy (Popper, 1959) with an implicit goal of establishing the truth (though not necessarily via formal logic), assumed to be hampered by a human inability to always perform more complex computations. What initial model is generated can be influenced by semantic knowledge, and how exhaustively the initial model is evaluated is determined by cognitive processing limitations and/or limited cognitive efforts). The mental models theory also adds computational elements ("extra-logical constraints") that fit the theory to known data (specifically, that conclusion must conserve semantic information, be parsimonious, and assert something new). In mental models the processes are now more vaguely specified than in the mental rules account and no longer bound so rigidly to deductive competence, but the essential idea of deduction supplemented by additional processes remains unchanged. Furthermore, although the purpose for which reasoning exists has changed – from finding logical truth to finding any kind of useful and true conclusion – this is more of a shift in emphasis than a theoretical chasm. In contrast to mental rule theories, Johnson-Laird has promoted mental model theory as being simple to refute in principle (e.g., Johnson-Laird et al., 1994), but it is frustratingly difficult to refute in practice due to the vague nature of the mental model's procedures (Rips, 1986).

Research on models and rules

Both the mental rules and mental models views tend to focus on the syntax of the reasoning situation, as opposed to the content of the reasoning situation, when conducting research. This can easily be seen by looking at some of the reasoning items that studies from either of these perspectives use:

> If there is a red or a green marble in the box, then there is a blue marble in the box.
> Which is more likely to be in the box: the red marble or the blue marble?
> (Johnson-Laird, Legrenzi, Gorotto, Legrenzi, & Caverni, 1999, p. 64)

> IF Betty is in Little Rock THEN Ellen in is Hammond.
> *Phoebe is in Tucson AND Sandra is in Memphis.*
> IF Betty is in Little Rock THEN (Ellen is in Hammond AND Sandra is in Memphis).
> (Rips, 1994, p. 105)

It does not matter what contents are in the above sentences; what matters are the connecting terms (and, or, not, if, then) and their relative positions. In fact, the contents in the above tasks are specifically designed *not* to relate to anything that people normally encounter in the real world. Thus, although mental models and mental rules could be adequate explanations of how people reach conclusion in tasks like the above examples, reasoning in the real world is almost never about marbles in boxes or four strangers' locations in four cities. Instead, people reason about the situations, events, and people in their lives, and the contents (details about the situation, event, or person) are as important – if not more important – than the connecting terms. For these traditional views, however, reasoned inferences that are based in some way on the content of the reasoning task rather than on the logical connecting terms are often called "content effects" and are actually viewed as problematic.

Research done on the nature of content effects, from a domain-general viewpoint, have tended to produce fairly general explanations. For instance, one major explanation for content effects is the belief bias: the tendency to either accept conclusions known to be true or desirable even if they are logically unwarranted or reject conclusions known to be false or undesirable even if they are logically demanded (e.g., "All dangerous drugs are illegal; Cigarettes are dangerous drugs; Therefore, Cigarettes are illegal"; Evans, Barston, & Pollard, 1983; Markovits & Nantel, 1989; Newstead & Evans, 1993; Newstead, Pollard, Evans, & Allen, 1992; Oakhill & Garnham, 1993). Although there certainly is a phenomenon that is well described by the existence of belief biases, the use of this general explanation to resolve any type of inference that does not fit with a domain-general theory of reasoning seems suspect. First of all, this creates a situation in which nearly all research results can be explained *post hoc* (e.g., either a person reaches the correct conclusion by the ascribed process, or she reaches the incorrect conclusion because of some belief bias). Second, a belief bias is more of a label for what is occurring than it is an explanation of why it occurs, and specifically, it does not provide much guidance on when and why different beliefs will tend to bias reasoning processes in everyday life (Vadeboncoeur & Markovits, 1999). Third, the explanation of belief biases seems to cover a vast range of inference types that may include processes more complex than beliefs simply overriding deductive competence. Fourth, and perhaps most important, reasoning in the real world is always about something; it is always rich with content. People (aside from working logicians) do not just "reason" in an abstract manner. We use reasoning to understand the behaviours of others. We reason to understand why our car won't start. We use reasoning to decide upon our own behaviour. Although people seem to be able – with some effort – to reason about "If A, then B; given B is true; what follows?" it is not a usual human activity.

In summary, domain-general accounts of human reasoning may provide an explanation of how people solve fairly abstract reasoning tasks in laboratories, but the work of describing real-world, everyday reasoning (sometimes called "practical reasoning"; Audi, 1989) is largely shunted to accessory mechanisms or simply dismissed as content effects of little theoretical significance. The fact that there may be problems with a domain-general account of human reasoning, however, does not automatically lead to the conclusion that reasoning must be domain specific. It is also necessary to show that there are good reasons in favour of domain specificity as the more plausible explanation.

WHY DOMAIN SPECIFICITY?

Over the years, different people have argued for increasingly domain-specific abilities in various areas of psychology, with the fields of perception and psycholinguistics having the oldest histories of recognized domain-specific abilities. Within these fields, the tools of brain lesions (accidental and experimental), comparative animal studies, and computer modelling have shone an intense light on the modular structure of perception and language (e.g., Gardner, 1974; Gopnik & Crago, 1991; Kolb & Whishaw, 1990; Pinker, 1984, 1994; Pinker & Bloom, 1990). From line detectors and motion detectors, to a universal grammar and the sensory and motor homunculi – it has been continually revealed within these fields that the mind must have a functionally domain-specific cognitive architecture simply to account for the things that people manifestly do.

More recently, similar levels of modularization have been proposed within other areas of psychology. Researchers in the field of developmental psychology, for example, have developed theories and experimental support for domain-specific cognitive abilities that infants have at birth (Hirschfeld & Gelman, 1994), as well as domain-specific abilities that have developmental sequences (e.g., the Theory of Mind Module [ToMM], Baron-Cohen, 1994, 1995; Leslie, 1987). A more pervasive view of domain specificity is proposed by a general perspective known as *evolutionary psychology*. In one sense, evolutionary psychology is simply the study of psychology while taking into account the information known about evolutionary biology and the evolutionary history of the species being studied (i.e., anthropology and archaeology). Evolutionary psychology is furthermore often regarded as entailing some specific conclusions about how the mind is designed and how it works. These basic premises of evolutionary psychology are not shared universally (see, e.g., Holcomb, 2001), but this specific view of evolutionary psychology is important for several reasons: (1) it is clearly the dominant evolutionary view in the research field of human reasoning, (2) it strongly contrasts with the domain-general views of human reasoning, whereas many other evolutionary views can be understood as intermediate positions, and (3) it is clearly enunciated in terms of first principles derived from evolutionary biology and other fields. These first principles that form the foundation of evolutionary psychology are used to generate the conclusions that the mind is domain specific on a very extensive scale (sometimes called multimodular or even "massively modular"), that these domain-specific modules should be species-typical and common to nearly all people, and that the domains should map onto specific aspects of the world.

Evolutionary selection pressures and modularity

Look at your thumb for a minute. The human thumb is a remarkable and unique human evolved adaptation. At some point in evolutionary history, our ancestors began using tools. Those who had slightly better tool-handling skills were able to dig out more food, defend themselves a bit better, and attack opponents or prey with weapons a bit more accurately. These slight advantages had some partial basis in genetics, so these good early tool users passed on their predispositions to their children. Generation after generation the slightly better tool users survived and helped their children survive better than the slightly inferior tool users. The result today is a thumb that is physically different from the other digits, can directly oppose the other digits, and that has muscles specifically for tool use (Marzke & Wullstein, 1996). The forces that created the human thumb over thousands of generations are called evolutionary selection pressures (they select, by differential survival and reproduction, the individuals in a species that are better adapted to that species' environmental circumstances). The human thumb – the result of evolutionary selection pressures – is an evolved adaptation.

One of the necessary features of an evolutionary selection pressure is that it must be based on some aspect of the environment that posed a challenge to the species in question (e.g., the advantages of tool use included obtaining food to prevent starving, and defence against large predators). If there was no selection pressure "for" a particular adaptation, then the adaptation could not arise. The environment is not just generally a dangerous place, though; it is made up of all sorts of rather specific dangers and problems. There are dangers from large predators (lions, tigers, and bears), small predators (viruses and other pathogens), failing to satisfy your own needs (food, shelter, etc.), and even from conspecifics that mean you harm. In other words, evolutionary selection pressures are typically based on specific problems (i.e., dangers, threats, dilemmas) in the environment. Specific problems, to be effectively and efficiently solved, require specific solutions.

Figure 13.1 The fact that the human body and mind is a collection of domain specific adaptations is illustrated by the absurdity of the opposite alternative.

This basic property of the evolutionary process is a specific example of the principle described earlier, in which it was discovered by computer scientists that problem-solving systems have to be specific to the problem domain in order to be "strong" systems (i.e., able to solve the problem reliably, accurately, and efficiently). There are other examples of this principle as well. Philosophers recognized it as a general problem of induction (Quine, 1960), Chomsky (1975) recognized it in the domain of language acquisition as the "poverty of the stimuli", it is known in the field of artificial intelligence as the "frame problem", and in developmental psychology it motivates the idea of developmental "constraints". In fact, even within the field of logic there is some recognition that specific types of situations call for correspondingly specific forms of reasoning. Evaluating the truth of a conclusion derived from material statements calls for propositional logic; evaluating the violation of social rules calls for deontic logic.

The conclusion from all this is that one of the fundamental tenets of evolutionary psychology is that evolutionary selection pressures led to domain-specific adaptations, and therefore to a mind that is composed of many specific cognitive adaptations (sometimes called modules, leading to the label of multimodular, or massively modular, mind).

A universal human nature

No two people are completely alike; even identical twins can think, act, and to some extent look different from one another. At a certain level, however, all human beings share a common and universal human nature. Part of this universal human nature is the opposable thumb, and the ability to walk bipedally, and the capacity to learn language. From a biological and evolutionary standpoint, humans are all part of a single species and therefore there are certain features that all of us have and that define us as that species. Some people are more aggressive than others, some people are more intelligent than others, some people walk faster than others. But it is universal of all humans that we engage in aggression, thinking, and walking. Furthermore, all these characteristics are part of our human nature because they were developed over evolutionary history in response to various selection pressures. An extension of the fundamental tenet of a multimodular mind is that all normally developing humans have this multimodular cognitive structure, by virtue of being human. Certainly specific individuals can utilize different cognitive abilities (modules, adaptations) to greater or lesser extents than other individuals, but the only persons who should entirely lack one of these abilities are individuals with traumatic brain damage or developmental disorders, or who were raised in extremely unusual environments.

The environment of evolutionary adaptation

What is an "extremely unusual environment"? The answer, from an evolutionary perspective, is not based on the current world in which we all live.

Because our minds are the products of millions of years of evolution (that is, millions of years of evolutionary selection pressures producing adaptive solutions in the form of cognitive mechanisms), the benchmark "normal" environment is something called the environment of evolutionary adaptation (or EEA). The EEA is the world in which our ancestors lived. Many people generate images of the African savannah or a tropical rainforest as the EEA, but that is somewhat misleading. The evolutionary history of humans did not take place in one location, but across an array of settings, across millions of years. In fact, the EEA is a *statistical composite* of all the different environments in which our human, hominid, primate, and mammalian ancestors lived. Thus, while the EEA almost certainly includes savannah and forest environments, neither is even approximately a complete description. In some ways the generality of the EEA is limiting – one cannot say exactly in what particular environment humans evolved (Lewontin, 1990). The EEA is also, however, quite informative: humans did, at some points in evolutionary history, live in different environments and we should expect adaptations for these different environments to co-exist in human nature. There are also aspects of the human EEA that have reliably existed for many thousands (or millions) of generations: humans have lived in a world with physical objects, gravity, food, predators, prey, and other humans. Studies in cultural anthropology are useful not only for the information they provide about the different physical and social environments in which humans live, but also because they tell us some of the universal features of human environments (Brown, 1991).

WHAT ARE THE DOMAINS?

Having made a case for the insufficiency of domain-general models of reasoning and provided reasons to support the idea that human reasoning should be expected instead to be domain specific, one immediately paramount question is how to split human reasoning into domains. Although general principles of the evolutionary process and of information processing can tell us that domain specificity is the likely structure of the human mind, it does not tell us what the specific domains are within this structure. This is an issue, essentially, of deciding how best to carve nature at its joints.

The most widely recognized evolutionary approach to domain-specific human reasoning is that of Cosmides and Tooby, who clearly indicate that their overall view postulates the existence of many computational reasoning abilities within different domains (see, for example, Cosmides & Tooby, 1992, pp. 179–180). So what specific elements in our evolutionary history can be expected to have constituted selection pressures recurrent enough to have created their own reasoning processes? Put another way, what cognitive tasks have humans faced that could have been important, enduring, and complex enough to have evolved their own reasoning processes? Making a list of this sort is fraught with conceptual and practical issues and debates, not the least of which is that there can be disagreement about specific items being added to or removed from the list. There are also problems about specifying the level of detail at which one should "carve" different domains from each other (Atkinson & Wheeler, 2001; Sterelny & Griffiths, 1999). Steen (2001) has constructed a much larger list of cognitive adaptations: abilities for which arguments have been made that they are evolved parts of human nature, and in some ways the current list can be viewed as a subset of that (similarly tentative and prospective) list. Specifically, the following list attempts to identify some areas in which there are both theoretical reasons to expect, and experimental evidence to support, the existence of cognitive adaptations that have as part of their functionality some type of reasoning/inference procedure that is invoked within that domain. And in particular, this list focuses on "higher-order" reasoning processes that are partially or fully under conscious control, which is usually the type of reasoning studied under the topic of human reasoning ("lower-order" inferential processes such as recovering visual depth from retinal information can be considered as "reasoning", but not with the meaning usually considered by human reasoning researchers).

Physical interaction domains

From a very young age, people appear to have an intuitive understanding about physical (i.e., non-living) objects and how they behave. Even infants understand that items which move as a unit are whole objects, that objects do not move on their own (i.e., no action at a distance), and that objects generally obey basic laws of causality (e.g., classic Newtonian mechanics; Spelke, 1990; Spelke, Breinlinger, Macomber, & Jacobson, 1992). Older children and adults understand that objects have properties (rather than the opposite relationship), that one object can have several properties along different dimensions, and that different objects can have the same property without being the same in other ways. For example, people think it sensible to say "all rocks are grey" but not "all grey things are rocks", and "All rocks are grey; my shirt is grey" does not mean "my shirt is a rock".

In many ways human reasoning based on intuitive physics and the nature of objects appears to be a plausible toe-hold that can be used to learn abstract and non-intuitive reasoning processes such as formal deductive logic. Intuitive physics, which dominates many areas of everyday thinking (because most things in the world are physical objects) may also contribute to the appeal of ideas such as the mental models theory of reasoning, in which there is an implied analogy of "constructing" mental models as if they were physical entities.

Children also develop specific ideas about the nature of biological organisms, as opposed to non-living objects (artifacts; Gelman, 1988; Gelman & Markman, 1986; Keil, 1986; 1994, 1995). Biological entities are seen as intentional agents and as having an "essence" that cannot be altered. For example, most people have no objection to "If a soup can is filled with birdseed, punched with holes for access, and hung from a tree, it is a birdfeeder" – regardless of what the can was before or what it previously contained. Children over the age of about 7, however, will reject the analogous idea that "If a black cat is painted with a white stripe and smelly stuff is put in a pouch inside it for squirting at other animals, it is a skunk".

There are several established cognitive adaptations that involve the evaluation of foods in regards to what is (and is not) safe to eat. These adaptations include a learned taste aversion system (Garcia & Koeling, 1966), motion sickness (visual/vestibular discrepancies can indicate the ingestion of a toxin, leading to regurgitation of recently eaten food; Yates, Miller, & Lucot, 1998), and pregancy sickness (to avoid the ingestion of teratogens in the first trimester; Profett, 1992). While these adaptations certainly involve some forms of inferences (e.g., from sickness to dislike of certain foods), they are relatively subconscious and therefore have only some resemblance to human reasoning as it is usually considered (i.e., higher-order, conscious, and willful inferences). It does appear, though, that evaluations of food can involve conscious reasoning processes as well, particularly in the service of evaluating the social suitability or appropriateness of a food for consumption (Occhipinti & Siegal, 1994; Rozin, Fallon & Augustoni-Ziskind, 1985)

Language and intention domains

Language has long been an area in which domain-specific abilities are thought to exist (Chomsky, 1975). There are many implicit reasoning processes involved in language (e.g., for conjugating verbs and forming tenses) but there are also some higher-level reasoning processes. There is evidence that specific forms of reasoning exist, beginning in childhood, for individuals to infer the meanings of novel words (Pinker, 1984, 1994) For example, children (and adults) tend to infer that a new word provided in reference to a novel item refers to the entire object, but a new word that refers to an item that already has a label is assumed to refer to some part or property of the whole object (Markman, 1987, 1990). Reasoning processes tied to language have been recognized as being relevant to human reasoning generally (e.g., Braine & O'Brien, 1991, 1998; Brooks & Braine, 1996), but within a domain-general approach these effects have largely been seen as phenomena that either impair or extend beyond "correct" reasoning performance. The point here is that these reasoning processes can be better understood and appreciated if viewed as domain-specific inference mechanisms for language development and use.

People reason about intentionality, including at the most basic level of whether or not something has intentions. If something has self-propelled movement then people tend to spontaneously infer that it has intentions (i.e, it has beliefs and desires that guide its actions; Dasser, Ulbaek, & Premack, 1989; Premack, 1990). People use eye direction as an indication of what specific things an individual has an interest in or wants or desires (Baron-Cohen, 1994, 1995; Lee, Eskritt, Symons, & Muir, 1998). The basic rule that even young children use is that if someone gazes directly at something, they want/are interested in that thing. People also use facial expressions in a similar manner to infer the emotional states of other individuals (e.g., Knutson, 1996; Segerstrale & Molnar, 1997). At a higher level of consideration there is the ability to reason generally about the state of another's mind (called mindreading, or the theory of minds module; Baron-Cohen, 1994, 1995). This mindreading ability includes reasoning about false beliefs (e.g., Mary thinks there is a King of France), deception (Tom told Mary there is a King of France), and second-order belief states (Tom thinks it is funny that Mary thinks there is a King of France). Furthermore, there are reasoning processes that have been suggested to exist in order to manage and use information about the sources of information (e.g., Information from Tom is unreliable; Tooby & Cosmides, 2000).

Social interaction domains

Many specific categories, or domains, of social interactions also involve specific and adaptively specialized reasoning processes. The most well-studied area of domain-specific social reasoning is that of social exchanges (also called social contracts).

Cosmides and Tooby (Cosmides, 1989; Cosmides & Tooby, 1989, 1991, 1992, 1997) proposed that people possess, as part of the evolved architecture of the human mind, the abilities to initiate, recognize, and evaluate social exchanges: situations in which two people agree (i.e., form a contract) to exchange items for mutual net benefits. These social contracts can be stated in ways that can be analyzed according to deductively correct responses (such as the example at the beginning of this chapter), but the theory predicts that people will eschew formal deduction for the responses that are adaptive within the specific domain of social contracts. Several studies have found that social contract contents, but not similar non-contract contents, lead to the selection of the "cost not paid" and "benefit taken" as those that could violate the conditional rule, regardless of whether these are the deductively prescribed selections or not (Cosmides, 1989; Cosmides & Tooby, 1992).

Similar areas of domain-specific social reasoning have subsequently been proposed, including reasoning about social threats (Rutherford, Tooby, & Cosmides, 1996) and reasoning about precautions and hazard avoidance (Fiddick, Cosmides, & Tooby, 1995, 2000; Pereyra, 2000). In both these areas there is now experimental evidence to support reasoning processes that are not only adaptive within these specific situations, but are different both from social exchange reasoning and from each other.

Finally, there are reasoning processes that have been hypothesized to exist for specific domains having to do with social groups and social networks. Research by Cummins (1996, 1999) has found that the now established findings of domain-specific social contract reasoning are also influenced by the social status of the participants. She has suggested that this reflects collateral (or alternative) reasoning processes that involve the negotiation of social dominance hierarchies. Other research on reasoning about social groups has found specific patterns of inferences that are made in relation to coalitional markers (i.e., the physical indicators such as ribbons, badges, and cards that people use to identify themselves as group members; Brase, 2001). For example, when people are told "If a person is a member of the Fishermen Club, then he wears a silver badge" and "This person wears a silver badge", they are very likely to conclude that "This person is a member of the Fishermen Club" (which is deductively invalid; compare to the earlier example of a grey shirt/grey rock).

This is almost certainly not a complete list, nor it is a list that is even at this time a foundational list of certain reasoning domains. It is, for better or worse, an initial cataloging of suggestions that have been made by several different researchers regarding evolved domain-specific reasoning abilities. Like a mock-up construction of a car, or a model of a building before it is actually cast in steel, brick, and cement, this tentative list allows us to see the overall effect and the further implications and issues that arise from domain-specific reasoning.

Properties and interactions of reasoning domains

There have been some confusions, debates, and misunderstandings about how these various domains of human reasoning function, both singularly and in connection with one another. One area in which confusion sometimes occurs has to do with the borders of each domain in which reasoning processes are proposed to exist. Initial reactions to Cosmides and Tooby's work on reasoning about social exchanges illustrate this confusion well. Some argued that any finding of very good reasoning abilities that occurred outside the context of social exchanges would invalidate the theory of domain-specific abilities for reasoning about social exchanges (Cheng & Holyoak, 1989; Manktelow & Over, 1991; Rips, 1994). This argument may be the result of an interpretation of social exchange reasoning as a domain-general theory of human reasoning – i.e., the claim by Cosmides (1989, p. 200) that "no thematic rule that is not a social contract has ever produced a content effect that is both robust and replicable" was read as being a claim that the context of social exchanges was the only domain in which facilitation could ever exist. A closer reading of that very article, as well as both earlier and subsequent writings, shows clearly that this more extensive interpretation was never intended. Instead, what had been proposed is the multimodular mind described earlier.

Another initial reaction to the social exchange theory of human reasoning was to question some of the specific findings of facilitated reasoning that were claimed to be situations of social exchanges. For example, people tend to reason much better about the conditional rule "If you are drinking beer, then you are over 21 years old" than a similar rule (e.g., "you are drinking beer, then you are eating pizza"). How can a person's age be an item being exchanged? If, as it seems reasonable to assume, one cannot trade in one's age for a drink, then this is not an example of a social exchange, and there must be something other than social exchange reasoning going on. The problem here is not that of trying to have social exchange theory account for all types of good reasoning (as above), but rather of constraining the scope of application of social exchange reasoning to a very narrow area. This problem raises an important issue created by modularity: How widely (or narrowly) are modules applied?

Sperber has outlined – and provided terminology for – how cognitive modularity can be expected to work in terms of this scope of application issue – that is, how to think of module domains and the application of each module's mechanisms. First of all there is the *proper domain* of a cognitive module. The proper domain is the class of situations making up the specific adaptive problem that those cognitive abilities evolved to solve. In other words, the proper domain is "all the information that it is the module's biological function to process" (Sperber, 1994, p. 52). A social exchange situation clearly within the proper domain for social exchange reasoning would be something like, "If you watch my child for an hour, then I will feed you lunch": there are clear benefits exchanged in such a way that both parties can end up with a net gain in their own estimation. Many modular abilities are not tightly scope-limited to their original adaptive function, however, and it is therefore also useful to consider what is called the *actual domain* of a cognitive module. Because humans are able to conceive of aspects of the world – and particularly the social world – in a non-literal fashion, it is possible to invoke the functional machinery of a cognitive module in a situation that is not actually within the original (i.e., proper domain) scope of that module. Specifically, a modular ability (including some reasoning processes) can sometimes be invoked by a situation that manages to meet the module's input conditions, even if meeting those conditions is achieved by prior processing of the situational information by other systems (e.g., the beer-drinking rule discussed above relies on a conceptual interpretation of being "over 21 years old" as a cost paid in waiting for the benefit of being allowed to drink beer. (see also Brase & Miller, 2001, on reasoning about sexual harassment situations as being perceived as either social exchanges or threats).

Sperber (1994) additionally points out that a sub-part of this actual domain of application for modular abilities is what he calls the *cultural domain*. The cultural domain is made of those situations that people have purposefully designed so as to meet a specific module's input conditions, in order to reliably invoke the inferential machinery of that module. For example, the invention of money in cultures around the world appears to be a method of capitalizing on our ability to reason quite well (that is, adaptively) about social exchanges, while at the same time overcoming the inherent limitations of a barter economy (by creating a general intermediate item to transfer costs and benefits across individuals). The cultural domain of social exchange reasoning thus now extends to cover a bewildering array of situations, rather than just situations in which two people have rather specific items to exchange.

One can think of these proper and actual domains as concentric circles of light, the inner circle (proper domain) being a more intense light than the outer (actual domain). The different modular abilities can then be envisaged as multiple instances of these concentric circle arrangements, sometimes even with parts of these circles overlapping (Brase & Miller, 2001). This is not an unreasonable arrangement to propose as existing within the human mind, and in fact similar arrangements are known to form parts of the architecture of the mind (e.g., visual cues for perception of depth; Holway & Boring, 1941). This arrangement does bring up new issues to be resolved, or rather it gives a new intensity to issues that were implicitly raised before. It is now apparent that the precise input conditions for each form of domain-specific reasoning must be specified, and these specifications should at least try to be clear about the proper and actual scopes that can satisfy each input condition (e.g., see list in Cosmides & Tooby, 1992, p. 177).

Another area in which it is increasingly imperative for theories of domain-specific abilities to be clear is in the ontogeny of the ability. Because domain-specific reasoning abilities are proposed to be universal aspects of human nature (i.e., species-specific and reliably developing), they are often supposed to be heavily biologically determined. The underlying thought is a testament to the power and influence of the cultural relativism viewpoint; any ability that is proposed to be universal among humans must be biologically determined because otherwise cultural factors would quickly change or eradicate it. The problem with this position is that cultural factors simply are not universal trump cards for any and all aspects of human physiology, behaviour, and thought. Within any domain there are aspects that are heavily influenced by genetic and biological factors and other aspects that are much less influenced by genetics or biology. The human ability to produce language, for example, involves universal human features that require very little in terms of environmental input (e.g., a descended larynx, vocal cords, and suitable oral cavity need only proper nutrition, oxygen, and use to develop), and other universal human features that require more substantial environmental inputs – e.g., the universal language acquisition device requires information inputs from the environment about the which phonemes, morphemes, words, and syntax are utilized in the ambient language system(s) (Pinker, 1994). Neither strong cultural relativism (or environmental determinism) nor strong biological determinism will ever carry the day. The only responsible – and in fact the only feasible – position to take is that the functional development and subsequent operation of domain-specific abilities are canalized by biology and guided by the environment (Cummins & Cummins, 1999).

CHALLENGES TO AN EVOLUTIONARY APPROACH

The evolutionary approach to reasoning is controversial along several fronts. Some of these sources of controversy have been covered already (for example, the challenge to domain-general approaches). There are other challenges, however, some deriving from the very idea of using an evolutionary approach, and others deriving from certain implications within the evolutionary approach.

Objections to the use of evolutionary theory

The evolutionary approach is not the only perspective that has proposed the existence of domain-specific reasoning abilities. The theory of pragmatic reasoning schemas (PRS: Cheng & Holyoak, 1985; Cheng, Holyoak, Nisbett, & Oliver, 1986; Holyoak & Cheng, 1995; Kroger, Cheng, & Holyoak, 1993) proposes that evolutionary considerations are not necessary for the development of domain-specific reasoning abilities. This theory holds that "people reason using knowledge structures that we term pragmatic reasoning schemas, which are generalized sets of rules defined in relation to classes of goals" (Cheng & Holyoak, 1985, p. 395). Pragmatic reasoning schemas produce domain-specific reasoning mechanisms via inductive learning, with no reference to evolutionary selection pressures or adaptations. Instead, specific reasoning schemas are created by individual experiences with recurring types of situations. For instance, the production rules for the permission schema are:

(1) If the action is to be taken, then the precondition must be satisfied.
(2) If the action is not to be taken, then the precondition need not be satisfied.
(3) If the precondition is satisfied, then the action may be taken.
(4) If the precondition is not satisfied, then the action must not be taken.

While these schemas are claimed to be "not equivalent to any proposed formal or natural logic of the conditional" (p. 397), the permission schema (along with the also proposed obligation schema) generally describes situations of deontic logic.

Two aspects of the theory of pragmatic reasoning schemas are troublesome in comparison to evolutionary accounts of domain-specific reasoning. First, there is little theoretical guidance about the scope and limits of these reasoning schemas: Why do situations of permission and obligation and not other classes of goals and situations so definitely lead to reasoning schemas? If other classes of goals and situations do create reasoning schemas, how does one limit the number of schemas created in order to avoid something approaching the representation of thousands or even millions of goals and situations, each with their own unique reasoning schema? The second, and actually related, trouble with the theory of pragmatic reasoning schemas is that the knowledge structures, schemas, or production rules (i.e., computational processes and constraints) are explained as the result of induction: Ordinary life experiences are distilled into general reasoning processes. This explanation is troublesome because, for a large number of general goals (e.g., language, vision, and concept learning), there is a great deal of evidence that it is improbable – if not impossible – for induction alone to provide the basis for human performance (e.g., Gelman, 1990; Pinker, 1979; Wexler & Culicover, 1980; see, however, Holland, Holyoak, Nisbett & Thagard, 1986).

Another objection to the use of evolutionary theory is more general. Gould and Lewontin (1981; see also Lewontin, 1990) have criticized the use of evolutionary theory to create hypotheses about evolved adaptations (including cognitive adaptations) on the basis of a claim that there is not enough understanding of the evolutionary histories of species to draw even tentative conclusions about functional designs. They have summarized this criticism by labelling adaptationist explanations as "just so" stories (i.e., analogous to Rudyard Kipling's children's stories about how various animals got their properties). There are some useful cautions to take to heart in Gould and Lewontin's arguments (e.g., the need for experimental research to support theories), but overall the stronger criticisms of the adaptationist approach in general have been extensively rebuked several times over (Borgia, 1994; Buss, Haselton, Shackelford, Bleske, & Wakefield, 1998; Queller, 1995; Tooby & Cosmides, 1992). Gould and Lewontin's objection nevertheless reappears occasionally without any reference to the documented problems with this view (e.g., Johnson-Laird et al., 1999; see comment by Brase, 2002).

Issues within an evolutionary approach

Evolutionary theories of human reasoning achieve several useful and important ends: they provide a novel explanation for several phenomena, they make significant and new predictions about how people reason, and they move the field of psychology into closer compatibility with other fields such as biology and anthropology. Evolutionary theories about human reasoning, and specifically the notions of domain specificity and a multimodular structure for the mind, also raise new questions and issues that must be dealt with if such an approach is to ultimately prosper.

One issue that arises based on the assumption of a multimodular mind is the need for some higher-level organization and functional integration of these modules. For example, if there are, even modestly, dozens of domain-specific reasoning abilities (i.e., modules) in the mind, then something needs to exist that cognitively organizes these different modules, determines what information is sent to which modules, and maybe even influences where the results of module functions are then sent. This sounds something like a domain-general, content-independent reasoning ability itself, and some researchers have identified this as a crucial area in which multimodular descriptions of the mind are seriously inadequate (Samuels, 1998). This certainly is a crucial issue, and one that deserves to be given considerable attention. It is not, however, a problem that invalidates the idea of a multimodular mind and it is certainly not a problem that is impossible to solve (e.g., see Barrett, 2002; Brase, 2003).

Another issue that emerges with the consideration of a multimodular mind is the issue of what exactly is a "module". For instance (and with some liberty with terminology), people have talked about a "cheater detection" module, which is a specific aspect of what some have called the "social exchange reasoning" module, which others have argued is part of a "permissions and obligations reasoning" module. At what level (or levels) do modules exist? Atkinson and Wheeler (2001) have dubbed this the *grain problem* of evolutionary psychology; some modules are proposed at a very fine-grained level whereas others are proposed at more coarse-grained levels. Do these different proposals now stand in opposition to each other? Are we to allow modules to exist within larger modules? How about modules that partially overlap with several other modules? In some respects these issues may be semantic; we do not seem to have the theoretical or scientific language yet to talk about certain possible solutions to this problem. Other aspects of the grain problem, however, highlight further topics that need to be addressed regarding the functional organization and structure of a multimodular mind.

Lastly, there is an implication of domain-specific, evolutionary approaches to human reasoning that has not been considered very much at all. For many people the study of reasoning is defined in reference to the ideas of deduction, formal logic, and general abilities. In other words, the study of human reasoning is the study of human cognition in relation to these benchmark ideas. The domain-specific, multimodular conception of human reasoning belies this unitary benchmark, replacing it with benchmarks based on adaptive functionality within each domain. In practical terms, this means that research on reasoning will need to interact much more with areas such as social and developmental psychology when developing theories of "correct" reasoning.

ACKNOWLEDGEMENTS

The author thanks Sandra Brase for her unstinting advice and support, and David Farley for permission to reproduce his work in Figure 13.1.

REFERENCES

Atkinson, A. P., & Wheeler, M. (2001). *Evolutionary psychology's grain problem and the cognitive neuroscience of reasoning*. Paper presented at the Human Behaviour and Evolution Society, London, 13–17 June.

Audi, R. (1989). *Practical reasoning*. London: Routledge.

Baron-Cohen, S. (1994). How to build a baby that can read minds: Cognitive mechanisms in mindreading. *Cahiers de Psychologie Cognitive/Current Psychology of Cognition, 13*, 513–552.

Baron Cohen, S. (1995). *Mindblindness: An essay on autism and theory of mind*. Cambridge, MA: The MIT Press.

Barrett, H. C. (2002). *Enzymatic computation: A new model of cognitive modularity*. Paper presented at the Human Behaviour and Evolution Society, New Brunswick, New Jersey, 19–23 June.

Borgia, G. (1994). The scandals of San Marco. *Quarterly Review of Biology, 69*, 373–375.

Braine, M. D. S. (1978). On the relation between the natural logic of reasoning and standard logic. *Psychological Review, 85*, 1–21.

Braine, M. D. S., & O'Brien, D. P. (1991). A theory of if: A lexical entry, reasoning program, and pragmatic principles. *Psychological Review, 98*, 182–203.

Braine, M. D. S., & O'Brien, D. P. (1998). *Mental logic*. Mahwah, NJ: Lawrence Erlbaum Associates Inc.

Braine, M. D. S., O'Brien, D. P., Noveck, I. A., Samuels, M. C. et al. (1995). Predicting intermediate and multiple conclusions in propositional logic inference problems: Further evidence for a mental logic. *Journal of Experimental Psychology: General, 124*, 263–292.

Brase, G. L. (2001). Markers of social group membership as probabilistic cues in reasoning tasks. *Thinking and Reasoning, 7*, 313–346.

Brase, G. L. (2002). Ecological and evolutionary validity: Comments on Johnson-Laird, Legrenzi, Girotto, Legrenzi and Caverni's (1999) Mental model theory of extensional reasoning. *Psychological Review, 109*, 722–728.

Brase, G. L. (2003). The allocation system: Using signal detection processes to regulate representations in a multi-modular mind. In K. J. Gilhooly (series Ed.) & D. E. Over (Vol. Ed.) *Current Issues in Thinking and Reasoning. Evolution and the psychology of Thinking: The debate* (pp. 11–32). Hove, UK: Psychology Press.

Brase, G. L., & Miller, R. L. (2001). Sex differences in the perception of and reasoning about quid pro quo sexual harassment. *Psychology, Evolution and Gender*.

Brooks, P. J., & Braine, M. D. S. (1996). What do children know about the universal quantifiers all and each? *Cognition, 60*, 235–268.

Brown, D. (1991). *Human universals*. New York: McGraw-Hill.

Buss, D. M., Haselton, M. G., Shackelford, T. K., Bleske, A. L., & Wakefield, J. C. (1998). Adaptations, exaptations, and spandrels. *American Psychologist, 53*, 533–548.

Cheng, P., & Holyoak, K. (1985). Pragmatic reasoning schemas. *Cognitive Psychology, 17*, 391–416.

Cheng, P. W., & Holyoak, K. J. (1989). On the natural selection of reasoning theories. *Cognition, 33*, 285–313.

Cheng, P. W., Holyoak, K. J., Nisbett, R. E., & Oliver, L. M. (1986). Pragmatic versus syntactic approaches to training deductive reasoning. *Cognitive Psychology, 18,* 293–328.

Chomsky, N. (1975). *Reflections on language.* New York: Random House.

Cosmides, L. (1989). The logic of social-exchange – has natural-selection shaped how humans reason – Studies with the Wason selection task. *Cognition, 31,* 187–276.

Cosmides, L., & Tooby, J. (1989). Evolutionary psychology and the generation of culture. 2. Case-study – a computational theory of social-exchange. *Ethology and Sociobiology, 10,* 51–97.

Cosmides, L., & Tooby, J. (1991). Reasoning and natural selection. In R. Dulbecco (Ed.), *Encyclopedia of human biology, Volume 6* (pp. 493–503). La Jolla, CA: Academic Press.

Cosmides, L., & Tooby, J. (1992). Cognitive adaptations for social exchange. In J. H. Barkow, L. Cosmides, & J. Tooby (Eds.), *The adapted mind: Evolutionary psychology and the generation of culture* (pp. 163–228). Oxford: Oxford University Press.

Cosmides, L., & Tooby, J. (1997). Dissecting the computational architecture of social inference mechanisms. In *Characterizing human psychological adaptations (Ciba Foundation Symposium #208)* (pp. 132–156). Chichester, UK: Wiley.

Cummins, D. D. (1996). Dominance hierarchies and the evolution of human reasoning. *Minds and Machines, 6,* 463–480.

Cummins, D. D. (1999). Cheater detection is modified by social rank: The impact of dominance on the evolution of cognitive functions. *Evolution and Human Behaviour, 20,* 229–248.

Cummins, D. D., & Cummins, R. (1999). Biological preparedness and evolutionary explanation. *Cognition, 73,* B37–B53.

Dasser, V., Ulbaek, I., & Premack, D. (1989). The perception of intention. *Science, 243,* 365–367.

Evans, J. St. B. T., Barston, J., & Pollard, P. (1983). On the conflict between logic and belief in syllogistic reasoning. *Memory & Cognition, 11,* 295–306.

Fiddick, L., Cosmides, L., & Tooby, J. (1995, June). *Does the mind distinguish between social contracts and precautions?* Paper presented at the meeting of the Human Behaviour and Evolution Society, Santa Barbara, CA.

Fiddick, L., Cosmides, L., & Tooby, J. (2000). No interpretation without representation: The role of domain-specific representations and inferences in the Wason selection task. *Cognition, 77,* 1–79.

Garcia, J., & Koelling, R. A. (1966). The relation of cue to consequence in avoidance learning. *Psychonomic Science, 4,* 123–124.

Gardner, H. (1974). *The shattered mind.* New York: Vintage.

Gelman, S. (1988). The development of induction within natural kind and artifact categories. *Cognitive Psychology, 20,* 65–95.

Gelman, S. (1990). Structural constraints on cognitive development: Introduction to a special issue of *Cognitive Science*. *Cognitive Science, 14,* 3–9.

Gelman, S. A., & Markman, E. M. (1986). Categories and induction in young children. *Cognition, 23,* 183–209.

Gopnik, M., & Crago, M. B. (1991). Familial aggregation of a developmental language disorder. *Cognition, 39,* 1–50.

Gould, S. J., & Lewontin, R. C. (1979). The spandrels of San Marcos and the

Panglossian program: A critique of the adaptationist programme. *Proceedings of the Royal Society of London, 250*, 281–288.

Hirschfeld, L. A., & Gelman, S. A. (Eds.). (1994). *Mapping the mind: Domain specificity in cognition and culture.* New York: Cambridge University Press.

Holcomb, H. R. III (2001). *Conceptual challenges in evolutionary psychology: Innovative research strategies (Studies in cognitive systems: Volume 27).* Amsterdam: Kluwer Academic Publishers.

Holland, J., Holyoak, K., Nisbett, R., & Thagard, P. (1986). *Induction: Processes of inference, learning, and discovery.* Cambridge, MA: MIT Press/Bradford Books.

Holway, A. F., & Boring, E. G. (1941). Determinants of apparent visual size with distance variation. *American Journal of Psychology, 54*, 21–37.

Holyoak, K. J., & Cheng, P. W. (1995). Pragmatic reasoning about human voluntary action: Evidence from Wason's selection task. In S. E. Newstead & J. St. B. T. Evans (Eds.), *Perspectives on thinking and reasoning: Essays in honour of Peter Wason* (pp. 67–89). Hove, UK: Lawrence Erlbaum Associates Ltd.

Johnson-Laird, P. N. (1983). *Mental models: Towards a cognitive science of language, inference, and consciousness.* Cambridge, MA: Harvard University Press.

Johnson Laird, P. N. (2001). Mental models and deduction. *Trends in Cognitive Sciences, 4*, 434–442.

Johnson-Laird, P. N., & Byrne, R. M. J. (1991). *Deduction.* Hove, UK: Lawrence Erlbaum Associates Ltd.

Johnson-Laird, P. N., & Byrne, R. M. J. (1993). Precis of *Deduction. Behavioral and Brain Sciences, 16*, 323–380.

Johnson-Laird, P. N., Byrne, R. M. J., & Schaeken, W. (1994). Why models rather than rules give a better account of propositional reasoning: A reply to Bonatti and to O'Brien, Braine, and Yang. *Psychological Review, 101*, 734–739.

Johnson-Laird, P. N., Legrenzi, P., Girotto, V., Legrenzi, M. S., & Caverni, J-P. (1999). Naive probability: A mental model theory of extensional reasoning. *Psychological Review, 106*, 62–88.

Keil, F. C. (1986). The acquisition of natural kind and artifact terms. In W. Demopoulos & A. Marras (Eds.), *Language learning and concept acquisition: Foundational issues.* Norwood, NJ: Ablex.

Keil, F. C. (1994). The birth and nurturance of concepts by domains: The origins of concepts of living things. In L. A. Hirschfeld & S. A. Gelman (Eds.), *Mapping the mind: Domain specificity in cognition and culture* (pp. 234–254). New York: Cambridge University Press.

Keil, F. C. (1995). The growth of causal understandings of natural kinds. In D. Sperber, D. Premack, & A. J. Premack (Eds.), *Causal cognition: A multidisciplinary debate. Symposia of the Fyssen Foundation* (pp. 234–267). New York: Clarendon Press/Oxford University Press.

Knutson, B. (1996). Facial expressions of emotion influence interpersonal trait inferences. *Journal of Nonverbal Behaviour, 20*, 165–182.

Kolb, B., & Whishaw, I. Q. (1990). *Fundamentals of human neuropsychology, 3rd Ed.* New York: Freeman.

Kroger, J. K., Cheng, P. W., & Holyoak, K. J. (1993). Evoking the permission schema: The impact of explicit negation and a violation-checking context. (Special Issue: The cognitive psychology of reasoning). *Quarterly Journal of Experimental Psychology: Human Experimental Psychology, 46*A, 615–635.

Lee, K., Eskritt, M., Symons, L. A., & Muir, D. (1998). Children's use of triadic eye gaze information for mind reading. *Developmental Psychology, 34*, 525–539.

Leslie, A. M. (1987). Pretense and representation: The origins of "theory of mind". *Psychological Review, 94*, 412–426.

Lewontin, R. C. (1990). The evolution of cognition. In D. N. Osherson & E. E. Smith (Eds.), *An invitation to cognitive science: Vol. 3. Thinking* (pp. 229–246). Cambridge, MA: MIT Press.

Manktelow, K. I., & Over, D. E. (1991). Social roles and utilities in reasoning with deontic conditionals. *Cognition, 39*, 85–105.

Markman, E. M. (1987). How children constrain the possible meaning of words. In U. Neisser (Ed.), *Concepts and conceptual development: Ecological and intellectual factors in categorization.* Cambridge: Cambridge University Press.

Markman, E. M. (1990). Constraints children place on word meaning. *Cognitive Science, 14*, 57–77.

Markman, E. M., & Hutchinson, J. E. (1984). Children's sensitivity to constraints on word meaning: Taxonomic vs. thematic relations. *Cognitive Psychology, 20*, 121–157.

Markovits, H., & Nantel, G. (1989). The belief bias in the production and evaluation of logical conclusions. *Memory & Cognition, 17*, 11–17.

Marzke, M. W., & Wullstein, K. L. (1996). Chimpanzee and human grips: A new classification with a focus on evolutionary morphology. *International Journal of Primatology, 17*, 117–139.

Newell, A., & Simon, H. A. (1972). *Human problem solving.* Englewood Cliffs, NJ: Prentice-Hall.

Newstead, S. E., & Evans, J. S. B. T. (1993). Mental models as an explanation of belief bias effects in syllogistic reasoning. *Cognition, 46*, 93–97.

Newstead, S. E., Pollard, P., Evans, J. St. B. T., & Allen, J. L. (1992). The source of belief bias effects in syllogistic reasoning. *Cognition, 45*, 257–284.

Oakhill, J., & Garnham, A. (1993). On theories of belief bias in syllogistic reasoning. *Cognition, 46*, 87–92.

Occhipinti, S., & Siegal, M. (1994). Reasoning and food and contamination. *Journal of Personality and Social Psychology, 66*, 243–253.

Pereyra, L. (2000, June). *Functional variation of the hazard management algorithm.* Paper presented at the meeting of the Human Behaviour and Evolution Society, Amherst, MA.

Pinker, S. (1979). Formal models of language learning. *Cognition, 7*, 217–283.

Pinker, S. (1984). *Language learnability and language development.* Cambridge, MA: Harvard University Press.

Pinker, S. (1994). *The language instinct.* New York: William Morrow & Co.

Pinker, S., & Bloom, P. (1990). Natual language and natural selection. *Behavioral and Brain Sciences, 13*, 707–784.

Popper, K. R. (1959). *The logic of scientific discovery.* New York: Harper & Row.

Premack, D. (1990). The infant's theory of self-propelled objects. *Cognition, 36*, 1–16.

Profet, M. (1992). Pregnancy sickness as adaptation: A deterrent to maternal ingestion of teratogens. In J. H. Barkow, L. Cosmides, & J. Tooby (Eds.), *The adapted mind: Evolutionary psychology and the generation of culture* (pp. 327–365). Oxford: Oxford University Press.

Queller, D. C. (1995). The spandrels of St. Marx and the Panglossian paradox: A critique of a rhetorical programme. *Quarterly Review of Biology*, *70*, 485–490.

Quine, W. V. (1960). *Word and object*. Cambridge, MA: The MIT Press.

Rips, L. J. (1986). Mental muddles. In M. Brand & R. M. Harnish (Eds.), *The representation of knowledge and belief. Arizona colloquium in cognition* (pp. 258–286). Tucson, AZ: University of Arizona Press.

Rips, L. J. (1994). *The psychology of proof: Deductive reasoning in human thinking*. Cambridge, MA: The MIT Press.

Rozin, P., Fallon, A. E., & Augustoni-Ziskind, M. (1987). The child's conception of food: The development of contamination sensitivity to disgusting substances. *Developmental Psychology*, *21*, 1075–1079.

Rutherford, M. D., Cosmides, L., & Tooby, J. (1996, June). *Adaptive sex differences in reasoning about self defense*. Paper presented at the meeting of the Human Behaviour and Evolution Society, Chicago, IL.

Samuels R. (1998). Evolutionary psychology and the massive modularity hypothesis. *British Journal for the Philosophy of Science*, *49*, 575–602.

Segerstrale, U. C., & Molnar, P. (1997). *Nonverbal communication: Where nature meets culture*. Hillsdale, NJ: Lawrence Erlbaum Associates Inc.

Simon, H. A. (1973). The structure of ill-structured problems. *Artificial Intelligence*, *4*, 181–201.

Spelke, E. S. (1990). Principles of object perception. *Cognitive Science*, *14*, 29–56.

Spelke, E. S., Breinlinger, K., Macomber, J., & Jacobson, K. (1992). Origins of knowledge. *Psychological Review*, *99*, 605–632.

Sperber, D. (1994). The modularity of thought and the epidemiology of representations. In L. A. Hirschfeld & S. A. Gelman (Eds.), *Mapping the mind: Domain specificity in cognition and culture* (pp. 39–67). New York: Cambridge University Press.

Steen, F. F. (2001). *Evolutionary psychology: Evolutionary theory, paleoanthropology, adaptationism*. Retrieved 18 November 2001 from http://cogweb.ucla.edu/EP/

Sterelny, K., & Griffiths, P. E. (1999). *Sex and death: An introduction to philosophy of biology*. Chicago: University of Chicago Press.

Tooby J., & Cosmides, L. (1992). The psychological foundations of culture. In J. H. Barkow, L. Cosmides, & J. Tooby (Eds.), *The adapted mind: Evolutionary psychology and the generation of culture* (pp. 19–136). Oxford: Oxford University Press.

Vadeboncoeur, I., & Markovits, H. (1999). The effect of instruction and information retrieval on accepting the premises in a conditional reasoning task. *Thinking and Reasoning*, *5*, 97–113.

Wexler, K., & Culicover, P. (1980). *Formal principles of language acquisition*. Cambridge, MA: MIT Press.

Yates B. J., Miller A. D., & Lucot J. B. (1998). Physiological basis and pharmacology of motion sickness: An update. *Brain Research Bulletin*, *47*, 395–406.

14 The proof of the pudding is in the eating

Translating Popper's philosophy into a model for testing behaviour

Fenna H. Poletiek

Popper's philosophy of falsificationism has a monopolistic position in the psychological study of human testing. Scientists and ordinary people alike should test their hypotheses with the intention to eliminate them. Falsificationism, as Popper's (1935) philosophy is globally called, was proposed as a reaction to "logical positivism", whose main defects were being dogmatic and making use of the unjustified method of "inductivism". According to logical positivism, hypothesis testing is an activity aimed at finding empirical support for one's hypothesis. The core objective of science, in this view, was that hypotheses should be supported by as much empirical evidence as could possibly be found.

Popper's counterintuitive idea of falsificationism had a great appeal to European philosophers, and it became especially influential after his book *Logik der Forschung* (1935) was translated into English in 1959 (as *The logic of scientific discovery*) and after Popper's move to University College London. Peter Wason then imported the idea into experimental psychology. Wason (1960, 1966) developed the famous experimental hypothesis-testing tasks aimed at observing whether human subjects do what Popper prescribed for scientists: hypothesis testing by falsification. Interestingly, Popper, instead of applauding Wason's attempts to use his idea in everyday situations, was quite negative about this psychological application. This negative attitude is understandable because Popper meant his philosophical proposal as a logical programme prescribing under which formal conditions scientific knowledge would grow. The programme, having its foundation in logical theory, was therefore meant to be in principle immune from empirical results about how scientists, let alone ordinary people, actually test their hypotheses.

Despite Popper's anti-"psychologism", Wason's experimental programme had an enormous influence on the psychology of reasoning. The two tasks developed in this programme (the rule discovery task, 1960, and the selection task, 1966) were used and varied in hundreds of studies, and resulted in many converging and diverging findings on human hypothesis-testing strategies (Evans, 1989; Evans & Over, 1996). The diversity of these findings, and their interpretation against the background of Popper's philosophy, are the subject of this chapter. How should falsificationism be understood? How did psychologists translate the philosophy of science in their experiments? And to which problems does this translation lead?

Originally, Wason's experiments seem to indicate that people do not behave as falsificationists, and explanations were sought for the apparent verificationist behaviour (Evans & Wason, 1976; Johnson-Laird & Wason, 1977; Wason, 1960, 1977). Some studies still interpret hypothesis-testing behaviour as biased by verification (Kareev, Halberstadt, & Shafir, 1993). However, a growing number of authors doubt the robustness of this "confirmation bias" (Evans & Over, 1996; Klayman & Ha, 1987, 1989; Poletiek, 2001). Wetherick (1962), Klayman and Ha (1987), and Poletiek (2001) asked why behaviour in these tasks cannot simply be interpreted as a wish to confirm what the subject believes. An important argument to consider in interpreting an apparent confirmation bias is whether it would be really rational and helpful to behave like a falsificationist in these tasks. In such tasks, might confirmation be a reasonable strategy as well (Klayman & Ha, 1987; Oaksford & Chater, 1994)?

A further psychological problem in interpreting the behaviour of subjects in hypothesis-testing tasks was how to operationalize falsification behaviour. Although Wason had clear definitions of falsification and confirmation behaviour, it is questionable whether these do justice to Popper's philosophy and whether they satisfy logical demands (Klayman & Ha, 1987; Wetherick, 1962). Moreover, it appears to be difficult to think of a falsification strategy in the first place. If we agree that falsifying testing is testing in a manner that allows falsifications to show up, is it possible then to arrange our test in such a way that we can realize this, without cheating? In other words, realizing falsifying results from our tests presupposes that we *know* where to find them beforehand, which is in conflict with the idea of performing a test (Poletiek, 1996). Finally, what exactly is the difference between such a strategy, if it can be defined, and its opponent: the confirmation strategy?

The goal of this chapter is to analyze the principle of falsification in the context of its application in psychology. I will argue that some problems with applying this principle follow directly from the very philosophy of Popper. Other problems with using the concept of falsification are specific to its application in psychology. As a possible solution to the empirical and conceptual problems discussed, I will propose a probabilistic view of falsificatory behaviour, which is perfectly consistent with Popper's definition of a falsifying test, but not with his prescriptive testing attitude. The surprising implication of this solution is that it does not differ from its rival: the confirmatory view of hypothesis testing (Poletiek, 2001). The focus of the present chapter, therefore, is to disentangle a number of theoretical problems of falsificationism, by working out its implications in behavioural terms. By doing so, the usefulness of falsificationism in the psychology of hypothesis testing is evaluated.

TWO-FACED FALSIFICATIONISM

An important aspect of the philosophical argument for falsificationism is its twofold justification. The first justification is that it is logical. Indeed, according to classical propositional logic, it is impossible to definitely induce the truth or confirm a hypothesis by a limited number of observations, because we can never know whether and how much disconfirming evidence there is that we did not find. Induction leads to unwarranted claims about the truth status of hypotheses, according to propositional logic. It is possible, however, to definitely prove a hypothesis to be wrong, with a finite number of observations. We only need one such observation to make a definite inference as to the falsity of the hypothesis. This logical argument is repeatedly used by Popper and illustrated by the famous "black swans" example. If we want to test the hypothesis that "all swans are white", we only need one black swan to show it to be wrong, but we can never come up with enough white swans to definitely show that it is true (assuming of course that the set of swans in the world is infinitely large, and therefore the hypothesis is a "universal" one). Hence, the testing behaviour that falsificationism prescribes is to look for a black swan, rather than collecting ever more white ones.

The second justification of falsificationism is psychological, or "moral". This is the anti-dogmatic argument. When testing our ideas, we should not behave dogmatically, conservatively, or try to confirm (again) what we already believe. This argument bears on the attitude a hypothesis tester should have regarding his or her own beliefs. A substantial part of Popper's defence of falsificationism (1959/1974) is psychological in nature. In falsificationism, science is ideally represented as constantly putting one's own beliefs to the most severe tests, rather than trying to look for supporting data.

The justification of falsificationism is not without problems, however. For example, the logical aspect of falsificationism is neutral with regard to the content of the hypothesis tested: it merely prescribes that the tester look for potential rejections. The psychological justification, however, does address the content of the hypothesis: it prescribes that the tester constantly question those hypotheses believed to be true. The tension between the logical and the psychological justification is exemplified in the significance test procedure (see also Krueger, Gigerenzer, & Morgan, 1987). In this procedure the scientist is requested to bring in enough evidence to satisfy a conventional statistical criterion in order to reject a hypothesis. However, the hypothesis she is supposed to reject in this procedure is not the one she believes best describes nature, but, on the contrary, the one that is believed by her opponents in a scientific discussion. In this virtual discussion, she has subsequently to convince this forum that they are wrong. Thus, the logical aspect of falsificationism is applied in the significance test, but the psychological one is not, because the hypothesis at test is not the scientist's own belief. The result is a mix that only logically but not psychologically corresponds to falsificationism as meant by Popper.

In the early years of psychological research in hypothesis testing, this dualism was already visible. Some researchers focused on the logical aspect, others on the psychological one. Snyder and Swann (1978), for example, performed social hypothesis-testing experiments. Participants had to determine whether a fictitious person was "introverted". They tended to perform tests that they expected to result in support of the introversion hypothesis. This strategy was interpreted in terms of verification by social stereotyping: we tend to look for evidence supporting our prior beliefs. This interpretation is an example of a violation of psychological falsificationism. However, the strategy used by the participants is not irrational from a logical falsificationist point of view, because any test that falsified the introversion hypothesis would suffice for its rejection. Violation of logical falsificationism was investigated specifically with Wason's rule discovery task and, even more explicitly, with the selection task. Actually, in the rule discovery task, the violation of the falsification principle was interpreted originally as both a logical problem and a psychological problem of human reasoning. That is, the search for confirming evidence was explained both as a lack of insight into the value of falsifying evidence and as an unwillingness to reject what one believes to be true (Wason, 1960). In later studies, the second explanation, often called the motivational explanation in the experimental literature, was abandoned (Evans, 1989). An important finding casting doubt on the motivational explanation of irrational testing behaviour, was that participants correctly inferred the falsity of their hypotheses after having observed an inconsistent test result (Wason, 1969; Wason & Johnson-Laird, 1970). Thus, on the one hand, participants tend to induce the truth of a hypothesis after having observed a limited number of observations supporting it. But, on the other hand, they also reject hypotheses when inconsistent evidence shows up. Rather than displaying an erroneous testing strategy, what participants actually did wrong was that they "spoke too soon" in the hypothesis-testing tasks (Klayman & Ha, 1989).

In conclusion, falsificationism has two justifications: it is both logically and psychologically better to look for rejections of one's belief. However, the two principles do not always coincide. Logically correct falsifying behaviour is not necessarily psychologically correct, and vice versa. Experimental findings about hypothesis-testing behaviour, although originally interpreted as incorrect logical and psychological testing behaviour, seem to show a more complex picture of the human hypothesis tester, as both willing and able to look for new evidence for his or her hypotheses, and rejecting it when inconsistent evidence shows up. The main limitation is a tendency to induce the truth or acceptability of a hypothesis on the basis of a limited number of confirmations, seemingly violating the logical falsification principle. Humans tend to succumb to the attractiveness of inductions. But what about falsificationism itself?

FALSIFICATIONISM AND INDUCTION

Everyday hypothesis testers tend to induce at some point the truth of a hypothesis from observed evidence. Apparently, they can hardly avoid inferring a conclusion from what they see, apart from rejecting unsupported guesses. Science is no different. In the significance test procedure, efforts have been made to guarantee the Popperian line of thinking. However, in following this line, we end up by rejecting a hypothesis nobody has ever actually committed themselves to, and with a persuasive suggestion that we can trust the alternative hypothesis. This "unPopperian" result of the procedure, however, is precisely what makes it meaningful. From a psychological point of view, no scientist is interested in all these rejected null hypotheses, or memorizes them as the "state of knowledge in the field", even if, from a logical point of view, this huge collection of rejected hypotheses is all there is. Clearly, not only do human hypothesis testers and real scientists tend to make inductions to eventually confirm a hypothesis, but even falsificationism cannot do without it. Even more, as I will argue hereafter: falsificationism's benefits can only be argued for with reference to its inductive benefits. Falsificationism is good *because* it leads to the best inductive verifications, and precisely *not* to the best falsifications.

The relation between Popper's falsificationism on the one side, and inductive verification on the other, can be elucidated by analyzing the respective measures developed by Popper. These measures are "severity of test", being a measure for the falsifying potential of a piece of evidence, and "degree of corroboration", which is the value of a piece of evidence to "corroborate" a hypothesis (Popper, 1963/1974). "Severity of test" is the value of a piece of evidence representing one of the possible results from a test, and supporting the hypothesis tested. For example, the hypothesis H can be tested with a test with possible outcomes e and f, whereby observation e supports H and observation f falsifies H. As the evidence e deviates more from what is expected under background knowledge, it represents a more severe test for hypothesis H. The three parameters of the definition of test severity are: H, the hypothesis, e, the piece of evidence, and b, the background knowledge. The severity function is called S:

$$S(e,H,b) = \frac{p(e|H \text{ and } b)}{p(e|b)} \qquad (1)$$

The second measure is the "degree of corroboration" of a hypothesis. This value refers to the *extent* to which a piece of evidence corroborates the hypothesis at test.

$$C(H,e,b) = S(e,H,b) \qquad (2)$$

Popper directly derives the degree of corroboration from the severity of test. The order of the parameters changes (Popper, 1963/1978).
Thus,

$$\frac{p(H|e \text{ and } b)}{p(H|b)} = \frac{p(e|H \text{ and } b)}{p(e|b)} \tag{3}$$

In his philosophical argumentation, Popper (1963/1978) carefully differentiates this measure from concepts such as "degree of confirmation", "support", or "revision of belief", which are concepts issuing from the rivals of falsificationism: confirmation philosophies of science. The word "corroboration" expresses less persuasion than "confirmation", in order to fit better within the falsification theory, and to avoid association with confirmation theories. This distinction, however crucial in the philosophical respect, fades away in the formal definition. The degree of corroboration of a hypothesis H by a piece of evidence *e* is thus *exactly the same* as the test severity it represents for H.

Even more, the degree of corroboration is exactly the same measure as the "degree of confirmation", or "revision of belief" in confirmation theories. Degree of confirmation of a hypothesis by evidence *e* is defined in both Bayesian theory (Howson & Urbach, 1989), and Logical Positivism (called the "relevance ratio", Carnap, 1950), as the ratio of the probability of hypothesis H, given the evidence *e*, to the unconditionalized probability of the hypothesis H. Thus, the degree of corroboration is *equivalent to* the degree of confirmation. By force of this equivalence, the degree of confirmation is also equivalent to the degree of severity of test (3). This is the far-reaching consequence of the formalizations of severity of test and degree of corroboration that Popper (1963/1978) proposed. Interestingly, due to this formalization, not only can the formal equivalence relation between his theory and its rival be demonstrated, but it also opens the possibility of these principles (degree of confirmation and severity of test) being equivalent in terms of behaviour. Besides the formal equivalence, the falsificationist standard also becomes indistinguishable from the confirmationist one, at the *behavioural* level. At a behavioural level, the question is: what piece of evidence should we prefer in order to *behave* as a good falsificationist, and which one in order to behave as a good confirmationist, i.e. to make good inductions? The striking answer is that the same evidence should be looked for because, by implication of the equivalence between the severity of test and the degree of confirmation, the evidence that maximizes the severity of test necessarily maximizes the degree of confirmation.

The difference between the two principles lies mainly in the abstract background and the philosophical history. Also, both measures look at the testing process from a different angle. In the severity function, the falsifying element lies in the risk that is taken regarding the probability of getting a falsification out of the test; that is, the risk of *not* obtaining support *e*, and therefore, being forced to reject the hypothesis. As this risk increases, the severity of *e* increases. And Popper wants us to take this risk, in our test choice. In the degree of confirmation function, the accent lies on the potential of evidence *e* to increase our belief in the hypothesis H, *after* it is observed. So, the severity function thus provides a pre-test perspective and the degree of confirmation a post-test perspective. Severity refers to behaviour in choosing the test; degree of confirmation refers to the induction following the test. Popper's philosophy is oriented on the pre-test phase, and explicitly not on the second. Verificationists deal with the second phase. But, severity and degree of "corroboration" ("confirmation") being fully equivalent, maximizing one function necessarily leads to maximizing the other (Poletiek, 2001).

There is also a non-formal version of the argument that falsificationism cannot do without induction that can be made. This can be illustrated by examining the characteristics of one of the most prototypical cases of falsification testing: the famous Michelson and Morley finding about the velocity of light, that corroborated Einstein's relativity theory. Other examples have the same characteristics, however. The prediction chosen to test the theory was highly unlikely given the relevant background knowledge available at that point. The Michelson–Morley finding was a clear case of testing relativity theory the falsificationist way, because this finding was highly *unexpected* a priori, and therefore the test could be expected beforehand to falsify the theory predicting it.

The first characteristic of this successful example of a falsifying test is that it seems to provide a better proof for a hypothesis because the predictions tested are so surprising a priori. This is intuitive: if Michelson and Morley's finding had not been so unexpected, it would have been felt as constituting less of a strong case for Einstein's relativity theory. The surprisingness of an eventually supporting piece of evidence is represented in the denominator of Popper's definition of test severity (1). The second characteristic of this and other exemplary cases of falsificationism is that the falsification did not actually come about. Thus, the Michelson–Morley experiment *did* produce the observation predicted by relativity theory, however unexpected beforehand. Thus, the falsifying test, although expected to produce a result that was consistent with the available background knowledge and inconsistent with the theory to be tested, surprisingly produced the unexpected result. In other words, one of the great examples of falsificationism in science actually failed to do what it was supposed to do, namely to falsify the theory at test. This seems true for all such examples: the stories always end up with a fortunate confirmation.

This last characteristic of the success of testing by falsification is less trivial than it might look at first sight. It is quite striking for two reasons. The first reason is that these examples cannot but reflect the exceptional cases out of the total history of good falsifying hypothesis testing. Suppose that all scientific theories are tested in this manner. By definition, they will mostly result in actual falsifications. Thus, the benefits of falsificationist testing are exemplified not by cases that result in the pursued and expected falsification, but by those cases in which the actual falsification failed and the test resulted in a confirmation. But, on the basis of the very strategy of falsificationism, namely looking for the falsifications, it follows that for every case producing a confirmation, probably hundreds of cases ending up with such a falsification must have taken place in anonymity.

The second reason why the "selection bias" in the choice of examples of good falsificationsim is important is that falsifying testing borrows its very merits from the confirming result, as was already argued in the formal analysis. The superiority of a testing strategy aimed at falsifying the hypothesis lies in the *failure* of this attempt, and the high degree of corroboration of the actual confirming test result. The high probative value of the confirming evidence arising from a falsificatory test is a direct consequence of looking for falsification. This is reflected by our intuition about the significance of the Michelson–Morley experiment. By contrast, keeping silent about falsifying test cases that resulted in the expected falsification is striking because these cases can be shown to be particularly insignificant. Indeed, in these cases the brave falsificationist tester is left behind with an observation that is at odds with his or her hypothesis, but which does *not* establish its falsity either. This can be explained by the inverse relation between the possible evidential value of confirming and falsifying instances issuing from a test (Poletiek, 2001). That is, as the severity of a possible test outcome to support the hypothesis H increases, the severity of the other possible outcome from the same test, the one that falsifies H, decreases.

This relation between the value of a confirmation and of a falsification implies a paradox for the Popperian hypothesis tester. This paradox is that the more you try to behave according to the prescriptions of falsificationism, the worse off you are if you "succeed". It is only if you find an unexpected confirmation that you will benefit from your choice. Popper does not warn the reader of this side effect of falsificationism. Instead, Popper proposes that actual refutations should not be undervalued in science. They are to be seen as important contributions to knowledge. However, the falsifying tester has little to be happy about if he finds the falsification he pursues, because the refutation is not convincing, and no journal will accept his paper describing such a result. The exemplary success stories of falsificationism disguise its important shadow side, because they actually failed to falsify the theory at stake.

To sum up, falsificationism cannot do without inductive confirmation. Any test situation is an anticipation of the evaluation of a hypothesis in the light of the possible results of the test to be performed. Falsificationism is actually justified by the valuable confirmations it provides. Even if induction is tactically reduced to "corroboration" in the actual practice of falsifying testing, it plays the main role. Falsificationism is exemplified by cases from the history of science in which unexpected confirmation of the theory was responsible for the advancement of knowledge. And it seems that falsificationism is not always the rational way to behave in everyday testing either.

Indeed, the relation between falsifying testing and inductions not only holds for science. The same intuitions occur in everyday reasoning. Suppose you have the chance to buy a 10-year-old car of make R. You want to test your assumption that R is a good make for your purposes. Your choice is between two tests: consulting the local R-cars dealer and consulting the P-cars dealer. The falsifying test prescription for this hypothesis is that you should consult the P-cars dealer. If you choose the P-cars dealer, a confirmation of your hypothesis is quite unexpected. Rather, you expect to hear that R-cars are not that good, and that you had better go for a P-car. But suppose that the P-cars dealer actually confirms, to your surprise, that R-cars are good cars. You would be highly convinced of your hypothesis and buy the R-car. However, the most probable outcome of your test is that the P-dealer is negative about R-cars. But then, you would still be in much doubt about the car precisely because you got the information you already expected. By contrast, consulting the brand R-dealer will make you expect that you will see your assumption confirmed, but this will have little impact on your beliefs. However, if the R-dealer, surprisingly, is negative about R-cars, this falsification will definitiely change your mind! The relation between a falsifying test strategy and the inductive power of an actual confirmation, arising from such a test, implies that the more we try to obtain falsification, the less well off we are if we get it. This is felt in both scientific and everyday hypothesis-testing situations.

TRANSLATING POPPER IN PSYCHOLOGY, BUT NOT FALSIFICATIONISM

Falsificationism has been argued to be inextricably bound to induction. The merits of falsificationism were even shown to be justifiable by the fact that it can ultimately lead to strong *verifications*. In general, the less probable of the two possible outcomes will tell us most about the "truth" of a hypothesis. This relation is specified in Popper's severity of test function. The core of falsificationism, however, is its normative component: the hypothesis tester should choose the test that will most probably lead to a falsification: she should *maximize* the severity of the test selected to test her theory. However, the normative aspect is not adequate as an empirical model, for both theoretical and practical reasons. I will argue, however, that the formal aspect, i.e., the relation between test choice and the properties of its outcome as specified in the severity of test formula, provides a useful basis for modelling hypothesis-testing behaviour. Next the problems of normative falsificationism in practice are dealt with.

Given the relation between the a priori test properties and the actual test results, hypothesis testing can be seen as the choice of one test among a number of possible tests, each having probabilities and values attached to the confirming result (predicted by the hypothesis) and the falsifying result. This choice is between a test having either a high probability of a weak confirmation or a low probability of a strong confirmation. Describing test behaviour in terms of this choice implies that it is a decision problem. As in the decision theoretic framework, the tester makes a "preposterior" consideration about how reliable he wants the outcome to be with regard to the confirmation and the falsification of the hypothesis at hand. The hypothesis tester considers how confident he wants to be that a future confirmation will prove his hypothesis to be true or a future falsification will prove his hypothesis to be false. As in decision theory, pragmatic considerations also play an important role in this decision, for instance utilities regarding a wrong "decision" (Friedrich, 1993). For example: the price of a rejection of the hypothesis on the basis of a falsification, while it is actually true.

Consider how this might apply to the hypothesis tester with his R-car. If he absolutely wants to avoid the risk of buying a wreck, he might choose the test giving him the most improbable, but also most reliable, confirmation, i.e., consulting the P-cars dealer. However, if he is prepared to take some inconveniences for granted, because he urgently needs a car anyway, he might go for the test with the most probable but less useful confirmation: asking the R-dealer. Only if this results in unexpected falsification will he cancel the purchase. In the example, the hypothesis testing boils down to setting the demands we put on each of the possible results. This form of testing behaviour clearly goes beyond the distinction between "falsifying testing" and "confirmation bias". It is more sophisticated. It represents testing as solving the dilemma of either maximizing the probability of a confirmation at the cost of its reliability or maximizing the probability of a falsification at the cost of its reliability. In other words, either you maximize the risk of having a falsification and the value of a confirmation, or you maximize the chance of having a confirmation and the value of a falsification.

In most everyday hypothesis-testing situations, this dilemma is intuitive, as shown in the car-buying example. Interestingly, the mere search for one outcome, falsifications or confirmations, although the way testing behaviour was modelled by researchers for years, is *not* straightforward to the naïve hypothesis tester. Poletiek (1996) showed that when participants were asked to "look for falsifications" in the rule discovery task, they felt unable to obey this instruction. However, Poletiek and Berndsen (2000) showed that participants in a realistic testing task felt they could make a sensible choice between tests when they were aware of both the probability of the possible test results *and* their related values, to evaluate the hypothesis. Summarizing, Popper's model for testing, in which the relation between the probability and the test outcome is specified, is a useful model for representing human testing behaviour, because it involves both the probability and the probative value of the anticipated test result. Therefore, the considerations an everyday tester is faced with when choosing a test can well be represented with the severity of test measure (1) provided by Popper (1963/1978).

Now, how useful is the normative aspect that more severe tests are always better (i.e., falsificationism strictly speaking) as a model for testing behaviour? First, the two justifications of the falsificationist standard are argued not to hold in everyday testing situations. Second, it can be questioned whether the standard of falsification is actually efficient in increasing our knowledge, in practice. The logical argument for falsification, that one falsifying observation allows one to definitely reject a hypothesis, stems from a propositional logic framework. In this framework, which is an abstract mathematical system, the outcome can have two values: true or false. A hypothesis cannot be "somewhat true". This logical assumption, however, does not always correspond to intuition in everyday hypothesis testing. For example, in the car-buying story, we felt that a falsification from the P-cars dealer, i.e., the P-cars dealer says that R-cars are no good, is less of a definite rejection than the same answer from the R-cars dealer. The fact that our confidence in the value of the hypothesis may decrease or increase to varying degrees is at odds with the two-values assumption of propositional logic. Thus, the assumption that a hypothesis, after being tested, is either true or false with nothing in between is clearly too strong an assumption for modelling human testing behaviour.

The psychological aspect of normative falsificationism, prescribing that the test should be chosen in such a way as to maximize the probability of rejecting the hypothesis, rather than trying to find support, becomes theoretically awkward when we realize that this is perfectly consistent with the confirmation theories it attacks. Indeed, confirmation theories of testing and their formalizations show a similar relation between the expected observation on the one hand and its value to evaluate the hypothesis tested, on the other. In the confirmation-theoretical framework, the observation that confirms the hypothesis best is the one that increases the probability of the hypothesis most, relative to how much we believed it already. This property is equivalent to its severity, i.e., its unexpectedness *per se*, and its potential supporting value. Hence, in the framework of confirmation theory, consulting the P-dealer would also result in the best confirmation, because if he says that R-cars are good, this result will most increase your belief in the hypothesis that R is good. Also, in both frameworks, the confirming outcome is less expected.

Thus, the contrast between falsificationism and confirmationism fades away when we analyze exactly what these strategies do; that is, if we ask what a tester should *do* if he wants to be a good falsificationist and what a tester should do if he wants to be a confirmationist. The conclusion is that they have to make the *same* test choice. The Popperian argument against confirmationism seems to represent this position as: "look for the most probable confirmations, regardless of their values". In this reasoning, an inductivist would advise you to consult the R-dealer because you probably will hear from him what he already believes. This is a caricature of confirmation theories, however. These theories actually define the inductive power of an observation as increasing its probability *in comparison* to what the tester already knows. In these theories, the formal expression of the degree of confirmation could be shown to be equivalent to Popper's degree of corroboration (3). Indeed, the degree of confirmation is not merely the probability of a theory given the observation, but the ratio of this probability to the probability of the theory before the test [see (3)]. However, increasing the probability of a hypothesis is exactly what severe evidence does as well, by force of its degree of corroboration. Thus the best "falsifiers" also are the best confirmers in the end. But in that case, the falsificationist standard becomes pointless if it equates with confirmation theories.

Finally, a number of findings on human hypothesis-testing behaviour suggest that a "successful" falsifying strategy, resulting in a sequence of actually falsified hypotheses, is not efficient *per se*. Poletiek (2001) related the number of falsifications obtained after successive tests to performance in Wason's rule discovery task. Participants obtaining more falsifications of their hypotheses about the rule discovered the true rule less often than participants having more confirmed hypotheses. Since participants rejected their current hypothesis after each falsification, they were set back after each rejection, and they felt they had too few chances left to explore new hypotheses. As Klayman and Ha (1989) suggested, hypothesis testing might better proceed by starting with a low-risk testing strategy, i.e., coming up with tests having a reasonable chance of resulting in a confirmation. After some weak supporting evidence has been gathered, and some confidence in the hypothesis built up, a more risky strategy might be adequate, to explore more precisely the limits of the hypothesis. But much will depend on one's goal, prior knowledge, the costs of multiple tests, *et cetera*. In sum, having a new idea, immediately submitting it to the most severe test, and obtaining many successive falsifications in a search process is not an efficient strategy *per se* to discover how close to the truth one is. The usefulness of such a rigorous test choice will normally depend on how sure we are that our hypothesis is right, of the costs of having it incorrectly rejected, or incorrectly accepted, and of the costs of testing (Van Wallendael, 1995).

CONCLUSIONS

We have evaluated various aspects of falsificationism, in the light of its possible contribution to the psychology of hypothesis testing. The falsificationist standard was argued to be problematic, not only because of its historical weakness in describing how scientists and everyday testers actually proceed when they test their hypotheses, but also because of its very logic. The analysis led to three major conclusions. First, falsificationism is intrinsically related to confirmationism, and it basically borrows its merits from its inductive success. Second, falsificationism can be shown to be equivalent to confirmation theories, because good falsifying testing is choosing tests that necessarily also satisfy good testing according to confirmation theories. Third, falsifying evidence actually becomes less informative the more it is the result of a stricter falsificatory test choice. This paradox was argued to be inherent in the falsificatory theory. A falsificatory test is most fruitful when it unexpectedly results in a confirmation a posteriori. In other words, falsificationism's success results from its failure. Apart from these theoretical considerations, from a pragmatic point of view repeatedly observing falsifying evidence is not the sure way to increase knowledge. It leads to a sequence of refutations, which repeatedly sets the tester back. The confirmatory alternative would involve a sequence of low-value confirmations slowly consolidating the theory. One might also follow a strategy somewhere in between. For example, "binary search" involves testing first one half of the set of alternatives, then half of the set left over, *et cetera*, until the hypothesis is narrowed down most closely to the true state of nature.

Falsificationism is a proper model for modelling hypothesis-testing behaviour, however, especially the severity of test measure. This model expresses that a test can be characterized by its probability of resulting in a confirmation and its power to confirm the hypothesis. But describing test choice in these terms is no different from the confirmations model. The result of this "merger" of the two classical rival views on testing is a unified model that can represent testing behaviour in a very intuitive way, as was shown above, and it provides a good point of departure for the study of human hypothesis testing, both everyday and expert.

The criticism of the concept of confirmation bias does not imply that no errors in actual testing behaviour can occur. For example, since the *a priori* test choice dictates the value of the different posterior possible outcomes of a test, the value of an actual test result may be under- or overestimated. For example, if a test is chosen with a high probability of a supportive result, this result, if actually found, should be seen as a weak proof of the truth of the hypothesis. If, however, the hypothesis tester overestimates this probative value, then an unwarranted induction is made. Imagine that you would be absolutely convinced that your R-car is the best choice after having heard this from an R-car dealer. The cost of such a reasoning error might be that you pay too high a price for it. Slowiazcek, Klayman, Sherman, and Skov (1992) showed that hypothesis testers tend to weigh the values of both severe and weak tests equally. This bias was found in experimental tasks in which the relation between test properties prior to testing and the properties of the outcomes were not very intuitive due to the formal presentation of the stimuli. Nonetheless, this result indicates an important possible pitfall of everyday hypothesis testing. People may assign too much value to observations from weak tests, as in the car example. Or, in contrast, people might underestimate the value of a confirmation from a severe test. For example, people convinced that they have a serious illness might underestimate the value of a medical test result that contradicts their idea, continuing to worry about their possible illness. These reasoning biases do not involve biased test choice, but a misinterpretation of the evidence given the properties of the test delivering it. Also, in expert situations, the value of evidence from a test can sometimes be inaccurately assessed. A salient case is jurisdiction. In the legal context, the value of evidence gathered has to satisfy an explicit criterion: it has to be beyond reasonable doubt. Given the importance of the decisions, the assessment of the probative value of a piece of evidence on the basis of the test – or investigation – it comes from, must be highly accurate. However, even in expert legal reasoning, the value of the evidence is sometimes highly over- or underestimated (Wagenaar, Van Koppen & Crombag, 1993). The cases described in Wagenaar et al. nicely illustrate the usefulness of analyzing test behaviour in terms of the a priori properties of the test, the a posteriori result of the test, and the relation between the two.

REFERENCES

Carnap, R. (1950). *Logical foundations of probability*. Chicago: University of Chicago Press.
Evans, J. St. B. T. (1989). *Bias in human reasoning*. Hove, UK: Lawrence Erlbaum Associates Ltd.
Evans, J. St. B. T., & Over, D. E. (1996) *Rationality and reasoning*. Hove, UK: Psychology Press.
Evans, J. St. B. T., & Wason, P. C. (1976). Rationalization in a reasoning task. *British Journal of Psychology*, 67, 479–486.
Friedrich, J. (1993). Primary error detection and minimization (PEDMIN) strategies in social cognition: A reinterpretation of confirmation bias phenomena. *Psychological Review*, 100(2), 298–319.
Howson, C., & Urbach, P. (1989). *Scientific reasoning*. Chicago: Open Court.
Johnson-Laird, P. N., & Wason, P. C. (1977). A theoretical analysis of insight into a reasoning task. In P. N. Johnson-Laird & P. C. Wason (Eds.), *Thinking*. Cambridge: Cambridge University Press.
Kareev, Y., Halberstadt, N., & Shafir, D. (1993). Improving performance and increasing the use of non-positive testing in a rule-discovery task. Special Issue: The cognitive psychology of reasoning. *Quarterly Journal of Experimental Psychology Human Experimental Psychology*, 46A(4), 729–742.
Klayman, J., & Ha, Y. (1987). Confirmation, disconfirmation, and information in hypothesis testing. *Psychological Review*, 94(2), 211–228.
Klayman, J., & Ha, Y. (1989). Hypothesis testing in rule discovery: Strategy, structure, and content. *Journal of Experimental Psychology Learning, Memory, and Cognition*, 15(4), 596–604.
Krueger, L. E., Gigerenzer, G., & Morgan, M. S. (1987). *The probabilistic revolution, Vol. 2: Ideas in the sciences*. Cambridge, MA: MIT Press.
Oaksford, M., & Chater, N. (1994). A rational analysis of the selection task as optimal data selection. *Psychological Review*, 101(4), 608–631.
Poletiek, F. H. (1996). Paradoxes of falsification. *Quarterly Journal of Experimental Psychology Human Experimental Psychology*, 49A(2), 447–462.

Poletiek, F. H. (2001). *Hypothesis testing behaviour*. Hove, UK: Psychology Press.
Poletiek, F. H., & Berndsen, M. (2000). Hypothesis testing as risk taking with regard to beliefs. *Journal of Behavioral Decision making, 13*, 107–123.
Popper, K. R. (1935). *Logik der Forschung*. Wien: J. Springer Verlag.
Popper, K. R. (1959 / 1974). *The logic of scientific discovery* (3rd Ed.). London: Hutchinson.
Popper, K. R. (1963 / 1978) *Conjectures and refutations* (4th Ed.). London: Routledge & Kegan Paul.
Slowiaczek, L. M., Klayman, J., Sherman, S. J., & Skov, R. B. (1992). Information selection and use in hypothesis testing: What is a good question, and what is a good answer? *Memory and Cognition, 20*(4), 392–405.
Snyder, M., & Swann, W. B. (1978). Hypothesis-testing processes in social interaction. *Journal of Personality and Social Psychology, 36*(11), 1202–1212.
Van Wallendael, L. R. (1995). Implicit diagnosticity in an information buying task. How do we use the information that we bring with us to a problem? *Journal of Behavioural Decision Making, 8*(4), 245–264.
Wagenaar, W. A., van Koppen, P. J., & Crombag, H. F. (1993). *Anchored narratives: The psychology of criminal evidence*. London: Harvester Wheatsheaf.
Wason, P. C. (1960). On the failure to eliminate hypotheses in a conceptual task. *Quarterly Journal of Experimental Psychology, 12*, 129–140.
Wason, P. C. (1966). Reasoning. In B. M. Foss (Ed.), *New horizons in psychology I* (pp. 135–151). Harmondsworth, UK: Penguin.
Wason, P. C. (1969). Regression in reasoning? *British Journal of Psychology, 60*, 471–480.
Wason, P. C. (1977). Self contradictions. In P. N. Johnson-Laird & P. C. Wason (Eds.), *Thinking*. Cambridge: Cambridge University Press.
Wason, P. C., & Johnson-Laird, P. N. (1970). A conflict between selecting and evaluating information in an inferential task. *British Journal of Psychology, 61*, 509–515.
Wetherick, N. E. (1962). Eliminative and enumerative behaviour in a conceptual task. *Quarterly Journal of Experimental Psychology, 14*, 246–249.

15 Constructing science

Sandy Lovie

LOGOS: IN THE BEGINNING WAS THE WORD

The whole of the scientific enterprise is suffused with reasoning and the related process of argumentation. From the initial choice of theoretical context and the researcher's position within it, to the production of the consequent detailed hypothesis and the selection of variables in order to translate this into a testable form; from the choice of equipment and how it is to be used, to the interpretation of the outcome of the study and its relationship with the context in which the work was devised, working scientists have to continually justify their choices both to themselves *and* to the community of scientists to which they belong. In general, therefore, I want to argue that *reasoning in context* is central to both the belief processes of science and to its practices. Even open-ended pursuits such as blue-sky, exploratory, or curiosity-driven research still require the originator to persuade others (and themselves!) at some stage of the game of the meaning of the results that they believe they have found. This chapter is designed to introduce the reader to the range of modern approaches by certain social sciences, including psychology, to this central aspect of science.

There is one fundamental point that I would like to make about the orientation of my account: this is that all aspects of scientific reasoning, and related aspects of it such as the stating and developing of theoretical positions, or the actions and practices to explore such settings, are all expressed as *text in context*. I follow the pragmatic linguist Jacob Mey in arguing that "Wording the world is seeing, not just looking at it to make sure it's there" (1993, p. 301). I also agree with him that language/text symbolically represents not just the beliefs, ideas, and knowledge that make up science, but also the actions that augment, support or materially exemplify such beliefs etc. Thus, the extended key is science as *texts of belief and action in context* (see Watson & Seiler, 1992, for more of interest here; also the two-volume collection of the unpublished work and lectures of Harvey Sacks, 1992). And finally, and again echoing Mey, such texts are social and collective in what they mean and represent, including the existence or necessity for collective change: "language is a social activity, and a change in language is a way of telling the world that it has to change as well" (Mey, 1993, p. 314). Let me illustrate some of these initial themes in a case study from the early days of the biochemical study of memory.

CUTTING PLANARIAN, AND *THE WORM RUNNERS' DIGEST*[1]

For many psychologists, a belief in the biological basis of all behaviour is both natural and inevitable. Their argument is deceptively simple: since we are all a product of our biological ancestry through the process of Darwinian evolution, so all that we are and do must also be accountable within such a framework. Thus, all social behaviour, all perceptual judgements, all memory, learning, and thinking must ultimately be explicable through a range of biological mechanisms. This reductionist move will be illustrated in the rather bizarre story of James McConnell and the conditioned flatworms, or planarians, which mixes drama, farce, and fundamental principles of scientific reasoning in the one study.

The 1950s saw the advent of modern genetics, with its increasing subservience to the explanatory power of complex and sophisticated biochemical processes. No longer could it be portrayed in the simple-minded way that allowed people like the biologist/politician J. B. S. Haldane to scribble down on the back of an envelope which of his near and far relatives he would be more or less inclined to save on the basis of how many genes they had in common with him! All of this had been swept away by the breaking of the genetic code by Watson and Crick in 1953, and their account of the key biochemical structure of cellular DNA and, with the microbiologist Brenner, the way in which DNA synthesizes biologically potent proteins via the action of RNA (see Andersen & Cadbury, 1985, for a semi-popular, first-person account of some of this material). The possibility that a biomolecular story could be advanced for such basic psychological processes as memory seemed to be little more than an extension of this exciting work. James McConnell was a bit better placed than most to jump aboard this particular nascent bandwagon, since he had, by the mid-1950s, begun training simple, free-swimming flatworms of the genus *Planaria*, and had then cut them up to see which of the two regenerated halves would retain the training: would it be the top half, or "head" end, which contained a simple neural knot, or the bottom one, which had no such neural cluster? (The odd finding was that *both* regenerated flatworms appeared to do equally well!)

The training regime used by McConnell was designed to condition the planarians to emit a particular piece of behaviour in reaction to a light, in this case a curling up movement of the body accompanied by a turning of the "head" end, which Collins and Pinch call the "scrunch" reaction (1998a, pp. 6–7). McConnell attempted to link the scrunch to the light by associating a noxious US (an electric shock) with the light CS, using a classical conditioning paradigm of the Pavlovian kind. The training regime, including the reliable detection of any conditioning, proved to be a difficult undertaking, with a steep learning curve for all the experimenters. For example, flatworms will spontaneously scrunch without any apparent external stimulus, or to a range of stimuli *including light alone*. Hence the observer needs to take into account the base-rate of scrunches and the time relations between the light CS and the scrunch response (now defined as the CR) or, even better, only to try to condition the animal when it has been swimming calmly in the test trough for some reasonable time. Thus the ability to distinguish between spontaneous scrunches and conditioned ones, and the ability to detect calmness in a swimming flatworm, all became essential and painfully acquired experimenter skills. Not too surprisingly, McConnell and his assistants showed a wide variation between themselves and over time, with only 45% successful conditionings being reported in the 1950s, while the same regime of 150 pairings of light and shock had generated a 90% conditioning rate by the 1960s.

As Collins and Pinch note, such a variation over time and people provided much valuable ammunition to McConnell's critics, since a phenomenon so elusive that it could only be observed or induced by a limited number of people might not exist at all, and could be accounted for by some other mechanism, including falsification of the records! There is also the matter of the slime trails left by the flatworms as they move about. As Collins and Pinch point out, where choice points in the swimming troughs (for instance, a simple right/left branching) might be used as part of the training, there then existed possible confusion over the interpretation of the flatworm's behaviour, since shocked flatworms leave stronger slime trials than non-shocked flatworms, while flatworms will normally follow the stronger slime trial whatever the stage or content of the training regime (1998a, pp. 10–11). Thus the effects of differential sliming could overlay any conditioned responses.

Finally, McConnell pursued the new developments in genetics more directly by injecting RNA extracted from conditioned flatworms into non-conditioned flatworms, on the grounds that since RNA provided the major mechanism for creating new proteins from DNA, so such a fundamental and robust biochemical process must also form the biological basis for memory (see Bower & Hilgard, 1981, pp. 510–514, for a more detailed account of the workings of RNA, and a partial justification for its use as an encoder for the storage of complex phenomena such as memories). In these latter studies, McConnell had claimed considerable success, thus encouraging others to enter the field, in particular the pharmacologist George Ungar (see Collins & Pinch, 1998a, pp. 15–25, for an insightful analysis of Ungar's work and the controversies that it provoked). Further, insofar as the work of Ungar attracted additional criticisms, so McConnell's work using RNA could be tarred with the same brush.

Here several challenges both explicit and implicit to McConnell's earlier experiments can be detected, as can the ways in which they were handled, that is, how the argumentation surrounding the studies was developed jointly by the critics (real, imagined, or role played) and McConnell. For instance, to those who attacked the reality of the phenomenon, McConnell would underline the increasing success over time in conditioning their flatworms, while he mounted a robust attack on those laboratories that could not replicate the flatworm studies by pointing to "differences in personality and past experience amongst the various investigators" (quoted by Collins & Pinch, 1998a, p. 11). These latter factors were apparently important determiners of success since flatworms should not be pushed too hard, and "[it is necessary to] treat them tenderly, almost with love . . ." (McConnell, 1965, p. 26; also cited in Collins & Pinch, 1998a, p. 11, their square brackets). As far as the issue of sliming was concerned, at least three distinct strategies were adopted by McConnell: cleaning the troughs between animal training sessions, or replacing the troughs with new ones between sessions, or working with uniformly pre-slimed troughs whose slime had come from non-experimental flatworms (Collins & Pinch, 1998a, pp. 10–11). We can thus detect a number of ways in which critics, real or self-created, were rebutted, for example, by criticizing the practices – including, apparently, the attitudes – of the non-successful laboratories, by varying the confounding factors in the apparatus, and by pointing to the rising success brought about by improvements to the experimental routines (and, by implication, the increased level of skill among the observers, and the uniformity and consistency of the application of best experimental practice). And all of these counters were expressed as text in the appropriate, often high-status, journals.

Collins and Pinch also indirectly indicate the textual nature of the process when they discuss the content of McConnell's most notorious publication, the *Worm Runners' Digest* (now something of a cult item on the internet). This lively and irreverent publication carried many of McConnell's early planarian results from the 1950s, and as a result had the unfortunate effect of reducing the status of this material. Even McConnell's attempt to fix the *Digest* by bolting his newly created (and refereed) *Journal of Biological Psychology* to its front end did little to make the flatworm results, or any of the other material, more respectable (Collins & Pinch, 1998a, pp. 12–13). However, even though McConnell continued to generate controversial and heavily criticized research, he did not abandon his commitment to the biochemical basis of memory and was only forced to close his laboratory in 1971, and thus discontinue his work, because the money just plain dried up, whilst Ungar died still believing in the same essential proposition. How can I, as a psychologist, capture McConnell's and Ungar's stubborn resistance in the face of the heavyweight and prestigious opposition cited by Collins and Pinch (1998a, pp. 18–21)?

A MINIMAL PSYCHOLOGY FOR SCIENCE IN CONTEXT

Since this is a chapter in a book on the psychology of reasoning, I feel under some obligation to give an indication as to what kind of model of the reasoning person/scientist I am assuming. This is not an elaborate one of the kind beloved by the cognitive architectural school of thought, but looks a lot like the dynamic and process-based one of the schemata lobby, with the added *frisson* of a collective self made up of significant others *and their conceptual positions*, all available for role playing by the self (see Stevens, 1996, for a recent and broad-based introduction to modern notions of the self). This self is also assumed to be capable of reflexivity, that is, the ability to question or undermine or re-examine its own presuppositions and their rhetorical basis (see the volume edited by Woolgar, 1988b, for a classic treatment of reflexivity in the social sciences, especially Woolgar's own contribution, "Reflexivity is the ethnographer of the text"; see also Stevens, 1996, particularly Chapter 4). Further, if one accepts the notion of a *collective* self, then reflexivity also means the ability of the self to critically examine other people's conceptual positions as well as its own, although this is complicated by the orientation that the self takes to such positions. In other words, if you are positively committed to a particular position, then it will be more difficult to reflexively undermine it than it would be if you had adopted either a neutral or negative attitude to the material. This notion of commitment is equally shared by sociologists of science, and philosophers of science sympathetic to Thomas Kuhn (see Kuhn, 1970; also Barnes, 1982, for a commentary from the social sciences). In some ways, reflexivity has much in common with the psychological notion of *metacognition*, insofar as both imply the ability of the self to distance itself from its immediate concerns in order to comment on them. As far as the most appropriate structuring principle for any stored representations are concerned, Frederick Bartlett's original notion of the schema as a dynamic, adaptive, and social process would seem to be the most appropriate one here (see Shotter, 1990, for a re-evaluation of the essentially anthropological nature of Bartlett's initial conception of the schema, and the role that the neurologist Henry Head's own conception of the schema played in Bartlett's thinking).

Thus, for my purposes, a minimal psychology would consist of a collective self, capable of both reflexivity and moral evaluation, and therefore able to form a variety of commitments (*positive, neutral, or negative*) to significant portions of the world, and drawing on (but limited by) a dynamically organized and socially shaped schematic memory system, which is itself a reciprocally generated product of these same processes of reflexivity, evaluation, and commitment. The science produced by such a psychology is one that adopts a particular point of view (epistemologically speaking), and is formed by action, negotiation, and persuasion within such a dynamic context. It would not, in general, be analyzable from a strictly logical standpoint, nor would it conform to any simple-minded realist doctrine, for instance, that such and such a scientific finding was entirely *independent* of the work of the observer. Let me illustrate a fair percentage of these points in my next case study, that of Percival Lowell and the photographs of Mars.

PERCIVAL LOWELL AND THE ULTIMATE PROOF OF LIFE ON MARS

For most scientists, an invitation to address that prestigious body the Royal Society of London would be a considerable high point in their professional lives. So it is not too surprising to find this august body being enthusiastically regaled in 1905 by the American astronomer and businessman Percival Lowell with what he claimed was incontrovertible *scientific* evidence of the existence of sentient (and hardworking) beings on Mars, our nearest planetary neighbour. It is, of course, the case that Lowell and his associates at the Flagstaff Observatory in Arizona had studied Mars for many years before this meeting and had amassed an enormous number of drawings and instrument readings of the planet, but what Lowell paraded in triumph before the Royal Society was the *photographic* proof of the canals on Mars,[2] and with it, the final vindication of even the most outrageous of his speculations about this distant world. He could scarcely contain his glee at the persuasive power of the material: "To make the canals of Mars write their own record on a photographic plate, so that astronomers might have at first hand *objective* proof of their reality, has long been one of the objects of this observatory. The endeavour has at last succeeded." Lowell's account then goes on to distinguish between at least two groups for whom the evidence would be somewhat differently received: "Unnecessary as such corroboration was to the observers themselves, it is different with the world at large; for the work of the camera at once puts the canals in a position where scientists in general, as well as astronomers in particular, are able to judge the phenomena" (both selections taken from Lowell, 1906, p. 132; my emphasis).

These two quotations provide support for several of the cross-linking themes on scientific reasoning that I will pursue in this chapter: first, that any argumentation in science is always from a particular knowledge position or *point of view* (see Harman, 1986, and Brannigan, 1981): in our present case, Lowell presupposes the *reality* of the Martian canals (note that his paper is entitled "First Photographs of the Canals of Mars" without the slightest trace of irony, while we have already seen his claim that "... the canals of Mars write their own record on a photographic plate ..."). Second, that there are scientific instruments and practices (here telescopes and cameras, and associated usages) whose output is simultaneously beyond debate and independent of the observer (and consequently that there are instruments and practices that are most definitely *not*). Here the *photographic* record of the Martian canals (together with the practices that simultaneously both generated the material *and* warranted its quality) represents such an objective source of knowledge. Third, that science must create and differently address its various audiences, strongly implying that important parts of scientific reasoning are concerned with persuasion. Lowell's explicit distinction between the two main recipient groups of the photographs, for example, shows that he recognized the *rhetorical* nature of his presentation to the Royal Society, as is also revealed by later parts of the report.

INTERLUDE: ARGUMENTATION AND STS

My take on reasoning in science, therefore, bears only a passing resemblance to the way that scientists are supposed to operate in their argumentation, that is, as propositional machines obeying logical rules. My contention, on the other hand, is that scientists operate in complex contexts made up of beliefs, knowledge, judgements, and action, that they advance, explore, and defend a conceptual position, whether empirically, theoretically, or *morally* derived, which is based on elements (and their understanding) of these contexts, and that they justify their conclusions with respect to that position and within whatever context they find themselves. This amounts to what I can only describe as a kind of *practical reasoning*,[3] although I would also want to emphasize the fundamentally *social* nature of such a process, from the source and nature of the context to the means whereby the adopted position is created and defended; from the way that the position is expressed to the form that any conclusions drawn from its exploration and testing are stated and justified. Although this might seem to imply that scientists have complete control or say over all parts of this process, there are always unforeseen elements and consequences at each stage, simply because of the inherent ambiguity and uncertainty of meaning attached to any context or action. Consequently, all positions (and the components that create, defend, or extend them) are potentially underminable by others (or even by the individual scientist, if he or she is sufficiently reflexive, or self-critical). Ongoing systematic, scientific change is, therefore, brought about by collectively negotiated and agreed-on processes designed to advance propositions about the world, including those designed to defend such propositions against any undermining. Note that this latter process also implies the possibility of any world view having to be re-ordered (or re-negotiated) in the face of what is taken by *all* sides to be a successful challenge.

The problem for many people is that such an outline does not seem specific to the received view of science. For example, it sounds suspiciously like what happens under current adversarial systems of justice, or indeed the heated arguments around the breakfast table as to when Sara *actually* returned the previous night (or was it early this morning?) after a visit to the coolest club in the Universe. Surely science has to be above or, at the very least, different from such things! My evidence for arguing that there is nothing basically different between all these forms of argumentation is contained, first of all, in the considerable body of participant observer work by many social scientists on the routine, day-to-day work of professionally employed scientists (see Lovie, 1992, for a coverage of the classical work on the subject). Other work that I find equally convincing is the analysis, again by social scientists, of historical and contemporary accounts of science by scientists themselves (see, for example, Collins & Pinch, 1993, 1998a, 1998b; Gilbert & Mulkay, 1984; Gross, 1996; also Knorr-Cetina, 1981; Latour & Woolgar, 1986; Shapin, 1994; Shapin & Shaffer, 1985). There is also a growing radical tradition in social psychology stemming from the work of Billig (1987) and others, which argues for a rhetorical and discursive approach to all social behaviour. This approach has latterly been applied to the actions and output of scientists (see, for instance, Soyland, 1994, and Potter, 1996; see also chapters in Shadish & Fuller, 1994). You should, therefore, take it that I want the current chapter to be viewed as situated within these several traditions, one of whose collective names is the (Social) *Study of Technology and Science* (or STS).[4]

RETURNING TO MARS

But let me get back to Lowell and his photographs by pointing to some of the *pragmatic* aspects of the material I have quoted, where I take pragmatics to be the study of language as *the creation of meaning and action in context and in interaction* (see Thomas, 1995, for more, or Mey, 1993). For example, the term "*canals on Mars*" is actually shorthand for both Lowell's long-held belief in the existence of Martian life and for the complex arguments that he mounted to support this view, and therefore acts a little like the *implicature* rules in pragmatics (see Mey, 1993, pp. 99–106). Thus, if the canals actually existed in the form believed by Lowell, then many things would follow, for example, since they were too regular and too systematic to be natural, so they had to be the product of intelligent life, which had constructed them to act not only as a way of carrying irrigation water around the planet, but also as means of transportation across the enormous expanses of the planet's surface.[5] In addition, the appearance of many nodes or *oases* linking up adjacent canals suggested a coherent and fully interconnected transport system, as did the apparent lack of any unconnected canals or isolated nodes. The reality of the canals also suggested that the consistent and seasonal colour changes that swept over large areas of the Martian surface defined by the canals (a phenomenon long noted by Lowell and other astronomers) were, in fact, caused by predictable alterations in the appearance of the enormous acreage of crops being grown and harvested by the Martians themselves. Here the canals took the form of boundaries and separators of the cultivated areas, while also acting as a means of moving essential irrigation water released on a seasonal basis from the polar ice caps. Thus, according to Lowell, the Martians were consummate civil engineers, well able to construct complex and interconnected networks of kilometre-wide trenches running for hundreds, perhaps even thousands, of kilometres from the ice fields across the Martian surface. A further implication of the seasonal changes in colour across the planet was that the Martians were farmers on a gigantic scale, easily handling the planting, nourishment, and harvesting of crops covering many hundreds of hectares of land. Indeed, so convinced was Lowell of the contemporary reality of the Martian race, including its evident triumphs and the many material pressures on it, that he felt able to speculate about the nature of Martian morality and even their social order. This he believed was arranged in a hierarchy similar to that in Plato's Republic, with statesmen/scientists and engineers at the top, and workers at the bottom (see Lovie, 1992). And all of this flowed from accepting the objective reality of the canals from the photographic evidence! Thus the elaborated context of the simple phrase *"The canals of Mars"* simultaneously supported and exemplified Lowell's complex and strongly held certainties about the planet and its inhabitants.

The rest of Lowell's paper is concerned with legitimating and objectifying the truth contained in the photographs in the sense of morally justifying the design and properties of the instruments used at Flagstaff, and the practices adopted by Lowell's assistant, Lampland, who actually took the photographs. I will only briefly cover this part of the paper, since there are more details and a commentary to be found in Lovie (1994). First, Lowell claims that the 24-inch reflector telescope used by Lampland was "the most space-penetrating glass at present in use", since it was able to detect more stars in a particular quadrant of the sky than the competition at the Lick Observatory and the Washington Naval Observatory (Lowell, 1906, pp. 132–133). The superior quality of the glass forming the telescope lens is particularly singled out for mention, as is the unusually steady and transparent air at Flagstaff during the photographic sessions. The latter was supplemented by Lowell's claim to have an exhaustive knowledge of the air currents playing about the observatory, thus collectively underlining the superior quality of both the viewing and the photographic experience. All of these points were employed to rhetorically justify the tiny telescope apertures used during the camera work, which (so Lowell claimed) minimized the blurring of the image and hence allowed both the human observer *and* the camera to detect the same detailed structures on the surface.[6]

Again, Lowell drew his audience's attention to the large number of photographs taken over the comparatively short period when Earth and Mars were at their closest, that is, during their so-called *opposition*. This serves to further legitimate the information by pointing to its optimum timing and to its abundance, where the latter provided enough overlapping knowledge to allow the astronomers to correct for variations in the air currents around Flagstaff, and any intermittent technical problems with the apparatus. Thus, Lowell and his assistant had more than enough material to select only the strongest and least controversial evidence for the correctness of their views, where Lowell writes "These plates, *when sufficiently good*, all show the canals . . ." (1906, p. 134; my added emphasis on the *moral* nature of the material). Lowell maintains, however, that while the photographs have a useful public role in persuading a wider audience than the Flagstaff Observatory of the reality of the canals, "The eye is able to go much further than the camera . . .". In consequence "That the camera confirms, *as far as it can go*, the eye observations at Flagstaff, should lead any *unprejudiced* mind to consider very seriously the probability of their being correct beyond" (both quotations from 1906, p. 134; my added emphases). Notice the careful rhetorical coupling of *"unprejudiced"* and *"mind"*, with the obvious implication that all those who were unable to see the canals as clearly as Lowell were, *irrationally* biased against the Flagstaff view.

REASONING IN SCIENCE AND TWO PHILOSOPHICAL INPUTS

Although I have excluded traditional logic as a useful way of describing the actual processes of science, what I have not laid out in any detail is what I think is a reasonable alternative. Consequently, this section will outline two complementary approaches that I believe capture in a more systematic fashion much of what I have already sketched out. But I would initially like to offer a context for these approaches.

First of all, I do not believe that it is possible to offer a single formal or formalized theory of scientific reasoning that will apply universally to all areas culturally designated as science, any more than it is possible to prescribe a single, common, and overarching scientific method. This does not mean, however, that I can be easily dismissed as one of those rascally relativists so beloved of the more conservative wing of the scientific press. Nor does it mean that I am arguing that people (including scientists) are intrinsically irrational; I am, for instance, no supporter of Feyerabend's notorious claim that "In science, anything goes" (1970, p. 26). Rather, I believe that scientists are contextually bound and understood, and that rationality, any rationality, has to take account of this boundedness. Further, since I have also argued earlier in the chapter that the context is a social product, so I could be counted as a less than radical *social realist* where I take reality, any reality, to be *collectively* constructed. This allows me to analyze science as the product of skilled and expert persons, whose major aims include making sense (within the context of their knowledge, beliefs, and actions) of what they find, and then persuading others (where these could include both expert *and* lay audiences) of the rightness of the sense-making that they have achieved, even if this means negotiating changes to the context and their take on it. Thus scientists, like all people, are sense-making, rhetorical beings working within a collectively constructed and dynamically changing context of knowledge, beliefs, and actions, rather in the fashion of Head and Bartlett's schemata (see also my earlier remarks on minimal psychology).

What I believe I am putting forward is not so much a detailed and fixed set of rules as to how scientific reasoning is performed, since I do not believe that any such thing exists, but a general framework within which scientific reasoning can be studied. Thus, for me, scientific reasoning consists of three major steps: the positing and justification of an idea drawn from a particular context and a point of view within it; the laying out and grounding of a set of actions and practices to test this idea; rounded off by an equally well-justified interpretation of the results of these actions offered in the light of the original idea and context. Scientific reasoning, therefore, consists of both cognitive and rhetorical work, and the instrumental manipulation of the material world, all situated within a dynamic and interactive context, with *all* the parts formed by collective, social processes.

I want to briefly discuss two approaches from the philosophy of action and reasoning which embody much of this thinking: the first, by Stephen Toulmin, dates from 1969, and is contained in his book *The uses of argument*, while the second is more recent and is by Gilbert Harman (1986) from his book *Change in view: Principles of reasoning*. Both authors eschew formal logic as a model for argumentation or reasoning, and instead offer an alternative that they claim both encompasses most practical, everyday arguments *and* allows for a degree of systematization and formalization of reasoning. Thus in Toulmin's book we find the following general format for any argument:

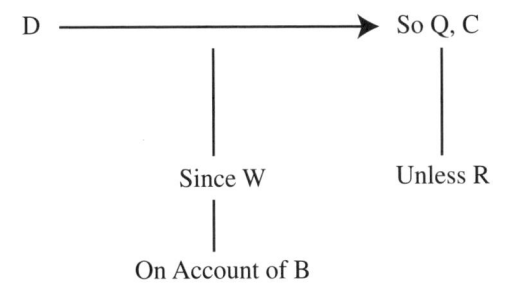

```
D  ─────────────▶  So Q, C
│                  │
│                  │
Since W           Unless R
│
│
On Account of B
```

where D is an assertion or datum, W is a truth warrant for the datum, B is the backing for the warrant W, Q is the qualifier for the conclusion (or C), which might in turn be challenged by the existence of a rebuttal (or R item).

Toulmin's example is a little banal, but reasonably convincing: Harry was born in Bermuda (D), *so presumably* (Q) he is a British citizen (C), *since* a man born in Bermuda is usually a British citizen (W), *on account of* the existing legal statutes and precedents (B), *unless* both his parents were not citizens of Bermuda at his birth, or he had subsequently obtained American citizenship, etc. (R). It is worth noting that Toulmin took the adversarial rules of the British courtroom to be a model for such reasoning, although it is easy to detect a strong strand of rhetoric and reflexivity in the structure and components of the process, where one is interested in establishing a point of view against all comers, including the possibility (reflexively obtained) of having to reverse the current argument in the face of certain convincing additional data, for instance, that Harry was indeed a naturalized American. For Toulmin, therefore, anyone actively engaged in argumentation would need to know not just the simple inference from datum to (qualified) inference, but also the support in depth of the inference (warrants and backup), as well as the grounds for challenging the inference (the rebuttals). In other words, anyone undertaking an argument structured in such a form would not only be versed in practical inference or reasoning and in reflexivity, but would also be willing to alter the argument in the light of new information. Of course, reflexivity could also be used to strengthen a challenged argument, in that it could be used either to undermine the opposition or to find deeper, additional support for it, or even to find evidence apparently unrelated to the original argument by re-expressing it and its supporting evidence in another way. Reflexivity, in other words, can open up the possibility of new insights and hence the recasting of all aspects of the argument. Further, given that one concedes the existence of reflexivity as a part of the dynamic of science, then one might also concede the more general point that science is a matter of rhetoric and negotiation.

The major problem with Toulmin's book for my present purposes is that the notion that logic does not, or need not, play a role in argumentation was so novel at the time that he had to spend most of the treatment establishing this contention on many philosophical fronts, thus confining his formulation of the argument to a single if meaty chapter (1969, Chapter 3, "The layout of arguments"). I also believe that Toulmin's somewhat ambivalent attitude to psychology and what it can or cannot do for philosophy, from the principles of probability to epistemology, would make him a difficult bedfellow in the current enterprise, in that his layout of arguments owes little to any explicit psychological insights, although some psychologists have found his formulation useful for their own purposes (see, for instance, Bromley, 1986, on the case study method). However, my second writer, Gilbert Harman, is known to be much more sympathetic to a certain kind of psychology, as a careful reading of his 1986 text shows. As with Toulmin, Harman provides a useful diagram of the processes of reasoning, which he characterizes as *Change in view*, that is, reasoning is all about a reasoned alteration of one's take (and action) on the world in the light of new or altered circumstances.[7] His story of the unfortunate Mary who comes down to breakfast determined to consume a plate of Cheerios, but then finds that there are none to be had and concludes that this is because her room-mate Elizabeth had already finished them off, and, as a consequence, then elects to eat Rice Krispies instead, provides a neat, if milk-soaked, example of this process.

More formally, therefore, any reasoner following Harman's prescription will (i) determine on a reasoned course of action to achieve an end (Cheerios for breakfast), (ii) behave according to this action plan by selecting appropriate means to accomplish it (open kitchen cupboards, check fridge for milk etc.), and then (iii) carry it out, unless (iv) encountering not intended conditions (no Cheerios, hence the inference that Elizabeth ate them all before Mary appeared), which might then lead to (v) a change of plan and a consequent change of action (have Rice Krispies instead of Cheerios for breakfast). In Harman's scheme, Ends (E) and Means (M) are intended, while both the Side Effects (S) of the Means and the Consequences (C) of the Ends might not be intended but might be foreseen. The diagram below (based on Harman's original on p. 97 of his 1986 treatment) illustrates this reasoning structure (and points to its similarities to Toulmin's analysis):

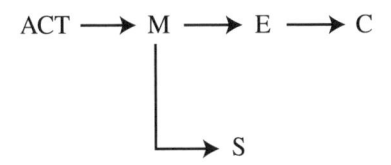

$$ACT \longrightarrow M \longrightarrow E \longrightarrow C$$
$$ \downarrow$$
$$ S$$

The quasi-psychological principles supplied by Harman which help determine this account of reasoning are all to do with the *timing* of acceptable or unacceptable inferences, thus generating the principles of *Immediate Implication* and *Immediate Inconsistency*, where one is more likely to favour the former, but will vigorously seek to avoid the latter. These are supplemented by the principle of *Clutter Avoidance*, a kind of cognitive economy that determines the number and relevance of the beliefs that one might produce or hold during reasoning. Harman also distinguishes between the *Maxims of Reflection* (a close relation of reflexivity) and *Principles of Revision*, where the former are concerned with the evaluation and generation of beliefs, while the latter determines the actions actually implied by such reasoned revisions, although Harman also concedes that reasoning, in his sense, might be almost automatic (1986, pp. 1–2). It is not too difficult, therefore, to appreciate both the cognitive psychology determinants of his system, and how it might provide a useful descriptor of most forms of reasoning, including that used by science. In general, therefore, both Toulmin and Harman argue that reasoning takes place within a context familiar to the reasoner, that the reasoning process asserts a justified or appropriate *something* (a fact and/or action) that has *consequences*, but whose truth (of the *something–consequences* link) can also be challenged by alternative circumstances or conditions (again, *ultimately* meaningful within this context) which may then lead to a change of view or conclusion or action. Thus, as I have argued before, reasoning is dynamic but context-bound.

Let me illustrate some of these novelties by an episode from the history of palaeontology (the study of human fossil remains), that of the notorious Piltdown Man. Although most modern accounts of this episode tend to emphasize the forgery aspects of the discovery (see the brief treatment in Broad & Wade, 1985, pp. 119–121, and their references to the earlier literature), the sociologist of scientific discovery, Brannigan (1981, pp. 164–166), has cast his remarks on the case as an example of the effects of change of view. Thus, during the time of the greatest influence of the finds, that is, from the publication of their discovery in 1912 to the mid-1920s, when more scientifically acceptable fossils began to appear from African sites, the skulls of Piltdown Man were considered good evidence for the existence of the so-called "missing link"[8] between ourselves and the fossil apes. However, when strong evidence began to emerge in the 1950s that the remains had actually been created from modern human skulls joined to equally modern ape jaws (with both suitably stained to make them look old), so the veracity of their initial discoverer, Charles Dawson, had begun to be questioned, including the sudden "re-discovery" that he had also been accused of plagiarizing an earlier author in writing his history of Hastings Castle.[9] Thus, the undoubted problems with the original interpretation of the skulls had been played down during the time that most of the scientific establishment had been committed to the reality/meaning of the Piltdown findings, while the change of view brought about by the discovery that they had been faked had forced a completely new interpretation of the "facts", including the moral status of the original messenger!

Evidence for such a change of view can also be found in the recent account by Judith Hooper of the evolutionary implications of the wing colouring of the peppered moth (2002). This rather drab insect also became, in the mid-1950s, the "missing link" in the Darwinian story when the moth collector Bernard Kettlewell (working under the influence of his Oxford mentor the committed Darwinian E. B. "Henry" Ford) published experimental data showing the adaptive advantage of *melanism* (blackening) over *non-melanism* in their wings. The experiment itself consisted of the release of many hundreds of melanated and non-melanated moths into a heavily polluted wood on the Cadbury Estate a few miles from Birmingham, UK. On the basis of day-by-day recapture, Kettlewell then attempted to work out the survival rates of each type over time. Almost immediately, this work was recognized as providing apparently unassailable evidence for Darwinian evolution in action, where the source of the critical environmental event (pollution) was taken to be the (historically recent) Industrial Revolution of the early 1800s. Thus the adaptive effect of the pollution was, as it were, to select those genetic elements within the moth's repertoire of inherited characteristics that blackened the moth's offspring, thus making them much more difficult to see against the blackened bark of a polluted tree by predators such as birds. On the other hand, if the characteristic had not been selected or expressed, then the lighter-coloured, non-melanated moths would be that much more obvious to any predator. More precisely, what Kettlewell had reportedly showed was that "... black moths survived twice as well as light-coloured moths on the darkened tree trunks of a polluted wood near Birmingham" (Hooper, 2002, p. 116). This result, together with photographs of *dead* (or artificially arranged) light- and dark-winged moths with their wings spread out and carefully posed against various coloured barks, became the standard fodder of biological textbooks pushing the Darwinian line as against the hated doctrine of the Lamarckian inheritance of acquired characteristics.

However, beginning with the work of Ted Sargent in the mid-1960s and culminating with a major review of all the extant material by Michael Majerus in 1998, just about all the supporting features of Kettlewell's major 1953 study had been shredded: peppered moths of all colours do not normally alight on the bark of trees; birds are not major predators of peppered moths (or indeed of moths in general), hence undermining the argument for the advantages of melanism; even if they actually ate them, bird vision is not like human vision, hence the colouration of the moth's wings is of less relevance. Even the photographs of the moths (including those by Kettlewell) give a completely erroneous picture of how *live* peppered moths actually arrange their wings at rest – these are typically folded over each other, never spread out as in the illustrations, thus making them less of a target for predators (see Hooper, 2002, especially chapter 11, for more details). Consequently, if Darwinian theory is to be preserved as the only explanation for the existence of so-called "*industrial melanism*", then a much more complex mechanism is required to account for its early appearance in the history of the peppered moth. More relevant for my current argument is that most if not all of the counter-arguments were not exactly unfamiliar to the participants, that is, that they drew on common knowledge within the moth collectors' tight circle. However, given that the evidence seemed to supply the almost unique picture of Darwinian evolution in demonstrable action, so the peppered moth, like the Piltdown Man, seemed to supply science with one of the very few missing links in the Great Chain of Being. To argue against both instances was, therefore, to achieve a kind of *reasoned* Harmanian change of view. This alteration would also generate new knowledge, not a simple re-ordering of the same material, since it is based on a newly achieved *and quite different* conceptual foundation and its attendant commitments. But what has modern psychology got to say about the processes of scientific reasoning?

BUT WHERE IS THE PSYCHOLOGY?

There is, of course, a further and peculiarly psychological aspect to this chapter which says that this STS stuff is all very well in its place, but what sort of *experimental* work does it lead to? My reply is not encouraging to what has already been attempted in the areas that might be termed the cognitive study of science. Thus, the efforts by the late Herbert Simon to find out how the 17th-century astronomer Johannes Kepler discovered the elliptical nature of the orbits of the planets, by asking students from various academic backgrounds to attempt to solve the problem after having been given some general information as to how it might be solved and some sample data points, do not impress me in the slightest, if only because four of the fourteen students solved the puzzle in a brief period of time, while stupid Kepler took over 20 years to come up with the answer! (See Qin & Simon, 1990, for more details; also Klahr & Simon, 1999, 2001.) I am equally unimpressed by a similar study by Kevin Dunbar, which also used students to solve a simplified version of the classic studies by Monod and Jacob on how genes control other genes, research that had gained the pair a Nobel prize in 1965. Here 40 students, already familiar with basic genetics, were given elementary instruction in biochemistry and microbiology, and were then faced with computer-simulated, if somewhat simplified, versions of some of the problems that Monod and Jacob tackled. Many of the students (who had been given either 90 minutes or an hour to come up with a solution, depending on which experiment they had been allocated to) were, at the end, judged to be sufficiently close to the expected result for Dunbar to conclude that they had indeed discovered what the Nobel laureates Monod and Jacob had struggled to find in over 20 years of hard work. Again, one could ask what relevance is any of this to the understanding of actual scientific work, particularly as it completely ignores the vast historical, cultural, and geographical gulfs between the original work and its attempted replication by a modern American student sample. What both studies seem to me to be about is not scientific discovery *per se*, but the role of background knowledge and training on elementary problem solving, which, from the students' point of view, appeared to involve tackling a series of open-ended problems, but which were, in fact, profoundly *close-ended*, at least as far as the experimenters, with their realist scientific ideologies, were concerned. This was not really the exploration of the truly unknown, but a heavily prompted and goal-shaped journey down a well signposted road with an unproblematic endpoint: you could even turn it into a test of ability for the scientifically inclined!

I am, however, much more impressed by those very few workers (not always psychologists) who have bravely used psychological notions in an exploration of actual scientific work: the social and cognitive psychology equivalents of the micro-sociologists of science whose work I have recounted earlier. This, it seems to me, is the more useful way to go, since it treats the rich and multi-faceted data of actual scientific belief and practice as a *sacred resource* that has to be accounted for *retrospectively*.[10] The one figure that I want to discuss under this heading is Ronald Giere, who has adopted a nice line between realism and relativism as his philosophy of science (a position that he calls *constructive realism* – see Giere, 1988, especially chapter 4), and the notion of *bounded rationality* from Simon (1983) for his intellectual tool kit. In Giere's view, bounded rationality implies that people (and scientists) can make sensible decisions about their world, even if it is recognized that what they know or can assume about it is limited or contextualized. Thus people, while being characterized as constrained sense makers, are still *sense makers* in that they actively *choose* between theories, earlier accounts, equipment, practices, and outcomes, *and* justify their decisions to themselves and others. This general orientation and method is applied by Giere to two major scientific efforts: one contemporary – the workings of a particle physics laboratory, particularly in its involvement with a problem in what Giere calls "relativistic Dirac models of the nucleus" (1988, p. 191: note that this section of the book also contains extensive background material to the problem); and one historical – the geological puzzle linking continental drift and sea-floor spreading. In both cases, Giere suggests that the positions adopted by what he terms the various "cognitive agents" in the accounts are, in part, a product of their pre-existing intellectual and professional contexts and experiences, and, in part, also derived from their interaction with other, similarly formed agents, where these "negotiations" are couched in, and conducted through, a common language and set of technical practices (see, for example, Giere, 1988, p. 277, final paragraph).[11] Although Giere and I differ on many points, I am happy, as a social realist, to agree with this characterization of the working scientist and scientific reasoner!

POSTSCRIPT

What I have attempted to do in this chapter is to lay out an alternative way of thinking about reasoning in science and related areas, one based not on science as the exercise of narrowly defined logical or rational principles, but on a construal that emphasizes the context-boundedness of scientific beliefs and practices, while also underlining the collective, rhetorical, and reflexive nature of scientific skills. The major question is how can psychologists operate fruitfully in this new, socially constructed scientific world? The answer cannot lie in the laboratory, but through methods that respect both the work and the person, and the past. This can only mean the deployment of qualitative methods such as the analysis of discourse in all its expressions (conversation, text, mathematics, etc.) and human action in its material and culturally determined settings, all in the service of a Toulmin/Harman approach (or something very like it) to human scientific reasoning. What I believe psychologists can contribute is our fundamental concern with the individual in their socialized and acculturated forms, drawing on insights gained, for instance, from social psychology, psycholinguistics, and social cognition to complement current work in STS. It will not be easy, but the way forward, I submit, is now clear.

NOTES

1 This account of the work of James McConnell and the planarians has been heavily influenced by the "Golem" study of the same material by Collins and Pinch (1993/1998a).
2 The use of the term *canals* by Lowell, rather than *channels* implies the artificiality of the structures. It is also worth noting that the many commentators who have accused Lowell of deliberately mistranslating the distinguished 19th-century Italian astronomer Schiaparelli's term *canali* as canals, when it actually means channels, do not seem to have realized that in Italian at least *canali* can mean both channels *and* canals. One might therefore conclude that in using so ambiguous a term Schiaparelli was, scientifically speaking, sitting on the fence over the issue of the nature of the phenomenon, a position most definitely not occupied by Lowell!
3 That is, the kind of reasoning that is used every day as distinct from formal or theoretical reasoning. Such reasoning is also intimately connected with (reasoned) action or behaviour, a point succinctly made by Audi: "Practical reasons might be said to be reasons for acting; theoretical reasons might be described as reasons for belief" (1989, p. 2). Practical reasoning has also been used to model *moral* or *evaluated* actions or behaviour, thus making its study of increased value here, since I would want to argue that the scientific order is also a *moral* one – that is, since scientists evaluate their actions and beliefs, so this in turn provides an additional structuring element for their world view.
4 Now, STS might seem to challenge the received view that science is the observer-independent uncovering of uncontroversial, objective "facts", a view held by most lay people and scientists (including many psychologists), but I want to argue that the issue is less straightforward than so stark a contrast between the received view of science and STS might imply. Thus, if we follow the received view we are immediately faced with the paradox that science, while obviously undertaken by people, has somehow to be rendered *independent* of them. Now, the triumph achieved over individuality and subjectivity is said to be due, in part, to the checks and balances that monitor and shape science, while the generally sceptical atmosphere that is supposed to pervade scientific education and practice is claimed to add additional reflexive safeguards to the work. Further, all of these processes are said to justify the *realistic* nature of most scientific reports, with their absolutist tone and grammatical forms which rely heavily on indirect speech and third-person reporting. There may indeed be a list of names at the head of all scientific papers, but it would be wrong to think that they were the *onlie begetters* of the work reported therein!

But surely this process of de-individuation is essentially social and collective, where scientific practices and communication are all dictated by the culturally determined view as to what *currently* constitutes science. If this seems to have a point, then STS could be of some considerable use, and with it my argument for scientific reasoning as a form of practical reasoning not unlike what might go on in a court of law, or at a rather tense breakfast table the morning after the night before!

There are, of course, many intermediate positions that can be and have been adopted between the objectivist view of science and its construal as a purely social construct, or more radical still as a construct *per se* – see, for instance, Giere, 1988, or Collins and Pinch, 1998a, or Woolgar, 1988a – but the increased richness of the resulting analyses of science have more than justified this messy post-positive upheaval!

5 Although Mars is about a third the size of Earth, there are no significant bodies of unfrozen water on its surface, except at the poles, although very recent observations have suggested that there may be enormous volumes of water some distance *below* the surface. Consequently, the dry land area of the planet is considerable, relative to its size.

6 It is worth adding something about Lowell's astronomical practices here. He invariably observed Mars during daylight hours. This helped him to observe the behaviour of the air currents at Flagstaff and to correct for them if necessary. Also he (and his assistants) drew Mars at times close to when the photographs were taken, so that the two sources of images could mutually inform and support each other (see Lovie, 1994, for more on this).

7 Harman has argued that classical forms of logic such as the syllogism (which he refers to as *argument* or *proof*) do not really count as reasoning in that the conclusions are directly and unambiguously implied by the premises, hence in a non-trivial sense nothing new is achieved (see Harman, 1986, pp. 3–6; also his Chapter 2). Rather, reasoning for him is going from the known to the unknown, from one take on the world to another. It is not about the (logical) coverage, extension, and implication of pre-existing content, but about the often rapid and *holistic* reconstruction of the world brought about by adopting a newly changed view of it.

8 The scientific necessity for the existence of the "missing link" was thought to follow from the Darwinian system of evolution, although Darwin himself had never used such crude terminology.

9 It is also the case that Brannigan points to other counter-counter-revisionist treatments which sought to rescue Dawson's reputation (1981, p. 166), thus pointing to the role that differential assumptions make to the differential interpretation of what appears to be the same set of "facts".

10 This was pretty much the way that the pioneer of conversational analysis, Harvey Sacks, viewed naturally occurring language (Sacks, 1992, Vol. 1, pp. 802–805).

11 I should also like to mention a couple of other works whose message both reflects and extends Giere's efforts. The first is by Martin Rudwick (1985) whose celebrated treatment of a key finding in the history of 19th-century geology (the recognition of a new epoch, the *Devonian*, in the history of the Earth) points explicitly to the socially negotiated nature of scientific discovery. The book also underlines the role of *material culture* in the process – in his case, the speed and efficiency of the British postal service, and the existence of a spatially linked network of researchers and museums in the London area. My second is by Peter Galison (1987) which explores the complex social and technical negotiations that lie behind the conclusion of certain experiments in 20th-century particle physics: "Experiments begin and end in a matrix of beliefs" (1987, p. 277). Galison also points to the existence of collective or community beliefs which shape and buttress the forms of persuasive argumentation that, he claims, advance the field.

REFERENCES

Andersen, P., & Cadbury, D. (1985). *Imagined worlds: stories of scientific discovery*. London: Ariel Books/BBC.
Audi, R. (1989). *Practical reasoning*. London: Routledge.

Barnes, B. (1982). *T. S. Kuhn and social science*. London: Macmillan.
Billig, M. (1987). *Arguing and thinking: a rhetorical approach to social psychology*. Cambridge: Cambridge University Press.
Bower, G. H., & Hilgard, E. R. (1981). *Theories of learning* (5th Ed.). Englewood Cliffs, NJ: Prentice Hall.
Brannigan, A. (1981). *The social basis of scientific discoveries*. Cambridge: Cambridge University Press.
Broad, W., & Wade, N. (1985). *Betrayers of the truth: Fraud and deceit in science*. Oxford: Oxford University Press.
Bromley, D. B. (1986). *The case-study method in psychology and related disciplines*. Chichester, UK: Wiley.
Collins, H., & Pinch, T. (1993/1998a). *The Golem: What you should know about science*. Cambridge: Cambridge University Press.
Collins, H., & Pinch, T. (1998b). *The Golem at large: What you should know about technology*. Cambridge: Cambridge University Press.
Dunbar, K. (1993). Concept discovery in a scientific domain. *Cognitive Science, 17*, 397–434.
Feyerabend, P. (1970). Against method: Outline of an anarchistic theory of knowledge. In M. Radnor & S. Winokur (Eds.), *Analysis of theories and methods of physics and psychology*. Minneapolis: University of Minnesota Press.
Fuller, P. (1997). *Science*. Buckingham, UK: Open University Press.
Galison, P. (1987). *How experiments end*. Chicago: Chicago University Press.
Giere, R. N., (1988). *Explaining science: A cognitive approach*. Chicago: Chicago University Press.
Gilbert, G. N., & Mulkay, M. (1984). *Opening Pandora's box: A sociological analysis of scientists' discourse*. Cambridge: Cambridge University Press.
Gross, A. G. (1996). *The rhetoric of science* (2nd Ed.). Cambridge, MA: Harvard University Press.
Harman, G. (1986). *Change in view: Principles of reasoning*. Cambridge MA: MIT Press.
Hooper, J. (2002). *Of moths and men: Intrigue, tragedy & the peppered moth*. London: Fourth Estate.
Klahr, D., & Simon, H. (1999). Studies of scientific discovery: Complementary approaches and convergent findings. *Psychological Bulletin, 125*(5), 524–543.
Klahr, D., & Simon, H. (2001). What have psychologists (and others) discovered about the process of scientific discovery? *Current Directions in Psychological Science, 10*(3), 75–79.
Knorr-Cetina, K. (1981). *The manufacture of knowledge*. Oxford: Pergamon.
Kuhn, T. S. (1970). *The structure of scientific revolutions* (2nd Ed.). Chicago: Chicago University Press.
Latour, B. (1999). *Pandora's hope*. Cambridge, MA: Harvard University Press.
Latour, B., & Woolgar, S. (1986). *Laboratory life* (2nd Ed.). Princeton, NJ: Princeton University Press.
Lowell, P. (1906). First photographs of the canals of Mars. *Proceedings of the Royal Society of London, Series A, 77*, 132–135.
Lovie, A. D. (1992). *Context and commitment: A psychology of science*. London: Harvester Wheatsheaf.
Lovie, A. D. (1994). Context and commitment: The psychology of science as rhetoric. *Mexican Journal of Behaviour Analysis, Monograph Issue, 20*, 5–34.

Majerus, M. E. N. (1998). *Melanism: Evolution in action*. Oxford: Oxford University Press.
McConnell, J. V. (1965). *Failure to interprete planarian data correctly: A reply to Bennett Calvin*. Unpublished manuscript, Ann Arbor, MI: University of Michigan.
Mey, J. L. (1993). *Pragmatics: An introduction*. Oxford: Blackwell.
Potter, J. (1996). *Representing reality: Discourse, rhetoric and social construction*. London: Sage.
Qin, Y., & Simon, S. (1990). Laboratory replication of scientific discovery process. *Cognitive Science, 14*, 281–312.
Rudwick, M. J. S. (1985). *The great Devonian controversy*. Chicago: Chicago University Press.
Sacks, H. (1992). *Lectures in conversation, Vol. 1 and 2*. Oxford: Blackwell.
Shadish, W. R., & Fuller, S. (Eds.). (1994). *The social psychology of science*. New York: Guilford Press.
Shapin, S. (1994). *A social history of truth*. Chicago: Chicago University Press.
Shapin, S., & Shaffer, S. (1985). *Leviathan and the air pump: Hobbes, Boyle and the experimental life*. Princeton, NJ: Princeton University Press.
Shotter, J. (1990). The social construction of remembering and forgetting. In D. Middleton & D. Edwards (Eds.), *Collective remembering*. London: Sage.
Simon, H. (1983). *Models of bounded rationality*. Cambridge MA: MIT Press.
Soyland, A. J. (1994). *Psychology as metaphor*. London: Sage.
Stevens, R. (Ed.). (1996). *Understanding the self*. London: Sage, Open University.
Thomas, J. (1995). *Meaning in interaction: An introduction to pragmatics*. London: Longman.
Toulmin, S. (1969). *The uses of argument*. Cambridge: Cambridge University Press.
Toulmin, S. (2001). *Return to reason*. Harvard, MA: Harvard University Press.
Watson, G., & Seiler, R. M. (Eds.). (1992). *Text in context: Contributions to ethnomethodology*. London: Sage.
Woolgar, S. (1988a). *Science: The very idea*. Chichester, UK: Ellis Horwood.
Woolgar, S. (Ed.). (1988b). *Knowledge and reflexivity*. London: Sage.

Author index

Abelson, R.P. 44
Adams, E.W. 86
Adelman, L. 31
Ajzen, I. 270
Alksnis, O. 172
Allais, M. 46
Allen, J.L. 258, 313
Almor, A. 108, 120, 162
Anand, P. 301
Andersen, P. 350
Anderson, J.R. 4, 45, 57, 58, 62, 64, 257, 261
Anscombe, G.E.M. 164–165
Aristotle 1, 5, 6, 49, 163–165, 166, 168, 172, 190, 217, 234–237, 241
Arnauld, A. 231, 238
Atkinson, A.P. 318, 326
Audi, R. 164–165, 166, 167–168, 169, 313, 366
Augustoni-Ziskind, M. 319
Aumann, R.J. 291
Austin, G.A. 36

Bacharach, M. 291, 295, 297–298
Baddeley, A.D. 185
Bailenson, J. 279
Ball, L.J. 252
Ball, T.M. 185
Ballard, D. 69
Balzer, W.K. 29
Bara, B.G. 192, 193, 204, 214, 231
Barclay, J.R. 189
Barnes, B. 353
Baron, J. 273
Baron-Cohen, S. 314, 320
Barr, D. 34

Barres, P. 197
Barrouillet, P. 197
Barrett, H.C. 326
Barsalou, L.W. 186
Barston, J.L. 158, 247, 313
Bartlett, F. 282, 353, 359
Bayes, T. 27
Beatty, J. 55
Begg, I. 230, 235
Bell, V. 201, 204
Benthin, A. 268
Bereiter, C. 282
Berndsen, M. 342
Bernieri, F. 31
Berry, D.C. 254–255
Berry, M. 268
Beyth-Marom, R. 60
Biederman, I. 188
Biller, B. 269–270
Billig, M. 356
Binet, A. 185
Binmore, K. 300, 304
Björkmann, M. 16
Black, J.B. 188
Bless, H. 269–270
Bleske, A.L. 325
Block, N. 112
Bloom, P. 314
Bochensky, I.M. 217, 234
Bolton, N. 243
Boltzmann, L. 180
Boninger, D.S. 276, 280–281
Boole, G. 55
Borgia, G. 325
Boring, E.G. 323
Bourmaud, G. 80

Bower, G.H. 185, 352
Bowerman, M. 120
Braine, M.D.S. 52, 60, 67, 84, 112, 115, 116, 120, 122, 190, 203, 216, 232–234, 253, 310, 319
Brams, S.J. 299
Brannigan, A. 355, 362, 367
Bransford, J.D. 189, 272
Brase, G. 7, 8, 321, 322–323, 325, 326
Brehmer, A. 31
Brehmer, B. 19, 27, 29, 31
Breinlinger, K. 318
Brentano, F. 11
Brewer, W.F. 188
Broad, W. 362
Bromley, D.B.
Brooks, P.J. 4, 319
Brown, D. 317
Bruner, J.S. 36
Brunswik, E. 2, 3, 4, 7, 8, 11–36,
Bucciarelli, M. 193, 200, 204, 215
Buchel, C. 260
Buck, E. 65
Bühler, K. 11–12, 17
Burton, A. 243
Buss, D.M. 325
Byrne, R.M.J. 2, 46, 52, 67, 76, 77–83, 84, 87–91, 97, 128, 135, 145, 146, 153, 158, 171, 173–174, 187, 194, 195, 197, 198, 199, 200, 203, 204, 246, 254, 255, 276, 310, 311

Cacioppo, J.T. 276, 281
Cadbury, D. 350
Campbell, R. 300
Cantor, J.B. 4, 120
Cara, F. 67, 120, 136
Caramazza, A. 188
Carnap, R. 338
Carreiras, M. 193, 195
Carriedo, N. 202, 253
Caverni, J.P. 82, 204, 312
Chadwick, R. 34
Chaiken, S. 269
Chammah, A.M. 299
Chan, D. 62
Chase, W.G. 187
Chasseigne, G. 29
Chater, N. 3, 4, 7, 52, 57, 60, 61, 62, 63–66, 67–68, 75, 86, 98, 108, 135–136, 143, 159, 162, 169, 170, 186, 281, 334
Cheng, P.W. 5, 64, 90, 97–103, 118, 120, 134, 161, 170–171, 321, 324
Cherubini, P. 99, 200
Chomsky, N. 51, 127, 316, 319
Christal, R.E. 259
Chrostowski, J.J. 100
Chua, F. 62
Clark, H.H. 187
Clark, K.L. 52
Clibbens, J. 245, 252
Cohen, L.J. 48–49, 256
Colbourn, C. 161
Collins, H. 351–353, 356, 366, 367
Colman, A.M. 7, 8, 288, 295, 297–298, 299, 304
Cooksey, R.W. 30
Cooper, R.W. 296
Copi, I. 139
Cosmides, L. 5, 7, 97, 98, 101, 103, 120, 128, 134, 145, 149, 161, 162, 170–171, 260, 309, 317, 320–321, 323, 325
Cox, J.R. 96, 99, 100, 133, 134, 160
Cox, R.T. 51
Crago, M.B. 314
Craik, K. 5, 179–180, 182–184, 203
Cramer, K.M. 275
Crawford, V.P. 295
Crick, F. 350
Crivello, F. 260
Crocker, M. 57
Crombag, H.F. 345
Culicover, P. 325
Cummins, D.D. 143, 161, 162, 167, 170, 172, 321, 324
Cummins, R. 324

Danziger, K. 13
Dasser, V. 320
Daston, L. 55
Davidson, D. 43, 54
Davis, R. 188
Dawson, C. 362
de Finetti, B. 50
DeJong, D.V. 296
de Kleer, J. 188
Deutsch, M. 300
Dewey, J. 11

Dias, M.G. 4, 112, 120
Dienes, Z. 254–255
Dietrich, E. 186
Dieussaert, K. 200
Dipboye, R.L. 297
Doherty, M.E. 2, 7, 8, 14, 16, 25, 27, 29, 30, 31, 34
Dolan, R.J. 260
Doyle, J. 52
Dreman, D. 268
de Vooght, G. 195, 253
Dunbar, K. 34, 364
d'Ydewalle, G. 186, 195, 200, 253

Eagly, A.H. 269
Ebbinghaus, H. 2
Edgington, D. 83, 86, 87
Edwards, W. 31
Ehrlich, K. 188
Ellsberg, D. 294
Erickson, J.R. 191
Ericsson, K.A. 250
Eskritt, M. 320
Espino, O. 193
Euler, L. 217, 220–224, 230–231, 237
Evans, J.StB.T. 2, 4, 6, 27, 46, 51, 53, 60, 63, 64, 65, 67, 75, 76, 78, 80, 83- 87, 90, 96, 97, 98, 133–134, 137, 157, 158–159, 160, 197, 200, 204, 241–261, 313, 333–334, 336

Fairley, N. 167, 172–174
Fallon, A.E. 319
Fangmeir, T. 195
Faraday, M. 34–35
Feeney, A. 86
Feibelman, J.K. 281
Feldman, J. 69
Feyerabend, P. 358
Feynman, R.P. 180–181
Fiddick, L. 120, 166, 320
Field, H. 112
Fillenbaum, S. 137, 276
Finucane, M. 268
Fischhoff, B. 60
Fisher, R.A. 45, 301
Flaton, R. 269
Foddy, M. 299
Fodor, J.A. 44, 52, 66, 67, 112

Forbus, K. 188
Ford, E.B. 362
Ford, M. 193, 215, 216, 231–234, 237, 238
Forsythe, R. 296
Franks, J.J. 189
Frege, G. 55, 181
Frenkel, E. 13, 27
Friedrich, J. 342
Fuller, P. 356
Funder, D.C. 31

Gale, A.G. 252
Galison, P. 367
Galton, F. 242
Garavan, H. 34
Garcia, J. 319
García-Madruga, J.A. 200, 202, 253
Gardner, H. 314
Gardner, M. 217
Garey, M..R. 68
Garnham, A. 2, 158, 189, 200, 253, 313
Gebauer, G. 137, 142
Gelman, S. 314, 318, 325
Gentner, D. 188
Gentner, D.R. 188
Gentzen, G. 111, 112
Gergonne, J. 224–231, 233, 237, 238
George, C. 62, 258
Gerrard, M. 268
Gibson, J.J. 20
Giere, R.N. 365, 367
Gigerenzer, G. 2, 3, 13, 28, 32, 36, 51, 55, 57, 58, 97, 101, 103, 162, 256, 260, 335
Gilbert, G.N. 356
Gillies, D.B. 304
Gillis, J.S. 29, 31
Ginsberg, M.L. 68
Girotto, V. 67, 82, 99, 100, 120, 136, 161, 197, 204, 253, 261, 281, 312
Glasgow, J.I. 188
Gleicher, F. 276, 280–281
Glenberg, A.M. 189
Goel, V. 260
Goldstein, D. 51, 57, 58
Goldvarg, Y. 198, 199, 204
Gonzales, M 261
González, M. 204
González-Labra, J. 253

374 *Author index*

Gooding, D. 35
Goodman, N. 48, 49, 127
Goodnow, J.J. 36
Goodwin, R.Q. 249
Gopnik, M. 314
Gould, S.J. 325
Graesser, A.C. 272
Grainger, B. 60
Grassia, J. 27
Green, B. 188
Green, D.W. 6, 7, 8, 64, 120, 134, 137, 143, 204, 268–269, 270, 274–275, 281, 282
Grice, H.P. 228
Griggs, R.A. 96, 99–100, 120, 133, 134, 160, 235
Griffiths, P.E. 318
Grootendorst, R. 275
Gross, A.G. 356
Grosset, N. 197
Guttiérez, F. 202

Ha, Y. 334, 336, 344
Haddock, G. 270
Hadjichristidis, C. 86, 91
Halberstadt, N. 334
Haldane, J.B.S. 350
Halford, G.S. 188
Haller, H. 295
Halpern, J.Y. 202
Hamm, R.M. 27
Hammond, K.R. 14, 25, 26, 28, 29, 31, 33
Hamscher, W. 188
Handley, S.J. 65, 83, 200, 202, 204, 252, 254, 260, 261
Hanson, N.R. 130
Harman, G. 3, 8, 112, 164, 169, 172, 355, 359–362, 363, 365, 367
Harper, C.N.J. 65, 204
Harris, G. 230, 235
Harsanyi, J. 45, 290, 292, 295
Haselton, M.G. 325
Hasson, U. 203
Hastie, R. 269, 281
Hayes, P. 68
Hayes, P.J. 188
Hayes-Roth, B. 184
Head, H. 353, 359

Hegarty, M. 188
Hempel, C. 139
Henkemans, F.S.
Henle, M. 2, 243, 256
van der Henst, J.B. 200, 201
Herma, H. 16
Hesse, F.W. 273
Hilbert, D. 55
Hilgard, E.R. 13, 352
Hirschfeld, L.A. 314
Hitch, G.J. 185
Hoch, S. 137
Hoffrage, U. 32, 260
Hogg, M. 299
Hogge, J.H. 26
Holcombe, H.R. III 314
Holland, J.H. 183, 188, 325
Holway, A.F. 323
Holzworth, R.J. 29
Holyoak, K.J. 5, 90, 97–103, 118, 120, 134, 161, 170–171, 188, 270–272, 274, 321, 324, 325
Honzik, C.H. 184
Hooper, J. 362–363
Horn, L.R. 228, 238
Houdé, O. 260
Howson, C. 54, 338
Hug, K. 97, 101, 103, 162,
Hughes, M. 134
Hull, C.L. 18
Hume, D. 165–166, 172, 287
Humphrey, G. 11
Hunt, R.M. 188
Hunter, W.S. 18, 21
Huttenlocher, J. 191

Inhelder, B. 190, 243
Iyengar, S. 269

Jackson, S. 96, 99
Jacobson, K. 318
James, W. 11
Jeffrey, R. 200
Jessop, A. 57, 60
Johnson, D.S. 68
Johnson, M.K. 272
Johnson-Laird, P.N. 2, 5, 52, 55, 60, 65, 67, 77–83, 84, 87–91, 122, 128, 133, 135, 138, 141, 143, 145, 146, 153,

160–162, 171, 173–174, 181, 182, 186, 187, 189, 190–204, 214, 215, 231, 243, 245, 246, 249, 253–254, 255, 257, 276, 281, 310, 311–312, 325, 334, 336
Jonsen, A.R. 164, 166, 167–168
Joyce, C.R.B. 29

Kagel, J.H. 288
Kahneman, D.E. 36, 46, 51, 55, 89, 276, 334
Kamiya, J. 15, 18
Kamp, H. 181, 189
Kant, I. 165–167, 172
Kao, C.F. 281
Kareev, Y. 334
Karttunen, L. 122, 189
Keil, F.C. 318
Kenny, A.J.P. 169, 170
Kettlewell, B. 362–363
Keynes, J.M. 45
Kilpatrick, S.G. 167
Kimmel, M.J. 288
Kintsch, W.A. 189
Kirby, K.N. 60
Kirlik, A. 20
Kitchin, R.M. 184
Klahr, D. 34, 364
Klauer, K.C. 64, 197
Klayman, J. 334, 336, 344, 345
Kleinbölting, H. 32
Kleindorfer, P.R. 50
Knauff, M. 195
Kneale, M. 111, 235
Kneale, W. 111, 235
Knorr-Cetina, K. 356
Knutson, B. 320
Koelling, R.A. 319
Köhler, W. 182
Kohlberg, L. 166
Kolb, B. 314
Kosslyn, S.M. 185, 248
Krauth, J. 247
Krebs, J.R. 57
Kroger, J.K. 99–101, 103, 324
Krüger, L. 55
Krueger, L.E. 335
Kruglanski, A.W. 270
Kuhn, D. 269, 273, 277, 281
Kuhn, T.S. 127, 129, 151–152, 353
Kuipers, B. 188

Kunda, Z. 270, 282
Kunreuther, H.C. 50
Kurz, E.M. 11, 12, 13, 14, 25, 28
Kusch, M. 11
Kyllonen, P. 259

Laming, D. 137, 142
Larkin, J. 60, 62, 86, 188
Larking, R. 120
Latour, B. 356
Le, Q.A. 270–272
Lee, K. 320
Lear, J. 235
Leary, D.E. 11
Lecas, J.F. 197
Legrenzi, M. 82, 133, 146, 160, 204, 281
Legrenzi, P. 82, 133, 146, 160, 204, 253, 281, 312
Leibniz, G.W. 6, 217, 218–219, 222, 231
Lemmon, E. 139
Lepore, E. 112
Lepper, M.R. 269
Leslie, A.M. 314
Lewis, C.I. 139
Lewis, D. 83, 87
Lewis, D.W. 291, 295
Lewontin, R.C. 317, 325
Liebrand, W.B.G. 299
Light, P. 161
Lindem, K. 189
Lindley, D.V. 45
Lindsey, S. 269
Liu, I. 62
Lo, K. 62
Loar, B. 112
Lombardo, V. 210
Lord, C.G. 269
Lovie, A.D. 8, 356, 357, 367
Lowell, P. 354–358, 366
Lubart, T. 172
Lucas, E.J. 252
Luce, R.D. 290
Lucot, J.B. 319
Lukasiewicz, J. 216, 235
Luria, A.R. 185
Lynch, J.S. 245–246, 249

McCarthy, J.M. 52, 68
McClelland, A. 268

McClelland, J.L. 68
McCloskey, M. 188
McCloy, R. 269, 273, 274–275, 276
McConnell, J.V. 350–353, 366
McCulloch, W.S. 187
McDermott, D. 45, 52
McEleney, A. 204
MacGregor, D.G. 268
MacKay, D.J.C. 68
McManus, I. 204, 275
Macnamara, J. 190
Macomber, J. 318
Maier, N.R.F. 184
Majerus, M.E.N. 363
Mandler, G. 242
Mandler, J.M. 242
Maniscalco, C. 31
Manktelow, K.I. 2, 4, 7, 64, 90, 91, 129, 133, 137, 139, 158, 159, 160, 161–162, 167, 170–171, 172, 204, 256, 257, 321
Marcus, S.L. 84–88
Margolis, H. 137
Markman, A.B. 186
Markman, E.M. 318, 319
Markovits, H. 197, 313
Marr, D. 56, 148, 187
Marvin, B.A. 31
Marzke, M.W. 315
Maxwell, J.C. 180–181, 182
Mazoyer, B. 260
Mazzocco, A. 99, 197
Means, M.L. 273
Mehta, J. 296
Mellet, E. 260
Mertz, C.K. 268
Meseguer, E. 193
Messick, D.M. 299
Metzler, J. 185
Mey, J.L. 350, 356
Meyer, M. 189
Miles, J.N.V. 252
Miller, A.D 319
Miller, D. 89
Miller, G.A. 36
Miller, R.L. 322–323
Milson, R. 57
Minsky, M. 44
Molnar, P. 320
Monaghan, P. 148

Montague, R. 127, 138
Moran, P. 268
Moray, N. 188
Moreno, S. 202
Morgan, M.S. 335
Morgenstern, O. 45, 51, 288, 290, 303–304
Morley, E. 200
Moutier, S. 260
Muckli, L. 268
Muir, D. 320
Mulkay, M. 356
Mullet, E. 29
Murray, D.J. 13
Mynatt, C.R. 34

Nantel, G. 313
Nash, J.F. 289, 290–295, 298, 299, 302, 304, 305
Neisser, U. 242
Nersessian, N. 35
Neth, H. 202
von Neumann, J. 45, 51, 288, 290, 303–304
Newell, A. 133, 187, 202, 215, 310
Newstead, S.E. 2, 46, 65, 76, 97, 158, 197, 202, 235, 246, 257, 313
Newton, E.J. 252
Neyman, J. 45
Nguyen-Xuan, A. 162
Nicole, P. 232, 238
Nisbett, R.E. 49, 120, 188, 250, 324, 325
Noveck, I.A. 97, 99–101, 104, 118
Nozick, R. 300–301

O'Brien, D.P. 4, 5, 7, 8, 84, 97, 99–101, 104, 111, 112, 113, 116, 118, 120, 122, 190, 203, 253, 319
O'Connor, R.O. 29, 37
Oakhill, J.V. 2, 158, 189, 200, 253, 313
Oaksford, M.R. 3, 4, 7, 52, 57, 60, 61, 62, 63–66, 67–68, 75, 86, 98, 108, 113, 135–136, 143, 159, 162, 169, 170, 186, 243, 334
Oberauer, K. 83, 86, 90, 197
Oberlander, J. 193, 231, 233–234, 236
Occhipinti, S. 319
Oestermeier, U. 273
Olan, J. 260

Oliver, L. 120, 324
Ormerod, T.C. 198, 200
Osherson, D.N. 190
Ottati, V. 269
Over, D.E. 3, 4, 5, 6, 8, 27, 53, 57, 60, 61, 62, 64, 75, 80, 82, 83–87, 90, 91, 96, 98, 139, 157, 158, 159, 161–162, 167, 170–171, 172, 204, 241–242, 248, 251, 254, 256–261, 321, 333–334

Paivio, A. 185
Paris, J. 68
Park, B. 269
Park, J.R. 297
Pascal, B. 167, 169
Patzig, G. 217, 235–236, 237
Peacocke, C. 112
Pearl, J. 68
Pearson, T. 27
Peirce, C.S. 5, 179–181,
Pennington, N. 281
Pereyra, L. 320
Perham, N. 261
Perky, C.W. 185
Peters, E. 268
Peterson, D.M. 150
Petty, R.E. 276, 281
Pham, L.B. 270–272
Piaget, J. 17, 138, 166, 190, 243
Pickering, M. 57
Pinch, T. 351–353, 356, 366, 367
Pineau, A. 260
Pinker, S. 314, 319, 323, 325
Platt, R.D. 100, 120
Poletiek, F.H. 6, 8, 130, 334, 338, 340, 342, 344
Politzer, G. 5–6, 67, 80, 122, 162, 235
Polk, T.A. 202
Pollard, P. 158, 247, 257, 313
Porter, T. 55
Popper, K.R. 4, 8, 12, 128, 129, 131, 132, 133, 136, 139, 151, 311, 333–347
Potter, J. 356
Premack, D. 320
Preston, E. 269
Profet, M. 319
Pruitt, D.G. 288
Putnam, H. 183
Pylyshyn, Z.W. 44, 52, 68, 185, 248

Pyne, R.A. 64

Qin, Y. 364
Quattrone, G.A. 302
Queller, D.C. 325
Quine, W.V.O. 43, 54, 112, 316

Radford, J. 243
Raiffa, H. 290
Ramsey, F.P. 3, 50, 86–87
Rapoport, A. 299
Rawls, J. 49
Real, L.A. 258
Reber, A.S. 242, 254–255, 259
Reilly, B.A. 31
Reilly, J.S. 120
Reiser, B.J. 112, 185
Reiter, R. 52
Richardson, J. 198
Riggs, K. 150
Rips, L.J. 52, 60, 84–88, 190, 202, 203, 253, 273, 279, 310, 311–312, 321
Rist, R. 172
Rith, C. 260
Roazzi, A. 4, 112, 120
Roberge, J.J. 243
Roberts, M.J. 200, 252
Roese, N.J. 89
Rohrbaugh, J. 31
Rood, B. 245, 252
Roose, J.E. 31
Ross, T.W. 296
Roth, A.E. 288
Rouse, W.B. 188
Rozin, P. 319
Rucci, A.J. 13, 15
Rudwick, M.J.S. 367
Ruff, C.C. 195
Rumain, B. 112
Rutherford, M.D. 320
Ryle, G. 242

Sachs, J.S. 189
Sacks, H. 350, 367
Samuels, R. 326
Santamaría, C. 193, 195, 199, 200
Sargent, E. 363
Savage, L.J. 51
Savary, F. 146, 199

Scardamalia, M. 282
Schaeken, W. 186, 195, 200, 253, 311
Schank, R.C. 44
Schilling, S.G. 26
Schlick, M. 11–12
Schneider, S. 299
Schoemaker, P.J.H. 50
Schooler, L.J. 57
Schooler, T.Y. 269
Schroyens, W. 186, 200
Schwartz, D. 188
Scott Edwards, C. 280–281
Segerstrale, U.C. 320
Seiler, R.M. 350
Selten, R. 28, 45, 292–293, 295
Sen, A.K. 289–290
Severson, H. 268
Shackelford, T.K. 325
Shadish, W.R. 356
Shafir, E.B. 300
Shafir, D. 334
Shaffer, S. 356
Shannon, C. 14, 36
Shapin, S. 356
Shapiro, D.A. 133, 141, 159
Shaw, V. 273
Shepard, R.N. 185, 187
Sherman, S.J. 345
Sheu, C.F. 64
Shotter, J. 353
Siegal, M. 319
Simmons, C. 268
Simon, D. 270–272, 274
Simon, H.A. 28, 36, 57, 58, 188, 250, 310, 364, 365
Simon, S. 364
Singer, M. 272
Skov, R.B. 345
Skyrms, B. 50
Sloman, S.A. 86, 108, 120, 162, 242
Sloutsky, V.M. 198
Slovic, P. 46, 268
Slowiaczek, L.M. 345
Smedslund, J. 17, 256
Smith, C. 180
Smith, D.G. 41
Smithson, M. 299
Snyder, M. 336
Sonino, M. 204

Sowa, J.F. 181
Sowden, L. 300
Soyland, A.J. 356
Spelke, E.S. 318
Sperber, D. 67, 120, 136, 143, 227, 322
Stalnaker, R. 3, 83–87
Stanovich, K.E. 157, 159, 242, 259–260
Starmer, C. 296
Steedman, M.J. 191, 192
Steen, F.F. 318
Stein, E. 61
Stenning, K. 1, 4, 5, 6, 7, 8, 63, 113, 135, 136, 139, 140, 142, 144, 145, 146, 148, 149, 153, 159, 189, 193, 216, 231, 233–234, 236–237, 243
Stephens, D.W. 57
Sterelny, K. 318
Stevens, A.L. 188
Stevens, R. 353
Stevenson, R.J. 62, 86, 87, 189, 258
Stewart, T.R. 27, 31
Stich, S.P. 49, 59, 61
Stirk, J.A. 298
Störring, G. 185, 193, 213–216, 217, 231, 233–234
Stratham, A. 276, 280–281
Sugden, R. 291, 295, 296, 297
Sutherland, E.J. 64, 172
Sutherland, N.S. 59
Swann, W.B. 336
Swijtink, Z. 55
Symons, L.A. 320

Tabossi, P. 195
Tagart, J. 245
Tasso, A. 197, 204, 276
Teigen, K.H. 89
Thagard, P.A. 49, 188, 281, 325
Thom, P. 235–236
Thomas, J. 356
Thompson, V.A. 202, 261, 275
Thorndike, P.W. 184
Todd, P. 3, 28
Tolman, E.C. 5, 12–13, 15, 18, 21, 184
Tooby, J. 120, 134, 145, 162, 260, 309, 317, 320–321, 323, 325
Torrens, D. 275, 281
Toulmin, S.E. 6, 8, 138, 164, 167, 168, 273, 359–362, 365

Trabasso, T. 272
Tschirgi, J. 137
Tucker, A.W. 298
Tucker, L.R. 26
Tversky, A. 36, 46, 51, 55, 276, 300, 302
Tweney, R.D. 2, 7, 8, 11, 13, 14, 15, 34, 35, 100

Ulbaek, I. 320
Ullman, D.G. 30, 31
Ungar, G. 352–353
Urbach, P. 54, 338

Vadeboncoeur, I. 313
Vandierendonck, A. 195, 253
van Dijk, T.A. 189
van Eemeren, F.H. 273, 275
van Koppen, P.J. 346
van Lambalgen, M. 1, 4, 5, 6, 7, 8, 135, 136, 139, 140, 142, 145, 146, 153
van Lange, P.A.M. 299
van Wallendael, L.R. 344
Vardi, M.Y. 202
von Frisch, K. 184
von Winterfeldt, D. 31
Vosniadou, S. 188
Voss, J.F. 273

Wade, N. 362
Wagenaar, W.A. 346
Wakefield, J.C. 325
Walton, D.N.
Walton, I. 153
Wänke, M. 269–270
Wason, P.C. 2, 4, 6, 34, 55, 60, 63, 95, 123, 127–130, 132, 133, 134, 135, 136, 137, 138, 141, 142, 143, 151, 157, 159, 160, 170, 186, 194, 198, 241, 243, 245, 246, 247, 248–251, 253, 259, 333–334, 336
Watson, G. 350
Watson, J. 350
Webber, B.L. 189
Weinstock, M. 269
West, R.W. 157, 259–260
Wetherick. N.E. 231, 334
Wexler, K. 325
Wheeler, M. 318, 326
Whishaw, I.Q. 314
Wiener, N. 14
Wigton, R.S. 31
Wilhelm, W. 83, 86, 90
Wilke, H.A.M. 299
Wilkins, M.C. 158–159, 247
Williams, B. 287
Williams, B.C. 188
Wilson, D. 227
Wilson, T.D. 250, 269
Wise, M.N. 180
Wittgenstein, L. 138, 182, 186
Woods, W. 112
Woodworth, R.S. 14, 15, 20
Woolgar, S. 353, 356, 366
Wu, J. 62
Wullstein, K.L. 315

Yachanin, S.A. 100
Yang, Y. 199, 200
Yates, B.J. 319
Young, R. 57, 188
Yule, P. 135, 216, 233–234, 236–237

Zago, L. 260
Zajonc, R.B. 267
Zimbardo, P.G. 297

Subject index

Abstract tasks 2, 97–98,137
Affect *see* Emotion
Animal behaviour 57, 58, 184, 258
Argumentation 6, 8, 145, 267–285, 349, 352, 355–356, 359–362

Bayesian theory 63, 135–136, 147, 296, 338
Belief bias 247–248, 253, 257, 313

Common knowledge 44, 290–291, 295–296
Computational tractability 57–58
Conditionals 3–4, 5, 75–94, 95–125, 135–138, 243–246, 312
    causal 172–175
    counterfactual 75, 84–85, 87–90, 91, 277
    deontic 3–5, 75, 90–92, 96–110, 117–121, 139–141, 161–162, 171, 173, 174
    descriptive *see* indicative
    indicative 3, 5, 75, 76–87, 91, 96–97 103–104, 106, 107–108, 118–120, 137–138, 139–141, 310
    material *see* Material implication
Constancy 12, 16–18, 20
Context 9–9, 12, 17–18, 34, 349–350, 353–354, 356, 365

Decision making 4, 7, 8, 33, 43, 46–48, 50, 54, 68, 75, 91, 169, 171, 257, 258, 268–272, 287–308, 342
Domain-specificity 4, 7, 66, 97,120–121, 134, 309–310, 313–326

Dual processes 6, 27, 157, 241–266, 273–276

Economics 57, 59
Emotion 149, 150, 268–269
Evolutionary explanation 7, 11, 50, 128, 130, 134–135, 143, 146, 149, 161, 170, 171, 255, 260, 261, 309–331, 350, 362–363
Everyday inference 46–50, 53–55, 75

Falsificationism 4, 7–8, 17, 129, 132, 136, 151, 311, 333–347
Fast and frugal heuristics 2–3, 27–28, 32–33, 58

Game theory 7, 8, 45, 68, 287–308
General-purpose reasoning processes 4, 120, 145, 309–313, 315,

Hypothesis testing 59, 129–131, 132–133, 151, 333–347

Information gain 3, 57–59, 63–64, 133, 135–136

Lens model 13, 14, 15, 23–27, 32, 34
Logic 3–6, 51, 52, 54, 55, 61–62, 67, 69, 76–77, 87, 110–111, 128, 129–131, 134–135, 137–138, 143, 144–146, 148–153, 181, 186, 190, 200, 204, 232–233, 235–236, 243–244, 247, 256, 309–312, 324, 333, 334, 335–336, 337, 343, 344, 355, 358, 359–360, 365
    mental *see* Mental logic

Subject index

Logicism 3, 75, 80, 92, 213, 243

Matching bias 133–134, 243–247, 249–250, 252
Material implication 4, 76–84, 110–112, 135–136, 138–139, 146, 174
 paradoxes of 77–83, 139
Mental logic 4, 5, 52, 60, 84–87, 110–117, 120, 135, 190, 203, 232–234, 243, 253, 310–313
Mental models
 in argumentation 267, 275–282
 probabilistic 2–3, 32–33
 theory of 5, 6, 52, 60, 65, 67, 76–83, 87–91, 135, 145–146, 148, 152, 179–212, 214, 215, 219, 222–223, 253–254, 255–256, 310–313
Modularity *see* Domain-specificity

Optimality 57–60, 63, 135–136, 157

Philosophy of science 7–8, 128–133, 151–153, 333–335, 337–339, 353
Pragmatics 4, 5, 95–125, 136, 141, 144, 226, 227, 258, 259
Pragmatic reasoning schemas 97–101, 103, 118–119, 134, 170–171, 321, 324–325
Probability 4, 13, 14, 16, 28, 45, 50–51, 55, 60–66, 69, 75, 82–83, 85–87, 91, 92, 169, 171–172, 204, 260–261, 290, 291–292, 293, 296, 342
 conditional 62, 63, 64, 85–86, 91, 301, 303
 heuristics model 64–66
 learning 29

Rational analysis 3, 45, 55–60, 63–64
 see also Representative design
Rationality 8, 43–74, 136, 203, 204, 287–308, 365
 bounded 28, 36, 58, 288, 365
 dual 44–45, 53, 60–61, 157, 159, 256–260
 formal 46, 50–55
Reasoning
 causal 172–175, 204, 301

conditional 3–4, 8, 61–63, 76–92, 95–125, 196–203, 243–246, 249, 312, 320
deductive 3, 34, 61, 181, 190–204, 213, 252, 256, 258, 310–313
deontic 4–5, 64, 90–92, 96–110, 117–118, 120, 134, 139–143, 146, 149, 161–162, 170–174, 204, 320–321, 322, 324–325, 326
illusions 146, 199, 204
inductive 333, 335, 337–341, 344
motivated 267, 270–272
practical 5, 157–177, 313, 355
pure 5, 157–177
scientific 33–35, 349–369
spatial 184, 186, 194–195
strategies 149, 180, 193, 200–203, 204, 214–215, 231–234, 287–308
syllogistic 5–6, 64–66, 158–159, 164–165, 190–193, 213–240, 247–248, 275, 281, 311
theoretical 5, 157–177
Reflective equilibrium 49
Relevance 67, 136, 143, 227, 251–252
Representative design 2, 19–20, 33

Semantics 4, 78–82, 86, 95, 110–113, 115, 117, 127–128, 135, 137–143, 146–148, 151–153, 189, 190, 199–200, 204, 226, 254, 311
Semantic information 79–80
Social contract theory 7, 97, 98, 101–102, 103, 134, 149, 161, 162, 170–171, 499, 320–322, 326
Social interaction 7, 8, 287–308, 320–321, 355–356
Social judgement theory 14, 33

Truth tables 76–77, 110, 244–246, 252

Utility 4, 58, 75, 91–92, 98, 171, 288–291, 296–298, 301–303, 342
Wason's selection task 4–5, 6, 34, 60, 63–64, 90, 95–125, 127–153, 159–162, 170–171, 198, 244, 246–247, 249–250, 251–252, 260, 333
 deontic version 4–5, 64, 90, 95–96, 97–110, 134, 139–142, 161–162
Wason's 2 4 6 (rule discovery) task 34, 333, 334, 336, 342, 344